ANCIENT NORTH AMERICA

With 345 illustrations

BRIAN M. FAGAN
ANCIENT NORTH AMERICA

THE ARCHAEOLOGY OF A CONTINENT

THAMES AND HUDSON

To Colin Ridler
With gratitude for his encouragement and insights

Picture research by Imogen Graham

Typeset by Bookworm Typesetting in Linotype Slimbach
Printed and bound in the United States
by R.R. Donnelley and Sons Company

CONTENTS

Preface
page 9

Preface

Ancient North America is a narrative account of what is known of the diverse prehistoric societies of North America, from first settlement before 12,000 BC up to European contact and beyond. It is based on a complex archaeological record that is buried in thousands of books, articles, mimeographed reports, and brief notes in literally dozens of languages, also on many years of field and museum visits, attending conferences, and discussions with colleagues working in every corner of North America. Some brief remarks about the nature of this book are appropriate.

I assume that the reader has some basic knowledge of the fundamental principles and terminology of archaeology, obtained either in a college or university course or through avocational or practical experience. To start from the beginning would require a far longer book than this already lengthy one. Readers anxious to acquire such knowledge are referred to widely available textbooks on the method and theory of modern scientific archaeology. This book has been written in such a way as to keep terminological labels and other technicalities to a minimum. The text is referenced, but only sufficiently so for the reader to delve more deeply into the technical literature when desired. In most cases, the reference given is that of a key synthesis or report that provides comprehensive citations for further reading.

Inevitably, a book like this is a constant compromise between the harsh dictates of space and the need to be comprehensive. There are many places where it has been necessary to compress local and regional data in the interests of brevity and clarity. This has led to unavoidable over-generalizations and simplifications in some places, as I have tried to balance accuracy with economy. Further examination of more specialist references will quickly introduce you to the real complexities of what is, at times, a frustrating and complex literature.

Many local cultural terms have been omitted. In places, we have summarized these for reference, but, again, every effort has been made to keep such terms to a minimum in the narrative. This is partly because of space considerations, and also because many of them are of extremely local application. Archaeology, by its very nature, is a local subject with many narrow concerns and local culture-historical problems. These are more appropriately addressed in more detailed regional syntheses than this one.

A major theoretical ferment has engulfed archaeology in recent years, as prehistorians have grappled with the complex problem not only of describing the past, but of explaining it as well. It would be folly for this book to be encased within a rigid theoretical doctrine, and I have made no attempt to do so. Part I gives a summary account of some of the major theoretical developments in North American archaeology, and we introduce many more specific controversies and theoretical insights at appropriate moments in later chapters. In this way, we balance narrative description with explanation, the broad sweep of North American prehistory with more descriptive concerns.

I strongly believe, however, that North American prehistory must be interpreted in terms not only of world prehistory, but also in the context of later world history. It is for this reason that the closing chapter of the book examines the archaeology of post-contact North America, some of the catastrophic cultural changes that overtook native American societies after European exploration and settlement. We have tended to be isolationist in our perspectives on prehistoric North America, and I hope this book helps counteract such intellectual tendencies.

Much North American archaeology is now carried out under the general guise of what is commonly called "Cultural Resource Management" (CRM). I make no attempt to describe the approaches or history of this kind of archaeology here, nor to critique it. These are tasks more appropriate for a more specialized volume. CRM has resulted, however, in the creation of an enormous "grey literature" on North American archaeology. This literature is commonly mimeographed or desktop-published for limited distribution, sometimes even for confidential record. As a consequence, much vital new evidence is effectively lost to the wider archaeological community, or available only to a narrow coterie of local fieldworkers. Few of these reports are available to a wider audience, let alone the scholarly community as a whole — who are often simply unaware of them. I am acutely conscious that there may be inaccuracies in the book as a result, through no fault of my own.

I have carefully avoided using unpublished data in this book, unless, of course, I have the written permission of the excavator to do so. Unpublished data is unverified in the scientific eye, and I have no option but to omit it here. *It must be stressed, therefore, that this book is written from published sources only*, not from verbal or conference reports, or unavailable grey literature. This reflects the reality of archaeology in the public arena, even if a mass of unpublished data contradicts the published record. No responsible chronicler of prehistory can do otherwise. Effectively the database of North American archaeology available to the public, or any archaeologist, is tragically, and unnecessarily, incomplete because of dilatory publication and limited circulation of many field reports.

Our story is very incomplete, tantalizingly so, at a time when North America's past is under siege from collectors, looters, and the ravages of industrial civilization. Even unprecedented tourist traffic is taking its toll of archaeological sites. As I hope this book shows, the archaeological record of prehistoric North America is a fascinating chronicle of brilliant human achievement. Please, dear reader, do all you can to discourage collecting and looting, to convince everyone that this record is precious, finite, and worth preserving! It would be a great tragedy if our grandchildren cursed us roundly for letting it vanish. There is a real chance they will do so.

Acknowledgments

Dozens of colleagues have assisted with this book, in the field, in museums, libraries, and university departments, even on the shores of the Arctic Ocean and in hot pools along Idaho rivers. It is impossible to thank all of them individually. I only hope they find the end-product of these deliberations worthwhile. This book is immeasurably better as a result of everyone's help, and I am deeply grateful.

I am indebted, too, to the many friends who reviewed all, or portions of, the draft manuscript. They were generous with opinions, insights, and trenchant criticism. Among the many reviewers were Douglas Bamforth, Cindy Bettison, Jefferson Chapman, Linda Cordell, Dale Croes, Michael Glassow, Michael Jochim, John Johnson, Jack Lobdell, Allen McCartney, Robert McGhee, George Michaels, James O'Connell, Terry Rudolf, Vincas Steponaitis, and William Turnbaugh. Thank you, one and all!

Lastly, a word of thanks and appreciation to my colleagues at Santa Barbara, who have been a constant source of intellectual stimulation and ideas for more than twenty years. I value our association more than I can say.

Santa Barbara, California

BRIAN FAGAN

A Note on Radiocarbon Dates

Until very recently, few North American archaeologists quoted radiocarbon dates calibrated with the tree-ring chronology. For this reason, all radiocarbon dates quoted in this book are radiocarbon ages, except where otherwise specified. Calibrated chronologies are quoted in special columns in chronological tables.

For convenience, the following calibration table is provided, based on commonly used data in Jeffrey Klein, J. C. Lerman, P. E. Damon, and E. K. Ralph, "Calibration of Radiocarbon Dates: Tables Based on the Consensus Data of the Workshop on Calibrating the Radiocarbon Time Scale," *Radiocarbon*, 1982, 24 (2) : 103-149.

Radiocarbon Date Calibration Table

Radiocarbon Age	*Calibrated Age Range*
AD 1500	AD 1300 to 1515
1000	870 to 1230
500	265 to 640
1	175 BC to AD 235
500 BC	820 to 400
1000	1530 to 905
1500	2345 to 1660
2000	2830 to 2305
2500	3505 to 2925
3000	3950 to 3640
3500	4545 to 3960
4000	5235 to 4575
4500	5705 to 5205
5000	6285 to 5445
Before 5500	Outside accurate calibration range

PART ONE

BACKGROUND

"None of the dead can rise up and answer our questions. But from all that they have left behind, their imperishable or slowly dissolving gear, we may perhaps hear voices, 'which are now only able to whisper, when everything else has become silent,' to quote Linnaeus."

BJÖRN KURTEN
How to Deep-Freeze a Mammoth (1984)

CHAPTER 1

DISCOVERY

In about the year AD 982 (the exact date is disputed), Norseman Eirik Thorvaldsson the Red sailed west from Iceland to explore the mysterious lands that sometimes appeared distantly on the far horizon when the winds blew from the north. Three years later, he and his men returned with glowing tales of a fertile, uninhabited land where fish were plentiful and the grazing grass lush and green. Eirik named it the Green Land, a name retained to this day.

Eirik persuaded 25 shiploads of settlers to sail for Greenland in 986. They founded tiny, remote Brattahlid in the southwest, and the so-called Western Settlement at Godthaab some 400 miles (644 km) to the north. For centuries, these tiny hamlets were bases for Norse wanderings far to the north, among ice-bound fjords and islands on the fringes of the Arctic Ocean, and west 186 miles (300 km) across the Davis Strait to Baffin Island, Labrador, and beyond.

The restless and adventurous Greenlanders farmed, kept cattle and sheep, fished, and were skilled hunters who took game on land and sea. Above all, they were seamen, who explored every nook and cranny of southwestern Greenland. Very early on, it seems, bold young men ventured far north toward the arctic ice, and across the Davis Strait to the *Ubygdir*, "the unpeopled tracts," new lands beyond the western horizon.

Only the faintest records of these western voyages have come down through the centuries. They survive in two fragmentary Icelandic sagas, often called the Vinland Sagas, written at least 200 years later. *The Saga of the Greenlanders* and *The Saga of Eirik the Red* are tantalizingly vague and contradictory accounts of extraordinary voyages. Unfortunately, it is almost impossible to separate historical fact from fantasy, geographical information from vague description written and copied several times over (Wahlgren, 1986).

The Saga of the Greenlanders tells how a young merchant named Bjarni Herjolfsson comes home to Iceland from Norway with a full cargo. He finds that his father has moved to Greenland with Eirik the Red, sets out to visit him, but the voyagers become lost in a wilderness of North Atlantic fog. Days or weeks later, they encounter a low, forested coast, which faces east. Bjarni realizes that this cannot be Greenland, so he turns north, sights more forested land a few days later, then an island with mountains and glaciers. Herjolfsson turns east, sails across Davis Strait, and reaches Greenland safely.

(Opposite) Routes of the early European explorers in and around North America.

Perhaps some 15 years later, in the 990s, Leif Eiriksson, son of Eirik the Red, sets out on a journey of exploration to the west. He sails across to the icy island that was Bjarni's last landfall, then voyages southward until he is well below the latitude of southern Greenland. Eiriksson and his 35 followers winter in a sheltered location where they are amazed and delighted to find wild grapes and grapevines growing. They survive an unusually mild winter, explore the countryside, load up with timber and return home to Greenland. Leif Eiriksson names the new lands: *Helluland*, "Slabrock Land," perhaps Baffin Island and northern Labrador, *Markland*, "Forest Land," probably central Labrador and Newfoundland, and *Vinland*, "Wineland," to the south, whose location is a matter of vigorous controversy. In a meticulous analysis of the sagas, Erik Wahlgren (1986) has argued persuasively that Eiriksson wintered over somewhere near Passamaquoddy Bay, close to the border between Maine and New Brunswick. The grapes that so enraptured his men were wild grapevines that are common in New England. Others believe, on the basis of a 16th-century Icelandic chart, that Vinland was Newfoundland, and that Eiriksson simply embellished his account with wild grapes to encourage prospective settlement (McGhee, 1984).

Leif Eiriksson never returned to Vinland. His brother Thorvald followed in his footsteps, mounting an expedition that lasted two years. He appears to have explored the Bay of Fundy, was killed in a clash with local people, and buried there. A visiting Icelandic merchant named Thorfinn Karlsefni was next in Vinland. He took a 60-person expedition back to Leif's winter settlement and traded with some visiting Indians. There was fighting and men perished on both sides. After two winters, Karlsefni sailed back to Greenland, probably sometime around 1012. More sporadic and unrecorded Norse voyages to Labrador probably ensued in the following three centuries, ventures in search of timber, which was in short supply in Greenland (McGhee, 1984).

Norse Settlement in North America

Archaeologists have searched diligently for traces of Viking settlement in North America. There have been the usual archaeological fantasies — stones inscribed with Norse runic script and mysterious towers in New England and the celebrated Kensington Stone discovered in Minnesota in 1898. None stand up to scholarly scrutiny (Wahlgren, 1986).

The logical place for such sites would be Labrador or Newfoundland, and it is at L'Anse aux Meadows in northern Newfoundland that the only known trace of Norse settlement has come to light. Helge Ingstad and Anne Stine discovered the remains of eight sod-walled structures on a terrace overlooking a shallow bay (Ingstad, 1977; 1985). These turf houses contained Norse artifacts such as a spindle whorl and a needle hone. One of the houses was too long to have been covered by a single roof. It consisted of several dwellings built together, perhaps forming a kind of sleeping hall. The settlement had a work shed, a smithy situated well away from the houses, and a possible bath house, also four turf boat sheds, perhaps once roofed with sod-covered rafters or branches. There are signs of both earlier and later native American settlement on the site.

L'Anse aux Meadows, in northern Newfoundland. (Above left) Aerial photograph of the marine terrace at Epaves Bay, showing partially excavated house-sites. (Above right) Layout of the site: A-D, houses; E, work shed; F, large house; v, natural deposit of iron ore; w, charcoal kiln; x, forge; y, boat sheds; z, cooking pits. (Left) Three sod houses reconstructed by Parks Canada. One is a long-house, others a small dwelling and a workshop. The reconstructions are based on archaeological data and information from other Viking sites.

L'Anse aux Meadows is a shallow bay, but a site with one major advantage — ample grazing for cattle. It lies at a strategic point, surrounded by water on three sides, an excellent base for exploring the St Lawrence Valley, if such a Norse enterprise was ever contemplated. Radiocarbon dates from the dwellings date the settlement to about AD 1000, but the precise identity of the builders is unknown.

No other indisputable traces of Norse settlement have come to light in North America. A Norwegian penny dating to between AD1065 and 1080 was found at the Goddard site on the coast of Maine's Penobscot Bay. As far as can be established, this penny reached the site during the 12th or 13th centuries, probably as a result of indirect trading contacts with Inuit people far to the north (McGhee, 1984).[1] Some disputed long-house foundations on Ungava Bay, across Davis Strait from Brattahlid, are almost certainly of Inuit manufacture, and not the work of Norsemen.

As early as the 12th century, Norsemen had sporadic contacts with Inuit groups living in the Canadian Archipelago and along the western

---

[1]For the purposes of this book, the term Eskimo is used to refer to Alaskan maritime peoples, while Inuit is used for their Canadian Arctic relatives.

Clues to a Norse presence in the High Arctic. (Above) Wooden figurine of a Norseman found in a Thule (Inuit) house at Okivilialuk. (Above right) Fragment of Norse woollen cloth from Skraeling Island.

Greenland coast, in the Nordrsetur (the central west coast), the area around Disko Bay, and probably much further north (McGhee, 1984). A scatter of Norse artifacts have come from Inuit settlements in the High Arctic — especially from the Ellesmere Island area. These include non-Inuit copper and iron fragments, pieces of woollen cloth, chain mail, and carpenters' tools, also boat nails and rivets, even carvings that give impressions of Norsemen. There are Norse stone cairns, some reworked bottom sections of casks, and a single runic inscription from Kingiqtorsoaq high on Greenland's western coast, probably dating to 24 April 1333.

The Norsemen called the Inuit Skraelings. "They possess no iron, but use walrus tusk for missiles and sharpened stones instead of knives," we learn from the *History of Greenland*, a work based on a 13th-century manuscript (McGhee, 1984). Contacts between Norse and Inuit were probably sporadic, the result of summer bear- and walrus-hunting expeditions far to the north. Walrus ivory was the medium in which Greenlanders paid their annual tithe to the church in distant Norway, on some occasions at least 400 tusks annually, far more than could be obtained around the Greenland settlements.

As far as we can tell, the contacts between Inuit and Norse were sometimes friendly, occasionally violent, apparently rarely prolonged. In all probability, the Norse came in touch with both Inuit and American Indians, the latter Beothuk, Algonquian-speakers who were summer visitors to the Labrador coast and Newfoundland (McGhee, 1984; for archaeology, see Chapter 21). Norse artifacts have come from as far afield as the western shores of Hudson Bay and latitude 79°N, 500 miles (819 km) north of the Kingiqtorsoaq rune stone. That is not to say that the Norse themselves actually traveled this widely, for many prized exotica may have passed along Inuit barter networks.

However, the Norse did not cononize North America. In AD 1000, Europe was not ready to, or capable of, settling the lands to the west. The tough and resourceful Norsemen could survive on Greenland coasts. However, they lacked the sheer numbers and the resources to expand and maintain pioneer settlements, to confront and compete with much larger indigenous populations. Nor were there strong motives for colonization — no religious persecution at home, no promise of great wealth to attract the greedy adventurer. Eventually, even Greenland proved beyond their capabilities. Norse civilization survived there until around 1500, progressively debilitated by increasing arctic cold that brought Inuit hunters further south, by economic deprivation and competition for game resources, and perhaps by declining birth rates and sheer cultural isolation from the homeland. There were occasional hostile visitors, too, perhaps even some piracy, for Basque whalers from northern Spain had been sailing in Greenland waters since at least 1372.

Eventually, the Norsemen quietly withdrew, leaving two geographical legacies behind them for later explorers – the term "Skraeling" and two place names: Markland, a land of forests, and Promontorium Winlandiae, a land of vines — actually northern Newfoundland. Their epic journeys survived in European consciousness as hints of exotic peoples living at the very edge of the known world. "There are animals of such enormous size that the inhabitants of the inner islands use their bones and vertebrae in place of wood in constructing houses. They also use them for making clubs, darts, lances, knives, seats, ladders, and, in general, all things which elsewhere are made from wood ..." Thus did the great Arab geographer al-Idrisi write of the North Atlantic and its rich fisheries in his *Nuzhet al-Mushtaq*, written in about AD1150 (McGhee, 1984). Like the medieval geographers, al-Idrisi relied not only on first-hand experience, but travelers' accounts from every corner of the world. Perhaps, among these accounts, he heard vague stories of northern whale hunters from the far north. Were these "inhabitants of the inner islands" Inuit hunters, native Americans from the Canadian Arctic, living at the extreme edge of the known medieval world? If al-Idrisi was indeed writing of Inuit peoples from North America, the tales of their whalebone houses had probably reached him through many hands from Norse sources in Greenland and Iceland.

The first, fleeting contacts between Inuits, native Americans and Western voyagers did nothing to alter hunter-gatherer cultures that had been evolving in a vast, isolated continent for more than 12,000 years. Centuries were to pass before Westerners again voyaged along North American shores.

The Search for a Strait

On 12 October 1492, Christopher Columbus, Admiral of the Ocean Sea, sailing under the Spanish flag, set foot on San Salvador in the Bahamas. There he found naked people, "very well made, of very handsome bodies and very good faces." Columbus himself believed he had found the outlying islands of east Asia, and called the inhabitants of the new lands "Indios," Indians. The Admiral's explorations brought a torrent of settlers to the Caribbean, settlers who came to "serve God and get rich." They soon encountered an astounding diversity of different peoples — simple hunters, village farmers, and magnificent civilizations like that of the Aztecs of highland Mexico. When Hernan Cortés and his soldiers gazed down on the great Aztec capital at Tenochtitlán in the Valley of Mexico in 1519, they marveled at a gold-laden civilization that rivaled those of Christendom in its magnificence.

Only seven years after Columbus' death in 1506, conquistador Vasco Nuñez de Balboa trekked across Central America and gazed on the Pacific. The Indies were not part of China at all, but what "we may rightly call a New World more densely peopled and abounding in animals than Europe, or Asia, or Africa." For years afterward, Europeans had but two ambitions in the New World — to find another gold-rich civilization, and a navigable strait to China.

Just as the last Norse colonists vanished in southern Greenland, Genoese-born John Cabot sailed west from Bristol, England, in search of a short, northern route to the Indies (Morison, 1971). The *Mathew* sailed in 1496, made landfall on Newfoundland, coasted down the west coast, and discovered the rich cod fisheries of the Grand Banks. Cabot encountered no human beings, but observed snares and nets, presumably belonging to Beothuk groups.

Two years later, Portuguese explorer Gaspar Corte Real sailed northwest from the Azores and made landfall on "a land that was very cool and with big trees," almost certainly Newfoundland. He returned the following year. His men kidnapped 57 Beothuk Indians, who "live together by fishing and hunting animals, in which the land abounds, the skins of which they use for garments and also make houses and boats thereof." The people lived in "rocky caves and thatched huts." After their first experience with Europeans, the Beothuk retreated to the interior and were very hostile to later visitors.

The next quarter-century saw the ice-bound and foggy north with its forested, rocky shores fade into relative oblivion. Only cod fishermen penetrated northern waters, people with little interest in exploration or the local inhabitants. Everything else was eclipsed by the brilliant discoveries that followed on Columbus far to the south. Then, in September 1522, Juan Sebastian del Caño in the ship *Vittoria* anchored at Seville in Spain, carrying just 18 of the 239 men who had set out on Ferdinand Magellan's epic circumnavigation of the globe. He had sailed into the Pacific through the stormy Magellan Strait at the southern tip of South America. Spanish and Portuguese explorers had now covered the entire east coast of the Americas from Florida to Patagonia, but had been unable to find any other strait north of Magellan's. On most maps of the time, Newfoundland floated in the North Atlantic, without any seeming link to the lands further south. Thirteen degrees of latitude from Maine to Georgia remained unexplored. Here, surely, lay either a strait to the west, or, even better, open sea that would carry European mariners to the "happy shores of Cathay."

In January 1524, the French gentleman explorer Giovanni da Verrazzano sailed west from Madeira (Morison, 1971). Instead of dropping down to the West Indies, he sailed well north of Columbus' track just over 30 years before. About 1 March, he made landfall at Cape Fear, North Carolina, then sailed up the east coast as far as Newfoundland. He encountered many friendly Indian groups along the way, mostly simple farmers and fishermen, wearing leaves or skins. The people of Casco Bay, Maine, apparently more familiar with foreigners, were less welcoming. "They used all signs of discourtesy and disdain, as was possible for any brute creature to invent, such as exhibiting their bare behinds and laughing immodestly." Verrazzano named this coast *Terra Onde di Mala Gente*, the "Land of Bad People," in revenge.

The prospect of a northern route to China brought Jacques Cartier, French Master Mariner of Saint-Malo in Brittany, to Newfoundland in April 1534. He returned to France five months later, having sailed completely around the Gulf of St Lawrence, where his men lived off great auk meat, salmon, and other fresh fish, goose eggs and wild strawberries. He was accompanied by two Huron Indian teenagers, a chief's sons, who were to act as guides on his second voyage. Cartier returned a year later to penetrate deeper into the Gulf. His Huron guests knew the great river well, all the way upstream to modern Quebec. It was, Cartier realized, a highway to the interior. "No man has been to the end, so far as they had say," he wrote.

Cartier made contact with Huron people living near modern Quebec, and arrived at Hochelaga, the site of present-day Montreal, on 2 October 1535. There, more than 1000 Indians greeted him, bringing gifts of corn bread and performing welcoming ceremonies. They lived in a fortified village surrounded by corn fields, partly situated on the grounds of today's McGill University. The fortifications consisted of palisades with two redoubts "garnished with rocks and stones, for defense and protection." There were 50 bark and wood houses inside, each with several rooms and a central fireplace, grouped around a central plaza. The people were in a constant state of readiness, for their home was close to the militant Five Nations of the Iroquois, notorious for their sudden raids. Cartier was impressed by his friendly reception in what were the golden days of race relations along the St Lawrence. They were not to last. When Cartier returned in an abortive attempt to found a colony, the Huron were hostile, attacked his settlement, and killed at least 35 people. For more than a half-century, the Huron were left alone, as exploration and settlement faltered.

Raleigh's Virginia

On 27 April 1584, two ships slipped out of Plymouth, England, on a voyage of reconnaissance along the more southern coasts explored by Verrazzano 60 years earlier. Philip Amadas and Arthur Barlow sailed at the behest of Walter Raleigh, who held letters patent from Queen Elizabeth granting him permission to colonize an unspecified area of North America. Four months later, the two vessels anchored close to Nag's Head in present-day Virginia. They soon came in contact with the local Powhatan Indians, Algonqian-speakers, "very handsome, and goodly people," who entertained them royally (Morison, 1971). "The soil," Barlow wrote enthusiastically if mendaciously, "is the most plentifull, sweete, fruitfull and wholesome of all the world." All this was good publicity for prospective colonists and for royal ears. Queen Elizabeth I knighted Walter Raleigh and allowed him to name his prospective colony Virginia.

In April of the following year, Sir Richard Grenville led an expedition of five ships and about 500 men, including 108 prospective colonists, to Virginia. This time, Raleigh sent along a scientist, Thomas Hariot, an Oxford mathematician, and an artist, John White. The settlement was a complete failure, but Hariot and White had ample opportunity to visit several Indian settlements. White sketched the people and their villages with astounding, if romantic detail. Hariot's *Briefe and True Report of the New Found Land of Virginia* appeared in 1588. Illustrated with White's sketches, it became a basic source of information on American Indians for more than a century (Rountree, 1989) (illus. p. 22).

Despite later efforts, no permanent colony was established in Virginia until that at Jamestown on the Chesapeake in 1607. That effort succeeded both because of sustained economic support from England, and because the colonists exported tobacco back home. A year later, Samuel de Champlain established a colony at Quebec on the St Lawrence, 12 years before the Pilgrim Fathers landed at Plimoth in New England. The first two

The Algonquian village of Secotan in Virginia, sketched by John White in about 1585. A romanticized view of the American Indians that shows many details of daily life.

decades of the 17th century saw the era of permanent European colonization in North America finally begin – with catastrophic effects on the native peoples that lay in the white settlers' paths.

Spanish Explorations in the Southeast

A century earlier, however, the Spanish had tentatively explored North America from the south — from New Spain (Mexico) and the Caribbean. Not that this exploration had followed immediately upon the conquest of Mexico, for it took 10 years and innumerable military campaigns to subdue the Indian population of Central America. The lust for gold intensified as more and more territory was opened up to European exploitation. Vast land masses lay to the north of wealthy Mexico. Did these also contain fabulous riches? Applicants willing to lead expeditions into the unknown importuned the Spanish Crown for permission to find out (Fagan, 1977).

The first man to sail north from the Indies was a soldier named Ponce de Leon, who landed near present-day Palm Beach, Florida, in 1513 (Fagan, 1977; Silverberg, 1968). He was searching for the mythical "Fountain of Youth," that chroniclers insisted was to be found on an island north of Cuba. His search was fruitless, the country sandy and low-lying, the local inhabitants fierce and unfriendly. Six years later, Alonso Alvarez de Piñeda entered the Mississippi River estuary, where he spent six weeks. The area was quite densely populated, but devoid of gold.

The sinister and red-bearded Panfilo de Narvaez followed Piñeda north, but landed to the east, in what is now Tampa Bay. There his men obtained some gold objects that fired their greedy imaginations. Sending his vessels to find a better harbor, Narvaez set out to march west along the coast with 260 men, promptly losing touch with his ships. The soldiers constructed temporary boats, but these foundered off the mouth of the Mississippi. The last vessel was cast ashore off modern Galveston, Texas. Only a junior officer named Alvar Nuñez Cabeza de Vaca, two soldiers, and a black slave survived. The five men withstood incredible hardships, and walked all the way from Texas to New Spain. Their report gives little information on the country and its inhabitants, except for an impression of poverty-struck people living in a dry environment. Again, there were no signs of gold or great treasure.

In 1537, the wealthy conquistador Hernando de Soto came home to Spain after making a small fortune under Francisco Pizarro in Peru (Garcilaso de la Vega, 1951). He was restless for further adventure, and lobbied for the governorship of Cuba and Florida, which he obtained. By 1539 this remarkable adventurer had raised a force of 622 men and had landed in Tampa Bay. De Soto hoped to find a kingdom as wealthy as that of the Aztecs or Inca. His only objectives were gold, the acquisition of wealth, and colonization.

Tampa was unpromising. The local people lived in "a town of seven or eight houses, built of timber and covered with palm-leaves. The chief's house stood near the beach on a very high mount made by hand for defense; at the other end of the town was a temple, on top of which perched a wooden fowl with gilded eyes." The surrounding countryside was flat and swampy, and no metals were to be found.

De Soto set off through marshy terrain until he reached higher ground. His soldiers treated the local people brutally, burning villages, then seizing food stocks and adults as slaves. Eventually, the conquistadors reached the large settlement of Cofachiqui, where an important female chieftain greeted him in a shaded canoe. Apparently terrified of the Spaniards, she ordered that all yellow and white metals in her domains were to be laid before the foreigners. Large quantities of copper were forthcoming, also sheets of mica, which local artisans fashioned into fine ornaments. The Spaniards asked for freshwater pearls, but were told they were imported from far away. In desperation, the chieftain directed them to the "upper part of the town," where a temple covered the burial place of long dead chiefs and their relatives. The soldiers looted the burials. Some 350 lbs (158 kg) of discolored freshwater pearls were divided between them.

During their journey to Cofachiqui, the conquistadors had passed many abandoned villages, as if the local people had lived there for a long time. Three miles (4.8 km) from Cofachiqui lay Talomeco, a larger settlement with the usual artificial earthen mounds upon which a temple and the chief's house formerly stood. The temple was still standing, a structure over 100 ft (30 m) long and 40 ft (12 m) wide, with a steep roof of reeds and split cane adorned with sea shells. The Spaniards forced their way in and wondered at wooden statues mantled with pearls, at enormous bundles of skins and dyed cloth. There were caches of copper-bladed ceremonial weapons, battle axes and clubs, delicately inlaid bows and arrows, wooden and woven cane shields, all of the finest workmanship — but no gold.

The taciturn and inflexible De Soto was so obsessed with the yellow metal that he ordered his men westward over the Blue Ridge Mountains into what is today Tennessee. Hardships multiplied. Choctaw raiders

The brutality of this Spanish attack on a Florida Indian village in the 1590s recalls the harshness of De Soto's expedition half a century earlier.

attacked the party. More than 150 men perished in a counterattack to recover lost baggage. The conquistadors wintered near the Yazoo River in Mississippi, where they encountered "fine looking" Indians in a fleet of canoes that "appeared like a famous armada of galleys." Next spring, De Soto led his men through the Ozarks into eastern Oklahoma. There they heard stories of "many cattle," whose skins the local Indians gave them in abundance as bed covers. But they never set eyes on the bison themselves.

Finally, De Soto realized that the gold-laden kingdoms over the horizon were a fiction. He headed southeast toward the Gulf of Mexico. The journey was a harsh one, through unfriendly territory occupied by suspicious Indians. De Soto himself perished of fever, but half of the 622 men who had set out with him managed to reach Cuba.

De Soto's expedition put paid to any dreams of fabulous, golden kingdoms in the north. Apart from two abortive French expeditions to Florida in the 1560s, the Mississippi Valley and the Southeast with their elaborate chiefdoms were left in peace for over a century. By the time the 16th-century Spaniards encountered them, many large Indian settlements had been abandoned, as if the population had declined sharply. Some archaeologists believe this may have been the result of epidemics of exotic diseases like smallpox that spread across the interior long before the Indians had direct contact with Europeans (Ramenofsky, 1987). (This is a controversial subject, see Chapter 22.) The large earthworks built by some of these people were to puzzle white settlers and scholars for generations.

The French in Florida. (Above right) Chief Athore in 1564 shows French explorer René de Laudonnière a stone pillar erected by a previous French expedition two years before. The pillar (labeled "F" in the sketch map above left) bore the coat-of-arms of the King of France. The scene of friendship and harmony by artist Jacques le Moyne de Morgues may have been used to recruit emigrants to the New World.

The Seven Lost Cities of Cibola

When Alvar Nuñez Cabeza de Vaca reached Mexico City overland from Texas in 1536, his tales of a harsh and arid land to the north astounded the gold-hungry colonial government of New Spain. So greedy were they that they shrugged aside Vaca's tales of suffering. Ever since Cortés and Pizarro had plundered Mexico and Peru, there had been talk of the fabled Seven Cities of a mythical land named Cibola, cities founded as long ago as the 8th century by a legendary bishop from Lisbon (Fagan, 1977). Where, then, were these cities, if they were not to be found in Mexico or Peru?

Hawikuh pueblo, a Zuñi settlement in New Mexico, photographed in the late 19th century.

When Vaca returned with vague rumors of large towns to the north, towns crowded with Indians and rich in gold and silver, the authorities were goaded into action. The Viceroy of Mexico sent Franciscan friar Fray Marcos de Niza in search of the cities, a man said to have "great experience in the affairs of the Indians." He was accompanied by Esteban, the black slave who had traveled with Cabeza de Vaca as a guide. They were a curious pair: the sober priest and the jaunty, freed slave who journeyed in great style, dressed in ribbons and feathers, for he had acquired somewhat of a reputation as a sorcerer among the Indians.

The expedition was a disaster. Esteban explored far ahead of the main caravan, sending back optimistic messages along the way. After a 15-day desert crossing, his party arrived at a Zuñi pueblo in what is now New Mexico, only to be massacred by the inhabitants. Marcos claimed that he heard of the killings from a survivor, then traveled secretly within sight of the pueblo, where he gazed undetected at "a faire citie," with many houses "builded in order . . . all made of stone with divers stories, and flatte roofs, as farre as I could discerne." The people were light skinned, possessed "emeralds and other jewels," and used "vessels of gold and silver, for they have no other metal, whereof there is greater use and more abundance than in Peru."

As can be imagined, Marcos' report fueled the flames of gold lust when he returned to Mexico City with "more feare than vituals." The friar was a good storyteller, and embellished his report at every opportunity. In fact, historians are almost certain that he turned and ran, never penetrating much further north than the Gila River in southern Arizona, a long way from Zuñi country. Marcos' stories fell on fertile ground. In February 1540, Francisco Vasquez de Coronado, a competent young nobleman and royal courtier, led a much larger expedition in Marcos' footsteps: 225 horsemen, 60 foot soldiers, and a motley crowd of slaves and Indian allies marched north, with Fray Marcos as their guide (Fagan, 1977).

Coronado and his men found themselves traveling along Indian trails through harsh, dry country. Horses and men suffered greatly in the shimmering heat, but emerged from the desert within reach of six Zuñi pueblos. These were the "Seven Lost Cities," a disappointing sight to the conquistadors. "It is a small, crowded village," wrote Pedro de Castaneda, Coronado's chronicler, of Hawikuh pueblo, "looking as if it had been all crumpled up together. There are haciendas in New Spain which make a better appearance at a distance." Marcos' celebrated city was little more than a glorified village. Coronado routed the defenders in less than an hour. The hungry soldiers made a beeline for the storehouses, where they found "much corn and beans, and fowl." Of gold and precious stones there were no signs.

In the months that followed, Coronado explored much of the Southwest — without finding any gold. His men entered Hopi country, penetrated as far as the Grand Canyon, and visited Pecos Pueblo close to modern Santa Fe, a settlement so large it could field 500 warriors. The town "is square, situated on a rock, with a large court or yard in the middle, containing the steam rooms," reported Pedro de Castaneda. "The houses are all alike, four stories high. One can go over the top of the village without there being a street to hinder." The houses could be entered only by means of ladders from the roofs, with doors that led into the passages.

Conquistador Hernando de Alvarado was sent onto the plains that lay east of Pecos to investigate stories about strange animals like cows with hairy skins. Alvarado and his men were soon surrounded with enormous herds of bison, "the most monstrous thing in the way of animals that has ever been seen or read about." Later, Coronado himself ventured onto the plains and deep into Kansas, where he encountered Plains Indians who relied on bison for food, hunting them in game drives or at water holes.

Barely a hundred men marched into Mexico City in the fall of 1542, when the dispirited expedition returned home. There were only a handful of Indian blankets and turquoises, and a wealth of new geographical knowledge, to show for more than two years' arduous traveling. It was half a century before attempts were made to settle the arid, gold-less Southwest. Even then, the Spanish hold on these remote lands was tenuous at best, although Catholic missionaries and explorers had traveled widely through the region by the late 18th century.

"A Young People, Younger a Thousand Years..."

Columbus and his successors revealed a vast continent teeming with new forms of animal and plant life, and with a bewildering diversity of human societies both simple and complex (Fagan, 1987a). Who were these "Indians," exotic, feathered people that Columbus paraded before the Spanish court, people according to Pope Alexander VI "well disposed to embrace the Christian faith?" Where had these strange humans come from and why were they so diverse? Soon, Europeans back home could see a surprisingly wide variety of native Americans, shipped back by explorers, missionaries, and slavers. The Aztec nobles and acrobats from Mexico, who spellbound the Spanish Court in the 1520s, were a far cry from North Americans "clothid in beastys skinnys" who ate raw meat and had the manners of "brut bestis." In contrast, John White's Virginia Indians were depicted as friendly, noble-minded people, who did not abuse nature. The Inuit of the far north were apparently hardier. Martin Frobisher brought back a man and woman from Baffin Island in 1576. The hunter obligingly paddled his skin kayak on the River Avon near Bristol and shot ducks with his bow and arrow.

The 16th century saw a torrent of speculation about the origins of the American Indians, speculations about ancient Carthaginian migrations, about the Ten Lost Tribes of Israel exiled by Assyrian King Shalmaneser in 721 BC (Wauchope, 1972). There were more serious observers, too, like the celebrated Dominican Friar Bartolomé de las Casas, a champion of the Indians, who wrote that "there is not a great argument that the people of these islands and continent are very ancient." But he, and other historically minded religious scholars, turned to the only historical sources available to them — the Scriptures. They believed that all American Indians were related to familiar ancient societies in the Scriptures, like the Tartars, Scythians, and biblical Hebrews.

The Elizabethan philosopher Francis Bacon, on the other hand, marveled "at the thin population of America, for you must accept your inhabitants of America as a young people: younger a thousand years, at least, than the rest of the world."

An Inuit man captured by explorer Martin Frobisher in 1576.

Whatever their antiquity, everyone agreed that the Indians had come from the Garden of Eden. How, then, had they reached the Americas? Had they sailed across a vast ocean, or had they walked? Siberia was still a geographical blank in the 16th century, the Bering Strait between Asia and Alaska unknown. In 1589, Jesuit missionary José de Acosta published a remarkable work, his famous *Historia Natural y Moral de las Indias* (Fagan, 1987a; Willey and Sabloff, 1980). It was entirely possible, he wrote, that "men came to the Indies driven unwittingly by the wind." However, he believed that most of the Indians had reached the New World in the same manner as the unfamiliar beasts that abounded in the Americas – by land. He theorized that small groups of "savage hunters driven from their homelands by starvation or some other hardship" had taken an overland route through Asia to their present home. There were, he argued, "only short stretches of navigation" involved. At first, Acosta wrote, only a few Indians settled in the Americas. But they were successful. Their descendants developed not only agriculture, but elaborate states like those of the Aztecs and Inca. Acosta calculated that first settlement had taken place as much as 2000 years before the Conquest of Mexico.

It was to be a century and a half before Russian explorer Vitus Bering sailed through the Bering Strait in 1728, and seven decades after that before North American archaeology was born. By that time, Western explorers had penetrated all the oceans, and encountered a myriad of unfamiliar human societies on remote shores. The Age of Enlightenment had made science fashionable in the intellectual circles of 18th-century Europe. Captain James Cook had mapped much of the Pacific, and the Russian scientist Pfefferkorn was able to state in 1794 that "it is almost certain that the first inhabitants of America really came by way of the strait." Not that such sober observations quenched the wild fire of speculations about the ancient Americans. They were the background to the first archaeological researches in North America.

Further Reading

Fagan, Brian M. 1977. *Elusive Treasure*. Charles Scribners, New York.
A popular account of early archaeological research in North and Central America. Copiously illustrated.
Morison, Samuel Eliot. 1971. *The Discovery of America. Volume 1: The Northern Voyages*. Oxford University Press, New York.
This is the definitive account of early explorations of the North American shoreline by a master of historical analysis and narrative.
Sabloff, Jeremy A. and Willey, Gordon R. 1980. *A History of American Archaeology*. Freeman, San Francisco. 2nd ed.
The standard work on the history of American archaeology for the serious student. Lavish illustrations and comprehensive bibliography.
Wahlgren, Erik. 1986. *The Vikings and America*. Thames and Hudson, London and New York.
An authoritative, closely argued essay on the Viking exploration of North America.

CHAPTER 2

CULTURE HISTORY AND NORTH AMERICAN ARCHAEOLOGY

When Thomas Jefferson retired to his Virginia estate in 1791, he settled down to complete a long questionnaire from the French Government, seeking information on his home state. What plants and animals flourished in Virginia? What minerals, products, and industries were to be found? What was known of the native inhabitants? His famous *Notes on the State of Virginia* was the result, a lengthy treatise that discussed, among other things, the "aborigines," and the first archaeological investigation in the United States (Jefferson, 1797).

The First Excavation
1782

Jefferson was an influential member of Philadelphia's coffee house society, one of many intellectuals who speculated about American Indian life, about abandoned towns and earthworks said to exist out west. He was a friend of the celebrated botanist William Bartram, who traveled widely through the Southeast in the 1770s, through country still densely inhabited by Indian tribes. The Cherokee, Bartram noted, built their meeting houses on large artificial mounds, as much as 20 ft (6 m) high. They did not build these earthworks, for they found them "in the same condition as they now appear." Bartram thought the mounds were the work of Biblical peoples (Fagan, 1977) .

Bartram was by no means the only person theorizing about the mounds. Many travelers believed that the Indians were incapable of building such elaborate earthworks. Rather, they theorized, Toltec Indians from Mexico had erected them before migrating southward. Others argued for Welshmen, for some lost race that had occupied North America long before the Indians had arrived.

Jefferson listened to these hypotheses and resolved quietly to test them by digging into a small mound by the Rivanna River. His trenches revealed layers of burials and artifacts of Indian origin, separated by levels of stones and earth. Jefferson observed the strata with care, and remarked: "That they were repositories of the dead, has been obvious to all; but on what occasion constructed, was a matter of doubt." This was probably the first stratigraphic excavation anywhere, and was unique not only for its time but for generations afterward (Willey and Sabloff, 1980).

The moundbuilder controversy. The Great Serpent Mound, Adams County, Ohio (above), was one of the many mounds accurately mapped for the first time by Ephraim Squier (below) and his colleague Edwin Davis in the late 1840s. But they continued to believe in a mythical race of moundbuilders.

The Myth of the Moundbuilders
1770s to 1894

After 1815, a flood of settlers poured over the Alleghenies, clearing farmland and exposing mounds, enclosures, and other exotic earthworks. The land itself was largely depopulated, the result, probably, of devastating 16th- and 17th-century epidemics of exotic European diseases. The newcomers were convinced that golden treasure lay in the mounds, and dug for their fortunes. They found no gold, but dozens of skeletons and exotic artifacts such as carved soapstone pipes, mica silhouettes of birds and animals, and fine copper ornaments and artifacts. The finds caused an intellectual furor, a wave of sentiment for theories of a "lost race" of white Moundbuilders, who had once settled and conquered the fertile lands of the Midwest. Such wild theories appealed to the romantically inclined, to people who believed that American Indians were incapable of building anything as elaborate as a burial mound.

Meanwhile, a few scholars and antiquarians set out to acquire more information about the earthworks and their builders. Caleb Atwater, the postmaster of Circleville, Ohio, spent his ample leisure time exploring the mounds near his home town and described them in a two-part paper published in 1820 that separated observation from pure speculation. Atwater's descriptions were accurate enough, but his theories a product of his time: migrating Hindus from India had built the mounds, then moved on to Mexico (Atwater, 1820; Willey and Sabloff, 1980). Only a few observers, like Dr James McCulloh, an armchair antiquarian, argued that the Indians were the Moundbuilders. By and large, their findings were ignored.

In 1839, a pioneer physical anthropologist, Samuel Morton, published his famous *Crania Americana*, in which he analyzed eight Moundbuilder skulls and compared them with modern Indian crania. He stated that they represented but a single race, even if he distinguished between "Toltecs" and the "Barbarous" on purely cultural grounds (Morton, 1839).

Just under a quarter-century after Caleb Atwater's report appeared, two Ohio antiquarians, E.G.Squier and E.H.Davis, completed one of the first scientific monographs published by the newly founded Smithsonian Institution. *Ancient Monuments of the Mississippi* was a comprehensive, descriptive work, with plans so accurate that they are still used today (Squier and Davis, 1848). Squier and Davis' descriptive research was remarkable for the time, but they still referred to the "great race of Moundbuilders," and believed that the American Indians and their ancestors were incapable of building the earthworks.

Although most antiquarians believed in exotic moundbuilders, a growing minority of influential scientists thought otherwise. Foremost among them was Samuel Haven, the Librarian of the American Antiquarian Society. In 1856, Haven published a remarkable essay, *Archaeology of the United States*, in which he surveyed everything that was known about the prehistory of North America, and the origins of the American Indian. A judicious and dispassionate observer, Haven set the tone for all future scholarly enquiry into the native Americans. His conclusions were admirably cautious. "We desire to stop where evidence ceases," he stated at the outset. The Indians were of high antiquity, he

The moundbuilder controversy. Three scientists, Samuel Haven (below left), John Wesley Powell (below center), and Cyrus Thomas (below right), were among those instrumental in proving beyond doubt that the American Indians themselves had built mounds such as those at Marietta, Ohio (left, a sketch by Squier and Davis).

Frederick W. Putnam (far right) and other archaeologists photographed on a mound near Fair Grounds, Chillicothe, Ohio, in 1883. Putnam has been called the "professionalizer of American archaeology" for his work as an excavator, and as an administrator or founding father of several North American museums and departments of anthropology.

believed. "All their characteristic affinities are found in the early conditions of Asiatic races," he wrote. Haven set the stage for a new era of systematic, much more scientific, research into the North American past.

The Moundbuilder controversy dragged on from the 1850s into the late 1890s, kept alive by continual amateur diggings and by the publication of often bizarre tomes that added new, and ever more offbeat, chapters to the ancient saga (Silverberg, 1968). Meanwhile, however, professional science grew hand in hand with the establishment of new universities and colleges, and thanks to the increasing influence of government agencies such as the US Geological Survey. Both the Survey and Harvard University's Peabody Museum played an important role in the controversies surrounding Stone Age settlement in North America (Fagan, 1987a).

The Smithsonian Institution's Bureau of Ethnology was founded in 1879, thanks to the lobbying of John Wesley Powell, the first man to traverse the Grand Canyon by boat. The Bureau was founded specifically to recover rapidly vanishing information about American Indian peoples in the far west. Under Powell's Directorship, it also embarked on ambitious archaeological programs on a broad geographical scale (Silverberg, 1968; Judd, 1954).

Powell moved into Moundbuilder studies because Congress insisted in 1881 that he spend the then large sum of $5000 annually on mound investigation. Forced to sponsor archaeological research, he appointed Cyrus Thomas, an entomologist from Illinois, to head a Division of Mound Exploration in 1882. At first Thomas believed in a "separate Moundbuilder race," but fortunately, he realized that he would have to embark on an extensive campaign of survey and excavation, both to support his hypothesis, and to save hundreds of earthworks from imminent destruction. He and his assistants fanned out over the Midwest, surveying, digging, studying artifacts, and making plans of sites large and small. The steady flow of data from the excavations soon convinced Thomas that the mounds were the work not of a "separate race," but of prehistoric Indians, the ancestors of modern populations. His monumental report appeared in the 12th *Annual Report* of the Bureau of Ethnology in 1894, a description of hundreds of sites, thousands of artifacts, and a pioneering effort at studying the prehistoric past by working back from known modern sites and artifacts as a basis for comparison with earlier cultures.

With the publication of Thomas' great work, every serious scholar of North American prehistory accepted that the moundbuilders were native Americans. All modern research into these peoples is based on this fact.

First Descriptive Efforts
1874 to 1914

The 40 years between 1874 and 1914 saw the first systematic descriptions of prehistoric pottery styles in eastern North America, early attempts to define the criteria for establishing the date of the first Americans (Chapter 4), and stratigraphic excavations in prehistoric shell middens on the East Coast and by the German-trained archaeologist Max Uhle along the California coast. As early as 1880, Canadian geologist John Dawson of McGill University in Montreal attempted to link prehistoric artifacts with the Huron village of Hochelaga, visited and described by Jacques Cartier in 1535 (Willey and Sabloff, 1980).

Such research stemmed from the logical subdivision of anthropology into three subdisciplines – ethnography (today part of cultural anthropology), which dealt with living peoples, physical anthropology, which studied their biology, and archaeology, the study of the ancient native Americans. Close links between archaeology and cultural anthropology were forged by John Wesley Powell at the Smithsonian from the very beginning. Cyrus Thomas' work on the eastern mounds with its rich finds of artifacts and human remains confirmed the importance of a joint anthropological and archaeological approach to the prehistory of the American Indian. This perspective, soon taught at Harvard, Pennsylvania, and Berkeley, was in sharp contrast to European approaches, where the three disciplines of anthropology developed separately and archaeology was thought of as an extension of history. At the time, there was some scholarly logic in this, for American archaeologists were investigating the prehistory of non-Western peoples, not of the Romans and indigenous Europeans who formed a historical continuity with the modern inhabitants of that region of the Old World (Willey and Sabloff, 1980).

This close association with cultural anthropology has been a powerful catalyst for North American archaeology, providing a rich reservoir of modern analogies for interpreting the archaeological record, and offering chances to work back from the known present into the unknown past. It has also offered theoretical perspectives on prehistoric times that are of great benefit to a discipline that is an unrivaled way of examining and interpreting human cultural change over very long periods of time indeed.

For most of the late 19th century, the doctrines of biological and social evolution were extremely fashionable in anthropological circles. In an era when human progress was a watchword, anthropologists theorized that human societies everywhere had passed through successive stages of universal evolution. These theories culminated in the brilliant researches of lawyer turned anthropologist Lewis Henry Morgan. Morgan (1877) proposed no less than nine stages of linear social evolution, beginning with simple Savagery, and progressing from there through successive stages of Barbarism, culminating in Civilization. Morgan's unilinear evolutionary scheme proved popular, but was soon abandoned, as it was far too simplistic to explain the great diversity of American Indian groups.

Cushing, Bandelier and the Southwestern Pueblos

The earliest archaeological investigations in the west were at the hands of government scientists or members of private expeditions, often surveyors who came across abandoned pueblos and dry caves where surprisingly well-preserved prehistoric artifacts were to be found. Serious research began with two remarkable pioneers, Smithsonian anthropologist Frank Cushing, and Adolph Bandelier, a Swiss-born mine engineer who became an anthropologist.

Frank Cushing arrived at Zuñi pueblo in 1879, intending to stay for three weeks. He stayed for four-and-a-half years, learnt to speak the Zuñi dialect fluently, and, through participant observation, recorded an extraordinary wealth of information about pueblo life. Cushing was not an archaeologist, but he collected a rich lode of Zuñi oral tradition about earlier times that made him realize that the best way to study prehistoric times was by working back from the present into the past (Cushing, 1882-83).

Adolph Bandelier arrived in the Southwest in 1880. A mine administrator and amateur anthropologist, Bandelier had come under the influence of Lewis Henry Morgan, who obtained a grant for him to work in the west. For 12 years, he wandered from pueblo to pueblo on a mule, carrying all his worldly possessions in a saddle bag. At pueblos like Pecos, he recorded centuries of Southwestern history, oral traditions and local histories that reached back into prehistory. He soon realized that the way to study early pueblo history was to work back in time, "from the known to the unknown, step by step" (Bandelier, 1884).

(Above) Frank Cushing: Zuñi war chief and US Government ethnographer. Cushing was a pioneer of participant observation in anthropology and became famous for his descriptions of Zuñi life.

(Right) A scene of Zuñi life: decorating pottery, from Cushing's My Adventures in Zuñi. *During this process "no laughing, music, whistling, or other unnecessary noises were indulged in," he wrote. The potters believed the sound would enter the clay and cause the vessel to shatter when fired.*

Franz Boas and "Historical Particularism"

By the 1890s, evolutionism was in considerable disrepute among many anthropologists, partly because of slavish insistence on Morgan-like universal stages, and also because of extravagant claims by its proponents. The result was a strong reaction against any form of evolutionary theory, especially simplistic, linear schemes of human progress. A new generation of anthropologists led by the great fieldworker Franz Boas insisted on factual evidence, data on cultural traits collected from systematic field investigation. Boas and his many students devoted years to the meticulous collection of cultural data throughout North America, founding a school of American anthropology known as "Historical Particularism." The result was a stifling intellectual climate, where any form of search for cultural change was a low priority. The effects on North American archaeology were serious.

On the face of it, one might have expected archaeologists to resist this current of anti-evolutionism. However, there were compelling reasons not to do so. In the first place, everyone was convinced that the American Indians had settled in their homeland only a relatively short time ago. Under the strong guidance of the strong-willed, indeed authoritarian, personalities of archaeologist William Henry Holmes and physical anthropologist Ales Hrdlička at the Smithsonian, almost every prehistorian accepted that the earliest human settlement of the New World had taken place no more than about 4000 years ago (Meltzer, 1983). Thus, there had been little time for significant cultural change.

Stratigraphic observation was also in its infancy, for few North American sites were thought to have multiple layers. Nor had North American scholars developed the excavation or analytical techniques to observe cumulative, small changes in human culture over even short periods of time. In brief, archaeologists were hardly in a position to rebut the historical particularists (Willey and Sabloff, 1980). And when they started to use stratigraphic techniques and the Direct Historical Method, they began to develop their own conceptual frameworks quite separately from cultural anthropology.

William Henry Holmes in an ocean of "paleoliths," c.1890. This carpet of flaked stone was, Holmes discovered, a recent Indian quarry, like many of the supposed ancient chipping sites uncovered in the late 19th century.

Ales Hrdlička investigates a prehistoric skull.

The Birth of Culture History
1914 to 1940

Culture history, the reconstruction of the prehistoric past, is based on two fundamental principles that were enumerated in the early years of this century. The first was inductive research methods, the development of generalizations about a research problem that are based on numerous specific observations. The second was what is called a "normative" view of culture. This is the notion that abstract rules govern what cultures consider to be normal behavior. The normative view is a descriptive approach to culture, which describes it during one long time period or throughout time. Archaeologists base all culture history on the assumption that surviving artifacts, such as potsherds, display stylistic and other changes that represent the changing norms of human behavior throughout time. Culture history resulted from careful stratigraphic observation, meticulous artifact classifications and orderings, and accurate chronologies (Fagan, 1987b). The culture-historical approach resulted in a descriptive outline of North American prehistory in time and space that took generations to assemble.

Stratigraphic Observation was introduced to North American archaeology in about 1914 and came into universal use during the next two decades. This was the time when the principles not only of stratigraphic observation, but also of seriation (artifact ordering in a time sequence) became allied with artifact typology and classification. The result was the first culture-historical syntheses of major culture areas of North America.

Nils Nelson was a large, earthy Scandinavian archaeologist who was trained by the great anthropologist Alfred Kroeber at Berkeley. As a young man, he had visited French cave excavations and worked with eminent scholars like Hugo Obermaier and Henri Breuil, experiences that convinced him of the importance of stratigraphic excavation. Working for the American Museum of Natural History in 1914-16, young Nelson excavated in the Galisteo Basin area of New Mexico, an area where Bandelier and another pioneer, Edgar Hewett, were convinced that there had been "cultural transformations in prehistoric times." A series of excavations at San Marcos and other pueblos provided stratigraphic proof of different pottery styles, but Nelson's sequence was incomplete until he excavated the 10-ft (3-m) deep middens at San Cristobal. There he described a sequence of changing pottery styles, from black-and-white painted that was common in earlier levels to glazed, then painted-and-glazed forms (Nelson, 1916).

The Direct Historical Method. Nelson's Galisteo research was a major breakthrough, and a foundation of what became known as the Direct Historical Method, working from the present into the past. The first large-scale application of stratigraphic methods came with Alfred V. Kidder's classic excavations at Pecos pueblo (Kidder, 1924). Kidder had been trained at Harvard and had taken a course in field methods with Egyptologist G.A. Reisner, a leading excavator of the day. He had also traveled in the Near East and observed modern European excavation methods at first hand. These he now applied at Pecos after 1916, in the largest excavation so far conducted in North America, dissecting refuse

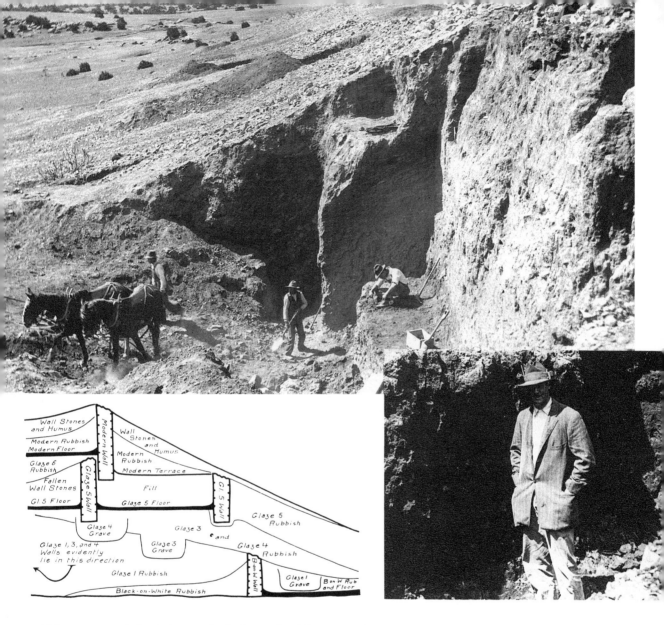

middens over 20ft (6m) deep at both the Fork Lightning and Pecos sites. Kidder excavated with careful controls, assembling selected potsherd samples at first, then digging further trenches with meticulous care. After several seasons of work, he constructed a stratigraphic sequence of pottery styles for each pueblo, confirming the general sequence from the Galisteo Basin, and ultimately creating a regional sequence for Southwestern prehistory (Kidder, 1924).

Thus was born a careful sequence of research strategies for developing culture histories that were to be applied by dozens of North American archaeologists in coming years – preliminary site survey, selection of criteria for ranking these sites in chronological order, then comparative study of these criteria, followed by a search for, and excavation of, stratified

Pecos excavations in 1916 with (inset) A.V. Kidder at the site, and his cross-section drawing of Pecos refuse stratigraphy with building walls and floors. Different ceramic styles found in the different layers are indicated by "Glaze 5," "Black-on-White," etc.

sites. Finally, more survey and additional excavations to confirm the results and refine cultural and stratigraphic findings.

The Direct Historical Method became even more formalized by important researches elsewhere in North America during the 1920s and 1930s. It was used in New York State as early as 1916 to relate prehistoric settlements to historic Iroquois villages. However, the greatest impetus came from excavations by W.D. Strong and Waldo Wedel in Nebraska (Strong, 1935, 1940; Wedel, 1938, 1961). These two archaeologists started with a rich lode of historical information collected by anthropologists and amateur historians. They excavated historic Pawnee sites, then went on to dig settlements from the contact period and from remoter prehistory. The results were extraordinary, for the application of the Direct Historical Method revealed dramatic cultural changes on the Plains, shifts from bison hunting on foot to horticulture in river valleys, then back to bison hunting again, this time on horseback. Strong's monograph *Nebraska Archaeology* became a model for such research in many areas of North America.

Classification. Typology and artifact classification were fundamental to the emerging culture history of North America. The first systematic attempts to classify prehistoric pottery were at the hands of William Holmes of the Bureau of Ethnology in the 1890s (Holmes, 1903). He worked on potsherds from mounds and other eastern sites, while early Southwestern archaeologists like Hewett and Nelson wrestled with different pottery types from their excavations in the Galisteo Basin and elsewhere. These early attempts at classification were basically descriptive taxonomy. As excavations in the Southwest introduced at least a degree of chronology into stratigraphic sequences, archaeologists were forced to refine their typologies to take account of change through time. Inevitably, since it was the most common artifact, the humble potsherd became the yardstick of classification, a kind of changing marker that was used to subdivide prehistoric times into ever more minute subdivisions (W. and H.S.Gladwin, 1931; Sayles, 1936).

The Pecos Classification. Kidder's Pecos excavations added much new data to Southwestern archaeology, and Kidder himself called a conference at the pueblo in 1927, where the leading archaeologists working in the area came together to develop a standardized classificatory scheme and chronology for the Southwest. From this, the first Pecos Conference – they are held annually to this day – emerged a chronological classification of Southwestern cultures that has survived, albeit in modified form, until today.

The earliest peoples identified in the Pecos classification were the "Basketmakers" of the Four Corners area, people who lived in pithouses and surface pueblos and were incipient farmers and hunters. There were two stages of Basketmaker culture, followed by five Pueblo periods, each distinguished by changes in architecture, community arrangement, pottery styles, and other artifacts. Pueblo IV and V straddled the first centuries of European contact and the transition from historical to modern Pueblo culture.

The Pecos classification was developed at a time when Southwestern chronology was still relatively imprecise. When more precise dates were forthcoming, it became apparent that the Pecos periods were better thought of as stages, which developed at different times in different local areas.

Furthermore, the classification was better suited to the northern Southwest than to areas further south.

The Gladwin Classification. In 1934, Harold and Winifred Gladwin proposed another kind of culture classification, this time, a framework based on three broad "roots," the major cultural regional subdivisions of the Southwest: Basketmaker (later to be called Anasazi), Mogollon, and Caddoan (later named Hohokam). Each root was divided into "stems" which were major geographical areas. For example, the Basketmaker root contained "San Juan" and "Playas." Stems were split into even smaller units known as "branches." Each branch delineated a culture area within a stem such as "Chaco" or "Kayenta." These branches were divided into "phases," and generally named after local geographic features. Phases were units, defined by comparing individual culture traits from different sealed levels at different archaeological sites. The Gladwin classification grouped archaeological cultures by using culture traits, linked in space and time by a branching scheme that was almost genetic in nature – the assumption was that everything had started from a single root, then branched outward in a gradual evolution of Southwestern culture.

Gordon Willey and Jeremy Sabloff (1980) refer to the Pecos classification as "Chronologic" and the Gladwin scheme as "Chronologic-Genetic," a fairly apt description. The two systems were by no means incompatible, for the Gladwin hierarchy was a regional and local one, and the Pecos classification a useful way of generalizing over the entire area.

The Midwestern Taxonomic System. While Gladwin was wrestling with roots and stems in the Southwest, a group of Midwestern archaeologists under the leadership of W.C. McKern was developing a classificatory scheme for eastern North America. This was the famous Midwestern Taxonomic System, sometimes called the McKern Classification (McKern, 1939).

Midwestern archaeologists grappled with very different problems from those in the Southwest, notably an apparent lack of stratified sites and much poorer conditions of preservation. However, they had access to enormous numbers of artifacts from every millennium of local prehistory, most of them without provenience, collected by private individuals and professional excavators alike.

The McKern scheme dealt not with time and space, but entirely with artifact classifications. Its architects assumed that formal similarities between artifact forms signified both cultural origins and cultural history. They proposed a taxonomic hierarchy that began with *components*, a unit of a culture complex that could be a site, or a distinct layer in a site. Several components were then grouped into a *focus*, components that shared high frequencies of similar culture traits. Foci were classified into *aspects*, broader groupings where there were still many culture traits in common. The highest levels in the McKern Classification were the *phase*, the *pattern*, and the *base*, all of them founded on increasingly more generalized cultural traits.

The Midwest Taxonomic System started off as just that — a taxonomic scheme, with no explicit chronological or spatial contexts at all. It was much criticized by Southeastern archaeologists, who had acquired a great deal of valuable time and space data during the great River Basin Surveys carried out during the Depression. These ambitious surveys involved large quantities of data that was described minutely by James A. Ford and others (Ford and Willey, 1941). In time, however, the Midwestern system was found so effective that its rapidly multiplying taxonomic categories began to acquire chronological and spatial dimensions.

Seriation. The Midwestern system required, and still requires, precise methods for ordering artifacts through time — seriation. Seriation is based on two assumptions: that cultural change is gradual, and usually from the simple to the more complex, and that similarity between artifacts is a measure of their cultural relationship. The first American scholar to demonstrate the effectiveness of seriation was anthropologist Alfred Kroeber, who wrote a classic paper on prehistoric potsherds he had collected from eighteen sites in the desert near Zuni pueblo (Kroeber, 1916). He seriated these into six sub-periods by style and frequency of occurrence, arguing that his seriation showed that the cultural history of the Zuñi region resulted from "a steady and continuous development on the soil."

Leslie Spier (1917) refined Kroeber's work the following year and was the first person to use the term "seriation." His researches caused seriation to become standard archaeological practice in North American archaeology, not only for classifying potsherds, but also for pueblo architecture,

James A. Ford's stylized seriations of pottery type frequencies. The table illustrates different vessel types and tries to correlate pottery sequences from northeast Texas, Louisiana, and Florida.

stone tools, and other artifact forms. The Arctic archaeologist Henry Collins used both stratigraphic observation and the associations of prehistoric Eskimo settlements with ancient beach lines as a chronological framework to seriate bone and ivory tool forms over many centuries (Collins, 1937). One of the young fieldworkers with him was James A. Ford, who took seriation back with him to the Southeastern United States, where he developed elaborate artifact-based chronological schemes between the 1930s and 1960s.

As time went on, many important area syntheses appeared, each of them adding to the emerging, and increasingly bewildering, diversity of North American prehistory (for examples, see Collins, 1940; Deuel, 1935; Ford and Willey, 1941; Kidder, 1924; McGregor, 1941; Strong, 1935; and many others). From these pioneer syntheses emerged the fundamental principles of culture history and nomenclature that are in use today, among them chronological schemes like the familiar Archaic-Woodland-Mississippian terminology of the Eastern Woodlands (Griffin, 1946).

The 1920s through the early 1950s saw North American archaeologists focusing on sites, artifacts, and chronologies, with any form of speculation or theoretical discussion considered not only unnecessary, but intellectually unsound. Archaeology was basically a descriptive, historical methodology that paid lip service to anthropology. Many anthropologists considered it peripheral to their research. "Archaeology ... is always limited in the results it can produce. It is doomed always to be the lesser part of anthropology," wrote anthropologist E. Adamson Hoebel in a revealing and devastating comment of the day.

Dating North American Prehistory
1901 to 1960

We should not be surprised that the archaeologists of a half-century ago were preoccupied with chronology. Their preoccupation was similar to colleagues in every part of the world, simply because there were no reliable ways of dating the prehistoric past. Until the 1920s, all absolute chronologies for prehistory in North America were based on intelligent extrapolation from historical records, and on guesswork, instinct, and an assumption that the first human inhabitants of the Americas were of relatively recent date (Meltzer, 1983). Artifact typology and seriation merely ordered cultural material in a relative chronological sequence, without being anchored to "true" dates.

The bastions of the short chronology crumbled in 1924, with the well-known discoveries at Folsom, New Mexico, that proved that early native Americans had hunted extinct forms of Plains bison. Soon estimates of 10,000 years for Folsom were considered not unreasonable, but there was still no accurate method of dating even recent archaeological sites. Even such comprehensive syntheses as those of Ford and Willey (1941) in the Southeast were based on very short time scales indeed, in the order of 2000 to 3000 years. It was the development of two accurate, easily applicable chronological methods that was to prove to be the catalyst for new approaches to North American archaeology. In both cases, these methods came to archaeology from the hard sciences.

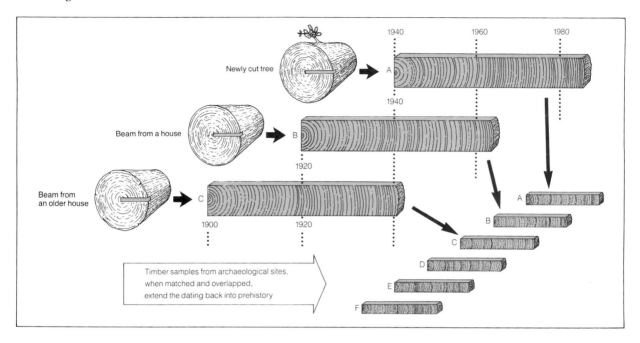

Dendrochronology: using tree-ring sequences to date North American archaeology.

Dendrochronology. Astronomer A.E. Douglass of the University of Arizona, Tucson, was interested in tree-rings as a means of dating sunspot activity. He began his research in 1901 with live trees, then searched for wooden beams preserved in prehistoric pueblos. By 1929 he had two tree-ring sequences, the one extending back from the present through Spanish contact into late Pueblo times, the other a chronology that was not anchored to historic trees, which covered a long period of earlier prehistoric times. Douglass searched hard for the beams that would link his two tree-ring sequences, and eventually found a charred log of AD 1237 in a pueblo at Show Low, Arizona. Once he had secured his master tree-ring chronology, Douglass could apply dendrochronology (tree-ring dating) to prehistoric sites simply by comparing the ring sequences from their beams with the master sequence.

By the mid-1930s, later Southwestern prehistory had an accurate chronology. Basketmaker II dated to before AD 500, Basketmaker III between AD 500 and 700, and the four Pueblo stages from AD 700 to 1600.

Dendrochronology was an important advance, albeit a local one, for the chronology it produced could not be expanded far beyond the Southwest and contiguous arid areas. It is only in recent years that more sophisticated methods have enabled the development of tree-ring chronologies based on oak trees and other temperate species in the Midwest and elsewhere, chronologies that act as a useful check on radiocarbon dates. The new tree-ring dates showed Southwestern scholars that the various periods of the Pecos classification were more stages of cultural development than precise time periods. For the first time, the archaeologist could study not just rigid cultural sequences, but such phenomena as rates of cultural spread and change, also minute changes in rainfall over long periods of time.

Radiocarbon Dating. Other than for the Southwest, dating the prehistoric past was more-or-less a matter of intelligent guesswork and careful extrapolation backward from sites of known age. Then, in 1949, University of Chicago chemist Willard Libby (1955) published the new and revolutionary radiocarbon dating method. This operates on the principle that the radioactive carbon in the atmosphere is, and was, absorbed by all living organisms. This absorption ceases when they die, and a steady, and measurable decay of carbon then begins. Libby tested his new method with objects of known age like ancient Egyptian boats, then extended his tests to charcoal and other organic materials excavated in association with prehistoric artifacts. He found that he could date sites up to 40,000 or more years old. By the mid-1960s, radiocarbon dating was a routine procedure in every corner of the world.

It is no exaggeration to say that radiocarbon dating revolutionized North American archaeology. Within a few years of Libby's announcement, radiocarbon dates had shown that human beings had lived in the Americas for at least 11,000 years. Other samples filled in the chronological vacuum between Paleo-Indian and much later sedentary cultures such as the Mississippian of the Eastern Woodlands. The radiocarbon revolution was far more profound than merely an opportunity to date cultural sequences from all corners of the continent. It enabled the archaeologist to look at the rate of cultural evolution with far greater precision. It was a chance to compare rates of change in different places and in different environments, and an opportunity to compare prehistoric developments in widely separated areas. For the first time, one could move beyond simple cultural sequences and study the complex processes that triggered cultural change. Libby's discovery laid the foundations for the dramatic theoretical and methodological advances of the 1960s. The radiocarbon revolution took hold at a time when the sciences began to have an increasing impact on North American archaeology. Tree-ring dating was further refined, and is now used as a method of studying very fine-grained climate change in the Southwest. New, but still somewhat experimental, dating methods have been developed, among them paleo-magnetism, obsidian hydration, and thermoluminescence (for details of dating methods, see Fagan, 1987b; Renfrew and Bahn, 1991).

Science and Archaeology
1950 onward

By the 1950s, many North American archaeologists had realized that the sciences had much to offer prehistoric archaeology. Fossil pollens offered opportunities to study ancient environments, animal bones a chance to examine prehistoric subsistence activities. Closer collaboration with geologists, biologists, botanists, and other scientists led to numerous interdisciplinary research projects, which studied the evolution of human cultures against a backdrop of major climatic changes over the past 15,000 years (for a summary, see Willey and Sabloff, 1980). This collaborative research has yielded detailed results, especially when geomorphologists, pollen experts, paleontologists, and archaeologists cooperate in the field, as has been the case with the study of the Bering Land Bridge (see Chapter 4).

The development of quantitative approaches to artifact analysis, increasing use of computers, aerial photography, and remote sensing from space — these are but a few of the scientific methods that have had a profound effect on North American archaeology since the 1960s (for details, see Fagan, 1987b; Sharer and Ashmore, 1987).

Method and Theory in American Archaeology

These experiments coincided with an explosion of archaeological research after World War II, partly as a result of massive federal flood control projects that had started before the war and continued into the 1950s. These works led to a great deal of salvage archaeological work carried out in advance of dam building, projects such as the Glen Canyon project in Utah (Jennings, 1966). Much more basic culture-historical data flowed from these projects, and also from important, purely academic researches of the 1940s and 1950s.

All these researches led to a proliferation of historical and developmental syntheses of North American prehistory, the most famous of which was Gordon Willey and Philip Phillips' *Method and Theory in American Archaeology*, published in 1958. This classic work drew on years of gradually evolving area syntheses from the Southwest, the eastern United States, and on ideas developed in Mesoamerica and Peru. In it, Willey and Phillips referred to five broad developmental, or culture, stages, based not only on technology, but on economic data, settlement patterns, art traditions, and social factors, too. Chronology was less significant. These stages were:
— The Lithic (Paleo-Indian and other early cultural manifestations in the New World),
— Archaic (post-Ice Age hunter-gatherers),
— Formative (village agriculture and/or sedentary life). There were two additional stages that did not exist in North America:
— Classic (urban development),
— Postclassic (imperialistic states such as the Aztec and Inca).

The Willey and Phillips scheme created a ferment of discussion, and was rejected by some archaeologists out of hand, and modified by others (Willey and Sabloff, 1980). Many scholars were unhappy with the strong evolutionary undertones of the work, an approach that had long lain dormant in American archaeology. The book was a sign of the times, for archaeology was on the move. Now the stage was set for new approaches that did not merely describe the past, but attempted to explain *why* prehistoric American cultures had changed, and *how* they had adapted to their very diverse environmental settings.

A Study of Archaeology

In 1948, W.W. Taylor published *A Study of Archaeology*, a detailed critique of archaeological approaches of earlier years. Taylor singled out Kidder's Southwestern research for attack, describing it trenchantly as a "comparative chronicle." Kidder never reconstructed life in the past, nor did he use

North American archaeologists commonly subdivide prehistoric times into broad cultural stages that are a terminological relic from earlier attempts at culture-historical reconstruction. Like the Three Age System in the Old World, the terms have little more than very general theoretical application in our data-rich scientific environment. Since they are still commonly used, and occur frequently in the pages of this book, we should define them in general terms here.

Two terms used throughout North America:

Paleo-Indian. Human cultures ancestral to later, Archaic developments. This very generalized term subsumes the first Americans, the Clovis people, and other pre-Archaic groups. In strictly chronological terms, the boundary between Paleo-Indian and later cultures is usually about 8000 years ago.

Archaic. Archaic cultures evolved from Paleo-Indian ones, to the point that the boundary between the two is often impossible to draw. Archaic peoples hunted smaller, more varied animals, placed greater emphasis on plant foods, and developed a toolkit for processing same. They also created increasingly diverse, and often specialized, adaptations to local environments. Archaic cultures survived in some parts of the western United States until modern times.

Two other terms are commonly used in the Eastern Woodlands culture area:

Woodland. Woodland subsumes many local adaptations. Generally, the label Woodland implies hunter-gatherer societies augmented with some cultivation, manufacture of some pottery, also more elaborate tools and art traditions, and cemetery burials, often associated with earthen mounds and more elaborate ritual and trade activities.

The Woodland continued in many areas of the east until European contact, but by AD 800 the **Mississippian** tradition replaces it in the Midsouth, between the Mississippi River and the Appalachians (see Chapter 20).

TABLE 2.1

Commonly Used General Subdivisions of North American Prehistory

his data to discuss functional matters, Taylor alleged. Not that Kidder alone was singled out for criticism. Taylor swept a broad brush across North American archaeology, accusing its practitioners of being more concerned with artifact classification and chronology than with culture change or social behavior in the past. He proposed a new, "conjunctive" approach that used all possible lines of research to work on specific archaeological problems, problems with far wider focuses than merely pottery classification and chronological sequences, everything from settlement patterns to food remains.

Predictably, *A Study of Archaeology* raised many academic hackles, for many archaeologists sincerely believed that archaeological data was too

TABLE 2.2

Culture-Historical Terminology

Major North American language groups (below right). The early 20th century photographer Edward Curtis made a priceless record of American Indians (below, Yellow Owl [Mandan]; bottom, Sitting Bear [Arikara]).

There is no absolutely agreed upon terminology for North American culture history. However, the following hierarchy of terms is in wide use, and is employed in this book:

Component. A culturally homogeneous stratigraphic unit within a site. A settlement occupied but once will consist of a single component, but one occupied four times will have four. Components occur at one location. To produce a regional chronology, one must synthesize components from different sites, using the next analytical step:

Phase. Similar components from more than one site. They are limited to a locality or region and span a relatively limited amount of time. Distinctive culture traits distinguish one phase from another. Phases enable one to establish regional contemporaneity, but, as time goes on and more discoveries are made, may be broken down into more and more precise sub-phases.

Archaeological Regions. Normally defined by natural geographic boundaries, archaeological regions usually display some cultural homogeneity. They are often defined by natural geographic features as well – for example, the Santa Barbara Channel region.

Culture Area. These define much larger tracts of land, and often coincide with broad ethnographic culture areas identified by early anthropologists. The Southwestern United States is one such area, in turn subdivided into distinctive sub-areas (see Chapter 13).

North American archaeologists also use two units that synthesize archaeological data over wide areas:

Horizon. Horizons link a number of phases in neighboring areas that

Eskaleut
Athabaskan
Wakashan
Salishan
Penutian
Algonquian
Siouan
Iroquoian
Muskogean
Hokaltecan
Azteco-Tanoan
Caddoan

0   600mls
0   1000km

The map shows numbered regions and named groups. Labels visible include:

ARCTIC OCEAN, GREENLAND, EAST GREENLAND ESKIMO, WEST GREENLAND ESKIMO, BAFFINLAND ESKIMO, POLAR ESKIMO, CENTRAL ESKIMO, Cape Dorset, LABRADOR ESKIMO, NASKAPI, BEOTHUK, MONTAGNAIS, MICMAC, 1a, 1b, HUDSON BAY, YUIT, NORTH ALASKAN ESKIMO, BERING STRAIT, Point Hope, KOTZEBUE ESKIMO, NORTON SOUND, Anaktuvuk, MACKENZIE ESKIMO, COPPER ESKIMO, SOUTH ALASKAN ESKIMO, Yukon R., KOYUKON, Kuskokwim R., INGALIK TANAINA, TANANA, KUTCHIN, HARE, CARIBOU ESKIMO, ALEUT, CHUGACH, AHTENA, EYAK, TUTCHONE, DOGRIB, YELLOWKNIFE, SLAVE, CHIPEWYAN, SWAMPY CREE, CREE, OJIBWA, TLINGIT, KASKA, TAHLTAN, Skeena R., Nass R., SEKANI, BEAVER, HAIDA, Queen Charlotte Is., TSIMSHIAN, CARRIER, 1b, ALGONQUIN, OTTAWA, ABNAKI, PENOBSCOT, BELLA COOLA, SHUSWAP, Fraser R., THOMPSON, SARSI, PLAINS CREE, PLAINS OJIBWA, 8, KWAKIUTL, NOOTKA, COAST SALISH, KUTENAI, FLATHEAD, BLACKFOOT, ASSINIBOIN, MANDAN, Missouri R., MENOMINEE, WINNEBAGO, FOX, HURON, IROQUOIS, MASSACHUSET, MAKAH, CHINOOK, 9, YAKIMA, NEZ PERCE, WASCO, Columbia R., TENINO, HIDATSA, ARIKARA, CROW, TETON DAKOTA, YANKTONAI DAKOTA, SANTEE DAKOTA, POTAWATOMI, ERIE, MAHICAN, PEQUOT, DELAWARE, SUSQUEHANNOCK, NANTICOKE, TILLAMOOK, COOS, KAROK, YUROK, HUPA, KLAMATH, YANA, BANNOCK, PAVIOTSO, SHOSHONE, CHEYENNE, YANKTON DAKOTA, IOWA, OMAHA, PAWNEE, MISSOURI, MIAMI, TUTELO, VIRGINIA ALGONQUIAN, YUKI, POMO, 5, MAIDU, WASHO, MONO, Great Basin, YOKUTS, UTE, ARAPAHO, 2, KANSA, ILLINOIS, SHAWNEE, CHEROKEE, CATAWBA, YUCHI, NORTH CAROLINA ALGONQUIAN, TUSCARORA, MIWOK, COSTANO, PAIUTE, Colorado R., NAVAJO, HOPI, KERESAN, TANO, KIOWA, OSAGE, CHICKASAW, CREEK, CUSABO, CHUMASH, SERRANO, ZUNI, COMANCHE, WICHITA, CADDO, CHOCTAW, GABRIELINO, LUISENO, TIPAI, MOHAVE, YAVAPAI, YUMA, MARICOPA, PIMA, TANO, APACHE, Gila R., Salt R., 7, TONKAWA, NATCHEZ, BILOXI, 4, SEMINOLE, TIMUCUA, PAPAGO, Rio Grande, Pecos R., ATAKAPA, CHITIMACHA, CALUSA, GULF OF CALIFORNIA, GULF OF MEXICO, 3, MISSOURI, ILLINOIS

---

contain rather general cultural patterns in common. In some parts of the world, all-embracing religious cults may transcend cultural boundaries and spread over an enormous area. Their distinctive artifacts, like those of the famous Chavín art style of Peru (900 – 200 BC, can be identified in phases hundreds of miles apart.

Tradition. A widespread term in North American archaeology. It is used to describe a lasting artifact type, assemblages of tools, architectural styles, economic practices, or art styles that last much longer than one phase or even the duration of a horizon. Tradition implies a degree of cultural continuity, even if shifts in cultural adaptation have taken place in the meantime. A good example is the so-called Arctic Small Tool tradition of Alaska, dating to as early as 2000 BC (see Chapter 8). The small tools made by these hunters were so effective that they remained in use until relatively recent times.

Names of major groups and the main culture areas of North America: 1a Arctic, 1b Subarctic, 2 Great Plains, 3 Eastern Woodlands, 4 Southeast, 5 California, 6 Great Basin, 7 Southwest, 8 Northwest Coast, 9 Plateau. For the purposes of this book, 1a and 1b have been grouped as the Far North, 3 and 4 as the Eastern Woodlands, and 5, 8, and 9 as the Far West.

limited for anything much more than classification and description. On the other hand, a significant number of scholars chafed under the narrow restrictions of culture history (J.A. Ford, 1952; Spaulding, 1953). In 1958, Gordon Willey and Philip Phillips wrote that archaeologists had used such explanatory terms as "acculturation" (the assimilation of one culture by another) and "diffusion" (the spread of culture traits and ideas from one culture to another), but only in very local contexts. Few people had attempted generalizations, indeed "so little work has been done in American archaeology on the explanatory level that it is difficult to find a name for it." They proposed the term "processual interpretation" for such attempted explanations.

The publication of *Method and Theory in American Archaeology*, and of *A Study of Archaeology* mark an important watershed in North American archaeology, the end of a period of transition from arid culture-historical studies to a new era that focused not only on questions of "how," but on questions of "why" as well. With their insistence on multi-dimensional, problem-oriented research, more imaginative hypotheses, and their cautious flirtation with the then unrespectable notion of cultural evolution, these landmark essays paved the way for the theoretical debates and scientific approaches that now dominate North American archaeology.

Further Reading

Fagan, Brian M. 1977. *Elusive Treasure*. Charles Scribners, New York.
A popular introduction to the history of American Archaeology, which focuses on the Moundbuilders and Southwestern archaeology in the context of this book.

Meltzer, David J. 1983. "The Antiquity of Man and the Development of American Archaeology," *Advances in Archaeological Method and Theory*, 6: 1-51.
A detailed essay on the controversies surrounding the antiquity of humankind in North America, which contains an invaluable account of the emergence of government archaeology in North America.

Sabloff, Jeremy A. and Willey, Gordon R. 1980. *A History of American Archaeology*. Freeman, San Franciso. 2nd ed.
The best comprehensive source on the early history of North American archaeology. Especially strong on the development of culture history and classification.

Silverberg, Robert. 1968. *Moundbuilders of Ancient America: The Archaeology of a Myth*. New York Graphic Society, Greenwich, Connecticut.
A well-researched and vividly written account of the Moundbuilder controversy for the general reader.

Willey, Gordon R. and Phillips, P. 1958. *Method and Theory in American Archaeology*. University of Chicago Press, Chicago.
The classic essay on culture history in American archaeology. Essential reading for any serious student of the subject.

CHAPTER 3

EXPLAINING PREHISTORIC CULTURAL CHANGE

The theoretical and methodological revolution that overtook archaeology in the 1960s began with three major developments that took hold in the preceding decade — cultural ecology, settlement archaeology, and environmental reconstruction.

Evolution, Cultural Ecology and the Environment

During the 1940s and early 1950s, anthropologist Julian Steward searched for ways of identifying common cultural features in societies distributed in many parts of the world. In so doing, he assumed that certain basic types of culture would develop in similar ways under similar conditions. Steward was by no means the first anthropologist to think in terms of multilinear cultural evolution, but he added a new dimension to the discussions of cultural change — that of the natural environment. He looked to it for causes of cultural change, and spent much time studying the relationships between environment and culture, calling his new approach "cultural ecology."

Cultural ecology is based on three fundamental assumptions. First, similar adaptations may be found in different cultures when their environments are similar. Second, no culture has ever achieved an adaptation to its environment which has remained unchanged over any length of time. Third, differences and changes during periods of cultural development in any area can either add to societal complexity, or result in completely new cultural patterns (Steward, 1955).

Steward applied cultural ecology to the study of a fundamental question: why does the adjustment of human societies to different environments result in certain distinctive types of behavior? Thus, to diffusion, the spread of culture traits and ideas, and evolution, he added a new concept — changing adaptations to the natural environment. In other words, the study of culture change involved not only human cultures, but their changing environmental conditions as well. This entailed not only studying ancient environmental change and cultural adaptations, but shifts in human settlements on the natural landscape over long periods of time.

Steward himself was one of the first anthropologists to study human settlement patterns, in his case the distribution and annual ranges of Shoshone hunter-gatherers in the Great Basin. It was he who encouraged

TABLE 3.1

Stages of Socio-Cultural Evolution

All theories of cultural evolution are based on the premise that human societies have changed over long periods of time, and that the general trend throughout prehistory has been toward a greater complexity of human culture and social institutions. How, then, does one classify North American societies before European contact? The most widely accepted classification divides human societies into four broad categories – bands, tribes, chiefdoms, and states. This classification has won wide acceptance, but is much criticized for its arbitrary rigidity. Many archaeologists prefer a broader grouping:

Pre-State Societies. Societies on a small scale, based on the community, band, or village, which vary greatly in their degree of political integration. These societies lack the highly stratified class structure and other characteristic features of ...

State-Organized Societies. Societies on a large scale with centralized social and political organizations, class stratification, and intensive agriculture. States have complex political structures and many permanent government institutions, with social inequality a reality. The Maya and Aztec civilizations of Mexico were state-organized societies.

Although the issue is much debated, it is safe to say that all prehistoric North American societies fell in the pre-state category. Only the Mississippian of the American Bottomlands was close to the critical economic, political, and social thresholds of an emerging state. Pre-state societies can be divided arbitrarily into three broad categories. *It should be stressed, however, that these categories are far too rigid to reflect anything more than the most general reality, and are little more than labels of convenience.*

Bands. Autonomous and self-sufficient groups that consist of fairly small numbers of people, usually a few families. This form of organization is highly adaptive for hunter-gatherers, people constantly

Harvard archaeologist Gordon Willey to carry out a large-scale survey of changing settlement patterns in the Virú Valley on the Peruvian coast in 1946, generally agreed to be the study that launched similar research all over the Americas (Willey, 1953). During the 1960s, important settlement surveys were carried out in the Southwest and other areas, many of them as a result of Cultural Resource Management projects.[1]

Environmental reconstruction was even slower to come to North American archaeology. This may be because there were no known spectacular waterlogged sites in North America at the time, sites that

[1]Cultural Resource Management, the investigation of North American archaeology as part of the inventorying, salvage, and management of archaeological sites, is now the dominant context for archaeological research north of the Rio Grande. We cannot cover this complex topic here. For a full discussion of the legislation, history, and current directions of CRM, see Fagan, 1987b.

on the move with band size varying constantly. Band societies are egalitarian, leadership coming from experience and personal qualities rather than political power.

In general terms, more complex pre-state societies are a form of transitional society between simple bands and elaborate, state-organized societies in their social and political complexity:

Tribes. Egalitarian societies, like bands, but ones that have achieved a greater level of social and cultural complexity, also mechanisms to accommodate more sedentary living, the need to redistribute food, and to organize some communal services. While some complex hunter-gatherer societies can be classified as tribal, most tribes were associated with village farming. Political, religious, and social authority is basically egalitarian, communal decisions being based on public opinion. The basic social and economic unit is the household, the nuclear family, and close kin that produce and store food. These kin links provide effective mechanisms for social control.

Chiefdoms. Societies headed by important individuals with unusual ritual, political, or entrepreneurial skills. In many cases, it is hard to distinguish them from tribes. Society is still kin-based, but is more hierarchical, with power concentrated in the hands of powerful kin leaders, who are responsible for redistribution of resources. Chiefdoms tend to have higher population densities, to display the first signs of social ranking, often reflected in more prestigious material possessions. Chiefdoms vary widely in their elaboration, the degree of elaboration depending on many complex factors, including the distribution of the population over the landscape. Judging from their elaborate ritual artifacts and the large public works under their control, the major Mississippian chiefdoms were extremely elaborate societies, with complex social, religious, and political hierarchies.

(Below) Waldo R. Wedel, left, with George S. Metcalf at an archaeological site in Rice County, Kansas. (Bottom) Emil Haury, left, with Vance Haynes at the Paleo-Indian Lehner site, Arizona.

spurred pollen studies and other ecological approaches long used on Scandinavian sites, and in the 1950s at Starr Carr in northeast England (Clark, G., 1954).

Waldo Wedel, a Plains archaeologist, was one of the first North Americanists to attempt environmental reconstructions, interpreting Plains subsistence patterns against a backdrop of changing environmental patterns on the grasslands (Wedel, 1953). Emil Haury at Ventana Cave in the Southwest, Jesse Jennings in Utah, and Robert Heizer in California were some of the other scholars who attempted descriptive rather than interpretive analyses of prehistoric environmental conditions, even of ancient diets (Willey and Sabloff, 1980).

Steward's new cultural ecological approach was, perhaps, the most important theoretical development in North American archaeology in a century, even if his work could be faulted on several grounds, not least because he lacked a holistic, truly ecological view of prehistoric cultures.

Processual Archaeology

As younger scholars started examining the delicate and ever changing relationships between human societies and their prehistoric environments, they cast around for theoretical models, borrowing models from biologists, ecologists, even sociologists. The impact of philosophers of science like Thomas Kuhn and Carl Hempel, and of general systems theory, began to be felt in archaeology (Binford, 1983). Systems theory was particularly attractive as a conceptual model, for it allowed an archaeologist to think of human cultures as complicated systems of interacting elements, such as technology and social organization, which interacted in turn with the ecological systems of which they were a part. This approach allowed archaeologists to prepare far more detailed and meticulous descriptions of their sites, and helped in the development of much more sophisticated research designs for survey and excavation.

During the 1960s, Lewis Binford, now of the University of New Mexico, published a series of papers in which he argued for more rigorous scientific testing, for the development of independent methods for testing propositions about the past (for a summary, see Binford, 1983). These, he said, must be far stricter than the time-honored value judgments arrived at by assessing the professional competence of the archaeologist who did the work. He urged the use of formal scientific methods, an approach that soon came to be called the "new archaeology."

Binford argued for the use of formal research designs, for scientific approaches that provided interaction among old data, new ideas, and new data. This was a collection of observed data that would enable archaeologists to pose research hypotheses. Working hypotheses were nothing new in archaeology, but Binford's approach was different because he advocated that these hypotheses be tested *explicitly* against archaeological data collected in the field, and against other hypotheses that had been rejected. Once a hypothesis was tested against raw data, it could join the body of reliable knowledge upon which further, more precise, hypotheses could be erected.

Binford and his many disciples also challenged the assumption that because the archaeological record is incomplete, reliable interpretation of the non-material and perishable components of prehistoric society and culture was impossible. Their argument was that all artifacts found in an archaeological culture occur in meaningful patterns that are systematically related to the economies, kinship systems, and other contexts within which they were used. Moreover, all these artifacts were at the mercy of transient factors such as fashion or decorative style, each of which itself had a history of acceptance, use, or rejection within society. Thus, artifacts are far more than material items. Rather, they reflect many of the often intangible variables that went into determining the actual form of the objects preserved. "Data relevant to most, if not all, of the components of past sociocultural systems *are* preserved in the archaeological record," Binford insisted (Binford and Binford, 1968).

The debates over what came to be known as "processual archaeology" raged fast and furious in the 1960s and 1970s. Some scholars argued that archaeology was a science, whose objective was to study basic laws of human behavior. Other archaeologists viewed archaeology as examining the activities of past human beings, as a discipline that was less a science than a historical discipline with its own limitations, resources, and explanatory methods (Flannery, 1973a; Spaulding, 1973). Everyone agreed, however, that mathematical models, statistical approaches, and rigorous scientific methods would become ever more important.

The fervor of debate and controversy has quieted considerably in recent years, partly because many of the basic tenets put forward by Lewis Binford and other scholars are now widely accepted. Processual archaeology, with its strongly materialist and ecological approach, has become a mainstream framework for much North American archaeology. The scientific method is widely used. Research designs are far more sophisticated than those of a generation ago. Highly technical scientific techniques like isotope analysis and remote sensing are commonplace. But frustration remains, for many of the rich theoretical expectations of the 1960s remain unfulfilled (Dunnell, 1982).

North American archaeologists today seem divided into two broad groups: those who write about "theoretical issues" and concentrate on concepts, methods, and techniques, which are occasionally applied to a body of data, and those, perhaps most archaeologists, who carry out empirical studies of much the same type that have been done for generations. More "scientific" methods may be used, true, but the effect is often superficial. Little integration seems to link the two groups. In this sense, the "new archaeology" of the 1960s has failed. In baffled frustration, many North American archaeologists have even wondered whether archaeology is, in fact, an atheoretical discipline. They are misguided in such an assumption. Even a superficial glance at the history of other, more mature, disciplines suggests that archaeology, like the other social sciences, is undergoing the same kind of change that biology went through a generation ago — a serious attempt to assemble a body of theory for archaeology as distinctive as that for physics and other established sciences (Meltzer, Fowler, and Sabloff, 1986).

Part of the current theoretical debate in archaeology revolves around the relationship between the archaeological record of the present, and the human behavior of the past. Archaeology is unique among the sciences in that it relies on inference for interpreting the past. We can study that past only by means of material evidence that has been changed by centuries, even millennia, underground. How, then, can we explain the archaeological record? Ethnographic analogy, middle-range theory, ethnoarchaeology, and experimental archaeology are among the approaches being explored for this purpose.

The Problem of Ethnographic Analogy

Analogy is based, ultimately, on the Direct Historical Method, the notion of working back from the present into the remote, prehistoric past (Wylie, 1985). North American archaeologists use analogy on many levels. In a simple one, someone infers that carefully pressure-flaked Paleo-Indian points are spearheads, because there are ethnographic records of peoples making broadly similar points for the tips of lances. This form of simple, and commonly used, analogy is a far cry from claiming analogies between the ways in which a prehistoric culture used the spearpoint and the ways in which a living society uses it. To do the latter is to assume that the relationship between the form and the function of the artifact has remained static over the centuries. If you explain the past simply by analogy with the present, then you are assuming that nothing new has been learned.

Direct historical analogies are highly effective with historic sites, such as, for example, the Colonial village at Martin's Hundred, Virginia, where textual sources provided valuable analogies about house ownership and other details of the archaeological record (Nöel-Hume, 1982). Such analogies are highly effective with recent prehistoric sites, also, but lose much of their effectiveness as one moves back further in prehistoric time.

At one time, ethnographic analogy was regarded as *the* way to interpret the prehistoric past. Today, the selection of appropriate analogies from the ethnographic literature is seen as only one step in the quest for interpretation. Processual archaeologists like Lewis Binford use three interlocking approaches to try and achieve the end of having the present serve the past – middle-range theory, ethnoarchaeology, and archaeology by experiment.

Middle-Range Theory, Experimental Archaeology and Ethnoarchaeology

It was Lewis Binford who posed the fundamental question: "The archaeological record is contemporary; it exists with me today and any observation I make about it is a contemporary observation." How can one make inferences about the past unless one knows "the necessary and determinant linkages between dynamic causes and static consequences"? The new body of bridging or "middle-range" theory (a term derived from sociology) is often called "actualistic," and is designed to treat the relationships between statics and dynamics, between behavior and material derivatives. It is actualistic because it studies the actual coincidence of both static and dynamic in cultural systems in the only time frame in which this can be achieved — the present. Middle-range theory involves studying the processes by which the archaeological record comes into being, the many natural and humanly-generated phenomena that transform an abandoned habitation with its collapsing huts, for example, into the scatter of artifacts, structures, and other finds made by the late 20th-century archaeologist. These are known as site formation processes (for a full discussion, see Schiffer, 1987). Middle-range theory is also formulated through controlled experiments with replicas of prehistoric artifacts, by studying living systems (ethnoarchaeology), and through the use of historical or ethnohistorical records (see Part Seven) (Binford, 1983; Fagan, 1987b).

Controlled experiments can be a fruitful, if often limited, source of data to test middle-range theory (Coles, 1973). Much early experimentation went into the mechanics of stone tool manufacture, and into such esoterica as prehistoric archery (Pope, 1923). Today's experiments are more focused, carried out under controlled conditions, and often have very long-term goals. They include replications of prehistoric stone tool reduction strategies, such as those used to make Paleo-Indian projectile points, experiments with maize cultivation in the Southwest, and with the construction and then controlled burning of Mississippian houses in the Midwest. All of these controlled experiments are designed to give archaeologists the kind of objective data that will be needed to understand the static archaeological record, as studied in the dynamic present.

Ethnoarchaeology, sometimes called "living archaeology," is the study of contemporary societies to aid in the understanding and interpretation of the archaeological record (Gould, 1978). By living in, say, an Eskimo hunting camp and observing the activities of its occupants, the archaeologist hopes to record archaeologically observable patterns, knowing what activities brought them into existence. The first ethnoarchaeological projects, among such people as the San of Africa's Kalahari Desert, or the Australian Aborigines, focused on specific artifact patternings, and on studies of hunter-gatherer encampments that might provide ways of interpreting the very earliest scatters of human artifacts and animal bones in East Africa (Yellen, 1977). A major focus of more recent work has been to develop archaeological methods of inference to bridge the gap between past and present.

Lewis Binford carried out living archaeology among the Nunamiut people of Alaska, hunters who gain over 80 percent of their subsistence from caribou hunting. As part of his formulation of middle-range theory, he wanted to find out as much as he could about "all aspects of the procurement, processing, and consumption strategies of the Nunamiut Eskimo and relate these behaviors directly to their faunal consequences" (Binford, 1978). Binford chose to concentrate on animal bones rather than artifacts, because, although the bones were not humanly manufactured, their use patterns were the result of cultural activity.

The Nunamiut depend more heavily on meat than any other surviving hunter-gatherers. Binford estimated that each adult only ate about a cup and a half of vegetable foods a year, supplemented by the partially digested stomach contents of caribou. In an environment that has but a 22-day growing season each year, the Nunamiut rely on stored food entirely for

Experimental archaeology. Lithic expert Jeffrey Flenniken demonstrates the making of a Folsom point replica. A hammerstone (top left) reduces the large obsidian cobble to a series of flakes suitable for point manufacture. Using careful percussion and pressure flaking (top right), the projectile blank is shaped until the final channel flake can be removed using a punch, resulting in the finished artifact (above).

Ethnoarchaeology: Lewis Binford's research among the Nunamiut of Alaska. (Above) Binford's map of Nunamiut hunting territories before and after the 1910 crash of the local caribou population. The people's response to food stress was to triple the territory they covered to obtain food. Note the location of Anaktuvuk Pass, where Binford carried out detailed research. (Right) Map of the Anaktuvuk Pass area showing, among other sites, the three locations illustrated on these two pages: Tulugak Lake, Hunting Stand R&B (no. 6 in the key), and the Mask site. (Above right) Hunting Stand R&B revealed a caribou skin-bed where a man slept while his partner watched for game.

MASK SITE
OBSERVED LOCALIZATION OF ACTIVITIES
AFTERNOON JUNE 5

CARIBOU SKIN-SLEEPING

EATING/TALKING

CRAFT ACTIVITIES

WATCHING FOR GAME

ACTIVE HEARTH

N

SCALE IN METERS
0   2

*Nunamiut ethnoarchaeology
(continued). (Above) "Soldier rocks"
were used by the Nunamiut to form a
caribou drive line running up the
mountainside east of Tulugak Lake in
Anaktuvuk Pass. (Left) Binford's
drawing of various Nunamiut activities
observed by him at the Mask site,
Anaktuvuk Pass, on a spring afternoon.
Studies such as this have helped
ethnoarchaeologists assemble a mass of
empirical data to aid in the
interpretation of archaeological sites.*

eight and a half months a year, and partially on it for an additional month
and a half. Fresh meat is available for only two months a year. Thus, factors
such as the bulk of caribou carcasses and the logistics of carrying meat to
and from storage places were of vital importance. Binford soon realized
that the linkage between the facts of caribou anatomy and the realities of
the Nunamiut lifeway were the only way in which he could make a
meaningful analysis of the animal bones they discarded.

Thanks to studies of actual Nunamiut hunting, of their intimate
knowledge of caribou anatomy, and of existing and "archaeological" camps

and caches, Binford assembled an enormous mass of empirical data on human exploitation of animals that was applicable not only to the Nunamiut and other caribou hunters, but to the interpretation of archaeological sites elsewhere. He showed how local cultural adaptations could be, how the Nunamiut depended on interacting topographic, climatic, logistical, and other realities. In the end, he drew several important conclusions from his study, which are of fundamental importance to interpreting North American prehistory:

— The continuing dynamics of a local adaptation can result in considerable variation in archaeological sites.
— There may be considerable interregional variations within a culture, which are reflected in different archaeological remains. Yet, the inhabitants of one site were well aware of the general cultural variations displayed at other locations nearby.
— The adaptive strategies and the factors affecting the peoples' decision-making may remain constant, even if the archaeological remains show great variability.
— Most important of all, changes in stone tool frequencies or pottery forms may reflect no significant change in adaptation at all. It is impossible to tell without understanding the strategies behind the local adaptation through time. And such understandings can be obtained only from sites where food remains and other such data are available.

The Nunamiut and other such ethnoarchaeological studies have shown that not all variability in the archaeological record is directly related to cultural similarity and difference. Research of this type is predominantly functional, behavioral, and ecological in its general approach. As we shall see in Chapter 4, it has profoundly affected archaeological studies of prehistoric hunter-gatherers in North America.

Functionalism and Structural Archaeology

We are now going through a prolonged period of theoretical fumbling, searching for a new body of archaeological theory for North American archaeology that will truly give us new models for interpreting the past (Binford, 1986; Moore and Keen, 1983). One such fumbling is an assault on functionalism in archaeology.

Functionalism, the notion that a social institution within a society has a function in fulfilling all the needs of a social organism, is a concept that has been integral to much anthropological thinking since the late 19th century. Functionalists assess any aspect of a society according to its contribution to the total working of society. Functionalism has long been a controversial topic among anthropologists, but is inextricable from the notion of systems and cultural systems, concepts that are fundamental tenets of processual archaeology.

This functionalist approach has been criticized by some archaeologists, who believe processual archaeologists place an overemphasis on equilibrium between culture and environment and the idea that most change has to come from outside the system (Hodder, 1982). Under this argument, function and utility are inadequate ways of explaining social and cultural systems, for many archaeologists distinguish between culture on the one hand and adaptive utility on the other. "There is much more to culture than functions and activities. Beyond functioning and doing there is a structure and content which has partly to be understood in its own terms, with its own logic and coherence," writes Ian Hodder (1982). He argues that processual archaeology stresses the identification of variability in human culture, and in so doing has tended to think of adaptation in general rather than of adaptation in individual historical context. Systems are seen as being in equilibrium or disequilibrium, populated by human beings, who, as individuals, are minimally important. Processual archaeology is based on the assumption that prehistoric institutions were rational in their dealings with their environments. Hodder believes that structuralism offers a more productive approach.

Hodder defines "structure" in an archaeological context not as a set of relationships between components of a cultural system (a way in which it could be used, interchangeably with "system"), but as "codes and rules according to which observed systems of interrelations are produced." For example, he (1982) studied the Nuba agriculturalists of the Sudan, and showed that all aspects of their material culture, including burial customs, settlement pattern, and artifact styles, could be understood within the context of a set of rules that perpetuated their beliefs in "purity, boundedness, and categorization." Hodder argues that many studies of areas like the Southwest have explained the structure of human societies in terms of social functions and adaptive values. But in fact the studies hint that there is more to culture than observable relationships and functional utility. Hodder writes of a set of rules, which he likens to those operating in chess, which are followed as people go about the business of survival, adaptation, and making a living.

Structural archaeology borrows from cultural anthropology such theoretical ideas as structuralism, symbolic analysis, and Marxism (Leone, 1986). These structural concepts are all very well in theory, but few archaeological studies anywhere, let alone in North America, have yet provided convincing accounts of the relationships between the structural archaeologists' "codes" and social and ecological organization.

The new fascination with structural archaeology has flared at a time when North American archaeologists are beginning to wrestle with the problems of developing a theory of social practice for understanding the relationships among structure, belief, action, and the material remains they ultimately generate. Structural archaeology is one of many reactions against the logic-based and deductive approach of processual archaeology, a sign that North American archaeology, as a cultural and historical discipline, with its systems and explicitly scientific approach, is about to undergo further exciting, and perhaps radical, change.

The Future Direction of Theory in North American Archaeology

Where does the future of North American archaeology lie? Few archaeologists agree on this point. Clearly, both evolutionary theory and ecology will be important in the study of cultural change and the birth of more complex pre-Columbian societies. Processual archaeologists have long understood that individual human actions and decisions are an important part of human history. These actions and decisions are made within a framework of checks and balances that are not only cultural and biological but also environmental. Processualists regard the understanding of these frameworks, in order to establish the circumstances under which cultural process takes place, as one of their primary tasks.

In many ways the biologist and the archaeologist are facing the same problem: How do forms, whether living or cultural, emerge and stabilize? Yet archaeologists have done little so far to explore the thinking of modern evolutionary biologists, who have made giant strides in recent years in accounting for the behavior of animal species. Archaeology badly needs a general theory capable of generating scientific explanations within a historical framework, and of integrating them into a systematic, coherent body of knowledge (Dunnell, 1980). Progress in this direction is still minimal, and this ambitious agenda is likely to be the major aim of research into the 21st century.

Further Reading

Binford, Lewis R. 1983. *In Pursuit of the Past*. Thames and Hudson, London and New York.
  Lewis Binford's own synthesis of his approach to archaeology, which helped revolutionize North American archaeology in recent decades.
Coles, John. 1973. *Archaeology by Experiment*. Heinemann, London.
  A general account of experimental archaeology in many parts of the world.
Fagan, Brian M. 1990. *In the Beginning*. Scott, Foresman, Glenview, Illinois. 7th ed.
  A widely used basic textbook on archaeology, which discusses major theoretical approaches in archaeology. Recommended for the beginner.
Jennings, Jesse D. 1988. *Prehistory of North America*. Mayfield, Palo Alto.
  A basic account of North American prehistory designed for beginning students. Strong on culture history.
Meltzer, David, Fowler, Don, and Sabloff, Jeremy A. (eds.). 1986. *American Archaeology Past and Future*. Smithsonian Institution Press.
  Critical essays on many aspects of contemporary American archaeology, which probe basic topics in this chapter. A "must" for any serious student.
Renfrew, Colin and Bahn, Paul, 1991. *Archaeology: Theories, Methods, and Practice*. Thames and Hudson, London and New York.
  A new textbook with a strong emphasis on the application of different methodological approaches.
Sharer, Robert, and Ashmore, Wendy. 1987. *Archaeology: Discovering Our Past*. Mayfield, Palo Alto.
  Another popular textbook on archaeological method and theory. Strong American emphasis.

PART TWO

THE PALEO-INDIANS

*"In this isolated land [the past]
has been a hoary hermit, to the
very verge of the newest
creations of nature and the
latest institutions of man. The
flint utensils of the Age of Stone
lie upon the surface of the
ground ... The peoples that made
and used them have not yet
entirely disappeared."*

SAMUEL HAVEN, 1864

YEARS AGO	NORTH-EAST ASIA	NORTH AMERICA			
		ALASKA	WEST	PLAINS	EASTERN WOODLANDS
				EARLY PLAINS ARCHAIC	MIDDLE ARCHAIC
8000			WESTERN EARLY ARCHAIC		
9000		PALEO-ARCTIC TRADITION			EARLY ARCHAIC
				Paleo-Indian occupations defined by unfluted points	DALTON
10,000	SUMNAGIN CULTURE		Blackwater Draw		
11,000	?	Dry Creek II Dry Creek I	SAN DIEGUITO	FOLSOM CLOVIS CULTURE	EASTERN FLUTED TRADITION
12,000			Manis		
13,000			Fort Rock		
14,000	Mal'ta DYUKHTAI CULTURE	Bluefish Caves			Meadowcroft ?
		No securely dated human settlement recorded			

Note on Chronological Tables
These tables are intended as a general guide only. Not all sites, phases or cultural terms used in the text appear in these tables.

The following key is used throughout the tables:

——————— Well-established chronology. Time span may continue beyond the line.

———————| Limit of the chronology is generally agreed.

— — — — — Chronology doubtful.

CLOVIS A name in capital letters is an archaeological culture, horizon, or tradition.

Meadowcroft A name not in capital letters is an archaeological site.

CHAPTER 4

FIRST SETTLEMENT

After five years' research on the problem of the first Americans, this author was moved to write that "Anyone studying the first Americans sets sail in hazardous academic seas, beset on every side by passionate emotions and contradictory scientific information." This most fundamental of issues in North American archaeology is among the most controversial, and we summarize the main areas of agreement and disagreement in this chapter (for a detailed analysis, see Fagan, 1987a; Kirk and Szathmary, 1985; Meltzer 1989, also the essays in Carlisle, 1988).

Stone Age Hunters in Asia
30,000 to 14,000 years ago

Despite some unsubstantiated claims to the contrary, only anatomically modern humans, *Homo sapiens sapiens*, settled in the Americas. Their arrival was the end result of cultural developments in northeast Asia and much further afield (Fagan, 1987a, 1990).

There is general agreement that modern humans spread widely over the Old World and into the Americas as part of a general expansion of Stone Age hunter-gatherers into arctic latitudes after about 40,000 years ago, during the last cold snap of the Würm glaciation[1]. No one knows exactly when Stone Age groups adapted to the vast, treeless arctic plains that stretched northeast from eastern Europe and the Ukraine during the late Würm, but it was at least 35,000 years ago. These plains extended into arid central Asia and Siberia, places of limited glaciation, nine-month winters, and endless steppe-tundra, a distinctive, open landscape with sparse, arid grass and cottonwood scrub cover. Small, local river valleys and drainages may have supported stands of willow brush, with deltas and coastal flats near large lakes and some sea coasts. This arctic landscape supported a remarkable diversity of game animals — mammoth, woolly rhinoceros, musk ox, steppe bison, reindeer, and wild horse, animals that were the staple of Stone Age hunters for millennia.

It was *Homo sapiens sapiens* who developed the technology and the social institutions that enabled widely scattered hunting bands to live

---

[1]The last glaciation is known as the Würm in the Old World, and the Wisconsin in North America. This terminology is used here.

In order to survive the bitter winters of the west Eurasian plains at the height of the last Ice Age, modern humans cooperated in the construction of substantial base camps. The 18,000-year-old Mezhirich site, on the Dnepr River in the Ukraine, has yielded the remarkably complete remains of oval dwellings built out of mammoth bone. Partially dug into the ground for insulation, these structures would have had a final roof covering of hides and sod.

permanently in this extremely cold environment with its widely dispersed game herds (Soffer, 1984). Each group covered very large distances, resulting in a rapid expansion of Stone Age hunters over the steppe-tundra from the west. The concentrations of game animals changed constantly through the year, so human populations would gather and disperse according to the season, and the need for cooperative hunting. The result was remarkably standardized Stone Age culture over enormous areas.

Mal'ta and Dyukhtai. Two major clusters of Stone Age sites provide our best clues to Stone Age settlement in Siberia. One lies near Lake Baikal in the Trans-Baikal, typified by the Mal'ta settlement, occupied between about 25,000 and 13,000 years ago. The Mal'ta people were mammoth hunters, whose dwellings and lifeway were strongly reminiscent of big-game hunters in the Ukraine far to the west (Gerasimov, 1935).

The second cluster comes from the Middle Aldan Valley in extreme northeast Asia. Here Yuri Mochanov has excavated Dyukhtai Cave, where mammoth and musk ox hunters lived between about 14,000 and 12,000 years ago. Mochanov (1977) has also investigated some open sites occupied by the same people, which he claims date to as early as 18,000 years ago, perhaps even to 35,000 years ago. Unfortunately, Mochanov's early dates come from much churned-over river terrace deposits and may be very unreliable.

Most American and Soviet archaeologists believe that the Dyukhtai culture is no older than about 18,000 years ago, and that it was widespread

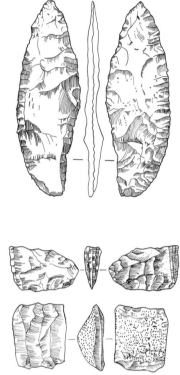

over northeast Asia about 14,000 years ago. The Dyukhtai toolkit includes well-made bifacial (bifacial: flaked on both sides) projectile heads and knives, large stone choppers that probably served as butchery tools, and numerous wedge-shaped and disc-shaped cores used to produce small "microblades," used as stone inserts for hunting weapons.

Most Dyukhtai sites date to the closing millennia of the Würm glaciation. They lie between the Angara River in the west, as far south as the Amur Valley on the Manchurian border, on the coastal plain of the Sea of Okhotsk, even in the Kamchatka Peninsula, and perhaps in Japan. There are also late Stone Age sites with microblades in northern China that date between 30,000 and 15,000 years ago, reaching an even higher level of technological sophistication between 15,000 and 10,000 years ago (Chung and Pei, 1986). In short, Dyukhtai-like microblade technology was widespread in northeast Asia during the late Würm, even if there was widespread local variation on a common technological tradition. Some Dyukhtai-like artifacts, including microblades and the wedge-shaped cores used to produce them, also occur in Alaska, across the Bering Strait, but they appear to be of later date than in Siberia. There were also biface traditions in maritime northeast Asia and Japan, but it is still not clear how these relate to early biface assemblages in Alaska.

Does this mean, then, that the first Americans originated, ultimately, among late Stone Age hunting traditions in northern China and inner Asia? We can evaluate this hypothesis from two directions, one biological, the other archaeological.

Northeast Asia: map of relevant sites (above left), and Dyukhtai tools (above) from Verkhene-Troitskaya, Siberia (a biface, top, and two wedge-shaped microblades; length of biface 14 cm).

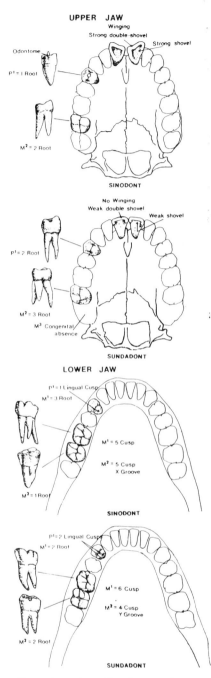

Dentochronology: Sinodonty and Sundadonty. Sinodonts display strong incisor shoveling (scooping out on one or both surfaces of the tooth), single-rooted upper first premolars, and triple-rooted lower first molars.

Sinodonts and Amerinds

Physical anthropologist Christy Turner (1984, 1986) has examined the teeth of thousands of ancient and modern individuals from Old World and New, specimens going back as far as 25,000 years ago and to Paleo-Indian times. He points out that prehistoric Americans display fewer variations in dental morphology than do eastern Asians, and their crown- and root-trait frequencies are similar to those of northern Asians. The three "Sinodont" (Chinese-like teeth) groups share incisor shoveling, double-shoveling, single-rooted upper first pre-molars, and triple-rooted lower first molars, among other features.

Sinodonty only occurs in northern Asia and the Americas, not among the Mal'ta people of Lake Baikal, or in the Stone Age Ukraine. Turner argues that northern Chinese may have evolved from a southeast Asian population, people they resemble more closely than the eastern Siberians and native Americans who evolved in turn from the northern Chinese. He used statistical calculations based on dental morphology to date the approximate moments at which Sinodont populations split off from the ancestral Chinese groups. The first of these divergences, Turner believes, led to the migration of Sinodonts into Mongolia about 20,000 years ago, and across the Bering Strait about 14,000 years ago.

Turner's dental work gains support from both genetic and linguistic researches. A team of American geneticists has collaborated on a study of the variants (called Gm allotypes) of one particular protein found in the fluid portion of the blood, the serum. All proteins drift, or produce variants, over the generations, and members of an interbreeding population will share a set of such variants. Thus, by comparing the Gm allotypes of two different populations one can work out their genetic "distance," which itself can be calibrated to give an indication of the length of time since the populations last interbred (Suarez, Crouse, and O'Rourke, 1985).

The research team sampled thousands of Indians from four cultural groups in western North America, and found their Gm types divided into two groups. One large group shared the same grouping with over 14,000 Central and South American Indians, and is thought to result from a single, early migration of hunter-gatherers, who evolved later by cultural differentiation. Two later migrations brought the present-day Athabaskan and Eskimo-Aleut populations to North America. Such Gm allotype data as comes from Siberia appears to link all three groups with northeastern Siberia.

Back in 1956, the Stanford linguist Joseph Greenberg proposed that most North American and all South American languages were part of a single, large "Amerind" family. Aleut-Eskimo and Na-Dene were quite separate linguistic groups, making a total of three for the whole of the Americas. Greenberg then spent years compiling a vast database on the vocabulary and grammar of American Indian languages, which confirmed his belief that there were three linguistic groups that corresponded to migrations into the Americas. Greenberg estimates that his Amerind group arrived before 9000 BC, Na-Denes around 7000 BC, and that Aleuts and Eskimos diverged about 2000 BC (Greenberg and others, 1986; Greenberg, 1987).

There is substantial, if superficial, agreement between the biological and linguistic evidence. What, then, of the archaeological data? At present, there is no solid evidence for Siberian sites dating to earlier than 18,000 years ago, and sophisticated microblade sites appear to be later than that. There are suspected technological links between northern Chinese and Siberian microblade sites, but these are still ill-defined. The only possible link may be a very general, adaptive one. Paleontologist Dale Guthrie believes (1982) that Dyukhtai microblades were inset into antler shafts as slotted points. He links the distribution of microblade production to that of reindeer hunting. Could it be that this inset-weapons system emerged in China and other parts of eastern Asia, in Siberia, and northwestern America, as a widespread adaptation to tundra conditions, where migratory reindeer herds roamed? Perhaps, he argues, the widespread microblade tradition reflects a widely shared and successful material culture that emerged at the very end of the last glaciation and flourished well into Holocene times.

The most likely ancestors for the first Americans were Sinodont late Stone Age hunter-gatherers with a dental and genetic morphology remarkably like that of the modern American Indians. They subsisted off big-game, smaller animals, perhaps fish and sea mammals, and some wild vegetable foods. At some point, a few of these people, perhaps no more than a few families, walked (see below) or paddled eastward across the Bering Strait into North America. David Meltzer has argued persuasively (1989) for migratory "dribbles" of early settlers, for many tiny population movements, some of which failed. On these general points, there is little disagreement. The date of first settlement is another matter, for archaeologists divide sharply into two schools of thought — those who believe settlement took place well before the end of the Ice Age some 15,000 years ago, and those who argue for first occupation at, or after, 15,000 years ago.

Beringia

Some 18,000 years ago, when world sea levels were more than 300 ft (91 m) lower than today, a vast, low-lying landmass known to geologists as Beringia linked Siberia and Alaska. Central Beringia was an exposed coastal plain, denuded and dissected by many rivers, that covered the floors of the Chukchi Sea and the northeast Bering Sea. This was the famous Bering Land Bridge, commonly believed to be the land route by which human beings first reached the Americas (Hopkins and others, 1982).

The Bering Land Bridge has a complicated geological history, known both from land-based studies and deep-sea cores. These cores show that the last glaciation began about 100,000 years ago, with a gradual cooling trend that exposed the land bridge from about 75,000 to 45,000 years ago. A lengthy period of less cold climate ensued from about 40,000 to 25,000, when the land bridge was no more than a narrow, periodically flooded isthmus. Bitter cold returned as sea levels fell about 25,000 years ago. This time, the land bridge lasted until around 14,000 years ago, when rapid post-glacial warming began. During this last period of intense cold, the windy land bridge stretched from Asia to Alaska, and covered much of the Chukchi Sea. Its southern coastline extended from the Gulf of Anadyr in Siberia to the Alaskan Peninsula in North America.

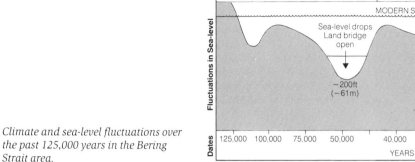

Stages	HIGH-LEVEL PELUKIAN BEACHES	HAPPY INTERVAL		BOUTELLIER INTERVAL	DUVANNY YAR INTERVAL	ICE AGE ENDS	POST-GLACIAL
Climate	COOLING	SHORT WARMER PERIOD	VERY COLD	INTERMEDIATE CLIMATE	VERY COLD		WARMING TREND

MODERN SEA-LEVEL

Sea-level drops
Land bridge
open

−200ft
(−61m)

Sea-level drops
Land bridge
open

−300ft
(−91m)

Fluctuations in Sea-level

| Dates | 125,000 | 100,000 | 75,000 | 50,000 | 40,000 | 30,000 | 20,000 | 10,000 |

YEARS AGO

Climate and sea-level fluctuations over the past 125,000 years in the Bering Strait area.

As sea levels rose at the end of the Ice Age, the geography of the land bridge changed dramatically. The Bering Strait and Gulf of Anadyr were submerged when the sea level rose to −157 ft (−48 m). Much of the Siberian coastline assumed its modern appearance about 10,000 years ago, but the North American coastline was still up to 63 miles (100 km) offshore at the very threshold of modern times.

The low-lying land bridge was no landscape of gently waving grass, where half-naked hunters pursued big-game from Asia into a new continent. Beringia was a treeless, arctic land, covered with a patchwork of very different types of vegetation. Palynologists are sharply divided on the nature of this plant life. Paul Colinvaux of Ohio State University (1980) thinks the land bridge was sparse tundra, "a dusty plain, stretching to the horizon, vegetated between the bare patches with a low mat of sedges and grasses looking like a drier version of arctic plain." An arctic tundra fauna lived on the plains, a fauna somewhat similar to the rodents of the modern tundra. Such large mammals as existed were outliers of much larger populations that lived in more hospitable terrain in neighboring Asia and Alaska.

Palynologist Steven Young (1982) and paleontologist Dale Guthrie (1982) take a less pessimistic view. They think that the land bridge was part of a now vanished ecosystem where many different animal species lived in productive harmony, just as they do on the African savanna today. Young and Guthrie argue that the land bridge was a mosaic of steppe rather than tundra, with shallow ponds and swamps in the center and south, where grass-dominated wetlands might have attracted large herbivores in summer. Several large rivers, among them the Anadyr and the Yukon, once crossed the land bridge. They would carry huge amounts of spring and summer glacial meltwater, creating great floodplains, where abundant fodder would have grown. The land-bridge environment was somewhat drier and more steppe-like than modern-day Alaska, an environment capable of supporting large mammals (Matthews, 1982).

Whether or not all the animals in this fauna existed together in Beringia at one time is highly uncertain. Matthews argues (1982) that bison, caribou, mammoth, and horse, also two forms of musk ox, a wild sheep, and arctic predators made up a mammalian community with twice as many

Beringia (untinted area of map, above left) and its bestiary. The Ice Age bestiary is known from fossil discoveries, frozen animal carcasses, and Eurasian cave paintings and engravings. (Above) Ice Age deposits all the way from Europe to Siberia and Alaska yield the remains of – from top to bottom – woolly mammoth, steppe bison, wild horse, and reindeer/caribou, all seen here as depicted by Upper Paleolithic artists in southwest France. (Left) Paleontologist O.W. Geist examines a hide fragment and bones from the partial carcass of an extinct bison (Bison crassicornis) found during gold mining operations on Dome Creek, near Fairbanks, Alaska, in 1951. The hide was subsequently radiocarbon-dated to around 31,400 years old.

species as that of the modern tundra. The land bridge could have supported a diversity of herbivores, provided it had sufficient variety, and quantity, of plant communities to do so. It never teemed with game animals, for they were probably scattered through the landscape, concentrated at dozens of special sites, in lowland meadows and near rivers. They would have succeeded one another, utilizing patches of the bare, treeless environment in an endless succession of grazing patterns that persisted as long as the continental ecosystem of the land bridge remained intact.

Hardly surprisingly, no archaeological remains have yet come from the floor of the Bering Strait, so we can only assume that there was once a sparse human population dwelling on the land bridge, preying on the great herbivores that lived there. There may have been coastal settlements on the southern shores, too, settlements flooded by rising sea levels, where people might have taken fish and sea mammals. However, without effective canoe technology, they would have been severely limited in their ability to take maritime resources[1]. In all likelihood, the first Beringians were big-game hunters, practicing a lifeway that had already flourished for thousands of years on the steppe-tundra. When human beings first set foot on the land bridge remains a complete mystery, but, given the present dates for Dyukhtai sites in Siberia, it may have been after 18,000 years ago. And, at some point afterwards, some of these people hunted their way across to higher ground in the east and ultimately into the Americas. At present, it is not possible to give an even slightly precise date for this crossing. Alternatively, it may have been a response to the rapid flooding of the land bridge after 14,000 years ago.

First Settlement of Alaska and the Yukon Territory

About 18,000 years ago, glaciers covered the Alaska Range and the Alaska Peninsula, as well as the Brooks Range, but much of the land immediately east of the Bering Strait was dry and ice-free. Some archaeologists believe these ice-free areas of Alaska were uninhabitable during late Wisconsin. Others have considered Alaska little more than a passageway, a "natural highway" to more temperate latitudes. In fact, a sparse arctic population spread over this vast arctic landscape, adapted to it in many ways, and evolved distinctive cultures over very long periods of time indeed (Giddings, 1960). Unfortunately, the archaeological potential of Alaska and the Yukon has hardly been tapped. The level of speculation about first settlement vastly exceeds the amount of archaeological data. Only a handful of sites give us clues (Fagan, 1987a; Morlan,1978).

Bluefish Caves lie in the Keele Range of the Yukon Territory. Some 15,000 years ago, the caves lay within sight of windswept glacial lakes. Here Jacques Cinq-Mars (1978) unearthed a layer of tightly packed glacial, wind-blown loess accumulated as birch trees became more frequent between 14,000 and 12,000 years ago. The loess contained mammoth, horse, bison, and caribou, and a large pile of Ice Age mammal bones lay

[1]We assume here that the first Americans crossed into Alaska on foot. For the arguments against an open-water crossing, see Fagan 1987a.

outside Cave I. The same cave yielded some stone tools, including some biface trimming flakes, microblades, a wedge-shaped core, and other tools. Bone collagen radiocarbon dates from the bones gave readings between about 15,000 and 12,000 years ago. If the Bluefish dates are correct, then people making microblades that would not be out of place in the Dyukhtai tradition of Siberia were living in North America by 12,000 years ago, perhaps somewhat earlier.

Dry Creek on the Nenana River Valley in the northern foothills of the Alaska Range contains two radiocarbon dated levels. The earliest, Dry Creek I, dates to about 11,200 years ago, and contains some cobble and flake tools, also broken blades, thin bifacial knives, and points. Roger Powers compares the artifacts to tools from the Kukhtyi III site in eastern Siberia, a site belonging within the Dyukhtai tradition (Powers and Hamilton, 1978). Dry Creek II above dates to about 10,700 years ago, and contains microblades and other artifacts associated with such technology.

Dry Creek I is still almost unique as a possible forerunner of the microblade traditions that were widespread in Alaska after 11,000 years ago. These are subsumed under a so-called Paleo-Arctic Tradition, described in Chapter 8 below. William Powers and John Hoffecker (1989) include Dry Creek I in the so-called Nenana Complex, assemblages that contain bifacial tools, but no microblades, dating in the Nenana Valley to between 11,800 and 10,500 years ago. Nenana Complex sites lie along outer river terrace margins, well-drained locations close to water, and offering good observation posts. They reflect short-term occupation of the valley, perhaps while hunting large mammals. Powers and Hoffecker stress that the Nenana Complex is a local term, applying only to the immediate vicinity of the northern foothills of the Alaska Ridge.

At present, there is no evidence for the human settlement of Alaska and the Yukon before 15,000 years ago. This raises the possibility that eastern Beringia was settled only when Stone Age people retreated to higher ground as the land bridge was submerged after 14,000 years ago. If the paucity of sites is any guide, the initial human population was tiny. Only after about 11,000 years ago do a variety of microblade, Paleo-Arctic occupations appear throughout Alaska. Apparently, earlier occupations were by people who were not microblade makers, suggesting to Powers and Hoffecker that the first settlers migrated from the maritime regions of Asia where bifaces were made during the late Ice Age, and microblades may be later. In contrast, the Siberian interior was dominated by the microblade tradition of the Dyukhtai culture from at least 18,000 years ago. Whatever the actual direction of migration, however, what is known from the archaeological evidence meshes well with what we know of the human biology and linguistic history of the first Americans.

Nenana Complex tools from Dry Creek, Alaska. Clockwise, from top left: small triangular point, large triangular point, end scraper on a blade, and lanceolate point (length of end scraper 5 cm).

Ice-Free Corridors and Continental Shelves

During the late Wisconsin, when the Bering land bridge was exposed for the last time, northern North America was mantled by the vast Cordilleran and Laurentide ice sheets. The Laurentide was centered on Labrador and the Keewatin areas of Canada, a complex glacial mass fused into a single

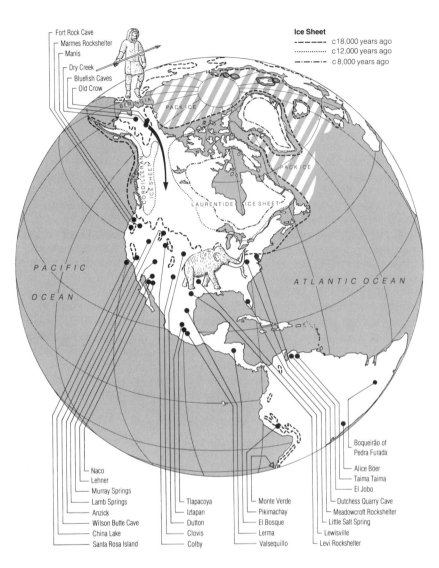

Ice Sheet
- - - - - c 18,000 years ago
· · · · · · c 12,000 years ago
- · - · - c 8,000 years ago

Fort Rock Cave
Marmes Rockshelter
Manis
Dry Creek
Bluefish Caves
Old Crow

BERINGIA

PACK ICE

CORDILLERAN ICE SHEET

PACK ICE

LAURENTIDE ICE SHEET

PACIFIC OCEAN

ATLANTIC OCEAN

Boqueirão of
Pedra Furada
Alice Böer
Taima Taima
El Jobo
Dutchess Quarry Cave
Meadowcroft Rockshelter
Little Salt Spring
Lewisville
Levi Rockshelter

Naco
Lehner
Murray Springs
Lamb Springs
Anzick
Wilson Butte Cave
China Lake
Santa Rosa Island

Tlapacoya
Iztapan
Dutton
Clovis
Colby

Monte Verde
Pikimachay
El Bosque
Lerma
Valsequillo

Major early archaeological sites and other locations in the Americas during the last stages of the Ice Age, when human colonization took place. The routes that humans used to move south are still uncertain. One much discussed and controversial route is shown here: the widening corridor between the Cordilleran and Laurentide ice sheets.

icebound wilderness with an ever-changing margin that extended from the Atlantic coast, along the southern shores of the Great Lakes, into southeastern Alberta. The mountain ranges of Alaska and British Columbia were also heavily glaciated, forming the Cordilleran glacial complex in the west that extended to about 30 miles (48 km) south of Seattle by about 14,500 years ago. For at least 10,000 years after 25,000 years ago, these icy barriers would have inhibited travel between Beringia and the ice-free zones to the south.

In the 1950s, Canadian geologists reported that Cordilleran ice did not fuse with the western margins of the Laurentide, creating an "ice-free corridor" between them. This corridor passed into the popular imagination, and became, in some peoples' minds, a kind of Paleo-Indian superhighway to the south, where mammoths and people traveled. This appealing picture is a geological myth, for the boundaries of the ice sheets are slowly being mapped, revealing only a partial corridor, and one that was very inhospitable indeed (Rutter, 1980). Rugged terrain, mazes of meltwater lakes, crumbling rocks, and only the scantiest of vegetation and few game animals — there were few incentives to travel through this ice-free zone at the height of the late Wisconsin. If human beings did travel south, the most likely times for them to do so would have been either before the last glacial maximum beginning 25,000 years ago, or soon after 15,000 years ago, in early Holocene times (Porter, 1988).

If the ice-free corridor was an unlikely migration route to the south, what about other paths? Canadian archaeologist Knud Fladmark has uncovered traces of human occupation on the Queen Charlotte Islands of British Columbia, and suspects that human occupation of this region may date to as early as 10,000 to 12,000 years ago. He points out (1983) that the Pacific coast of North America was relatively warmer and more productive than other shores. Perhaps, he speculates, the ice-free Pacific coast could have sustained human life, especially societies that used skin boats and other technological innovations adapted to the pursuit of marine mammals. Unfortunately, there is no evidence that such societies existed in late Wisconsin Beringia, although, of course, their settlements may have been submerged by rising sea levels. Although early coastal settlement is possible, such occupation on a large scale seems unlikely, for everything we know about the Paleo-Indians suggests that they were terrestrial hunters and gatherers, with a lifeway adapted at least in part to the pursuit of large Ice Age mammals.

The Case for Human Settlement Before 15,000 Years Ago

Those who believe that the human settlement of the Americas took place before 15,000 years ago, either during the late Wisconsin, or even earlier, are faced with the problem of documenting such activity in stratified, properly dated archaeological contexts. It is only fair to say that no archaeological site dating to earlier than 15,000 years ago in any part of the New World has received complete scientific acceptance — for a variety of highly complex reasons (for discussion, see Bednarik, 1989; Bryan, 1986; Fagan, 1987a; Lynch, 1990; Meltzer, 1989, among others).

The most widely discussed claims for early settlement come not from North America, but far to the south, from northeast Brazil and northern Chile. Among the numerous rockshelters from the Piaui area of northeastern Brazil is Toca do Boqueirão da Pedra Furada, a large rockshelter with a stream channel cutting through it. There is abundant evidence for later prehistoric occupation in the shelter, artifacts such as knives and scrapers made on exotic chert or flint. The putative earlier occupation consists of "crude" artifacts made on local rocks such as quartz and quartzite that are extremely hard to identify as being of human manufacture. Charcoal from the stream-deposited lower levels has been dated to as early as 40,000 years ago, and is claimed to come from hearths, which may, in fact, be the result of natural brush fires (Guidon and Delibrias, 1986; Lynch, 1990). Boqueirão da Pedra Furada bristles with unanswered questions — what were the forces that fashioned the artifacts from the stream-deposited lower levels? Is the charcoal from these levels naturally formed, or the result of human activity? Why did the earlier inhabitants of the shelter prefer coarse quartz and quartzite when much finer-grained rocks were available a short distance away? Excavations continue at other nearby sites, but in the meantime, Pedra Furada is far from convincing.

Monte Verde in northern Chile has been exhaustively investigated by Tom Dillehay, a site lying alongside a low-lying creek that, according to radiocarbon dates, was occupied by people living off game animals and vegetable foods some time around 12,000 years ago, and perhaps even earlier, some 30,000 years ago (Dillehay, 1988; Dillehay and Collins, 1988). The upper occupation is said to include wooden huts, hearths, and a wishbone-shaped structure, associated with bone and stone artifacts. The site lies in a good environment for natural carbonization, and was hardly an ideal place to camp, leading Lynch to query whether the site was in fact a site at all — or perhaps a natural deposit accumulated by the local creek (Lynch, 1990). The artifacts are very simple, some "little modified from their natural state" (Collins and Dillehay, 1986), and it is by no means certain that all of them are humanly manufactured. Even if one accepts the later Monte Verde occupation as being a human occupation, there must be serious doubts about the 30,000-year level, which Dillehay himself has described with open-minded, scrupulous care as a level containing "carbonized wood" (Pino and Dillehay, 1988). To date, no large-scale excavations have exposed these horizons.

Neither Monte Verde nor Pedra Furada, nor any of the other Central and South American sites claimed as evidence for pre-15,000-year-old settlement, stand up to rigid scientific scrutiny. There is even debate as to what constitutes valid criteria for establishing such occupation (Bray, 1988; Fagan, 1987a). Perhaps most significant of all, we still lack the clusters of dated sites and indisputable pre-Clovis artifacts either in North or South America that would document consistent ways in which such people adapted to their new homeland. After more than a century of research, we must begin to question whether they actually exist — especially since evidence for settlement contemporary with Pedra Furada or Monte Verde is almost non-existent in North America before about 12,000 years ago. The few early sites north of the Rio Grande are quickly summarized:

Meadowcroft Rockshelter in southwestern Pennsylvania was occupied from at least 12,000 until nearly 700 years ago, and perhaps from much earlier. James Adovasio (1982, 1984) excavated this large shelter meticulously between 1973 and 1977, revealing no less than 11 strata, dated by more than 70 radiocarbon samples. The lowest level containing traces of human occupation is known as Stratum IIa. Adovasio and his colleagues divide this into three subunits. The uppermost dates to between about 10,950 and 7950 years ago. It is separated from Middle Stratum IIa by a layer of rock spalls from the roof and walls of the shelter. This middle zone accumulated between about 12,950 and 10,950 years ago, while the lowermost subunit, again sealed by rock spalls, has yielded seven radiocarbon dates ranging from 19,600 to 13,230 years ago.

9N   8N   7N   6N   5N   4N

GROUND SURFACE

VI

XI

IX

VII

V

IV

III

IIb

IIa

IIa

I/IIa
INTERFACE DEPOSITS

𓆸 ROOT

▨ UNEXCAVATED

╱ CHARCOAL LENS

▢ SANDSTONE

-·-·- PROGRESSIVE DRIPLINE

|— I METER —|

Note: Strata VIII and X lens
out west of the illustrated
sections.

JOEL GUNN JAN 76
N.L. YEDLOWSKI MAY 89

*Meadowcroft Rockshelter,
Pennsylvania. (Above) Overhead view
of excavations near the beginning of the
seven-year project in 1973. The large
rock at left was once part of the shelter's
roof. (Left) Portion of the stratified
layers of Meadowcroft Rockshelter, with
layer IIa at the base.*

Meadowcroft Rockshelter, Pennsylvania. (Left) Miller lanceolate (unfluted, lance-shaped) projectile point, length 4.4 cm (Center and right) small prismatic blades from Paleo-Indian occupation levels, length of each c. 4 cm.

The geologist and archaeologist Vance Haynes (1980) and other critics questioned the dates from the earlier strata, arguing there was a danger they contained large percentages of soluble humic acids, or "dead" carbon in the form of coal particles. The reason the humates were earlier is because acids in groundwater were permeating, or had in the past permeated, Stratum IIa. Other critics suggested that there might have been stratigraphic mixing in the lower levels. Adovasio and his colleagues (1990), in a line-by-line rejection of these criticisms, publish not only accelerator dates from the lowest (pre-human) level and from later strata that are consistent with other readings, but also produce a conservative averaging of the radiocarbon chronology. This gives a minimum age for the presence of humans in the 12,000-to-10,600 years ago range. An averaging of the six deepest dates associated with cultural materials suggests humans were at Meadowcroft between about 14,555 and 13,955 years ago. This, as Adovasio and his colleagues point out, does not argue for "any radical extension of the 11,500 year 'baseline'." Perhaps people were present at Meadowcroft 2,000 to 3,000 years before the Clovis time horizon.

Some critics of Meadowcroft believe that the small samples of flora and fauna from the early levels are types that flourished in the area *after* the ice sheets retreated. Adovasio counters by pointing out that the site lies in a sheltered region that could have fostered a more temperate ecology. Whatever the precise date of first occupation, Meadowcroft is one of the earliest well-documented archaeological sites in North America.

Other Early North American Sites. A scatter of 12,000-year or older sites are found elsewhere in North America. The most coherent western US evidence comes from Washington, Oregon, and Idaho, at sites dating back to 12,000, perhaps 14,000 years ago. These locations include the Manis mastodon kill of some 12,000 years ago from near Sequim, Washington, and the Fort Rock Cave in south-central Oregon. Here, a gravel layer under an occupation level of 11,000 years ago seals two poorly worked obsidian projectile points and some flakes dated to as early as 13,250±720 years ago.

Claims of earlier human settlement from California and Texas have either been based on conflicting field evidence or have not withstood close scientific scrutiny (for a summary, see Dincauze, 1984; Fagan, 1987a). Some spectacular finds from Florida sink holes are thought to date to as early as 12,000 years ago (see Chapter 6).

At present, the earliest securely dated human settlement in North America dates to about 14,000–12,000 years ago, this despite more than a century of intensive search. Only the tantalizing Meadowcroft finds offer a possible hint of earlier occupation. Many archaeologists, while quite prepared to accept a considerably earlier date for the first Americans, believe that initial settlement of Alaska took place at the very end of the Wisconsin glaciation, with a fairly rapid spread southward into ice-free North America during the next few millennia. All this is, of course, little more than a theoretical scenario. There is only one certainty: about 11,500 years ago, the Clovis culture appears, marked by a veritable explosion in the number of archaeological sites throughout North America, from the California deserts to the Eastern Woodlands.

Clovis Culture
c. 11,500 to 11,000 years ago

The Clovis culture lasted for about half a millennium, from about 11,500 to 11,000 years ago, a radiocarbon dating so precise that 21 dates from the Lehner and Murray Springs sites in Arizona give a mean reading of 11,000±200 years ago, a remarkably consistent result by radiocarbon standards. Everything points to their having been successful, efficient big-game hunters.

At the end of the Wisconsin and during the millennia that followed, the areas in the rain shadow of the western mountains of North America were dominated throughout the year by the dry mid-Pacific air mass. The Plains were an area of seasonal extremes during the Late Wisconsin, a place where big-game species like the mammoth and large Ice Age bison adapted to conditions where growing seasons were short and intense. The grasslands provided high-quality nutrients in the dry fall and into the winter, sustaining large herbivores during the lean months. These grasslands were becoming drier in Early Holocene times, at the time they were home to scattered bands of Clovis people, who ranged over enormous territories. Within a few centuries, small groups of Clovis people had spread throughout North America. They camped on low terraces along rivers and streams, in places where big-game came to feed, to obtain water. Some Plains groups favored perennial springs and waterholes, while others visited caves and rockshelters, some probably winter encampments.

It would be a mistake to think of the Clovis people as merely big-game hunters, even if the bones of larger animals are normally those that are preserved. Undoubtedly they took not only big Ice Age species, but medium-sized animals like deer, and small rabbits and other mammals as well. They must, also, have exploited wild plant foods in spring, summer, and fall, as well perhaps as fish and other aquatic resources when the occasion arose. While the hunting of large mammals was important, and the people wandered far and wide in search of them, we can be sure that there were many distinctive adaptations to locally plentiful and predictable resources, which are not yet reflected in the archaeological record. Many bands may have lived on coastal plains, on now sunken continental shelves, where, conceivably, they relied heavily on marine resources.

Judging from Plains sites, the Clovis people were especially fond of mammoth and bison. Mammoth bones occur at almost every kill site known. These lumbering beasts were attractive quarry for many reasons. A single animal could provide meat for weeks on end, and if dried, for much of the winter, too. Hides, tusks, bones, and pelts were used to make household possessions and weapons, for shelter, even clothing. Precious fat from the internal organs could be melted down and used for cooking and burning in lamps — just as it had thousands of years before on the steppe-tundra of Eurasia.

We do not know whether the hunters attacked mammoth individually or in groups. Most Clovis mammoth kills lie on low ground, near creeks, springs, or ponds. The hunters could have ambushed the animals at watering places, spots where the soft ground impeded movement. Our only analogies can come from modern elephant populations in the tropics. There, herds are highly mobile and respond quickly to fluctuations in food availability. Their matriarchal social organization means that they wander in family units, a pattern that allows the development of traditions of resource-oriented movements. Generation after generation, the elephants

Excavations at the Murray Springs Clovis site, Arizona.

would return to the same salt licks, waterholes, trails, and favored patches of vegetation. It is hardly surprising to find hunting sites close to permanent water supplies in an arid landscape.

Clovis hunters were obviously shrewd observers of mammoth behavior. Vance Haynes believes (1966) they followed matriarchal groups for weeks on end, observing the behavior of individual elephants with great care. They would then catch individuals off guard and cull the herd one by one at the same location over the years, perhaps in a place like Lehner, where 13 mammoth carcasses were found. George Frison has experimented with stone-tipped Clovis spears on dead African elephants in Zimbabwe, Central Africa. He found that Clovis weapons could indeed inflict lethal wounds, especially if the hunter stood still and took careful aim. He argues that the hunters worked in pairs, the one attracting the beast's attention, while the other loosed off a spear. Such an approach means concentrating on individual beasts, and positioning oneself carefully for the kill. Most probably, the Clovis people took individual animals.

Eleven bison died at Murray Springs, Arizona, yielding enough meat to support as many as 50 to 100 people, perhaps many fewer. A single mammoth, from Naco in Arizona, had no less than 8 Clovis points in its carcass, four times more than any other known kill. Perhaps it escaped wounded, only to die later. If each point belonged to an individual hunter, then at least 8 men attacked the beast or 4 if each fired off two spears. Vance Haynes believes that the hunters may have represented about a fifth of a band of about 20 to 40 men, women, and children. Not that the Clovis people used all the meat they butchered. Whenever they killed a mammoth, they only partly dismembered the carcass, taking away some choice parts with them. At Clovis itself, Murray Springs, and the Colby site in Wyoming, they created piles of disarticulated bones, perhaps left as winter meat caches. Bison carcasses were more heavily utilized and less was left at the site.

Clovis Technology. Clovis toolkits were highly effective, lightweight, and portable, as befits people who were constantly on the move. Their stone technology was based on precious, fine-grained rock that came from widely separated rocky outcrops, outcrops that were exploited for thousands of years afterwards by later peoples. Some of the stone came from sources more than 186 miles (299 km) away. These included alibates, a form of banded, agatized dolomite from the Canadian River area of Texas. Translucent dark brown chalcedony came from the Knife River Valley of North Dakota and Manitoba. There was chalcedony from Ohio, volcanic obsidian from the Yellowstone Park region. The hunters traveled long distances to obtain rock, and, judging from Eastern Woodlands sites (Chapter 6), exchanged it over considerable distances. Sharp-edged stone was vital, for effective procurement of other raw materials such as bone, hide, sinews, even wood, depended on an adequate supply of fine-grained rock to kill and process big-game and cut down trees.

Clovis stone workers used a careful reduction process that started with large bifaces and branched out into smaller artifacts with maximum economy and logical efficiency. The bifaces themselves were not only a "bank account" of potential artifact blanks, but served as heavy butchery knives and choppers into the bargain. These were constantly flaked as

Clovis points found with the mammoth skeleton at Naco, Arizona, four times the number discovered with any other such kill. This suggests the animal may have got away from its hunters only to die somewhat later.

Experimental archaeology has played an important role in Paleo-Indian archaeology. Here Bruce Huckell of the Arizona State Museum makes the initial skinning cut with a biface into the hide of a deceased circus elephant.

Clovis points from the Lehner site, Arizona (left), and Blackwater Draw (right). Length of Lehner point c.9 cm.

butchery proceeded. At Murray Springs, Bruce Huckell of the Arizona State Museum pieced together clusters of thin bifacial trimming flakes to reconstruct the bifaces that produced them. At the same site, a few projectile points and other tools, and thousands of thinning and sharpening flakes, lay among the dismembered carcasses. Only 36 finished tools came from the entire site, presumably because the hunters conserved their best artifacts and took them away for reuse. The ratio of finished tools to waste flakes was 6:10,000, a startling demonstration of the high value Clovis people put on fine-grained rock.

The fluted projectile point is the most celebrated, distinctive part of the Clovis toolkit. Judging from modern experiments, they were time-consuming to prepare, so the hunters resharpened them again and again when they were damaged in the chase. Exactly how the points were hafted is unknown, but the men probably carried a series of them mounted in wooden or bone foreshafts that worked loose from the spear shaft once the head was buried in its quarry. Besides projectile points, the Clovis people used bifacially trimmed points and other woodworking and butchering artifacts, as well as flakes used simply as sharp-edged, convenient tools in their struck-off form.

Clovis Origins. There are isolated hints of human settlement south of the ice sheets earlier than 11,500 years ago, at places like Meadowcroft Rockshelter, but none of these sites prove that there were indigenous ancestors for Clovis. The evidence is simply too sparse and the range of tools too inadequate to suggest a local origin for the highly developed Clovis technology. Vance Haynes (1982; 1987) argues that the Clovis people came originally from north of the ice sheets and migrated south in pursuit of big-game at the very end of the Wisconsin glaciation, as the glaciers melted and the ice retreated.

Are there, then, archaeological links between Clovis artifacts and Stone Age tools made in the far north at a much earlier date? Distinctive Clovis points with or without fluted bases are found in all the Canadian provinces and throughout North America. However, no securely dated prototypes that are widely accepted as such have come to light in Alaska or the Yukon, except in later sites or in poorly dated contexts. Perhaps the Clovis point was an indigenous development, first fabricated in temperate North America and not in the Arctic at all.

The microblade and wedge-shaped core traditions of Alaska are really no earlier than Clovis itself, and at many sites perhaps a millennium or so later. Only Bluefish Caves and Dry Creek I offer hints of an ancestral occupation in the far north, and there are too few artifacts from either location to make meaningful comparisons. However, Vance Haynes and German archaeologist Hansjurgen Müller-Beck argue (both 1982) that the mammoth was to the late Stone Age hunter what the reindeer is to the Lapplander or the caribou to the inland Eskimo. They both believe that general similarities between Clovis stone and bone tools and those from classic mammoth hunting sites in eastern Europe and the Ukraine mean that the first settlement of the New World was part of a big-game hunting tradition that spread across Russia into northeast Asia.

This line of thinking agrees well with Turner's dental calculations for the land bridge crossing. However, modern native Americans display Sinodonty, a feature found not at Mal'ta and other late Stone Age sites in the west, but in northern China and Asia generally. Did, then, the ancestral populations come from the south in Asia? The inconsistency between the two points of view may not be important, for northeast Asia was environmentally highly diverse, a region that may have supported a far more varied population than just big-game hunters, peoples with distant cultural roots in the far east as well as in the west. It is not illogical to argue that Clovis derived ultimately from late Stone Age cultural roots, even if details of their technological ancestry remain enigmatic. This ancestry may always remain somewhat of a mystery, for the archaeological signature is but transitory, indeed, the earliest Americans may have used artifacts that bore no resemblance to those that ultimately came into use south of the ice sheets.

Unfortunately, our knowledge of the Clovis people comes from kill sites rather than habitations, so our picture of these primeval hunters may be somewhat skewed. However, everything we know about their culture is strongly reminiscent of late Stone Age hunters in the Old World. The people lived in small bands, ranged over enormous distances, and relied significantly on big-game hunting (Fladmark and others, 1988). They shared the same basic cultural traditions and toolkits over vast areas, giving at least a superficial impression of cultural standardization. Haynes (1982) hypothesizes that the ancestors of the Clovis people wandered south from eastern Beringia, pursuing their favorite quarry, the mammoth. Eventually they reached the Canadian prairies, where they encountered new mammoth species and a greater bounty of other big-game species. And there the Clovis culture, basically a late Ice Age phenomenon, emerged before 11,500 years ago, to spread and flourish all over North America and further afield for more than 500 years.

Clovis and Megafaunal Extinctions

The Clovis people hunted in all corners of North America until about 11,000 years ago, when they abruptly vanish from the archaeological record, to be replaced by a myriad of different local hunter-gatherer cultures. By an intriguing coincidence — if coincidence it be — the disappearance of Clovis coincides with one of the great mysteries of vertebrate paleontology, too — the mass extinction of Ice Age big-game animals, the megafauna. Inevitably, this has led to speculation that Clovis people overhunted these mammals and drove them into extinction. Therein lies a major controversy in Paleo-Indian studies (Fagan, 1987a; Martin and Klein, 1984; Mead and Meltzer, 1986).

Everywhere in the world, the end of the Ice Age saw massive, even catastrophic, extinctions of big-game species, including the mammoth, the mastodon, giant sloth, and many camel species, to mention only a few. During the 1960s, Paul Martin of the University of Arizona developed a provocative hypothesis. He argued that an exploding population of big-game hunters, fanning out over a virgin continent, rapidly drove the megafauna into extinction through wasteful hunting methods and before the fauna learned defensive behaviors. The result was a human population crash following the big-game extinctions (Martin, 1967; 1973).

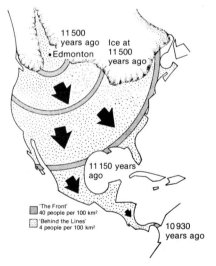

Paul Martin's hypothetical scheme for the rapid spread of the first hunters through the Americas. As local extinctions occurred at the "front," so the hunters moved on.

Martin's theory provoked opposition from those who believe that drier climatic conditions at the end of the Ice Age led to mass starvations in game populations and to eventual extinction. Others argue that as the climate dried up, so water tables fell and reliable water supplies were hard to come by. Mammoth were still to be found, but the hunters had to cover far greater distances to take them. There may always have been low human population densities, so there was no population crash when extinction took place, but, instead, a steady, slow growth, one that brought neighboring bands together in cooperative hunts, this, and other developments, leading to far greater cultural diversity in later centuries.

Most likely, a complicated set of factors spelled the extinction of the American megafauna, and probably Clovis hunters were one of the factors involved (for full discussion, see Fagan, 1987a; Mead and Meltzer, 1986).

Whatever the cause of megafaunal extinction, the later Paleo-Indians adopted far more diverse adaptations to their new homeland, a process that was to continue for the rest of prehistoric times and long after European contact.

Further Reading

Bryan, Alan L. (ed.). 1986. *New Evidence for the Pleistocene Peopling of the Americas*. Center for the Study of Early Man, Orono, Maine.
Essays containing valuable information on claims for very early settlement of the Americas, also on later sites.
Carlisle, R. (ed.). 1988. *Americans before Columbus: Ice Age Origins*. Department of Anthropology, University of Pittsburgh, Pittsburgh, Pa.
A volume of conference papers that examines first settlement from a multidisciplinary perspective.
Dincauze, Dena. 1984. "An Archaeo-Logical Evaluation of the Case for Pre-Clovis Occupations," *Advances in World Archaeology* 3:275-324.
A carefully argued evaluation of claims for early settlement on a site-by-site basis.
Fagan, Brian M. 1987. *The Great Journey*. Thames and Hudson, London and New York.
An account and evaluation of the evidence for first settlement. Aimed at both specialist and general reader.
Greenberg, Joseph, Turner, Christy, and Zegura, Stephen. 1986. "The Settlement of the Americas: A Comparison of the Linguistic, Dental, and Genetic Evidence," *Current Anthropology* 27,5:477-497.
This comparison makes a strong, and well-documented, case for Paleo-Indian settlement at the end of the Ice Age.
Hopkins, David M. and others (eds.). 1982. *The Paleocology of Beringia*. Academic Press, New York.
Essays that seek to reconstruct the environment and ecology of Beringia and the Bering Land Bridge, also its fauna and inhabitants. Authoritative, but technical.
Shutler, Richard (ed.) 1983. *Early Man in the New World*. Sage Publications, Beverly Hills.
Wide-ranging articles on first settlement, including progress reports on sites excavated since the appearance of Bryan (1978).

CHAPTER 5

HUNTER-GATHERERS AND THE HOLOCENE

By 9000 BC, scattered hunter-gatherer populations lived in every corner of North America, direct descendants of the first Stone Age settlers of the New World some millennia earlier. These isolated groups, small in size, armed with but the simplest of hunting technology, flourished at a time of continual, and rapid Early Holocene climatic change. These changes, and perhaps the Clovis hunters, decimated the big-game that had been one of the staples of the first Americans. Undoubtedly, many groups perished as their primeval quarry became scarce and starvation stared them in the face. But one of the most formidable of all human qualities is an ability to adapt to radically new circumstances, to seize opportunities as they come along. Thus it was that a great diversity of hunter-gatherer societies developed during the later centuries of the Early Holocene and throughout the warmer millennia of the Middle Holocene that followed.

These Paleo-Indian, and, later, Archaic societies enjoyed a great variety of lifeways. Some, Plains hunters, remained big-game hunters right up to European contact many centuries later. Others adapted to harsh desert environments in the west, subsisting off seasonal plant foods and small game. Others settled near marshes, lakes, and perennial streams, on sea coasts and by wide estuaries, where the bounty of aquatic resources and waterfowl enabled them to develop sedentary lifeways and more complex societies. Still others hunted deer and other game throughout the Eastern Woodlands, with the greatest population densities again near sea coasts and in resource-rich river valleys. These societies displayed a remarkable variety of adaptations to North American environments over more than 12,000 years of prehistoric time. Some survived as hunter-gatherers into modern times, while others became full-time food producers in the closing millennia of prehistory. In a real sense, a major part of the study of North American prehistory is the study of the archaeological record of hunter-gatherers.

Although the Eskimo, Inuit, Athabaskans, and other North American hunter-gatherer societies have survived into historic times, archaeology generally has probably contributed more to our knowledge of such societies north of the Rio Grande than any other subdiscipline of anthropology (Bettinger, 1987). These archaeological and anthropological studies have prompted major theoretical debates about North American hunter-gatherers and some basic concepts that are of fundamental importance for interpreting the archaeological record. In this chapter, we examine notions of "foragers" and "collectors," and of optimal foraging strategy that are central to interpreting prehistoric hunter-gatherer societies at all levels of complexity. Later, at intervals in the text, we discuss some of the theories that have been advanced to account for the emergence of more complex societies in some parts of prehistoric North America.

Hunter-Gatherer Theory

When they have engaged in theoretical discussion, students of hunter-gatherers have tended to do so in comparative, evolutionary, and materialist terms (this summary is based on Bettinger, 1987). From the early 1900s up to the 1960s, they depicted hunter-gatherers as primitive societies, unable to rely on predictable food supplies, constantly in danger of starvation, and, as a result, underdeveloped in their cultural and social institutions. Under this Darwinian form of model, they were the least-developed stage of human culture.

During the 1960s, a series of thorough field studies, especially that of Irven De Vore and Richard Lee among the !Kung San of the Kalahari Desert in southern Africa, led to radically new perceptions of hunters and gatherers. Archaeologists now discovered that hunters do not necessarily die young, nor do they constantly struggle against food shortages and an alien environment. No longer could one explain hunter-gatherer society as backward, or in strictly Darwinian terms. So they turned to contemporary anthropological theory, to cultural ecology and functionalism. These new approaches stressed the importance of understanding local environments. Under this new rubric, hunter-gatherer behavior became rational, adaptive, and functioned as a result not only of individual behavior, but of that of the group as a whole. Consciously or unconsciously, all hunter-gatherer behavior had an underlying logic—sustain long-term internal group equilibrium.

As we saw in Chapter 3, this ecological model of hunter-gatherers was based on general and sometimes vague systems models, assumptions that band societies operated as cultural systems within the larger ecological system of which they were part. By the 1970s, many researchers were trying to develop better links between theory and field data through combining archaeological and ethnographic observations in ethnoarchaeology. It was this approach that prompted Lewis Binford's Nunamiut Eskimo research (1978), described briefly in Chapter 3, and the development of his so-called "forager-collector" model of hunter-gatherer societies.

The Forager-Collector Model

Binford's model is based on the assumption that, where access to resources is limited for many months of the year, or where a group has but a limited area to exploit, then hunter-gatherers will take measures to extend the economic utilization of these resources (Binford, 1983). If such limitations are absent, then people are unlikely to try such extension strategies.

Foragers. In warmer environments, there are no serious seasons of relative shortage. Thus, there are few incentives for storing and saving resources beyond those needed for immediate consumption. People will tend to exploit the resources within walking distance of their camps, in the case of the San about a two-hour walk. When these resources are exhausted, they move their camp site to a new location. The sizes and duration of their camps and residential bases depend on the productivity of the local environment. Binford calls this a "foraging system," where the population is said to "map" onto resources, moving its camps to allow people easy access to them. There is no mismatch between the distribution of food supplies and population distributions.

Collectors. What happens when there are sharp seasonal contrasts, when the availability of food supplies differs from one month to the next, often dramatically? The Plains Indians, for example, live in an environment where food supplies are very sparse during the five winter months. Some form of efficient food storage technology is essential in this environment. As we have seen, the same is true of the Nunamiut. Under both these circumstances, and in many other climatically more severe areas of North America, people had to obtain their food in bulk, accumulate a surplus sufficient to meet storage needs for the hungry months. Such hunting strategies require advance planning and organization. Hunter-gatherers living under these circumstances use what Binford calls "collector systems."

Paiute women in Arizona wearing basketry caps and carrying burden baskets for foraging.

Large-scale food storage has some serious disadvantages. It anchors the population to the bases where they store their food, thereby making it harder for them to shift their settlements to match the changing distributions of animal and plant foods. Furthermore, food resources are never uniform. This creates further inconsistencies between food supplies and residence patterns. The hunters often respond by hunting and foraging enormous quantities of food at periods of maximum, and predictable, abundance, often in groups. The Plains Indians would conduct bison drives during the fall, then spend several days camped by their kills while they skinned and butchered the animals, dressing the hides, drying many pounds of meat, and pounding much of it to make pemmican, a mixture of pounded flesh and fat that was easy to eat on the move. The Nunamiut not only store food in special "caches," they also organize their hunting technology in such a way that they can store it with the game meat, a process called "curation" — saving tools in anticipation of future use. Such forms of hunting require efficient technology that is portable, and sometimes hard and costly to manufacture, phenomena that make it cost effective to curate the resulting specialized artifacts.

Collector systems involve a more structured relationship between hunter-gatherer populations and their food resources. Task forces move from centrally located residential bases to obtain specific resources. People respond to lean periods by having sophisticated storage systems, and to the mismatch between their base sites with their storage pits and available resources by careful organization of specialized hunting and gathering tasks at specific locations. Collectors tend to live in more diverse settlements, where many activities take place, and to occupy specialized hunting camps at different, specific times of year, and at the same locations

The collector model: Plains Indian bison hunters disguised as wolves approach their quarry in George Catlin's famous sketch of 1876.

that are visited again and again. In contrast, foragers respond to shortages and resource exhaustion by moving their camps much more frequently.

The forager-collector model is a useful conceptual framework for studying North American prehistory. However, it should be noted that there is, in reality, a broad continuum of hunter-gatherer societies, with the forager-collector model representing two possible extremes. Only very rarely were hunter-gatherer societies exclusively foragers or collectors.

Optimal Foraging Theory

Hand-in-hand with more sophisticated models of foragers and collectors goes another fundamental notion, that of optimal foraging theory. Optimal foraging theory, a set of theories about how people make rational decisions about limited resources, came to anthropology from biology. Its principles also form a central core of microeconomics (Bettinger, 1987). From the archaeological perspective, optimal foraging theory assumes that, under certain well-defined circumstances, human decisions are made to maximize the net rate of energy gain. These decisions can revolve around diet or breadth of diet, around where to forage, the amount of time spent on different activities, or on settlement location or group size (Bettinger, 1987; E.A.Smith, 1983; Winterhalder and Smith, 1981). The most common applications of optimal foraging strategy in North American archaeology revolve around diet models.

The basic diet model argues that hunter-gatherers confront a range of animal and plant foods in their daily round. These resources vary greatly in abundance, both in the amount of energy they produce, and in the effort required to acquire and process it from each resource unit once it has been selected. Every hunter-gatherer society has to select a combination of resource items that maximize net energy intake per unit of foraging time, that is, the amount of energy captured less the amount expended in the chase or while gathering. Three assumptions lie behind this model:

— Under most normal circumstances, the amount of time and energy needed to extract energy from a resource and the amount it yields are fixed commodities;

— When decisions about dietary alternatives are made, normally those with a higher rate of energy return will be selected;
— A food resource is either on the optimal set of choices "list," or it is not.

This model and its assumptions of fixed extraction costs and benefits has but one variable factor — the abundance of food resources in the environment. If all resources were infinitely abundant, one's choice would revolve around two variables, the time needed to acquire resources and their energy benefits. So one would choose only the item that yielded the highest possible energy intake rate under optimal circumstances. If one had to select more than one resource, one would exploit a combination of items with the highest rates of potential return. Under this rubric, resources can be "ranked" by energy return per extraction time. The hunter-gatherer would logically not choose to pass over a higher ranked resource to exploit one with fewer benefits — there is no benefit in doing so. Therein lies the nub of optimal foraging theory — the implication that the hunter-gatherer uses all higher-ranked resources when available.

This is fine in a world where everything is infinitely abundant. In practice, resources vary greatly in distribution and abundance, and, thus, in the time needed to search for them. For example, in the resource-rich Northwest Coast region, salmon runs occur in well-defined areas and at predictable seasons, whereas deer are solitary animals that are less predictable, but available all year round. The hunters' choices revolved around the need to acquire large quantities of dried fish to store for winter consumption, while acquiring game and other foods when the opportunity arose. For some coastal peoples without watercraft, whales, the most highly prized resource of all, may strand on the beach so rarely that the cost of searching for them may exceed the benefits, resulting in a lower overall rate of return. This rate can be calculated by subtracting the amount of energy required to locate and process a resource from its ultimate energy benefits.

The resource-rich Northwest Coast region: Indians spearing salmon at the Colville Falls on the Columbia River in a painting by Paul Kane, c.1850.

A new twist to optimal foraging theory now enters the picture. When a hunter in the Eastern Woodlands is hunting, say, deer, the most highly prized game, he may encounter a teeming rabbit warren on the way, rabbits being the second or third highest ranked food resource on his mental list. He stops and takes six rabbits, and forgets about deer, deciding on a new course of action based on anticipated energy consumption and immediate food needs at the time he encounters the warren. In this case, exploitation of the food resource is independent of its abundance, what optimal foraging theorists call a "contingency model" (for summary, see Bettinger, 1987). Such models are important, for they imply a basic reality that repeats itself again and again in North American archaeology: as food resources decline in abundance, the time required to search for them increases, and the breadth of the hunter-gatherer diet widens to compensate for this reality. Conversely, as resources become more abundant, so does selectivity increase.

Relatively few North Americanists have applied optimal foraging theory to their research, except in the Great Basin. In two important papers, Robert Bettinger and Martin Baumhoff have used this general model to produce a theoretical continuum of hunter-gatherer strategies in the Great Basin that approximates to Binford's "forager-collector" sequence (see Chapter 11) (Bettinger and Baumhoff, 1982, 1983). This model is useful, for it specifies quite precise relationships between Great Basin populations and food resources, and settlement and subsistence patterns.

On the face of it, optimal foraging strategy seems an attractive model for interpreting prehistoric hunter-gatherer societies in North America. There are, however, important criticisms that can be leveled at this approach. First, is it best to measure the efficiency of hunter-gatherer societies in strictly energy terms? What about nutrition and other important variables? Second, should one treat hunting and gathering as "an endless string of individual responses to momentary contingencies rather than as an overarching plan or strategy?" (Bettinger, 1987). Third, what kinds of genetic mechanisms or learned behaviors could cause people to hunt or gather in optimal fashions? (For a detailed discussion, see Bettinger, 1987.)

There is a close relationship between optimal foraging strategy and middle-range theory (Chapter 3), for both are grounded in the same principles of economic utility and rational behavior by hunter-gatherers. Both are limited theories that are ultimately governed by more general theories, which are still not completely defined. Both, however, are useful in seeking to explain the bewildering diversity of hunter-gatherer societies that developed in North America after first settlement.

"Resource-Stress" and Hunter-Gatherer Diversity

The end of the Ice Age caused major adjustments in North American hunter-gatherer societies, characterized by two broad trends. First, everywhere — even in the richest game areas — people tended to broaden their resource base. They hunted a greater variety of animals, even species as small as edible rats. Domesticated dogs and the bow and arrow made hunting more efficient and effective. Many groups must have regularly burnt off forests as a way of increasing prime grazing land for game.

Second, in time, many also developed special technologies to process seeds and other edible plants. Mortars and pestles came into widespread use, pounding devices that helped extend the food supply by reducing otherwise inedible cartilage or masses of small bone to edible pulp, by macerating food for the very young or aged, and by pulverizing toxic starches such as acorns for leaching. Regular boiling of food rendered plants with toxins edible, and could be used to extract hitherto inaccessible fat, marrow, and meat from animal bones. Fishing techniques improved, too, and fish became a regular part of the diet in areas where they were readily taken from shore, and later from canoes. In time, many societies developed specialized toolkits — hooks, fishing spears, and nets — for exploiting oceans, lakes, and rivers. Shellfish became an important supplemental food, although they provide relatively little protein. (It takes 83,422 mussels to make up the protein equivalent of a deer.)

In areas with poor-to-moderate resources, such as much of the Eastern Woodlands outside major river valleys, coasts, and lake basins, the Great Basin, and the far Western interior, highly mobile groups greatly diversified their food sources — as optimal foraging strategy would predict.

Again, as optimal foraging theory predicts, groups who lived in regions where food supplies were plentiful and seasonally predictable tended to specialize, to focus their attention on a few resources to the virtual exclusion of others. For example, after about 4000 BC, the maritime peoples of the Northwest Coast took thousands of salmon during spring and fall runs and developed an effective drying and storage technology to preserve them for lean months. Fish were much more important than game animals.

Seed-gathering technology: California Pomo Indian woman collects seeds with a beater and basket.

Vigorous controversy surrounds this important transition in hunter-gatherer life at the end of the Ice Age. Were these changes the result of chronic imbalances between population and food resources, as some archaeologists have argued? Or did major climatic change cause the transition? The climatic explanation is suspect simply because the entire Ice Age was a period of constant, and often dramatic, climatic change. One can readily understand such long-term change causing severe stress on local populations, but why did not earlier major change result in the same kinds of cultural shifts earlier in prehistory?

The population hypothesis assumes that steady, if usually slow, growth has characterized North America since first settlement, that this growth was a "general phenomenon." Put in very simple terms, this "bottle model" suggests that North America's population grew throughout prehistory. Then, after about 2000 BC, population densities overflowed in some areas of abundant and predictable resources, requiring new food-getting strategies, including the deliberate cultivation of wild plant foods.

The "bottle model" falls down on several counts. Why or how is human population growth different from that of other animals? Many living hunter-gatherer populations have maintained stable populations over long periods of time, using both child spacing and other devices to control their numbers. Why should we argue that prehistoric hunters were any different in keeping their populations in balance with their resource bases? How can we explain how areas like the Near East, which have been occupied for at least 700,000 years, should have a population pressure crisis at the same moment as the Americas, which have been occupied at most for 15,000 to 20,000 years?

No hunter-gatherer group could avoid periodic imbalances between population and available food resources. Dramatic short-term climatic changes, also long-term ones, may create famine conditions, whatever the local population density. Canadian archaeologist Brian Hayden (1981) argues that hunter-gatherer populations tried to control the amount of stress they would experience by modifying their behavior in response to changing conditions. He believes periodic resource stress was the most important motive for cultural change, a need to minimize the immediate effects of food shortages and cultural instability.

Usually, hunter-gatherer groups dealt with stress by using established strategies and hunting or foraging techniques. On occasion, however, they developed new and more efficient ways of obtaining and using food, perhaps, for example, by exploiting spring salmon runs with newly developed barbed spears, and by drying the fish in enormous numbers for later consumption.

Hayden takes his arguments a stage further. These newly efficient ways of obtaining or using food mostly involved more effective ways of obtaining the game or plant foods they had exploited before, or by diversifying to exploit large-bodied animals that were dangerous or more difficult to obtain. This required more diverse, more specialized toolkits adapted to all kinds of hunting quests, some of them very high-risk indeed. In time, all large bodied animals would have been exploited, so the hunters adopted another strategy. They began harvesting very small species such as rodents and birds, animals that were predictable enough, but often very hard indeed to procure economically, especially with simple hunting tools. Some of them, such as, for example, waterfowl, would require complicated processing and special storage methods to make them economically viable.

These small resources were, Hayden believes, vital to cultural evolution. They were relatively inexhaustible, had a much higher biological productivity than larger species. This provided a much more stable and abundant resource base in those local areas where they were abundant. In turn, this led to major changes in the hunter-gatherer cultural system. Settlements became more sedentary, more permanent, population densities rose, resulting in more competition for resources and social prestige, and eventually to some form of ranking within society.

The Hayden "resource-stress" model regards hunter-gatherers of whatever economic level in long-term evolutionary terms. The archaeological record from areas like the Great Basin and California, for example, tends to support the notion of continuity. The Great Basin was first occupied by human beings by at least 10,000 BC. The total population was very small and widely scattered until about 4000 BC, and in some areas remained tiny right into historic times. Some more favored areas of the Basin with abundant, relatively predictable resources witnessed population increases after 4000 BC. The number of archaeological sites now increased, specialized toolkits for processing seeds first appeared in considerable numbers, just as they did in other continents. By the time of European contact, most groups in the arid and semi-arid areas of the Basin and the far west generally relied heavily on plant foods, which they exploited in many specialized ways, making use of staggered harvests and careful storage strategies. In more favored areas, especially near perennial wetlands, late prehistoric hunter-gatherer adaptations were highly localized, often complex, and based on a wide range of land management strategies. These included deliberate burning of hunting and foraging grounds, exploiting a very wide range of animals and plants, and intensive exploitation of wetlands. In well-watered areas such as Nevada's Humboldt Sink, the people often lived in sedentary settlements. It should be emphasized, however, that the Hayden resource-stress model is necessarily a simplification of very complex processes. It has been criticized as providing only a partial explanation as to what actually took place.

Until recently, archaeologists tended to assume that the development of agriculture and animal domestication was a revolutionary trend in human history. Under this argument, food production involved major, dramatic changes in human culture and settlement patterns, including sedentary villages and radically new toolkits. If, however, one thinks of the development of hunter-gatherer societies in evolutionary terms, then it is reasonable to argue that the deliberate cultivation of wild plants was a logical extension of gathering them. As we shall see in Chapter 17, certain hunter-gatherer groups living in food-rich Eastern Woodlands environments with predictable and seasonally abundant resources began deliberately cultivating native plants as a means of *supplementing* their vegetable diet, in some areas at least as early as 2000 BC. These far-from dramatic strategies were successful and persisted for many centuries, without any major changes in hunter-gatherer life, while, at the same time, settlements became more permanent, human society somewhat more complex, territorial boundaries more precisely set. To societies like these, and to many in the Southwest, the adoption of cultivation was a simple and thoroughly logical strategy to supplement natural food supplies, a strategy that could be pursued without the need for new artifacts or major energy expenditure. It was not until much later, some 2000 years ago, that rising population densities led to the large-scale growing of maize and beans, subsistence activities that had much more profound consequences for American Indian societies. These were the innovations that, millennia after the first cultivation of native plants, transformed not only the natural environment but many of North America's human societies as well.

Before examining this diversity, however, we must describe some of the major climatic changes that transformed North America after the Ice Age.

Holocene Climatic Change in North America: The West

To understand cultural change over the 12,000 years or more of North American prehistory means studying the major environmental changes during the Holocene (Holos is the Greek word for "recent," the Holocene meaning postglacial times), both at the local and continent-wide level, using pollen analysis, tree-rings, glacial moraines, and many other sources (Wright, 1981).

An airline passenger flying over western North America would not be blamed for thinking of much of this vast region as utterly dry, uninviting desert lapping rugged mountains and the broad reaches of the Pacific Ocean. In fact, the west includes hundreds of diverse and sometimes rich coastal and interior environments. A wide range of edible animals and plants are to be found in greatly varying abundance throughout the interior

Temperate rainforest

Tropical rainforest

Undifferentiated Caribbean formations

Desert

Scrub steppe

Undifferentiated prairie, grassland, scrub steppe and desert

Glaciated area

Exposed continental shelf

Steppe-tundra savannah (glacial times). Tundra (modern)

Undifferentiated alpine formations

Temperate deciduous forest

Coniferous forest (Taiga)

Undifferentiated tropical deciduous forest and grassland

The North American environment: glacial.

west. The Pacific coast abounds in aquatic resources of every kind, sometimes in almost overwhelming bounty. On the coast and inland, the types of food resources vary infinitely, not only in variety and abundance but in availability from one local environment to the next.

The west is an environment where the signatures of Ice Age and later climatic change are writ not only in mountain glaciers and great ice sheets but many obscure, diffuse ways — in pollen diagrams from dried-up lakes, in deep-sea cores, in tree-ring fluctuations, and in many esoteric climatic archives (Aikens, 1981). For instance, the humble desert packrat gathers plant materials within a very confined area, typically about 98 to 328 ft (30 to 100 m) from its den. These dry middens contain beautifully preserved plant remains that provide a superb portrait of local vegetation. Since the middens contain organic materials that can be radiocarbon dated, sequences of small packrat middens from caves, rockshelters, and other contexts can provide unrivaled pictures of long-term vegetational change. For instance, packrat middens from Chaco Canyon in the Southwest tell us that Douglas fir, Rocky Mountain juniper, and limber pine were dominant trees in the area between 8500 and 7300 BC. In dramatic contrast, piñon-juniper woodland covered the area when packrats flourished in the Canyon between 3500 and 2500 BC (Betancourt and Van Devender, 1981).

The hundreds of small jigsaw pieces go to make up the climatic mosaic of the desert west, most of them, like the packrat middens, of a very local nature. They provide a very different and far more complex picture of Holocene climate than advances and retreats of ice sheets or rising sea levels. The effect is rather like a series of snapshots from dozens of obscure locales, where *local* climatic changes as small as a minor shift in rainfall patterns could have dramatic short- and long-term effects on *local* populations.

In reality, archaeologists examine Holocene climate in western North America at two levels. The first is within the context of a broad context of Holocene climatic change all over the west. The second is a mosaic of studies that provide ways of studying the effects of changing resource availabilities triggered by local climatic changes.

In general, the weather systems that control the diverse climates of the west have probably remained much the same through the entire Holocene and may only have varied during the height of the Wisconsin glaciation (Madsen, 1982). The resource mix depends, and has depended, not only on local environmental conditions, but on biological changes in local environments caused by fluctuations in rainfall and temperature during the entire Holocene. Most climatologists subdivide the western Holocene into three broad regimens, with many local variations (Antevs, 1948; Aikens, 1983).

Late Wisconsin (c.23,000 years ago to 10,500 BC). The height of the Wisconsin glaciation occurred throughout the west between about 16,000 and 12,000 BC. Summer temperatures in the Great Basin were much cooler, with tree lines between 1640 and 3280 ft (500 and 1000 m) lower.

Early Holocene (c.10,500 to 6500 BC). Between 10,000 and 8000 BC western glaciers receded and montane ice caps were reduced, woodlands and basin lakes diminished, and the Ice Age big-game vanished. Basically modern environmental conditions were reached just after the Early Holocene, between 6000 and 5000 BC. The actual rate of climatic change may have been slower in some more southerly areas, where vegetational changes were less extreme, but the evidence is still uncertain. From the archaeological point of view, what is important is that the first human settlers of the west and their immediate successors lived in a constantly changing, indeed transitional, environment. Over more than five millennia, the distribution of water supplies changed radically, major ecosystems like piñon-juniper woodland were on the move. Sea levels rose rapidly, flooding estuaries and coastal plains. It is difficult, then, to compare Paleo-Indian and Early Archaic societies to more recent western hunter-gatherer groups, for they lived in transitional environments that were very different from those of today.

The North American environment: modern.

Middle Holocene (6500 to 2000 BC). The Middle Holocene (sometimes called the Altithermal (Antevs, 1948)) was a period of major cultural change in many parts of the west, change that coincided with a general rise in temperatures, sometimes to higher levels than today. Many of the large interior lakes dried up, making surviving freshwater marshes and lakes of the greatest importance to hunter-gatherer populations. Piñon woodlands vanished in the southern Great Basin and expanded in more northerly areas. But the highly diverse environment of the west makes it virtually impossible to generalize about the effects of warmer Middle Holocene conditions. Some areas may have been abandoned completely, while others only a few miles away may have become exceptionally favorable under warmer conditions. There were certainly cycles of higher rainfall that affected human settlement. However, to correlate environmental change from one site to another, let alone one physiographic region to the next, is a virtual impossibility. One can only examine the archaeological and environmental record in units of a millennium or more, hoping to discern major climatic and cultural developments.

Earlier generations of archaeologists argued at great length about the effects of the Middle Holocene warm-up on human populations in the western interior. Jesse Jennings of the University of Utah has spent much of his career working on Great Basin prehistory and on major cave excavations spanning thousands of years. He stresses that what he calls the "Desert Culture" of the Great Basin was a very stable phenomenon that lasted for thousands of years. Environmental changes even of some magnitude had little change on this long-established adaptive pattern (Jennings, 1957; 1964). Two other veteran archaeologists, Martin Baumhoff and Robert Heizer, have taken the opposite viewpoint. So severe was the aridity during the Middle Holocene, they argue, that much of the interior desert west was abandoned between about 5000 and 2500 BC (Baumhoff and Heizer, 1965). More recent research has shown how very diverse western environments were during the Holocene. Most archaeologists now argue against widespread depopulation. They agree that while some areas may have been abandoned during the Middle Holocene when water supplies dried up, others were still occupied, sometimes even more intensively than before.

Late Holocene (2000 BC to the present). The Late Holocene (sometimes called the Medithermal (Antevs, 1948)) may have seen three colder episodes, some expansion of freshwater lakes, and a slight lowering of tree lines in some areas of the west. Again, the effects of environmental diversity are hard to measure. In some areas, upland resources may have been enhanced, while some lakeside areas were flooded by rising water, thereby reducing marsh areas available for human exploitation. There is, however, agreement that the basic animal and plant communities throughout the west were firmly established during the Late Holocene, ushering in a period not of climatic transition, but of fundamental stability.

The precise effects of the climatic episodes that punctuated the Late Holocene are still imperfectly known. There is evidence from the Great Basin, for example, of a rainfall increase by 2000 BC, a dry cycle around the time of Christ, and two further wetter intervals between about AD 400 and 1300 in the northern Great Basin and between about AD 950 and 1250 in the Southwest (Aikens, 1983; Mehringer, 1977).

Eastern North America

Much of temperate eastern North America is now farmland and secondary forest, but was largely deciduous forest at the time of European settlement. This enormous area is known to archaeologists as the "Eastern Woodlands," a region of great botanical and environmental diversity. Today, taiga, spruce-birch-pine boreal forest, extends north from the northern shores of Lake Superior. It covers the once-glaciated pre-Cambrian Shield from the edge of the western plains prairie in Minnesota eastward to the St Lawrence River. South of the Great Lakes, the boreal forest gives way to prairie-parkland from Iowa to the Appalachians far to the east. Deciduous forests dominated by sugar maple, beech, and yellow birch surround much of the Great Lakes and extend into the northeast. Hemlock and white pine are also common. As one moves south, red maple and hickory forest gives way to oak-pine woodland and southern mixed forest with its grassy vegetation and numerous swamps. Like the west, Holocene times are conventionally, and arbitrarily, subdivided into three stages (Delcourt and others, 1985).

Late Wisconsin (c.23,000 years ago to 10,500 BC). At the peak of the Wisconsin glaciation, some 18,000 years ago, the Laurentide ice sheet extended south of the Great Lakes, with a belt of treeless tundra between 62 and 37 miles (100 to 60 km) wide south of the ice. Boreal jack pine forest extended more than 1075 miles (1700 km) south of its present border across much of the eastern interior and Atlantic coastal plain at 34°N. It was here that a steep boundary between temperate and boreal ecosystems existed, the climatic Polar Frontal Zone that separates prevailing Arctic and Pacific air masses from the predominance of the Maritime Tropical Airmass. Warm-temperate oak-hickory-southern pine forest persisted across the Gulf and lower Atlantic coastal plain. The water table was so low that sand dune scrub covered much of the Florida peninsula. With the possible exception of Meadowcroft Rockshelter (Chapter 4), human settlement is unknown.

Early Holocene (c.10,500 to 6500 BC). About 14,000 BC, the first signs of warming appeared, accelerating after 12,000 BC, with the boundary between Late Wisconsin and Early Holocene conventionally drawn at 10,500 BC. As the Laurentide ice sheet retreated rapidly, cool-temperate tree species spread northward, dominating vegetational cover throughout the mid-latitudes of the Eastern Woodlands. A surge of glacial meltwater coursed down the Mississippi, diluting the salinity of the Gulf of Mexico. The tundra retreated northward with the ice. Spruce forest, a transitional zone between tundra and boreal forest, expanded across the newly deglaciated landscape.

By 8000 BC, the Laurentide ice sheet had retreated from the Great Lakes region. There was still tundra along the St Lawrence and in New England, with open spruce forest in Canada's Maritime Provinces, in New England, and Manitoba. Spruce-jack pine forest extended from Wisconsin to New York. Mixed-conifer-northern hardwood forest expanded northward over much of the Midwest, with oak-hickory and mixed hardwood forests to the south and east.

These vegetational changes were important to human settlement, because boreal spruce and pine forests offer few wild vegetable foods and even sparser game populations. In contrast, oak and hickory forests yield bountiful harvests of nuts and more diverse game resources. Under such changing circumstances, the animal species more capable of adapting to a broad range of potential environments were favored. And, of course, the Paleo-Indians and their Early Archaic successors were among them.

Middle Holocene (c.6500 to 2000 BC). The Middle Holocene is sometimes called the Hypsithermal (the equivalent of the West's Altithermal). It was marked by warming and increasing aridity, perhaps the result of stronger prevailing warm dry, westerly air flows that may have led to greater incidences of summer drought. Prairie, oak savannah, and oak-hickory forests shifted eastward as the mixed hardwood forest was reduced in extent. The boundary between forest and prairie reached its easternmost limit about 5000 BC. Sea levels reached their modern levels by 3000 BC, by which time basically modern vegetation patterns were established throughout the Eastern Woodlands. This was a period of rising population densities and increasingly diverse Archaic adaptations.

Late Holocene (c. 2000 BC to the present). The climate and vegetation of the Late Holocene were essentially similar to that of the present time. There have been minor fluctuations in temperature and precipitation in climatically sensitive areas, and along boundaries between ecological zones, to be sure, but the overall resources available in the Eastern Woodlands did not change dramatically. For example, the southern frontier of the boreal forest moved southward because of increased rainfall and a cooling trend. The prairie peninsula retreated westward, too.

The Late Holocene saw Late Archaic and Woodland peoples begin to cultivate native plants. It is during the Late Holocene that the first signs of substantial modification of natural vegetation by humans appears in pollen diagrams. Occasional maize grains have been found in Southeastern pollen samples dating to the time of Christ. The Delcourts' researches in the Little Tennessee River Valley have revealed high percentages of pollen associated with cleared land after about AD 450, and final deforestation of the area by Europeans in 1756 is well documented (Delcourt and others, 1986).

As many Ice Age geologists have pointed out, it is a mistake to think of Holocene climatic change as a series of rigid events that affected all corners of the world at the same time. Deep-sea cores and pollen samples have shown that the world's climate has been changing constantly over the past 700,000 years, and the past 20,000 years have been no exception. The actual peaks of extreme glacial conditions or full interglacial warmth have been few and far between. For over 60 percent of the time, environmental conditions have been transitional between extreme glacial and non-glacial regimes – just as they are today, and have been throughout North American prehistory. From the very earliest days of human settlement, hunter-gatherers, and later farmers, lived in a constant state of dynamic development and cultural change, as they adapted to local environmental changes. It is these many trajectories of continuous cultural change that we examine in the chapters that follow.

Further Reading

Bettinger, Robert. 1987. "Archaeological Approaches to Hunter-Gatherers," *Annual Review of Anthropology* 16:121-142.
  A useful survey article on hunter-gatherer theory. An excellent historical survey which makes fundamental points, and includes a critique of optimal foraging strategy.
Binford, Lewis R. 1977. *Nunamiut Ethnoarchaeology*. Academic Press, New York.
  This widely quoted case study in ethnoarchaeology is a mine of information on caribou hunters.
Bryant, Vaughn, and Holloway, Richard (eds.). 1985. *Pollen Records of Late-Quaternary North American Sediments*. American Association of Stratigraphic Palynologists Foundation, Dallas.
  Definitive summaries of pollen researches and paleoenvironmental reconstructions in all parts of North America.
Hayden, Brian. 1981. "Research and Development in the Stone Age: Technological Transitions among Hunter-Gatherers," *Current Anthropology* 22, 5:519-548.
  Discusses resource diversification among hunter-gatherers. A thought-provoking article that has caused considerable debate.
Winterhalder, B. and Smith, E. (eds.). 1981. *Hunter-Gatherer Foraging Strategies*. University of Chicago Press, Chicago.
  This volume serves as an introduction to optimal foraging strategy in hunter-gatherer studies.
Wright, H.E. (ed.). 1983. *Late-Quaternary Environments of the United States, vol. 2: The Holocene*. University of Minnesota Press, Minneapolis.
  Authoritative essays on Holocene climatic change, including two articles on the archaeological record.

CHAPTER 6

LATER PALEO-INDIAN CULTURES

When the Ice Age megafauna vanished about 9000 BC, Paleo-Indian groups throughout most of North America diversified away from big-game hunting. Some bands adapted to increasingly arid conditions in the west and placed major emphasis on plant foods. The sparse Paleo-Indian population of the Eastern Woodlands pursued deer and other forest game, also relying on seasonal vegetable foods. Only on the Great Plains did big-game hunting remain a viable lifeway, a lifeway that was to survive into historic times (Fagan, 1987a).

Unfortunately, our knowledge of these later Paleo-Indian cultures is very inadequate. Throughout North America, their archaeological signature is usually little more than a confusing multiplicity of projectile points and small scatters of scrapers and other generalized artifacts. The most complete information comes from bison kill sites on the Plains that may give a skewed impression of Paleo-Indian life. One has an impression, however, of a relatively generalized hunter-gatherer lifeway, with considerable standardization of material culture over thousands of square miles of sparsely populated, but varied terrain. It was only later, in Archaic times, that more specialized, often highly local adaptations arose.

Post-Clovis Paleo-Indians on the Plains
c.9000 to 6000 BC

About 9000 BC, a vast tract of arid grassland extended from the frontiers of Alaska to the shores of the Gulf of Mexico. This was the "Great Bison Belt," which lay in the rain shadow of the western mountains. It was dominated throughout the year by the dry mid-Pacific air mass. Spring and early summer rains supported, and still support, short grasses that keep much of their biomass beneath the soil. This retains moisture at the roots, so grazing animals like bison find high-quality nutrients in the dry autumn. Bison succeeded where other Ice Age animals failed because they diversified to become short-grass feeders as this type of grassland expanded in postglacial times (McDonald, 1981). By 8500 BC, the Plains Paleo-Indians, once broad-spectrum big-game hunters, turned to bison hunting instead.

The bison hunters moved around in small family groups most of the year. They tended to return to the same springs and other favored locations

Excavations at the Lindenmeier site by Frank Roberts, c.1936,

on higher ground year after year. There they would camp for a few days, dig a fire pit, perhaps erect a temporary shelter depending on the weather conditions, make some stone tools or process some meat, then move on (Bamforth, 1988; Frison, 1978). Nevertheless, some locations like Lindenmeier, Colorado, were exploited on a regular basis, thereby anchoring the people to specific points on the landscape. Communal kills were concentrated from fall to spring. Apparently, many did not involve large-scale processing of meat for later use, as if there was sufficient food to support large groups of people during the summer months. Thus, one can argue for a lifeway that involved at least some seasonal aggregation and dispersal of Plains populations (Bamforth, 1988).

Almost certainly, Paleo-Indian population densities were considerably lower than those of later prehistoric times. In most areas, groups had to remain widely dispersed and constantly mobile in their quest for game. Some of their mass kills appear to have produced more meat than the groups could use, for their high degree of mobility may have had another adaptive feature as well. The hunters needed to maintain social contacts with a considerable number of other widely separated social groups, if nothing else to provide mates (Wobst, 1974; Bamforth, 1988).

Most excavated later Paleo-Indian locations are kill sites that tell us much of the drama of hunting bison on foot. They may also give us a misleading impression of bison hunting as a kind of macabre orgy of mass game drives, of people herding dozens, if not hundreds, of beasts to their death. In fact, conducting bison drives is a difficult art, especially on foot. Most likely, a combination of solo and cooperative hunting ensured a

(Opposite) Later Paleo-Indian sites of North America.

regular supply of bison flesh, strategies that survived far beyond Paleo-Indian times (Chapter 7) (Frison, 1978).

When left alone, bison soon become less fearful of humans. Subjected continuously to pursuit, however, they become unpredictable and far harder to drive. If Paleo-Indian hunters were anything like historic bison hunters, they watched their prey constantly. They were probably careful to pursue the herds intermittently, driving them small distances, giving them time to calm down. Modern bison can be moved a mile or so without trouble; then they start to break and run, when it is almost impossible to stop them. Thus, large-scale game drives probably required careful orchestration and organized cooperation.

A mass bison drive demanded intimate knowledge of the surrounding countryside. The topography of the approach to the selected trap or jump had to stampede the animals in a predictable direction. Judging from 18th- and 19th-century accounts, the hunters were careful to "arrange" the layout of the approach in such a way that the drive direction was controlled. A skilled group of hunters could subject their quarry herd to gentle influences over periods of days, moving them a little way in the right direction when conditions were favorable. They would line the approach with decoys, with shouting men, while hunters dressed in bison hides would approach the unsuspecting animals. Once the drive began, the hunters would run and shout, even wave skins at the thundering herd. Clouds of dust rose from the plain as the sheer mass and weight of the herd forced the leaders over a precipice to their deaths, or into a corral lying under a low cliff or at the mouth of a narrow defile.

Bison jump on the northern Plains. A diorama commissioned by the Montana Historical Society.

Many hunts may have taken place in favored locations, places used more than once, intermittently over the millennia. The Folsom type site in New Mexico was a place where several bison were killed, probably in late fall or early winter. At Lindenmeier, 46 miles (74 km) north of Fort Collins, Colorado, generations of bison hunters of about 8800 BC camped in a small, well-watered valley near the Plains grasslands. On the basis of careful analyses of bone and stone artifact scatters, Ed Wilmsen believes Lindenmeier was visited by at least two semi-autonomous groups, who cooperated in bison hunts and regular social transactions (Wilmsen and Roberts, 1978).

The Casper site in Wyoming of about 6000 BC showed how the hunters used a parabolic sand dune with steep, loose sides to trap a herd of about 100 bison during a late autumn hunt (Frison, 1974). They drove the animals into the curve of the steep-sided dune, animals that may have been grazing near a natural pond nearby. The bisons' hooves sank into the loose sand. As the beasts panicked, the hunters moved in to kill them as fast as they could. Each hunter, or group of hunters, would select a single animal, and aim deliberately to thrust their spears through the rib cage into the heart.

George Frison took a typical Hell Gap projectile point (see below) that had been found on the surface and mounted it with a sinew binding in a slotted pine shaft, bonding the haft with pine pitch without using a foreshaft. He thrust and threw the 11-ft (3.3-m) long spear into the carcass of a domesticated ox. Frison found that an extremely hard thrust would penetrate the rib cage and hide, sometimes even reaching the heart, causing an extremely lethal wound. Occasionally, the point would break, but it was easily sharpened for re-use later. The haft was strong enough not to break, even after the hardest thrust. A skilled hunter with a long spear that gave him some distance from his quarry could deliver very lethal blows in short order without endangering himself unduly.

The Jones-Miller site in extreme eastern Colorado contains the remains of several hundred animals, which may have been killed over a period of some months, perhaps a single winter. Dennis Stanford (1978) believes the bison may have been driven into a specially constructed corral, where they were dispatched under the watchful eye of a waiting shaman. He found traces of a stout wooden pole near the corral. An antler flute and a miniature projectile point lay nearby. Stanford believes the wooden upright may have served as a shaman pole, the nearby artifacts as part of the priest's paraphernalia.

The Olsen-Chubbock site 16 miles (25.7 km) southeast of Kit Carsen, Colorado, on the central Plains offered a unique chance to record a Paleo-Indian bison hunt of about 6500 BC (Wheat, 1972). The hunters had located a large bison herd and stampeded them into a dry gully. The leading bison arrived at the steep edge and were swept on by the animals behind them. About 157 beasts were immobilized and trampled to death in the dry defile. Ten animals were pinned with their heads down and their rumps up. Two lay on their backs. Most of the skeletons lay where they had perished, facing south. Given the excavator Joe Ben Wheat's reasonable assumption that the hunters approached the herd from downwind, the wind would have been blowing from the south on the day of the hunt.

Once the stampede was over, the hunters faced many hours of arduous work. First, they maneuvered the carcasses into a position where they could be cut up at the edge of the arroyo. The bison wedged at the bottom were butchered where they lay. The butchers worked in teams and cut up several animals at once. They rolled the animals on their bellies, slit the hide down the back, and pulled it down the flanks to form a carpet for the meat. Then they removed the blanket of prime flesh on the back, the forelimbs, shoulder blades, hump meat, and rib cage. They probably ate the

The Casper site, Wyoming. (Above left) Looking into the northeast and leeward end of part of the trough of the old parabolic sand dune containing the Casper site bison. (Above) Close-up of butchered bison skeletons.

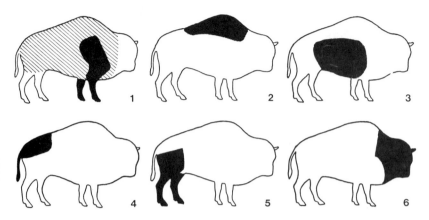

The Olsen-Chubbock site, Colorado: a reconstruction of Paleo-Indian butchery methods. The hunters skinned the bison down the back to get at the layer of tender meat (hatched area) just beneath the surface. When this was removed, the bison's forelegs and shoulder blades could be cut free (1), exposing the much-prized hump meat (2) as well as the rib meat and inner organs (3). The next step was to sever the spine and take off the pelvis (4) and hind legs (5). Finally the neck and skull were cut away as a single unit (6), their tough meat being dried and converted into pemmican.

tongues and some internal organs as they went along, piling the bones in the arroyo.

The Olsen-Chubbock hunters butchered 75 percent of the animals they killed, acquiring about 54,640 lbs (24,752 kg) of meat in the process. They also obtained 5400 lbs (2449 kg) of fat and 4000 lbs (1812 kg) of edible internal organs as well. The meat from this prehistoric hunt may have sustained over 100 people for a month or more.

As George Frison argues (1978), the Paleo-Indians knew their prey so well that they did not necessarily require natural arroyos, sand dunes, or low cliffs for their game drives. Rather, they relied on their stalking skills and on infinite patience to maneuver the bison on their own terms. Perhaps this is why large kill sites such as Olsen-Chubbock are rare phenomena (see also Frison and Todd, 1987).

Post-Clovis Material Culture on the Plains

For thousands of years, Paleo-Indians all over North America, and not just on the Plains, relied on a very simple, highly portable material culture that changed very slowly over a 3000-year period, from before 9000 until at least 6000 BC. Projectile points of different type usually constituted between 10 and 20 percent of the toolkit. At least seven forms of later Paleo-Indian Plains projectile point alone are known after 9000 BC, all apparently descended from the fluted Clovis head. To what extent these represent actual cultural differences is a matter for discussion (Knudsen, 1983). Side and end scrapers (20 to 54 percent) were invariably the most common tools. Knives were another characteristic Paleo-Indian artifact, tools that are easily confused with projectile point blanks or even finished heads. The most famous on the Plains is the so-called Cody Knife, an asymmetrical implement up to 3.9 in (10 cm) long with a transverse cutting edge, usually with a shoulder on one side. Some of these artifacts were made from broken projectile points (Irwin and Wormington, 1970).

***Folsom** (9000 to between 8500 and 8000 BC).* The Folsom tradition with its distinctive fluted point follows Clovis on the Plains. Folsom projectile heads have been found over an enormous area of the Plains, in the

Southwest and the far west, and east of the Mississippi in the Great Lakes region and New Jersey. Everyone assumes that the Folsom tradition originated in Clovis, but no intermediate projectile point forms have been radiocarbon dated or found in a stratified context. One possible candidate is the so-called Goshen Complex at the Hell Gap site in southeastern Wyoming, undated, but thought to lie between 9000 and 8800 BC (Irwin-Williams and others, 1973).

Undisturbed sites like Lindenmeier or the Folsom type site itself are rare. Most locations were kill sites where small or large numbers of bison were taken, often within a relatively short period of time. For example, the Lipscomb site on the Southern Plains contained the remains of 50 bison (Schultz, 1943), but it is not known whether their killing was a single event. Perhaps the best-known Folsom site is the Hanson settlement near chert and quartzite outcrops in the northern Bighorn Basin of central Wyoming (Frison and Bradley, 1981). Three hard-packed areas may have been the remains of circular lodge structures, radiocarbon dated to at least 8000 BC. The animals eaten at Hanson included bison, mountain sheep, deer, marmot, and cottontail rabbit, ample proof that the Paleo-Indians took many more animal species than just bison. Folsom may, in fact, include other traditions, such as the Midland, which is thought to date to between 8700 and 8400 BC (Agogino, 1969; Wendorf and Kreiger, 1959).

After Folsom. The late Plains Paleo-Indian traditions that follow on Folsom are defined very largely by stratified, *unfluted* projectile point forms, sequences that appear to apply to quite broad areas of the Plains. There were several contemporary Paleo-Indian occupations on the Plains after Folsom times, some of them oriented toward open plains bison hunting, others adapted to hunting and foraging in foothill and mountain areas at

Some of the major Plains Paleo-Indian projectile forms.

Approximate Chronology of Major Plains Projectile Types							
Years Ago	11,000 – 12,000	10,500	10,000	9500	9000	8500	8000
Point Type	Clovis	Folsom	Midland Firstview, San Jon Agate Basin	Hell Gap	Alberta	Frederick-Firstview Cody Knife Scottsbluff Eden	Jimmy Allen Cascade
	Clovis	Folsom	Midland Agate Basin	Hell Gap		Frederick Scottsbluff Eden	

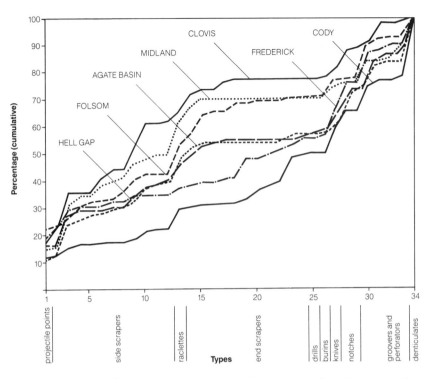

Cumulative curves of the percentages of different Plains Paleo-Indian artifact types, constructed by Irwin and Wormington.

the edge of the Plains. Projectile point forms include Alberta, Cody, Frederick, Eden, Scottsbluff, and many others, sometimes linked together under the general label of Planó cultures. The reader is referred to more specialist works for details (Frison, 1978; Irwin and Wormington, 1970; Wheat, 1972).

Irwin and Wormington (1970) constructed a series of cumulative curves of the percentages of different artifact types, to compare the various toolkits in their samples. The cumulative graphs for Clovis, Folsom, and Midland were very similar, with Folsom and Midland being the closest, especially in scraper inventories. Hell Gap and Agate Basin form a second, very closely similar, group, both containing more specialized tools than the first one. Frederick and Cody are the latest of the samples, and they form a third group, marked by even more specialized tools.

Joe Ben Wheat (1972) argued that different projectile forms were in use on the northern, central, and southern Plains. He proposed grouping post-Folsom assemblages from the central and southern Plains into a single Firstview Complex. However, more recent analyses argue for a more complex sequence of Plainsview and Fairview forms (Johnson and Halliday, 1980).

Culture Change on the Plains

Given that we have mainly stone artifacts to work with, it is hard to study Paleo-Indian cultural change on the Plains. Douglas Bamforth (1988) has shown that Early Holocene climatic change reduced the overall abundance of large animals over much of the Plains. At the same time, the size and mobility of the herds increased. The primeval Clovis population was widely dispersed, with relatively rare mass hunts. In contrast, with more game, Folsom groups came together for communal hunts more regularly, especially at preferred locations. As conditions became drier after Folsom times, herd distributions became less predictable, so the hunters used many more locations, engaging in communal hunts as and when the opportunity arose, on a far less predictable basis. Thus, argues Bamforth, social complexity should have increased from Clovis to Folsom times, and decreased thereafter.

Clovis and Folsom points are harder to manufacture than later Paleo-Indian points, which boast of no fluting. However, Folsom heads are thin, well-flaked, and fluted with a single channel flake along most of their length (Wormington, 1957), apparently requiring more skill on the part of the stone worker than the Clovis head. If this is so, then Folsom groups may have relied more heavily on elaborate tools, perhaps another sign of greater social complexity and of a degree of specialized production (Bamforth, 1988). It is noticeable that high-quality stoneworking declines at the end of the Paleo-Indian period (Hayden, 1982). This may reflect circumstances where essentially modern climatic conditions forced most members of society to make their own tools, under circumstances where it was difficult to maintain a more complex social structure.

One can theorize that as a patchwork of more predictable food resources developed over the Plains during Folsom times, it tended to favor larger and more regular concentrations of human populations (Bamforth, 1988). In turn, these human societies became more complex. Whether this provocative theory and the models derived from it hold up in the future depends on more sophisticated analyses of stone technology and animal bone fragments than have hitherto been undertaken on the Plains.

Paleo-Indian Occupation in the West

Everything points to an extremely sparse human population in western North America before about 9000 BC. Most recorded Paleo-Indian sites are little more than surface scatters of stone artifacts, including Clovis fluted points. One of the earliest may be Borax Lake near Clear Lake in northern California, which may date to as early as 10,000 BC (Meighan and Haynes, 1970). Fluted points are widespread in the west and many Paleo-Indian sites lie on gravel bars or higher ground, often close to former marshy deltas or streams that once fed large lakes.

Some of the best Paleo-Indian evidence comes from the Southwest, where higher rainfall filled some low-lying basins with large lakes. Vegetation patterns were very different, with widespread boreal forests and little temperature variation between winter and summer. There was apparently plentiful water and grazing grass for large herbivores to range widely over the Southwestern landscape. With such environmental diversity, it is hardly surprising to find considerable variation in Paleo-Indian projectile forms, some of which resemble those of the Plains to the east (for a full discussion of different traditions, see Cordell, 1984).

Students working in a Cody level (c. 4800 BC) at Blackwater Draw, Arizona.

Some Southwestern locations were visited for many centuries. Blackwater Draw is a shallow valley in the Llano Estacado that extends from eastern New Mexico into west Texas. Today, dry playas of the Llano only carry water after heavy rains and sand dunes line either side of the valley. This is grassland country, with occasional trees and shrubs, as it was in 10,000 BC. There were shallow ponds in the valley between 9000 and 8000 BC, which became marshes in later millennia (Wendorf and Hester, 1975). Clovis people hunted in Blackwater Draw between 9500 and 9200 BC, leaving some of their artifacts by a spring. The small mammals of the time suggest a climate with mild winters and cool summers.

Folsom and Midland points are stratified above Clovis artifacts in the Draw, with Folsom implements occurring in a diatomaceous earth (chalk-like earth filled with freshwater diatoms) deposit laid down between about 8500 and 8300 BC, at a time of greater rainfall. Later Paleo-Indian implements lie in silts that were laid down at a time when conditions became drier at the end of Paleo-Indian times (Haynes, 1975).

If conditions were somewhat wetter and there was more standing water in Clovis times, it would have been possible for the sparse human population to range far and wide, to achieve a similarly highly mobile lifeway. At Blackwater Draw, for example, the hunters obtained fine-grained rock from up to 186 miles (300 km) away, either through exchange, or by actually traveling to the source across all manner of landscapes. The Folsom inhabitants may have enjoyed a high degree of mobility, a mobility that followed from pursuing widely dispersed bison populations, also other animals and plant foods. At Blackwater Draw, for example, no less than 78 percent of the Folsom points found in the valley were made from Edwards Plateau chert, only obtainable some 186 miles (300 km) away. Perhaps the hunters were obtaining their large cores of raw material from one location as they followed bison and other animals moving along the valley.

The San Dieguito Complex hunter-gatherer culture from both the western parts of the Southwest and southern California was broadly contemporary with the occupation of Blackwater Draw (Warren, 1967), perhaps dating to as early as 9000 BC and flourishing until after 8000 BC. San Dieguito may represent a once broadly distributed hunting culture that flourished over much of southern California as far north as the Death and Owens Valleys. William Wallace believes it originated in the Great Basin (Wallace, 1978; Warren and True, 1961). It emerged in an area where drowned river valleys were commonplace along the coast, so the exploitation of marshlands and lakeside resources was probably important. For example, various forms of leaf-shaped and shouldered projectile points have come from the dried up shores of Lake Mojave in the Mojave Desert. This was an ideal location for Early Holocene hunters, for the shores must have teemed with game and plentiful vegetable foods.

Along the southern California coast, people were exploiting fish and marine mammals, as well as shellfish, perhaps as early as 8000 BC. At that time the Pacific shore was some miles further offshore, and is now submerged under higher sea levels. One has a strong sense of cultural continuity from late Paleo-Indian into Archaic times throughout the west. As western environments became drier and resources more localized, the Paleo-Indians developed ever more diverse local adaptations and much greater cultural diversity, as well as highly varied population densities. In much of southern California, for example, drowned river valleys persisted until as late as 3500 BC, accounting for a continued human presence in these regions, while population densities apparently fell further north.

Paleo-Indians in the Eastern Woodlands

Around 8600 BC, only a thin scatter of human beings lived in eastern North America, the descendants of a few early Paleo-Indian families who had hunted their way eastward perhaps 1500 years earlier. They are sometimes classified under the general label "Eastern Fluted Point Tradition" (Meltzer, 1988). These Paleo-Indians hunted and foraged over thousands of square miles of tundra, coniferous forest, and deciduous woodland, mostly in river valleys, near lakes, swamps, and perhaps sea coasts where game and other food resources were most abundant. One or two families would form a small band, occasionally encountering neighboring groups during the brief summer months, times when wives were exchanged, initiation ceremonies held, fine-grained rock and finished projectile points exchanged.

Like their distant western relatives, eastern Paleo-Indians were constantly on the move. They left hundreds of fluted points (many of them, in fact, probably hafted knives) behind them, all the way from Nova Scotia to Florida. In fact, fluted projectile points are much more common east of the Mississippi than in the west. They also display far more variation in size, shape, and technique of manufacture. The Paleo-Indian archaeology of the Eastern Woodlands, like that of the Archaic, is largely based on these artifacts.

As we have seen, there were at least two major environments in eastern North America during the Early Holocene — a northern tundra and spruce parkland and a more southern complex of boreal and deciduous forests. The Paleo-Indians who lived in the more northern regions would necessarily have exploited caribou, the only significant Holocene game species capable of providing sufficient food for long-term human occupation. More southern groups living in forest areas must have been both hunters and gatherers, people who exploited both forest game and wild plant foods (Meltzer, 1988). It is hardly surprising that Eastern Fluted Point Tradition sites and artifacts show great variation.

At least seven distinctive Paleo-Indian fluted point styles are known from the Northeast alone, the earliest of which is somewhat similar to the western Clovis form. There are fluted points with constricted edges, some with pentagonal shapes, others are long, and almost triangular. Generations of archaeologists have classified and labeled eastern Paleo-Indian points, naming them after the sites or areas where they were found — Debert, Bull Brook, Cumberland, and so on. As on the Plains, the problem is to decide what these stylistic variations mean in cultural and functional terms. In general, however, eastern fluted points are so basically similar to Clovis and Folsom points from the west that they are assumed to be of approximately the same age.

As the Ice Age megafauna vanished, the easterners turned to more diverse subsistence strategies. The Early Holocene environment of the

Eastern Woodlands was far more diverse than that of the west. In some areas, especially large river valleys, there may have been plentiful seasonal supplies of nuts and fish that allowed people to live for the summer and fall in larger base camps, but such bounty was highly localized. Tens of thousands of square miles of Early Holocene woodland were but sparsely endowed with vegetable and aquatic resources. The only viable adaptation was one based on the pursuit of game of all sizes, often solitary species like deer that had to be hunted and trapped over very large hunting territories indeed. In archaeological terms, the result is a superficial uniformity of basic hunting toolkits over an enormous area, with, however, significant local variation (Meltzer, 1988).

The close similarities between fluted points throughout the east argues for a rapid expansion of Paleo-Indian hunters over the centuries. Despite very low population densities and constant mobility, neighboring bands kept in touch with one another over long distances, probably through marriage and kin connections. We know this because of finds of exotic, fine-grained rocks in artifact scatters in many parts of the east. Some rocks were highly prized: Knife River chalcedony from North Dakota, Upper Mercer cherts from Ohio, Peoria and Burlington flints from Illinois. We know from many excavations that fine-grained rock was passed from hand to hand, from one band to another over hundreds of miles, perhaps as gifts. So constant was the exchange of fine-grained rocks that it was to be thousands of years before an equivalent level of interaction was ever reached again, perhaps not until Hopewell times, some 8000 years later.

The rapid spread of early Paleo-Indian culture is hardly surprising, for the carrying capacity of the woodlands was very low. There were no earlier inhabitants to resist the arrival of newcomers. At first there was plenty of hunting territory for everyone, even with the sparse populations concentrated in more favorable hunting and foraging areas. When population pressure on local resources became too intense, a son or daughter's family could simply branch off into new country nearby. In time, of course, the prime territories would be filled to the limits of their sparse capacities, so people no longer had the luxury of moving into new, unexploited terrain. By this time, in some areas perhaps as early as 8000 BC, environmental constraints came into full play, so more focused adaptations based on local game and vegetable resources emerged, reflected in the archaeological record by regional variations in projectile points and other artifacts. Many Paleo-Indian groups were initially generalized foragers, who developed into regional cultures in late Paleo-Indian and Early Archaic times throughout the east (Meltzer, 1988; Meltzer and Smith, 1986) (Chapter 16).

Northeastern Sites. Unfortunately, only a handful of dated sites chronicle Paleo-Indian occupation in the Eastern Woodlands, several of them close to the northern frontiers of the Early Holocene landscape (Meltzer, 1988). About 8600 BC, the Debert site on the Nova Scotian tundra was occupied again and again by a small band of between 15 and 50 people, who hunted caribou and perhaps exploited sea mammals (MacDonald, 1968). They probably dwelt in simple wood and skin structures like recent sub-arctic hunting peoples. Debert may have been an important base camp, for the diverse artifacts suggest a wide variety of activities – everything from butchery to hide processing and wood-working. The contemporary Bull Brook site near Ipswich, Massachusetts, is another large fluted point site with artifacts, animal bones, and floral remains apparently concentrated in at least 45 circular areas, perhaps distributed in a large semi-circle about 295 ft (90 m) across (Byers, 1954). Many of the Bull Brook artifacts are made from chert from the west, from the Hudson valley or Pennsylvania, as if the inhabitants were involved in gift exchanges with people further inland.

Most Paleo-Indian sites were much smaller, like Vail in northwest Maine, where a group made a kill and camped on the bank of the Magalloway River. The stone workers made fluted points and other tools from raw material found between 15 and 18 miles (24 and 28.9 km) away.

William Ritchie points out (1969) that the thin scatter of fluted points in the Northeast tends to follow the major river systems, such as the Ohio, Allegheny, Susquehanna, and Delaware. In central and southwestern New York State over 30 percent of all fluted points come from locations on, or close to, former lakes. Ritchie believes that large, fertile valleys, coastal plains, and their surroundings supported the largest populations of game animals and the people who preyed upon them.

Paleo-Indians in the Northeast: indented-base fluted points from the Debert site, Nova Scotia (length of left specimen 11.3 cm).

Mid-South. Further south, many Paleo-Indian camps were probably little more than temporary hilltop hunting locations, places visited for short times at regular seasons, as much part of the people's large territorial range as the quarries where they obtained their chert. The hilltop Shoop site in the Susquehanna drainage near Harrisburg, Pennsylvania, may be one such camp (Witthoft, 1952; Cox, 1986). In Paleo-Indian times, the hill probably overlooked the open tundra and thin forest of the river valley, offering a commanding view of the surrounding country. Most of the artifacts and waste flakes from Shoop were of Onondaga chert, quarried more than 186 miles (300 km) up the Susquehanna Valley to the north. John Witthoft identified 11 artifact concentrations, each about 32 ft (10 m) across, located on separate hilltops about 328 ft (100 m) apart. The site is estimated to date to about 9000 BC.

River valleys were favored locations, too. The Shawnee-Minisink camp on a terrace of the Delaware River near Stroudsburg, Pennsylvania, was occupied by Paleo-Indians some time between 8700 and 8500 BC (McNett, 1985). The Paleo-Indian level lies below approximately 9.8 ft (3 m) of soil and is isolated from later Archaic and Woodland occupations by over 5 ft (1.5 m) of sterile overburden. Shawnee-Minisink is one of the few Paleo-Indian sites to yield evidence for fishing and foraging. The excavators used flotation techniques to recover hackberry, wild plum, grape, blackberry, ground cherry and goosefoot, as well as some tiny fish bones, from the abandoned hearths. These vegetable foods are abundant in late summer and early fall. The Shawnee-Minisink group may also have harvested salmon that spawned in the Delaware and its tributaries in fall.

William Gardner's excavations of a series of interrelated northern Virginia Paleo-Indian sites known as the Flint Run complex are especially important, for they document human occupation in this area from about 9500 to 6500 BC (Gardner, 1974; 1976; 1977). The major sites — the Flint Run Quarry, Thunderbird, and Fifty — lie within a three-quarter square mile area on the Shenandoah River's South Fork. The Thunderbird site lies on the Early Holocene bank of the Shenandoah, a series of floodplain

MAINTENANCE CAMP
(Fifty)

BOG

BASE CAMP
(Thunderbird site)

REDUCTION STAT
(Lockhart)

QUARRIES

SOUTH FORK OF THE SHENANDOAH RIVER

Paleo-Indians in the Mid-South: Thunderbird site and Fifty site, Virginia. (Above) South Fork of the Shenandoah River. The Thunderbird site is located on the floodplain on the river's right bank. (Above right) Locations and functions of the various sites. (Below) Excavators using a mapping frame to map Clovis level activity areas at the Thunderbird site.

encampments scattered over an area almost 500 ft (152 m) long by 250 ft (76.2 m) wide. The location is thought to have been a base camp with many uses, a place where the local jasper was fashioned into finished artifacts and tool blanks. Gardner plotted the distributions of stone artifacts and identified different activity areas — places where hunting tools were fabricated, living areas often situated with reference to wind and sunlight and availability of food resources.

Thunderbird and the stratified Fifty site chronicle 3000 years of the Flint Run complex, a long sequence of seven phases of intermittent occupation that began with Clovis people after 9500 BC, with the only apparent cultural change the appearance of edge-notched projectile points about 8000 BC, perhaps the moment when atlatls (throwing sticks used to extend the range of a spear) came into use. The sites also document a cultural continuum from Paleo-Indian into Archaic life.

Gardner believes that Thunderbird was a central base for a mobile Paleo-Indian population hunting within a broadly prescribed territory, then returning regularly to the same location, where fine-grained jasper was abundant at nearby quarry sites. The people used their floodplain base camp again and again, perhaps in the summers when they gathered with other bands to quarry and trade jasper and socialize. The same form of territorial mobility based on a quarry and game-rich area may have occurred elsewhere at places like the Williamson and Dismal Swamp locations in southeast Virginia, where considerable densities of projectile points lie near outcrops of fine-grained rocks.

The same phenomenon marks the flint outcrops of Tennessee and Ohio, where points are also abundant. Away from these favored locations with their quarry sites and hunting base camps, the density of points, and presumably of Paleo-Indian population, drops sharply. This "centrally-based wandering" model may not apply in the Northeast. Debert, Bull Brook, and other sites in this region are far from quarry locations. They may have been large hunting camps where the people hunted caribou that ranged over large distances.

Midwest. Paleo-Indian fluted points and other artifacts have been found near the Great Lakes, sometimes lying on Early Holocene shorelines. These include the Potts site inland of the southeastern corner of Lake Ontario, located on a promontory overlooking what were marshy lowlands after about 9500 BC. The Barnes site in central Michigan to the west may have been a hunting camp, perhaps used no earlier than about 9200 BC — the date is disputed.

In Ontario, William Roosa, Peter Storck, and others have found a series of undated fluted point sites on the ancient Lake Algonquin shoreline in Ontario, perhaps temporary camps left by generations of a single band ranging along ancient beaches on the eastern side of the Huron basin (Roosa, 1965; Storck, 1984). Parkhill, near London, Ontario, was once a lakeside camp that Roosa estimates to have housed between 45 and 74 people grouped in small families, perhaps caribou hunters (Roosa, 1977). The excavators could isolate separate debris concentrations, perhaps the remains of individual tents. Roosa analyzed the artifacts and debris so thoroughly that he claimed to be able to identify the individual work of different stone workers. Parkhill is undated, but pollen from the site compares closely with radiocarbon-dated pollen samples found in a 8900 – 7900 BC context elsewhere.

The greatest concentrations of fluted points in Ohio and Indiana are to be found in the southern parts of each state. They are also widespread in southern Illinois and southern Wisconsin, but few locations have been dated.

Paleo-Indians in the Midwest: projectile points from Ohio. (Top row) Lanceolate points from the Sawmill site, Erie County. (Second row) Fluted and unfluted lanceolate points from the Mathewson site, Hardin County. Length of specimen top left 7 cm.

Southeast. More than 120 isolated fluted Clovis or Folsom-like points have come from the central Mississippi Valley, mostly from northeast Arkansas (Morse and Morse, 1973). Once again, the Paleo-Indian population was probably sparse and concentrated in resource-rich areas, at a time when the climate was cooler and drier, quite different from the lush environment of today. Many Southeastern Paleo-Indian settlements of 8000 BC are probably submerged below modern sea levels. The interior populations were sparse and concentrated near rivers and sink holes, where game would also feed. At a time of lowered sea level, present-day southeastern Florida rivers left large sink holes that could be exploited by animals and humans. Carl Clausen, Wilburn Cockrell, and other archaeologists have recovered a wealth of paleoenvironmental information from them (Clausen and others, 1979).

At Warm Mineral Springs in Sarasota County, Wilburn Cockrell discovered a human burial on a ledge in a sink hole. The skeleton was 42.6 ft (13 m) below the modern water level. The dead man had been deposited in an earthen grave that had subsequently been submerged. A shell spearthrower hook lay with the skeleton. This burial was radiocarbon dated to about 8300 BC. Some further human remains have come to light beneath a 9.8 ft (3 m) ledge at the Springs, in the same clay layer as the bones of a ground sloth, a saber-toothed tiger, and other extinct species. These people were exploiting not only large game, but animals as small as the raccoon and the frog, also plant foods. Some of the Warm Mineral Springs occupation may date to before 9000 BC.

An even more spectacular find came from Little Salt Spring not far away. The collapsed shell of an extinct giant land tortoise that had been killed with a wooden stake thrust between shell and plastron lay broken and carbonized 85.3 ft (26 m) below the sink-hole lip. The stake has been radiocarbon dated to before 9000 BC. The excavators believe the tortoise was impaled with the stake, then turned over and cooked in its own shell. Portions of an immature mammoth, an extinct sloth and bison, another turtle, and several other mammals and birds, lay nearby. By 8000 BC, the water level had risen to 36 ft (11m) below the lip, and white-tailed deer had

MODERN
WATER-LEVEL

87 feet
(26·5m)

WATER-LEVEL 12,000 YEARS AGO

LEDGE

Little Salt Spring, southern Florida, contains archaeological remains dating back some 12,000 years. A Paleo-Indian apparently fell into the spring. He must have swum to a dry ledge just above the water level of the day. His remains were found there together with those of a turtle he probably cooked for food. When the meat ran out, he simply starved to death.

become common prey. Little Salt Spring also yielded the head of a boomerang-like artifact made of oak, remarkably similar to those made by modern Australian Aborigines.

Most likely, the Paleo-Indians who visited the sink holes camped for short periods around major water sources, lingering to consume their prey after making a kill. Since water supplies were irregular and widely dispersed, the hunter-gatherer population may have exploited huge territories to support a very low population density per square mile. Perhaps greater population densities flourished near the now-submerged coasts.

Social Organization and Settlement Patterns

We still know virtually nothing about Paleo-Indian social organization anywhere in North America, of the kin and marriage ties that linked one isolated band to its neighbors. Sharing, social flexibility, egalitarian status — these were probably vital necessities in Paleo-Indian life. The realities of Early Holocene woodland environments would have led to a constant state of social flux within bands consisting of only a few adults and children. A single hunting accident could have wiped out all the hunters in a single band in a day, leaving the survivors with only one recourse — joining a neighboring band. Perhaps, then, we can speculate that many highly mobile Paleo-Indian bands were patrilocal and exogamous. This meant that the men remained with the same band into which they were born, while the women married into neighboring groups. The intricate kin relationships between neighboring bands also facilitated the exchange of vital commodities like the fine-grained rock that made the best projectile points.

The archaeological evidence for Paleo-Indian settlement is so incomplete that it is well nigh impossible to reconstruct a detailed model of subsistence and settlement patterns anywhere in North America. It has even been argued that their lifeway was quite unlike any modern hunter-gatherers, on the grounds that population densities were so low that no one could rely on the specialized environmental knowledge of their neighbors (Kelly and Todd, 1988). Did, for example, the Paleo-Indians wander from camp to camp without any major base, or did they hunt within large territories on a seasonal basis, "anchoring" their annual round on one much-visited location, which served as the focus of a "centrally based wandering system?" Judging from the Flint Run Complex sites in the Eastern Woodlands, raw materials like jasper may have indeed served as "anchors" for centrally based wandering systems, but perhaps only in a few, relatively rich resource areas.

In the Southeast, archaeologists like Albert Goodyear and Michael Schiffer have espoused models that make a fundamental distinction between long-term settlements and shorter-term occupation sites. The former are often called "base camps," places where "maintenance tasks" were carried out. They were locations visited repeatedly over the generations, where people would live for longer periods of time at certain seasons of the year. Sites like Bull Brook and Thunderbird may have been such base camps, favored places close to especially bountiful hunting grounds or near groves of nut-bearing trees.

In archaeological terms, base sites would yield a far wider range of Paleo-Indian artifacts than a short-term occupation site, where a narrow range of "extractive activities" took place. Hunting or butchery sites or quarries come under this latter category, as do places where people gathered to harvest nuts in season, to make stone or wood artifacts, or to trap birds. The base camp and shorter-term sites can, of course, be subdivided into many categories, categories based on the duration of occupation, season of the year in which they were customarily used, and so on. Unfortunately, these models are very difficult to document from sites where preservation conditions are poor, and where the precise functions of many artifacts, especially scrapers, are difficult to establish. Even when microscopic techniques like edge-wear analysis are brought to bear on surviving stone tools, one cannot be sure whether the entire range of the material culture, and the activities associated with it, are represented in the archaeological record.

As we have seen, perhaps the most valid models for the Eastern Woodlands are those developed from sites in the Carolina Piedmont area of the Southeast and from locations like Thunderbird. There the first settlers may have exploited large hunting territories. Each band returned regularly to a residential base camp located on or near a floodplain where there was considerable environmental diversity. For much of the year the people relied on more transitory sites in less favored floodplain or inter-riverine areas, places that overlooked regular hunting grounds or that allowed them access to fine-grained rock.

Such a settlement pattern was adaptive as long as population densities were low and there were big-game animals to hunt, also local harvests of wild vegetable foods in spring, summer, and fall. The Paleo-Indians must have depended on a highly flexible social organization, adaptive because of far-reaching kin ties and marriage alliances that allowed each band access to fine cherts and other resources hundreds of miles away through gift exchange. As the Early Holocene climate continued to warm up, the megafauna vanished, and many hunting territories filled up, their successors had to adapt to new environmental circumstances that challenged their hunting and foraging abilities to the full.

If there is one overall trend in Paleo-Indian adaptations, it was toward increasing cultural diversity. At the end of Paleo-Indian times, western hunter-gatherers were already pursuing very diverse subsistence strategies, relying heavily on plants and non-migratory small game. Plains bands still depended heavily on big-game, on regular bison kills. Eastern groups relied on deer and small game as staples, also on seasonal plant foods as supplements. In all areas, one can reasonably and generally assume, as optimal foraging theory does, that subsistence strategies were based on the notion of maximizing a range of food resources that were mentally ranked by the Paleo-Indians in terms of energy return. One can assume that the availability of these staple ranked foods had a considerable effect on the rate of population growth and on the population density levels that developed. Thus, conditions existed for very different population growth rates in east and west (Stuart and Gauthier, 1981).

On the Plains, population growth and expansion must have depended on fluctuations in bison populations dictated by constantly varying, and often abrupt, expansions and contractions of local range land. Thus, overall population growth would be slow, but with constant, often sudden, movements into bison-rich areas. In the west, the people were dependent on much more diverse game and plant resources. Again, slow population growth would result, but population growth that would soon reach an equilibrium point at a relatively low density, except, perhaps, in the most resource-abundant areas. Eastern Paleo-Indians lived in locally very diverse environments with generally low population densities in vast areas where the carrying capacity was very low. Only in local areas where food resources were predictable and seasonally more abundant than usual did populations rise to higher levels. As we shall see, in both east and west, these local concentrations of hunter-gatherer populations were to develop complex adaptations during the Archaic.

Further Reading

In addition to the sources cited for Chapter 4:

Frison, George. 1978. *Prehistoric Hunters of the High Plains*. Academic Press, New York.
  Frison's thorough analysis is the standard work on Plains Paleo-Indian cultures.

Irwin, H.T. and Wormington, Marie. 1970. "Paleo-Indian tool types in the Great Plains," *American Antiquity* 325:24-34.
  A still fundamental paper on Paleo-Indian projectile point typology.

Meltzer, David J. 1988. "Late Pleistocene Human Adaptations in Eastern North America," *Journal of World Prehistory* 2, 1:1-52.
  A technical synthesis of the evidence for Paleo-Indian settlement in the Eastern Woodlands. Good on the Eastern Fluted Point Tradition.

PART THREE

THE GREAT PLAINS

"The new people asked Inktomi what they should eat. Inktomi did not want people to eat his friends, so he created buffalo ... He taught the men how to kill the buffalo, and how to skin the animals. He showed them how to make knives to remove the skin, and he taught the women how to make scrapers and how to scrape the skin so it was soft and pliable. He showed the people how to butcher the buffalo and what parts could be eaten."

Assiniboine Creation Legend

CALIBRATED DATES	RADIOCARBON AGES	THE PLAINS		CLIMATIC STAGES
Modern times	Modern times		Horses introduced to Plains (after 1640) Onate expedition (1598)	
AD 1541 —	AD 1541 —	PROTOHISTORIC PERIOD LATE PREHISTORIC PERIOD	Coronado expedition (1541)	LATE HOLOCENE
			Communal bison hunting reaches greatest intensity after AD 550	
175 BC – AD 235 —	AD 1 —		Bow and arrow introduced to the Plains Pottery appears (*c.* AD 500)	
		LATE PLAINS ARCHAIC		
1530 – 905 BC —	1000 BC —			
2830 – 2305 BC —	2000 BC —	MIDDLE PLAINS ARCHAIC		
3950 – 3640 BC —	3000 BC —		McKean Complex on Northwestern Plains Head-Smashed-In site first in use	
5235 – 4575 BC —	4000 BC —	EARLY PLAINS ARCHAIC		MIDDLE HOLOCENE
6285 – 5445 BC —	5000 BC —			
outside accurate calibration range	6000 BC —		Olsen-Chubbock site Bison hunting assumes predominant importance	
	7000 BC —	PALEO-INDIANS		EARLY HOLOCENE
	8000 BC —		Extinction of Ice Age megafauna	
	9000 BC —			

CHAPTER 7

BISON HUNTERS ON THE PLAINS

During the early 19th century 27 tribes of horse-mounted Indians dominated the Great Plains. All of them were either nomadic buffalo (bison) hunters subsisting almost entirely off Plains game herds, or semi-nomadic farmers, who relied on crops for a substantial part of their diet. These groups were of diverse biological and linguistic origin, but they shared a common culture based on the horse, a culture that valued bravery in war and ardent militarism.

Such colorful cultures were the stuff of which legends were made. Years of spectacular raids and battles against encroaching white settlers gave the Plains Indians a villainous but warlike reputation. Reports of these many skirmishes by traveling correspondents and small town reports gave the "feathered brave" an air of romantic invincibility that was grist to dime store novelists' pens. Without conscious effort, thousands of 19th-century Americans absorbed inaccurate and misleading stereotypes of Indians in the far west, images of fierce, colorfully dressed and mounted Indian braves and their romantic squaws.

The stereotypes persisted in the circus ring and later in the movies. William F. (Buffalo Bill) Cody employed a large troop of Plains Indians and a band of cowboys to tour eastern cities in his famous Wild West Show (illus. p.119). Bands of gaily painted warriors in bright robes dashed around the arena on their "Indian ponies." They wore glamorous regalia and showy war bonnets with twin tails, attire that was, in fact, never worn to war but only on ceremonial occasions. The warriors attacked covered wagons and stage coaches, only to be gunned down by dashing cowboys who arrived at just the right moment to dispatch the pesky redskins. To add authenticity to his shows, Cody engaged veteran warriors such as the Dakota leader Sitting Bull, men who had recently featured in well-publicized skirmishes on the Plains.

The Wild West show gradually gave way to the circus and the Western movie. Many western stories that appeared in that bastion of Middle Class America, the *Saturday Evening Post*, became Hollywood films, and later television shows. The Indians that formed the backdrop to the story were almost invariably dressed in Plains costumes, even if the plot unfolded at a location thousands of miles away from the open grasslands.

Generations of western tales and movies led not only to persistent stereotypes of Indian society, but also to the widespread assumption that Plains Indian culture was static over long periods of time. The Plains

A CONGRESS OF AMERICAN INDIANS, REPRESENTING VARIOUS TRIBES, CHARACTERS AND PECULIARITIES OF THE WILY DUSKY WARRIORS IN SCENES FROM ACTUAL LIFE GIVING THEIR WEIRD WAR DANCES AND PICTURESQUE STYLE OF HORSEMANSHIP.

peoples were frozen, as it were, in the form in which they flourished during the stirring years between 1830 and 1880, the decades of white expansion into the far west.

Spanish adventurers first encountered the Great Plains in the mid-16th century. They reached the grasslands after hundreds of miles of scrub-covered countryside and marveled at the prodigious numbers of "wild cows" that roamed the Plains. Fur traders from eastern Canada explored the northern reaches of the treeless country. It was late 18th-century British fur traders who first called the treeless grasslands the Great Plains. American explorers of the 1800s were less sanguine, considering the central plains unfit for human habitation: "The Great American Desert."

Most 19th-century authorities were content to accept the judgment of the great anthropologist Lewis Henry Morgan — that American Indians only settled the harsh Plains when they acquired the horse and the rifle. He claimed the grasslands had been uninhabited by human beings until about 1000 BC. Then a few groups had moved to the edge of the Plains and remained there until the Spaniards brought horses to the Southwest. The Indians had embraced these strange beasts with enthusiasm, then settled rapidly in buffalo country where they flourished until European contact.

The Folsom discoveries of the 1920s and other archaeological finds proved that the Plains had been continuously occupied by hunter-gatherer

A stereotyped image of Plains life. In the late 19th century Buffalo Bill's Wild West Show promised "wily dusky warriors giving their weird war dances."

(Opposite) Archaeological sites of the Great Plains referred to in the text.

peoples for at least 10,000 years. As we saw in Chapter 6, the Great Plains may have been one of the earliest environments settled in North America. That chapter described Paleo-Indian settlement on the Plains; we must now examine later adaptations to this diverse and challenging environment.

The Plains Environment and Climatic Change

The Great Plains cover an enormous area of North America's heartland from the Rockies in the west to the Eastern Woodlands near the Mississippi. They are a grass sea that covers about a half-billion acres from Canada in the north to Mexico's Rio Grande in the south. The Plains are a vast area of low to moderate relief with relatively low rainfall. They were, and still are, a harsh place to live, with often brutally hot summers and long, bitterly cold winters. The original native vegetation was perennial grasses, with trees limited to stream valleys and occasional higher ground.

The actual boundaries between the Plains and neighboring environments are often blurred. Sometimes one can literally draw a line between the Rocky Mountain foothills and the Plains. In other places, long mountain ridges finger into the open country, forming intermontane basins that obscure the boundary. The eastern frontiers of the Plains pass imperceptibly into the Eastern Woodlands as annual rainfall rises and short grass prairie gives way to tall, lusher grasses, then woodland.

Flying over the Plains at 40,000 feet gives a misleading impression of environmental homogeneity over hundreds, if not thousands, of miles. One can drive for hours across gently rolling landscape, over seemingly drab, unchanging plains. Then one encounters an unexpected stream, a local spring, or a deep gully that alters the entire environment. It is then one realizes that the Plains are a very diverse environment, where complicated changes in climatic conditions produce major variations in local rainfall and climate.

The Great Plains lie in the rain shadow of the Rocky Mountains, their climate dominated by three major air masses that usually move across North America from west to east. Mild Pacific air from the west has lost most of its moisture by the time it crosses the Great Basin and Rockies. On the Plains, it meets moist, warm subtropical air from the Gulf of Mexico and cold, dry arctic air moving southward from Canada. A strong westerly air flow over the Plains enhances arid conditions over the western Plains. But there are constant local changes caused by ever altering air mass circulation patterns that weaken prevailing westerlies and allow moist tropical air over the grasslands. The result is constant variations in plant and animal distributions throughout the Plains, an environmental characteristic that has persisted through thousands of years of prehistory, and, indeed, much earlier into geological time.

During the Early Holocene, after forest developed on newly deglaciated land, continued climatic warming led to major vegetational changes, with spruce forests giving way to prairie grasslands as early as 9000 BC (Wright, 1983). Further east, a brief interlude of deciduous woodland in a parkland landscape also gave way to open prairie about 7500 BC. In some places in the extreme east of the Plains, deciduous woodland survived until about 5000 BC.

This boundary between prairie and woodland is especially important, for pollen samples provide strong evidence for a progressive decrease in moisture as the dry Pacific air masses shifted position when the Laurentide ice sheet retreated across central and eastern Canada. This meant that dry, cold arctic air flowed less frequently over the Plains. During the Early Holocene, the deciduous forest was dominated by elm and other cooler weather trees, with warmer-loving oak much less widely distributed than in later times.

Vegetation is the most important factor in controlling the distribution of animals, and it is noteworthy that most large Ice Age animals became extinct before 8000 BC, just as these major vegetational changes were taking place. Some paleoecologists believe that the increased seasonality at the end of the Ice Age may have led to shorter, warmer winters with cooler summers than today. This would have allowed temperate trees like ash and oak to mingle with spruce and other colder-loving trees, creating a greater range of habitats for a more diversified mammalian fauna. The warming climate set in motion a series of progressive environmental changes that resulted in a form of dynamic equilibrium during the Middle Holocene. (It should be noted that much climatic change was highly localized. The literature is complex: for example, for the southern plains, see Bryant and Holloway, 1985.)

The increasingly dry conditions peaked during the Middle Holocene, when the prairie/deciduous forest border was more than 62 miles (100 km) east of its present position. This so-called Prairie Peninsula reached its maximum extent between 6000 and about 3000 BC, but changed its position somewhat, probably in response to fluctuations in the lingering Laurentide ice sheet on the Labrador Plateau far to the north. The Peninsula is a mosaic of prairie and forest, its shift to the east during the Middle Holocene signaling the more frequent occurrence of warm, dry westerly air flow across the Plains.

The eastward expansion of the Prairie Peninsula coincided with Ernst Antevs' so-called Altithermal episode of 6000 to 2500 BC (Chapter 5). This was when temperatures and dry conditions reached their Holocene maximum on the Plains, to the point that some scholars have argued that the grasslands were completely devoid of human habitation because of the dry conditions. This seems unlikely, for there is evidence of Altithermal occupation at several major bison kill sites including Hawkens and Head-Smashed-In (see below). Bison population densities may at times have been much reduced, but we can be certain that the animals were a constant resource on the Plains, although arid conditions impacting on grazing range may have reduced herd populations considerably or affected vital seasonal migration patterns.

Some idea of the localized conditions that affected bison hunting can be gained from Vaughn Bryant's palynological researches in southwest Texan caves (Bryant and Holloway, 1985). Bonfire Shelter is located hundreds of miles south of the Great Plains, and is the southernmost site in North America where mass bison hunts took place. There are two discrete zones of bison bones in the shelter, each apparently representing repeated bison jumps over relatively short periods, perhaps no more than 50 to 100 years. The earliest bone deposit resulted from Paleo-Indian hunts, the later one from another episode of repeated game drives in about 500 BC. What happened during the 7500 years that separated the two bone beds? Bryant's pollen samples revealed that the Bonfire Shelter region enjoyed good grass cover only twice since 10,000 BC. Each of these periods coincided with a layer of bison bones, each time when it was possible for the area to support large herds of grazing animals. At other times, the grass cover was much reduced, suggesting that opportunistic hunters followed the bison into the Bonfire Shelter area, and chose that ideal location for their hunts. Throughout prehistoric times, survival depended on careful observation of changing grazing conditions, and of bison movements. (For a survey of paleoenvironmental evidence in the southern Plains area and further afield, see Bryant and Holloway, 1985).

Prehistoric people appear to have responded to dry conditions by diversifying their subsistence strategies. The Cherokee Sewer Site in northeast Iowa consists of three stratified cultural horizons in an alluvial fan at the edge of the Little Sioux River. Each horizon is associated with bison butchery, dating to about 6400, 5300, and 4350 BC respectively (Shutler and others, 1974). The small animal bones, gastropods, and pollen samples from the Cherokee site show that the local climate was drier than today in about 4400 BC, with slightly higher mean winter temperatures. There may also have been some diversification of hunting economies. The Coffey site in northeast Kansas dates to about 3100 BC, a place where people not only exploited bison, but hunted deer, shot waterfowl, and foraged for many species of wild vegetable foods. Sites like Mummy Cave in northern Wyoming (Wedel and others, 1968) (occupied as early as 7000 BC) and Medicine Lodge Creek, 99 miles (160 km) to the east (Frison and Wilson, 1975), also reflect a more diverse subsistence strategy at the edge of the Plains during the Altithermal. Other locations, like the Hawkens site in Wyoming, were the scene of communal hunts, another strategy for maximizing the hunt (Frison, 1978).

Bison and Humans

For most of prehistory, the Great Plains were a favorable habitat for large, gregarious herbivores. At the time of first European contact, a north-south belt of short grasses such as *Bouteloua* and *Bucloe* flourished in the west beyond the 100th meridian. This grass was well adapted to dry soils and a short growing season in an environment under the rain shadow of the Rockies where as little as 14.7 in (37.5 cm), or less, precipitation fell every year. The rainfall rises gradually as one travels eastward, reaching 24.6 in (62.5 cm), to as high as 39 in (100 cm) on the tall bluegrass prairie, sometimes called the *needlegrass-pronghorn-grama grass* biome (Shelford, 1963). This was the heart of the bison's range, the animal that was the staple of human diet on the Plains. Not that the staple was a reliable one. The amount and distribution of annual rainfall was especially important to bison, for grass production was not uniform over the Plains. So the grazing animals shifted location from one year to the next, following fresh, green spring grass. The condition of the graze was vital, for successions of dry years with short grass could force the bison to grub close to the ground, wearing out and breaking their teeth on the soil and grass stems. As the teeth wear down, the grinding surfaces become less efficient, until the

American buffalo from the National Zoological Park: this animal served as the model for the $10 bill.

animal can no longer feed itself and dies. Thus, human populations were constantly on the move, following bison herds on their annual range.

Bison colonized North America long before the Wisconsin glaciation. Primeval forms often reached enormous sizes, with great horns measuring 6 ft or more (2 m) from tip to tip. The smaller Wisconsin long-horned form, *Bison antiquus*, was distributed between Alberta and Texas, but also as far afield as California and Florida. After the Ice Age, bison became more abundant, also decreasing in size. A postglacial type, *Bison occidentalis*, invaded the Plains and came into contact with the much larger *antiquus* form. From their genetic mixing evolved the Plains bison, *Bison bison*.

Ice Age steppe bison had a very short spring calving period, for their young had to be reared before the next harsh winter. In contrast, *Bison bison* has a longer rutting season that covers more than a month. As post-Ice Age bison adapted to the short grasslands, the "Great Bison Belt," their winter mortality declined, the breeding season lengthened, and they became much less selective eaters. So they flourished while other large mammals came under increasing stress. The arid, western Plains were always inhabited by hunter-gatherers, who were concentrated along stream valleys and near springs. They supplemented bison meat with other food resources, among them pronghorns, deer, elk, bears, and other small animals. Fish and shellfish were occasionally important, as were seasonal wild vegetable foods such as the prairie turnip (*Psoralea*), groundnuts (*Apios*), ground beans (*Amphicarpa*), sunflowers, and Jerusalem artichokes, as well as seasonal fruits.

The mixed and tall-grass prairies of the eastern Plains supported soils that were more suitable for horticulture. Fertile, easily cultivable river bottoms enabled many eastern Plains groups to grow substantial food surpluses that were used in trade with non-farmers to the west (for a full discussion of the rise of agriculture, see Chapter 14). Agriculture took hold in these regions about 500 years before European contact, with farming being combined with seasonal bison hunting. The agricultural traditions of the eastern Plains have close ties to contemporary cultures in the Mississippi Valley and further afield. But the basic cultural roots of many of these groups lay in big-game hunting traditions that flourished for thousands of years on the Plains.

Plains Archaic Traditions
c. 5600 BC to *c.* AD 500

Plains Indians moved around in small bands in a highly mobile lifeway, where relatively few locations were exploited on a regular basis (Chapter 6). As Douglas Bamforth has argued (1988), there was probably some seasonal aggregation and dispersal of Plains Paleo-Indian populations. To some degree, too, population movements depended on the availability of fine-grained rock for making the large bifaces that were the sources, in turn, of the flakes used to make fluted and other projectile points. As we have seen, too, this mobility was adaptive, for it may have enabled each band to maintain social contacts with others (Wobst, 1974).

Population densities were lower than in later times, too, the hunters relying heavily on their stalking skills and on patient observation during the chase. Earlier, Paleo-Indians were less selective in their killing, whereas later groups took mainly cow and calf herds. Perhaps mass bison kills were much rarer than they were to become in later prehistory, when both technology and hunting methods became more efficient, apparently more standardized. There is some reason to believe, too, that Paleo-Indian groups lacked the manpower to butcher all the animals they took in occasional mass drives, even when hunting cooperatively with others. Not that they may have wanted to waste meat. In some cases, the hunt may have taken place in winter, so the hunters let the carcasses freeze, then lived alongside their kill for some time (Reher and Frison, 1980; Kelly and Todd, 1988).

There were probably substantial differences in bison adaptations and game densities in different areas of the Great Plains. Recent and historical records show, for example, that bison herds in the drier southwestern Plains would have been smaller, fewer, and more mobile, less predictable in their movements than those to the northeast. Using ethnographic records and a sophisticated climatic index, Douglas Bamforth has argued (1988) that the more complex Plains societies were indeed in those areas where favorable climatic conditions should have supported larger, less mobile, and more predictable bison herds.

The Paleo-Indians gave way to much more varied Archaic hunting traditions on the Plains after 8000 BC, traditions associated with gradually more sophisticated bison procurement methods. With the onset of the warmer and drier climate of the Middle Holocene in about 6000 BC, the human population of the Plains may have fallen considerably, although earlier hypotheses of complete abandonment, based on lack of sites, seem too extreme.

There are few areas where even an incomplete framework of Plains Archaic culture is known, with the best-researched sites occurring on the Northwestern Plains, upon which this summary is based (Frison, 1978).

Early Plains Archaic
c. 5600 to 3000 BC or later

The onset of the Plains Archaic is marked by an abrupt change in projectile point forms from lanceolate Paleo-Indian types to characteristic side-notched Archaic points. The side notch was an important innovation, for the notches presumably allowed a much tighter and stronger binding of head to foreshaft or spear handle. That the change was effective is shown by the rapid spread of the innovation over the Plains.

The point changeover is well documented at Mummy Cave close to the Shoshone River near Yellowstone National Park in Wyoming, in an occupation level dating to about 5600 BC. Similar side-notched points have been recovered from other sites such as the Medicine Lodge Creek location and the stratified Sorenson site in Bighorn Canyon (Husted, 1969).

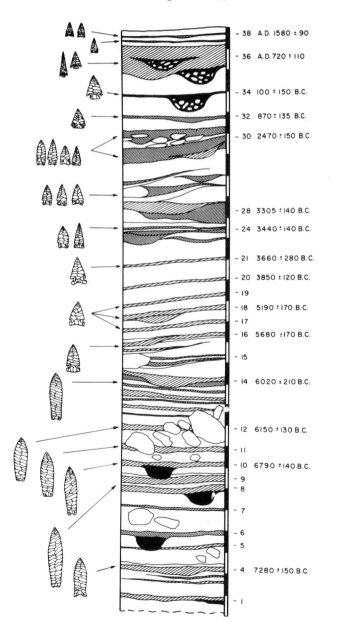

Mummy Cave, northwestern Wyoming: stratigraphic profile showing periods of human occupation separated by layers of silt. Projectile point forms illustrated at left show the change from Paleo-Indian lanceolate forms to side-notched and then stemmed forms, starting about 5600 BC.

Again, there are several, still little known, local variations of Early Archaic projectile points, which are fundamentally of local interest (see Frison, 1978). There seems to have been a proliferation of different forms toward the end of the Early Archaic. By all indications, Early Archaic hunter-gatherers lived in much the same way as their predecessors, even if they relied on a wider variety of game and vegetable foods. The famous Head-Smashed-In Buffalo Jump in Alberta was in use in about 3500 BC. Levels of this approximate age contain Mummy Cave style Early Archaic projectile points.

The Hawken site in Wyoming of about 4400 BC records an Early Archaic hunt where bison were driven up a narrow arroyo until they reached the knickpoint barrier. Hawken was used at least three times, and, judging from the bison jaws, in early or mid-winter. The hunters were taking both mature beasts and driving nursery herds, but the killing was tough work. At least 300 projectile points were found among the bones, many of them broken by the brutal impact against struggling animals. Many of the Hawken points had been reworked again and again, with carefully ground bases and needle sharp tips that penetrated hides and muscles very effectively.

Middle Archaic
c. 2900 to *c.* 1000 BC

During the Middle Plains Archaic, northwest Plains groups appear to have moved onto the open Plains and into the interiors of intermontane basins, also increasing their emphasis on plant foods. These moves are associated with the sudden appearance of the so-called McKean Complex as early as 2900 BC (Kornfeld and Todd, 1989). In the Bighorn Basin, for example, the people now commonly used sandstone grinders to process wild vegetable foods, as well as roasting pits that were often used again and again for centuries. This is not to say that the Plains people of this region gave up hunting bison all together. Rather, they developed a hunter-gatherer adaptation that relied on carefully planned scheduling of economic activities throughout the year, activities closely tied to seasons of wild plants and the annual movements of game herds. Each band may well have ranged over a wide area annually.

The label McKean is somewhat controversial, on the grounds that it may disguise greater cultural elaboration. McKean at present subsumes not only the lanceolate McKean point with indented base and convex blade edges, but numerous variations on this artifact theme. Judging from the highly localized and distinctive points found with several Middle Archaic bison kills, it may be that some almost-McKean forms may, in fact, have been used for highly specialized activities.

The Middle Archaic also saw the appearance of large numbers of stone circles, circles between 11 and 24 ft (3.3 − 7.3 m) in diameter that may have been the bases for circular lodges or tipis. However, they may have served many other purposes as well (Kehoe, 1960; Hoffman, 1953). Many of them were used for very short periods of time, perhaps only a few days or weeks, sometimes single circles, at others concentrations of hundreds, often located on higher ground or along stream terraces. Unfortunately,

Two McKean projectile points from Signal Butte.

nearly all of them are devoid of artifacts, except for the occasional flake or broken projectile point.

Middle Archaic sites include not only bison kills but seasonal camps where mule deer and some mountain sheep were taken. About 2500 BC, bison remains become more common in many northwestern Plains sites. There were now major shifts in bison procurement throughout the Plains, for the people now mainly hunted them in the fall. These hunts were often concentrated at favored locations that were used again and again. The resulting carcasses were processed very thoroughly, and much of the meat made into pemmican, as if the emphasis was on long-term storage, apparently less important in earlier times. The hunters still used tried and tested methods employed by their remote ancestors, especially the arroyo trap system. Bison jumps were also used, witness the Kobold site in southern Montana that remained in use right into late prehistoric times. Kobold is a 25-ft (7.6-m) high sandstone bluff close to well-watered grazing land. The arroyo below the cliff is wide and spacious, ideal for butchering large numbers of animals. The terrain is favorable for game drives, allowing but one approach to the bluff, an approach that was controlled even more closely by rows of stone piles, at least in late prehistoric times. Judging from the many broken bones among the bison remains, many of the animals were killed by the precipitous fall, and fewer projectile points were present than at Hawken, for example. There are four Middle Archaic kill sites in this general Powder River area. Frison (1978) believes that the people of the area conducted communal bison hunts during fall and winter, and perhaps in early spring, collaborating to kill large numbers of beasts, not only for fresh meat but also for dried flesh that was stored for use during cold periods when hunting was impossible.

Middle Archaic hunters are known, also, to have made use of artificial corrals, like the enclosure dating to about 2500 BC found at the Scoggin site north of Rawlins, Wyoming. Scoggin lies at the end of a natural gap in a long ridge astride a route that bison took when going to water. The site was ideal, for the stampeding beasts could be driven over a short steep slope into a specially constructed stone and wood corral. The walls were probably covered with hides preventing the animals from seeing out and trying to force an exit.

The jump-off point at the Kobold site, southern Montana.

Besant projectile point from the Muddy Creek site, length c. 9 cm.

Late Plains Archaic
c.1000 BC to AD 500

Once again, the changeover from Middle to Late Archaic is marked by projectile point innovations rather than by any significant alteration in lifeway. The distinctive Pelican Lake point appears, a corner-notched point with wide, open notches that form sharp points as they intersect both the edges and base. Pelican Lake sites occur in southern Saskatchewan, and bison kills by these people are dated to between about 1000 and 700 BC at Head-Smashed-In, Alberta.

In the third century AD, a highly sophisticated Late Archaic bison hunting culture emerged on the Northwestern Plains, a culture known by characteristic, long-sided and dart-like Besant projectile points (Wittlaufer, 1955; Frison, 1971). These people used much more complicated bison corrals built of logs set in deep post holes known from two Wyoming locations. The Ruby site lies on a dry tributary of the Powder River, while Muddy Creek is on a small side stream of the North Platte River.

The Ruby corral was placed on the low-lying stream bed in such a way that the stampeding animals did not see the enclosure until the last minute. The hunters also used natural features like ridges and arroyo banks to "funnel" their quarry toward the pen. Significantly, it is just at the moment when the bison would have sighted the corral that projectile points first appear, as if the hunters were goading the animals on toward the entrance. The Ruby hunters were real experts at handling stampeding animals, for to steer them into the corral required pursuing and prodding the fast-reacting bison at just the right moments.

The corral bears a surprising resemblance to modern cattle corrals. Almost certainly the hunters erected pairs of stout posts separated by the diameter of the horizontal timbers wedged between them. The result was a strong structure that could withstand the onslaught of penned animals, even if they could see out. The Ruby corral was built on a slope, and the lowest wall was subjected to the most stress. Frison observed that it had been rebuilt several times, strengthened perhaps, as this was the place where the animals could be crowded for slaughter purposes. The excavators found bison ribs and jaws that were used for digging the post holes into the soft, sandy soil. The builders used juniper wood, perhaps burning off suitable poles rather than cutting them down, also using dead timber. Frison estimates 20 hunters would have taken between 10 and 14 days to build the Ruby corral, final drive lane, and wings. He believes that this substantial investment of time and labor was made with the intention of using the corral over a long period of time.

The downslope side of the corral was filled with bison bones to a depth of over a foot (0.3 m), so many animals were killed there. A so-far unexcavated processing area covering at least 10,000 sq. ft (929 sq. m) lies about 1000 ft (304.8 m) up the arroyo. Nearby, also, lay what appears to have been a ceremonial structure formed by the intersection of two arcs of circles each about 33.5 ft (10.2 m) in radius. The outline of the 39-ft (11.8-m) long structure was delineated by post holes, with the ends oriented on a north-south axis. Five post holes across the 15 ft (4.5 m) widest axis separated the structure into two enclosures, at least one of which was roofed. Eight male bison skulls lay at the southern end. Frison believes the stout building was a form of shaman's structure, where the priest who supervised corral construction sang and smoked to invoke his spirit helpers (Frison, 1971). Judging from both historical accounts and archaeological observations at other sites, ritual observances played an important part in communal bison hunting.

The Muddy Creek site corral was also built on sloping ground, a structure about 40 ft (12.2 m) in diameter. It lay upslope from extensive, fertile grazing tracts, and was hidden from view by a low ridge until the very last moments of a drive. Both this, and the Ruby corral, were designed to handle relatively small numbers of bison, perhaps a nursery herd of about 25 beasts. The teeth from both sites suggest they were used in fall and early winter, when calves were 5 to 8 months old (Frison, 1978).

These sites chronicle much more sophisticated bison hunting methods that were introduced to the Plains during the Late Archaic. Now the hunters were less dependent on the arroyo trap and the jump. Instead, they constructed skillfully contrived artificial corrals that could be set up in a much wider variety of optimum locations, corrals that were erected with the aid of the powerful supernatural forces that governed human life on the Plains, forces that were still invoked 1800 years later, when Europeans spilled onto the grasslands.

Bison Jumps

Communal bison hunting on foot reached its greatest prehistoric intensity after AD 550, during a period that saw the bow and arrow reach the Plains, perhaps from the northwest. George Frison (1978) argues that the bow and arrow was not that much more effective than stone-tipped spears unless it penetrated the animal through the ribs. However, the stone points could be made from more easily obtainable rocks, and arrow shafts were easier to make than long, well-balanced spears to be launched with the atlatl. The bow had a longer range, and many arrows could be carried in a convenient quiver without the need to mount new foreshafts all the time. Furthermore, the bow was easier to handle, for the hunter could adopt any stance, take his time aiming, and do so from a slightly greater range. The bow was adopted quite quickly, but still did not solve the problem of driving and controlling the movement of the quarry. As time went on, the hunters made increasing use of bison jumps, high bluffs approached by long lines of stone piles, over which they could stampede large herds. These drive lines served as markers for the stalkers moving the herd into position.

Bison jumps were sited at strategic locations, such as convenient bluffs, precipitous cliffs, sink holes, and other natural features that, combined with one another, made for a suitable killing site. Unlike a corral, a successful jump hunt depended on a large number of animals, so that the pursuers could stampede them, moving close together at a high rate of speed. The mass of animals then prevented the leaders from turning aside, as would happen with a small herd. Frison, with his extensive experience of cattle ranching and herding, points out that 10 mounted and well-trained cowboys should be able to maneuver 100 head of buffalo into the proper place and stand a better than even chance of stampeding them over a cliff, if conditions are favorable.

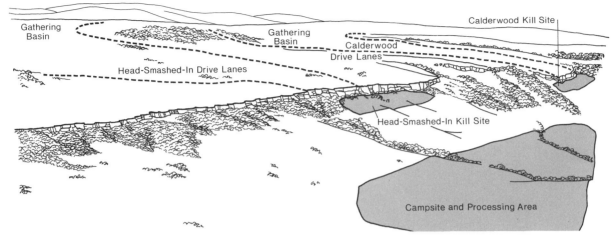

Gathering Basin

Gathering Basin

Calderwood Kill Site

Calderwood Drive Lanes

Head-Smashed-In Drive Lanes

Head-Smashed-In Kill Site

Campsite and Processing Area

Head-Smashed-In, Alberta, is among the oldest, largest, and best preserved of the western Plains buffalo jump sites. (Top) Major features of the site and the neighboring Calderwood site, including gathering areas where the hunters maneuvered the herds into position, drive lanes, and kill and processing areas. (Above) Reconstruction of a bison jump at the Head-Smashed-In kill site.

The classic bison jump sites of the northwest Plains document bison jumps and the drive lines of stone piles associated with them in great detail. Locations such as Glenrock, Big Goose Creek, and Vore, Wyoming, document how the hunters moved herds over distances of several miles to their deaths. At Vore (Reher, 1974), the excavators used layered pond sediments in the sink hole "jump" to estimate that five bison hunts took place, each after a period of higher rainfall, spaced at about quarter-century intervals over a 140-year period after about AD 1550. Frison wonders whether these higher rainfall cycles improved the grazing grass, which led to better breeding conditions, a better calf crop, and ultimately a minor population explosion. This created optimum conditions for communal bison kills.

The famous Head-Smashed-In buffalo jump in western Alberta was used for more than 7000 years. Six streams feed into a shallow basin in the plains surrounded by higher ground. A large creek forms the only entrance. More than 500 stone cairns up to a foot (0.3 m) high mark drive lines as much as 5 miles (8 km) long leading to the sandstone cliff that formed the jump. Deep deposits of bison bones lie below the cliff, dating back to as early as about 5400 BC.

This type of bison drive was still in use when Hudson Bay Company trader Peter Fidler spent six weeks among the Piegan Indians in 1797. He witnessed many bison drives as he camped among them at one of their drive pounds. At one drive, the hunters killed more than 250 beasts and would have taken more. But "when the wind happened to blow from the pound in the direction of the tents, there was an intolerable stench of the large numbers of petrified [sic] carcasses, etc. on which account the reason of our leaving it."

Mass kill sites like Olsen-Chubbock and Head-Smashed-In represent relatively unusual events in Plains life. For such mass hunting strategies to be successful, the bison density would have had to reach a critical level, a density only reached at certain times of the year, when patterns of animal migration permitted it. Many communal hunts may have been annual affairs, or conducted after periods of higher rainfall as we have seen, when the bison population increased.

John Speth's excavations at Garnsey, New Mexico, reveal that prehistoric Plains hunters were expert observers of their prey. About AD 1550, a group of hunters visited a small gully where they knew bison would congregate in late March or early April. Instead of just killing every animal on sight, they tended to concentrate on the male beasts. Speth (1983) believes this was because males are in better condition in the spring, and their bone marrow has a higher fat content. Hunters everywhere prefer fatter meat, for it is an important source of energy and essential fatty acids. In spring, such flesh was hard to come by, for the herds were still recovering from the lean winter months. So the hunters selected male beasts at Garnsey, only consuming the choicest parts with higher fat content from the few cows they killed.

Late Prehistoric Period
c. AD 500 to the 16th century

The Late Prehistoric period begins with the introduction of the bow and arrow, reflected in the appearance of side-notched projectile points designed for use on light arrows. The earliest of these side-notched points are the so-called Avonlea forms named after a site in Saskatchewan. Avonlea was a highly organized kill site, one where the hunters were killing large numbers of bison not only to satisfy their own needs, but, perhaps, to produce surplus meat and by-products for exchange with horticultural societies at the edges of the Plains. This exchange pattern persisted right into the historic period.

Several pottery traditions appear on the Plains during this period, a useful chronological marker, most of them introduced from outside. Such wares include Shoshonean and Crow pottery, also Woodland vessels in the east. Predictably, Fremont and Pueblo wares are found in areas contiguous to the Great Basin and Southwest respectively (Chapters 12 and 15).

The great efficiency of late prehistoric bison hunting can be seen at the Wardell site and other locations. Wardell, in Wyoming's Green River Basin, was a bison corral from about AD 350 to 1050 (Frison, 1973). Over the centuries, local hunters used it to intercept bison moving between nearby grazing and water supplies. The corral lay at the foot of a steep cliff at the confluence of two arroyos, strengthened by slopes on three sides. At least 1000 bison were killed here over five centuries, many of them processed at a butchery camp nearby. The killing took place in fall, using bows and arrows. Much of the meat was dried or made into pemmican on-site, for stone heating and cooking pits abound. Everything points to economical butchery, with little going to waste. Frison believes the hunters lived off antelope, rabbit, and other game as well as fresh bison meat while processing their kills.

Without horses, prehistoric bison hunters were dependent on ever-changing herd densities for successful communal hunts. Individual or small group hunting would be far more adaptive with lower densities, for bison drives have a high failure rate and a herd could move out of foot range if allowed to escape unless herd densities were unusually high. In the final analysis, everything depended on the hunters' knowledge of bison habits and of their natural behavior. Larger hunts were surrounded by complex shamanistic rituals. These prepared both humans and bison for the hunt, and controlled the direction and conduct of the drive. Such controls were an essential part of the organization of game drives, for

(Above) Two Avonlea points, from the Glenrock and Wardell sites respectively, lengths c. 4.2 cm. (Below) Shamanistic rituals: detail of a Mandan okipa *(or buffalo dance) in the 1830s, depicted by the Swiss artist Karl Bodmer.*

success depended on the animals being kept together in tight formation, pushed along at top speed, and headed in exactly the right direction. Judging from Dennis Stanford's discovery of shamans' artifacts at a Paleo-Indian kill site, the same basic rituals sustained bison hunts for thousands of years. It was only when Europeans introduced the horse and the rifle to the Plains that the age-old hunting patterns changed and the bison virtually disappeared.

Protohistoric Period
16th century AD to modern times

In AD 1541, at about the same time a small band of hunters was killing bison at Garnsey, New Mexico, Spanish conquistador Francisco de Coronado ventured eastward from Pueblo Indian country in the Southwest from Pecos onto the Plains, in search of rumored Indian gold. One of his captains had traveled east the year before, emerging onto vast grasslands where his men were surrounded by enormous buffalo herds. Coronado's chronicler Pedro de Castañeda remarked on their "extremely large bodies and long wool." The conquistadors had some difficulty killing the large beasts, until they discovered that it was safer for their horses if they used their pikes from a distance.

Coronado traveled east for 37 days, traveling over featureless plains without landmarks except occasional lakes and buffalo wallows. The huge herds of domesticated animals that traveled with them obliterated their tracks, so the soldiers erected bones and cow dung to mark their route for the rear guard. The Spaniards soon encountered Plains Indian groups who depended entirely on the buffalo for their livelihood. At one point in northwestern Texas the soldiers came across a huge pile of buffalo bones by a salt lick that was a "crossbow shot long," about 12 ft (3.6 m) high and 18 ft (5.4 m) across, eloquent testimony to the hunters' expertise. After 48 days of exhausting riding across what is now the northern Texas Panhandle and into Oklahoma and Kansas, the Spaniards reached a place they named Quivira, actually a location somewhere near Great Bend, Kansas. There they found Wichita Indians living in grass lodges, in country "with mesas, plains, and charming rivers with fine waters," also plenty of wild fruit and buffalo. Coronado returned without gold, but left one momentous legacy behind him — the horse.

Just over a half-century later, on 15 September 1598, Juan de Onate, the first Spanish colonizer of New Mexico, sent an expedition of 60 officers and men to explore the plains that lay to the east. They found enormous herds of "cattle" roaming over "some extremely level mesas that extend for many leagues." They were hairy animals with black horns "similar to those of the *bufalo*" (the Asiatic buffalo or wild ox).

Occasional Indian settlements dotted the Plains. One was "A ranchería of 50 tents made of tanned skins which were very bright red and white in color. They were round like pavilions, with flaps and openings, and made as neatly as those from Italy. They are so large that in the most common ones there is ample room for four individual mattresses and beds." The buffalo hide was soft and pliable, so well tanned that not even the heaviest rain passed through. "To carry these tents . . . the Indians use medium sized, shaggy dogs, which they harness like mules. They have large droves of them, each girt around the breast and haunches, carrying a load of at least one hundred pounds. They travel at the same pace as their masters. It is both interesting and amusing to see them traveling along, one after the other, dragging the ends of their poles. . . ."

A few days later the Spaniards tried to drive buffalo for themselves. They built a corral of large cottonwood logs, a task that took three days. The wings leading to it were so large that they blithely assumed they would trap hundreds of beasts. Next day they set out to drive an enormous herd toward the corral. The herd moved toward the corral at first, but suddenly stampeded straight for the horsemen. Confusion reigned as the horsemen frantically dodged the charging animals. There was no way the Spaniards could take the buffalo alive. Despite the confusion, they shot a large number, with the loss of three horses. Many of their steeds were slashed by razor sharp horns.

The Spaniards soon developed a healthy respect for Plains bison. "There is no one so melancholy who if he were to see them a hundred times would not laugh heartily just as soon or marvel at the sight of such fierce beasts." They admired the way the Indians killed drinking bison with a single shot with bow and stone-tipped arrow, hiding in brush shelters near their favorite water holes. They saw some arrows with "large bone tips, although only a few, as the flint is better for killing the cattle than the spear."

The Plains peoples who came in contact with the Spaniards were Apache, people who had separated from their northern Athapaskan ancestors long before European contact, perhaps as early as AD 600. They arrived on the southern Plains sometime between AD 1450 and 1525. In the late 1600s, Apachean groups were living over a wide area of the western Plains, some of them part-time horticulturalists. To the north, the Blackfoot and Assiniboine inhabited the Canadian Plains, Arapahoe and Gros Ventre in what is now North Dakota, with Kutenai and Flathead close to the Rocky Mountains, venturing only occasionally onto the Plains. The Kiowa controlled the eastern Black Hills along the Little Missouri River to the south. Their Crow neighbors had originally been part of the horticultural Hidatsa along the Missouri River. They had split off from them at an unknown date, perhaps about AD 1400, and now occupied the Bighorn Mountains in northeastern Wyoming, also adjacent areas of Montana and the Dakotas.

The Shoshone were Numic speakers, who had moved out of the Great Basin through the mountains of Utah and Wyoming onto the Plains at some time after the 15th century. They may have occupied most of the northwestern Plains from Wyoming to the Canadian border before the introduction of the horse. Two other groups of Numic speakers lived on the High Plains in the 16th century — the Ute and Comanche. The latter split off from the Shoshone after their migration onto the Plains. The Ute expanded out of the Rockies at about the same time as the Shoshone did.

All of these groups hunted on foot. The causes of tribal movements before European contact are poorly understood. Those since 1650 are closely connected to the introduction of the horse to the Plains, European expansion, and to the ability of different tribes to obtain firearms.

It took about a century for horses, "mystery dogs," as the Indians called them, to reach the northern Plains. Horses were commonplace long before

French traders bartered firearms for furs in the northeastern Plains: a well-armed Cree Indian with his family, depicted by Peter Rindisbacher in 1821.

Indians hunting bison by Karl Bodmer (1843).

firearms, a reflection of strict Spanish policies that forbade the trading of muskets to the Indians. The Plains people obtained horses through barter and through theft. In contrast, the French fur traders in Canada and along the Mississippi had few horses but plenty of firearms and ammunition that they traded for furs. As a result, there tended to be more horses on the southwestern Plains, and more firearms to the northeast.

The Plains Apache obtained large numbers of horses after 1650, soon developing a form of mounted warfare that gave them marked military superiority over their neighbors. Horses reached Caddoan groups to the east by 1700, the Comanche and Ute at about the same time. The Shoshone of Montana and Wyoming were raiding the Blackfoot and Crow on horseback by 1730. They expanded to the south at the expense of the Apache, settling by the banks of the Arkansas River by about 1725. Constant tribal wars, raids, and stealing had the Blackfoot mounted by 1740.

The Assiniboine and Cree were armed by English Hudson's Bay traders after 1670. By the mid-18th century, firearms were relatively commonplace throughout the Plains. Tribal movements were now dependent on the military capabilities of each group, with the stronger triumphing at the expense of the weaker. The Shoshone, for example, were driven from the Plains in the late 18th century.

One major effect of the introduction of the horse was an enhanced ability on the part of the mounted hunter to locate bison (Osborn, 1983). In other words, areas of the Plains that supported dispersed bison populations that could not be exploited effectively by hunters on foot were now suited for mounted, more complex hunting societies to exploit. The horse extended the range of the hunter and his ability to carry large quantities of meat. Plains groups were now less dependent on the year-by-year, season-by-season fluctuations of bison herds, for they could cover enormous distances in search of their quarry.

Many more hunters now exploited the Plains herds, slaughtering more and more every year. In time, the herds moved west across the Plains from the Missouri River, as they were decimated. Bison robes and hides were in demand, hunting became harder as the beasts became more wary of humans. But even with the horse, food supplies were always chancy. Many bands relied on the sedentary villages in major valleys for grain during the lean months. This in turn placed severe strain on the farmers, for the women were often diverted into preparation of bison hides, raids often depleted granaries, and crop failure brought a village close to starvation.

The horse put the nomadic groups of the Plains in a strong position. They could either live off their farming neighbors, or could trade bison meat and hides for grain when it suited them. The nomadic population of the Plains grew as the bison dwindled. Some formerly sedentary groups like the Dakota and Cheyenne became nomads, joining others like the Blackfoot and Comanche, who had been hunting for centuries. The Bison Belt became an economic battleground, as fierce war parties raided and counter-raided each others' camps, to seize horses and loot food stores in a constant cycle of attack and retaliation.

Douglas Bamforth believes (1988) that there was an ecological context for the changing balance of power on the Plains. Military advantage was obviously important, for warfare was constant, and the ability to defend oneself the key to survival. This ability depended on numerical strength — concentrating large numbers of people in the largest camps possible, even if many raids were on a small scale. To do this, one had to have the ability to support oneself in the Plains environment. The communal hunt was a time when large numbers of people came together at one location, providing not only more food, labor and hunting skills, but also information, information on the whereabouts of bison herds. The hunters could even work several corrals or jumps at the same time. Larger concentrations of population meant more marriage partners, also access to trade goods obtained from a wide geographical area. The number of a leader's followers depended on his skills in war and in the chase. Ambitious individuals could manipulate the communal hunt to their advantage, to obtain power and prestige, more followers, and, eventually their groups would obtain long-term military advantage.

Bamforth argues that the mechanisms for social control that could flow from increased aggregation may have given some societies the longer-term military edge. This is reflected in the uniformly northeast-southwest pattern of recent tribal migration on the Plains, and in the absence of expansion from the east onto the southern Plains. It is no coincidence that the more complex groups who moved onto the Plains were those who lived adjacent to areas where such complex groups could support themselves. The most complex of these groups lived in the Black Hills area of the north, the area most suited to them. In contrast, the peoples living on the margins of the less productive southern Plains did not expand far onto the grassland steppe, perhaps because they could not subsist there, or preserve their existing social order.

The changeover to horses, and to a certain extent the rifle — a weapon that made people dependent on European traders — led to a chronically imbalanced and unstable way of life. In archaeological terms, the increasing value of European imports is reflected in occasional finds of glass trade beads, metal arrow points, and some locally made iron spear heads. In social and cultural terms, the changes were far more radical. The millennia-old communal values that stressed cooperation for survival gave way to highly individualistic doctrines that pitted biological family against biological family, with little concern for the common welfare. Individual fortunes could change almost overnight as a result of a successful raid. The wealth obtained in battle could be used to promote family status. The ranks of individuals changed constantly, as hunter vied with hunter for the allegiance of followers and fellow warriors. A flamboyant, almost frenzied era of Plains life dawned, one where most nomadic groups believed old age was evil, that it was better for a man to die in battle.

The combination of horses and firearms was a volatile mixture in the hands of ruthless warriors. The Blackfoot of the northern Plains were among the last hunters to receive the horse, in about 1740. They acquired guns from the Cree to the east at about the same time. Living as they did in a strategic position where they could control the spread of horses and firearms, the Blackfoot took to the warpath. They became masters of the lightning raid. A war party would swoop down, drive away horses, slaughter people without mercy and vanish over the horizon. By 1850, Blackfoot territory extended from the North Saskatchewan River to what is now Yellowstone National Park.

Plains Indians at a rendezvous, their tipis stretching away into the distance – detail of a 19th-century painting by A.J. Miller.

The Blackfoot rose to prominence as European fur traders and settlers pressed onto the age-old Plains hunting grounds. Fur traders were among the first to sow the seeds of wholesale bison slaughter, for they gladly exchanged firearms for beaver pelts. Now white hunters with their repeating rifles joined the fray, leaving thousands of wasted carcasses rotting on the Plains. Like the beaver, the bison began to dwindle, affected, also, by exotic cattle diseases. Then the railroads spread over the prairies. During the 1860s and 1870s, special excursion trains took hunters into a sea of bison. The great herds of thundering animals, with their seemingly inexhaustible supplies of meat and hides disappeared almost overnight. And, at the same time, the last vestiges of the primeval North American hunting life vanished in an orgy of 19th-century musketry. Only a handful of buffalo survived, to form the nucleus of the managed herds that graze on the Plains today.

A few European travelers were fortunate enough to witness Plains bison hunts before horses became commonplace. Fur trader Alexander Henry watched expert Assiniboine hunters set out on foot in 1776. "They were dressed in ox-skins, with the hair and horns. Their faces were covered, and their gestures so closely resembled those of the animals themselves, that had I not been in the secret, I would have been as much deceived as the oxen," Henry wrote.

The decoys slowly lured the herd toward the corral. Dogs were muzzled, men and women surrounded the corral. The decoyers bellowed like buffalo as the herd paused to feed about a half-mile away. As the bison approached, the decoys fell back until the leaders were inside the jaws of the pound. Then the hunters pounced as the leaders scrambled to safety. The slaughter continued until evening, ensuring ample meat supplies for the winter months ahead. But the Assiniboine hunt was the end of a big-game hunting era that extended back to the very beginnings of North American prehistory, to the time when a handful of hunting families set foot in a virgin continent. The same basic cultural traditions might have continued for millennia, had not Europeans intervened.

Further Reading

Bamforth, Douglas. 1989. *Ecology and Human Organization on the Great Plains*. Plenum Press, New York.
   An innovative study of cultural diversity on the Plains based on a multidisciplinary perspective.
Frison, George. 1978. *Prehistoric Hunters of the High Plains*. Academic Press, New York.
   The definitive work on the archaeology of the northwest Plains that has wide applicability elsewhere. Comprehensive references to many fine excavations.
Speth, John. 1983. *Bison Kills and Bone Counts*. University of Chicago Press, Chicago.
   This remarkable study gives invaluable perspectives on bison hunting.
Wheat, Joe Ben. 1972. "The Olsen-Chubbock Site: A Paleo-Indian Bison Kill," *Memoirs of the Society for American Archaeology*, 26.
   An exemplary monograph on a famous mass bison kill of 6000 BC.

PART FOUR

THE FAR NORTH

"The lakes melted, and the hunter wondered, 'What did the Snow Man mean when he said he was going to help me?' He began to hunt, and he saved all the fat from the animals he caught and stored it in bladders. He also cut lots of wood, which he arranged in deep piles. And he went on all summer and into the fall storing grease and piling up wood. He did not know why he did these things. Something seemed to impel him…"

Northern Athabaskan legend

CALIBRATED DATES	RADIOCARBON AGES	ALASKA			EASTERN ARCTIC	SUB ARCTIC
		ALEUTIANS	KODIAK AREA	BERING STRAIT AREA		
Modern times	Modern times	MODERN ALEUTS	MODERN ESKIMO GROUPS		MOD. INUIT THULE → POST-CLASSIC CLASSIC	MODERN ATHABASKAN-SPEAKING GROUPS
			KONIAG	→ PUNUK BIRNIRK		
AD 870–1230 —	AD 1000 —	Chaluka		NORTON IPIUTAK THULE OLD BERING SEA	THULE EXPANDS	
		A L E U T I A N	K A C H E M A K	N O R T O N	D O R S E T	N O R T H E R N A R C H A I C	S H I E L D A R C H A I C	M A R I T I M E A R C H A I C
175 BC–AD 235 —	AD 1 —					
		T R A D I T I O N		CHORIS	ARCTIC SMALL TOOL TRAD. → S A R Q A Q	
1530–905 BC —	1000 BC —	Chaluka	K O D I A K T R A D I T I O N	ARCTIC SMALL TOOL TRADITION	PRE-DORSET INDEP. I	
2830–2305 BC —	2000 BC —			?	→	
3950–3640 BC —	3000 BC —		OCEAN BAY TRADITION			
5235–4575 BC —	4000 BC —			?	No human settlement	
6285–5445 BC —	5000 BC —					
outside accurate calibration range	6000 BC —	Anangula		PALEO-ARCTIC TRADITION	No human settlement	
	7000 BC —					

CHAPTER 8

EARLY ARCTIC CULTURES

For at least four centuries, the far northern reaches of North America have been a focus of intense interest, a challenge that has exercised a powerful spell on the Western imagination. The Europeans who first explored the Arctic had been raised in lands with fertile soils and long summers, where the enemies were late frosts and early winters. To these explorers, the geographical and social environments of the people of the north were a startling reversal of the human condition.

The distance that an English ship could penetrate into the Arctic during the ice-free summer months usually left her crew frozen into the territory of the Central Canadian Arctic, where the Iglulingmiut people used dog sleds and dwelt in snow houses. Their "igloos" and hunts became the "Eskimos" of popular imagination. The people of the north were seen as happy, optimistic hunters dressed in cozy furs, despite a harsh life of never-ending work and fatalism in an environment of impossible terrain and intolerable weather. This abiding stereotype was epitomized by Robert Flaherty's celebrated movie *Nanook of the North*, which appeared in 1922. This documentary told the story of a man pitted against the ferocious and unrelenting environmental odds of the frozen north. The film was an international hit in a naive, romantic era. When the hunter who had played Nanook starved to death in the Barren Lands a few years later, movie-goers as far afield as China mourned his passing.

The haunting stereotypes perpetuated by Europeans disguise a great diversity of thriving human cultures that extend back to the very earliest generations of prehistoric settlement in the Americas. Today, after more than 10,000 years of human settlement in the Far North, the mosaic of environments and societies in the North are much more elaborate than any scientific investigations have so far revealed. The northern peoples express differences between themselves in a myriad of ways — by the patterning of impressions left by sealskin boots, by pronunciations of words, by preferences for different hunting methods and camp sites. The archaeological record represents an inevitable blurring of cultural differences that persisted over many centuries.

At the time of European contact, arctic peoples were strung across the Far North from Attu Island at the extreme western end of the Aleutian Islands to the eastern shores of Greenland, more than 6800 miles (11,000 km) by reasonably direct boat and sled routes. There was considerable physical variation between them. The Eskimos and Aleuts of the west

One of the scenes from the movie, Nanook of the North *(1922).*

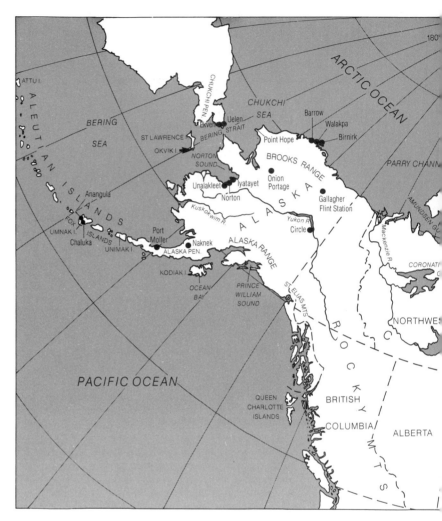

(Right) Major sites and regions of the Far North referred to in Chapters 8-9.

(Below) A generalized family tree of the Eskimo-Aleut languages, after Dumond (1987). The highest order of branches, shown on all but the three Siberian languages, indicates the presence of dialects.

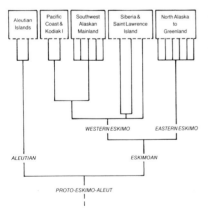

display some anatomical differences, but are generally considered to be the most Asian of all native Americans.[1] They have been classified as "Arctic Mongoloids," as have the peoples of northern Siberia. This type is distinct from that of most American Indians to the south.

Linguistically, all Eskimos and Aleuts belong within a single Eskimo-Aleut language stock (for a summary, see Dumond, 1987). However, there are differences between the Eskimoan and Aleutian branches, which have been likened to those between Russian and English in the Indo-European language group. When the first Russian explorers arrived, Aleutian dialects were spoken along the entire island chain and onto the Alaska Peninsula as far east as 159°W. Eskimoan flourished from there eastward to Kodiak Island and around the Alaskan coast and across Canada to Greenland.

[1]For the purely arbitrary purposes of this book, as explained in Chapter 1, the Eskimoan-speaking peoples of Alaska and the western Arctic are referred to as Eskimos, central and eastern groups as Inuit.

There are two distinct segments of Eskimoan. Western Eskimo includes at least five different languages and is centered in an area between the Chukchi Peninsula, Norton Sound, and Prince William Sound. Eastern Eskimoan is spoken from St Michael and Unalakeet northward and eastward all the way to Greenland. Eastern Eskimoan is so homogeneous that you can travel more than 6200 miles (10,000 km) and still use the same language whether you are on Baffin Island or on the shores of Attu in the far western Aleutian Islands. Linguists generally agree that Eskimo-Aleut languages are related to Siberian speech stocks, either to that of the Chukchi, close Siberian neighbors, or to the more widely distributed Ural-Altaic group found throughout much of Siberia.

Throughout the vast regions of the Far North, from Greenland across arctic Canada to Alaska, and along the Alaskan coast to the Alaska Peninsula, human societies at European contact practiced a highly varied hunter-gatherer economy based on the bounty of land and water. Sea mammals large and small, lake and river fish, caribou, musk ox, and small game supplemented by wild vegetable foods—most were available over wide areas and were taken with basically similar techniques. However, the emphasis of the hunting and gathering economy varied greatly from locale to locale depending on local environmental conditions.

The Arctic Environment

Alaska was joined to Siberia for much of the Wisconsin glaciation, part of the sunken continent of Beringia that formed a natural highway for human settlement of the New World (Chapter 4) (Hopkins, 1982). The Arctic Slope runs across the northern portion of the modern state of Alaska, separated from the interior by the Brooks Range that reaches an altitude of 9842 ft (3000 m) in a few places (Dumond, 1987). The Alaska Range, which includes Mount McKinley, forms another ridge across the south, merging into the Aleutian Range. These mountains extend southwestward along the Alaska Peninsula and become the 1000-mile (1600-km) Aleutian Island chain that stretches far into the Pacific. Two major rivers, the Yukon and the Kuskokwim, drain through the broken country and swampy lowlands of central Alaska into the Bering Sea from headwaters far in the interior. Vast numbers of salmon run up these rivers, a vital subsistence resource for the prehistoric (and modern) inhabitants.

Canada's Yukon Territory lies to the east, rugged country where the Rocky Mountains, the Coast Mountains, and the St Elias Range come together to form a massive backbone that extends south into what is now British Columbia. During the Ice Age, the mountain glaciers of northern and southern Alaska nearly joined in the Yukon, leaving the Alaskan interior nearly unglaciated during the Wisconsin.

East from the Yukon extends a vast tract of low-lying, undulating territory that was covered with the massive Laurentide ice sheet during the Wisconsin glaciation. The Canadian mainland surrounding Hudson Bay is fundamentally a shallow basin, with several large rivers flowing into the depression, among them the Churchill and Nelson from the west, the Great Whale and Eastmain from the east (Harp, 1976; Maxwell, 1985). The western rivers flow through an undulating plain covered in many places with glacial tills or marine deposits. To the east of Hudson Bay lies a rocky, glaciated plateau which lies at an altitude of about 984 ft (300 m) above sea level. The glacier-scoured and polished rocks of this area coincide with the Canadian Shield, made up of ancient pre-Cambrian rocks, devoid of most vegetation, and still glaciated in places.

North of the mainland lies the Canadian arctic Archipelago, covering an enormous area of the Arctic Ocean, and extending as far as Greenland. About a tenth of the islands are covered with permanent ice and mountain glaciers. The barren terrain is characterized by various land forms, but stands in contrast to the mountain chain along the fjord-indented eastern edge of the Queen Elizabeth Islands that reaches altitudes of nearly 10,000 ft (3048 m) in places.

Greenland lies to the east of the Canadian Archipelago, the northernmost landmass in the world, reaching to within 435 miles (700 km) of the North Pole and mantled with an enormous ice cap. This reaches the sea in places, but there is a fringe of ice-free territory along much of Greenland's deeply indented coasts.

The border between arctic and sub-arctic North America coincides approximately with the northern limits of the treeline, well south of the Arctic Circle. It is really a misnomer to call this a line, for in reality it is a broad transitional zone between the tundra and boreal forest. Archaeologist Elmer Harp puts it well (1978): "Approaching it [the treeline] from the north, one first encounters outlying isolated clumps of stunted conifers in sheltered valleys; these increase in size and density toward the south, until at last the closed boreal forest appears." Large-scale forest growth is impossible where the average temperature of the warmest month of the year, usually July, is below 50°F (10°C), and the arctic treeline coincides in general terms with the 50°F (10°C) isotherm for that month. This is, of course, an average temperature. Depending on location, actual summer readings can be much higher.

The northern climate is savage, with long, dark, and severely cold winters and brief summers with no more than about three frost-free months a year. Temperatures are never warm enough to allow total thawing of the ground, so permafrost occurs close to the surface, resulting in widespread summer bogs and swamps that make travel inland extremely difficult — to say nothing of the hordes of mosquitoes that torture both man and beast. Even at the southern edge of Labrador and Hudson Bay, sea ice rings coasts and islands for at least seven months every year. Mid-winter temperatures average below −25°F (−32°C) for weeks at a time, with winter storms with harsh northwesterly winds dropping them as low as −100°F (−73°C).

With such temperatures and only short summers, vegetational cover is sparse tundra at best, with occasional stands of dwarf willow, alder, and birch in sheltered locales. The early summer growth season is short and intense, as mosses, lichens, and other ground-hugging species grow rapidly in the long hours of welcome sunlight. In the Canadian Archipelago the protection is minimal and the sparse vegetation gives way to barren, rocky terrain.

Only a few species of land mammal flourish in the Arctic. The most common is the caribou, a gregarious species that occurs throughout the Far North, in several large herds west of Hudson Bay, and in smaller aggregations elsewhere. Musk ox thrive in Greenland, over much of the northern Archipelago and in remoter parts of the mainland. Other animals include hares, lemmings, arctic fox, wolves, and bears. Bird life is abundant, especially migratory waterfowl, which breed and nest in the Arctic during the summer.

Aquatic resources abound in northern waters, not only arctic char, salmon, and whitefish, but many species of sea mammals, including whales. For thousands of years, prehistoric peoples subsisted off a bounty of seal and walrus, developing specialized toolkits for sea mammal hunting throughout the Far North.

South of the treeline, the boreal forest, often called taiga, is virtually impenetrable, meaning that the traveler must traverse it along natural drainage systems (Harp, 1978). Spruce is dominant in the northern taiga, giving way to more hemlock, tamarack, and pine further south. Winters are just as severe as they are on the tundra, but there are more frost-free days and greater variety of land animals. Woodland caribou, moose, and migratory waterfowl were important food sources in prehistoric times. Fur-bearing animals such as the beaver and mink assumed great economic importance after European contact.

The biology of the Far North is far richer and more dependent on the cold than might appear. The open tundra is a perfect habitat for the lichens, grasses, and sedges that are the staple diet of caribou. The permafrost guarantees vast areas of shallow lake and swamp that never seep away, rich habitats not only for mosquitoes but many other insect species. They provide nourishment for many birds and fish. Throughout the Arctic and Sub-Arctic, the sunlight of spring and summer ensures that grasses and insects are turned into the protein upon which northern hunters depend.

Every year, millions of small seawater plankton, krill, shrimp, and tiny fish move into arctic waters. There they take advantage of the micro-organisms that have been growing at the base of the sea ice, organisms that are released into the ocean as the ice melts in spring and summer. Much larger creatures such as dolphins and whales feed on the small fry. The same food chain provides enough nutrients for a vast seal population year round.

Ironically, while southerners tend to think of the summer as the only bearable time in the Arctic, the warm months can be the most hazardous ones for the northern hunter. The tundra is awash in standing water, making walking and boat travel the only viable means of transport. Unpredictable summer storms can make canoe and boat travel slightly hazardous, and mosquitoes plague life ashore. The boreal forests are tangled with undergrowth, making tracking and snaring both hazardous and uncomfortable. Many interior groups tended to find more open camp sites in summer, which was a time for important social gatherings and relative inactivity.

The Paleo-Arctic Tradition
*c.*8000 to *c.*5000 BC

In 8000 BC, Alaska was still a cultural province of Siberia, as it had been in earlier times, occupied by peoples whose ultimate cultural roots lay to the west, in the Dyukhtai tradition of Siberia. Their microblades and other artifacts were part of a Stone Age cultural tradition that extended east from the Lena Basin in Siberia throughout most of the unglaciated area of Alaska and the Yukon, south and east along the Pacific coast, and perhaps as far south as British Columbia. After about 8000 BC, Dyukhtai gave way to the Sumnagin culture in Siberia, seasonal hunters and fisher folk who pursued both forest moose and tundra animals like the reindeer with a somewhat different technology from their predecessors (Dumond, 1987; Fagan, 1987a). A greater diversity of hunter-gatherer cultures also flourished in Alaska after 8000 BC. These cultures are subsumed under the Paleo-Arctic tradition.

The Paleo-Arctic tradition is a very shadowy entity, a patchwork of local Early Holocene cultural traditions that flourished over an enormous area of extreme northwestern North America for at least 3000 years, and longer in many places. Other terms such as the Northwest Microblade tradition,

Denali Complex, and Beringian tradition have been used to describe these same general adaptations, but "Paleo-Arctic" is the most appropriate, because it is the kind of general label that reflects a great variety of different human adaptations during a period of increasing environmental diversity and change (Dumond, 1987; West, 1981).

Undoubtedly, many Paleo-Arctic sites were buried by rising Holocene sea levels, perhaps a significant number of them in places where people exploited marine resources and lived in more permanent base camps. The settlements that survive are, for the most part, temporary land hunting camps where only stone tools survive.

Hardly surprisingly, the Paleo-Arctic is known mainly from stone artifacts — microblades, small wedge-shaped cores for making them, some leaf-shaped bifaces, also scrapers and graving tools. Perhaps the most distinctive stone objects are the wedge-shaped microcores. Their elliptical striking platforms were fashioned by removing a transverse flake. The stone worker then pressed off microblades at one end in such a manner that he made economic use of the precious raw material, ending up with a keel-shaped core. The tiny microblades were usually less than 2.5 in (6.5 cm) long, far smaller than classic Upper Paleolithic blades from Eurasia.

No Paleo-Arctic bone tools have survived, but we can assume that many microblades were used as sharp-edged barbs for hunting weapons, mounted in wood, antler, or bone points with slotted sides. Many microblades were snapped across, as if the mid-sections were used for this purpose. Paleo-Arctic stone workers also fashioned bifaces that were used both as tools and as cores for the production of larger artifact blanks. There is great variation in stone tool inventories from one Paleo-Arctic site to another. Some sites contain well-made stone projectile points, others no bifaces but many microblades, others a large inventory of scrapers. No securely dated early fluted projectile points have been reported from Alaska, but it is possible that rare fluted projectile points were part of the Paleo-Indian tradition.

The Paleo-Arctic tradition occurs throughout Alaska, and as far east as the west and southwest Yukon Territory. Wedge-shaped cores and microblades are known from the Icy Strait region of southeast Alaska, where they date to between 6000 and 2000 BC. They date to as early as 8000 BC a short distance further south, and also occur inland. The Queen Charlotte Islands off northern British Columbia were occupied by about 5000 BC, by people who manufactured microblades by striking them off much cruder cores (Fladmark, 1979). These bear little resemblance to the fine blades found further north, while microblades and crude cores have come from Namu on the British Columbia coast dating to as early as 7000 BC. Microblades were still being made in the Strait of Georgia region as recently as AD 400. Owing to rising sea levels, we do not know to what extent human settlement was focused on the coast, as it was in later millennia.

There are a number of early Alaskan sites that can be described as variations on the Paleo-Arctic tradition. These include Gallagher Flint Station in the north-central Brooks Range, the Groundhog Bay site from southeastern Alaska, and the Kagati and Ugashik Narrows locations in the southwest (Dumond, 1987), also the famous Anangula site from the Aleutian chain.

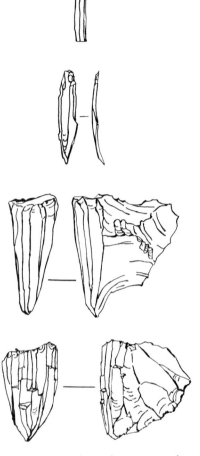

Paleo-Arctic tradition. (Top two rows) Two microblades from Ugashik Narrows, Alaska Peninsula. (Third and fourth rows) Two microblade cores from Onion Portage, Alaska. (Height of largest core 4.3 cm.)

Paleo-Arctic tradition from Anangula Island, Aleutians. (Right) Microcore and two microblades (height of core 3.7 cm). (Below) A core together with the refitted blanks struck from it.

Anangula is unusual in that it was occupied for a long period of time. The site lies on an islet off the coast of Umnak Island in the eastern Aleutians, about a third of the way along the Aleutian chain (Aigner, 1970), atop a 65-ft (19.8-m) cliff. The many radiocarbon dates range as early as about 6800 BC, but most of the occupation is probably later. The inhabitants made blade tools of various sizes, but few microblades in the Paleo-Arctic sense. There are signs of elliptically shaped houses that were partially dug into the ground and perhaps entered through the roof. Anangula was occupied when the sea level was at about its modern height and was only accessible by boat. This argues strongly for a marine adaptation at the site, an economy that relied on sea mammals and fish. However, none of the rather generalized stone artifacts from the site appear to have had specialized uses for sea mammal hunting. Judging from later sites, many such artifacts were probably manufactured of perishable bone and ivory.

Na-Dene and Aleut-Eskimos

Christy Turner's three waves of migration into North America at the end of the Ice Age.

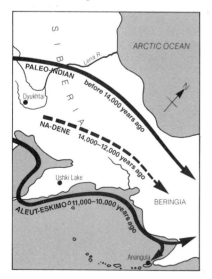

Physical anthropologist Christy Turner (1984) has attempted to reconcile the sparse archaeological evidence with information derived from dental morphology and linguistics. He believes that there were two post-Paleo-Indian migrations into North America across the Bering Strait. The earlier was of ancestral Na-Dene speakers, who came to the eastern shores of the Strait across the land bridge at the very end of its existence, between 14,000 and 12,000 years ago. These were forest hunters, he theorizes, people who used microblade-barbed, light hunting weapons against thin-skinned animals like the caribou. These were the people who manufactured the artifacts of the Paleo-Arctic tradition. According to Turner, these ancestral Na-Dene speakers spread south and west to Kodiak Island, to the Pacific Northwest Coast (Tlingit Indians are part of the Na-Dene group of languages), and far into the interior, where they became the Athabaskans. Later, some of them split off and moved southward to become the modern-day Navajos and Apaches.

Turner goes on to argue that later migration brought the maritime "Aleut-Eskimo," the ancestors of the later Aleuts and Eskimos, to Alaska via the exposed continental shelf off the Kamchatka Peninsula, perhaps some 10,000 to 11,000 years ago (Turner, 1987). Unfortunately, there are no archaeological traces of this population movement, for all sites are buried under the Bering Sea.

The Turner migrations have caused intense discussion among arctic archaeologists, who have raised all manner of theoretical, and archaeological, objections to them (for a detailed discussion, see Dumond, 1987). If Turner is correct, Na-Dene speakers spread widely through the interior and along the Northwest Coast early in Early Holocene times, while the ancestors of the Aleuts and Eskimos arrived somewhat later. The questions at issue are both complex, and bedeviled by a chronic shortage of definitive evidence. How long ago did arctic maritime culture evolve, the kind of adaptation associated with the historic Aleuts and Eskimos? Did these two peoples originate separately from the Na-Dene, or did the Na-Dene evolve as a hybrid between Paleo-Indians and Aleuts and Eskimos? And can we be sure that these groups, starting with the Paleo-Indians, actually arrived at different times? No one can pretend that there are easy answers, even if both linguistic evidence and researches into genetic markers support the notion of a single primeval migration into North America, followed by at least one, if not two, later population movements that were confined to the extreme Northwest of the continent.

Coastal Adaptations on the Pacific Coast: Ocean Bay and Kodiak
? earlier than 4000 BC to *c.* AD 1000

By 4000 BC, the Pacific Ocean had stabilized at more-or-less its modern level. As was the case elsewhere in North America, we find an increasing emphasis on coastal adaptations after this date. Judging from sites such as Anangula, the exploitation of ocean fish and marine mammals was almost certainly practiced along the Aleutian chain and on Kodiak Island at a very much earlier date (Dumond, 1987). Here, the climate is oceanic, with cool summers and relatively warm winters, where the mean temperature rarely falls below 20°F (−6°C). In this damp, often foggy environment, coastal waters teemed with sea otters, hair seal, and sea lion, with regular fur seal and whale migrations. The greatest population densities over the millennia concentrated near Kodiak and westward to Unimak Island, where whales were especially abundant. One would expect cultural uniformity over this entire area, but in spite of the relatively uniform ecosystem the ancient and modern populations fall into two major linguistic groups — Aleutian and Eskimoan. And therein lies a major controversy in arctic archaeology: when did Aleutians diverge from the Eskimoan stock of the mainland?

From the strictly archaeological point of view, it makes good sense to link the Aleuts and Pacific Eskimos into a single cultural unit, ignoring their linguistic differences and some major differences in material culture. Both Aleuts and Eskimos shared a relatively uniform ecological zone and many subsistence techniques and basic artifacts. The two-person skin kayak for open water hunting, multi-barbed harpoons for taking large sea

Eskimo two-person kayak, Nunivak Island, Alaska.

(Left) Ocean Bay tradition: large chipped-stone projectile point from Takli Island, length 15 cm. (Right) Kodiak tradition: polished slate dart or lance blade from the Takli stage, Alaska Peninsula, length 21 cm.

mammals, and many other bone and antler artifacts show close similarities, similarities that distinguish them from coastal peoples to the north. For instance, later northern peoples used toggling, not thrusting, harpoons. However, the stone implements fabricated by Aleuts and Eskimos show major differences, and provide one way of approaching the problem of distinguishing between the two groups in remoter prehistoric times.

Three major cultural entities have been identified over this large region after 4000 BC (Dumond, 1987). The first of these, the marine mammal-hunting Ocean Bay tradition, is found in the Kodiak Island region and may have spread westward from the mainland between 4000 and 2000 BC – the evidence is uncertain. These people used thrusting spears with large stone blades against large sea mammals, including whales, spears that were most likely coated with aconite poison from the Monkshood plant, a practice that was commonplace in historic times.

The long-lived Kodiak tradition lasted from at least 4000 BC until about AD 1000 and is known *not* from distinctive flaked stone artifacts, but from chipped-basalt and ground-slate tools (Clark, D.W., 1966; 1974). Unlike Ocean Bay, Kodiak sites are limited to the Eskimoan zone. The sea mammal hunting, salmon fishing, and caribou hunting culture associated with them appears to have originated in Ocean Bay, with the addition of techniques for working slate by grounding and sawing. Later Kodiak sites contain a wider variety of slate artifacts, many of them shaped by chipping before grinding and polishing. Perhaps the most characteristic is the transverse-edged knife known as the *ulu*, not found on earlier sites. Bone artifacts including barbed harpoon heads testify to the importance of sea mammal hunting.

The greater variety of bone and slate artifacts that appears during the Kachemak stage (*c.*500 BC to AD 1000) is part of a general trend along much of the Northwest Coast beginning in the early second millennium BC. The material culture of the Kodiak tradition became ever more elaborate until the first millennium AD, greater site density and increased midden accumulation indicating higher population densities. Common artifacts include notched net weights, also heavy, pecked stone lamps with human

Pecked and polished oval stone lamp with upper part of human figure inside, from Knik River, Cooks Inlet, Alaska. Drapery-like design on the outside in relief. Length 32 cm.

and animal figures carved emerging from the bowl. The Kachemak people practiced elaborate mortuary rituals, dismembering some of the dead, retaining some skulls as trophies, burying other people intact. Almost certainly, the inhabitants of Kachemak were Eskimos.

After about AD 500, cultural influences from both the Bering Sea area and from coastal regions to the southeast appear in Kodiak settlements. The Kodiak tradition evolved into the historical Eskimo-speaking Koniag culture of the region after AD 1000. This may have been an amalgam of Kachemak, Prince William Sound, and Thule cultural traits.

The Aleutian Tradition
*c.*2500 BC to AD 1800

The Ocean Bay tradition of the Kodiak region probably occurs in the Aleutian chain, but is not generally accepted as such. The earliest known human occupation in the Aleutians comes from the Anangula site. Anangula plays a critical role in Aleutian prehistory, and is the subject of three competing hypotheses (McCartney, 1984a). First, does this important site, with its emphasis on sea mammal hunting and long occupation dating back to about 6000 BC, represent ancestral Aleutian occupation in the islands? Some scholars, notably William Laughlin, one of the investigators of Anangula, believe that it does. This would imply an 8000-year linguistic, racial, and cultural continuum. Others argue that recent Aleut culture is a blend of later Eskimoid influences from the Alaska Peninsula and the older Anangula tradition. A third hypothesis contends that the Anangula people died out, to be replaced by a second occupation of the island chain by at least 2500 BC.

The first and second hypotheses both call, essentially, for cultural continuity, but one can argue with some justification that there is at present no archaeological evidence for cultural continuity between Anangula and much better documented later occupations. These latter form the Aleutian tradition, which began before 2000 BC and lasted until modern times. The third theory, the so-called Dual Tradition Model, argues that the basic stone technology of Anangula is very different from that of later Aleutian tradition industries, manufactured some 3500 years later. These two technologies, separated by many centuries, reflect quite different cultural traditions.

The Aleutian tradition is dominated by chipped stone artifacts rather than the slate so common in the Kodiak area, especially Ocean Bay-like stemmed points and knives. This is a core and flake tradition, with bifacially trimmed projectile points and tanged and untanged knives, that also contains adze and *ulu* blades. There are none of the blades and cores found in the Anangula site, and the bone industry is elaborate with strong Eskimoid influences (McCartney, 1984a). The absence of such Anangula tools as prismatic cores, gravers, and other artifacts is a powerful argument for a lack of cultural continuity, for such implements have never been found in contexts as late as 2500 BC. Alan McCartney and other scholars believe that Anangula is the isolated remnant of a much older Asiatic tradition that is very rare in northern North America, a tradition that predates the much later Aleutian.

Historic Aleut winter house. This form of large, semi-subterranean house was occupied by many related families, each with its own lamp and living space. Space was allocated on the basis of rank, the highest ranked occupant living on the eastern side of the house. The inhabitants used notched logs as ladders to enter and leave through the roof.

Aleutian tradition, Umnak, western Fox islands. (Left) Barbed harpoon head, length c. 10 cm. (Right) Ivory figurine, length 6 cm.

Everywhere the emphasis is on marine mammals and sea fish such as cod and halibut, also sea urchins and migratory animals like whales, especially in the eastern islands. Some settlements, like the Hot Springs site at Port Moller on the Alaska Peninsula, were occupied off and on for thousands of years, from as early as 2000 BC to about AD 1000. Here the houses were elliptical to rectangular, dug about 18 in (0.5 m) into the ground, roofed with driftwood and sod, and were probably entered through the roof.

In the western Fox islands, the Chaluka site on Umnak Island was occupied over a long period beginning in about 2000 BC. The early and middle periods of occupation last from about 2000 to 1000 BC, a settlement of semi-subterranean dwellings lined with stone slabs and whale bones with fire pits and some stone paving. The inhabitants made numerous chipped stone unifacial projectile points and apparently subsisted off sea mammals.

A thousand years or so later, some new occupants came to Chaluka, still living much the same lifeway and using chipped stone, including thick, bifacial and stemmed knives. Sometime between AD 1000 and 1500, slate implements came into use at Chaluka. What is striking, however, is that the basic lifeway remained very similar, with the same fundamental bone harpoon heads, spear points, chisels, awls, and ornaments in use throughout.

Sea mammal hunting and fishing communities also flourished further west on Amchitka and among the Rat Islands. Here, the people took large numbers of sea otters and hair seal, some migratory whales and fur seals, sea fish, ducks, geese, swan, and sea birds, also sea urchins and limpets. One excavated house was semi-subterranean, a sub-rectangular dwelling about 16.4 by 19.6 ft (5 by 6 m), radiocarbon dated to about AD 1500. A storage bench and depressed sleeping area surrounded a center section where a fire pit lay. As early as 600 BC, sea mammal hunters of the Aleutian tradition were living on the Near Islands, the extreme western Aleutians.

The Aleutian tradition continued to flourish into historic times, a tradition reflected by considerable stylistic variation in artifacts between one island and the next. These variations have been little studied (McCartney, 1984a).

Arctic Small Tool Tradition
c. 2000 to 800 BC

As early as Paleo-Arctic times, tiny groups of hunter-gatherers settled along the Alaska Peninsula and round Bristol Bay in the south, also on the eastern shores of the Bering Strait. By 2000 BC, a new and highly distinctive stone toolkit appears along these coasts, the Arctic Small Tool tradition. The new artifacts were indeed small, often diminutive blades or microblades, pointed at both ends, used as end or side barbs in antler or bone arrows or spear heads. The stone workers also made scrapers, graving tools and adze blades with polished working edges. Unfortunately, we know little of the organic components of the tradition, especially in the west.

The Arctic Small Tool tradition may have developed from Paleo-Arctic roots in Alaska. More likely, however, it was an intrusive culture, for possible prototypes for small, chipped bifaces, scrapers, and burins can be found in the Bel'kachinsk Stone Age farming culture of the Aldan River region of Siberia, dating to the third millennium BC. The Arctic Small Tool tradition may have resulted from a migration across the Bering Strait that introduced a new toolkit to Alaska sometime around 2000 BC (Anderson, 1968; Dumond, 1971; 1987). It is commonly believed to be associated with ancestral Eskimos.

The most important innovation brought to North America by Arctic Small Tool people was the bow and arrow, probably introduced from Asia in about 2000 BC. This weapon was highly effective against caribou and waterfowl, and spread rapidly not only through the Arctic and Sub-Arctic, but into continental North America. Bows were in use on the Canadian Plains by AD 200, and employed throughout the grasslands within a few centuries. They came to the Southwest at about the same time, perhaps a little later, and were in universal use by the late first millennium AD.

The Alaskan manifestation of the Arctic Small Tool tradition is sometimes called the "Denbigh Flint Complex," after the stratified finds at a temporary caribou hunting camp on Iyatayet Creek by Cape Denbigh on Norton Sound (Giddings, 1964), but the term has been loosely used in recent years and really only applies to the Denbigh region itself. Iyatayet yielded mainly microblades and small burins, graving tools whose spalls were sometimes mounted in antler or bone handles as tiny chisel blades. The site is remarkable for its numerous end and side blades, many of them carefully pointed at both ends, often with delicate workmanship.

Arctic Small Tool-style implements occur in the Brooks Range and as far south as the Alaska Peninsula. Some of these sites are little more than stone scatters, perhaps traces of hunting camps where a single tent was pitched. On the Peninsula, Small Tool camps lie along rich salmon streams, presumably to take advantage of summer runs. The people may also have hunted seal on the coasts. Several locations have yielded evidence of more permanent structures, among them the Kachemak Bay site, and also Onion Portage and the Brooks River site on the upper Naknek Drainage, where 14 sod-roofed houses have been excavated (illus. p.152). There, the inhabitants had dug roughly square pits into the subsoil, about 13 ft (4 m) on each side, with a sloped entryway on one side and a central hearth (Dumond, 1987).

Arctic Small Tool tradition, upper Naknek Drainage, southwestern Alaska. (Top row) Microblade and burin. (Second row) Projectile point and sideblade. (Length of sideblade c. 3.3 cm.)

Coronation Gulf Inuit using composite bows in the chase, photographed in 1913. The introduction of the bow and arrow allowed the hunter to shoot accurately 30 to 40 meters, although an arrow could fly as far as 120 meters. The men are clothed for summer conditions, the hair side of their paneled coats outwards.

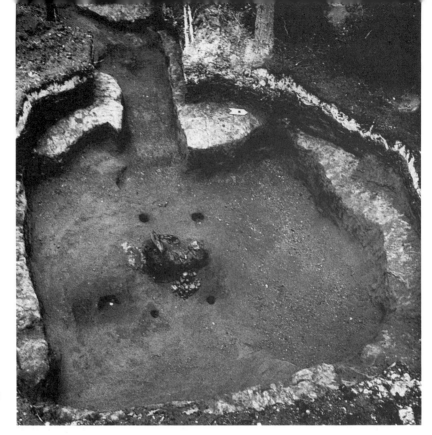

Arctic Small Tool tradition, southwestern Alaska. Excavated remains of a semi-subterranean house at Brooks River, upper Naknek Drainage, radiocarbon dated to about 1450 BC. A pile of fire-cracked pebbles lie beside the central hearth. Four holes may mark the locations of structural posts around the fireplace.

The western Arctic Small Tool tradition represents a cultural break from earlier Paleo-Arctic and interior Northern Archaic occupation. Apparently, the small indigenous population withdrew into the inland forests as Small Tool groups moved in. Both populations lived alongside one another for a long period of time.

First Settlement of the Eastern Arctic
*c.*2000 BC

At approximately the same time as their first appearance along the shores of the Bering Strait, Arctic Small Tool-using groups appear along the shores of the Arctic Ocean, among the islands of the Canadian archipelago, and in western Greenland (Maxwell, 1985). The tiny numbers of people who brought this technology eastward were the first human settlers of the Eastern Arctic. What caused this remarkable, and still largely undocumented, migration remains a complete mystery. The archaeology is confused by the changes in artifact forms that apparently took hold soon after the movement east. In general terms, however, the Arctic Small Tool tradition of the Eastern Arctic is divided into two stages: Independence I and Pre-Dorset.

Independence 1 Stage (2000 to 1700 BC). Independence Fjord forms part of Pearyland, an enormous arctic desert in northeast Greenland. Small tent rings marked by circles of large boulders lie along the shores of this, and neighboring, fjords, associated with scatters of stone tools, including the spalled burins that were used by Arctic Small Tool people for splitting and grooving bone and antler. These artifacts are quite similar to those from Cape Denbigh in the far west, but Independence I tools are larger, with many minor variations on smaller implements (Maxwell, 1985). There are bone needles, evidence for sewn clothing, pieces of bone arrowheads, and two harpoon heads with drilled holes for the line and slotted to receive a stone barb. These were not toggling harpoons, harpoons designed to detach from the head and twist in the wound, a later innovation. It was the barb that held the harpoon in the animal.

Danish archaeologist Eigil Knuth (1967) has recorded 43 settlements with 157 dwellings, all lying on old beach strands between 33 and 69 ft (10 to 21 m) above modern sea level. The highest density of settlements is around Independence Fjord, but elsewhere they average 8.6 miles (14 km) apart. Radiocarbon dates range between 1930 and 1730 BC. As many as 20 tents occurred at some locations, but most sites were no more than isolated dwellings. The tents themselves were probably fashioned of musk-ox hide. Covered with snow and equipped with a hearth and a passage-like storage area made of flagstones, they sufficed as winter homes.

Knuth believes the Independence I people were constantly on the move, mainly subsisting off musk ox, animals which wander in extensive, but restricted ranges, unlike caribou, which migrate along predictable routes every year. Occasionally, the hunters took sea birds, ring seal, arctic char, and other aquatic resources. Everyone lived in tiny hunting bands, perhaps no more than four to six people, existing without stone lamps or the technology needed to heat sea mammal oil. Their fuel was driftwood, occasional stunted willow branches, and the fat from musk-ox bones. With such heating sources and a food supply that was constantly on the move, the Independence I people had to be nomads, perhaps coming together in slightly larger groups during the two-and-a-half months of darkness in mid-winter. Moreau Maxwell (1985) gives a vivid description of their existence in the dark of winter. The houses may have been unbearably smoky when fires were lit, so perhaps they were only kindled to cook or thaw ice for water. "The bitter winter months might have been spent in a semi-somnolent state, the people lying under thick, warm musk-ox skins, their bodies close together, and with food and fuel within easy reach." Trips to the outside were kept to a minimum.

Spring and summer were the critical months, when the hunters had to accumulate large surpluses of dried fish, seal, and game meat for the winter. Knuth found one winter house with an impressive meat cache nearby – three fully grown musk ox, two calves, several hares, foxes, and fish, enough to provide about 6.6 lbs (2 kg) of meat a day for all the members of a family over a three-month winter. Perhaps about 200 people lived in this area of northeastern Greenland, a reasonable population density of about 1 person per 112 sq. miles (130 sq. km).

These Arctic Small Tool people lived nearly 750 miles (1200 km) further north than their distant relatives on the Bering Strait far to the west. Some of the sites are only about 434 miles (700 km) from the North Pole. The distribution of Independence I stage settlements extends south from Pearyland to Devon Island in the Canadian archipelago. Knuth traced Independence I stage sites 559 miles (900 km) south along Greenland's

Probable distribution of the Arctic Small Tool tradition in the Eastern Arctic.

east coast as far as Dove Bugt, the easternmost prehistoric settlement in the Americas. There is, however, considerable debate as to whether Independence I is a discrete culture in its own right.

Pre-Dorset (1700 to as late as 900–600 BC). Another Danish archaeologist, Jorgen Meldgaard, worked in the Melville Peninsula area west of Baffin Island. There he discovered more sites with Arctic Small Tool-like artifacts, that are often grouped with the so-called Pre-Dorset culture, with technological links to the Arctic Small Tool tradition. Equivalent artifacts have been found at other sites scattered throughout the southern portions of the Eastern Arctic, with at least one Melville Peninsula site being contemporaneous with the Independence I stage. There are many minor artifact differences between Pre-Dorset and Independence, although both appear to have common roots in the Arctic Small Tool tradition far to the west. Many arctic archaeologists believe they are both an integral part of the Tradition, not even separate cultures.

The relationship between Independence I and Pre-Dorset is much debated, mainly on the basis of a series of beach-side settlements in Port Refuge on Devon Island's Grinnell Peninsula in the Canadian archipelago. Here, seal hunters' tent sites lie on raised beaches, the earliest yielding microblades and other artifacts that resemble roughly contemporary Independence I forms from Pearyland, more than 497 miles (800 km) to the north. Some 300 years later, some other seal hunters camped on lower raised beaches, using Pre-Dorset-like harpoons.

Robert McGhee (1979) uses his Refuge Bay excavations to argue for two early migrations into the Eastern Arctic. The first was represented by the Independence I stage of the far northeast, the second by Pre-Dorset further south, a quite separate population that occurred some 300 years later. Moreau Maxwell (1985) believes that Independence I settlements may, in fact, exist in the south, but that they are obscured by later occupations in the rare places where people could pitch tents, places used again and again in later centuries. He argues for a single Arctic Small Tool migration that split into northern and southern waves. As time went on, different cultural traditions developed – Independence I in the High Arctic, northern Labrador, and perhaps in the Disko Bay area of Greenland, Pre-Dorset in the Foxe Basin and Hudson Strait region. Then, some centuries later, some Pre-Dorset groups moved north into places like Port Refuge.

The relationship remains unresolved, but recent research in the central Canadian archipelago has focused on differences between coastal and inland sites, also on seasonality (Bielawski, 1988). These excavations and surveys strongly suggest that seasonality may explain much of the variation in artifacts and dwellings between one region and another. Much earlier work is based on variations in artifact styles and dwellings, mainly from coastal sites. Small, dispersed Arctic Small Tool groups were capable of exploiting both coastal and inland resources, and did so in an apparently efficient and economical manner, covering large and harsh territories. Thus, the differences between Independence I and Pre-Dorset may be somewhat illusory, with all three forming not two or more separate cultures, but variations on the Arctic Small Tool tradition.

The Independence I occupation of the High Arctic ended about 1700 to 1600 BC, perhaps at a time of increasing cold after the Altithermal, the

Remains of a Pre-Dorset house at Refuge Bay. The circular depression in the ground marks the place where a tent or perhaps a snowhouse once stood. The vegetation inside the circle is feeding off nutrients in the refuse left inside the house more than 3500 years ago.

Holocene climatic optimum, that made these regions untenable for human settlement. In the south, the Pre-Dorset tradition flourished until between 900 and 600 BC (Maxwell, 1985).

One focus of early Pre-Dorset culture was an area centered on the islands in northern Hudson Bay, the northern and southern shores of Baffin Island, northern Labrador, and the west coast of the Foxe Basin. This has been called a "core" of Pre-Dorset occupation, but this concept is much debated (Bielawski, 1988). Further to the west, no early Arctic Small Tool sites have yet been reported between the Canadian/Alaskan border and Pelly Bay, some 1099 miles (1770 km) to the east.

This area is a region where no one food animal is dominant. Rather the number of these available species and the number of individuals within each species are sufficient to allow a diverse food supply throughout the year. These conditions are found through much of the Eastern Arctic, but are especially favorable in the northern Hudson Bay and surrounding regions (Maxwell, 1976). It is in this well-circumscribed area that archaeologists have been able to trace centuries of more-or-less continuous human occupation, from early Pre-Dorset up to modern Inuit occupation.

This region supported caribou migrations northward from the mainland along Melville Peninsula and across the ice to Bylot Island. There were resident caribou herds on Baffin Island, too, herds with their own migration patterns. Small musk-ox populations may have flourished in the region, as did five species of seal. Walrus and large bearded seal were common, as were migrating waterfowl, and smaller mammals. Harp seal migrations and whales passed through the Hudson Strait. This was an area where more permanent settlement was possible. The Igloolik site and other settlements literally followed descending sea levels down gravel beaches, from 203 ft (62 m) to 13 ft (4 m) above modern sea level. Over the centuries, local environmental conditions changed. Resources expanded and contracted, often with disastrous consequences for those who moved out into favored areas, where people starved when climatic conditions became more severe. Throughout the area, there was constant interaction between neighboring and more distant settlements, to the point that artistic styles and technological changes emerge almost simultaneously everywhere.

Inuit hunting seals at a breathing hole in the ice.

Subsistence. The Pre-Dorset people relied heavily on seals for their subsistence, hunting them at their winter breathing holes. This requires great patience and keen powers of observation. The hunter waits for hours for the moment when the seal comes up to breathe. A quick harpoon thrust snares the prey. Then the hunter rapidly widens the breathing hole with the chisel-like butt of his harpoon so he can drag the seal onto the ice before it carries the harpoon, and perhaps the hunter, into the water. This hunting method is most effective when there are enough hunters to keep watch on a number of breathing holes within a short distance. The thrusting harpoon used for ice hole hunting is also useful for taking bearded and ring seals at the edge of ice floes, and for stalking walrus and seals basking on the ice. It is not known whether Pre-Dorset people hunted sea mammals from light boats. If they did so, they would have needed lighter throwing harpoons, such as were developed to a high degree of elaboration by later Eastern Arctic peoples. Harpoon designs became

Trapping fish in weirs and dams was a technique used as early as Pre-Dorset times. Here Copper Inuit dressed in summer garb spear fish at a dam.

Pre-Dorset and Dorset harpoon heads. Their stylistic changes through time are useful chronological markers. The harpoon head top left dates to about 1700 BC, the specimen above right to about AD 1000.

increasingly sophisticated through time, and form a useful typological yardstick for rough dating of Pre-Dorset and Dorset sites (Maxwell, 1985).

Musk ox, caribou, polar bear, and small animals were taken with spears, and bows and arrows. The hunters probably made bows from fragments of driftwood, antler, and musk-ox horn carefully joined and bent to form small, recurved bows that were bound and backed with sinew. These weapons probably required expert stalking, for they may have been effective only at a distance of about 65 ft (20 m) or so. The hunters apparently used large dogs in the chase, for their bones have been found in Pre-Dorset middens.

The arctic char was an important food source, an anadromous species (fish that swim up rivers to spawn) that was taken in weirs and traps, then dried for use in the lean fall months before the ocean froze over. The people used leisters, barbed fish spears with trident heads that speared and held the wriggling fish, and could be sprung apart to release it on shore. (For details of the Pre-Dorset toolkit, see Maxwell, 1985: 90ff.)

Western Pre-Dorset. West of Hudson Bay, sizeable populations appear not to have developed until after the late 14th century BC, and they were predominantly hunters. The western region of Coronation and Amundsen gulfs may have been a dispersal area for hunting bands that pursued migrating caribou deep into the mainland interior. They were land hunters and fisher folk, only occasionally sealing on the coast. Some of these bands are thought to have followed caribou herds far south during a period of increasing cold between 1200 and 900 BC and may have penetrated far below the treeline, perhaps as far south as Lake Athabasca by 900 BC (Wright, 1972). Sparse Pre-Dorset populations occur across the interior of the Barren Grounds, as far as the modern settlement of Churchill on the western shore of Hudson Bay. Judging from the major shifts in the treeline in response to colder and warmer temperatures, these peoples' hunting territories fluctuated constantly.

Eastern Pre-Dorset. To the east, and in the core area, sea mammal hunting was more important. Pre-Dorset occupation may have been restricted to the northern one-third of the Labrador coast, from Hopedale to Cape Chidley, the population concentrated in favored areas (Fitzhugh, 1980; Jordan, 1978; Maxwell, 1985). The first settlement was almost as early as Independence I and Foxe Basin, about 1880 BC, with a peak settlement about 1500 BC, thereafter declining, with only very sparse occupation, if any, until the mid-8th century BC. Perhaps, argues Maxwell (1985), this was due to encroaching Indian populations.

Sarqaq Complex (c.1800 to c.300 BC). Across the Davis Strait from Baffin Island, Arctic Small Tool (Pre-Dorset) people occupied the Disko Bay area of eastern Greenland. This "Sarqaq Complex" is best known from the late Itivnera site, some 93 miles (150 km) inland from the coast. Itivnera, occupied between about 1250 and 340 BC, lies astride a migration route for caribou, the staple diet at the site. The earliest Sarqaq sites date to around 1800 BC, to about the time when Independence I occupation ceased. Some have argued that Sarqaq resulted from southern migrations from the bitterly cold Independence area.

Sarqaq was an Arctic Small Tool enclave for over 1000 years, marked in archaeological terms by high percentages of ground and polished tools, artifacts as small as arrow barbs manufactured mainly on silicified slate. Recent fieldwork in central-west Greenland has produced well-preserved animal bones, confirming that Sarqaq subsistence was based on sea mammal hunting, fishing, and caribou hunting. The relationship between Sarqaq, Pre-Dorset, and Arctic Small Tool is still somewhat uncertain, but they all form part of the same general arctic cultural tradition.

Archaic Hunter-Gatherers in the Sub-Arctic
c. 5000 BC to European contact

The Laurentide ice sheet was centered east of Hudson Bay and covered most of Sub-Arctic North America 15,000 years ago, then melted rapidly but not uniformly. The area southeast of Great Bear Lake was ice-free by about 8000 BC, the central Keewatin District some 2000 years later. The Great Lakes were ice-free by 9000 BC, south-central Quebec by 5000 BC, and the last traces of Laurentide ice vanished from the Labrador mountains by about 3800 BC. Only some scattered remnants linger in the Canadian archipelago and Greenland today (Campbell, 1962).

The spread of hunter-gatherer groups into this vast region was, in effect, a centripetal movement along the radii of progressively shrinking ice sheets (Harp, 1978). Newly deglaciated land would emerge from its icy mantle. Tundra vegetation and animals would migrate into the barren landscape. As the ice retreated north, so did taiga replace tundra in more southern areas. Human beings followed the game and the vegetation, often arriving somewhat later, for the bands had to surmount natural obstacles such as ice-dammed lakes or flooded lowlands. During the Early and Middle Holocene, two sparse, but important, population movements penetrated the Sub-Arctic. The first was from the west of Hudson Bay, the later one developed around the Great Lakes and spread along the St Lawrence Valley into the Quebec-Labrador Peninsula (see Chapter 16).

(Above) An Inuit hunter with caribou carcasses, Coppermine region, Northwest Territories, 1949. Some Sub-Arctic groups lived off the same migrating herds for generations.

(Below) Northern Archaic: Palisades complex projectile point, Onion Portage, Alaska, length 4.8 cm.

Northern Archaic (before 4000 BC to modern times). Some sparse Paleo-Indian settlement is recorded from the Canadian Shield area of the Sub-Arctic west of Hudson Bay, people who used projectile points reminiscent of Great Plains forms. As the taiga belt widened and separated the Arctic from temperate latitudes, new adaptations were necessary. It was during this period that the Northern Archaic developed, a cultural tradition thought to be associated with Athabaskans.

The Northern Archaic, which appears to be quite distinct from the Paleo-Arctic tradition of the Far North, has been identified as far northwest as the Arctic Ocean coastal plain north of the Brooks Range at Kuparuk Pingo (Lobdell, 1986) and dated to just after 4000 BC. Here the people took caribou and waterfowl, probably retaining cultural ties further inland. Northern Archaic hunters lived at Onion Portage, Alaska, by 4000 BC, with an artifact assemblage that included side-notched, often asymmetrical, projectile points, unifacial knives, and end scrapers (Anderson, 1968). The projectile points evolved into smaller forms over time and stemmed heads appeared. Northern Archaic hunting camps are widely scattered through the Brooks Range north to the Arctic Ocean coast, along the Yukon River downstream of the modern town of Circle, and into the central Alaskan Range, also close to the southwest Alaskan coast. Such settlements with side-notched projectile points also occur in the southwestern Yukon Territory and in the southwestern Northwest Territories of Canada, dating perhaps to as early as 3000 BC (Noble, 1971).

Shield Archaic (c.5000 BC to European contact). Caribou hunting was the primary activity on the northern fringes of the taiga to the west of Hudson Bay (Harp, 1961; 1962). Some Archaic bands were living on the shores of Great Slave Lake by 5000 BC, eventually to become the ancestral Athabaskans, ancestors of the Yellow Knife Indians who dwell there today. Further south and west elk, moose, and deer were staple prey. These adaptations changed little over many centuries, as Archaic populations rose slowly and more sedentary settlements developed in resource-rich areas where fishing or shellfish collecting were important (Dumond, 1987). This basic forest culture has been named the Shield Archaic by James Wright (1972, see Chapter 16). Such is the cultural continuity between ancient and modern culture over the entire Canadian Shield that he has argued on very slender grounds that these people spoke an Algonquian language and that they were ancestral to the central and eastern Algonquian peoples of historic times.

Immediately west of Hudson Bay, caribou hunting was always the staple, in the transitional country between the taiga and tundra, a landscape of plentiful lichens, marshes, and shallow lakes. Archaic bands could live on the edge of the forest, drawing on woodland resources and following migrating caribou herds into the more open barren lands in summer. This caribou adaptation survived into historic times, albeit with occasional incursions by Arctic Small Tool groups from the north. It was also the means by which human settlers first exploited the Barren Grounds during a period of warmer temperatures before 3500 years ago. Archaic groups settled in the Central Keewatin region, where they camped along rivers and lakes on caribou migration routes, ambushing their prey at crossings and other strategic spots. At least four major caribou herds are distributed across the Barren Lands today, each moving north and south along regular migration routes. The lives of the Archaic groups who preyed on these long-established caribou herds must have been governed by the movements of individual herds, in a long-lasting relationship between humans and caribou that endured for thousands of years — as it does today.

The Archaic peoples of the western Sub-Arctic shared a basic stone toolkit that varied but little throughout the region. The hunters used flaked stone lanceolate projectile points, discoidal biface knives, and various scrapers, also stone adze blades, basic artifacts for hunting and processing game. Here, as elsewhere in North America, stone projectile points provide some typological signposts. The Paleo-Indians used "Keewatin" lanceolate points with ground edges. These developed into various stemmed forms, as projectile heads became smaller.

Keewatin lanceolate point, Shield Archaic, Barren Grounds region.

Maritime Archaic (?7000 BC to modern times). The so-called Maritime Archaic is best known from Port aux Choix, Newfoundland (see also Chapter 16). Here, a community of Archaic sea mammal hunters flourished in the second and third millennia BC (Harp and Hughes, 1968; Tuck, 1970). More than 100 red ocher-adorned graves contained elaborate barbed bone points, open socketed toggling harpoons, and bone foreshafts. Many of the deceased had worn skin clothing adorned with shell bead ornamentation, also antler, bone, and ivory daggers. The Maritime Archaic occurs at many contemporary sites up and down the Atlantic coast from Maine to Labrador. The occupation was probably a seasonal one. During the winters, the people exploited elk, moose, caribou, and other land resources, as always the staple of Archaic life in the Sub-Arctic. The Maritime Archaic reached its apogee during the warmer centuries after about 4000 BC, and then waned when Pre-Dorset and Dorset groups moved southward along the Labrador coast in the first millennium BC and during the early Christian era.

The Archaic cultures of the Sub-Arctic slowly evolved into the native American groups that occupied the region at European contact. These include the Beothucks of Newfoundland, the Montagnais-Naskapi of Quebec and Labrador, the Cree and Ojibwa of the Hudson Bay lowlands, the Chipewyan west of the Bay, and other Athabaskan-speaking peoples to the northwest.

Further Reading

Damas, David (ed.). 1984. "Arctic," *Handbook of North American Indians*, vol. 5. Smithsonian Institution Press, Washington DC.
The authoritative compendium on the native peoples of the Arctic. An invaluable source book.

Dumond, Don. 1987. *Eskimos and Aleuts*. Thames and Hudson, London and New York. 2nd ed.
A superb brief summary of Arctic and Sub-Arctic prehistory.

Fitzhugh, William (ed.). 1988. *Crossroads of Continents*. Smithsonian Institution Press, Washington DC.
A joint Soviet-US exhibition of Siberian and Alaskan artifacts prompted this magnificently illustrated account of arctic peoples. Strongly recommended for the general reader.

McGhee, Robert. 1978. *Canadian Arctic Prehistory*. National Museums of Canada, Ottawa.
McGhee has written an excellent introductory account for the general reader.

Maxwell, Moreau. 1985. *The Prehistory of the Eastern Arctic*. Academic Press, New York.
Another authoritative synthesis, which focuses on both culture history and basic issues.

West, Frederick Hadleigh. 1981. *The Archaeology of Beringia*. Columbia University Press, New York.
A lucid, if sometimes controversial synthesis, which focuses on Paleo-Arctic and earlier settlement.

CHAPTER 9

NORTON, DORSET, AND THULE

Some time between 600 and 500 BC, the Pre-Dorset culture of the Eastern Arctic merged into the fully fledged Dorset culture, with its magnificent and distinctive art style. In the west, Arctic Small Tool people vanished in every part of Alaska, a process that may have taken several centuries. There was an apparent hiatus, still little understood, before new cultural traditions flourished along the shores of the Bering Strait.

The Norton Tradition of the Western Arctic
*c.*1000 BC to *c.*AD 800

Conservative Archaic cultural traditions survived for millennia in the Sub-Arctic interior, isolated cultures that persisted up to European contact and beyond. In the Western Arctic, however, major, almost revolutionary innovations in subsistence strategies radically transformed the ways in which prehistoric peoples exploited the maritime environment of the Far North. These innovations first appeared in the Bering Strait region, and, around AD 1000, spread into the Eastern Arctic.

The Arctic Small Tool tradition gradually disappeared along the Bering and Chukchi Sea coasts about 1500 BC, as late as 1000 BC in the south. There appears to have been somewhat of a cultural vacuum, for few sites along these shores date to the next few centuries. Then the more maritime Norton tradition appears, named after the bay of that name where it was first identified (Giddings, 1960). Norton is still poorly defined, and sometimes referred to as an "interaction sphere" not a tradition, on the grounds that considerable cultural interaction was involved over a large area (Dumond, 1982; Shaw and Holmes, 1982). Norton people used flaked stone tools reminiscent of the Arctic Small Tool tradition, but introduced technologies such as lamps for burning oil and clay vessels.

Origins. The Norton tradition is best known from the Alaskan shore of the Bering Strait, but there were strong cultural links with Siberia (Ackerman, 1982). Cord-impressed pottery occurs widely in northeast Asia and occurs in Norton sites, persisting right into the Christian era. Furthermore, contemporary Siberian chipped stone tools have strong ties with Arctic Small Tool forms, and included asymmetrical knives like Norton artifacts of the same general type.

Norton stage. Ivory-handled slate ulu *or woman's knife, c. 500 BC, length c. 10 cm.*

Closer to the Bering Strait, a maritime, Norton-like tradition with pottery, polished adzes, and projectile heads flourished on the Anadyr River during the second millennium BC, a culture adapted to fishing, sealing, and caribou hunting. Isolated finds of Norton-like pottery have been reported from the Chukchi Peninsula, too. Further south, sea mammal hunters had settled along the shores of the Sea of Okhotsk by the end of the first millennium BC, peoples with Norton-like stone artifacts and some pottery. "All in all it is fair to say that this was the period of greatest similarity between cultures of eastern Siberia and Alaska," writes Don Dumond (1987; see also Ackerman, 1982). Under this argument, the Norton tradition developed over a wide area of the Bering and Chukchi Sea coasts during the first millennium BC. This was a period of cultural and technological innovation that saw sporadic long-distance trading contacts across the open waters of the Strait, and some connections with prehistoric cultures in Siberia.

These developments coincided with a period of warmer Arctic temperatures and with great cultural diversity. About 700 BC, the climate had deteriorated considerably, a cold cycle that lasted for about five centuries. Now the Norton people moved south of the Bering Strait and settled throughout coastal Alaska north of Pacific waters. About the time of Christ, Norton sea mammal hunters migrated over the base of the Alaska Peninsula and exploited the rich waters of the northern Pacific from Takli Island and other locations, overwhelming the indigenous Kodiak tradition. These developments can be traced through at least three still ill-defined cultural stages — Choris, Norton, and Ipiutak (Dumond,1987; detailed essays in Shaw and Holmes, 1982).

Subsistence. Everything points to the Norton having been a culture that was oriented toward both land hunting and marine resources. Caribou and smaller mammals were still an important source of meat and antler for artifact manufacture, but marine resources were increasingly important. Norton groups settled near fish-rich Arctic Ocean river estuaries, and in the south up the banks of major salmon streams, where migrating fish could be trapped and speared. There can be no doubt that open water sea mammal hunting was a significant activity. Toggling-head harpoons of various sizes have come from Bering Strait sites, including some large enough for whaling purposes, artifacts that were essential for such activity.

Settlements. Hardly surprisingly, many Bering Sea Norton sites were occupied more-or-less permanently, great concentrations of substantial year-round dwellings. The Norton stage Safety Sound site near Cape Nome has yielded almost 400 house depressions, Unalakleet on Norton Sound itself almost 200. Not all the houses were occupied at once, of course, but they reflect dense, long-term occupation. At both these locations, people lived in square, permanent dwellings excavated about 20 in (50 cm) into the ground, with short, sloping entryways, central hearths, and pole and sod roofs. During the summer months, many groups used temporary hunting and fishing camps. The Ipiutak stage middens at Point Hope and elsewhere testify to the richness and elaboration of late Norton culture in the Bering Strait region. Certainly, later, Norton was based on year-round sea mammal hunting both in open waters and through the winter ice.

Choris Stage (*c.*1000 to 500 BC). Coastal sites north of the Bering Strait, found in Kotzebue Sound, on old beach levels at Cape Krusenstern, on the Seward Peninsula, perhaps in the Brooks Range, and at Onion Portage. Characterized by fiber-tempered pottery adorned with linear stamping all over the exterior surface. Lanceolate projectile points, oil lamps, considerable local cultural variation as if most communities were isolated ones (Dumond, 1987).

Norton Stage (*c.*500 BC to AD 800). Probably derived from Choris, and subsumes several local cultures in the Bering Strait area, the Ugashik and Naknek River drainages, and the Alaska Peninsula. Also occurs along the Arctic Ocean coast to extreme northwestern Canada. Caribou and small mammal hunting were important, but open water sea mammal hunting and fishing were of vital importance. More refined pottery with both Choris-type stamping and check stamps applied with ivory paddles. Stone seal oil lamps, cruder stone work, asymmetrical knives, slate projectile points, and many local artifact forms (Dumond, 1987; Giddings, 1964).

Ipiutak Stage (*c.*AD 1 to 800). A distinctive, highly developed form of Norton culture around Cape Krustenstern, Point Hope, and Point Barrow on the shores of the Chukchi Sea. Interior Ipiutak known from Brooks Range. No pottery, oil lamps, or ground slate artifacts. Far more sophisticated harpoon heads with elaborate decoration. Summer and winter sea mammal hunting important and much permanent settlement. The Ipiutak art tradition was lavished on bone artifacts – carvings of animals, human figures, some of which may recall Scythian and Siberian art motifs (Larsen and Rainey, 1948).

TABLE 9.1

Norton Tradition Stages

(Center below) Choris stage linear-stamped potsherd from Iyatayet, Cape Denbigh, height 14 cm; Choris stage projectile points, from a cache of about 60 points found at Cape Krusenstern, length of longest specimen 17.5 cm. (Center bottom) Ipiutak stage ivory object, perhaps a comb, c. AD 500, length c. 26 cm. (Below) Ipiutak stage engraved ivory "mask," found in a burial at Point Hope, probably once with a wooden backing.

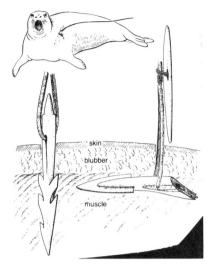

(Above) Harpoon technology. The non-toggling or "male" harpoon point holds an animal by its barbs (left). The toggling harpoon, a more complex design, was developed later for sea mammal hunting. The head toggles beneath the skin and blubber where it cannot be dislodged by ice, and is effective with heavier prey like walrus and whales.

(Below) Old Bering Sea stage toggling harpoon components and reconstructed assembly. The weight of the ivory harpoon head (left), foreshaft, and socketpiece (center) were counterbalanced by an ivory winged object (right) fixed to the butt of the harpoon.

The Thule Tradition
*c.*700 BC to modern times

In about 700 BC, the Norton inhabitants of St Lawrence and other Bering Strait islands developed an even more specialized culture, based entirely on the ocean. Like the Ipiutak people, these hunters were expert artists, who adorned their toggling harpoons and other weapons with elaborate and intricate motifs. The new sea mammal hunting technology with its efficient toggling harpoons and other ingenious devices was to revolutionize coastal life throughout the Arctic. This technology was the foundation of the Thule tradition (pronounced the Danish way — Tuleh).

No one knows whether such Thule innovations as working polished slate or the sophisticated toggling harpoon originated in the Bering Strait area or further south along either Asian or Alaskan coasts (Chard, 1974; Dumond, 1968). Whatever the origins of the new maritime culture with its new emphasis on whale hunting, it was the catalyst for the final chapter in Arctic prehistory. Dozens of Thule sites in the Western Arctic enable us to trace the outline development of this revolutionary culture

Old Bering Sea Stage *(c.200 BC to AD 800)*. The earliest Thule sites, subsumed under the Old Bering Sea stage, come from St Lawrence and Okvik islands in the Bering Strait (Collins, 1937; Rudenko, 1961). Occasional Old Bering Sea artifacts have been found on both shores of the Bering Strait, presumably as a result of sporadic trading with the mainland. Both kayaks, and *umiaks*, large skin boats, appear in the archaeological record for the first time.

Old Bering Sea toolkits are dominated by polished slate rather than flaked stone artifacts, including lanceolate knives, projectile heads, and the *ulu* transverse-bladed knife. Pottery is cruder, often gravel tempered, and decorated with broad corrugations. Bone and antler dominated local technology, including ivory harpoon heads and other harpoon parts, bird darts and fish spears, snow goggles, blubber scrapers, needles, awls, and mattocks, also walrus shoulder-blade snow shovels. The hunting artifacts also include important innovations that made for far more efficient hunting. The hunters now used harpoon-mounted ice picks for winter seal

Kayak hunting. (Above left) Regional kayak styles in historical times, reflecting a 2000-year-old tradition of kayak technology. (Above) Spearing fish from kayaks, a painting by H. Elliott, 1872. (Left) Use of floats enabled hunters to recover sea mammals such as these belugas, line and inflated float sill attached, photographed with a harpoon-wielding Eskimo in 1865.

hunting, also ivory plugs and mouthpieces for inflated harpoon line floats, floats that enabled them to recover larger sea mammals when dispatched. These were people who relied heavily on the ocean for subsistence, especially on seal and walrus, as the modern inhabitants of the Bering Strait islands do to this day.

Old Bering Sea artists lavished their skill on their socketed toggling harpoon heads, which is fortunate for the archaeologist, for the forms of these weapons changed but little through the centuries. However, the curvilinear dots, circles, and shorter lines of the Old Bering style are so distinctive that the style can be distinguished from later forms (illus. p.166). The art style from Okvik Island, one of the Punuk Islands, is often distinguished from the Old Bering style from St Lawrence Island and other locations (Rainey, 1941). Some believe Okvik is an earlier style that evolved into Old Bering, but radiocarbon dates suggest the two were contemporary phenomena, local variants of the same brilliant tradition.

Okvik

Old Bering Sea II

Old Bering Sea III

Punuk

Old Bering Sea art styles. Stratified house floors at St Lawrence Island, Alaska, revealed stylistic changes in Eskimo art. The Okvik flat, angular style dates to about 500 BC. Contemporaneous and later Old Bering Sea II and III styles were increasingly more ornate, more plastic, and curvilinear. After AD 500, Old Bering Sea art gave way to the simpler designs of the Punuk phase.

Across the Strait, at Uelen and Ekven, Soviet investigators have uncovered some richly decorated Old Bering Sea graves adorned with fine ivory artifacts, including harpoon parts, mattocks, and pots. Some graves were partially lined with whale bones, sometimes floored with wood. Conceivably, these were the sepulchers of important individuals, perhaps whaleboat captains, men of prestige who were owners of whale hunting *umiaks*. Such social distinctions are known to have been important in later centuries, and these may be the first signs of social differentiation in the north (Dumond, 1987; Larsen, 1968).

***Punuk and Birnirk Stages** (c. AD 800 to 1400 and later).* Harpoon styles and art motifs serve to distinguish two later Thule variants in the Bering Strait area, but variants that have a wider distribution than their Old Bering Sea predecessor (Collins, 1937; Geist and Rainey, 1936; Rudenko, 1961).

The Punuk stage is a development of Old Bering Sea, with a distribution that coincides closely with it, on the major Strait islands and along the shores of much of the Chukchi Peninsula. Artifact forms remain much the same, albeit with some elaboration of hunting weapons. Punuk art strongly recalls Okvik motifs, but became more geometric and eventually simpler as time went on.

Punuk settlements were larger and more common than earlier villages, settlements of houses that soon assumed the familiar 19th-century St Lawrence form. These were semi-subterranean, square or rectangular dwellings with wooden floors, sleeping platforms along the walls, and driftwood or whale jaw sides, the sod roofs held up with whalebone rafters.

Whale hunting was of great importance in Punuk life. Hunters in *umiaks* killed them in narrow ice leads during spring and fall, an enterprise that required skilled leadership, teams of expert boatmen and hunters, and usually the cooperation of several boats. The whaleboat captain, the *umialik*, played an important role in 19th-century village life, and probably in Punuk times as well. He was wealthy and an influential leader, often competing with his fellow captains in neighboring communities. It may be no coincidence that slatted bone armor now appears in Punuk villages, also a superior bow-and-arrow technology, based on sinew-backed bows of Asian form.

The Birnirk variant on the Old Bering Sea tradition developed between AD 500 and 600, along the shores of the Chukchi Sea from Cape Nome northward, also on the Siberian coast west from East Cape to at least as far as the mouth of the Kolyma River. Although the Birnirk people used much the same hunting weapons as Punuk and Old Bering Sea, they were no artists. Only rarely did they adorn their antler harpoons or other artifacts with any form of decoration, confining their artistic talents to concentric and spiral motifs executed on clay pots with bone paddles. They did, however, use sledges, of the same basic designs as were later used with dog teams. However, no traces of bone harness parts occur at Birnirk and other settlements, so they may have relied on man-hauling. As far as is known, the Birnirk people were sea mammal hunters who also engaged in fishing and whaling. Some of their sites, like those near Barrow and Point Hope, are situated close to whale-rich locales.

Thule Expansion in the West
AD 900 to 1100

Thule settlements were flourishing at Cape Denbigh on Norton Sound by AD 900, on Nunivak Island even further south a century later, and in the Naknek Drainage of the Alaska Peninsula by AD 1100. This spread was not necessarily a population movement, but more likely a diffusion of new artifact styles, more efficient house designs, and hunting methods to southern coastlines and river estuaries, much of it connected with seasonal sea mammal migrations. Some people may have moved into new areas, but everywhere the Thule tradition amalgamated with the older Norton.

Thule artifacts were in use close to the end of the Alaska Peninsula in about AD 1000, although the use of polished slate tools, a characteristic Thule trait, spread slowly throughout the Aleutian Islands thereafter. Thule gravel-tempered pottery, polished slate tools, and sunken dwellings replaced earlier Norton styles on the southern side of the Alaska Peninsula, too, resulting in a culture much closer to the Kodiak tradition of earlier times (Dumond, 1987). Here, as elsewhere, there were strong local preferences in harpoon styles and other artifact forms.

Throughout the Bering Strait and along the Alaskan coast from Barrow to the Alaska Peninsula, and far offshore to the islands and Siberian coast, communities of Thule sea mammal hunters were in constant, and regular, contact for many centuries. This led, inevitably, to a degree of linguistic and cultural standardization, and, perhaps, to the spread of Eskimo dialects to the Kodiak Island area, dialects spoken by modern Koniag people.

The Eskimo peoples of what is now Alaska, who came into contact with Europeans during the 18th century, all formed part of this powerful and long-lived cultural tradition.

The Dorset Tradition of the Eastern Arctic
550 BC to AD 1100

The Pre-Dorset culture of the Eastern Arctic developed into the Dorset tradition in about 550 BC, at a time when climatic conditions became colder after some centuries of warmer temperatures (Maxwell, 1985). Preservation conditions were poor in warmer, Pre-Dorset times, but permafrost has refrigerated many organic objects from Dorset sites, resulting in a far more complete knowledge of this remarkable Arctic culture.

(Opposite) Evolution of Punuk art, as exemplified by winged objects (harpoon butts) from St Lawrence Island. (Left) Early Punuk stage winged object in "butterfly" shape, width 16 cm. (Center) Middle Punuk trident-like winged object, width 10 cm. (Right) Late Punuk winged object with hardly any wings, resembling a coronet, width 7 cm.

Probable distribution of the Dorset tradition.

(Below) Dorset culture. (Left) Dorset artifacts. From upper left, clockwise: two styles of harpoon head, perhaps for different hunting tasks; a bone lance; a microblade knife in a bone-and-wood handle; a ground flint, burin-like tool in a similar handle; two styles of projectile point, and a ground-slate point; an ivory fish spearhead; a bone needle; and an ivory "ice-creeper," lashed on the foot to prevent slipping on smooth ice. (Right) Remains of a Dorset house on western Victoria Island, central Arctic, dating to c. AD 500.

With the Dorset tradition, we come to the outermost frontiers of modern Inuit legend, to fine threads of oral tradition that may extend back into the past more than 2000 years. Many Inuit legends refer to giants with enormous strength, to people called "Tunnit," legendary folk of long ago. Conceivably, these tales refer to Dorset hunters, people without dog sleds or bows and arrows, who hunted all manner of arctic game at close quarters with efficient thrusting spears and with none of the elaborate technological artifices of later times.

The actual archaeological evidence for the transition from Pre-Dorset to Dorset is limited to some isolated locations like the Killilugak site on Baffin Island, where Pre-Dorset and Dorset artifacts are found in an occupation level dated to about 600 BC (Maxwell, 1973). There are signs of continuous Pre-Dorset to Dorset occupation in northern Labrador, in sites where Pre-Dorset occupation passes into what is called the Groswater Dorset in about 850 BC, a culture centered around Hamilton Inlet (Fitzhugh, 1980).

In the High Arctic, some small groups reoccupied the area of northern Greenland and the Canadian archipelago abandoned by the Independence I people in about 1600 BC. Some 600 to 1000 years later, Independence II groups reoccupied the region in another warmer period, living in scattered dwellings lined along the same beaches as their predecessors, but at lower levels on the shore. Some of their stone artifacts, especially notched blades, recall Groswater Dorset (Knuth, 1967; McGhee, 1981).

The Pre-Dorset/Dorset transition can be explained in many ways. Was it the result of a population decline of Arctic Small Tool people in the Eastern Arctic about 3000 years ago, a decline that was followed by an expansion of Dorset peoples (McGhee, 1981)? Or was it a time when dwindling caribou herds in Quebec caused major adjustments in both population distribution and hunting methods (Fitzhugh, 1976)? Or was it, as Moreau Maxwell has argued persuasively (1980), a period of interregnum between two relatively stable lifeways that lasted some centuries?

Maxwell has created a possible scenario for the transition as follows: The impression is that the Pre-Dorset people were predominantly caribou hunters, while their Dorset successors were, above all, sealers. Maxwell notes that the bow and arrow vanished during the transition period, a hunting weapon that was useful for hunting caribou by stalking. Perhaps, he speculates, the Dorset people turned to new caribou hunting methods, driving them into shallow lakes and spearing them with stone-tipped spears. Perhaps, in time, the caribou herds were much reduced by the new methods or migration patterns changed. The new hunting methods were now inadequate, so the only solution was to turn to the coasts. The climate was becoming colder, so the people developed new, ice-hunting techniques that were successful in intensely cold winters, leading to the emergence of the Dorset tradition (for a full discussion, see Maxwell, 1985).

As for the Dorset tradition itself, Maxwell and others define it by a series of distinctive culture traits. These include rectangular, semi-subterranean buildings, many more triangular projectile points used for sealing, the appearance of a ground slate industry that manufactured notched knives and other utilitarian artifacts, distinctive harpoon head forms, and a rich artistic tradition with strong symbolic and magical undertones.

The Dorset Lifeway. Dorset people possessed no dog sleds, so their land travel range was restricted to the limits of human pulling and walking ability. They had no bows and arrows, nor throwing boards, just simple lances and harpoons. The hunters lacked sophisticated whale hunting gear, harpoon floats for pursuing sea mammals from kayaks, and, incredible although it may seem, even tiny stone drills for boring through bone and antler. The Dorset people had only small oil lamps and far from sophisticated winter houses. One marvels at their adaptive ability under such harsh environmental conditions, yet they managed to flourish for many centuries. In some ways they were even less prepared for arctic conditions than their predecessors (Meldgaard, 1962).

Like all Eastern Arctic peoples, the Dorset people were predominantly hunters, although they undoubtedly consumed berries and other plant foods in season (see discussion in Maxwell, 1985). They pursued caribou, musk ox, smaller land mammals, and some nesting birds, perhaps snared with nets on long poles. Seals were an important staple, and the hunters were not afraid to tackle such formidable animals as the walrus, narwhal, and even the occasional whale or polar bear — using a spear-based technology that put the hunter at very close range with his quarry, and in constant peril of his life. Such close quarters stalking and hunting requires not only remarkable skill but an intimate knowledge of animal habits during all seasons of the year.

A great deal depended on the design of Dorset harpoons. Later hunters used toggling designs, where the head slips off the foreshaft inside the wound, leaving only the head and line attached to the animal. Dorset harpoons were thrusting weapons, the heads bound to the foreshaft so that the shaft slid backward and the head came off attached to the line wedged in a split in the harpoon shaft. This design works much better at close quarters, when the hunter thrusts the head into the animal. Such weapons were probably effective for ice hunting, and had some limited use against basking seals pursued from kayaks.

Dorset art. (Left) Ivory bear with skeleton depicted, length 15.2 cm. (Right) Joined pair of ivory swans, the one at left 6 cm long.

Caribou hunting was probably a group effort involving carefully controlled game drives through rows of stone cairns or into shallow water where waiting spearsmen or kayaks dispatched the confused beasts. The staple fish was the arctic char, a species that is easily filleted and speared during seasonal runs. The Dorset fish spear was usually tipped with delicate ivory barbed heads that were used like harpoons, perhaps thrown rather than thrusted, unlike the elegant trident-like fish spears used by later Thule and Inuit peoples. These weapons required considerable skill and accuracy against fast-running fish that would be swimming over a rocky bottom.

Dorset Art. The Dorset art tradition is justly famous, especially for its life-like portraits of what were once living individuals (Taylor and Swinton, 1967). Dorset carvers worked with antler, bone, ivory, soapstone, and wood, depicting almost every arctic animal. More than half their carvings were of human beings or polar bears, sometimes highly naturalistic, sometimes merely stylistic impressions. The attention to minute detail is astonishing — complete polar bear skulls, tiny seals modeled complete with whiskers and tiny eyes. Unlike later Thule and Inuit artists, Dorset carvers and engravers usually ignored utilitarian objects and created work that had a strong ideological undertone. Masks, figurines, and plaques probably played important roles in funeral rites, and in shamanistic and magical ceremonies.

Human beings sometimes appear in distinctive portraits, in carvings that display rectangular or round eyes, outward facing nostrils, and a pug nose. This portrait may represent a living person, perhaps a famous shaman, who suffered from an infantile skull condition that made him stand out from his fellow priests. The Late Dorset site at Button Point on Bylot Island yielded wooden masks, one with simulated tattooing and at one time pegged-in hair and a moustache. There are smaller masks, too, no more than 2.3 in (6 cm) long, many with X incisions across the face, even dolls with detachable arms and legs. Small animal amulets to provide good fortune during the chase are common, often suspended on thongs or sewn to clothing. The carvers also made small ivory teeth plaques with ridges on the back, plaques that may have been worn over the mouth during shamanistic rituals.

The Dorset art tradition was a unique efflorescence over an enormous area of the Eastern Arctic, a reflection of basic ideologies that were to survive for many centuries. Without question, some of the fundamental spiritual beliefs of modern Inuit groups have their roots in the complex spiritual life of the Dorset people.

Evolution of the Dorset Tradition

The Dorset tradition is conventionally subdivided into Early, Middle, Late, and Terminal stages (for a full description of sites and artifacts, see Maxwell, 1985). Early Dorset culture may have developed in one core area and then spread rapidly over a much wider region. The most logical place is the northern Foxe Basin, where earlier prehistoric traditions flourished. There was such regular communication with other communities in the general area that cultural change must have been more-or-less simultaneous over a wide area (Maxwell, 1985).

The same basic lifeway flourished throughout Dorset times, but with constant adjustments in response to ever-changing cold and warm cycles. During Middle Dorset times, the climate was becoming progressively colder, so parts of the High Arctic and northern Labrador may have been abandoned. In some places, people may have chosen to live in more sheltered locations and in larger dwellings. Perhaps some groups of 2000 years ago moved out onto the ice, living in snow dwellings near favored sealing grounds.

By AD 100, the settlement pattern was changing. Many of the favorite locations in the core area around Foxe Basin were abandoned as populations along the south coast of Hudson Strait, and on Southampton and Victoria Islands, apparently declined. The surviving population adopted some minor technological changes — fresh needle designs came into use, soapstone lamps became oval rather than rectangular, and slate artifacts were less commonplace.

The populations of Newfoundland and the Labrador coast increased as people retreated from the north (Fitzhugh, 1980; Tuck, 1984). Many Middle Dorset settlements in these areas were small villages, some of them, like Port aux Choix, Newfoundland, semi-permanent locations where people fished and hunted throughout most of the year (Harp, 1976). Port aux Choix was also a base for hunting pupping harp seals in late winter, a place favored earlier by Maritime Archaic groups. One house midden from this site yielded a sample of 25,000 bone fragments, 98 percent of them from harp seals. Up to between 30 and 35 people lived at Port aux Choix, using a tool kit that has clear ties to northern Dorset, but with a strongly local flavor. The site was finally abandoned at about the time when temperatures warmed up again at the onset of Late Dorset times, *c.* AD 500.

The five or six centuries that followed saw a population increase, with an explosion in artistic skills, resulting in an art tradition that ranks among the best in prehistoric North America. The Late Dorset saw an expansion of relatively standardized arctic culture not only over the Foxe Basin area and into northern Labrador north of Nain, but into the High Arctic again. Many widespread communities appear to have participated in a vast cultural network, in which shamans may have played a leading role (Maxwell, 1985). Some sites, like Button Point on Bylot Island, may have been ceremonial centers. Button Point is rich in carved wooden figures, including life-sized ceremonial masks and wooden dolls of humans and stylized animals. There are fragments of drums, too. "It is easy to imagine nighttime ceremonies where rhythmic chants and drumbeats restored the sacred balance of nature," writes Moreau Maxwell (1985). "In the dimly lit houses, shamans, frighteningly masked, would manipulate little figures for magical protection from the only predators dangerous to humans — the giant polar bear and humans who were not part of the kinship web."

Late Dorset groups moved north in some numbers, establishing at least three significant village concentrations in the High Arctic (McGhee, 1976). They penetrated all the islands of the Canadian archipelago, and hunted as far north as land permitted. Many Late Dorset settlements at favored locations were reoccupied by later Thule and Inuit groups (Maxwell, 1985).

Dorset wooden doll body from Button Point, Bylot Island.

Terminal Dorset. The Dorset tradition reached its climax by AD 1000. A century later, it had all but vanished except in some isolated areas of Greenland and the Labrador coast. The conventional explanation is that Thule newcomers moved in from the west. With their superior hunting technology, more elaborate social organization, and vastly enhanced mobility by sled and boat, they took over Dorset hunting territories, assimilating the original inhabitants or driving them out to starve in marginal areas.

What actually happened? There is no archaeological evidence for sustained contact between Dorset and Thule, even if some artifacts like ivory sled shoes, snow knives for building snow houses, and the use of iron and soapstone, were culture traits borrowed by the newcomers from Dorset groups. Maxwell (1985) believes the explanation may lie in the radically different subsistence strategies employed by the two traditions. The Dorset people tended to hunt prey that was within walking distance of home, concentrating on the more easily taken, most abundant animals. Thule hunters ranged over much larger territories in their boats and with sleds. They exploited a wider range of food resources, were better organized, and had the ability to move in and take over, say, a seal migration route through a narrow defile miles from their base, thereby depriving the local people of the resource at a critical time of year. Over a few generations, the cumulative effects of such opportunism would have been felt in reduced reproduction and lower survival rates among Dorset populations. Exotic diseases from Asia may have played a role, too, diseases introduced by the Thule newcomers from distant Asian populations that spread like wildfire among Dorset groups, decimating communities in short order.

Nevertheless, deeply conservative Dorset and innovative Thule groups existed alongside one another in the Arctic for two or three centuries, the former virtually without change alongside the newcomers (Harp, 1976). There is a possibility, too, that the Dorset people endured into the 20th century. The Sadlermiut of Southampton Island kept themselves aloof from other groups, did not come in contact with Europeans until the 19th century, and were almost exterminated by an epidemic in 1902-3. Therkel Mathiassen (1927) learned they had spoken an exotic dialect, were expert stone workers, and were uninterested in trading for European copper, iron, and other commodities. Excavations on several Sadlermiut houses were inconclusive, yielding both Dorset and Thule artifacts (Collins, 1956; Taylor, 1960). So the Sadlermiut remain a mystery.

Probable distribution of the Thule culture in the Eastern Arctic.

The Thule Expansion into the Eastern Arctic
*c.*AD 1000

Sometime around the beginning of the second millennium AD, Thule people, perhaps speaking an archaic form of Inupiat language, began migrating to the east. By the 13th century, they had settled throughout the coasts of the Canadian Arctic and Greenland. Especially in the central and eastern Arctic, many scholars make a useful distinction between Paleoeskimos (Pre-Dorset and Dorset) and Neoeskimos (Thule/recent).

As we have seen, the Thule tradition had strong Norton undertones, with technology and subsistence strategies that resemble those of late Norton developments to the south of the Bering Strait — with one significant difference. Like their predecessors, Thule people subsisted off caribou and fishing, but they combined these activities with much more efficient exploitation of sea mammals, including whales. This expertise is reflected in great elaboration of specialized artifacts for such hunting. Thule men and women lavished great care and much time on their harpoons and domestic artifacts, making them highly efficient, very functional, and ingenious tools indeed. Thule art was impoverished, however, and decorated artifacts were much rarer than in Dorset contexts. Even their semi-subterranean dwellings were relatively energy efficient, with deep entrance tunnels below floor level. Cooking areas were usually close to the doorway, where the entry tunnel met the interior of the house. This elaborate cultural tradition flourished for several centuries after about AD 600 around the Bering Strait and along Chukchi Sea coasts, then spread very widely indeed, far eastward across the High Arctic.

The Thule culture of the Eastern Arctic was first identified during the highly productive interdisciplinary researches of Danish scholars between 1921 and 1924. A team of anthropologists, archaeologists, and natural scientists compiled a massive description of the Canadian Arctic which they published promptly in the 10 seminal volumes of the Thule Expedition (Birket-Smith, 1929; Mathiassen, 1927; Rasmussen, 1931, and others). All subsequent researches have built on these pioneer investigations. Therkel Mathiassen identified more than 100 Thule culture traits, a distinctive and highly effective toolkit for hunting on land, ice, and open water. Mathiassen argued that the tradition originated in northern Alaska or Siberia. Mathiassen claimed Thule hunting efficiency was based on three major innovations: the dog sled, the large skin boat, and the kayak. All of these enabled people to range over much larger hunting territories, to participate in widespread trade, and to transport heavier loads. Over many years of arduous fieldwork, this remarkable scholar not only hypothesized correctly about Thule origins, but traced almost the entire extent of the Thule migration, even interaction between Greenland Thule and newly arrived Norsemen from the east.

The Thule adaptation was infinitely more efficient and effective. Quite apart from their prowess at baleen whale hunting, an activity where one kill could feed several families for an entire winter, the leadership, craft specialization, and team organization needed to hunt whales spilled over

A Thule innovation, according to Therkel Mathiassen: the dog sled.

By Thule times, hunters in the Eastern Arctic were equipped with kayaks, like this man with his gear for open-water sea mammal hunting.

into the entire spectrum of daily life. Thule communities were better equipped to cooperate, to take concerted action, compared with more loosely knit, smaller Dorset groups. Their technology was far more effective, with dog sleds and large boats to carry even large groups to new hunting grounds and new settlement sites at short notice. Above all, Thule hunters were ingenious, well-equipped predators, capable of harvesting Arctic seas and coasts in almost any weather conditions (Maxwell, 1985).

Migration Theories. Many investigators have argued that the Birnirk stage of Thule culture on the shores of the Chukchi Sea was the base for the Thule migration (Collins, 1940; McGhee, 1970). Robert McGhee used Thule radiocarbon dates clustering around AD 1000 to trace the migration from Birnirk roots at the very end of that stage. There were no signs of population pressure in the Birnirk homeland. However, he pointed out that the migration occurred during a period of warmer temperatures throughout the Northern Hemisphere known as the Medieval Warm Period, which lasted from about AD 900 to 1200. This was a time when the southern boundary of arctic pack ice retreated northward in the Atlantic, allowing Norse seamen to expand to Iceland, onward to Greenland, and as far south as Newfoundland.

McGhee points out that the warmer temperatures also shrank the Beaufort Sea ice pack off the northern Alaskan coast, reducing the amount of sea ice in the Parry Channel across the Arctic archipelago. This would have allowed bowhead and Greenland whale populations to mingle, distributing abundant populations of these great mammals right across the north.

Whales migrate east along the Alaskan coast in spring, and west in fall, keeping to narrow ice leads close to shore. For centuries, prehistoric hunters watched these spring and fall leads and preyed on migrating pods with great efficiency. Some Thule Eskimo lived close to the ice edge – the demarcation between permanently frozen ocean and the boundary where the ice melted in summer. They hunted whales from this location, and were well placed to take early summer whales as the ice broke up. However, warmer temperatures caused the pack ice to retreat north, far from the coast. Since whales migrate close to the ice, the pods followed the pack, making conventional hunting methods far too dangerous. At the same time, reduced ice between the Canadian Arctic islands opened up the normal summering grounds of the bowhead whale to open-water hunting. So people could pursue whales for many months, and not just for short periods in spring and fall.

Open-water whaling required substantial modifications in hunting technique (McCartney, 1980; 1984b). The hunters had to sight the whales from ice-edge, land, or boat, then chase them with teams of kayaks and larger skin boats, dispatch their prey offshore, then tow the carcass to land. Open-water whaling became the hallmark of the Eastern Thule, a less productive hunting technique than the traditional ice-lead and ice-edge method, but one where the long season compensated for the lower productivity of the chase.

The whale hunters spread far and wide over the Canadian Arctic, founding widely separated settlements that were smaller (only a few as large as 25 to 35 houses) than those in the far west, for kayak and *umiak* teams from five or six families were far more effective than the teams of *umiaks* used close to land in the west. In the east, Thule hunters used kayaks to chase and locate whales (McCartney and Savelle, 1985). In both east and west, the *umiak* was the stable platform used for harpooning the whale.

Thule whale hunting was highly efficient. The successful hunters would tow their prey ashore, then butcher them, storing enormous quantities of meat and blubber for the winter. They would winter over in permanent peat-block houses that were occupied regularly for many years. Throughout the summer, they could move large amounts of meat and blubber from outlying areas to winter villages by boat or sled. The winter bases themselves were often built near coastal ponds, where abundant supplies of peat-blocks for house construction could be found.

Eastern dwellings tended to be less subterranean, often round. The sleeping platforms were stone-paved, with stone and whalebone forming walls and entrance tunnels, everything roofed with whalebone and sod. In some areas, ivory snow knives may be a sign that domed snow-block houses were in use.

There were other cultural differences, too. Pottery was used as far east as the Mackenzie River and sometimes further eastward. In many areas, soapstone vessels replaced ceramics, with large, crescent-shaped soapstone lamps favored over pottery versions. Most important of all, dogs tethered with sinew and ivory or bone harnesses now pulled ladder-like sleds with narrow runners, making for rapid winter travel on land.

The ease with which Thule people moved across the north is very striking, and may also be connected with other ecological changes related to warmer temperatures. As McGhee points out (1970), less pack ice may have fostered walrus and bearded seal populations, but it reduced the number of denning sites that were attractive to ring seals, the sea mammal that Dorset people depended upon most heavily. This may have helped the Thule people take over vacated Dorset hunting territories.

By no means everyone accepts McGhee's closely argued whaling model. Dennis Stanford (1976) excavated the Walakpa site west of Point Barrow, where he traced an evolving coastal culture from early Birnirk through a late Thule occupation of AD 1400. There was little evidence of whaling activity at Walakpa, where ring sealing was all important. Stanford observed a progressive reduction in seal bone size in the later levels, as if ring seals were being overhunted. He argues that a quest for new sealing grounds rather than whales sent Thule groups eastward.

Another hypothesis involves not only the Birnirk culture, but Punuk as well. Some Eastern Thule artifacts from Cornwallis and Ellesmere Islands in the High Arctic show striking connections with Punuk toggling harpoon heads from the Bering Sea (Collins, 1952; Schledermann and McCullogh, 1980; Yamaura, 1979). This whale and walrus hunting culture was in full swing by about AD 800 and may have been a major force in the Thule migration. Perhaps population pressure in the west and warring factions in northeastern Siberia caused some Punuk groups to move eastward, bringing their whale hunting expertise with them. Under this argument, the Thule migration into the Canadian Arctic was an amalgam of Birnirk and Punuk traits, brought about not only by warmer temperatures, but by population pressure and increased emphasis on whale hunting.

Despite general, and somewhat uncritical, agreement that the Thule migration took place about AD 1000, the dating is insecure. Radiocarbon dates are unreliable (Schell, 1983), so many workers have relied on seriations of harpoon head forms (Maxwell, 1985). Using the distributions of five early harpoon types, a possible early migration route follows a somewhat more southerly path than McGhee's hypothetical migration. The "harpoon route" follows the northern Alaskan shore into Amundsen Gulf and Victoria Strait, then north and east through Barrow Strait and Lancaster Sound. Emerging from the islands, the hunters turned north, along the east coast of Ellesmere Island and across Kane Basin into northwestern Greenland.

One could argue that the eastern sites with the most western traits are the earliest, sites like Nugdlit and Ruin Island in northwestern Greenland and on Skraeling Island, and others on eastern Ellesmere Island (Schledermann and McCullogh, 1980). These have been grouped into the so-called Nugdlit-Ruin Island phase (Holtved, 1954). House forms, harpoon heads, and other decorated items are said to recall western Thule. Many of the excavated houses also contain some Norse artifacts in wood, iron, copper, and cloth. Unfortunately, the radiocarbon dates from these fascinating sites are confusing. Some are too early for the Norse artifacts found with them, a few cluster in the 11th century, the widely accepted date for this phase, but the most reliable dates appear to belong in the 12th and 13th centuries. One could argue Nugdlit-Ruin three ways. First, all the radiocarbon dates are unreliable. Second, Thule people did not expand into the east until as late as AD 1200. Third, southerly regions of the eastern Arctic were colonized as early as the 11th century. Then, in the early 13th century, hunters with strong Punuk ties moved further north. There are some grounds for suspecting that the third hypothesis may be the most reliable one (for discussion, see Maxwell, 1985).

To summarize: most early Thule sites were probably occupied by groups whose ancestry lay in Birnirk communities along the northern Alaskan coast near Barrow. These communities had been influenced by new whale hunting techniques and innovative technologies developed by Punuk people, some of whom had moved into the Barrow area as a result of population pressure before AD 900. Perhaps, hypothesizes Maxwell (1985), it was a small number of Punuk groups who first followed whales along the summer pack to the east as far as the eastern parts of the High Arctic. Later in the same century, many more people, this time with Punuk and Birnirk artifacts, followed in their footsteps, settling along the southern shores of the Canadian Arctic. This was a much larger migration that resulted in the emergence of the true Eastern Thule tradition.

Classic Thule
AD 1100 to 1400

During the 12th and 13th centuries, Eastern Thule people increased their settlement of the High Arctic, but also expanded in the south. By the end of the 13th century, Thule people were living along Hudson Strait coasts, in the Hudson Bay region, on the shores of the Foxe Basin, along the mainland from the Mackenzie Delta to Melville Peninsula. Thule villages flourished across northern and eastern Greenland shores.

Alan McCartney (1977) first used the term "Classic Thule" to refer to winter settlements that depended on bowhead whaling, not only for food, but for building materials and artifacts as well. This label has been quite widely used by others (Maxwell, 1985). Many of these Thule groups lived in large semi-subterranean winter houses constructed of stone, sod, and whalebones. Some of these winter settlements were of considerable size and occupied for many generations, others little more than one or two winter dwellings. Four to six houses holding some 20 to 25 people appears to have been a widespread norm, an adaptive size for efficient hunting of available resources in many areas (McCartney, 1979; Maxwell, 1979). In summer, Thule groups moved into skin tents, the edges held down by circles of stones, the most ubiquitous archaeological sites in the Eastern Arctic today. Sometimes they would move only a short distance, perhaps to get away from the stench of rotting sea mammal carcasses that had been deep-frozen through the winter.

This sophisticated Arctic society maintained constant contact between dozens of scattered communities, and there may have been a continual drift eastward of more Alaskan groups, perhaps encouraged by reports of the favorable hunting conditions in the Canadian Arctic. Exotic materials were passed from community to community over enormous distances, among them copper and iron.

Northern peoples used iron long before European contact both along western Alaskan and Siberian coasts, and in the east. In the west, Okvik and Old Bering Sea peoples used iron in small quantities for carving knives, and for engraving other tools (Collins, 1937). Iron implements are also known from Birnirk and Punuk sites. All these occurrences date to the first millennium AD. The bone, antler, or ivory handles for iron blades are more common, suggesting that iron was a well-known, if scarce, commodity throughout the region. Most of this terrestrial iron probably came from the Amur River-Okhotsk Sea region, where it was being exploited as early as the first millennium BC. However, it was not until around AD 1000 that trade between the western and central Arctic picked up, perháps resulting in the movement of some Siberian iron eastward.

Both native copper and meteoritic and terrestrial iron were used in the central and eastern Arctic before European contact. Native copper came from southern Victoria Island and Coronation Gulf. Meteoritic iron from a large shower in the Melville Bay region, near Cape York, was used by Dorset people as early as the 11th century AD as substitutes for slate burins. Many Thule communities also used meteoritic iron. Non-meteoritic iron occurs in 13th- and 14th-century Thule sites, iron that is assumed to be of Norse origin (McCartney and Mack, 1973; McGhee, 1984). The trading distribution of metals was widespread, reaching the limits of Classic Thule population expansion during the 10th to 13th centuries. This trade coincided with the Norse expansion, and the iron, never common, was used in the Thule area not for engraving, but for projectile points and knife blades for butchery and sea mammal hunting. McCartney argues that metal was not only more widely distributed than appears from the archaeological record, but that it made possible the large whalebone artifacts that Thule peoples used long before there was direct European contact with Inuit groups. A form of what McCartney (1988) calls "epi-metallurgy" arose among late prehistoric Thule communities, a technology where metal was not manufactured, but bartered, then hammered into traditional artifact forms, a process that produced not only useful tools, but hardened their blades, making them more effective than slate prototypes.

Classic Thule culture is remarkable not only for its hunting skills, but for the extraordinary range of ingenious gadgets that the hunters developed for the chase. The Thule people were ardent technologists, as clever with their low tech life as we are with computers today. Thus, any report in a Classic Thule site is a weighty listing of myriad artifact traits, of whale and seal hunting gear, of specialized lances and harpoons used for pursuing game on land and sea. Like Birnirk in the west, however, Thule artistic endeavors were relatively modest, confined in the main to simple engravings on utilitarian artifacts such as combs, often Y motifs and straight lines. Sometimes, the engraver depicted humans and animals, even scenes of the chase. Three-dimensional figures in wood and ivory often depict women without arms or legs, often with topknot hairstyles. Tiny floating ivory carvings of loons and other birds are relatively commonplace, perhaps game pieces, or important ideological symbols, links between the people and the supernatural world (Sproull-Thomson, 1979).

(Below) Three scenes from Thule life incised on an ivory bow-drill from near Arctic Bay. Top, summer tents with men hunting with bow and arrow. Center, kayakers meet a swimming caribou. Bottom, whalers harpoon a spouting whale as bear skins dry in front of a tent camp.

(Below right) Classic Thule sea-hunting equipment included these harpoon heads.

Classic Thule technology made use of
many materials. Artifacts illustrated
here include, clockwise from the left:
an antler adze handle; a whalebone
adze head with polished stone blade; a
flensing knife with ground-slate blade;
an ulu with iron blade; a whalebone
snow knife, used to cut blocks for
snowhouses; a bone scraper for
preparing hides; an ivory engraving
tool with a small iron point; and a drill
bit with a ground-stone point.

Thule Subsistence. Thule whale hunters concentrated on bowhead whales, *Balaena mysticetus*, relatively placid creatures who swim slowly and often sleep near the surface (McCartney, 1980; 1984b; Savelle and McCartney, 1988). Their heavy blubber means that the carcass floats even when dead, a major advantage for hunters with skin boats. The average baleen whale can yield about 33,068 lbs (15,000 kg) of meat and outer skin, a delicacy among Inuit today. As little as 18,841 lbs (9000 kg) of blubber would provide heating, lighting, and cooking oil for months. The bones were invaluable for rafters and house walls (Savelle and McCartney, 1988).

The whalers used slate-tipped toggling harpoons attached to large foreshafts and wooden shafts. Entire sealskins formed the floats attached to the harpoon line that helped tire the harpooned whale. Judging from contemporary engravings, the sealskin and driftwood *umiaks* were manned by between four and seven or more people. The helmsman would

*Umiak and crew, Cape Prince of Wales,
Northwest Territories, 1927.*

approach the whale from the rear as it came up to breathe (Nelson, 1969). The harpooner in the bow would cast at a vital spot, the man behind him throwing out the floats. Several casts and a long fight might ensue, until the dead whale could be towed tail-first to a convenient beach or into shallow water, where butchering could proceed.

Bowheads were undoubtedly staples in coastal communities in whaling areas (Savelle and McCartney, 1988). While some other foods were consumed the sheer mass of whale meat and blubber probably overshadowed other supplies. Outside the whaling zones, the other classic arctic resources formed the diet — caribou, walrus, seals, and fish. Thule hunters with their more efficient technology and transportation took a wider range of prey than their Dorset predecessors, not only musk ox and smaller mammals like fox, but birds, clams, even bird eggs. However, predictable caribou migrations and seal harvests, especially of ring seal, often helped determine where winter settlements were located. The hunters took seals in open water from their kayaks, waited for hours at the ice edge or by breathing holes in winter. They would drive caribou into shallow lakes where waiting kayaks would kill the frightened animals. On land, they drove small herds through converging lines of stones piled up to resemble human beings, killing the stampeding beasts with recurved bows and arrows at a range of about 32 ft (10 m). Birds were taken with multibarbed spears or small whalebone bolasses, snared with gorges and hooks embedded in blubber. (For a full description of Thule subsistence and material culture, see Maxwell, 1985; Mathiassen, 1927.)

Postclassic Thule
AD 1400 to European contact

During the 12th and 13th centuries, Thule sites appear south of Parry Channel and along mainland coasts near Hudson Bay, in northern Labrador, and on Baffin Island, areas where whales were scarcer. The caribou, seal, and fish bones from these settlements argue for a slower settlement of less whale-rich areas, using the familiar subsistence strategies of the west. Thule settlements are also found far to the north, into the Independence Sound area of Pearyland in far northern Greenland. Eigil Knudsen made a dramatic discovery during the 1960s in Independence Sound in the very far north — an abandoned camp site of about AD 1450 with the remains of a wrecked Thule *umiak* nearby. Before walking away from their camp, and presumably perishing, for there is no settlement nearby, the hunters killed a whale, a narwhal, and bearded seal, in open water. Today, the area is ice-bound and never navigable by boat. Some time after that date, some Thule groups spread south along the Labrador coast as far as Hamilton Inlet.

This redistribution of population may reflect growing population pressure in the classic areas, but climatic change may have been a more important factor. The so-called Little Ice Age took place between AD 1400 and 1600, a time when glaciers advanced on Greenland and Baffin Island. Summer pack ice may have been so heavy that boat work was severely restricted, shortening the seasons for open-water whale hunting. The number of whales may have been smaller, too, for pods require open water

Eastern Arctic: open water whalers in skin kayaks and an umiak, 1905.

to breath every five minutes or so. Many Thule sites show that baleen whale hunting declined after AD 1400 in many areas (Schledermann, 1979). By the late 16th century, *umiak* and kayak whaling had ceased in the High Arctic. The people probably turned to fishing, musk-ox hunting, and fox trapping for much of their sustenance.

These may have been hard times. Moreau Maxwell (1960) excavated an isolated postclassic dwelling at Ruggles Outlet, on Lake Hazen in the interior of Ellesmere Island. A hunter took several foxes and a musk ox before he died. His widow buried him under some rocks outside the house. She was left alone and ate three sled dogs, then died on the sleeping platform inside the house. Climatic conditions became so severe that by AD 1600 much of the High Arctic was abandoned.

Further south, some whaling continued where open water conditions permitted. Ringed seal, caribou, and fish continued to be staples, with more regional variation than in earlier times. This may have been the time when local groups such as the Copper Eskimo, Netsilingmuit, and Ingloolingmuit emerged, the Inuit groups encountered by white explorers after the 16th century.

European Contact
AD 1000 onward

European contact began with the Norsemen, who settled in southern Greenland by AD 1000 and traded with the Inuit for furs, walrus ivory, and gyr-falcons (Chapter 1). The Norsemen may not have had much direct contact with Thule people, but their iron tools, smelted copper, cloth, and other trade goods were diffused far and wide through Eastern Thule territory down long-established exchange networks (McCartney and Mack, 1973; McGhee, 1978; 1981; Maxwell, 1985). Iron soon became a critical factor in Thule technology, for both imported European and natural meteoritic iron were employed to fashion iron-bladed knives, harpoon tips, and other artifacts.

Norse trade with the Thule collapsed by about 1480, and it was a century, in remoter areas much longer, before there were new contacts with Europeans. English voyager Martin Frobisher was the first to search for the elusive Northwest Passage. He made three voyages to the Baffin Island region, thought he had found gold but it was iron pyrites. Frobisher was followed by John Davis, Hendrick Hudson, and other explorers. Some of them had men killed in violent disputes with the Inuit. Others traded with friendly groups. These occasional contacts with Europeans had little effect on Inuit culture, except for the importation of rare foreign goods, especially iron tools. It was not until European ships managed to winter over successfully in the mid-19th century that significant populations of whalers, fur traders, even miners, arrived in the Far North. Within a few generations, many Inuit bands became heavily dependent on European trading stations for goods purchased with furs. In some areas, however, Inuit groups perpetuated prehistoric hunter-gatherer lifeways into the 1950s, when superpower rivalries led to the development of strategic defense networks in the Canadian Arctic.

Further Reading

In addition to the references at the end of Chapter 8.

Giddings, James L. 1964. *The Archaeology of Cape Denbigh*. Brown University Press, Providence, RI.
   A fundamental monograph, if now somewhat out-of-date.
   —1967. *Ancient Men of the Arctic*. Alfred Knopf, New York.
   An outdated, but fascinating, account of Arctic prehistory, which gives fine insights into working conditions in the Far North.

Harp, Elmer, Jr. 1978. "Pioneer Cultures of the Subarctic and the Arctic," in Jesse D. Jennings (ed.). *Ancient Native Americans*. W. H. Freeman, New York, pp. 303–371.
   An excellent synthesis of what little is known of Sub-Arctic prehistory.

Mathiassen, Therkel. 1927. "Archaeology of the Central Eskimos," *Report of the Fifth Thule Expedition 1921–1924*. vol. 4. National Museum, Copenhagen. Mathiassen is still an authoritative source on Thule culture.

Rudenko, S. I. 1961. "The Ancient Culture of the Bering Sea and the Eskimo Problem," translated by Paul Tolstoy. Arctic Institute of North America, Anthropology of the North, *Translations from Russian Sources*, 1.
   A Soviet perspective on the archaeology of the Berling Strait region.

Shaw, R. D. and Holmes, C. E. (eds.). 1982. "The Norton Interaction Sphere," *Arctic Anthropology*, 19, 2: 1-149.
   Important papers on the Norton tradition that describe recent research.

Tuck, James A. 1976. *Newfoundland and Labrador Prehistory*. National Museums of Canada, Ottawa.
   A useful handbook to the archaeology of extreme northeastern Canada, one of a series covering Canadian prehistory, province by province.

PART FIVE

THE WEST

"In the beginning, the earth was square and flat, and below its surface were four layers. All people, birds, and beasts lived in the bottom layer or world. Everything was in darkness. There was no sun, no moon. It was dark and it was crowded, but the people did not know how to get out. At last two boys pierced the roof of the lowest layer, making an opening ..."

Keresan Origin Myth

CALIBRATED DATES	RADIOCARBON AGES	WEST COAST		GREAT BASIN	SOUTHWEST	CLIMATIC STAGES
		NORTHWEST	CALIFORNIA			
Modern times	Modern times	MODERN GROUPS		MODERN GROUPS	MODERN GROUPS	
AD 870 – 1230	AD 1000	LATE PERIOD	AUGUSTINE LATE / BERKELEY / WINDMILLER ? / MIDDLE PERIOD / EARLY PERIOD ? / NORTH SOUTH	MIDDLE PERIOD / EARLY PERIOD / Many other variants	LATE ARCHAIC / MIDDLE ARCHAIC / EARLY DESERT ARCHAIC	HOHOKAM MOGOLLON ANASAZI / SOUTHWESTERN ARCHAIC	LATE HOLOCENE
175BC – AD 235	AD 1					
1530 – 905 BC	1000 BC	MIDDLE PERIOD				
2830 – 2305 BC	2000 BC					— — — —
3950 – 3640 BC	3000 BC					MIDDLE HOLOCENE
5235 – 4575 BC	4000 BC	EARLY PERIOD				
6285 – 5445 BC	5000 BC					
outside accurate calibration range	6000 BC					— — — —
	7000 BC			PALEO-INDIAN		EARLY HOLOCENE

CHAPTER 10

EARLY HUNTER-GATHERERS ON THE WEST COAST

The Spanish and English explorers who first sailed the western coasts of North America between the 16th and 18th centuries found themselves in one of the richest marine environments on earth. Here they encountered a great diversity of native American populations, not only small bands of hunter-gatherers, but elaborate, highly sophisticated societies, where people lived in large, permanent communities under powerful leaders. Ocean fishing and sea mammal hunting were important all along the West Coast, especially after about 4000 BC, but assumed particular importance along the Northwest Coast, and in central and southern California. Here, people developed highly specialized fishing and sea mammal hunting cultures that evolved into some of the most complex and elaborate hunter-gatherer societies in the world. The study of this remarkable cultural complexity has engaged archaeologists for generations.

Environmental Diversity

During the Early and Middle Holocene, the Northwest Coast became a strip of green, forested landscape that stretched from the mouth of the Copper River in Alaska to the Klamath River in northern California. Here the great mountain ranges of the interior were covered with vast stands of spruce, cedar, hemlock, and Douglas fir, trees that occurred in abundance throughout the coast. The Pacific and the rivers that flowed into it provided whales, porpoises, seals, sea lions, and dozens of fish species. Among these were halibut, some of which weighed up to a quarter of a ton. Herring, smelt, and candle fish swarmed in coastal waters. No less than five salmon species appeared in inshore waters each year, jamming rivers as they crowded upstream to spawn. Shellfish, waterfowl, some game like deer and fox, and wild plant foods were important elements in human diet throughout the coast. The rich and diverse coastal environment provided over 300 important edible animal species alone. The prehistoric inhabitants of the coast had an abundant cushion of natural resources to fall back on, in addition to the thousands of fish they could smoke dry and store in times of plenty.

At European contact, most human settlement along the Northwest Coast was concentrated on river banks or on the islands and shores of the coast, especially north of the Columbia River, where an abundance of fish and sea

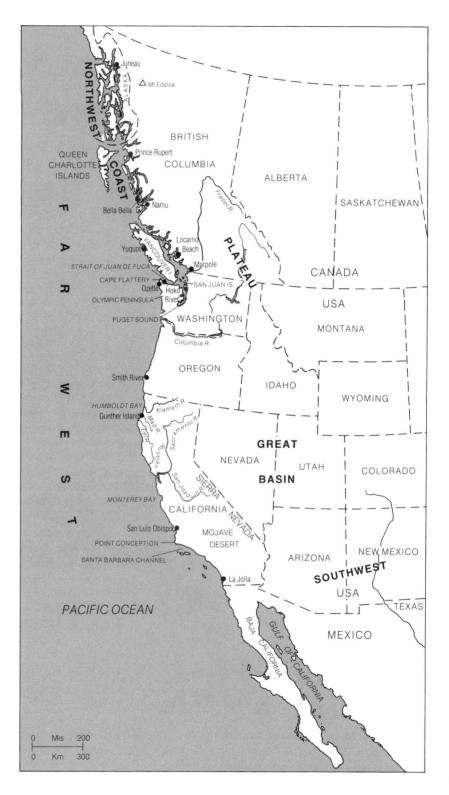

Archaeological sites and regions of the Far West.

(Left) Haida village photographed in the 19th century, with totem poles, large plank houses, and canoes.

mammals allowed relatively sedentary settlement. The damp, oceanic Northwest Coast climate provided abundant natural resources to create an elaborate material culture with only the simplest of tools. The dense forests of the coastal zone were rich in easily split, straight-grained softer woods like red and yellow cedar, fir, and spruce. The local carpenters used tough, polished rocks, shell, or antler blades in their adzes and chisels, taking advantage of the straight-grained wood to build large plank houses at winter villages and other important locations. They reserved some of their finest woodworking artistry for their canoes, large and small. Skilled canoe builders fashioned war and heavy load-carrying canoes from specially felled tree trunks and then carved and smoothed them carefully. The

(Below) John Webber, artist on Captain Cook's voyage, drew the inside of a Northwest Coast Indian house on Nootka Sound in the 1770s. Elaborately carved supporting posts can be seen at the rear of the house. Dried salmon and other fish were staples during the winter months.

(Right) Engraved and painted Haida storage box.

(Below) Portal pole, a carved entrance to a Haida house.

carpenters fashioned a magnificent array of wooden artifacts, large and small, adorning many of them with a heraldic art style that is among the most celebrated of American Indian art forms. Renowned ancestors, mythical birds, and humans appear on many boxes and small objects. Commemorative posts, portal poles, and great totem poles recounted family genealogies and celebrated the deceased. By the time Europeans arrived on the Coast in the 18th century, these flamboyant cultures had been flourishing for many centuries.

South of the Klamath River stretches more than 1242 miles (2000 km) of Pacific coastline, backed by the rugged Klamath mountains in the north, and by many separate and lesser coastal ranges from Oregon to central California. The Transverse Ranges abut the coastal mountains at the border of central and southern California, the only ones to run east-west in the state. These ranges rise from the Mojave Desert in the east. The western outliers jut from the Pacific, forming the offshore islands of the Santa Barbara Channel. To the south, the Peninsula Ranges form the spine of Baja California and extend north into the United States as far as the Los Angeles Basin. Three-quarters of inland California comprises the Great Central Valley, with flat lowlands drained by the Sacramento and San Joaquin rivers that merge into a great delta, pass through a gap in the coastal ranges, and ultimately flow into San Francisco Bay. The Lower Sacramento Valley region supported the highest population densities in prehistoric California. Relatively high concentrations also flourished in the Lower San Joaquin Valley.

This vast coastal region of great environmental diversity enjoys a generally Mediterranean climate, with the highest rainfall in the north and northwest, with some 15 in (38 cm) a year falling in the southern coastal regions, much less inland. In central and southern California, there are generally two seasons, a warm, wet winter and a warm, dry summer with ocean-moderated temperatures along the coast. There are many local climates, which affect the indigenous vegetational cover, and the distribution of animals.

California alone supports more than 30 natural vegetation types, which provided its prehistoric inhabitants with a variety of staple foods. Oak grassland covers the foothills of the Sierra Nevada, the Transverse ranges, and coastal mountains. It was a vital resource for prehistoric populations, for the oaks provided a bounty of acorns and the grasslands edible seeds. The same vegetation also supported populations of deer, rabbits, coyote, bear, and many bird species. Thick chapparal flourishes on steep, rocky slopes between the oak grassland and conifers at higher elevations. Unsuitable for human occupation, the chapparal did support deer and provided a variety of berries and wild plants.

From Monterey to the Oregon border and further north, redwoods grow in a narrow belt from sea level up to about 2000 ft (660 m) or more, nurtured by the moist air and fogs from the nearby Pacific. This highly varied zone supports a very diverse fauna, everything from Canadian elk to beaver, bear, deer, and many smaller mammals.

Everywhere, the rich and diverse coastal environment assured abundant and almost guaranteed food supplies for much of the prehistoric population (Heizer, 1964).

Prehistoric Food Staples

The peoples of coast and interior lived by hunting and gathering, subsisting in a patchwork of environments that provided local food resources of every kind. Only a handful of later prehistoric groups in interior southern California ever engaged in agriculture, growing maize, beans, and gourds – subsistence strategies derived from the neighboring Southwest. However, after about 1500 BC, some hunter-gatherer societies along the Pacific coast and in the Central Valley "managed" their wild food resources, sowing wild seeds, even irrigating favored food plants, and tending native root crops.

Three staple food categories comprised the diet of prehistoric peoples along the West Coast and immediately inland — large and small game animals, edible plants, and sea foods.

Prehistoric hunters stalked feeding deer and sometimes ambushed them, killing them with spear, and, after AD 500, with the bow and arrow. Pronghorn antelope (*Antilocapra americana*) grazed in large numbers in the Central Valley, as did tule elk. Every human group preyed on smaller game like coyotes, rabbits, and many species of rodents.

Acorns were the staple of staples in the far west after mortars and pestles made their appearance between 4000 and 3000 BC. Even in areas like the Northwest Coast where fish were abundant, acorns served as an important supplement. California peoples knew of many different oak species, some of which yielded more desirable acorns than others (Baumhoff, 1963). In many places, the foragers would travel a considerable distance to collect acorns from a preferred species, while ignoring large groves of less desirable oaks closer to home (Baumhoff, 1978).

The acorn was by no means the only wild plant staple eaten in prehistoric times, for many other plant foods served as secondary staples or supplements, especially in acorn-lean years. In southern California, for example, Buckeye (*Aesculus californica*) is a nourishing seed that, like the acorn, is poisonous unless the poison is leached out by pouring water over

Acorns (drawing below) were a staple food along the West Coast. They had to be carefully processed: (bottom) a Hupa woman leaches acorn meal in a basin of sand. A burden basket lies at the left, a basketry bowl in her hand, tightly twined to make it waterproof, and a cooking basket at the right.

the seeds. Since animals did not eat it, human beings never had to compete for seed with them, so it was a valuable food in lean years. Chia, sage seed (*Salvia* sp.), was especially plentiful along the southern California coast from Point Conception to San Diego. Harvest yields were small, so the seeds were combined with other famine foods in times of scarcity. People collected the seeds of many species of bunch grasses, also seasonal fruits and tubers, like, for example, the epos root, or yampa (*Perideridia* sp.). This edible root, widely eaten in northern California, had an aromatic, nutty taste when raw, and a flavor somewhat like that of a carrot when boiled.

So important were hunting and plant gathering to both coastal and inland peoples that they used deliberately set fires to control the growth of brush, promote the growth of seed-bearing grasses and other plants, and to improve game densities (Lewis, 1973). The prehistoric peoples of California had a considerable impact on the natural landscape by their use of fire (Timbrook and Johnson, 1982). They were well aware of the fire danger to valuable acorn crops posed by natural fires, spreading through dense brush from natural lightning strikes in the mountains. So they burned off the growth to prevent such accidents, and to foster deer populations. For example, modern experiments have shown that regular fires in chaparral increase the production of shrubs and herbaceous plants, with accompanying rises in deer populations. In one experiment, the summer deer density was 30 per square mile in an unburned area and up to 131 in a burned one (Biswell, 1967). By burning open areas in chaparral in spring and fall, hunter-gatherers could maximize the amount of edible vegetation along the edges of chaparral. New sprouts appear within three or four weeks of a spring burning, making excellent feed for deer, while fall burning ensures edible sprouts for humans the following spring.

Important staple foods came from the Pacific and the rivers that flowed into the ocean. Vast fish shoals and annual salmon runs contributed to dense populations along parts of the West Coast. King and Coho salmon, also steelhead trout, provided a bounty of fish along the Northwest Coast, and the Klamath, Smith, and Eel rivers in northern California. Annual runs occurred as far south as the Santa Barbara Channel and what is now the Los Angeles area. Many other fish species abounded off the coast, both in dense kelp beds and in deeper water. Bonito, tuna, yellowtail, and halibut were commonly taken from canoes close offshore. Sea mammals abounded on rocky outcrops and near kelp beds, also on the offshore islands. Harbor seals and sea lions were often clubbed on shore. Sea otters were another favorite prey. Inland river species provided abundant food sources along the Sacramento and San Joaquin rivers.

Vast shell middens line many parts of the West Coast, large whitish-grey mounds so densely packed with shell that only stunted vegetation grows on them. Abalone, clams, oysters, and sea mussels were collected where abundant. Northern groups also took Washington clams and bent-nosed macomas, while more southern shellfish included the abalone, Pismo clam, scallop, and California Venus clam.

The successful exploitation of sea foods depended to a considerable degree on the presence of good perennial streams, and on ready access to the shoreline. The sheltered, heavily forested, tidal waters of the Pacific Northwest were perfect for intensive sea mammal hunting and fishing.

Fishing for salmon with a plunge net on the Klamath River, California, before 1898.

Along California shores, north of San Francisco and south of Point Conception, for example, the coastline is relatively low lying with many streams and natural indentations to attract marine life and to provide shelter for those who live off them. The famous Big Sur coast of central California has steep cliffs that fall directly into the Pacific. Even here, shell middens are commonplace. The densest prehistoric coastal populations flourished in areas of easy access to the ocean, and, above all, in regions like the Santa Barbara Channel, where offshore islands protect the coastline from surf. Major riverine areas like the Lower Sacramento and Delta regions were also favored locations.

The great environmental diversity of the far west confronted prehistoric peoples with a patchwork of locally abundant food resources, resources that varied greatly in their availability. These patterns of resource availability had a strong influence on population density, settlement size, food-getting strategies, and on the degree to which local groups depended on one another. In the long term, this environmental diversity helped shape societies that were interdependent, passing both essential foods and exotic goods and materials through complex barter networks that linked Vancouver Island to the northern mainland, and extended from the offshore islands far into the Southwest, and from the northern coast to the Sierra Nevada and beyond. These trade networks carried acorns, salt, fish, shell artifacts, clothing, baskets, even dogs, over a network of trails that joined a myriad of small bands and larger societies with tenuous links. The obsidian trade was a vital element in these networks, as, in later times, was the use of beads made of clam shells or *olivella* as a form of simple "money." In late prehistoric times, regular trading provided some element of stability in diverse environments by reducing the risk of starvation when local food shortages threatened the stability of local populations (Ericson, 1977; Chagnon, 1970).

First Settlement of the West Coast
before 9000 BC to *c.*5000 BC

Stone tools from the Namu site. Clockwise from top left: bifacial point, chopper, grooved bola or sinker, microblades, and a microcore. Length of biface c.9.3 cm.

As elsewhere in North America, the evidence for first settlement is sparse, mainly in the form of scattered projectile points. The earliest settlement of the Northwest Coast was a complex process, probably involving both coastal groups from the north taking advantage of lower Early Holocene sea levels and other populations from the south, as people moved into formerly glaciated areas (Borden, 1975; Dumond, 1978; Fladmark, 1975). This complexity of early settlement is reflected in at least four known Early Period cultural traditions, identified by stone tools, along the coast and in the interior (Carlson, 1983). To what extent these represent actual cultural diversity is unknown.

Some Paleo-Indian groups hunted and foraged in the interior, while there are clear signs of maritime adaptations on the Queen Charlotte Islands and at places like Namu along the British Columbia mainland as early as 5000 BC. Some of these groups may have been ancestral to the Tlingit, Haida, and other Athabaskan-speaking peoples in the Northwest (Carlson, 1983). Carlson argues that as Northwest river waters warmed and lost their icy mantles, their up-river habitats became suitable for salmon spawning grounds. As lake-spawning salmon began spreading up-river, the prehistoric peoples who preyed on them also moved inland, into areas where they may have met expanding groups from the interior. From these complex movements emerged such historically known groups as the Salishan and Wakashan-speaking peoples of coast and interior today.

Further south, in what is now Oregon and California, initial Paleo-Indian settlement inland is chronicled by isolated fluted point finds. These groups were probably big-game hunters, who may have exploited wild vegetable foods, smaller animals, and marine resources as well. Grinding implements are rare on Paleo-Indian sites, as if intensive exploitation of wild vegetable foods was relatively unimportant (Wallace, 1978). Undoubtedly, foraging assumed greater importance after 9000 BC, with the vanishing of the Pleistocene megafauna, but the major shifts in subsistence strategies that occurred about this time are poorly documented anywhere in the far west. This is because many of the key artifacts used for plant or shellfish gathering are perishable items like baskets, skin bags, or wooden digging sticks. Only stone artifacts used for breaking up shells, and durable *manos* and *metates* survive. The latter grinding and milling implements become more common in western sites after 6000 BC, by which time shellfish collectors, fish and sea mammal hunting groups were flourishing along the California coast – as they had been doing for at least 2000 years.

The changeover is best documented along the southern California coast, where foraging sites occur from San Luis Obispo in the north to the Mexican border. The people still hunted some game and used stone projectile points, but judging from the abundant milling stones, much of their diet came from seeds and edible plants. The material culture from these sites tends to be somewhat monotonous, consisting of heavy, deep seed mills and heavy handstones. But settlement sites are much larger than in earlier times, associated with middens of considerable size. Here, as in the Pacific Northwest, the basic patterns of coastal adaptation that were to persist for millennia were already established by 5000 BC. These patterns depended to a considerable degree on the diversity of food resources available close offshore, in the coastal hinterland and along rivers or lakes, and in the interior.

Northwest Coast Middle Period
3500 BC to *c.*AD 500

Roy Carlson (1983) divides Northwest Coast prehistory into Early, Middle, and Late Periods, arguing for cultural continuity and increasing elaboration since before 8000 BC (see also Borden, 1975; Dumond, 1978; Fladmark, 1975). The Early Period saw the emergence of several local hunter-gatherer and maritime cultures, known mainly from stone tool assemblages, as mentioned above (Carlson, 1983).

With the beginning of the Middle Period in 3500 BC, the cultural diversity of earlier millennia gave way to greater homogeneity throughout the Northwest Coast except in basketry styles (Croes, 1989). The reasons for this are little understood, but may be connected with shifts in adaptations and rising population densities, with the stabilization of sea levels and environmental conditions during the Middle Holocene. There are signs of a higher level of interaction between neighboring groups, too, reflected in widespread trade in fine-grained, tool-making obsidian. Judging from X-ray fluorescence studies, much of the obsidian came from sources in eastern Oregon, reaching the Puget Sound region, Vancouver Island and the Gulf Islands, and the mainland as far north as Namu (Carlson, 1983). Mount Edziza in northwestern British Columbia, as well as local sources, provided supplies for prehistoric communities at the headwaters of the Yukon, near Juneau, Alaska, and throughout much of coastal northern British Columbia. These exchange networks, and others handling different commodities, may have contributed to the spread of ideas and culture traits throughout the coastal regions (Croes, 1989).

Even as early as 3500 BC, it is possible to recognize a nascent Northwest Coast cultural tradition that evolved continuously until European contact. Many sites of this period have been grouped together into the Charles Phase, centered on the Strait of Georgia area but representative of generalized cultural developments over a much wider area (Borden, 1975), even as far north as the Alaska Peninsula (Carlson, 1970).

The Middle Period is marked by a greater emphasis on maritime resources, especially salmon and halibut, and on a much wider range of woodworking and craft skills (Croes and Hackenberger, 1988). This was the time when the basic characteristics of historic Northwest Coast culture appeared — an emphasis on status and wealth, and on elaborate ceremonial, reflected in new art traditions (Carlson, 1983). Specialized woodworking tools became more common during the Middle Period, and finely made polished chisels and adze blades appeared by about AD 450. By this time, too, cedar bark was being fabricated into cloaks and other

Middle Period artifacts: (a) harpoon foreshaft, (b) stone adze or chisel blade, (c) scallop shell gorget, (d) labret or lip ornament, (e) chipped stone point, (f) ground slate point, and (g) chipped stone knife.

garments, basketry had reached a high level of sophistication, and planked houses were probably in use. Hunting and fishing technology now reached new levels of elaboration. Some 400 bent wood and composite fish hooks came from the Hoko River site on the Olympia Peninsula (Croes, 1988), arguing for more emphasis on offshore fishing, while many forms of stone, bone, and wooden projectile points were in use. Hunting of such animals as the elk, deer, bear, and beaver was important in many areas. Ocean and estuarine fishing certainly assumed greater significance during the Middle Period.

The Middle Period may have seen the accumulation of large food surpluses, surpluses that led to complex mechanisms for redistributing food and other goods throughout society. A few wealthy and powerful individuals may have controlled such redistribution as a way of acquiring personal prestige. One mechanism for doing this may have been ceremonial feasts, the ancestors of the elaborate *potlatches* of historic times. It is hard to identify such personages in the archaeological record. Some Middle Period burials from Namu, Prince Rupert, and elsewhere appear to have more elaborate grave furniture, to be the graves of more important people, but poor preservation makes the evidence tantalizingly uncertain. Some status artifacts such as labrets, lip ornaments, and gorgets worn at the throat, occur at many later sites, as do superbly flaked stone knives of a form that were used by important people in historic times. Middle Period art with its animal motifs carved on spoons and bowls recalls the prestigious crests that were commonplace in later times.

For all the relative homogeneity of Middle Period culture, there were important clusters of more elaborate culture in such areas as the Lower Fraser River Valley and the Gulf of Georgia, on the west coast of Vancouver Island, and along the central British Columbia coast. These are reflected in differences in toolkits, harpoon forms (Carlson, 1983), and in basketry and cordage (Croes, 1989). There are other artifacts such as stemmed projectile heads, tobacco pipes, and slate projectile points, that entered the narrow confines of the Northwest Coast during the Middle Period, with cultural influences percolating in both from Alaska and from the south.

Northern California Early Archaic
6000 to 1500 BC

Further south, the rocky and mountainous habitat of the northern California coast supported Archaic populations for thousands of years, populations that survived comfortably with little contact with neighboring culture areas. The people subsisted off wild vegetable foods, moving seasonally from one concentration of edible foods to another. They probably changed their highly flexible adaptations to accommodate plant distribution changes resulting from minor climatic fluctuations. The size of local bands seems to have varied considerably, with little of the elaboration found in later coastal and Sacramento Delta cultures.

In the San Francisco Bay area, early sites were located not only on bay and ocean shores but in hill country, and considerable distances inland. Some groups collected shellfish, but nothing like on the scale of later coastal societies.

Southern California Early Period
before 6000 to 1000 BC

The early prehistory of the southern California coast is best known from the Santa Barbara Channel region where Chester King (1984) distinguishes an Early Period that lasted from before 6000 until about 1000 BC. The Early Period has been broken down into three divisions, known locally as Ex, Ey, and Ez (Glassow, Wilcoxon, and Erlandson, 1987). Ex passed into Ey in about 4450 BC, with the final phase assigned to between 2350 and 1350 BC, but the chronology is little refined.

Early Period groups flourished at a time of steady sea level rise, so many important sites may be buried under the Pacific, or have been eroded away by rising sea levels. Some settlements were built on higher ground away from the ocean. On the offshore islands, people built semi-subterranean pithouses, leaving numerous seed-processing *metates* and *manos* behind them. The inhabitants sometimes buried their dead in red ocher-sprinkled graves. Other sites occur near coastal wetlands and on lower ground.

Early investigators believed that plant foods were more important than hunting or fishing during the Early Period. While it is true that basin *metates* and *manos* are common on sites of this period, shellfish were an important resource throughout these millennia. Judging from modern analogies, basin *metates* and *manos* were mainly used to process small nuts and seeds. Mortars and pestles appear in Ey and Ez sites, artifacts that may be associated with the introduction of acorns and other pulpy nuts and seeds into the diet (for discussion, see Glassow, Wilcoxon, and Erlandson, 1987).

Land and sea mammal hunting may have assumed greater importance as time went on. Deer and sea mammal bones are more common in later Early Period sites, coinciding with a change from crude, percussion-flaked

Southern California mano and milling stone, Topanga Complex. Length of mano 9 cm.

lanceolate projectile points to abundant side-notched and stemmed heads (Harrison and Harrison, 1966). The people used bone gorges and barbed, multi-part fish hooks to catch both shallow- and deep-water fish. Chester King (1981) believes that gorges and nets served to obtain inshore fish, while the larger, compound fish hooks, and perhaps harpoons, took deeper water fish like sharks, and dolphins, species more common in later times. Deep-water fish may have been taken more frequently on the islands, while mainland beaches were convenient places to net smaller species.

The Early Period settlement pattern was probably a balance between seasonal hunting and foraging, especially at the time of fall nut and seed harvests. However, shellfish, sea mammals, and fish of all kinds played an increasingly greater role, perhaps allowing the people to occupy base camps for long periods of time.

The origins of this early coastal tradition are still little understood. Glassow points out that the earliest solidly documented traces of Archaic occupation, dating to about 7000 BC, come from north of the Santa Barbara Channel, from the cool, foggy environment of Point Conception and further north, where the coast is rocky and conditions are slightly wetter. This region may resemble primeval Ice Age environments more closely than drier areas further south, but the field information is very sketchy (Glassow, Wilcoxon, and Erlandson, 1987).

This entire (Archaic) tradition owes much to earlier Paleo-Indian cultures, with new artifacts for seed processing grafted onto an existing material culture. Several authorities have pointed out that the earliest Early Period dates, and readings from equivalent sites near La Jolla, coincide with the early Altithermal, when inland lakes dried up and there was a major warming trend. Some inland foraging populations may have moved to the coast in response to increasing aridity in the interior.

Judging from a rise in site numbers, admittedly a somewhat tenuous yardstick to use, Santa Barbara Channel populations may have first reached significant levels about 6000 BC, with a drop in coastal populations between about 5000 and 3500 BC, the lowest density occurring between 4000 and 3500 BC. Coastal populations rose relatively rapidly after 3500 BC, at a time coinciding with the first use of mortars and pestles, perhaps with more intensive acorn exploitation, certainly with a greater emphasis on fishing and sea mammal hunting. Similar patterns are thought to occur elsewhere in southern California (Glassow, Wilcoxon, and Erlandson, 1987).

About 4000 BC, sea temperatures cooled considerably, but the land vegetation was still that of a warm, arid climate. Sea levels were rising, drowning the seed-rich coastal plain. The gradual reduction of these seed communities between 5800 and 4000 BC may have contributed to the shift to acorn harvesting as a major element in human subsistence, oaks having become more frequent than in the Early Holocene.

Did these changes in subsistence and settlement pattern result from major environmental change? There is a more specific question: did new subsistence strategies result from changes in availability and abundance of food resources (Glassow, Wilcoxon, and Erlandson, 1987)? The Early Period begins just as the pine and fern tree cover of the cooler and damper Early Holocene climate gives way to more open vegetation. The changeover took place about 5800 BC. As the early Ex phase ended, warm and dry conditions prevailed, with higher sea temperatures and a shift to oak forest and much more open vegetation. During Ex times, sea levels were up to 49 ft (15 m) lower than today, with dry land extending more than half a mile (l km) from the present mainland. The coastal plain would have been much larger than today, and may have supported grasslands and sage brush, which themselves would have produced productive harvests of small seeds, the seeds processed with basin *metates* and *manos.*

The period between about 5800 and 4000 BC coincides with warmer ocean temperatures, a time when peak temperatures would have inhibited the growth of the coastal kelp so typical of the California coast today. Kelp forests support large inshore fish populations, important prey for sea mammals. A reduction in kelp beds may have diminished near-shore fish populations, also the sea mammals that preyed on them, removing part of the local resource base. Perhaps this was responsible for low population densities during part of the Altithermal. By the same token, the population growth after 4000 BC may coincide with an increase in the productivity of the inshore marine habitat as kelp beds reappeared.

Why did the people of the coast take advantage of this enhanced productivity? Why was similar increased productivity not taken advantage of much earlier, during the Ex phase? Glassow and his colleagues argue that while the timing of subsistence changes may have resulted from environmental shifts, additional factors may have played an important role. One was a relatively rapid population increase during the Ey and Ez phases of the Early Period. As populations grew, the overall energy cost of providing food for everyone would also increase. More effort would have been needed to obtain food, perhaps triggering a shift to new food sources that may have required a greater time and energy investment to catch or process (Glassow, 1978). One could argue in theoretical terms that optimal foraging strategies applied, as they may have done in the Great Basin (Chapter 12), but the data is still insufficient.

There are, however, some obvious signs of change. Both large sea mammals and deer were favored resources as long as they were fairly easy to obtain. As population densities rose, these same resources probably became scarcer, requiring more energy to collect. For example, seals and sea lions that frequented convenient beaches are an easily hunted resource. But once the hunters had to mount special expeditions to remoter outcrops frequented by the animals, the hunting cost rose rapidly.

Fishing, too, has varied costs. Catching inshore fish by hook and line in tide pools or from outlying rocks is a cheap way of catching food, but the yield is usually low. Canoes would be needed to exploit the rich kelp beds close offshore, but the yields would be much higher. However, building and maintaining boats requires considerable, and constant effort, as does sewing and repairing seine nets to be used from shore or canoe. Sea craft more substantial than a reed raft would have been adaptive for the catching of larger fish like halibut or sharks as well, species with a high meat yield per specimen landed.

Acorns are the most obvious example of a higher cost food resource, for the elaborate processing procedure has been documented from ethnographic observations. Both seeds and acorns have a major advantage: they are easily stored for long-term use (illus. p.198), as foods that can be drawn upon in lean winter months. Both require considerable collecting and processing effort, but acorns probably came into widespread use when

Acorn storage: the Nisenan village of Yupu near Yuba City, showing acorn granaries and large, dome-shaped, earth-covered dwellings. Illustration from Gleason's Pictorial Drawing Room Companion *(1882).*

population growth as well as rising sea levels reduced seed harvests, making harder-to-process plant foods a competitive, easily stored resource for feeding more people.

During the Early, and especially the Middle, Holocene, coastal peoples expanded the breadth of their diet, a diet that probably included small amounts of most food resources from the very beginning. It was only when populations grew and traditional staples became scarcer that people turned to alternative, more costly sources.

This broadly distributed Archaic lifeway survived into later millennia, adapting to changing climatic conditions, and devising far more diverse subsistence strategies. Notable among these was a much greater focus on acorn harvesting, fishing, sea mammal hunting, and shellfish collecting. This development was a factor in the emergence of some of the most sophisticated, and densely packed hunter-gatherer societies to flourish in the prehistoric world, societies described in the next chapter.

Further Reading

Borden, Charles E. 1975. *Origins and Development of Early Northwest Coast Culture to about 3000 BC.* Archaeological Survey of Canada, Mercury Series, no. 45.
An overview of Northwest Coast prehistory as known in the mid-1970s.

Carlson, Roy (ed.). 1983. *Indian Art Traditions of the Northwest Coast.* Archaeology Press, Simon Fraser University, Burnaby, British Columbia.
Essays on the prehistoric background to Northwest Coast art, which range widely over archaeological and historical issues.

Heizer, R. F. and Whipple, M. A. 1971. *The California Indians: A Source Book.* 2nd ed. University of California Press, Berkeley.
A carefully selected series of essays on California Indian societies of great use to the general reader.

Moratto, Michael J. 1984. *California Archaeology.* Academic Press, New York.
The definitive account of California prehistory, which is widely used as a teaching text. Technical, at times demanding, but authoritative.

CHAPTER 11

LATER PREHISTORIC SOCIETIES
OF THE PACIFIC COAST

Emerging Cultural Complexity on the Northwest Coast
*c.*1000 BC to modern times

The Late Period of Northwest Coast prehistory arbitrarily begins in about AD 500, the culmination of continuous cultural evolution along the coast since at least 3000 BC. The staples behind this long process were fishing, shellfish collecting, seà and land mammal hunting, and some plant gathering. They provided the resource base for a great elaboration of Northwest culture, reflected in intensive economic specialization, relatively high population densities, and considerable sophistication of social and political organization.

The causes of this elaboration have been the subject of much speculation (Croes and Hackenberger, 1988; Fladmark, 1975). Many authorities speculate that it was connected to a combination of a greater focus on anadromous and offshore fish, population growth, and local resource depletion. Efficient exploitation of resources required centralized authority in the form of socially prominent people who managed territories they owned, coordinated their work forces of extended families and associates, and redistributed the resulting food resources (Ames, 1981; Fladmark, 1975). Unfortunately, few archaeological sites along the Northwest Coast provide stratigraphic or organic information to document this important cultural trend. One exception is Hoko River.

Hoko River Site Complex. These sites lie near the northwest tip of the Olympia Peninsula, (illus. p. 200); Croes and Blinman, 1980; Croes and Hackenberger, 1988; Croes, 1988). There are two sites close to the ocean. The first is an up-river waterlogged and dry camp site area dating to between 1000 and 200 BC, the second a river mouth site within a large rockshelter, occupied from about AD 1000 to 1850, after European contact. The former belongs to the Middle Period, which is thought to reflect "a more specific adaptation to the coastal environment" than earlier cultures (Mitchell, 1971). The artifact inventory from this settlement includes over 400 cod and halibut offshore fishing hooks, complete with floats and cordage leaders, indicating an early specialization in such fisheries. The fish bones include 52 percent flat fishes, 20 percent cod, and 16 percent salmon, all of them caught offshore. Traces of fires and wooden racks on shore are convincing evidence for the drying of catches (Croes, 1988).

The bone tools from the nearby Late Period Hoko River rockshelter are very different from the artifacts found at the earlier site up-river. Bone is now the dominant technology for making artifacts, as it was elsewhere along the nearby Gulf of Georgia. Over 800 years of occupation, the inhabitants took an average of 10 percent cod, 59 percent salmon, and only 5 percent halibut, probably consumed in dried form. The rockshelter was probably used in fall and early winter when salmon could be taken. Shellfish and mussels were also a significant part of the diet.

Subsistence and Cultural Elaboration. Dale Croes and Steven Hackenberger (1988, where the full arguments appear) have used the Hoko sites with their excellent preservation to develop elaborate models of the relationships between resources and evolving human cultures along the Northwest Coast. On the basis of these predictive models, they argue for small and widely dispersed Northwest coastal populations until about 3000 to 2000 BC. At first there was slow population growth, they believe, followed later by rapid growth and expansion into new hunting territories. Group sizes increased relative to hunting territory, with subgroups moving into new lands both on the coast and inland. Many of them relied on intensive seasonal hunting and on storage of summer and fall food resources. Somewhere between 2000 and 1000 BC, population growth may have begun to stabilize and plateau, with more intensified exploitation of fishing territories and shellfish resources. Not much food may yet have been stored, for people may have relied heavily on reliable winter food sources like shellfish, to the point of overexploitation.

As populations continued to grow, albeit much more slowly, and shellfish populations were depleted, Northwest Coast groups turned to new storage technologies as a logical alternative to strict population controls. During spring and early summer, offshore flatfish and halibut were taken in large numbers and dried for later consumption. These fish have the advantage of being easier to take and process, as well as being of predictable occurrence. Initially at any rate, the people may have relied more heavily on spring and summer resources like salmon, which they could dry for winter consumption, both because they were relatively predictable and abundant, and also because the spring and summer sunshine was more dependable than that later in the year.

Croes and Hackenberger believe that spring and summer bottom fisheries were the first major intensification of coastal resource use. Then, between about 400 BC and AD 500, resource storage assumed ever greater importance as a solution to continuing population pressures and fluctuations in local food resources. Many groups now made a logical extension to earlier storage practices, placing an increasing emphasis on summer and fall resources that were also stored. This was the time when anadromous salmon assumed ever greater importance, with more and more settlement concentrated in strategic river and estuary areas, where

(Above) Zoomorphic carving on (?) whale bone, probably representing a bird figure, found near the base of the Hoko River rockshelter trench excavation. Makah elders believe it may be a hair pin, pushed through the hair bun typically worn on the back of the head by fishermen.

(Opposite) Hoko River sites, Washington. (Top left) Map showing the two site locations, an earlier upriver camp and a later rockshelter site. (Top right) Halibut hook as it was found at the wet site. Note the bone barb, the Indian plumb wood shanks, and two-strand spruce root leader attached. (Center right) Makah fisherman displays a modern replica of the Hoko halibut hook, used to catch a fish close offshore. (Center left) Hoko rockshelter excavations in progress. (Bottom) Reconstructed Makah canoe used for the halibut fishing experiment at Hoko River.

salmon runs were seasonally predictable. Marpole sites, for example, are concentrated along river banks and estuaries, perhaps flourishing at a time when salmon fishing reached its height.

During the final centuries of prehistoric times, Northwest Coast groups further intensified their maritime procurement strategies by concentrating more heavily on offshore fisheries. At Hoko Rockshelter and Ozette on the Olympia Peninsula, there is great elaboration of offshore, jigging (hook-and-line), and trolling (used with a towed line) fish hooks, as if the inhabitants were venturing close offshore to catch large numbers of fish before they entered rivers in summer and fall. Sea mammal bones become more common at Hoko after AD 1000, together with the bone harpoons used to take them.

Croes and Hackenberger believe that the major artifact changes along the Northwest Coast during the Holocene are linked to major shifts in subsistence strategies. They argue in terms of economic stages or "plateaus," underlain by an early period of exponential population growth that led to territorial circumscription about 2000 BC, and eventually to critical resource stresses. In particular, they argue that overexploitation of shellfish resources, followed by an increased emphasis on stored and alternative foods, was an important factor in the emergence of complex maritime culture on the Northwest Coast, and perhaps elsewhere.

This model is a convincing one, but a model still based on relatively few sites, and few where preservation conditions are good. It has important implications for understanding the emergence of more complex social and political institutions on the Northwest Coast.

Most arguments about emerging cultural complexity in the Northwest assume that the efficient use of anadromous fish like salmon required careful organization and management of the resource – to organize labor for catching, gutting, and drying the fish, also for carrying it from the rivers to nearby villages (Fladmark, 1975). As Croes and Hackenberger have pointed out (1988), however, the need to intensify the use of bottom fish and anadromous species during the Middle Period did not in itself require the development of centralized authority to manage people and food supplies. Rather, they predict that food resource depletion combined with a rapid growth of extended families led to the ownership of well-defined territories. Access privileges to the fisheries and other food resources within these areas varied from family to family, with those who controlled access acquiring greater wealth and social ranking than less fortunate people. Thus, they argue, differential access to precious food resources resulted in a need to manage their exploitation and allocation. These resources, while relatively predictable, fluctuated in their availability from year to year. Social ranking, the ownership of territory, and ritualized redistribution of food and other commodities at ceremonial feasts (*potlatches*) were, in the final analysis, adaptive ways of coping with fluctuations in the food supply.

The Croes and Hackenberger hypothesis is flexible enough to accommodate another major variable in the complexity equation — that of the individual. Technically, many Late Period Northwest Coast societies can be defined as chiefdoms, chiefdoms that were dominated by powerful clan leaders, very often individuals with exceptional entrepreneurial and leadership powers. (Another classification terms them "Big Men" polities

(Johnson and Earle, 1987).) Their authority and power depended on their ability to attract followers and to retain their loyalty, through their control, acquisition, and redistribution of resources. It may be that the emergence of complex hunter-gatherer societies on the Northwest Coast depended to a considerable degree not only on the careful management of fluctuating food resources, but on the proper training of the elite individuals who inherited the rights to control particular territories. Unfortunately, it is almost impossible to trace the emergence of social ranking in the archaeological record of the Northwest Coast, but there are some hints of its existence as early as 1000 BC at the Hoko "wet/dry" settlement. There, Croes found remains of conical basketry hats with both distinctive knob-shaped and flat tops. At the Ozette site and in historical Makah Indian society, commoners wore flat-topped hats, while the higher-ranking owners of family territory had knob-topped forms. He believes that similar hat styles and rank differentiation were in use 2500 to 3000 years earlier, in the Middle Period (Croes and Hackenberger, 1988).

Late Period and Links to Historic Peoples
AD 500 to modern times

The boundary between the Middle and Late Periods of Northwest Coast prehistory is a purely arbitrary one, for there is strong evidence of cultural continuity throughout the entire Northwest Coast from Alaska to extreme northern California over a long period of time. Nineteenth-century ethnographies and historical accounts tell of the great diversity of Late Period Northwest Coast culture (Barnett, 1955; Boas 1905–1909, among others), the emergence of which is little known from the archaeological record.

Some archaeological sites document historic cultures during earlier times. For example, the Middle Period Marpole culture of southern Vancouver Island, also the San Juan and Gulf Islands, developed from earlier, Locarno Beach roots about 400 BC and flourished until about AD 400 (Matson, 1989). By this time, there are clear signs of differing social status, both in the value and amount of grave goods and in the presence of skull deformation, a characteristic of socially prominent birth on the Northwest Coast. Marpole art traditions and antler and bone artifacts are quite distinct from those of the Coast Salish, the people living in the area at European contact. Salish culture can be traced back to at least AD 1200, a culture that relied heavily on bone artifacts, and used side-notched arrowheads, probably introduced from the interior plateau to the east. Despite the major differences between Marpole and Salish, most authorities believe that the one developed into the other during the first millennium AD.

Nootka-speaking peoples flourished along the shores of the Strait of Juan de Fuca, and on the west coast of Vancouver Island. Basketry styles from Hoko River reflect 3000 years of Nootkan style at this location (Croes, 1989). The Yuquot site at Friendly Cove on that island documents a basic continuity of Nootka sea mammal and fishing culture from historic times right back into the Middle Period (Dewhirst, 1980).

Whaling became more important during the Late Period, as it was at the famous Ozette site on the Pacific coast south of Cape Flattery, perhaps the most important sea mammal hunting site for thousands of miles along the West Coast. Ozette lay at the back of a protected beach on the Pacific, an ideal place to hunt whales, fur seals, dolphins, and other deep-water fish, with plant foods, shellfish, and shallow fishing grounds close by. One late spring night about AD 1750, a massive mud slide cascaded over the village, smashing and burying at least four houses (Kirk, 1975). Preservation conditions under the mud are such that even fragile organic finds such as barkcloth, hide, and netting were preserved, giving a remarkably complete picture of Late Period culture at Ozette before European contact. Hundreds of fish hooks for cod and halibut, pieces of harpoons and whaling kit come from the Ozette houses, one of the most important archaeological sites in North America, and one where Northwest prehistoric life is being reconstructed in great detail.

Ozette art and artifacts show connections with that of other Nootka-speaking peoples, and with people living to the south, with Salish culture on Puget Sound. The decorated objects include wooden boxes, clubs, whale harpoons, bows, and a magnificent whale fin adorned with a mythical thunderbird outlined in sea otter teeth. The motifs are lively, mainly zoomorphic and anthropomorphic, with many complex geometric patterns that were reproduced on materials as diverse as bone and basketry.

To the north, Kwakiutl, Bella Bella, and Tsimshian-Haida-Tlingit country have yielded many Late Period fishing and sea mammal hunting sites (for summary, see Carlson, 1983). There is abundant evidence for continued

(Right) Ozette, Washington. Carved cedar representation of a portion of a whale's back, including the closed fin. One surface is decorated with more than 700 sea otter teeth. This object was probably used in whale hunting ceremonies, and is unique in the archaeological record, although Cook recorded one on his voyage. Length c.1 m long.

(Opposite) Ozette, Washington. (Above left) Carved panel depicting Thunderbird and Wolf found in a broken state on the floor of a house. (Above right) Carved detail of a whalebone club. (Below left) Oil dish in the shape of a human figure. (Below right) This club was probably used for killing seals after harpooning.

cultural growth and elaboration over at least 4000 years, processes at first accelerated, then drastically interrupted, by European contact — by Russians in 1741, by Spaniards in 1774, and by Captain James Cook four years later (Fisher, 1977).

The California Coast: Diversification and Regional Specialization

The Spanish explorers who first sailed the southern California coast in the 16th century found themselves in one of the richest maritime environments on earth. Great schools of tuna and other deep-sea fish, myriad shoals of sardines and lesser species, regular whale migrations, and enormous herds of sea mammals provided a bounty of different foods. They also encountered a great diversity of indigenous populations living along the Pacific coast, among the coastal mountains, and further inland. As late as 1769, when actual Spanish colonization began, some 300,000 Indians lived in what is now California, perhaps a greater number than in any area of comparable size anywhere in North America. But population densities varied greatly, from less than 0.5 a person/sq. mile (0.20/sq. km) in inland desert areas to more than 10.4 people/sq. mile (3.85/sq. km) in the biologically rich Santa Barbara Channel region of southern California (Cook, 1976).

California's later prehistoric cultures were remarkable for their intensive and often highly specialized hunting, gathering, and fishing activities. After 3000 to 2000 BC, the climate was essentially the same as today. The implements used on land and sea were basically the same all along what is now the Oregon and California coasts, with, however, major elaborations and local variations, depending on specific environmental challenges and needs. Rich acorn crops were important everywhere, on the coast and in the interior. Shellfish played a major role in the San Francisco Bay area, while the peoples of the Santa Barbara Channel region and further south exploited not only molluscs but sea mammals, and shallow-water and deep-sea fish. The intensive exploitation of acorns and marine resources led to the great elaboration of technology, art, and social organization in some areas, especially in the Santa Barbara Channel and the San Francisco Bay-Sacramento-San Joaquin Delta regions.

The people also enhanced the resources available to them by careful controlled burning, by husbanding and managing wild foods, and occasionally deliberately planting wild grasses and other plants to extend their natural availability. They also developed complex social mechanisms to regulate long distance exchange and the redistribution of resources — political alliances, kin ties and ritual obligations, and formal banking of resources among them. The pioneer California archaeologist Robert Heizer wrote (1964) of the "abundant and assured food supplies" that led to dense populations and permanent settlements in some areas of the California coast. These intricate coastal and riverine adaptations gave rise to societies that reached the effective limits of social complexity without adopting agriculture. They were still flourishing along the Pacific coast at the time of European contact.

Northern California

Any understanding of the later prehistory of northern California must take into account the linguistic history of the area. Not that this is an easy task, for California Indians spoke about 20 percent of the nearly 500 separate languages spoken in North America in the 15th century AD. There were 23 language families and isolated languages, making a total of some 90 languages that themselves formed innumerable dialects (Moratto, 1984). For our purposes, it is sufficient to assume that the Hokan and Penutian language stocks incorporate about 67 of the 90. Another, Uto-Aztecan, probably originated within California. Two others — Algic and Athabaskan — belong to stocks that are mostly distributed outside California. The Yukian stock is a mystery, unrelated as it is to any other group (Shipley, 1978).

Reconstructing culture history from language distributions is always a high-risk proposition. It is possible to draw some general conclusions. Hokan-speaking groups are commonly thought to be among the first settlers, partly because their languages show the greatest diversity and possible time depth. Before 4000 BC, the population of what is now California may have been almost entirely Hokan-speaking, except for the North Coast Ranges, where Yukian speakers lived (Moratto, 1984). There were considerable language shifts between 4000 and 2000 BC, especially among Uto-Aztecan groups in eastern California. In northern California, Penutian speakers may have moved into the marshy lower Sacramento Valley from the Columbia Plateau or Great Basin in about 2500 BC, a movement often associated with the so-called Windmiller Pattern (see below). Utian-speaking peoples spread and diversified in later centuries, expanding westward into the Bay area with its swamps and marshes soon after 2000 BC, where they came into contact with earlier Hokan people. In time, two traditions emerged and intermingled, the one a primeval one associated with Hokan, the other associated with the Penutians. They were to survive for 4000 years (Gerow, 1968).

The later linguistic prehistory of California is very complex, and beyond the scope of this book. The maps (illus. p. 208) summarize major language changes about 2000 BC – AD 1 and immediately before European contact. The reader is referred to Moratto's summary (1984) for an analysis.

The archaeology of northern California coastal areas is known mainly from shell middens, and from dense settlements in the Bay area and in the Sacramento Delta region. The outline sequence that follows is based on excavations at dozens of sites large and small. The North Coast is isolated and relatively mountainous, but it still came under influence from neighboring areas. The Yurok of the extreme northwest came under strong influence from the Northwest Coast peoples in Oregon and Washington, while groups living to the south were open to ideas and contacts from their California neighbors.

However, each local group had its own distinctive adaptation, with most of them forming what the great anthropologist Alfred Kroeber called "tribelets," small groups presided over by a local chief or headman, each with their own territory, often a local river drainage area. Each tribelet usually had a principal settlement, a ceremonial center, and several outlying camps used at different seasons of the year.

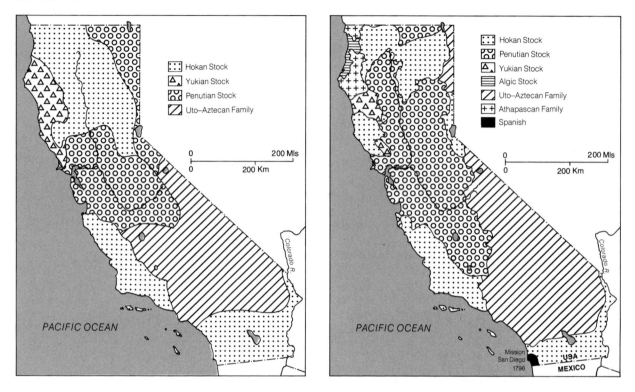

Probable distributions of language groups in California: (left) about 2000 BC to AD 1; (right) about AD 1000 to 1769.

Each group followed its own distinctive subsistence strategy, exploiting rugged terrain that was deceptively rich in both predictable marine resources and more dispersed game and plant foods. Michael Moratto and other California archaeologists talk in terms of "searchers" for dispersed resources, and "pursuers" of more predictable resources like anadromous fish. The people would shift from searcher to pursuer mode depending on the season, a shift that could mean major changes in social organization as isolated tribelets came together, usually in the fall, and cooperated with others in catching, cleaning, smoking, and storing salmon, or when netting enormous numbers of smelt on the fringes of sandy beaches each fall. Come winter, most groups resided in winter villages, relying heavily on foods stored during the bountiful summer months. This general form of lifeway was followed throughout the North Coast region, albeit with considerable local variation, depending on the distribution of resources and environmental circumstances.

***The Gunther Pattern** (?150 BC to recent times)* of the Humboldt Bay area and of the lower reaches of the Eel and Mad rivers was first identified from excavations at Gunther Island in Humboldt Bay. The artifacts from these excavations show strong influences from the Northwest Coast culture area to the north (Heizer and Elsasser, 1964). The Gunther Pattern is a specialized riverside and coastal adaptation that was brought into the area by ancestors of the Wiyot and Yurok peoples who lived there at European contact. Gunther sites with their distinctive barbed projectile points are concentrated along rivers like the Klamath and Trinity, also at strategic lagoons. The inhabitants relied heavily on seasonal salmon runs and other predictable marine resources, using mountainous areas for hunting and seasonal acorn harvesting. There are clear signs of long-distance trade in obsidian from sources at least 248 miles (400 km) away, and evidence for social ranking in Gunther cemeteries.

Gunther Pattern barbed projectile point, length c.3 cm.

Augustine Pattern (AD 200 to recent times). Further south, the Eel River region and the Russian River area are less mountainous, with some major rivers and large coastal lagoons, especially to the south. Here anadromous fish were less important and the people fanned out over the neighboring country in search of wild vegetable foods during the summers. With offshore marine mammal rookeries, seasonal fishing, some mollusc collecting, and inland foraging, the different bands adjusted their annual rounds and settlement patterns to ever-changing distributions and availabilities of animals and plants. This was the area into which the Augustine Pattern spread about 2000 years ago, a widespread culture in central California (see below) characterized by intensified hunting, fishing, and foraging, especially for acorns. A migration of Penutian-speaking Wintun peoples from the Sacramento Valley may have been a stimulus to the development of this Pattern (Fredrickson, 1973).

After AD 1400, dense populations congregated in many areas, populations that enjoyed highly developed long-distance exchange systems, elaborate ceremonial life, and a degree of social stratification. This elaboration appears to have resulted from population growth, favorable environmental conditions, and increased contacts between isolated populations.

Central Coast and San Francisco Bay

Widespread, but scattered, populations of hunter-gatherers lived in this large region before 2000 BC. These sparse populations lived on the coast and in the mountainous interior, with both hunting and plant gathering being important elements in the diet. In contrast, coastal resources seem to have been less important.

Windmiller Pattern (before 2500 BC to 2000 BC and later). About 2500 BC, people well adapted to riverine and marshland environments settled in the Sacramento Delta region. It is thought that these Penutian speakers may have originated in the Columbia Plateau or western Great Basin, settling in a bountiful, low-lying region where their successors were to flourish for more than 4000 years.

The Windmiller economy was focused on hunting deer, pronghorn, and rabbits, also waterfowl. The people fished for sturgeon, salmon, and other fish with spears and nets and lines, as well as gathering storable plant foods such as the fall acorn harvest. Almost certainly many groups hunted in the nearby Sierras during the summer months. Delta groups acquired obsidian from Coast Range sources, and also from the eastern side of the Sierra. They traded coastal shells and ornaments from the Pacific, and obtained other exotic materials such as quartz crystals. Windmiller burials and

Windmiller Pattern of Sacramento Delta region. Clockwise from top: large stone projectile point; ground-slate pin; charmstone of blue amphibolite schist.

cemeteries show evidence of considerable ceremonial, including the use of red ocher, with many bodies oriented toward the west (Fredrickson, 1973; Ragir, 1972).

The Windmiller Pattern spread widely in the Central Valley, also westward into the Bay area, forming the foundations of a cultural tradition that was to survive into recent times.

Berkeley Pattern (c.2000 BC to AD 300). Soon after 4000 years ago, new peoples moved into the Bay area, Utian-speaking peoples with a basically Windmiller culture. These were people adapted to estuaries, bays, and marshes with their diverse resources. This spread may have coincided with a great expansion of bayside and coastal marshlands, local environments that supported a bounty of fish and shellfish, large waterfowl populations, also game and many edible plant species (Bickel, 1978). By AD 1, numerous Berkeley Pattern villages flourished throughout the San Francisco Bay area, along the Central Coast, and in the Monterey Bay area, associated with exploitation of acorn and some shellfish collecting.

Judging from the larger site size, local populations were denser than in earlier millennia, but still egalitarian. Most people were buried with but a few utilitarian objects, except for occasional individuals associated with what are known from ethnographic records to be shamans' kits — bone whistles, quartz crystals, and charmstones (Fredrickson, 1973).

According to Tom King, the prehistoric Bay region of 2000 BC to the Christian era offered a wide diversity of environments, everything from oak woodland to grassland and marshland. Many Berkeley Pattern settlements were sited to take full advantage of this diversity, often lying near freshwater streams and marshlands. By settling in such ecotones, the people could exploit both inland and bayshore locations. Tom King (1970) argues that the earliest settlements were located in these prime locations, places where there were few gaps in the annual "harvest" of different resources. Later, smaller camps were established in the interior, the result, he argues, of dense populations splitting off to form satellite communities in more marginal lands. Eventually, each major community was surrounded by peripheral settlements, to the point that its territory was circumscribed, redefining the relationships between them. They may have shared resources, exchanged them, or even competed in war. Whatever the vehicles of interaction, the result would have been more formal social and political relationships, with the emergence of important kin leaders and non-egalitarian political systems (T.King, 1974).

Augustine Pattern (c.AD 300 to recent times). Between AD 300 and 500, the Berkeley Pattern gradually evolved into the Augustine Pattern, a pattern associated not with major population movements but with technological innovations such as the bow and arrow, harpoons, tubular tobacco pipes, and an unusual custom, that of burning artifacts in a grave before the body was interred (Fredrickson, 1973). These developments are associated with the movement of Utian-speaking Wintun (ancestral Patwin) peoples from the Sacramento Valley who displaced some of the Bay Miwok groups while settling among them.

Augustine communities supported large, dense populations in favored locations. They intensified hunting, gathering, and fishing to the point that their culture was much elaborated. After AD 1400, the number of Augustine settlements proliferated dramatically, settlements fostered by kin leaders who maintained constant ties with neighboring communities. An elaborate ceremonial involving secret societies and cults came into being. Inter-community exchange assumed such importance that clam shell disk "money" came into widespread use. This increasingly more complex cultural system survived until European contact and beyond, to disintegrate in the face of inexorable Spanish missionary activity.

Southern California Coast

"The natives are well appearing, of good disposition ... As to their government, it is by captaincies over villages ... They have cemeteries set apart for the burial of their dead. The god whom they adore, and to whom they offer their seeds, fruits, and all that they possess, is the sun ... Their houses, shaped like half-globes, are neatly built; each is capable of sheltering four or five families ..." (Fages, 1972 [1775]).

The Santa Barbara Channel and other parts of the southern California coast supported exceptionally sophisticated hunter-gatherer societies at European contact. These groups maintained long-distance exchange networks that carried sea shells, soapstone, and other exotica far into the interior as the Southwest. As in the Bay area, there is good reason to believe that the coastal adaptation evolved over a long period of time, in response both to an exceptional diversity of marine resources, and also to steady population growth over many thousands of years.

As so often happens in archaeology, it is the inconspicuous and tiny objects that are often the most revealing. Some of the most sensitive indicators of cultural change over long periods of time in California are shell beads and ornaments, which can be classified by size, shape, even by the relationships between their diameter and thickness (King, C., 1978; 1984). Fortunately, there are relatively complete historical records of the ornaments worn by different groups at European contact, which serve as a useful baseline for chronological studies.

There were two types of shell beads which were in use over wide areas of California. Some served as "money beads," bartered by everyone regardless of social status for food and other commodities over very wide areas. Others were ornaments of status, limited to those allowed to obtain them, or to people of inherited rank. The values of both bead groups differed considerably, often a function of the amount of manufacturing effort involved. For example, the small *olivella* shell was relatively easy to grind into beads, which were worn by the Chumash in strings or kept by the hundred in bags. Clam disk beads were another common form of money, widely used in central coastal California, but the Chumash used them for decoration and to mark status.

Further north along the Pacific coast, people relied less on shell money and used dentalium shell beads that were much less effort to manufacture. Chester King hypothesizes that many groups living in areas where there were relatively few important food resources with fluctuating harvest yields were able to regulate food shortages by political relationships and exchanges of food based on them. In contrast, the Chumash of southern

California lived in a highly varied environment with many local variations and fluctuations in food resources. Here shell money came into its own, creating what King calls a "monetized" economy, which was more efficient in evening out regional differences in food supplies from one year to the next. The peoples of central California used both shell money and political relationships to regulate their food supplies (Chagnon, 1970).

Chester King (1971, 1984) has used distinctive shell bead forms found in dated graves in the Santa Barbara Channel area to reconstruct a cultural sequence for the mainland and offshore islands (chart opposite). He recognizes three periods, each with different phases and further subdivisions (see King, C., 1971). The Early Period, already described, flourished from before 6000 BC until about 1000 BC. It was during the Early Period that the distinctive maritime adaptation in the Santa Barbara Channel area evolved. The direction of cultural changes was toward increasing complexity.

Middle Period (c.1000 BC to AD 1100). The cultural trends of the Early Period toward more maritime exploitation accelerate over these two millennia. Changes in beads and ornaments reflect a new role for such artifacts in local society. Originally they served an ornamental function. Now they may have been used as status markers in society, often exchanged or as a form of storable wealth. Seals, porpoises, dolphins, whales, swordfish, and shark bones now occur in coastal middens as well as thousands of shellfish remains. Bones of deep-water fish may be a sign that much more sophisticated watercraft, including plank canoes, may have been used for offshore fishing.

Late Period (AD 1100 to 1804). By this time, shell money was in widespread use throughout southern California. These were Hokan-speaking Chumash people, the immediate ancestors of the coastal groups encountered by the first European explorers and missionaries. The Chumash enjoyed a complex adaptation, not only to the bounty of the Pacific environment, but also to areas a considerable distance inland. Some groups exploited the oak-covered foothills seasonally, gathering acorn and seed harvests. As early as the Middle Period, other Chumash communities lived inland year-round, subsisting off deer, seasonal salmon runs, and a wide variety of plant foods.

There were probably close economic relationships between coastal and inland groups, for some inland villages have yielded the bones of marine fish and sea mammals. Perhaps families ventured to the coast to fish, or engage in other specialized activities at certain times of the year. Close kin ties, relationships between individuals of equal rank, and long-term trade relationships may have led to a constant exchange of food and other goods between coast and interior over many centuries. However, as Michael Glassow (1979) points out, we need much more environmental and archaeological data before we can define the interactions between coastal and inland Chumash groups, let alone those between immediate neighbors. Another source of information will be marriage patterns detected by using post-contact Spanish mission registers.

Chester King's detailed studies of shell beads and other ornaments (1984) make a compelling case for Chumash society having evolved in the Santa Barbara Channel region for over 7000 years. Over this long period of

Phase		*Olivella biplicata*	CLAM	MUSSEL	ABALONE EPIDERMIS	ABALONE NACRE	BLACK ABALONE NACRE & EPIDERMIS
Late Period	L3						
	L2b						
	L2a						
	Llc						
	Llb						
	Lla						
AD 1150	M5c						
	M5a	Conus					
Middle Period	M4						
	M3						
	M2b						
	M2a						
	Ml						
800 BC	Ez						
Early Period	Eyb						
	Eya						
	Ex	5 cm					

Chronological chart of shell bead types in southern California compiled by Chester King.

time, the local people transformed their culture from one based predominantly on plant foods, some hunting, also intertidal resources to one that relied heavily on fish and marine mammals. And, as time went on, the sheer richness and diversity of Pacific waters enabled them to adopt a more sedentary lifeway, and to achieve a much higher degree of social complexity and higher population densities than were to be found over most of western North America before Europeans arrived.

Chumash Culture

Thanks to the dedicated researches of the remarkable anthropologist John Harrington, we know a great deal about the Chumash (Harrington, 1942;

Hudson, T. and others, 1979). A brief description of their lifeways gives a useful impression of the sophistication and diversity of late prehistoric coastal adaptations in southern California (for summaries, see Landberg, 1965; Hudson, T. and Blackburn, 1983).

Spanish observers of the 18th and early 19th centuries reported that the Chumash peoples of the mainland and offshore islands were skilled navigators and expert fishermen, capable of navigating long distances over open water in their frameless, planked canoes. The mainland Chumash were described by one early Spanish missionary as "well formed and of good body, although not very corpulent." Neither men nor women wore many clothes. The men normally went naked except for a deerskin, bird feather, or fur cape in cold weather. The women wore knee-length, two-piece aprons of mule deerskin, or sea otter pelts. The Chumash made much use of body paint, the various designs serving to distinguish one group from another. They pierced their ears and wore necklaces of shell and stone.

Chumash villages consisted of well-built, dome-shaped dwellings made on a pole frame, settlements housing extended families of several dozen people. The occupants slept on sleeping platforms arranged in tiers along the walls, behind mats hung to give some privacy. Each village had one or two sweat houses and a nearby cemetery protected with a stockade, the graves marked with painted poles. Some Chumash settlements in the resource-rich Santa Barbara area housed as many as 1000 people and were centers for important ceremonies and trading activities. They served as political "capitals" over several lesser villages, even small "provinces," loose political confederations of communities large and small (Hudson and Blackburn, 1983).

Each Chumash village was ruled by a hereditary chief (*wot*) and his assistant. *Wots* served as war leaders and patrons of ceremonial village feasts. Once during the fall and at the winter solstice, outlying communities near and far flocked to major settlements for rich ceremonies that honored the earth and the sun. Chumash villages and provinces were constantly quarreling with one another over food supplies and territory, often over resources at the edge of one another's territory. Disputes over wives, social insults to chiefs (such as not attending a feast), and blood feuds were commonplace.

The Chumash exploited a great diversity of food resources, the importance of different foods varying from season to season. On the mainland, the people hunted mule deer year-round, especially in the late summer, stalking them near streams where lush grazing was to be found. They hunted and trapped every kind of small animal, even rats and squirrels. They dried seaweed and ate it in considerable quantities. "It may be said that for them, the entire day is a continuous meal," wrote one Spanish missionary marveling at the varied food resources enjoyed by the Chumash.

The annual acorn crop was a vital staple, gathered from the oak forests and foothills inland. The Chumash also ate other plant foods, including walnuts, wild cherry pits, pine nuts, yucca, and seeds from wild herbs and grasses, whose growth they fostered by deliberate burning. During the rainy season from November to March, people subsisted off dried meat, stored vegetable foods, and fish, also collecting shellfish like the abalone.

Come spring, the people would range far inland in search of fresh plant growth. The fishing improved with the warmer weather, peaking at the end of the summer and in early fall, when huge schools of tuna and other fish swarmed in open waters. Chumash fishermen rarely ventured beyond the outer edges of the inshore kelp beds, but even there they could benefit from this bounty. The fall brought the all important islay (wild cherry pits) and acorn harvests, when thousands of acorns and nut meats were stored away for the lean months ahead.

The Chumash achieved a level of social complexity that represents about the limit of such complexity possible without adopting agriculture. Like more complex hunter-gatherer societies elsewhere in North America, in the Pacific Northwest and the Eastern Woodlands, they were able to achieve this elaboration because of unusually favorable environmental circumstances. In the case of the Chumash, exceptional ocean bounty came from a natural hydrographic phenomenon known as upwelling. This upwelling is caused by the prevailing northwesterly winds that blow down the Pacific coast pushing surface water away from the shore. A submerged peninsula that runs southwest from Point Conception toward the outlying offshore islands intensifies the replacement of warmer surface water with colder

Reconstruction of Chumash village life: Santa Barbara Museum of Natural History diorama.

water from closer to the ocean floor. This upwelling replenishes surface layers with rich nutrients that foster plant growth and cause microscopic unicellular algae — photoplankton — to flourish. In spring, billions of spawning sardines feed on the nutrients and zooplankton that lie on the surface, moving inshore during the summer. Pelicans and larger fish like tuna and albacore feed on the sardines and other species. The Chumash were able to take hundreds of protein-rich ocean fish each summer from their canoes (Landberg, 1965).

Close inshore, the southern coast is protected by dense kelp beds, marine algae that greatly enrich the shallow water environment close inshore. The Indians could fish for at least 125 fish species like bass, halibut, and rock cod from small canoes based on sheltered bays. The greatest densities of archaeological sites are found close to kelp beds, even on relatively exposed coasts. Seals and sea lions abounded near the kelp and coasts. The coastal Chumash clubbed the seals as they lay sleeping on land, also took sea otters, and feasted off the meat of stranded whales, for eight species of these large mammals migrated through the Channel annually. Inland Chumash groups had relatively little access to marine resources.

This great resource diversity supported a relatively dense mainland and island population at European contact in the 16th century. Early Spanish records are vague on population estimates, but scholarly estimates place some 15,000 Chumash in the Santa Barbara-Ventura area, with the densest populations in the Santa Barbara region. The offshore islands were reached by a 17-mile(27.3-km) canoe ride and supported perhaps as many as 3000 people living in small fishing villages. The islanders traded shells and fish for plant foods and raw materials from the mainland.

Chumash culture was a maritime adaptation made possible by a specialized fishing technology that included planked canoes about 25 ft

A reconstruction by Travis Hudson and Peter Howorth of a plank canoe (tomol)*, used by both the Chumash and Gabrielino groups for fishing, sea mammal hunting, and transportation.*

(7.6 m) long paddled by three or four men (or more) with double-ended paddles (Hudson and others, 1978). Each plank was carefully shaped and fitted with stone and shell tools, secured in place with a mixture of hard asphalt and pine pitch, then sewn to its neighbors with vegetable fiber. The Chumash were also expert basketmakers, fashioning fine shell fishhooks, bone and wood artifacts, and stone mortars. They were artists, too, their petroglyphs and pictographs the most spectacular north of the Mexican border (Grant, 1965). Chumash shamans and specialists served as the artists, painting the walls of remote inland caves and rockshelters with abstract representations of the sun, stars, human beings, birds, fish, and reptiles. The meaning of the art is unknown, but at least some of it is connected with astronomical observances, and to a calendrical system. Some painted sites may have served as solstice observatories (Hudson, T. and Underhay, 1978; Hudson, T. and others, 1979).

This elaborate and sophisticated Chumash society maintained exchange contacts with other coastal communities to the south, also with peoples living far in the interior. The Gabrieleño occupied the Pacific coast areas now under the urban sprawl of Los Angeles and Orange County. They controlled valuable steatite outcrops on Catalina Island offshore, a soft stone ideal for making stone griddles and pots, which they traded widely. Further south, the Luiseño and nomadic bands of Diegueño peoples moved seasonally between coast and interior harvesting acorns, seeds, also shellfish and marine mammals, as well as fishing. The former's political organization was somewhat similar to that of the Chumash.

During late prehistoric times, some California Indian societies like the Chumash became highly stratified, with elites, office holders to assist chiefs, shamans, and commoners. The finely dressed chiefs lived in large houses, their establishments supported by their communities. Expert

(Below left) Chumash baskets. (Below right) Chumash rock art at the San Emigdio pictograph site.

traders, canoe builders, basket weavers, and other artisans also enjoyed considerable prestige, but social preeminence was reserved for one individual — the chief, who might marry several women to strengthen alliances with other tribelets nearby.

In other areas of North America, this emerging cultural and social complexity often foreshadowed more sedentary lifeways based on maize agriculture. But right up to European contact in the 16th century AD, the inhabitants of the Pacific coast and inland were still enjoying a hunter-gatherer lifeway that had begun to evolve as long ago as the Early Holocene. There is every reason to believe that they were perfectly familiar with maize agriculture and farming. However, the sheer bounty and diversity of the natural resource base made this subsistence strategy unnecessary.

Further Reading

In addition to the sources at the end of the previous chapter:

Heizer, R. F. 1978. *Handbook of North American Indians, vol. 8: California*. Smithsonian Institution Press, Washington DC.
  The *Handbook* volume on California is an admirable source of information on both later prehistory and California Indian societies before and after European contact.

Hudson, Travis, and Blackburn, Thomas. 1983. *The Material Culture of the Chumash Interaction Sphere*. Ballena Press, Socorro, California.
  The definitive account of Chumash material culture based on Harrington's notes and ethnographic collections.

Kirk, Ruth. 1975. *Hunters of the Whale*. Morrow, New York.
  A popular account of the Ozette site, which gives a wealth of information about this important Makah settlement.

Kroeber, Theodora. 1965. *Ishi in Two Worlds*. University of California Press, Berkeley.
  This classic tale of the last "wild" California Indian is a must for every student of California archaeology.

Landberg, L. C. W. 1965. *The Chumash Indians of Southern California*. Southwest Museum, Los Angeles.
  A straightforward description of Chumash culture based on archaeological, anthropological, and historical evidence.

CHAPTER 12

THE GREAT BASIN AND WESTERN INTERIOR

The European immigrants of the 1850s and 1860s who penetrated the mountain fastnesses of the Rockies and moved beyond Utah's Wasatch Mountains into the Great Basin encountered only scattered bands of Indians west of the mountains. Here, small groups of Western Shoshone, Paiute, and Washoe roamed the land on foot. They lived by hunting small animals and foraging for desert roots and seeds, in a land of dramatic contrasts – high mountains and arid plains, deep canyons and occasional bountiful lakes, territory completely different from the Great Plains to the east (D'Azevado, 1986). Mobility, flexibility, and detailed ecological knowledge – these were always the secrets of survival in the Great Basin from the earliest human settlement of this varied region before 9000 BC.

The Great Basin Environment

The Great Basin comprises about 400,000 sq. miles (1,036,001 sq. km) of the west between the Rocky Mountains and the Sierra Nevada. A definition on hydrologic grounds commonly used by archaeologists includes nearly all of Nevada and parts of California, Oregon, Utah, and Idaho. This is a region of great environmental diversity, of high mountains and intervening valleys, with the loftiest peaks and deepest valleys in the south and west. Climate, vegetation, animals and human populations display great variations with topography, the lower temperatures and higher rainfall totals occurring at high elevations. The lowest rainfall and severest evaporation is in the arid southwestern portions of the Basin, which support the sparsest vegetation. The mountains have somewhat wetter and more complex climatic regimens, with many ranges supporting relatively dense vegetation and lakes or ponds. Despite these variations, most of the Great Basin receives little rainfall, and, as in other areas of low precipitation, the amount varies dramatically from year to year. This means that the potential plant food supply can be as much as six times more plentiful in a wet year than in a dry (Hutchings and Stewart, 1953). As a result, the prehistoric and historic peoples of the Great Basin have always subsisted on a very broad range of food resources. To specialize in one particular resource is to invite disaster (Jennings, 1978b). Throughout prehistory, there have been great variations in group size, group stability, and degree of sedentary settlement, variations depending on the

(Right) The Great Basin showing sites and regions mentioned in the text.

(Below) Southwestern Great Basin, looking northwest from the Greenwater Range, Inyo County, California: a landscape of mesas and basins. The distant Funeral Mountains are tilted blocks of Paleozoic rocks.

availability of food resources and the subsistence adaptations that developed to exploit them (Madsen, 1982).

None of the Great Basin drains to the sea, so over 150 more-or-less closed basins have developed over millions of years. During the Wisconsin glaciation, many of the basins were filled to overflowing by cool snow meltwater, joined by fish-rich rivers, and linked by green belts of vegetation (Mehringer, 1986). Woodlands grew where there is now treeless, arid steppe. Camels, wild horses, and mammoth grazed on open plains and on the fringes of great marshes. Between about 10,500 and 8600 BC, Early Holocene lakes shrank, many rivers dried up, and the lusher vegetation retreated northward and to high elevations. Most subsequent climatic shifts have been relatively minor.

The Great Basin became increasingly arid during the Middle Holocene, a time of rapid climatic fluctuations. Temperatures rose until about 4000 to 3000 BC, and drier conditions persisted until modern times. Not that climatic conditions were stable, for dramatic changes in local environments were possible even within the confines of a single year. The diverse environments of the Great Basin were dynamic and ever-changing, affecting human populations in many dramatic, cumulative ways. Everywhere, resource distribution was patchy, with highly productive areas separated from sparser environments. The environmental realities of the Basin resulted in constant population movements, basically conservative hunter-gatherer adaptations, and a broad, if varied, cultural continuum over wide areas. Some groups lived in exceptionally rich lake-side or marshy environments. They dwelt in larger, more sedentary camps for most of the year, perhaps enjoying more complex social organization. At the other end of the continuum were tiny family groups, constantly on the move, living off seasonal foods at widely separated locations. For all this variation, the same basic hunter-gatherer material culture remained in use throughout the Basin for thousands of years.

A viable, but generalized, model of Great Basin subsistence and settlement assumes such a continuum of human settlement, with differences in subsistence and settlement patterns being due to different optimal extraction strategies in areas of highly varied resource availability (Madsen, 1982). David Madsen uses this model to hypothesize that the earliest sites in the Basin were found in areas with the greatest concentration and productivity of resources, such as lake and riverine marshes. Relatively permanent settlements were primarily associated with such rich habitats. Following initial settlement, he believes there was population growth in productive environments, resulting in expansion into less productive environments.

Tree-ring studies from timber 2000 years or more old show that changing lake levels, treeline shifts, dune activity, and both earthquakes and volcanic eruptions could affect human populations in important ways. Game distributions would change, trade routes be cut off by deteriorating climate, vegetational cover be decimated by a sudden volcanic eruption. All of these, and many other local phenomena, made highly flexible and mobile adaptive strategies essential in all but the most favored of Great Basin environments.

Wherever prehistoric peoples lived in this vast area, they utilized a wide array of food resources. The utilization of these resources varied from

Great Basin plant staples. (Top) Colorado piñon. (Center) Honey mesquite, Prosopis juliflora, *with fruit. (Bottom) Mature pods of the screwbean,* Prosopis pubescens.

region to region, and from millennium to millennium, as a result of local and more widespread climatic changes. For instance, the distribution of piñon pines changed drastically during the Holocene, and peoples' exploitation of these vital nuts fluctuated dramatically through time. Human groups settled in every kind of high and low altitude imaginable. Regional surveys have identified many complex settlement patterns. For instance, detailed archaeological surveys of the Raft River mountains of northwestern Utah and the Goose Creek mountains of northeastern Nevada investigated all manner of prehistoric sites, everything from large caves to tiny open air camps (Wylie, 1971–72, quoted from Harper, 1986). Wylie found that no less than 82 percent of the sites investigated lay between 5000 and 7000 ft (1524 to 2133 m) above sea level, a diverse environment that supported sagebrush, juniper-piñon, and mountain brush. People seem to have avoided the hot and inhospitable deserts, where only 11 percent of their settlements were found. A further 7 percent lay above 7000 ft (2133 m), in high altitude environments that were inaccessible much of the year. Most of the medicinal plants known to have been used by Indians and found in these sites came from the favored zone. Rigorous environments above and below the foothill zones of the Great Basin tended to concentrate much of the prehistoric population and game animals in areas where most forage was to be found, and where winters were relatively benign.

The foothill zones supported not only deer and other game, but the plant foods upon which the Great Basin people depended (Jennings, 1978b). For thousands of years, the inhabitants used a variety of technologies for obtaining and processing plant foods of many kinds (C. Fowler, 1986). The seeds of nut pines, especially piñons, were much prized, especially in the central core areas of the Basin. During the early fall, the people used long poles to gather green cones by the thousand, carrying them to central processing stations in large baskets. They pit-roasted the cones until they opened and the seeds were partially released. Next, the foragers beat the pile of cones with sticks, or tapped individual cones against a flat anvil with a hammerstone. The extracted seeds were then given a preliminary parching in an open, fan-shaped tray, shelled with a flat grinding stone, and ground before being eaten in gruel form, mixed with hot or cold water.

Abundant piñon harvests were the rule in three-to seven-year cycles, so the people stored thousands of cones in open pits under piles of stones, grass- or bark-lined pits, or skin bags. Stored in this way, cones could last four or five years (Steward, 1943). By the same token, piñon groves were so important a resource that many groups considered different groves family property. Acorns were gathered on the western, southern, and eastern fringes of the Basin, and were less important than piñons. Mesquite (*Prosopis juliflora*) and screwbean (*Prosopis pubescens*) are desert plants found in the Mojave and Sonoran deserts. Their fresh pods were taken in the spring and eaten raw as snacks. In late summer and fall the people gathered dried-up pods, placed them in large tree-stump mortars and ground them to a fine powder. The bean meal was dried thoroughly in baskets, where it formed large cones that could be stored in pits for long periods of time. Like piñons, mesquite bean meal was a staple for many Great Basin people.

Agave (*Agave utahensis*) are natives of the hot southern deserts of the southern Great Basin and the Southwest. The plants were harvested in spring just before they flowered and the leaves baked in a communal pit for 24 hours. The sweet, dark mass of agave was then pounded into large, flat cakes that were used to flavor meat and vegetable stews.

Perhaps the most vital artifacts in the Great Basin were the wooden digging stick, the flat *metate* or grinding stone and the small stone muller. These simple artifacts enabled people to process an enormous range of seeds, plants, and tubers with the simplest of technologies. The people would harvest stands of grasses by knocking the seeds into baskets or gathering them by hand. Hardwood digging sticks assumed great importance when harvesting root crops, especially in the northern Basin, where biscuit roots (*Lomatium* spp), yampa (*Perideridia*), and other tubers were abundant in spring. Berries and other fruit were important crops wherever they were found, sometimes gathered by the women with special chest-mounted baskets. Most berries were sun dried and stored in pits and bags. Many plants had not only food value but important medicinal uses as well.

Below the foothill zones, river banks, marshes, and lakes acted as magnets for human settlement, offering a great diversity of food resources. People camped near the water for much of the year, except, perhaps, during summer when mosquitoes and other insects are a plague. Such areas were highly localized, but were always of the greatest importance to communities residing in their vicinity. Marshes were especially productive, not only because of their plant foods, but for their diverse game populations. Elsewhere in the Great Basin game is rarely seen, for the animal species of the deserts and mountains tend to be solitary and secretive, and invisible to

Hopi man from the Southwest using a digging stick, c.1915. Similar forms of artifact were used for excavating wild tubers for thousands of years in the Great Basin.

anyone but an expert tracker. But the marshes abound in wildlife. In spring, a visit to any large Great Basin marsh means a "sky likely to be full of raucous birds representing as many as 40 species with each individual intent on intimidating and expelling the intruder from the nesting ground" (Harper, 1986). Areas like the Humboldt-Carson Sink in Nevada have been major breeding and nesting grounds for waterfowl for thousands of years. It is no coincidence that some of the Great Basin's major archaeological sites are found near such marshes.

Bird hunting was most common in marshy areas where major north-south flyways for migrating waterfowl passed. Both land and water birds were taken with nets suspended on sticks, or driven into netting tunnels. The hunters often used blinds to shoot birds, luring waterfowl with finely made tule reed decoys. Some expert fowlers swam up to their prey wearing a duckskin helmet or a mound of reeds. They would then grab the unsuspecting bird by the legs.

Not only waterfowl, but a diverse mammal fauna lived in the same marshes. Muskrats, rabbits, and many other rodents abounded. Grasses, wild vegetables and many rhizomes were harvested at the marsh margins in spring and fall, while tule reeds (*Scirpus acutus*) made fine mats, and other plants such as dogbane and milkweed provided ideal fibers for cords and basketry.

The forests and meadows at higher elevations were attractive hunting grounds for deer, pronghorns, and bighorn sheep in summer, as well as yielding harvests of gooseberries, strawberries, and other plant foods. The hunters used many techniques, sometimes stalking their prey in skin disguises, using snares and traps, and with cooperative game drives.

Throughout the Great Basin, prehistoric people fished in lakes and rivers, large and small. Along the Snake and Truckee rivers, for example, the fishermen built platforms out from the bank to fish with dip nets or spear their catch. Large gill nets harvested trout, chub, and other species in shallow waters, while basket traps and rock or brush dams were effective in many situations. Sometimes, women would even scoop fish from still water with shallow baskets.

With such a diversity of environments and altitudes, it is difficult to generalize about Great Basin hunter-gatherer diet in prehistoric times. The lake- and river-side peoples of Pyramid Lake and Walker River in Nevada may have obtained as much as 50 percent of their diet from fish, and a further 20 percent from large and small game, with the balance coming from wild plant sources. In contrast, the inhabitants of the Owens Valley region of the Sierra Nevada relied on wild plants for over half their food, the rest being game meat, with fishing accounting for but 10 percent. Whatever the Great Basin environment, wild plant foods provided a significant, and often the dominant, part of the diet. These were foods that tended to be low in protein, elements that had to be obtained from meat or fish. Such a diet makes the carbohydrates from plant foods of much greater importance than usual. Perhaps it is significant that pine nuts were a staple over so much of the Basin, for they are a valuable protein source, also exceptionally high in both fats and carbohydrates.

In such a diverse series of environments, where food resources are both patchy, and subject to cycles of plenty and scarcity, it is hardly surprising that the historic Great Basin peoples deliberately "managed" parts of their environment to increase its productivity and to conserve precious resources. Many groups burned the natural vegetation to increase natural yields of such plants as tobacco and a variety of seed-bearing grasses. Burning also served to increase available fodder for deer and other game, as well as helping drive prey toward waiting hunters. In historic times, several Great Basin groups such as the Shoshone not only burned the natural vegetation but scattered wild seeds as well (Steward, 1941).

Throughout most of the Great Basin the native Americans remained hunter-gatherers throughout prehistoric times, essentially preserving the Archaic lifeway right up to European contact in the 17th century AD. This general hunter-gatherer adaptation lasted for at least 10,000 years, from Early Archaic times onward. Even where agricultural economies did take hold, people still relied heavily on game and wild vegetable foods. However, as David Madsen (1982) and other authors have pointed out, it is a mistake to use the historic inhabitants of the Great Basin as ethnographic blueprints for interpreting earlier prehistoric cultures. Their adaptations were another example of the highly flexible, opportunistic way in which humans adapted to one of the most diverse environments in North America.

Conceptual Frameworks

For years, the Great Basin was regarded as peripheral to adjacent areas like California and the Southwest (Condie and Fowler, 1986; Fowler, D. and Jennings, 1982). The Pecos classification was transferred from the Southwest to the Great Basin, on the argument that culture traits spread from areas where they were most elaborately developed. Since there were some Southwestern traits to be found in the Great Basin, the area was considered tangential to mainstream cultural developments elsewhere.

The advent of radiocarbon dating showed conclusively that many Southwestern traditions were derived from much earlier cultures, some of which occurred in the Great Basin, a quite independent culture area in its own right. Jesse Jennings excavated the deep deposits of Danger Cave in Utah and used the long sequence of human occupation there to offer a new interpretation of Basin prehistory based on anthropologist Julian Steward's theory (1938) that ecological factors regulated population densities, local subsistence economies, and patterns of social organization in the region. Jennings formulated the concept of a Desert Culture that persisted for thousands of years, a culture whose behavior could be interpreted by using the general patterns of pre-European behavior proposed by Steward's pioneer work on Numic speakers in the Basin (Jennings and Norbeck, 1955; Jennings, 1957; Steward, 1938).

The Desert Culture concept came under attack from several directions. Some people argued that the Danger Cave sequence was too incomplete for such generalizations, that Jennings had ignored local variations (Baumhoff and Heizer, 1965). Furthermore, the Jennings model assumed that climatic change had been relatively uniform over large distances and over long periods of times, something that many archaeologists found it hard to accept (Fowler, D. and Jennings, 1982). The Desert Culture was a valuable idea, for it triggered a great deal of detailed local research. As a result, the

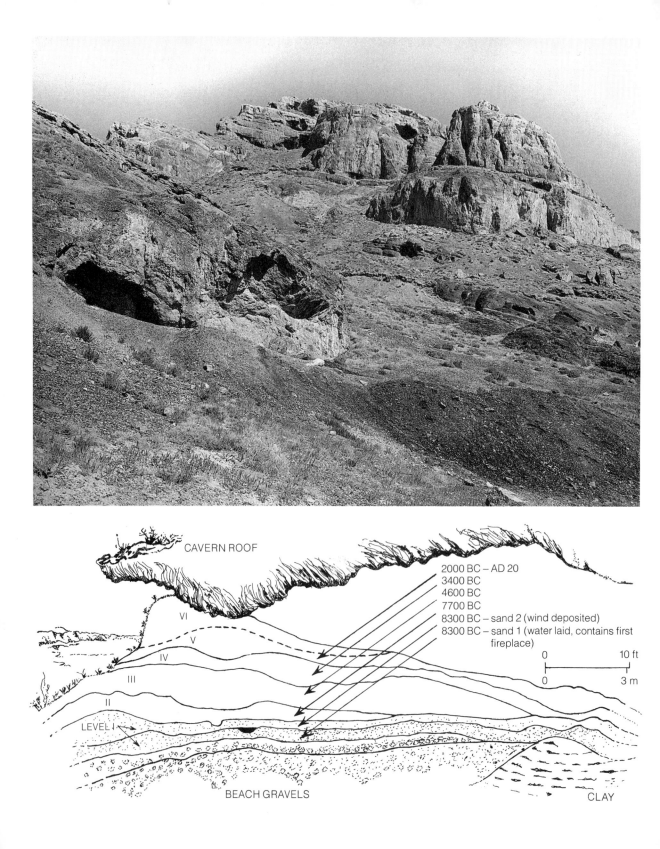

CAVERN ROOF

VI

V

IV

III

II

LEVEL I

2000 BC – AD 20
3400 BC
4600 BC
7700 BC
8300 BC – sand 2 (wind deposited)
8300 BC – sand 1 (water laid, contains first fireplace)

0   10 ft

0   3 m

BEACH GRAVELS

CLAY

Danger Cave, Utah. (Opposite) General view, and stratigraphic profile of the cave with estimated dates of layers extrapolated from radiocarbon from three laboratories. (Above left) Clockwise from top left: wooden knife handle; arrowshaft with broken projectile in place; twined matting; coiled basketry; milling stone; coarse cloth. (Above right) Gaming sticks, the longest 27 cm in length.

concept was abandoned, even by Jennings himself, being transformed into the Desert (or Western) Archaic. This coincided with a general, North America-wide Archaic culture stage, a time when prehistoric Americans hunted and foraged, a versatile adaptation that led to many local variations in toolkit and subsistence patterns – such as occur in the Great Basin and elsewhere.

For years, descriptive culture-historical approaches dominated Great Basin archaeology. In recent years, they have been replaced by descriptive ecological approaches, that also owe a debt to Julian Steward's ecological researches of the 1930s (O'Connell, and others, 1982). Research has shifted away from single sites to an approach focused on overall settlement-subsistence systems within individual valleys, watersheds, or sub-areas. A large site like Danger Cave or Hogup Cave in Utah, or Lovelock Cave in Nevada, may contain long sequences of prehistoric occupation, but the archaeological record in their deposits only represents a single stop in a complicated annual round of hunting and foraging. This approach has been highly productive in such areas as the Reese River Valley, Nevada (Thomas and Bettinger, 1976), in the Monitor Valley (Thomas, 1983), and in the Surprise Valley, California (O'Connell, 1975). These approaches have been combined with important advances in research design, simulation studies, and the use of sampling strategies. They have led to models that stress the basic continuum among prehistoric Great Basin societies, from small, family-based hunter-gatherer groups to much larger, more sedentary societies, perhaps with more complex social organization, that flourished in resource-rich areas (Madsen, 1982).

James O'Connell and others (1982) have argued that the descriptive ecological approach is a valuable strategy, but that it is unable to explain why the relationships between humans and their environment take the form they do. Thus, this approach cannot contribute to the comprehensive reconstruction of prehistoric behavioral systems that may have been quite unlike those known from historical Great Basin societies. Nor can descriptive ecology explain why prehistoric cultural systems change.

O'Connell and his colleagues argue that the unified, uniformitarian theoretical perspective of evolutionary ecology may provide a new approach. Evolutionary ecology is based on the proposition that variation in the behavior of individual organisms is shaped by natural selection.

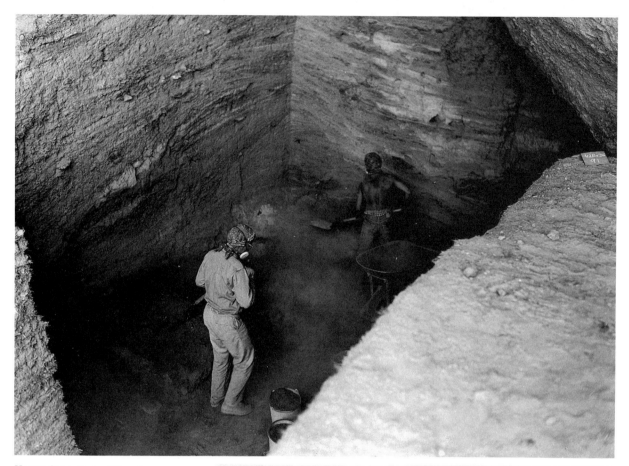

*Hogup Cave, Utah. (Above)
Excavations in progress. (Right)
Incised stones; the significance of the
incised patterns is unknown.*

Hogup Cave, Utah. (Above left) Elk tooth necklace. (Above right) Anthropomorphic figurines.

Thus, it identifies a single goal, the maximization of potential reproductive success, toward which all behavior is directed and in terms of which it can be predicted. An example of this approach is the use of optimal foraging strategy, a theoretical model that argues that the most efficient foraging strategies will be adopted by human groups – those that produce the greatest return in energy relative to time and effort expended (see Chapter 5). For example, seeds were added to Great Basin diet after 6500 BC, a dietary change that is widely agreed to be connected with Early Holocene climatic change. The mechanisms of the changeover are poorly understood. The optimal foraging model argues that resources can be ranked according to the ratio of gains made from consuming them (in calories) relative to the cost of collecting and processing them (measured in time). The proportions of resources exploited vary according to the abundance of the highest ranked ones. In the Great Basin, the extinction of Ice Age big-game, a high-ranked resource, may have led to the addition of more seeds to the diet, probably lower ranked food than game meat.

Research using evolutionary ecology is in its early stages, but such an approach may be peculiarly suitable for Great Basin conditions, where arid conditions often preserve a wide range of ancient food remains. With such complete preservation, optimal foraging strategy models may offer a way of making specific predictions about continuity and change in Great Basin prehistoric subsistence economies, integrating population densities, resource abundance, and technology. The same models may enable the archaeologist to identify precise information to test them in the field, information on resource ranking obtained from ethnographic information, historical records, or from experimentation with traditional tools and techniques. Once these rankings are developed, one can then try and trace their relative importance over long periods of time.

The description of Great Basin prehistory that follows reflects not only these new approaches, but the broad culture-historical framework that has been developed over generations of field research. As is the case in other parts of North America, this framework is based on stone artifact typologies, often projectile points (Table 12.1 next page; Thomas, 1981).

TABLE 12.1

Projectile Point Typology in the Great Basin

Projectile point typology in the Great Basin is complicated by considerable geographical variation, and substantial disagreements between local archaeologists. The so-called Berkeley Typological System was in widespread use until the 1970s (Hester, 1973, Heizer and Hester, 1978), but this has been revised in recent years. The scheme that follows relies heavily on David Hurst Thomas' researches in Monitor Valley, Nevada, and elsewhere in the western Basin (Thomas, 1981). His excavations and analyses quantified the original definitions so anyone could replicate them, and confirmed the original chronology proposed by earlier workers.

Corner-Notched Projectile Points

Gatecliff Series (*c.*3000 to 1300 BC). Medium to large contracting stem projectile points, further subdivided into: Split stem points with contracting stems and concave bases, commonly referred to as Pinto points and a contracting stem type with straight, pointed, or convex base. Some Gatecliff Series points may also predate 3000 BC.

Elko Series (1300 BC to AD 700). Large, corner-notched points with concave, straight, or slightly concave bases. Two widely recognized forms, one with corner notches, the other with ears on the base (O'Connell, 1967).

Rosegate Series (AD 700 to 1300). Small, corner-notched points, once known as Rose Spring and East Gate types. The two types grade into one another, the stem expanding slightly.

Unfortunately, there is such diversity of prehistoric populations in the Great Basin that it is impossible to construct a chronological framework that brings together neatly cultural connections across the desert west. Some scholars even argue that local adaptations are so diverse that it is pointless even to try. In the interests of convenience and clarity, we have superimposed four general prehistoric periods across the Great Basin (Jennings, 1986). (For more detailed regional descriptions, the reader is referred to the essays in Madsen and O'Connell, 1982.)

Side-Notched Projectile Points

Desert Series (post AD 1300). Desert Side-notched forms dating to after AD 1300 are small, triangular points with notches high on the sides. Large Side-notched forms may be older than the Desert form, but remain undated. This series subsumes many earlier point terms in the literature.

Unshouldered Projectile Points

The earliest unshouldered points are the Triple T Concave Base form, represented by a few specimens at Gatecliff Shelter and dated between about 3400 and 3200 BC. These have concave bases and rounded basal projections.

Humboldt Series (*c.*3000 BC to AD 700). Unnotched, lanceolate points with concave bases of variable size. There are numerous varieties of Humboldt Series point.

Cottonwood Leaf-shaped and Triangular (post-AD 1300). Round-based and small, unnotched triangular points. Cottonwood points are widespread through the Great Basin after AD 1300.

The above is a simple summary of a complex typological problem. For full details and distinguishing criteria, see Thomas, 1981.

Paleo-Indian
before 10,000 BC to 7000 BC

The first human settlement of the Great Basin dates to before 10,000 BC, but the exact date is uncertain (Chapters 4 and 6). Population densities remained extremely sparse for thousands of years, with most Paleo-Indian settlement centered around lakes and along river banks where game was more abundant. Judging from fossil finds in caves and rockshelters, wild horses, camels, bison, mammoth, and other species flourished in the Basin. As elsewhere, they became extinct by about 8000 BC (Grayson, 1982).

Early Desert Archaic in the Eastern and Northern Great Basin
*c.*7500 BC to 2000 BC

The major adaptive shift in Great Basin life came around 7500 BC with the beginning of the Early Archaic. The inhabitants responded to the increasing aridity, the extinction of Ice Age megafauna, and the localization of resources by exploiting a far more diverse food base. In particular, they relied much more heavily on processed seeds, a shift reflected by the appearance of milling stones and other processing artifacts in the archaeological record. As the climate continued to warm up and many lakes and marshes dried up, Basin groups adopted far more complex settlement patterns that had them making use of semi-permanent winter base camps with basic storage facilities. In the northern and eastern Basin, much data for Archaic occupation comes from lake-margin dry cave sites around the Great Salt Lake in Utah (Aikens, 1982; Madsen, 1982). Perhaps these represent a skewed view of Archaic life in the region, but wide-ranging surveys suggest that, in fact, much human settlement was concentrated near this and other large lakes (Aikens and Madsen, 1986). Many of these caves have remained completely dry for thousands of years. Three of them – Danger Cave near Wendover, Utah, on the Nevada border (Jennings, 1957), Hogup Cave 75 miles (120.6 km) northwest of Salt Lake City (Aikens, 1970), and Sudden Shelter in central Utah (Jennings and others, 1980) – provide an exceptional record of Archaic life.

These and other less well-known locations contain deep deposits of rock spalls from their ceilings, windblown dust, droppings and other leavings from bats, packrats, wild sheep, and other animals – and debris from repeated human occupation. The deposits accumulated over thousands of years, reaching depths of 11 ft (3.3 m) at Danger Cave, and up to 14 ft (4.2 m) at Hogup. The human accumulations include not only stone and bone artifacts and food remains, but objects made of hide, fur, feathers, horn, sinew, grass, wood, and bark. Desiccated human feces survive by the hundred, documenting actual meals eaten thousands of years ago. The inhabitants carried grass, twigs, seeds, and bulrushes into the caves, which appear in layers stratified one above the other, as if the sites were occupied intermittently over immensely long periods of time.

Danger, Hogup, and Sudden Shelter provide such a complete picture of early prehistoric occupation in the eastern Great Basin that they have been used to divide the local late Paleo-Indian and Archaic into three technological and chronological periods.

Bonneville Period (9000 to 7500 BC) takes its name from the great Ice Age lake of that name, now a dry basin that forms much of the eastern Great Basin. Human occupation was sparse at best, but a few people camped in Danger Cave, lighting fires on the clean, sandy floor and leaving a scatter of stone flakes and milling stones there about 9000 BC (Jennings, 1957).

The Bonneville period occupation may be contemporary with, or later than, the scattered Paleo-Indian settlement of the Basin. Many fluted and stemmed points have been found around the margins of Early Holocene lakes throughout the Great Basin, but the relationships between them are still confused. Aikens and Madsen point out (1986) that the Bonneville period dates to a time of considerable environmental change. It may have been a time of transition between Paleo-Indian big-game hunting and the long-lived Desert Archaic tradition that followed.

Wendover Period (7500 to 4000 BC). The Wendover is an Early Archaic cultural tradition named after the town of that name on the Utah/Nevada border. Unlike earlier Bonneville occupation, Wendover sites are found at many different altitudes and in a wide variety of environmental settings. Everything points to a mobile lifeway, in which settlement sites, often at familiar locations, were occupied at different times of the year. People hunted and foraged year-round, but the balance between these activities varied considerably at different seasons, with plant collecting assuming major importance at harvest time.

The lower levels of Danger and Hogup Caves testify to the great importance of plants in Wendover diet. The inhabitants relied heavily on pickleweed (*Allenrolfea occidentalis*), a low-growing succulent that flourishes on the edge of salt pans and dried-up lake beds. Large stands of pickleweed were a staple, but the people also collected cattails, bulrush, and other marsh plants, as well as many other species. They gathered the harvest in coiled and twined baskets, then dried or parched the gathered seeds in tightly woven basketry trays, tossing them with some hot embers. Then they hulled and ground the seeds with hand stones and milling slabs, perhaps making them into cakes or gruel (Aikens and Madsen, 1986).

The Wendover people who visited Hogup Cave hunted deer, pronghorn antelope, wild sheep, and bison. The cave deposits included 32 species of small animals and 34 of birds, many of which must have been taken and consumed by humans. Spearthrowers, stone-tipped and wooden spears, sometimes used with foreshafts, sufficed to dispatch many larger animals. The snaring and netting of rabbits, hares, and other rodents, also birds, was very important at Hogup during these millennia (Aikens, 1970). Judging from the fragments of nets and cordage in the deposits, the hunters used the same basic trapping methods that were employed in historic times. They would stretch long nets across narrow defiles, then drive dozens of rabbits into the broad traps with mass drives. Some simple loop snares came from Hogup, too, designed to catch the foot of a walking bird or of the many rodents that lived in the cave.

The hunters processed their quarry with stone-tipped knives and scrapers, not only consuming the meat but using animal byproducts to make leather containers, and the bones as awls and needles for sewing and basketry, also netmaking. The people wore simple clothing, such as blankets fashioned from rabbit fur and transverse strands of plant fiber. These multi-purpose garments could serve for both clothing and sleeping. Woven fiber sandals protected the feet (Jennings and others, 1980).

Black Rock Period (4000 BC to AD 500). After 4000 BC, population densities rose, and many more human settlements flourished near the Great Salt

Lake, also at higher elevations and in areas that were hitherto apparently unsettled. The Black Rock period saw a continued trend toward greater aridity, with shrinking lakes, and perhaps a decrease in the availability of food resources close to the water. Human populations may have responded by adopting an even more mobile lifeway and by making greater use of upland piñon-juniper resources as well as mountain sheep, deer, and rabbits taken at higher elevations. Much of this hunting may have been the work of small family groups ranging far away from more permanent lake-side settlements (Madsen, 1982).

The Black Rock period is named after the cave of that name close to the southern end of the Great Salt Lake at the foot of the Oquirrh Mountains (Madsen, 1983). In strictly technological terms, the changeover is marked by the appearance of new and highly characteristic Elko and Gypsum projectile point forms that replace earlier designs. Artifacts of this period abound not only at Danger and Hogup Caves, but at many new settlements.

Later in the period, about 2000 BC, the annual rainfall increased to effectively several times more than the Holocene average, with a resulting increase in local resource productivity. At the same time, lake levels rose significantly, sometimes flooding prized springs and marshes. At Hogup Cave, for example, the people were forced to change their subsistence activities significantly. Waterfowl and shore birds practically vanished from the deposits by about 1000 BC, for the marshy lake bed nearby had disappeared. The site was occupied more intermittently, seed utilization declined, and rabbits were less commonly taken (Harper and Alder, 1970; Aikens and Madsen, 1986; Mehringer, 1977).

Similar adjustments to subsistence activities may have occurred at Danger Cave and other settlements, but were by no means universal. The Desert Archaic lifeway persisted with local adjustments that reflected local environmental change. The people still relied heavily on a wide variety of plants and animals and used the same basic technology as their predecessors. About the most significant innovation came late in the Black Rock period, when the bow and stone-tipped arrow replaced the spear and atlatl. Projectile points became much smaller, even if they retained the same basic stem and corner-notched designs as their predecessors.

About AD 400 to 500, small amounts of pottery and occasional domesticated maize cobs appear in Black Rock sites, innovations that came to the eastern Great Basin and northern Colorado from sedentary horticultural societies in the Southwest. The new traits did not lead to any dramatic changes in Archaic life, for hunting and gathering still remained the subsistence staples, as they had for millennia. But piñon nuts became a major element in eastern Basin diet at about this time (Madsen, 1985). By AD 800, settled "Fremont" horticultural people had settled in many parts of the northern Colorado plateau and in the eastern Great Basin (Marwitt, 1986), and a new economy had taken hold in these long settled areas (see below).

Desert Archaic in the Western Great Basin and Interior California
*c.*5000 BC to European contact

The Desert Archaic traditions of this vast area were as diverse as those of contemporary groups to the east (Thomas, 1982; Elston, 1982; 1986). As in the east, the drying trend of the Early and Middle Holocene dried up many of the surface lakes, with temperatures reaching their maximum between about 3100 and 2200 BC.

Early Archaic (c.5000 BC to 2000 BC). The Early Archaic is poorly documented in the central and western Basin and may have begun sometime between 5000 and 4000 BC, somewhat later than in the north and east (Elston, 1986). Good archaeological data for characteristic Gatecliff series points come from only the latter part of this period, between 3300 and 1300 BC (Thomas, 1981). There is a possibility that the central and western Basin were unoccupied during the very Early Archaic. Big-game hunting may still have been important, but many finds of grinding equipment testify to the importance of seeds and plants in the diet.

The best evidence for Early Archaic occupation comes from the Carson and Humboldt Sinks of the Lahontan Basin. Human occupation of the Lahontan Basin intensified after 3000 BC, with intermittent use of the famous Lovelock Cave overlooking the Humboldt Sink starting as early as 2580 BC (Heizer and Napton, 1970).

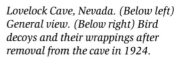

Lovelock Cave, Nevada. (Below left) General view. (Below right) Bird decoys and their wrappings after removal from the cave in 1924.

General map of the Carson Sink area
showing the location of Lovelock and
Hidden Caves. The heavy line delimits
the territory of the historic Toedökadö
people (see p.238).

Lovelock and other large caves were used predominantly as storage places or for burials by people living in residential base camps near lakes and sinks. Most such settlements are now marked by little more than small scatters of stone artifacts. The Cocanour locality on the Humboldt Sink has yielded two shallow, circular house depressions between 7.8 and 11.1 ft (2.4 to 3.4 m) across. The houses were surrounded with projectile points, scrapers, and other waste as well as *manos* and *metates*. Early Archaic

Toedökadö ("Tule Eaters") territory
● Hamlet (noted by DeQuille)
○ Hamlet, seasonal or abandoned (noted by DeQuille)

Stream
Lake
Intermittent salty water

Nevada
area of enlargement

5 0 5 mi. 15 20
5 0 5 km. 15 20
magnetic north at center of sheet
contour interval 1000 ft.

peoples in the Lahontan Basin apparently subsisted on a diet of fish, birds, cattails, and piñon nuts (Thomas, 1970). Pacific marine shells and obsidian from both western Nevada and California document barter networks reaching far over the coastal mountains to the west.

Middle Archaic (c.2000 BC to AD 500). The climate was now cooler and moister, with a resulting appearance of shallow lakes and marshes in areas where they had hitherto never existed. There were no great technological or subsistence changes, but local populations increased, with more diverse exploitation of food resources, and a trend toward repeated reoccupation of winter base camps and seasonal settlements. Trade in marine shells, obsidian from volcanic rocks north of the Owens Valley, and in other exotics became ever more important.

While mountain sheep hunting was important in the Central subregion, and both big-game hunting and seed collecting staples on the Sierra Nevada slopes, the best-documented Middle Archaic settlements come from the Lahontan Basin, where lakeshore and marsh environments were exploited intensively. In some areas, village-like settlements served as base camps for the exploitation of lake resources. Lovelock Cave has yielded a bounty of finds that testify to the diverse lifeway along the Humboldt Sink. The people caught fish of every size from minnows upward, especially Lahontan chub, with nets, traps, and bone fishhooks. They used life-like duck decoys made of tule reed, some even covered with fully feathered skins removed from real birds. Sometimes the hunters would swim close to waterfowl using stuffed necks and heads of water birds for the purpose. The dry cave deposits yielded feathers from pelicans, herons, ducks, and geese, also the nets sometimes used for taking them.

We know a great deal about Middle Archaic diet at Lovelock from human coprolites. Over 90 percent of the foods in the cave came from the Humboldt-Carson sink nearby. The plants included bulrush and cattail, also wetland grasses like *Elymus* and *Panicum* that were staples. The Tui chub, ducks, and mudhens were favorite foods. The abundance and diversity of food resources apparently made it possible for the inhabitants to live in the same area for most of the year. Many of the plant foods found at Lovelock were harvested in fall and stored for winter use. The cold season was a good time for hunting waterfowl and collecting rhizomes of water plants.

The interpretation of Great Basin lake-side adaptations as revealed in sites like Lovelock has led to competing hypotheses. One long-held "limnosedentary" view argues that the inhabitants of desert lake environments enjoyed such predictable and diverse resources that they rarely had to move from their bases, indeed enjoyed a virtually sedentary residence pattern (Heizer and Napton, 1970). Heizer, Napton, and others based their arguments on the coprolite analyses from Lovelock Cave, which revealed a local diet of which 90 percent came from the lacustrine resources of the Carson Sink (see also Madsen and Lindsay, 1977). A contrasting "limnomobile" hypothesis argues that statements about sedentary settlement are based on single sites, not on a series of locations that reflect subsistence activities throughout the year. Limnosedentary living could have been a feature of local life for only a few weeks, Lovelock being but a snapshot of a small portion of a regular seasonal round, critics argue. Furthermore, the excessive costs of obtaining, processing, and storing marsh resources like cattail seeds, waterfowl, and fish may have made them less satisfactory staples than foods like piñon nuts. Thus, the inhabitants of desert lake environments were as mobile as bands living away from the water.

David Hurst Thomas (1985) excavated the Archaic deposits of Hidden Cave immediately south of Lovelock Cave and the Carson Sink to test these competing hypotheses. This was a comprehensive regional investigation that involved not only reexcavating the cave itself, but modeling lacustrine resource and possible subsistence strategies through use of ethnographic and historical records. Thomas found that the historic Toedökadö combined both foraging and collecting, strategies forced upon them by distances between resources and competing seasons for gathering different foods. During the winters they maintained relatively stable home bases either near marshes or in the nearby uplands, depending on stored food supplies and the condition of the marshlands. In spring and summer, families moved out to forage for food at many scattered locations, coming together in fall at the time of the piñon harvests. The excavations in Hidden Cave itself were combined with a regional survey. The grasses, seeds, fish bones, and piñon nut remains from the deposits revealed a location where people visited in spring and summer, months when they also consumed some stored foods and fish carried over some distance, the remains of which were identified in coprolites. Hidden Cave was also a place where visitors stored artifacts such as projectile points and worked wood in carefully prepared caches. People also stored what can loosely be called

Excavations in progress at Hidden Cave, Nevada, in 1979.

"low-ranked" foods and spare foods in the cave, a reflection of a constant concern with possible famine. Some of these low-ranked foods may have been consumed on the march, to sustain energy along the trail. The cave contained few artifacts used for exploiting marsh-side resources – birds or fish – artifacts that were commonplace at Lovelock. Perhaps, argues Thomas, Hidden Cave was a spring/summer location, while Lovelock was occupied during the winter.

Thomas believes that both the limnosedentary and limnomobile hypotheses are too extreme to be viable interpretations of desert lake adaptations. Rather, he believes that Hidden Cave, and many other such locations, were visited for centuries, serving at times as a kind of warehouse, at times as a place where the dead were buried, and often as a summer camp where one could escape the oppressive heat. The visitors to this and other caves were both foragers and collectors, hunter-gatherers adapted to an environment where resources were widely separated, relatively predictable and sometimes storable, even if their yield fluctuated wildly. Under these circumstances, sedentary settlement was impossible, but long stays at some locations during the winter months were possible.

Late Archaic (AD *500 to European contact and beyond*). The climate of the western Great Basin became warmer and drier about the time of Christ, a trend that persisted for about 500 years. The change was relatively mild, but significant technological changes occurred. The bow and arrow replaced the spear and atlatl, with accompanying smaller and lighter Rose Spring and Eastgate projectile points, while pottery appeared after AD 1000. At the same time, people began to use much more elaborate plant processing equipment, a reflection, perhaps, of new subsistence strategies that involved exploiting a more diverse resource base and different ecological zones. Plant foods and small game like rabbits assumed great importance.

Some authorities believe the appearance of these new technological artifices may reflect the expansion of Numic speakers into the Great Basin from southern California within the past 1000 years (Lamb, 1958). A case can also be made for an indigenous, long-term development of Numic tongues in the Great Basin itself. However, as Bettinger and Baumhoff have argued somewhat controversially (1982), the more intensive subsistence strategies now in use slightly resemble those found to the west, in California, in historic times. These new strategies were higher in cost, sustained higher population densities, and made more use of hard-to-process small seeds and less of large animals. They believe that the competitive advantages of these new high-cost strategies may have facilitated the spread of Numic-speakers into the Basin.

The least-known area of the Great Basin is the extreme southwest, the vast area of the Mojave Desert. Dry, low-lying, and intensely hot in the summer, the desert offered meager fare for its prehistoric inhabitants, with only mesquites and agave providing dependable, nutritious staples. Human occupation spans at least 10,000 years, with two discernible trends: an increasing use of hill and mountain resources and a low reliance on processed seeds until surprisingly late, about 2000 years ago. In contrast, milling stones, the indicators of seed processing, appear as early as 10,000 years ago in the northern Great Basin and about 8000 years ago in California.

The high-altitude Alta Toquima site under investigation.

The Late Archaic throughout the western Basin is marked by a rising importance in plant gathering and processing, and by the exploitation of very diverse food resources. In the central subregion, the Alta Toquima village on Mount Jefferson documents a high-altitude base camp with substantial circular rock-walled houses and storage areas. Between about 2000 and 1000 BC, Alta Toquima was a hunting camp, but the later occupants lived there longer, processing plants as well as hunting. Perhaps both men and women visited the settlement, living there longer than in earlier centuries (Thomas, 1982). Another series of high-altitude sites comes from high in the White Mountains of eastern California. In the Grass Valley area of central Nevada, piñons were a staple, so abundant that many groups lived in comparatively sedentary villages, precursors of large Western Shoshone villages in historic times. The Owens Valley saw a decrease in upland hunting in favor of low-altitude settlement, a shift that coincides with historic Paiute culture, a culture that made use of irrigation to water wild plant stands. This adaptation required permanent settlement in the lowlands.

Throughout the western Great Basin, the Archaic adaptation involved gathering large surpluses of seasonal foods and storing them for winter use. This meant that the people often built substantial base camps with ample storage facilities, fanning out into special camps at different times of the year.

The Desert Archaic in all its diversity was an adaptation that was based on opportunism and flexibility, so much so that the same basic lifeway persisted for thousands of years. Lakes would dry up during cycles of arid climate. The people would adapt by moving away from the dried up basin and exploiting higher altitudes with apparently little effort or social change. When rainfall increased and lakes appeared, they would congregate along the marshy shores, adopting a new annual round that took advantage of the new diversity of food resources.

The Great Basin was never a stable environment, but a highly diverse one that changed constantly. Populations increased gradually over the millennia, exploiting new resources as they appeared, such as the piñon-juniper woodland that expanded over parts of the Basin after the Middle Holocene. As Robert Elston remarks (1986), the Archaic peoples of the western Great Basin resisted "change through change" with subtle technological innovations and intensive exploitation of a wide range of food resources. Had not European expansion disrupted and overwhelmed the age-old Archaic lifeway, it would have continued indefinitely.

The Fremont Culture and Great Basin Horticulture
AD 400 to 1300

About four centuries after Christ, more or less sedentary horticultural communities appeared in eastern Nevada, western Colorado, and southern Idaho, as well as much of Utah. These "Fremont" people lived in scattered farmsteads and small villages, their culture displaying some Southwestern pueblo traits (Marwitt, 1986). After nine centuries, these people disappeared and Archaic societies continued to flourish in the Great Basin until the arrival of European settlers. Ever since the days when the Great Basin was considered a periphery of the Southwest, the Fremont culture has generated controversy.

Origins. The "Fremont culture" was named by archaeologist Noel Morss after the river of that name in south-central Utah, a drainage where he located many farming sites (Morss, 1931). Morss and others recognized many Southwestern traits in Fremont culture, including pit houses, stone architecture, pottery, and maize cultivation. He believed that the local Archaic people adopted farming from Southwestern contacts, perhaps as a result of a population movement from the south. His ideas left many questions unanswered. Did the Fremont culture emerge from a Desert Archaic base, with an infusion of culture traits from the Anasazi region of the Southwest (Jennings, 1957)? Or did people actually migrate from the Southwest for a while, then return to their ancestral homeland centuries later (Wormington, 1955)? Or were they Great Plains people who moved into the Great Basin, then withdrew in the face of Numic-speakers expanding from the west (Aikens, 1967)? The controversy remains unresolved (for discussion, see Madsen, 1980).

It is difficult to develop a viable hypothesis about Fremont origins, for Fremont occupation appears at different times in different places. Melvin Aikens (1970) found a clear transition from Archaic to Fremont at Hogup Cave after AD 400. The people simply added pottery, maize, and other Fremont artifacts to their traditional Archaic culture without any apparent disruption of their lifeway. Elsewhere, Fremont occupation dates to as late as AD 800 to 900. So far, no one has been able to pin down the beginning date with any greater accuracy. This may be because different regional populations had different ethnic origins – in the Great Basin itself, on the Great Plains (for northern Fremont sites show strong Plains influence (Aikens, 1966)), or in the Southwest. David Madsen believes (1979) that there were two or maybe three groups in the Fremont area that shared little more than some common artifacts, perhaps acquired through trade, and some common religious beliefs expressed in rock art, or by anthropomorphic clay figurines. This theory is difficult to support with hard evidence, but it has the advantage of accounting for a wide range of beginning dates and for the great variation in Fremont culture.

Whatever the ultimate origins of the Fremont, there can be little doubt that there was a strong indigenous tradition in this farming culture, one that stemmed from the great environmental diversity of the Great Basin, and from the specialized nature of many of the Archaic adaptations in it.

Fremont Culture: clay figurines, from the Old Woman site. Height of tallest c.11.5 cm.

(Left) Fremont ceramic vessels from, left to right, Caldwell Village, Evans Mound, Snake Rock, and Evans Mound. Height of tallest c.27 cm.

(Center of page) Fremont bowl from Grantsville Mound (Ivie Creek Black on White); diameter 26 cm.

(Above) Fremont pipes from Evans Mound, top, and Nephi Mound.

(Left) Fremont moccasins from Hogup Cave, left, and Promontory Cave, right.

Fremont rock paintings from the Great Gallery, Barrier Canyon, Utah.

Regional Variation. Fremont culture displays so much variation that some authorities question whether the term has any practical use at all (Marwitt, 1986). However, Fremont persists, if only as a convenient label that subsumes a multiplicity of local cultural names. This local variation is characteristic of Fremont from its first appearance, presumably reflecting the great diversity of Basin environments and the Archaic cultures that flourished in them. John Marwitt (1970, 1986) has identified five major, but provisional, geographical variants of Fremont culture, variants distinguished by characteristic artifacts, subsistence patterns, and settlement patterns. Each has links to the others, but they are each a distinctive adaptation to local conditions (see Table 12.2).

The End of the Fremont Culture (c. AD 1250 to 1350). By the mid-14th century AD, most Fremont people had abandoned the Great Basin and the Colorado Plateau, except, perhaps in the north. The same droughts of the so-called Little Ice Age that affected the entire globe in the early second millennium and decimated Anasazi societies south and east on the Colorado Plateau eliminated maize cultivation as a viable subsistence strategy throughout the Fremont area.

Was population replacement also involved? Some scholars argue that there is no evidence for cultural continuity between Fremont peoples and historic, Numic-speaking groups like the Shoshone. They believe that Numic-speakers expanded into the Great Basin somewhere between AD 1250 and 1450. To have been ancestral Shoshone and Paiute as well as Fremont peoples, the Numic migration would have had to have taken place four to five centuries earlier – and there is no evidence that it did.

Given the great diversity of the Fremont culture, and the high degree of flexibility in Great Basin adaptations, it is most unlikely that all these many

All variants are distinguished by pottery styles, projectile points, and settlement types (after Marwitt, 1986).

Variants Confined to the Great Basin Itself (sometimes combined under the label "Sevier" (Madsen and Lindsay, 1977):

Parowan Fremont (before AD 900 to 1250). Maize farmers, also hunter-gatherers, centered in southwestern Utah, with a culture that shows strong Anasazi influence. Many large settlements of pithouses.

Sevier Fremont (*c.*AD 870 to 1250). Central-western Utah and eastern Nevada. Smaller communities than Parowan, many temporary settlements, many close to permanent water supplies and marshes. Maize agriculture and plant foraging both important.

Great Salt Lake Fremont (AD 400 to 1350). Hunting and plant gathering were more important than agriculture, for lakeside soils were too saline for farming. Few permanent settlements. The distinctive side-notched projectile points, pottery forms and bone artifacts of this variant are found around the Great Salt Lake, also as far away as the foothills of the Rocky Mountains in south-central Idaho.

Other Variants:

Unita Bay Fremont (AD 650 to 950). Occurs in the high altitude Unita Basin of northeastern Utah. Small pithouse hamlets, with deer hunting and plant gathering important in an area with short growing season.

San Raphael Fremont (AD 700 to 1250). Small settlements based on the Watsatch Plateau of eastern Utah and extreme western Colorado, where maize agriculture was very important. Sedentary settlement in an area where marshes were rare, in contrast to other regions where marshes allowed such settlement.

TABLE 12.2

Regional Variations of Fremont Culture

populations suffered a common fate. Each local group adapted to changing climatic conditions, to local environmental circumstances, to the arrival of new population groups. We know from Hogup Cave and other locations that Numic-speaking peoples replaced Fremont groups. At Hogup the newcomers made pottery and other artifacts that have clear links with historic Western Shoshone peoples. In other parts of the Great Basin, the same replacement pattern occurs. Initially, Fremont groups may have interacted with their successors, but in time earlier artifacts and cultural patterns vanished completely, for reasons that are still a mystery (Marwitt, 1986).

By the time of European contact, only a few groups cultivated maize on a limited scale, among them some Southern Paiute (C. Fowler, 1982), and some bands in the Mojave Desert. There were also some local groups irrigating, but not cultivating, native plants in the Owens Valley (Lawton and others, 1976). Hunting and gathering traditions honed over millennia of prehistoric time survived generations of sporadic contact with whites.

The harsh desert and rough topography inhibited European settlement and immigration. For instance, the Western Shoshone, who lived in the area between Death Valley, highland central Nevada, and into northwestern Utah, dwelt in one of the last areas of the United States to be settled by Anglo-European settlers. Many groups throughout the Basin were unable to survive the spurts of European development that disrupted their fragile ecology. But others had the time to develop responses to white settlement, to adapt to the radically different circumstances of a new era. Their material culture and subsistence patterns changed dramatically and rapidly, but many elements of traditional social organization and religious life survived into the 20th century.

Further Reading

Aikens, C. Melvin. 1978. "The Far West," *in* Jesse D. Jennings (ed.). *Ancient Native Americans.* W.H. Freeman, New York.
Summarizes the culture history of the Great Basin. Useful for the basic culture-historical sequence.
D'Azevado, W. (ed.). 1986. *Handbook of North American Indians, vol 11: The Great Basin.* Smithsonian Institution Press, Washington DC.
A fundamental source on the indigenous populations of the Great Basin and their prehistoric antecedents.
Madsen, David, and O'Connell, James (eds.). 1986. *Man and Environment in the Great Basin.* Society for American Archaeology, Washington DC.
An edited volume of articles that summarize theoretical, environmental, and cultural issues in the Great Basin. Very high quality papers reflecting state-of-the-art research.
Thomas, David Hurst. 1981. "How to Classify the Projectile Points from Monitor Valley, Nevada," *Journal of California and Great Basin Anthropology* 3,1:7–43.
Every classifier of projectile points should read this paper, which is of seminal importance to Great Basin archaeology.
——— 1983. *The Archaeology of Monitor Valley: I: Epistemology.* American Museum of Natural History, Anthropological Papers 58,1. New York.
An important statement about theoretical issues in Great Basin archaeology.
——— 1985. *The Archaeology of Hidden Cave, Nevada.* American Museum of Natural History, Anthropological Papers 61,1. New York.
A monograph describing excavations and a reinterpretation of desert lake sites in the Great Basin. Useful for its close theoretical reasoning.

CHAPTER 13

THE SOUTHWESTERN ARCHAIC

The area known as the "Southwest" is often defined as extending from Las Vegas, Nevada, in the west to Las Vegas, New Mexico, in the east, and from Durango, Mexico, in the south to Durango, Colorado, in the north (Cordell, 1984; Hunter-Anderson, 1987; Martin and Plog, 1973). What distinguishes the Southwest from neighboring areas of North America in archaeological terms is agriculture. Hunter-gatherer peoples flourished in the Great Basin to the north and in California to the west, and Plains bison-hunters to the east. The diverse peoples of the Southwest came to adopt radically different subsistence strategies, cultivating maize, beans, and squashes, using all manner of ingenious techniques to combat temperature extremes and constant water shortages. They were also responsible for some of the most spectacular architecture in prehistoric North America, adobe and stone buildings erected in caves or as multi-story pueblos, often occupied over many generations.

As Linda Cordell points out (1984), the Southwest can be defined culturally in two ways:
– By agriculture, a variety of farming artifacts and characteristic pottery styles, and also by multi-room villages with some public architecture.
– By the *absence* of formal social stratification, large cities, writing, and major, monumental architecture on the scale of such great Mesoamerican urban centers as Teotihuacan or Tikal.

Not that Southwestern peoples lived in isolation from their neighbors. They interacted with many groups near and far over long periods of time, through long-distance exchange networks that extended south to the Sea of Cortez and into Mexico, west to the Pacific coast where sea shells were to be obtained, and far north and east onto the Plains and north and west into the Great Basin. They acquired their basic crops, perhaps the art of pot making, and possibly some irrigation techniques from Mesoamerica, but adapted the techniques and ideas they received to the harsh environmental realities of the Southwest. (Some authorities believe both ceramics and irrigation were indigenous developments.) This was always a land of hot and dry landscapes where risk was a way of life, an adaptive reality where unexpected droughts could last for years on end. The secret to survival was flexibility, so Southwestern societies were in a constant state of cultural change, switching from a mobile lifeway to a more sedentary one when circumstances permitted and fostered more concentrated population densities. This was especially true in later prehistory, when there were

Sites and major cultural divisions of the Southwest.

centuries when large areas of the Southwest appear to have formed widespread economic and social systems. These larger units never lasted long in the face of variable rainfall and endemic drought. The people abandoned large centers and returned to dispersed villages again.

Southwestern Peoples

Despite generations of contact with Europeans, many descendants of the prehistoric population still flourish in their homelands, retaining their languages, important religious customs, and their value systems. There are four major cultural traditions, whose roots we shall trace in the next three chapters:

(1) Yuman-speaking peoples of the Colorado River Valley, the nearby uplands, and also of Baja California, living to the west. These groups practiced floodplain agriculture where possible, but relied heavily on hunting and gathering. The Yuma in particular were skilled warriors and active traders, maintaining exchange networks with the Pima in southern Arizona and with the Pacific coast.

(2) Pima, Papago, and other peoples living in southern Arizona, Sonora, and parts of northern Mexico. These are Uto-Aztecan speakers, who live in a vast territory that encompasses not only inhospitable deserts and rugged uplands, but some relatively lush river valleys. All these people live in what are commonly called *rancherias*, small hamlets housing several nuclear or extended families in separate dwellings.

(3) The Pueblo Indians of Arizona and New Mexico, who speak diverse languages but share much common culture. The Hopi live on and around mesas (tablelands) at the southern rim of Black Mesa, Arizona. The Zuñi, now living in one village, occupied six villages near the Zuñi River in New Mexico at European contact in the 16th century. East of Zuñi dwell the Acoma, Laguna, and various other Keresan and Tanoan-speaking groups. The various languages spoken by the Pueblo have roots in neighboring areas, Tanoan, for example, with the Kiowa-Tanoan language family that has relationships with Great Plains dialects (for details, see Cordell, 1984).

Woman of the Papago tribe, San Xavier Reservation, Arizona.

Pueblo groups tended to live in compact settlements rather than in *rancherias*, relying not only on various agricultural techniques, but heavily on hunting and gathering, too. Their villages were built of stone and adobe, often houses with interconnecting rooms for living and storage, some of multi-story design. All pueblos have special ceremonial rooms known as *kivas*. *(Kiva* is a Hopi word meaning "ceremonial room.")

There are important social, political, and religious differences between Pueblo groups. Among the Western Pueblo such as the Hopi, social

The compact settlement of Zuñi Pueblo.

organization above the level of the household is dominated by matrilineal, exogamous clans. In contrast, the Eastern Pueblo are organized around bilateral extended families and non-exogamous moieties. The moiety leaders coordinate tribal activities, as do ceremonial associations that cut across moiety lines. These broad generalizations disguise a great deal of cultural diversity within the Eastern and Western Pueblo, which can be ignored for the sake of this discussion.

(4)   Apache and Navajo peoples, Athabaskan-speaking peoples with an ancestral homeland far to the north in Canada. The ancestors of the Apache and Navajo probably entered the Southwest during the early 16th century AD, perhaps as early as AD 1450.

The Southwestern Environment

The Southwest straddles several major physiological zones, with rugged, parallel mountain ranges to the south and west, ranges separated by large basins, the lowest no more than 100 ft (30.5 m) above sea level. The central and north-central parts of the Southwest lie at high elevations on the Colorado Plateau, most of the land lying over 5000 ft (1524 m) above sea level. There are extensive tablelands (mesas), steep-sided canyons, and vast gorges, also volcanic deposits that were important obsidian sources in prehistoric times. To the east, the Southwest spills over into the southern Rocky Mountains, the ranges in this area providing a significant watershed for much of the region. Some farmers settled on the edges of the Great Plains, in major drainages like the Cimarron and Pecos rivers.

This highly diverse region has always enjoyed an arid to semi-arid climate, but a climate that is highly localized, making it hard to make any broad generalizations about Holocene climatic change. In the west, from

View looking north from the top of Hunts Mesa into Tse Biyi, Monument Valley, Arizona. Merrick Butte is near the center of the picture, which shows landscape typical of much of the Southwest.

Sonora, Mexico, through eastern California, Arizona, and north, rainfall comes twice a year. Winter storms from the Pacific bring soaking rain or snow to higher elevations between December and March, moisture that greens spring grazing areas. Most rainfall comes in July and August, short, intense thunderstorms that drift up from the Gulf of Mexico. To the east, from Chihuahua, Mexico through New Mexico, western Texas, and Colorado, July and August bring most of the year's rainfall in the form of Gulf thunderstorms. The position of the jet stream can have dramatic effects on the amount and distribution of annual rainfall, leading to unpredictable cycles of exceptional rainfall and drought.

In general, the desert areas in the south receive an average of less than 8 in (20 cm) of rain a year, while the uplands enjoy nearly 20 in (50 cm). But these are mere averages, which mask extraordinary variations in annual rainfall. Over much of the Colorado Plateau, farmers relied on springs and natural seeps, many of them emerging from natural contact lines between soft sandstones and impenetrable lower strata. The Rio Grande to the south and east was another matter. Irrigation was important along its banks, despite periodic floods that wiped out crops and entire settlements. The southern deserts support creosote brush and bursage, giving way in much of Arizona and New Mexico to higher ground that supports mixed grasses, shrubs, and open pine, piñon and juniper forest over about 7000 ft (2133 m). The Colorado Plateau supports arid grasslands at low altitudes, with widespread sage brush and open piñon-juniper woodland. The diverse vegetation of the Southwest includes many edible plants, among them agave, whose leaves and centers were roasted and stored. Sotol, yucca, cactus fruits, and cholla are important in desert regions. Wild onions and potatoes can be roasted and boiled. Many seasonal fruit such as hackberry and juniper assumed importance. Nuts and seeds are important supplemental foods, ground down and mixed with corn meal.

Desert vegetation, Maricopa County, Arizona.

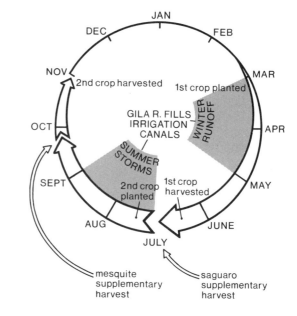

JAN

DEC   FEB

NOV   MAR

2nd crop harvested   1st crop planted

GILA R. FILLS
IRRIGATION
CANALS   WINTER RUNOFF

OCT   APR

SUMMER STORMS

2nd crop
planted   1st crop
harvested

SEPT   MAY

AUG

JULY   JUNE

mesquite
supplementary
harvest

saguaro
supplementary
harvest

Successful agriculture in the Southwest depends on careful use of scarce water resources. The diagram shows how the Pima Indians of southern Arizona, descendants of Hohokam people (see p. 254), schedule their plantings and harvests around rainfall seasons. The varying thickness of the arrows indicates seasonal variations in abundance of food.

Southwestern weather patterns are so erratic that many plant species remain dormant much of the time, making it hard to predict harvests and to collect adequate yields from one stand, forcing people to wander over large areas in search of edible plants. The animals that feed on the natural vegetation tend to be omnivorous feeders, including the ubiquitous mule deer, big-horn sheep in rugged terrain, and pronghorn antelope. Prehistoric hunters took many species of small animals, including jack rabbits, cottontails, gophers, prairie dogs, and voles. Birds were an important food source, as well as providing feathers for religious paraphernalia. Rivers, marshes, and small lakes, perhaps even humanly flooded agricultural land, are important habitats for migrating waterfowl. Some groups domesticated the turkey, everyone possessed dogs. But the staple for most Southwest peoples of the past 2000 years was maize agriculture.

Altitude, summer temperature, humidity, surface evaporation rates, and the length of the frost-free season all limited agriculture in the Southwest. This is an arid region, so maize requires longer to reach maturity, and hence a longer growing season. The hottest temperatures occur in the southern desert areas. There, the growing season is sufficient for maize cultivation, provided there is enough moisture. Temperatures decrease as one moves northward and onto higher ground. Agriculture is much riskier in mountain and high altitude mesa areas, where the growing season is often too short, and varies dramatically one year to the next. Local factors can be of vital importance for successful agriculture. For example, farmers can receive quite different crop yields and enjoy different growing seasons from one end or side of a deep canyon to another, simply because one flank may receive more direct sun than the other. Successful agriculture in the Southwest depended on careful use of scarce water sources and on minimizing risk of crop failure through careful placement of gardens.

Conceptual Frameworks

In Chapter 2, we saw how North American archaeology literally came of age in the Southwest, culminating in the brilliant stratigraphic researches of Alfred Kidder at Pecos Pueblo, New Mexico. When he started work in 1915, it was with the avowed ambition of tying together cultural developments in different areas. Pecos was an ideal site for the purpose, with the longest documented history of occupation of any pueblo on the Rio Grande. It was in use before the first Spanish visit in 1540, and was only abandoned in 1838 (Kidder, 1924; 1931). The so-called Pecos classification resulted from this work and Kidder's consultations with his colleagues, a developmental framework for the Southwest that has remained in use, albeit in modified form, ever since (Kidder, 1927).

The Pecos classification was based on architecture, pottery styles, tools, and to some extent on skeletal characteristics. It was developed at a time when tree-ring chronology was still in its infancy, for A.E. Douglass did not succeed in linking prehistoric and historic ring sequences until 1929. The scheme as originally proposed consisted of eight culture stages:
Basketmaker I was a pre-agricultural stage, a term no longer used, as this comes under the Archaic;
Basketmaker II (sometimes called Basketmaker), where people were farming and using spearthrowers;
Basketmaker III (sometimes called Post-Basketmaker). Pottery came into use, people lived in pit or slab houses;
Five Pueblo stages, I to V, which subdivided the rise of Pueblo culture right into historic times.

Kidder proposed this as a developmental, not a chronological scheme. Inevitably, it was modified by later research. For instance, the Basketmaker-Pueblo sequence was found to be characteristic of the northern Southwest, so Kidder proposed the term *Anasazi* to cover this northern tradition. The word "Anasazi" means "early ancestors" in Navajo, often translated as "old people." The Pecos classification has been much modified by ever more local researches in recent years, and suffers from being far too linear and ladder-like to reflect actual prehistoric reality, nor does it mirror the great diversity of prehistoric settlement now known to have existed throughout the Southwest. Furthermore, it is based on pottery styles often assumed to have been made at individual villages, and rarely traded from one area to another. In fact, there is mounting evidence that pottery was a commodity of often restricted production that was widely traded over large areas (Shepherd, 1965; S. Plog, 1980).

Today, we can think of Southwestern prehistory within a broad, culture-historical framework that begins with a Paleo-Indian tradition, subsuming human settlement before about 5500 BC. This is followed by the Southwestern Archaic, dating to between about 5500 BC and AD 200, then "later" prehistory, the time when the so-called Pueblo cultures flourished, when considerable regional variation is found in the archaeological record. Later prehistory is now divided into four major cultural traditions that are in turn subdivided into chronological phases. The four traditions are:

Anasazi (?AD 1 to modern times). The Anasazi tradition flourished in the northern Southwest and subsumes the old Basketmaker-Pueblo develop-

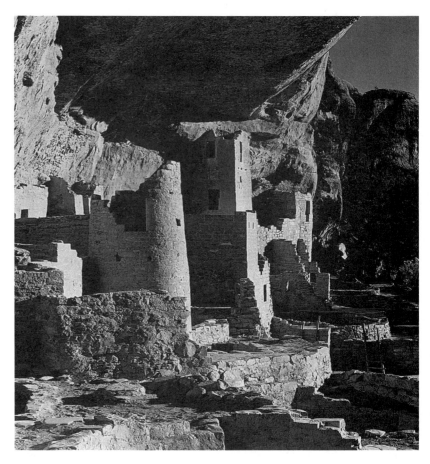

Part of Cliff Palace, Mesa Verde, among the finest of all Anasazi pueblo architecture. See p. 295 for a view of the whole site.

mental scheme. Such major developments as Chaco Canyon and Mesa Verde with their magnificent pueblo architecture lie within the Anasazi tradition.

Hohokam (c. AD 400 to 1500). The Pima word "Hohokam" means "those who have gone." The Hohokam tradition differs from Anasazi in its rectangular, single unit dwellings, low platform mounds, ball courts, cremations, and reliance on extensive irrigation systems, as well as in its paddle-and-anvil decorated pottery. This tradition flourished in the southern desert regions of the Southwest, and has been subdivided into as many as six periods at various times. Hohokam experienced considerable elaboration during its later history, maintaining trading connections with Mexico to the south. Irrigation canals, ball courts, platform mounds, and elaborate pottery, stone, and shell work are characteristic of Hohokam at the height of its development at Snaketown on the Gila River.

Mogollon (?250 BC to c. AD 1450). This tradition, centered on the mountains of that name in southeastern Arizona and southwestern New Mexico, is named after an early Spanish Colonial governor of New Mexico. The distinctive red-on-brown and polished red Mogollon ceramics are found over a large area from the Little Colorado River in the north well into Mexico in the south, and from Globe, Arizona, to El Paso, Texas, in the east. The Mogollon displays great variation, and has been divided into several stages on the basis of changing pit-house designs and ceramic styles.

Patayan (AD *875 to modern times*). The name Patayan comes from the Yuman, "old people," used to describe prehistoric cultures that once flourished west of the Hohokam region and north to the vicinity of the Grand Canyon. Patayan is a still inadequately defined entity. Various alternative terms have been proposed, together with several much discussed cultural stages (for a summary, see Cordell, 1984).

This very broad-brushed, general developmental scheme masks a great deal of cultural variation, and is not adequate to describe such variation accurately, nor to plot or evaluate the complex paths of culture change throughout the prehistoric Southwest. It was put together long before the advent of radiocarbon dating, and much of it developed while dendrochronology was still in its infancy. Nevertheless, the scheme is useful as a basic frame of reference. Generations of scholars have developed local chronological and cultural sequences under its umbrella. Tree-ring and radiocarbon chronologies and these frameworks have provided the basis for the much more sophisticated ecological, regional, and settlement studies that have been characteristic of Southwestern archaeology in recent years. A combination of all these approaches forms the portrait of Southwestern prehistory that follows.

Paleo-Indian Tradition
before 9500 BC

There is well-documented Clovis and Folsom occupation in the Southwest, associated with the bones of extinct big-game species (see Chapter 6). This includes several mammoth and bison kill sites, also the important Blackwater Draw locations (Wendorf and Hester, 1975; Haynes, 1975). Throughout Paleo-Indian times, the human population of the Southwest was small and very scattered, probably enjoying a generalized hunting and gathering adaptation. By the end of Paleo-Indian times, the hunter-gatherer populations of the region were pursuing very diverse subsistence strategies. In the east, bison were of importance, while San Dieguito peoples in the west may have relied more heavily on plant remains. In both areas, population growth was slow, but the long-term consequences of adopting quite different food-getting strategies were to prove significantly different, especially as far as sedentary settlement and population growth rates were concerned.

Southwestern Archaic
before 7500 BC to AD 200

As the Middle Holocene climate warmed up and vegetation patterns began to approach their present distributions, Southwestern people diversified their subsistence strategies even more, coming to rely more heavily on smaller animal species and especially on plant foods. The beginning of the Archaic coincided with drier weather in some areas of the Southwest, in part with the Altithermal (Chapter 6). Both pollens and packrat middens document more arid conditions, with Early Holocene forest cover giving way to desert scrub and more grassland around 6000 BC. This was a rapid, general change that saw woodlands retreat from the warm desert areas of the Southwest (Van Devender and Spaulding, 1979). After about 2500 BC, there may have been occasional cycles of higher rainfall, reflected in fluctuations in lake levels and local increases in forest cover. Whether these rainfall increases were widespread enough to call them a wet phase is uncertain.

The Southwestern Archaic is still a rather sparse entity, for the scattered archaeological remains of these millennia are overshadowed by the much more spectacular sites and material culture of the past 2000 years. Except in highly favored locations, too, Archaic bands exploited generally arid environments, where food resources were widely dispersed and where constant mobility was adaptive. Many Archaic encampments were highly transitory settlements, occupied for a few days or weeks at a time. Thus, the archaeological record is highly incomplete, except for occasional caves and rockshelters where dry conditions have preserved a wider range of artifacts, including such perishable items as basketry, fiber sandals, and fur blankets. However, the Archaic was a vital formative period in Southwestern prehistory, for it was during the later centuries of the period that some local groups adopted the deliberate cultivation of domesticated plants, among them maize (Cordell, 1984; Wills, 1989).

A "Gradualist" Model

In some respects, the study of the Southwestern Archaic has paralleled that of the Great Basin. As we saw in Chapter 12, the concept of a "Desert Culture," a long-lasting Archaic tradition sparked a new generation of research into Holocene climate change and human responses to changing conditions. Eventually, the Desert Culture concept was abandoned and replaced with more sophisticated formulations. In the southern Southwest, the term Cochise Culture was coined to cover a similar long Archaic occupation, and then elaborated into three general phases – Sulphur Spring, Chiricachua, and San Pedro (Berry and Berry, 1986; Sayles and Antevs, 1941; Sayles, 1983). As is inevitable, especially when archaeologists think in linear terms, there was a proliferation of new traditions, phases, and local variants. These reflected an increasingly complex and puzzling archaeological record.

These "gradualist" models assume that Southwestern Archaic hunter-gatherer traditions developed over as long as 5000 years, relatively stable adaptations to generally arid conditions and very varied local environments. In subsistence and adaptive terms, the Southwestern Archaic was seen as forming part of a much wider desert adaptation that flourished over much of the interior west, marked by a "specialized, successful way of life geared to the rigor and apparent biotic parsimony of the Desert West"

(Jennings, 1964). Throughout the Southwest a scattered Archaic population subsisted off small game and wild plant foods for a long period of time, under relatively stable climatic conditions, conditions far more stable than those of Paleo-Indian times. This may have led to a gradual population increase over the millennia, but with densities always remaining low throughout the area.

Clearly, there is a strong element of cultural continuity through the Southwestern Archaic, but the gradualist model is based on relatively unsophisticated views of desertic environments. A new generation of multidisciplinary research, using not only archaeological finds, but sophisticated climatic data, has shown that the Southwest and adjacent areas were settled by a very complex, multidimensional mosaic of Archaic hunter-gatherer societies. These many groups maintained the same *general* technological traditions for many thousands of years over wide areas, *but there was great local, and often short-term, variation*. This reality means adopting a very different approach to Archaic studies, one that focuses on reconstructing intricate jigsaws of local adaptations using data from both archaeological and climatic sources, then fitting these many local adaptations together into a wider, much more complex, picture (Berry and Berry, 1986). Such researches are still in relative infancy (Waters, 1986), but promise a much more complex picture of the Southwestern Archaic for the future. We must, however, summarize a general version of the gradualist sequence first, for it is still widely used in the literature and in the field.

The Picosa Culture
?before 7000 BC to AD 200

Cynthia Irwin-Williams (1967; 1968; 1979) argued for two levels of Archaic analysis. The first level was an integrative one. It identified traits that were common to many local cultures. For example, small *manos* and grinding stones occurred on Archaic sites throughout the Southwest. They were clear evidence for seed processing, an activity that was almost universal in the desert west. Most of the characteristics of the Southwestern Archaic fell into this integrative category. They were general traits defining a general stage.

Irwin-Williams then moved on to what she called an "isolative" level of analysis. This was a far more detailed comparison, where one tried to isolate specific traits such as characteristic projectile points that served to distinguish local cultures one from another, and to set up local culture-historical sequences through time. This was difficult with the Southwestern Archaic, for there were very few truly distinctive, local artifacts to work with. As is the case in other parts of North America, investigators have tended to emphasize projectile point forms for this purpose. This approach is a high-risk one, especially in the Archaic Southwest, where securely dated sites are few and far between, and where there are uncertainties as to the exact functional use of many projectile points. For instance, many are thought to have served as knives as well as spearpoints, and to have been modified several times during their useful life, perhaps for different purposes.

Despite these theoretical and methodological problems, Irwin-Williams developed a descriptive framework for the Southwestern Archaic, a framework that is still widely used in the literature (Irwin-Williams, 1968). She identified four interacting Southwestern Archaic traditions – Cochise, Oshara, Pinto, and Southeastern – collectively known as the Picosa culture. Normally, prehistoric cultures are named after geographical locations where they are first defined. In the Picosa case Irwin-Williams used an acronym developed from three of the four Southwestern traditions: *Pi* from Pinto Basin, *co* from Cochise, and *sa* from San Jose.

The Pinto Tradition *(?before 7000 BC until ?AD 500)* sometimes called the San Dieguito-Pinto, is the westernmost Archaic manifestation, extending from southern California in the west deep into southern Arizona. It is found within the Great Basin as far north as southern Nevada. Pinto apparently evolved from Paleo-Indian San Dieguito roots (Chapter 6) and is identified by "Pinto Basin" points with straight stems. The Pinto tradition survived for many thousands of years but is still largely undated.

The Oshara Tradition *(before 5500 BC to AD 600)* is centered in north-central New Mexico, the San Juan Basin, the Rio Grande Valley, southern Colorado and southeastern Utah (Irwin-Williams, 1973). The Oshara may have ancestral roots in earlier Paleo-Indian traditions, but these postulated roots are much disputed and the debate is unresolved (Cordell, 1984). Irwin-Williams dates the beginnings of Oshara to about 5500 BC and has developed a sequence of Archaic culture for Oshara in the Arroyo Cuervo area of north-central New Mexico. This sequence defines no less than six phases of occupation, each identified by projectile point forms and other less well-defined artifacts. Jay, Bajada, San Jose, Armijo, En Medio, and Trujillo – the successive phases chronicle local Archaic culture from its earliest manifestations right up until AD 600, by which time Anasazi culture is flourishing in the area. The Arroyo Cuervo researches are thought by Irwin-Williams to chronicle a long-term cultural development of the local Archaic into Pueblo-Anasazi culture.

The Southeastern Tradition is still poorly defined, and probably includes several local adaptations that evolved over long periods of time. Irwin-Williams (1979) considers this diverse tradition ancestral to later local Mogollon culture.

Southwestern Archaic projectile points. (Top) Pinto Basin point. (Second, third, and fourth rows) Bajada, San Jose, and Armijo points respectively. (Fifth row) Chiricahua Cochise points. (Bottom row) San Pedro Cochise points. Length of Pinto Basin point 3.7 cm.

The Cochise Tradition *(?before 7000 to c.200 BC)* lasted for a very long time, with its earliest manifestations perhaps occurring in the Paleo-Indian period at Sulphur Springs, Arizona, a site with disputed chronology (for detailed discussion of the Sulphur Springs phase, see Berry and Berry, 1986). Its two later phases, the Chiricahua and San Pedro, are much better known.

Chiricahua Cochise tools include a variety of projectile points and many seed-processing artifacts. The phase has been dated to between about 3500 and 1500 BC, but the chronology is open to doubt (Whalen, 1975; Berry and Berry, 1986), and has been formulated on the basis of occupations in Ventana Cave, near Sells, Arizona, and from other locations in the state, as well as in western New Mexico (Haury, 1950).

San Pedro follows the Chiricahua in the southern Southwest, characterized by large projectile points with corner or side notches and straight or
convex bases. Provisional radiocarbon dates have San Pedro flourishing
from about 1500 to 200 BC (Whalen, 1975). By this time, the Archaic
population of the Southwest appears to have grown, with groups exploiting
a wider range of environmental zones and sometimes living in larger,
perhaps more permanent, settlements. Some San Pedro sites contain oval
pit houses excavated about 1.6 ft (0.5 m) below ground level, dwellings
requiring sufficient effort to build that they must have been occupied for
some time. Without question, some San Pedro communities were
cultivating maize and other crops.

San Pedro occupations have been chronicled at many locations, among
them Bat and Tularosa Caves in New Mexico, as well as Cienega Creek,
sufficient to show that the later Mogollon tradition developed from the
earlier San Pedro Cochise (Martin, 1979). Emil Haury excavated the
Cienega Creek site, where he found San Pedro Cochise artifacts that he felt

San Pedro Phase oval pithouse.

documented cultural continuity not only to Mogollon, but to another later tradition, the Hohokam (Haury, 1950). As we shall see in Chapter 15, he has subsequently changed his mind, and believes that the Hohokam were people who migrated north from Mexico and were not descended from the Cochise (Haury, 1976). The question is still much debated (see Berry and Berry, 1986 for full discussion).

The tripartite subdivision of the Cochise is still ill-defined, to the point that there is a real question whether it, in fact, represents a continuous, unitary tradition of Archaic culture at all. The three stages are poorly dated, and sometimes with doubtful stratigraphic association. They probably represent an interrupted, rather than a continuous, sequence. In some places, they may have actually been contemporaneous (Berry and Berry, 1986).

A Population Movement and Climate Model

"It seems to me most appropriate to re-examine the cultural scene of the Southwest ... as a deep and wide zone of interpenetration of people and institutions, mainly originating elsewhere ..." Thus did geographer Carl Sauer (1954) describe the Pueblo occupation of the Southwest, but Claudia and Michael Berry (1986) argue, appropriately, that the same comment probably applies to the Southwestern Archaic. They point out that the complicated mosaic of Archaic settlement throughout North America cannot be understood on purely a local basis alone. This is especially true in the Southwest, where many projectile point forms used to subdivide different cultural stages were also in widespread use elsewhere. The Berrys have used 288 radiocarbon dates from 119 Southwestern sites to show that there were numerous gaps in Archaic occupation both on the northern Plateau and in the southern Basin and Range areas. These gaps should not be there, if the gradualist model is correct. There are peaks with many dates, as if there were bursts of cultural activity. If these gaps and peaks reflect actual reality, then the development of Southwestern Archaic culture was much more complex than hitherto suspected (for discussion of this model, see Berry and Berry, 1986).

The Berrys have developed a new model of population movement and climatic change that compares what is known of Holocene climatic change with this new, discontinuous Archaic chronology. They believe there was no one-to-one correlation between climatic variation and the intensity of prehistoric occupation in any given local area, that one cannot think purely in terms of drier conditions equalling lower population densities, and higher rainfall associated with higher numbers of people.

The new model is subdivided into three periods, which are purely arbitrary formulations, mere organizational devices, which do not imply continuous occupation.

Period I (8000 to 3000 BC). Almost nothing is known of the human populations of the Southwest during this long period of fluctuating warm-wet and cool-dry climate, for radiocarbon dated sites are rare. The Colorado Plateau, for example, may have been utilized on a transitory basis. The sparse population was probably concentrated around clusters of food resources, but even then occupation was probably intermittent. A number of distinctive projectile point forms are associated with this period, among them Pinto – generally agreed to be the earliest Archaic point in the eastern Great Basin and Colorado Plateau – Elko, Humboldt, and Northern side-notched (see Table 12.1).

Period II (3000 to 1000 BC). With the onset of a period of greater rainfall about 3000 BC, both the Plateau and the Basin Range were occupied more intensively, with a "peak" of cultural activity. There is a proliferation of new projectile point forms, including the Gypsum point with its contracting stem, which occurs as early as 2500 BC. Contracting stem points are found at Ventana and in the Trans-Pecos region of Texas, and are part of an Archaic culture there that has strong similarities to earlier Archaic assemblages from the Tehuacán Valley and elsewhere in Mexico. The Berrys believe that these similarities are the result of population movements from the Mexican highlands, where climatic conditions were deteriorating at the same time as they were improving in northern Mexico and the Southwest.

Period III (1000 BC to AD 500). Rainfall patterns changed fairly drastically about 1000 BC, as conditions became drier throughout the Southwest. It was during these protracted drought conditions that maize cultivation took hold among Archaic groups, during the so-called San Pedro stage of the Cochise culture. It is interesting to find another peak of radiocarbon dated sites just before 500 BC, as many Archaic groups became sedentary cultivators, centuries after the first introduction of maize to the Southwest (Chapter 14).

This model is a far more sophisticated formulation than the gradualist interpretation, based as it is on an emerging array of paleoclimatic data and hunter-gatherer theory. It is founded on notions that some areas were more productive than others, with productivity varying dramatically through time from one locale to another. In some areas like the eastern Great Basin, for example, long-term, successful adaptations were based on exploitation of lacustrine resources during dry spells, on upland plant foods during drought cycles. On the Plateau and in the southern Basin and Range of New Mexico and Arizona, it was not possible to develop such complementary strategies to accommodate climatic cycles, so these areas with their broadly similar food resources remained sparsely occupied until the higher rainfall conditions of Period II.

The Berry model also espouses not gradual change (although, obviously, this was a factor), but population movements. The process of Archaic population movements was an extension of the annual mobility characteristic of most hunter-gatherer groups. These expansions, contractions, and shifts in Archaic settlement were not conscious migrations. Rather, they followed the constantly changing annual availabilities of food resources, so their movements were short-term reactions to abrupt changes in resource availability. At times, they encountered new foods and developed new technologies to exploit them. But throughout the Southwest, and indeed the Great Basin, desert Archaic societies adopted conservative strategies that allowed them to feed themselves within local environments, adjusting to short-term minor changes within these, even when the Holocene climate in the longer term changed in major ways. Thus, the Berrys argue, we can trace migrations using tool forms like projectile points, because the peoples that used them were extremely conservative culturally.

Doubtless, the tentative Berry model will be criticized and much modified in the future. But whatever more sophisticated formulations and new data result, we can be sure that the Southwestern Archaic will be seen to be a far more complex phenomenon than we suspect, even today.

Further Reading

Cordell, Linda S. 1984. *Prehistory of the Southwest*. Academic Press, New York.
This important synthesis focuses on both cultural process and culture history. A definitive account.
Irwin-Williams, Cynthia. 1968. *Archaic Culture History in the southwestern United States*. Eastern New Mexico University, Portales.
A fundamental description of the Picosa Culture, by the archaeologist who formulated the concept.
Kidder, Alfred V. 1924. *An Introduction to the Study of Southwestern Archaeology, With a Preliminary Account of the Excavations at Pecos*. Yale University Press, New Haven.
Kidder's classic account was the first synthesis of Southwestern archaeology. Much outdated, but still invaluable as a historical document, and for its insights.
Lipe, William D. 1983. "The Southwest," *in* Jesse D. Jennings (ed.). *Ancient North Americans*. W.H. Freeman, New York, pp. 421–494.
Lipe's summary is widely quoted and is exceptionally well referenced.
Martin, Paul S. and Plog, Fred. 1973. *The Archaeology of Arizona*. Doubleday/Natural History Press, Garden City, NY.
Another basic synthesis of Southwestern prehistory that complements the Cordell volume.

CHAPTER 14

THE ORIGINS OF AGRICULTURE AND VILLAGE LIFE

Agriculture, the deliberate planting and harvesting of domesticated plants, seems, on the face of it, like a startlingly revolutionary invention. But, as the great English anthropologist Edward Tylor pointed out as long ago as 1883, "agriculture is not to be looked on as a difficult or out-of-the-way invention, for the rudest savage, skilled as he is in the habits of the food-plants he gathers, must know well enough that if seeds or roots are put in a proper place in the ground they will grow." We can be sure that Archaic peoples knew millennia before they felt any necessity to do so that deliberately planted seeds would germinate.

In the final analysis, plant production involves the deliberate manipulation of plants, intervening in their life cycle to make sure that some useful parts are available for eating or for some other use. There was no one single moment when prehistoric North Americans domesticated plants. Rather, plant domestication was part of a long continuum of human interaction with the natural vegetation that started with first settlement (Ford, 1985).

Foraging and Unintentional Tending. For thousands of years, Paleo-Indian and Archaic peoples foraged for wild vegetable foods in season, gathering nut harvests, harvesting wild grasses in river valleys, digging for tubers and roots. The very act of gathering vegetable foods can lead to unintentional tending of plants – accidental seed dispersal and trampling can benefit the wild resource. Intensive gathering of, say, larger seeds at the expense of smaller ones can also have unexpected genetic consequences, selecting against less desirable traits. These changes can be maintained over time, even if intensive human exploitation ceases. For instance, such accidental genetic changes may have caused the condensing of the lateral branches and tiny cobs of teosinte, the indigenous wild grass that is thought to have been the ancestor of domesticated maize.

In many parts of North America, hunter-gatherers used fire to encourage the regeneration of grasses and edible plants. The California Indians used fire to eliminate plant competitors under edible acorn oak trees, also to encourage growth of *Corylus* sprouts, much prized for basket manufacture. Deliberately set fires will select for certain species, but such techniques can hardly be called deliberate plant production.

Cultivation. Richard Ford argues that food production begins with "deliberate care afforded the propagation of a species" (1985), an activity he calls "cultivation." Such cultivation does not imply full domestication. But it does mean that people have disrupted the life cycle of a plant, usually to collect larger quantities of food or to enable them to obtain its products with greater ease.

Cultivation proceeds in several ways. Weeding, pruning, and otherwise tending plants is a commonplace practice in many parts of the world. Tending is a casual activity, usually removing competing vegetation around root plants or weeding the soil near important medicinal species, as is done in the Southwest. Usually, a higher yield results. Such techniques are, of course, impossible to identify from archaeological remains, but there is no reason not to assume that tending of wild plants was commonplace in Archaic times.

Tilling the soil with digging sticks (illus. p.223) or simple hoes tends to encourage the germination of naturally dispersed seeds. Grubbing the earth with a simple digging stick or hoe can increase moisture retention or aerate the ground. Many foragers use a digging stick to obtain tubers, removing lateral roots or bulbets at an early stage in growth. This very process could encourage further growth and tuber production. Again, such activities are impossible to identify from archaeological finds.

Transplanting takes the process of manipulation a stage further, the deliberate process of digging up plants and replanting them at a new location. Much transplanting is really a form of thinning out to enhance yields, but if a plant is moved to a new habitat, then the transplanter will have to care for it over its entire growth cycle. Such long-term care may lead to selection for new genetic characteristics and to hybridization with closely related plants. Historic American Indian groups regularly transplanted small herbs or shrubs, many of them ceremonial or medicinal plants. The transplantation was sometimes casual, sometimes to a space deliberately reserved for nurturing a variety of plants.

Sowing seed can be seen as a form of transplanting. It can be as casual as the deliberate dispersal of harvested seed to foster future growth. There are many more complex forms of sowing, like, for example, storing the dormant seed and then planting it in small plots cleared in advance, or sowing in completely different habitats. Procedures such as this can result in selection for useful traits, such as winnowing for large seeds, or planting all the seeds at once so they germinate simultaneously and are all harvested at the same time.

Cultivation of wild plants and potential domesticates that are undergoing genetic change does not necessarily produce stable crops. In all probability, early cultivation efforts were aimed at producing seasonal supplements to broad-based vegetable diets. The additional plant yields were a form of guarantee that the harvest would be at least partially bountiful, perhaps, also, eliminating the need for wide-ranging searches for additional foods.

All these forms of plant manipulation were in use for thousands of years, until people created new food plants through deliberate selection. At that point, humanly created plant communities became the dominant component in prehistoric diet.

Plant Domestication. Plant domestication is the final stage in the process of food production, the point at which cultural selection for useful traits results in new plants that depend on human beings for their existence.

Such plants cannot survive without human assistance, and may initially be a dietary supplement. However, as time goes on, they often become ever more important and more and more land is allocated to food production. The most important characteristic of domesticated plants is that one can increase their production by clearing a natural habitat and creating an environment favorable for growing a chosen domesticated plant. The result is what Ford calls "field agriculture," based on land where only a few species are grown in carefully chosen combinations that supplement each other, like maize with beans and squash.

"Waffle garden" at Zuñi Pueblo, New Mexico. Gardens such as these were an ingenious way of conserving moisture in the soil for growing domesticated plants.

Theories of the Origins of Agriculture

Few topics have generated so much theoretical speculation as the origins of agriculture. Modern theorizing began with the seminal work of the great prehistorian Vere Gordon Childe, who confined his researches to Europe and the Near East (1956). In a series of wide-ranging essays, he proposed two great watersheds in prehistory – the Agricultural and Urban Revolutions. To Childe, agriculture was a truly revolutionary invention, a development that changed the course of human history dramatically.

We now know that agriculture and animal domestication began in many parts of the world at about the same time, and that the changeover from hunting and gathering to food production was a long process involving a complicated set of interacting variables (Struever, 1971; Flannery, 1973b).

The most recent attempts to understand these processes have invoked such factors as population pressure and environmental stress (Stark, 1986). These hypotheses usually involve placing newly domesticated plants in their ecological and cultural context, in a theoretical environment that involves thinking of human cultures as cultural systems that interact not only with the natural environment, but as being made up of many different components that interact with one another (Redman, 1978).

The world's earliest farming societies emerged in Mediterranean and tropical environments. In contrast, North America is a continent of often dramatic winter and summer extremes, presenting difficult challenges to subsistence farmers in both the Southwest and Eastern Woodlands (Ford, 1985). In the east, for example, plant growth was dormant for many months of the year. So few vegetable foods were available for foraging. By the same token, the nut harvests and productivity of wild grass stands varied dramatically from year to year, so predicting food supplies was very hard. In the Southwest, irregular rainfall, many months of intense heat, and sometimes harsh winters, played havoc with wild vegetable foods.

In the Southwest, Archaic hunter-gatherer groups could overcome food shortage stress by covering large distances, by possessing knowledge of potential food sources over wide areas. They also concentrated on less preferred food plants, and sometimes exploited food sources like acorns that required a great deal of effort to prepare, and a greater energy expenditure by everyone involved. Another option was to respond to changed conditions by deliberately cultivating native plants, as happened in the Eastern Woodlands long before maize spread east (Chapter 18).

The Origins of Southwestern Agriculture

Maize (corn), squash, and beans were domesticated somewhere in Meso- or Latin America sometime before 5000 BC, centuries before they appeared in North America. Richard MacNeish's classic excavations in the Tehuacán Valley of central Mexico and in the Sierra de Tamaulipas in the northeast of the country have documented a changeover from hunting, gathering, and sporadic cultivation to a heavy dependence on farming that took many generations to complete (MacNeish, 1970). It was a considerable time before the cultigens spread to the Southwest.

Richard Ford (1981, 1985) has grouped the earliest Southwestern crops – maize, beans, and squash – into what he calls the Upper Sonoran Agricultural Complex. He points out that the crops within this complex had a long and complicated history before they reached the Southwest. They were cultivated in northern Mexico for some time before being introduced further north. Maize farming is an economic activity that may require sedentary living for much of the year, but we can assume that there were at least some sporadic contacts with nomadic hunter-gatherers living in desert regions to the north. Thus, it would have been easy for knowledge of plants, even gifts of seeds or seedlings, to pass from south to north. Such is the archaeological record that we shall probably never know what specific mechanisms diffused farming to the Southwest. The important point is that the *opportunity* for adopting the crops was probably present long before anyone thought it worth doing so. And domesticated plants had one major advantage: they might not be highly productive, but they were predictable. Cultivators of the new crops could control their location, and their availability at different seasons through storage. Under this argument, conditions favouring adoption of cultigens by Archaic groups could include both uncertainties about the productivity of the environment and changes in population densities (Wills, 1989).

The Southwestern climate was relatively stable during the Archaic, with a possible period of wetter conditions from about 2500 BC to about 100 BC. It was an environment where hunting and gathering were high-risk subsistence strategies, mainly because of highly variable rainfall distributions. Despite generally low population densities, local populations may have occasionally reached saturation point, resulting in food shortages. Wills (1989) argues that many Archaic populations grew rapidly as the distribution of piñons, desert succulents, and other valuable supplementary foods expanded during the arid Middle Holocene. The scattered hunter-gatherer population was mainly based on stream drainages, but as contrasts between vegetational zones became more pronounced as the climate became more arid, many groups developed a seasonal pattern of exploiting lowland resources during the winter and early summer, then moving to the cooler uplands to exploit piñons and other foods during mid-summer and fall. There was often repetitive use of the same, favored locations. Wills documents a northward shift of more numerous later Archaic settlements that paralleled a northward shift in piñon-juniper woodlands and savannas.

Wills also examined the distributions of projectile point forms through the Archaic in the central Southwest, and found that there was considerable emphasis on stylistic variation during the later part of the mid-Archaic, with less concentration on such features in favor of technological efficiency in the later Archaic. He notes that there are modern ethnographic analogies for the use of projectile point styles to convey social information, perhaps to reflect perceived, if not physical, territorial boundaries. Conceivably, then, the changing emphases on style may reflect decreasing success at foraging, reflected in a great need for information about one's neighbors, and for defining one's relationship with them in terms of control of resources. During the later centuries of the Archaic, groups were controlling resources in more formal terms, with specific territorial boundaries. Under these circumstances, more predictable food supplies would be an invaluable addition to Archaic diet.

Linda Cordell (1984) believes that Southwestern groups adopted agriculture when what she calls a "situation of regional imbalance" developed between local populations and local resources. Such situations could result from either environmental degradation or population increases. She believes that climatic changes during the Archaic were not sufficient to cause local degradation. Thus, rising population densities may have been a factor.

There are several possible ways in which rising population densities may have caused environmental degradation and the adoption of agriculture. Michael Glassow argues (1980) that sedentary populations in northern Mexico had been practicing agriculture since at least 1000 BC. Rising populations from such sedentary communities in the north, might, he believes, have moved over into the Southwest, placing pressure on indigenous hunter-gatherer groups. There were contemporary sedentary populations on the California coast, also, populations who may also have spilled over into the interior, again creating pressure on Picosa Complex peoples in the Southwest.

Another hypothesis points to the western Plains, where a dramatic increase in bison hunting during the Late Archaic may have led to the establishment of large, seasonal camps along the western margins of the flat country (Frison, 1978). The presence of these camps may have led to local resource shortages and resulted in some hunter-gatherer groups in the eastern Southwest planting crops to supplement reduced natural plant yields.

One could argue that foragers accept crops in order to become more effective foragers, not because they want to become farmers. Thus, one can argue that there were increasing environmental differences during the Archaic that saw the lowland and desert areas producing fewer resources for foragers, while the upland and northern regions were ever more seasonal in their food supplies. Wills (1989) suggests that lowland groups may have accepted crops to offset seasonal shortages in spring, for they could store the resulting grain. Upland groups might have accepted crops to allow them greater effective control over upland areas. If this view is correct, then lowland sites may one day yield cultigens slightly before they appear at higher elevations.

An increasing trend toward more sedentary settlement and a greater reliance on plant foods and more elaborate storage technologies may also have had an effect on diet. Perhaps, argue some authorities, it would be possible for such communities to assure a more balanced, even diet throughout the entire year, thus stimulating population growth (Binford 1968; Binford and Chasko, 1976).

Whatever the precise cause, the origins of horticulture in the Southwest appear to have resulted from an imbalance between population and available natural resources. In a sense, Archaic culture in the Southwest, as elsewhere in North America, with its elaborate seed-processing equipment, *manos* and grinders, was pre-adapted to agriculture. Had Southwestern peoples wanted to adopt agriculture as an opportunistic venture perceived to be of advantage, they would have done so much earlier, cultivating maize soon after it appeared far to the south. Ultimately, they adopted a low-yielding form of maize during the late second or first millennium BC, some time after it came into use in Mexico.

Maize Agriculture

Maize (*Zea mays*), sometimes called Indian corn, was the staff of life in the Americas at European contact, all the way from Argentina to southern Canada, and from sea level high into the Andes (Galinat, 1985; Mangelsdorf, 1974). Over the millennia, hundreds of races of maize evolved, each a special adaptation to every environment imaginable, from swamplands to intensely hot deserts. The crop was first domesticated somewhere in Mesoamerica, or perhaps even further south, perhaps from a common wild grass, teosinte (Beadle, 1980). The transition from wild grass to the maize cob probably took a very short time, perhaps a century or so, a

Maize, the staff of life in the ancient Americas. (Above left) Some 5000 years of the evolution of maize from the tiny corn cob on the left to an example on the right dating to about AD 1500. Modern corn is much larger and more productive than the earliest forms, which were possibly developed from a wild grass, teosinte, that still grows in Mexico. (Above right) Hopi woman shelling corn, Arizona.

shorter time span than that required to develop highly productive maize forms (Galinat, 1985). Richard MacNeish (1974) traced the gradual emergence of maize agriculture in the Tehuacán Valley, Mexico, and observed how the earliest maize cobs were of very small size. His excavations at Coxcatlán Cave and other nearby sites show that it took many generations for the farmers to create larger, more productive cobs that were capable of producing crop yields to support large agricultural populations.

Maize is a demanding crop, not a cereal that one can rely on to provide all one's food if one plants it casually, and simply return to harvest the resulting stand later, as one can many native plants like goosefoot. Maize also lacks one of the vital amino acids needed to make protein, and is only an effective staple when grown in combination with other crops like beans or squash that provide the necessary protein ingredients for a maize-based diet. Since most Southwestern groups continued to enjoy a highly mobile lifeway for at least a millennium after maize first appeared north of the Rio Grande, there is good reason to believe that it first served as a casual supplement to wild plant resources, especially in favorable areas where corn could be planted and then left largely untended, the process of cultivating it not being allowed to interfere with other subsistence activities.

Zea mays is a tropical cultigen, one that is always at risk in such northern latitudes as the Southwest. The hardy, low-yielding maize that first entered the Southwest was the so-called Chapalote form of *Zea mays*, a small-cob popcorn of great genetic diversity. Everyone agrees that Chapalote was the primeval Southwestern maize, but there is great uncertainty about the date of introduction (for a full discussion, see Upham and others, 1987). One scenario has Chapalote arriving in the Southwest early in the second millennium BC, a date perhaps supported by radiocarbon dates from the San Juan Basin in northern New Mexico (Upham and others, 1987). Despite these early dates, the archaeological evidence for the first appearance of Southwestern corn is still very scattered and comes mainly from caves and rockshelters (Wills, 1989).

There are accelerator radiocarbon dates on maize from the Tucson Basin of between *c.*800 and 500 BC, and other readings on maize and squash from the San Juan Basin to the north of *c.*1000 to 700 BC (Wills, 1989). Maize at Bat Cave is thought to date to about 1000 BC (Ford, 1981), and there are reports of maize pollen from Cienega Creek dated to an average of 500 BC. Block Cave in the Pine Lawn Valley of Arizona contains maize in Archaic levels dated to between 850 and 650 BC. Squash has been found in the same contexts (see Cordell, 1984; Ford, 1985; Upham and others, 1987). All these dates place the introduction of maize agriculture during a period of higher rainfall in the central and eastern Southwest, probably between 1500 and 1000 BC, perhaps some centuries earlier.

Shortly after its arrival, continues the same scenario, Chapalote was introgressed with the indigenous wild grass teosinte, creating a highly varied hybrid maize that appears at such well-known Southwestern Archaic sites as Bat Cave. The maize forms that resulted from this process of introgression often displayed more rows of kernels and large cob sizes, more productive forms that spread rapidly throughout the Southwest.

It was not Chapalote but radically different maize, Maiz de Ocho, which is thought to have been the key development in Southwestern life (Martin and Plog, 1973). Maiz de Ocho is adapted to dry conditions and yields large, more productive, flowery kernels that are easily milled. Until recently, it was commonly agreed that Maiz de Ocho had spread into the Southwest from northern Mexico even as late as AD 700, and then diffused from there to the Eastern Woodlands in about AD 1100. This was before Steadman Upham and Richard MacNeish excavated Roller Skate and Tornillo rockshelters in southern New Mexico. The latter yielded a radiocarbon date of 1225±240 BC, obtained from eight maize samples, including two complete cobs of an early form of Maiz de Ocho. All the maize fragments came from a single natural layer in the shelter. Two later levels at the same site contain Maiz de Ocho and date to 1029±130 BC and 652±60 BC respectively. Obsidian hydration dates from both Tornillo and Roller Skate tend to confirm these dates (Upham and others, 1987). It may be, then, that maize agriculture took hold at lower elevations earlier than in the uplands, but it is only fair to say that the dating of these sites still needs further testing (Wills, 1989).

These new dates raise the possibility that Maiz de Ocho evolved in, or near the Southwest, from earlier, highly variable Chapalote maize, including forms with a thick rachis (hinge) that held the kernel to the stalk. Maiz de Ocho may have resulted from a selection for a large kerneled corn, which was easier to grind, also for earlier flowering. Such an attribute was vital in the hot and arid Southwest, where growing seasons are often restricted by irregular timing and distribution of rainfall, leaving little time for large kernels to fill out. These characteristics of Maiz de Ocho were highly adaptive in North America, with its short growing seasons and very diverse temperate environments.

Hoeing around a maize plant.

Eight-rowed Maiz de Ocho dates to the 12th century AD in southeastern Colorado (Galinat and Campbell, 1967) and spread rapidly into the Eastern Woodlands at about that time. It was apparently preceded across the southern Plains into the Southeast by a small-cob 12- and 14-rowed race of hard flint corn, known as "Northern American pop". Eight-row maize dominated eastern agriculture after AD 1100. At European contact, Maiz de Ocho, often called "New England flint corn" grew from the Dakotas across to New England and up to the northern limits in southern Canada, places like the Gaspe Peninsula.

Southwestern farmers experimented with the genetically variable maize grown at higher elevations for many centuries. *Zea mays* is at the northern limits of its range in the Southwest, intolerant of too short growing seasons, weak soil conditions, and such hazards as crop disease and strong winds. The most important factors of all were soil moisture and water supplies. By careful seed selection, the farmers developed higher elevation varieties with elongated corn cobs and distinctive root structures, whose seeds could be planted at considerable depth, to be nourished by retained ground moisture. They became experts at selecting the right soils for cultivation, those with good moisture-retaining properties on north- and east-facing slopes that receive little direct sunlight. The farmers favored floodplains and arroyo mouths where the soil was naturally irrigated. They would divert water from streams, springs, or rainfall runoff to irrigate their crops. As with hunting and foraging, risk management was vital. So the cultivators dispersed their gardens widely from one another to minimize dangers of local drought or flood. They learned how to shorten the growing season from the 130 to 140 days needed in such a hot, arid environment closer to 120 days by planting on shaded slopes, planting in different areas, and at varying elevations. Over the centuries, a great diversity of highly effective dry climate agricultural techniques developed throughout the Southwest.

Squashes and beans also form part of Ford's Upper Sonoran Agricultural Complex. Squashes (*Cucurbita pepo*) appear in Southwestern sites after 1000 BC, and were all of the same variety until about AD 900, when other forms were grown. This versatile plant was used for containers and harvested for its seeds and fruit.

Common beans probably appeared in the Southwest by 500 BC, and became a widespread staple throughout the region. Beans were a very important crop in the Southwest and elsewhere in North America, especially when grown with maize, for, as we have remarked, the two complement each other (Kaplan, 1965). Beans contain a high level of the amino acid called lycene, which aids in the effective digestion of the protein found in corn. Not only that, but beans, being legumes, can return vital nitrogen to the ground, nitrogen that is depleted by maize. Thus, by growing maize and beans in the same garden, Southwestern farmers could maintain the fertility of the soil for longer periods of time (Castetter and Bell, 1942).

The factors that governed the acceptance of domesticated plants in the Southwest were very different from those in the Eastern Woodlands (Chapter 18). There, basically sedentary cultures adopted maize, beans, and squash at different times. In the Southwest, these three crops arrived at different times, adopted by small, mobile social groups, among whom crop cultivation required a major adjustment in settlement patterns and

Bean plants, Hotevilla Pueblo, Hopi, Arizona, c.1919.

hunting-foraging activities (Wills, 1989). The point is that the dispersal of domesticated plants into the Southwest was not just a matter of them being available for cultivation. Their adoption involved a conscious decision by individual, scattered, mobile Archaic hunter-gatherer groups to utilize these more predictable foods. This decision probably involved deliberate efforts by groups living at low elevations to enhance winter and springtime food supplies (Wills, 1989). Later, Wills speculates, maize and other crops were planted in the uplands, but as part of a different strategy – one that allowed people to monitor wild plant food resources at high altitudes while living off stored agricultural products. To argue that food production spread uniformly and immediately all over the Southwest is a gross simplification of very complicated processes.

The Lower Sonoran Agricultural Complex
AD 300 to 500

Another set of crops came to the Southwest from Mexico considerably later, between AD 300 and 500. These new crops, all plants that are tolerant of high desert temperatures, tended to require irrigation. This Lower Sonoran Agricultural Complex (Ford, 1981) includes sieva beans (somewhat similar to the familiar lima) and other bean varieties, cushaw squashes, pigweed, and cotton. Apparently, these crops were introduced to the Hohokam, who were already practicing irrigation agriculture in parts of the lower Sonoran desert. Their use was confined almost entirely to the hot regions of the south.

The Consequences of Southwestern Agriculture

The appearance of corn did not trigger a dramatic revolution in Southwestern life in the short term. The early corn was not very productive, and could be planted fairly casually without the careful tending needed to produce bountiful crops – at altitudes above 656 ft (200 m). Under these conditions it was probably about as high yielding as a stand of wild seeds. As Linda Cordell points out (1984), a plot of corn tended and harvested in a small garden would require less caloric energy to grow than wild seeds scattered in isolated locales over a wide area. This is not a problem when people hunt and forage over large territories. If mobility is restricted, however, then the advantage of stands of even low-yielding corn is considerable. Corn does not have as much food value as some wild foods, especially piñons and walnuts. But, as we have seen, piñon harvests in particular are subject to great cyclical variations, making them a less reliable food source than the newly cultivated crops.

The maizes grown in the Southwest were adapted to a wide variety of environmental conditions and were drought-resistant strains. Eventually, they became of staple importance to many Southwestern peoples, who became expert at growing maize using simple irrigation techniques or natural springs or seeps to water their crops and amplify sporadic rainfall.

The expansion of food production resulted from a long-term process of successfully manipulating crops. Serious maize agriculture in an arid region like the Southwest requires a great investment of time and energy, strong incentives for adopting more sedentary lifeways. As people settled down near their maize fields, they still relied on wild plant foods exploited in far smaller territories, territories restricted in size by their sedentary lifeway. The shortage of these wild foods in turn tended to encourage not only more cultivation, but the founding of new agricultural communities in neighboring areas where farming could be safely practiced.

The adoption of agriculture was not an inevitable process. The archaeological record of more than 2000 years of Southwestern farming shows cycles of expansion and contraction, of growing population densities within limited areas that suddenly dispersed over the landscape. At others, the expansion succeeded and stable farming populations survived over many centuries. Sometimes, the experiment failed and the land was abandoned. But once agriculture took hold in the Southwest, exclusive reliance on hunting and gathering was no longer a viable adaptation. And the farmers adapted to a high-risk agricultural environment with ingenuity and remarkable technological skill, skills that survived until European contact and beyond.

The Beginnings of Village Life in the Southwest
AD 200 to 900

The seven centuries between AD 200 and 900 saw the gradual spread of sedentary villages over much of the Southwest. These communities varied greatly in size, but were made up of individual oval to circular houses that were occupied over some length of time. In other parts of North America like the Midwestern river bottoms, sedentary settlements appear to have developed long before agriculture took hold. In the Southwest, agriculture was an essential prerequisite for abandoning a more mobile lifeway.

The term "sedentary settlement" conjures up images of quite large villages clustered near a patchwork of cultivated gardens, with much the same size of settlement being commonplace over considerable areas. In fact, Southwestern villages varied greatly in size, partly because of the highly diverse environment with its highly localized natural resources, and also because opportunities for cultivation varied greatly from one location to the next. Nowhere did the villagers subsist off agriculture alone. Wild plant foods were always of significant importance.

These early village communities, sometimes still grouped under the loose term "Basketmaker" over much of the northern Southwest (Chapter 2), owed much to their Archaic predecessors. At first, the people used simple, small *manos* and basin-like *metates* to grind both wild and domesticated seeds. In time they developed more elaborate grinders – large slabs or troughs worked with *manos* needing two hands to operate, presumably for grinding larger amounts of maize more efficiently. Stone technology remained much the same as in earlier millennia, except for the introduction of the bow and arrow, the latter tipped with small side-notched and stemmed stone projectile points. Michael Glassow (1972) believes that the appearance of the bow and arrow may have coincided with the rising importance of agriculture. It was a means of acquiring more game protein, for the bow and arrow enabled hunters to ambush a wide variety of game, shoot it from a greater distance, and to hunt in more wooded country.

One important innovation appears in the Southwest in about AD 200 – pottery. It is probably no coincidence that such containers first appear as farming and sedentary settlement become widespread. Too heavy for nomadic hunters, clay pots came into their own in village life. They were useful for storage and cooking over open fires, were strong and easily manufactured, and lasted for a long time.

In the north and in the mountains, the earliest villagers lived in pithouses, dwellings where part of the walls are formed from the sides of an excavated pit. According to Robin Farwell (1981), pithouses are thermally efficient, for the heat loss from underground structures is less than for above room pueblos. Farwell's calculations show that a pithouse required less manpower or fuel to heat in winter, a feature that would make them adaptive at higher altitudes.

Hopi woman making pottery in Oraibi village. She is using a coiling technique to build up the walls of the vessel.

Most pithouses were round or oval, up to 16.4 ft (5 m) across, their floors dug about 1.6 ft (0.5 m) below ground surface. They often contained storage pits or fire pits. As far as is known, the superstructures were usually a mud-covered framework of vertical poles set round the pit, the roof supported on strong post supports, or with a single cross-beam. Pithouse forms evolved into more-or-less standardized designs as the generations passed. Houses in the Mogollon region varied from round to rectangular,

The Mogollon Harris site, New Mexico. (Above) Plans and reconstructed cross-sections of an early round pithouse and a later rectangular pithouse. (Right) Plan of the village.

0 150 ft

0 50 m

with fire pits set into the floor in front of the sloping entryway. Anasazi area pithouses boasted of adobe walls that subdivided them into kitchens and living areas. Ventilators, air deflectors, and raised sleeping platforms were common features, as were roof hatches accessible with a wooden ladder.

Lower Sonoran desert houses were quite different, not pithouses as such, but rectangular or square houses built in pits. The floor was excavated up to 8 in (21 cm) below the ground, the roof and walls being formed of poles, reeds, grass, and mud. Small hearths lay just inside the entrances.

Early villages in the north varied greatly in size, from hamlets of merely two or three pithouses to large settlements that contained as many as 25 to 35 houses, perhaps sometimes many more. Everywhere, the houses were arranged without apparent order, associated with storage pits and cooking ovens. Settlements in the Hohokam area of the Sonoran desert were made up of loose clusters of houses covering much larger areas. At all but the smallest villages, one or more structures appear to have had special functions. These are usually pithouses, but ones that display unusual architectural features or greater dimensions than residential structures. For example, one circular pithouse at the Galaz site in the Mimbres Valley of New Mexico was 22.9 ft (7 m) across, with a floor area two and a half times that of nearby houses. Steven LeBlanc (1983) believes this is a kiva, for it has stylized adobe pillars close to the entrance ramp, exactly like those

Reconstruction of a Mogollon pithouse village from the Pine Lawn phase by the Chicago Natural History Museum.

Long-distance trade in luxuries. (Top) Copper bells found at Mimbres sites were imported from Mexico. (Above) Hohokam etched shell.

found in later Mogollon kivas. There are traces of what may have been ceremonial seats, flat stones set into the floor.

There were considerable differences in the size of early farming villages throughout the Southwest, also in the range of trade objects in various settlements, as well as in house size and storage capacity. Clearly, these differences have important implications for understanding early social and political organization. Were these villages independent entities, or were some of them linked by alliances or other political ties? In recent years, large-scale cultural resource management surveys have recorded thousands of early farming settlements large and small, and a great diversity of pottery styles and material culture from village to village. Do these represent differences in social organization? Despite occasional large centers, most settlements were little more than simply family households, the so-called *rancheria*.

Not that these were completely self-sufficient settlements. Anyone farming in the Southwestern highlands had to maintain constant contacts with the lowlands, as was the case with historic Mormon populations living in the area (Lightfoot, 1981; Plog, F. 1983). To argue that early Southwestern farming villages were autonomous, egalitarian, and completely self-sufficient appears to go against the environmental realities of the area. Any form of long-distance exchange of essentials and luxuries by farming cultures usually results in some form of ranked society. Modern Pueblo groups are far less egalitarian than often thought, a phenomenon that can also be observed in early Spanish records (Upham, 1982). Whether earlier Archaic, or even Paleo-Indian, societies were ranked is a matter of on-going debate.

Trade relationships probably played an important role in village social organization. Many essential commodities like obsidian, chert, and other raw materials were exchanged over considerable distances, sometimes even hundreds of miles (Green, 1982). Utilitarian artifacts like pots passed through many hands. Luxuries like turquoise, copper bells, and sea shells were exchanged over enormous distances, the former as far south as the Valley of Mexico. The trade was apparently highly organized and conducted by local leaders (Upham, 1982). For instance, Polvadera Peak near Santa Fé yields a fine obsidian that is found at many sites in Arizona, but they are always sites with more than 10 rooms, local or regional centers where large populations were concentrated. It is also believed that kivas may have served as centers for exchange systems (Plog, F. 1983).

Judging from historical records of intercommunity exchange in the Southwest, it involved a complex series of economic and social processes (Ford, 1985). It was conditioned by the great environmental diversity and the differences in productivity from one area to the next. With unpredictable rainfall, food shortages can result from poor piñon harvests or crop failure. Survival depended on gift exchanges between trading partners and friends, and on the social ties between them. So exchange equalized resources and also allowed the acquisition of valuable surpluses of luxury goods that might be traded later for food and other necessities. Every Southwestern group was dependent on others for ritual paraphernalia, items such as buffalo hides, red ocher, macaw feathers, sea shells, even coiled baskets used in naming ceremonies. The exchange could be between neighboring communities, along long, well-established trails that were in use for thousands of years, between friends or complete strangers, whose language one did not understand.

At first, exchange may have resulted from regular informal contacts, but in time these became more formalized. One set of rules and conventions applied to fellow villagers, normally based on notions of continuous sharing and mutual assistance, seasonal gambling, ceremonial redistribution, and trading parties. Everyone had access to local commodities and goods from afar. Exchange between neighboring communities often involved trading with relatives, or with non-strangers, with visitors bringing gifts in the expectation that they would be reciprocated in the future. Inter-community trading was constant, and sometimes took the form of informal markets, often on ceremonial occasions.

In recent times, southern desert villages would engage in inter-village entertainments where food and gifts were exchanged. These would distribute grain to needy communities, and also create trading friendships that could last for many generations. Long-distance trade was normally in the hands of men and conducted along a myriad of trails, some possibly marked by petroglyphs and shrines. One well-known, age-old trail brought Pacific sea shells from near Los Angeles across the desert to Needles, along the Gila River, and then along various branches to many villages and pueblos. A complex trail network linked the Plains, Great Basin, Sonora, the Southwest and California at European contact, most of them maintained not by parties of traders, but by chains of exchange and gift friendship that handled different commodities like sea shells, buffalo robes, and turquoise ornaments over enormous distances. Somewhat similar trail networks extended all over the Southeast after about 2000 BC. Exchange was an integral part of social relations, one that corrected economic differences, forged alliances and served as a basis for resolving disputes before warfare erupted.

Extensive cultural resource management surveys in many areas of the Southwest have changed earlier perceptions of prehistoric social organization. Prior to about AD 1100 most Southwestern sites averaged about three rooms. After 1100, the number increases to around 10. In both cases up to half the rooms were used for storage alone, with, perhaps, about 10 to 15 people living at each location. Most of these small communities were engaged in basic subsistence activities. They did not exist in isolation, for the inhabitants of each rancheria may have interacted with one another all the time, as well, perhaps, as maintaining ties with a common kiva, as is known to have happened in some areas of Arizona, or with one larger, central site. There were reciprocal ties between different communities that enabled individual households to acquire foodstuffs by exchange when shortages developed.

Occasionally, however, people lived in communities that formed more structured "alliances" (Upham, 1982), which shared some general characteristics:

– One or more central sites, even a central "zone" of clustered sites;
– Basically uniform architecture;
– Relatively homogeneous ceramic styles;
– Some signs of specialized craftsmanship;
– Regular trade and exchange;
– Some degree of social ranking or stratification.

On the Colorado Plateau, Fred Plog (1983) paints a picture of thousands of small, relatively autonomous farming communities that flourished for many generations. Occasionally, however, alliances appeared that drew these villages into larger, social and economic networks. These can be identified in the archaeological record by very homogeneous architecture and ceramic styles. Society became more complex, but never to the higher degree of stratification that developed to the south in highland and lowland Mexico. These alliances waxed and waned, but wherever they developed, they were associated with dramatic population increases.

The Plog hypothesis, with its emphasis on spatial rainfall variations and food scarcities, contrasts with other theories that argue for alliances developed in environmentally favorable areas. Its main weakness is the great difficulty of reconstructing how alliances were structured. Were expert traders and entrepreneurs or powerful kin leaders, "Big Men" in common anthropological parlance, responsible for political leadership? Or did some other social mechanism allow development of more formal ties between scattered communities? At the moment, we do not know. Whatever these mechanisms, however, the closing centuries of prehistoric times saw a dramatic efflorescence and elaboration of Southwestern culture.

Further Reading

In addition to the references for Chapter 13:

Ford, Richard I. (ed.). 1985. *Prehistoric Food Production in North America.* University Museum of Anthropology, University of Michigan, Ann Arbor. Wide-ranging essays by leading authorities on the origins of major North American crops. Strongly recommended.

Gumerman, George. 1984. *A View from Black Mesa.* University of Arizona Press, Tucson. A popular account of the Black Mesa area, scene of a major CRM research project in the Southwest.

Plog, Fred. 1974. *The Study of Prehistoric Culture Change.* Academic Press, New York. Plog examines the pithouse-pueblo transition in this much-quoted monograph.

Powell, Shirley. 1983. *Mobility and Adaptation: the Anasazi of Black Mesa, Arizona.* Southern Illinois University Press, Carbondale, Illinois. A study of agricultural strategies among village communities.

Vivian, R. Gwinn. 1974. "Conservation and Diversion: water-control systems in the Anasazi Southwest," *in* Theodore Downing and McGuire Gibson, *Irrigation's Impact on Society.* University of Arizona Press, Tucson, Anthropological Papers 25, pp. 95–112. Base-line article on water control and agriculture in the Southwest.

Wills, S.H. 1989. *Early Prehistoric Agriculture in the American Southwest.* School of American Research Press, Santa Fé, NM. Closely argued and impressive statement on the origins of Southwestern agriculture based on up-to-date evidence.

CHAPTER 15

THE RISE OF PUEBLO SOCIETY

If there is one broad theme in Southwestern prehistory, it is that of slowly evolving cultural continuity, continuity that extends back deep into Archaic times and persists right up through the eventful centuries of Pueblo culture that immediately preceded European contact in the 16th century AD. We must now examine some of the complex cultural processes that took hold in the Southwest after the emergence of village life early in the Christian era.

Pithouses remained in general use throughout the northern Southwest and the mountains until about AD 700. The next three centuries saw a change from pithouse villages to settlements made up of multi-room buildings constructed from adobe clay or masonry. In some areas, like Mesa Verde, Colorado, the change was a gradual one, with the first rooms being storage areas built behind pithouses. Later people moved into surface rooms, turning their old pithouses into kivas or ceremonial rooms. In other areas, the shift was a rapid one. The rate of changeover is so varied that no general cause like climatic change can be invoked (Cordell, 1984). Rather, an increased dependence on agriculture and more sedentary settlement followed from population growth. This dependence led to major changes in the ways food was stored and prepared, to the point that large grain stocks had to be husbanded each harvest time, not only surplus food but also the seed for the next planting season. Cooking and preparing food now took longer. These activities continued throughout the year, sometimes in inclement weather, and took up much more space than hitherto. Semi-subterranean houses were too small for the purpose, and it is hard to build interconnecting underground rooms without walls collapsing. So instead of constructing further below-surface rooms, the farmers erected above-ground structures for milling, storage, and other activities (illus. p.282). Such rooms were not so well insulated as semi-subterranean dwellings. In time the farmers built series of rooms abutting on one another, forming pueblos, a thermally relatively efficient way of living above ground in a climate with hot summers and cold winters. Such arrangements may have been more adaptive, but they were by no means universal. In many parts of the northern Southwest, people lived in dispersed or one- or two-room dwellings. Whether these differences are the result of using a variety of agricultural technologies or field systems is unknown.

The process may have been more complicated. Fred Plog (1974) used survey and excavation data from the upper Little Colorado River Valley and

Sites mentioned in Chapter 15.

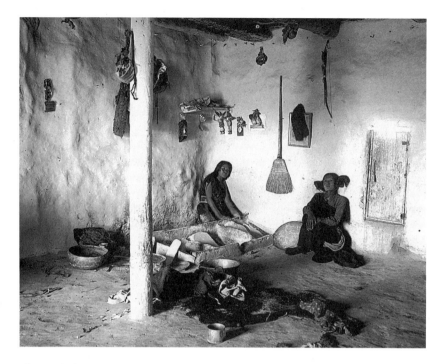

Interior of a Pueblo room: Hopi women grinding corn, 1895. The transition from pithouse to pueblo involved increasingly specialized use of space.

chronicled a population increase between Basketmaker and Pueblo times. He found that the people engaged in more and more diverse activities, and were more sedentary, after about AD 200. Three hundred years later, the pithouse villages were much larger, then progressively abandoned as people dispersed into smaller villages. This dispersal did not, apparently, coincide with a major climatic change, so Plog believes that the villages were too large and the social organization too simple to handle the complex environmental and social problems that developed over many generations. The concentration of people into larger communities may have resulted in more complex exchange networks, increased food sharing, and cooperation in hunting and foraging. These broke down when the population scattered, so individual communities turned to more dependence on agriculture as a more productive way of feeding smaller population densities. The Plog study shows how complicated the changeover from Basketmaker to Pueblo was – a change involving not only population growth, but new subsistence strategies and ways of integrating society into larger social units.

Between AD 750 and 900, village settlement expanded greatly throughout the northern Southwest, and especially on the Colorado Plateau. There was a great diversity of settlement, everything from large sites to tiny rancherias, representing a great heterogeneity of social organization and political life. Most scholars think of Southwestern prehistory over the past 1200 years in terms of cultural continuity between early village life and modern Pueblo Indian societies. Does this mean, then, that the same ideological and social structures and beliefs served for early villages as for modern pueblos? The question is much debated, but unanswered.

Many investigators relied on Indian migration tales and clan legends to theorize about the origins of matrilineal western Pueblo clans, approaches that were speculative at best. Then the great anthropologist Julian Steward (1955) approached the question from economic and ecological stand-points. The late farming villages of the San Juan drainage consisted of small clusters of houses located near one another. These, he believed, were a sign that the people relied heavily on agriculture. Had they been hunters and foragers alone, their settlements would have been separated by large hunting territories. Thus, he argued, the house clusters were occupied by unilateral groups living near their farm lands. As the population rose, small lineages split off and established their own house clusters relatively close to their former kin.

Among the Western Pueblo, the tending of crops may have been the work of women expanding foraging activities. Steward believed that the same form of organization pertained in early Pueblo settlements. Even when villages came together in larger settlements, each group maintained its own social and ceremonial identity. In early village times, when each cluster was not more than four or five houses, the basic social unit was the local lineage, a lineage consisting of a few families related by kin ties living together. In later times, this identity was maintained, with five or six rooms per kiva, everyone living in a system of exogamous clans. Then, as pueblos became larger after AD 1000 and there were many more rooms per kiva, the Eastern Pueblo lost their clan affiliations. In contrast, the Hopi maintained strong clan solidarity through ritual and other social devices.

Steward's model fitted well with the archaeological data of the 1950s, but he was at a loss to identify an ecological reason for people to cluster in larger settlements as time went on. He considered it was for defense. Today, we know that the dispersed household, rancheria pattern was much more widespread than Steward believed. Rather than defense, it seems possible that population pressure was the cause.

The Chaco Phenomenon
AD 900 to 1150

Chaco Canyon is a dramatic place, set in a stark landscape. The huge cliffs of the canyon glow yellow-gold in the sun, contrasting with the softer tones of desert sand, sage, and occasional cottonwood trees. Great shadows fall

Nineteenth-century artist's reconstruction of Pueblo Bonito, Chaco Canyon, New Mexico.

across the canyon as the sun sets, the grandiose landscape dwarfing the walls of the great pueblos that are camouflaged naturally against the high cliffs. A thousand years ago, flickering fires, barking dogs, and the echoing murmur of human voices would have greeted the evening visitor (Cordell, 1979; Frazier, 1986; Noble, D. 1984). Today, the ancient human settlements of the Anasazi, "the old people" (Chapter 13), are silent, an integral part of a spectacular desert landscape.

Beginnings. The Chaco sites document a dramatic increase in population density and cultural complexity that began about AD 900 and lasted two and a half centuries. During this time, the Chaco Phenomenon expanded from its canyon homeland to encompass an area of more than 25,000 sq. miles (64,750 sq. km) of the San Juan Basin and adjacent uplands. (Recent estimates more than double this area, and research continues (Lekson and others, 1988).) The people constructed large, well-planned towns, extensive road and water control systems, and outlying sites that were linked to the canyon by roads and visual communication systems. Many farmers still lived in small, dispersed villages. Many luxury items are found in Chaco sites of this period, items traded from afar: turquoise, the bones of exotic macaws ultimately from tropical forests, and copper bells, to mention only a few. So distinctive is this Anasazi efflorescence that it has been named the "Chaco Phenomenon."

Many intriguing questions surround the Chaco Phenomenon. How did such an elaborate efflorescence of prehistoric culture arise so suddenly, and collapse with such rapidity? What were the cultural processes that led to the sudden emergence of regional integration in this area of the Southwest? The Chaco area is a desert environment, with long winters, short growing seasons, and marginal rainfall. How could the Anasazi have developed such an elaborate culture in a high-risk environment, where the most one might expect were communities of widely dispersed farming villages? The number of residential rooms suggests a far larger population than could be supported by the available arable land. What activities in the Canyon prompted a much higher use and breakage of clay vessels than usual and the construction of many miles of long, wide roads through a sparsely vegetated desert where such constructions appear unnecessary?

The 32 sq. miles (82 sq. km) of Chaco Canyon contains not only 13 "towns" and great kivas, but more than 2400 archaeological sites ranging from potsherd scatters to large monumental structures (Hayes and others, 1981). These sites give us an outline culture history for the Canyon. Paleo-Indian and Archaic people hunted and foraged in Chaco Canyon. During the first millennium BC, semi-sedentary hunter-gatherers began to cultivate squash and corn in the Canyon. About AD 490, locally developed strains of corn and perhaps an increase in annual rainfall led to the appearance of the first sedentary villages in the Canyon area, among them Shabik'eshchee, a village farming (Basketmaker III) settlement of shallow, earth-walled pithouses with wood and mud roofs. Each pithouse had a stone storage hut behind it to store corn, squash, beans, and other foods. The largest village in the Canyon boasted of as many as 20 pithouses clustered close to one another.

During village (Basketmaker) times, the Chaco Canyon population was still small. Then, between AD 700 and 900, the Anasazi Pueblo Indians

The main sites in Chaco Canyon, New Mexico. The dashed line indicates the extent of the National Monument.

largely abandoned pithouses and now lived in surface, masonry dwellings. They were enlarged versions of the Basketmaker storerooms, often facing the southeast to take advantage of the winter sun for warmth. The clusters of rooms, known as pueblos, were shaped into small arcs, a layout that made each room equidistant from the circular pithouses in the center. These gradually became kivas, the focal points of ceremonial life. Despite these changes, the Canyon population was still very small, perhaps between 1000 and 1500 people.

Efflorescence. During the 10th century, tree-rings show that the Chaco Canyon climate was highly variable, with very unpredictable summer rainfall. This made maize and bean agriculture a chancy business, with highly variable yields from one area of the Canyon to the next. It was during this century that three large pueblos built at the junctions of major drainages came into prominence – Penasco Blanco, Pueblo Bonito, and Una Vida. They were semi-circular pueblos, with open plazas and kivas lying to the southeast. The buildings were much larger, some of them multi-storied. James Judge believes that the three sites may have served primarily as food storage areas, not only crops but wild plant foods and game meat obtained from nearby drainages. Perhaps these food supplies were grown or collected by different communities and pooled at these strategic locations for later redistribution, a mechanism for overcoming highly variable crop yields resulting from patchy rainfall.

During the 10th century, Chaco Canyon appears to have assumed a dominant role in the processing of turquoise into finished ornaments. Turquoise does not occur in the area, but the Chaco people had access to,

Cylindrical Anasazi vase with painted, polychrome decoration from Pueblo Bonito, c.AD 1200, height 20 cm.

and may even have controlled, sources near Santa Fé, New Mexico, about 100 miles (161 km) to the east and elsewhere. Many small Chaco villages contained turquoise workshops, and ritual ornaments in all stages of manufacture have been found among the more than 60,000 turquoise fragments found in the Canyon. Other ritual objects associated with Chaco towns include cylindrical vases, human effigy vessels, pottery incense burners, copper bells, sea shell trumpets, painted tablets and wooden effigies, also macaw skeletons, and elaborate inlaid decoration in selenite, mica, and turquoise on shell, wood, or basketry. Chaco itself may also have assumed an important role as ritual center in its own right. Whatever the religious role of the Canyon, it seems certain that the turquoise trade was of vital importance to its inhabitants, perhaps as a way of offsetting food shortages.

By about AD 1050, the Chaco Phenomenon was in full swing, a number of dispersed communities that interacted constantly with one another, linked by regular exchanges of essential foods and other commodities. Tree-rings show that the next 80 years were ones of generally good rainfall, a weather cycle that may have kept the system going longer than it might otherwise have done. Chaco Canyon's central role in the Phenomenon is not disputed, but exactly what this role was remains somewhat of a mystery. Between 1075 and 1115, the Chacoans built more structures in their Canyon than ever before. But the population was never large: estimates based on room counts range between 2000 and 10,000, with a recent estimate of 5600 being a reasonable guess. When reconstructions of the amount of available arable land are brought into play, there was only enough acreage to support about 2000 people. Perhaps, argue some

(Right, and opposite) Pueblo Bonito, Chaco Canyon: a photograph taken earlier this century, and a plan. One entered the pueblo by climbing ladders over the protective wall. The lower rooms were probably used mainly for storage.

archaeologists, the major sites were constructed to accommodate far larger influxes of people, who came to the Canyon occasionally, perhaps for regular religious observances.

The Chaco settlements are striking for their careful planning. Their actual construction must have involved well-organized labor forces to construct their average of 216 rooms, sometimes arranged in up to four stories. The ceilings are high, rooms well constructed with cored masonry covered on both sides with carefully selected ashlar, sometimes arranged in alternating courses of large and small stones to form patterns. These decorative veneers were covered with adobe plaster or matting. The great kivas were built with great care, roofed over with carefully dressed pine beams, many of them carried in from considerable distances away. This extravagance may reflect the religious importance of the major towns (Marshall and Doyel, 1981).

The nine larger settlements within Chaco Canyon all have at least one great kiva, and there are instances of isolated kivas associated with smaller settlements as well. The great kiva at Casa Rinconada is about 63 ft (19.2 m) across, and others are almost as large. The amount of labor involved in digging these subterranean chambers and constructing the walls, roofs, and antechambers must have been considerable, for some kiva walls were at least 11 ft (3.4 m) high. They are entered by a ladder or through recessed stone staircases, often through an antechamber beyond the stairs. Common kiva features include wall niches where offerings of beads and pendants were sometimes placed, encircling benches around the walls, pairs of masonry lined vaults, and a raised firebox in the center.

(Above) Plan of the great kiva at Casa Rinconada, Chaco Canyon, showing the subfloor passage, fire box, fire screen, parallel vaults or foot drums, seating pits for the roof-support columns, and the north antechamber rooms.

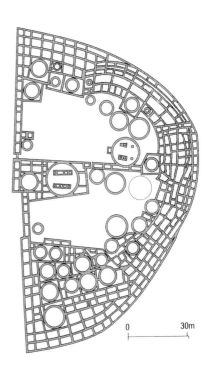

0   30m

The Bonito pueblos are remarkable for the small number of burials found within their precincts. Pueblo Bonito (illus. pp. 286–87) has more than 800 rooms, yet only between 50 and 60 burials can be associated with the town during its 150-year life (Hayes, 1981). Neil Judd once estimated that the settlement should have experienced between 4700 and 5400 deaths during the same period. The frequency of burials in Chaco Canyon generally is far smaller than elsewhere in the Southwest. Perhaps few people were buried within the sacred confines of the Canyon.

Beyond the general indications of farming, hunting, and foraging, we know little about the activities that took place in larger Chaco settlements. But there are some curious features in the archaeological record, especially from the Pueblo Alto site (Lekson and others, 1988). This large settlement was built between 1020 and 1060, but only 5 of the 85 rooms were actually inhabited. The remainder were large suites without interconnecting doors that may have had some social or political importance, or small, connected store rooms that opened not into the settlement with its plaza, but onto the adjacent road. These were inaccessible from within the pueblo. It is as if the residents had but limited control over these store houses. Pueblo Alto's trash middens yielded over 150,000 potsherds, a breakage rate quite out of proportion to the tiny population of the pueblo. Many of the vessels were made of clay imported from the Chuska area, some 45 miles (72.4 km) to the west. Unusually large quantities of animal bones and imported Washington Pass chert, also from the Chuska area, came from the same trash middens. The trash in the Pueblo Alto middens is layered, as if it was deposited intermittently, perhaps when people converged on Chaco for regular seasonal gatherings (Lekson and others, 1988).

Outliers. By AD 1115, at least 70 communities dispersed over more than 25,000 sq. miles (64,750 sq. km) of northwest New Mexico and parts of southern Colorado were linked through the socioeconomic and ritual networks centered on Chaco Canyon. Judging from other such networks, the trade and ritual activities of the Chaco Phenomenon were probably controlled by a small number of people. But whether these individuals formed a social elite with special privileges reserved to them, and them alone, or were simply members of an important kin group, is still uncertain.

Outlying sites display considerable cultural variation, but they share architectural features such as great or tower kivas with Pueblo Bonito and other large Canyon centers, and contain much Chaco pottery. They are connected to Chaco Canyon by a roadway or a signaling station system, arc-shaped stone structures on high ground so sited as to give line-of-sight visibility between one location and the next.

The Salmon Ruin near Bloomfield, New Mexico, reveals some details of how the system came into being. The foundations for the 290-room pueblo with its great kiva and tower kiva were laid out before any structures were built. It was constructed in three planned stages between AD 1088 and 1106 (Irwin-Williams, 1980). The distribution of local and Chaco vessels through the pueblo suggest that Salmon was founded by both local San Juan people and migrants from Chaco itself. Chaco pottery was associated with the tower kiva and associated rooms, as if there was a strong ideological component to the organization of what appears to have been an egalitarian community. It was, however, a site whose inhabitants had a "high degree of technical knowledge and specialization, and a centralized authority structure, tight social control, and membership in a central network economically and physically linked to the Chaco" (Irwin-Williams, 1980).

In a sense, outlying communities like Salmon were not colonies, but rather descendant communities, places that were often established in somewhat marginal agricultural areas as a result of population growth or factionalism within older communities. Some were formed to exploit nearby natural resources. The Pueblo Bonito-style· architecture used to build them often made dramatic use of the natural landscape, the buildings extending mesa cliffs, forming parts of canyon walls. Some pueblos stand in complete isolation in the harsh desert, what has been called a "human monument in the void of the desert plain." "It is as if the environment is personified with attributes of mythological character, and the placement of structures was dictated by Chacoan cosmography and sacred geography, balanced by certain economic considerations." (Marshall and Doyel, 1981).

The roads that connect outlying areas to the Canyon are remarkable for their straight courses. They do not follow contours, but change direction in abrupt turns, with stairways and ramps to surmount steep obstacles. These may be little more than toe holds, or elaborate stairways with wide steps cut out of bedrock or formed from masonry blocks. The roads themselves were sometimes cut into bedrock or through the desert soil to a depth of nearly 5 ft (1.5 m). At other times, the road makers simply cleared the vegetation and loose soil or stones from the pathway, lining some segments with boulders. The major roads were up to 29.5 ft (9 m) wide, secondary

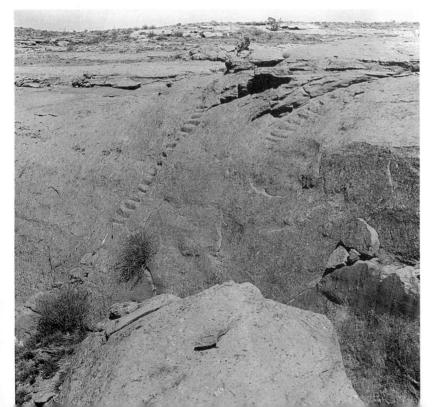

The Chacoan road system. (Left) Jackson Stairway, Chaco Canyon. (Below) Map of the road system, and outlying sites of the Chaco Phenomenon (black dots). Solid lines indicate roads documented by ground surveys, dashed lines segments known from aerial surveys.

routes about half that width. By using aerial photographs, fieldworkers have been able to trace roads extending from Chaco almost to the Colorado/New Mexico border and Aztec Ruins, some 50 miles (80.2 km) away. Other roads connect Chaco to natural resource source areas in modern-day Zuñi country and elsewhere. More than 250 miles (402 km) of roads have been traced so far, but the system may have extended as far north as the San Juan Range in the Rocky Mountains to the north, the Mogollon Mountains to the south, and from the turquoise mines near Santa Fé in the east to the Little Colorado River in the west. Current thinking suspects that the Chaco Phenomenon was the center of a vast regional system that extended far beyond the San Juan Basin (Lekson and others, 1988).

Chaco road construction must have involved the deployment of large numbers of people and considerable group organization. Unlike the trail systems that connected hundreds of prehistoric communities in the far west and in the Eastern Woodlands, these were wide, straight highways, whose significance still eludes us. Were they highways for transporting valuable natural resources to major pueblos? Or were they, as James Judge argues, pilgrim roads? Without draft animals or wheeled carts, the Chaco people had no use for formal roads for their everyday business. Originally, perhaps, people traveled from outlying communities to Chaco to acquire turquoise objects, to trade food for ritual paraphernalia. In time, this trade became institutionalized in regular ceremonies and festivals, where people gathered from many miles around for seasonal rituals, for exchange of food and other commodities, and where leaders from widely dispersed communities gathered to cement political and economic alliances.

Each member of the network would have complex obligations to fulfil, among them, presumably, the supplying of people to construct and maintain the road system, to transport wooden beams for building large pueblos in Chaco (more than 200,000 were needed to build them), and for many communal tasks. In other words, the Chaco system was a mechanism for integrating a large number of communities scattered widely in a harsh and unpredictable environment. By regulating and maintaining a large and far-flung exchange system, the leaders who controlled this intricate system were able to support far more people than the area would normally have carried, using a very simple agricultural technology to do so.

Gwinn Vivian has argued (1989) that the Chaco Phenomenon was not a complex, centralized society, but an "egalitarian enterprise," a variant of the San Juan cultural tradition that evolved increasingly more complex and closer economic, social, and ritual linkages between different groups. This complexity was not, however, a sign of centralized control, as some other authorities suggest.

The Chaco Collapse. The Chaco Phenomenon reached its peak between AD 1100 and 1130, at which point a prolonged drought cycle affected the San Juan Basin for 50 years. Tree-ring analyses show that dry year followed dry year, causing crop failures and reducing wild plant and animal resources in an area that was relatively marginal for agriculture at the best of times. By 1130, the Chaco system had probably been expanded to its effective limits by growing population densities. There was a population decline after 1130 until the next century.

The Chaco system collapsed, but the collapse appears to have been a natural one, in the sense that the people either moved to other, more productive areas where they maintained long-term alliances, formed independent, highly scattered communities, or simply remained in environmentally favorable areas. Some may even have reverted to the largely mobile hunter-gatherer lifeway of their Archaic predecessors.

Some communities still continued to flourish in the Canyon, and at outlying pueblos like Aztec and Salmon to the north, but they now show strong influence from Mesa Verde, both in kiva architecture and ceramics, among other features. Whether these changes were the result of migration from the Mesa Verde area (Vivian and Mathews, 1965) or simply the diffusion of ideas is a matter of discussion (Toll and others, 1980). Mesa Verde was the last remaining large population center in the general area at the time (see below), so the transfer of some culture traits is hardly surprising. Throughout the area once integrated by the Chaco system, the reorganized society that emerged from the prolonged drought cycle probably bore some resemblance to Pueblo Indian society in the area immediately before European contact.

The Chaco Phenomenon was a highly organized socio-political system that covered a large region of the Southwest. But whether this was a purely local development centered on Chaco itself, or just one manifestation of a development that occurred in many eastern Anasazi societies is a matter for debate. Most scholars believe that the Phenomenon was a response not to long-distance trading activities by professional merchants from far to the south in Mexico (Lister and Lister, 1981), but the result of the harsh economic constraints imposed by major imbalances between population densities and food resources in a high-risk agricultural environment (Cordell, 1984).

The Chaco Phenomenon was by no means the only centralized political and social system flourishing in the Southwest about 900 years ago, for there were other complex societies living in sharply contrasting ecological zones.

Hohokam and Snaketown
AD 900 to 1450

Another important regional system developed in the Hohokam area in the Gila and Salt River basins between about AD 900 and 1150. The Gila River flows from the eastern mountains into the Colorado River through mesquite studded desert landscape. Its prehistoric banks abounded in deer, cottontail, muskrat, and water birds, while fish were often plentiful. This was an ideal place for irrigation agriculture, and for hunting and foraging. The diverse resource base combined with maize agriculture sustained Hohokam people for centuries.

The Snaketown site (so called after the Pima Indian name Skoaquik, "place of snakes") lies on the upper terrace of the river. Wide expanses of undulating mounds distinguish the site from the surrounding countryside, mounds that have attracted archaeological attention since the late 19th century. Emil Haury (1976) conducted the most extensive excavations at Snaketown, investigating 167 houses out of the hundreds at the site. He

The Hohokam site of Snaketown, Arizona. (Right) Pottery bowl with flute players, diameter c.27 cm. (Below) The Snaketown ballcourt.

also dug into Mound 29, where he identified seven phases of Hohokam settlement, the earliest beginning in about AD 500. Snaketown reached its apogee in the so-called Classic period, between approximately AD 1100 and 1450, a time when the inhabitants built ball courts and large platform mounds with clay capping. During this time, Snaketown was an important regional center, based on a large irrigation system with an elaborate canal network on the terraces of the Gila. Between 650 and 1000 people may have lived in the settlement, which now covers more than 0.4 sq. mile (1 sq. km) and encompasses more than 60 trash-filled mounds.

Most Snaketown dwellings were pithouses, the larger ones being found in the central area, often clustered close together. Apparently, the large, earlier houses were occupied for long periods of time by extended families. In time, this residence pattern gave way to one with smaller dwellings with pole and brush superstructures that may have served single families. People reoccupied the same locations again and again, so the excavators found floor after floor stacked one above another. Above-ground adobe structures came into use during the Classic period. There was an inner habitation zone around a central plaza, surrounded by a series of mounds and two ball courts, then an outer habitation area.

Many of Snaketown's mounds were trash heaps that provided an invaluable record of human occupation over many centuries. During the Classic period, some trash mounds were capped with a thick clay layer. One was 50 ft (15.24 m) across and 3 ft (1 m) high. The end result was a form of platform mound, which Haury compared with platform mounds in Mexican sites.

The ball courts had floors excavated about 20 in (0.5 m) below the desert floor. The sandy soil was piled up on either side, together with earth brought in from elsewhere. Similar courts were built at other Southwestern locations, but it is not known whether they had any connection with the famous Mexican courts at Chichén Itzá and other major Mesoamerican centers.

Like Chaco, Snaketown was part of a settlement hierarchy that included irrigation canal networks that formed individual irrigation systems associated with large villages and smaller rancherias. Elaborate trading networks carrying shell ornaments and other commodities criss-crossed Hohokam country. The shell objects traded included *Strombus* trumpets, heavy bracelets, beads, and carved ornaments of several kinds, including etched and painted forms. Copper bells, macaws, and other exotic objects were also exchanged over wide areas, and far into Mexico. Over time, patterns of interregional trade changed considerably, beginning perhaps with simple inter-village bartering, then developing into formal trading expeditions and well-established trade routes. Fairs or markets may even have developed at some locations, centered on ball courts and large pithouses, even, perhaps, involving full-time traders.

Emil Haury once believed (1976) that Snaketown's exotic artifacts, ball courts, and platform mounds were culture traits that had been introduced from Mexico. He theorized that the Hohokam were immigrants from the south, who brought their pottery and irrigation agriculture with them. The newcomers soon influenced the life of the local people, and Hohokam's distinctive desert culture resulted. More recent fieldwork suggests local antecedents for Hohokam. In all probability, the Snaketown Hohokam was

Snaketown stone pigment mortar in the shape of a toad, length 12 cm.

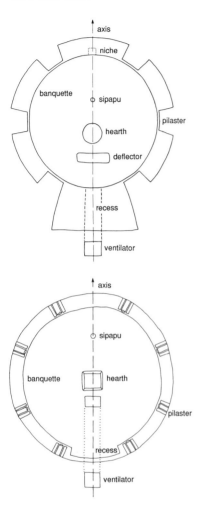

Differences in kiva architecture. (Top) Mesa Verde-style kivas in the northern San Juan Basin had a banquette-level recess on the south side which resulted in a distinctive keyhole-shaped outline to the structure. (Above) The Chacoan kiva had stone-and-log pilasters that rested on the banquette and supported the roof.

(Opposite) The Cliff Palace, Mesa Verde, Colorado.

an indigenous culture, perhaps originated in primeval Cochise Archaic roots, one that acquired greater complexity through time (Fish and Fish, 1977; Wilcox, 1985).

The relatively formal trade network that flourished in the Hohokam area after AD 1000 may reflect a common religious and belief system shared by scattered villages and larger centers, reflected in widely traded exotic objects. Judging from the distribution of ball courts, the trade networks extended from Gila Bend in the west to the Point of Pines area in the east, and from Tucson in the south to Flagstaff in the north. Within this area lived a wide diversity of farming communities displaying considerable cultural differences.

Snaketown declined in the 15th century, when the long-established settlement was abandoned. At Casa Grande (not to be confused with Casas Grandes below) and other later Hohokam sites, there are signs of Anasazi influence mixed with Hohokam artifacts. Haury and others believe, however, that the present-day Pima inhabitants of the area are descended from the Hohokam.

Mesa Verde and Mimbres
AD 500 to 1300

Between AD 900 and 1150, most of the Southwest was not part of the Chaco or Hohokam regional systems. There were a myriad of local cultural developments, where population densities were higher than usual, where soil and water conservation were practiced, and where some quite large settlements flourished. These were the areas between the regional systems, localized developments without the regional settlement hierarchies so characteristic of Chaco, and Hohokam, and, later, Casas Grandes.

Mesa Verde (AD 500 to 1300) covers an area north and northwest of the San Juan Basin (Noble, D., 1985; Rohn, 1977). This is a lusher environment that is wetter than much of the Southwest, with a natural juniper and piñon vegetational cover and many natural springs and seeps. As early as AD 950, there were significant differences between the Anasazi communities at Mesa Verde and Chaco, differences reflected in kiva architecture, burial practices, and perhaps ceramics. The Mesa Verde people used a different building technique, employing single- or double-coursed masonry for their kivas and pueblos.

Human occupation was probably sparse in the Mesa Verde area before about AD 575, but always greater than at Chaco. By AD 600, Basketmaker peoples were farming in the area. These Anasazi communities typically sheltered an extended family, villages of six to ten pithouses. Between 750 and 1150, the Anasazi Pueblo groups constructed surface villages made up of lines of post and mud rooms and associated subterranean pithouses. By the ninth century, these structures had become fully fledged pueblo complexes, that is to say, blocks of living and storage rooms, many of them as much as twice the size of earlier Basketmaker communities.

By 1100, the population of the northern San Juan region was concentrated in the Montezuma Valley, perhaps numbering some 30,000 people, mostly concentrated in villages of 1000 people or more. Of these,

only about 2500 lived in Mesa Verde. They became expert at conserving local water supplies. At the Mummy II location on Chapin Mesa, there are some 36 separate sites with 200 to 400 people situated near an artificial water supply (Rohn, 1971). This consisted of a stone-lined depression about 88.5 ft (27 m) across with high, artificial banks on two sides. A series of ditches brought water from a nearby catchment area through a feeder ditch 2637 ft (804 m) long. This impressive water control system supplied the domestic needs of hundreds of villagers.

Between AD 1200 and 1300, the focus of settlement moved south from the area around Mummy Lake to Cliff and Fewkes canyons (Rohn, 1977). By late Pueblo III times, Fewkes Canyon supported at least 33 habitation sites with between 530 and 545 rooms and 60 kivas, housing for 600 to 800 people. Cliff Palace, which was the largest settlement (illus. p.295), had 220 rooms and 23 kivas. People had moved from living in open locations to shelters and ledges in canyon walls, perhaps a defensive measure. Only a few precipitous trails led from the canyon to the plateau farmlands above.

Many Mesa Verde pueblos now boast of what appear to be defensive artifices, including walls that restrict access to ledges, large towers, and loopholes in walls flanking entries. However, there are no signs of warfare in the archaeological record. The nearby Montezuma Valley supported eight pueblos larger than the Cliff/Fewkes Canyon villages. One of them, Yellow Jacket, contains about 1800 rooms and probably housed some 2500 people, more than the whole of Mesa Verde. These settlements form a rough line running from northwest to southeast; other clusters of Pueblo population occur elsewhere in the Valley and in southeast Utah.

Both in Mesa Verde itself and in the surrounding country, large villages, almost towns, were homes for between 1000 and 2500 people, living in room clusters associated with kivas and other ceremonial buildings, also managed water supplies. The same communities were the focus of ceremonial life and exchange activities.

Although much of the population was apparently concentrated in the larger sites, there are few indications of social stratification. Cliff Palace appears to have been a focus of the Mesa Verde community, and there were some purely ceremonial sites, among them Fire Temple and Sun Temple. Fire Temple has been described as a modified great kiva, a rectangular structure at the foot of a cliff with antechambers, paired vaults, a bench, and raised firebox (Cassidy, 1965). In contrast, Sun Temple is D-shaped, with two massive stone walls enclosing two kiva-like structures ventilated by subsurface ventilators similar to those used at Chaco Canyon (Rohn, 1971; Cordell, 1984).

Many of the Mesa Verde sites were excavated long before modern archaeological methods came to the Southwest, so information on the social organization of the Mesa Verde people is sadly lacking. Arthur Rohn's excavations at the Mug House, a 13th-century 94-room cliff dwelling in Wetherill Mesa, provide some useful insights. He was able to show that the earliest inhabitants of the site built a series of rooms and a kiva associated with a trash heap and a single courtyard. Later on, the site grew to four house clusters, two within the Mug House Cave itself, two situated close by. Towards the end of the occupation, these four household clusters came together into a single pueblo that may have been divided into two parts separated by a wall (Rohn, 1977). The Mug House community

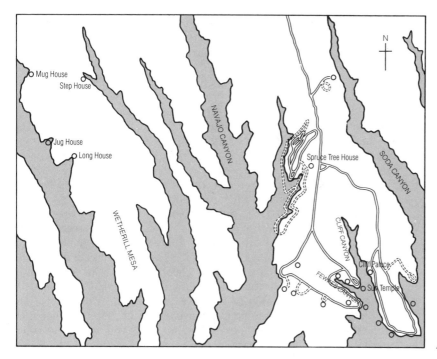

Map of the Mesa Verde area.

was not marked by any pronounced social differentiation, and, as Rohn argues, may have consisted of the inhabitants not only of this larger pueblo but of people living at nearby small settlements as well.

Mesa Verde's pueblos were constrained by the caves and rock overhangs under which they sheltered. Nevertheless, some communities reached considerable size. Judging from the numerous kivas, some of them multiple structures, there was considerable ritual activity, and there were numerous occasions when the inhabitants of different communities organized large labor parties to carry out sophisticated water control works and other communal projects. Everywhere in Mesa Verde, the emphasis appears to have been on individual communities, not on the kind of larger-scale regional integration so characteristic of Chaco, and the Hohokam area.

The 12th and 13th centuries saw the culmination of four centuries of rapid social and political development in the Mesa Verde region. About AD 1300, the entire San Juan drainage, including Mesa Verde, was abandoned by Puebloan peoples. They moved south and southeastward into the lands of the historic Hopi, Zuñi, and Rio Grande pueblos, where they retained the same basic community organization, with villages, perhaps better called towns, that never exceeded about 2500 inhabitants. There were larger pueblos elsewhere in the 14th century.

Frank Cushing and other early anthropologists commented on the elaborate ceremonial life among more sedentary Pueblo peoples like the Zuñi. Many of these ceremonies made use of astronomical observations, sometimes a place-specific horizon calendar (Williamson, 1981). By standing in a particular place and observing the sun's cycles throughout the year, priests were able to correlate their agricultural and ceremonial calendars to sunrise and sunset points on the surrounding horizon. Cushing watched a Zuñi sun priest at his astronomical observations. "He slowly approached a square open tower and seated himself just inside on a rude, ancient stone chair, and before a pillar sculptured with the face of the sun, the sacred hand, the morning star, and the new moon. There he awaited with prayer and sacred song the rising of the sun," he wrote. "Nor may the Sun Priest err in his watch of Time's flight; for many are the houses in Zuñi with cores on their walls or ancient plates imbedded therein, while opposite, a convenient window or small port-hole lets in the light of the rising sun, which shines but two mornings in the three hundred and sixty-five on the same place" (Cushing, 1882–83). Horizon calendars are still used by Hopi and other Pueblo Indians (McCluskey, 1977).

There can be little doubt that similar calendars and other astronomical observations were in use during prehistoric times. The Hovenweep pueblo structures in Colorado were erected by a group of Anasazi related to the Mesa Verde people in the late 12th and mid-13th centuries. They include round, square, or D-shaped towers that were originally two or three stories high. At least one of these towers, Hovenweep Castle, has a room with special sun-sighting ports aligned with the summer and winter solstices. Nearby Holly House contains petroglyph panels with symbols that may represent the sun and other heavenly bodies. There is also possible evidence for astronomical observation in Chaco Canyon, at Casa Rinconada and Pueblo Bonito (Williamson, 1981). As far as can be determined, Southwestern prehistoric astronomy was entirely solar, with considerable emphasis on the solstices. (For North American archaeoastronomy generally, see T. Hudson and Underhay, 1978; Williamson, 1981; 1984.)

Mimbres (AD 1000 to 1130). Mimbres sites lie along the river of that name in southwestern New Mexico. Between AD 1000 and 1130, Mimbres potters created magnificent painted ceremonial bowls adorned with geometric and pictorial designs (LeBlanc, 1983). These superb examples of prehistoric artistry are usually found in Mimbres burials, usually inverted over the head of the deceased, ceremonially "broken" by a small hole in the base. Unfortunately, these fine vessels have become a highly prized item on the illegal antiquities market and many Mimbres burials have been decimated by looters.

The Mimbres people lived in settlements of up to 150 rooms that consisted of single story, contiguous and rectangular rooms built of river pebbles and adobe. The pueblos grew gradually into groups of room clusters loosely grouped around an open plaza. At the well-known NAN Ranch and Galaz sites, the pueblo room clusters grew according to household needs, rooms sometimes being subdivided and remodelled (Shafer, 1982). Ceremonial structures included large, rectangular and semi-subterranean kivas somewhat like those of earlier Mogollon people, sometimes with entry ramps and ceremonial offerings under the floors. Smaller, quadrilateral kivas entered through the roof may have been used by small kin groups rather than the community as a whole.

The elaborate domestic pottery fabricated by Mimbres women gives the impression that the people enjoyed an elaborate ceremonial life. For all this apparent elaboration and craft skill, there are few signs of the long-distance trading contacts found at Chaco Canyon or Snaketown. Most ceremonial activities appear to have taken place at the community and household level, reflecting a relatively isolated, egalitarian pueblo society.

Both Mesa Verde and Mimbres boast of large settlements that give an impression of a much more nucleated society than was, in fact the case. Both cultural traditions display distinctive architectural and pottery styles that were widely used within relatively small areas. In fact, neither Mesa Verde nor Mimbres are typical of the very dispersed settlement patterns that were characteristic of much of the Southwest between AD 900 and 1150. For example, the Rio Grande Valley from about Albuquerque northward was relatively sparsely inhabited during these centuries, mostly by people living in small, pithouse villages, some of them perhaps seasonal settlements (Wendorf and Reed, 1955; Blevins and Joiner, 1977). These appear to have been isolated communities, with no contacts with the Chaco system.

Between AD 900 and 1150, Southwestern agricultural societies displayed great cultural variation. Some of them lived in more nucleated settlements. They enjoyed standardized agriculture, craft specialization, and participated in widespread trading networks. These more hierarchical systems are quite different from the more egalitarian patterns found elsewhere. The Mesa Verde and Mimbres people often dwelt in larger pueblos that consisted of conglomerations of formerly more dispersed settlements. These were still relatively egalitarian societies, while many Southwestern groups continued to live in dispersed pithouse villages, many of them seasonal bases for people who still relied on hunting and gathering as well as farming for their subsistence. In the centuries that followed, it was the aggregated and more dispersed cultural systems that survived, while the

Mimbres ceramics. (Above left) Bowl painted with enigmatic human figures, possibly representing the contrast between life and death, or male and female. The hole through the base "killed" the object, helping release the vessel's spirit into the next world. Diameter c.30 cm. (Above right) Bowl showing the Guardians of the Four Directions. Diameter c.30 cm.

nucleated systems at Chaco and elsewhere collapsed, for reasons that are still little understood.

The Abandonment Controversy

When Europeans first came on the spectacular ruins of Chaco Canyon and Mesa Verde, they were mystified by the long-abandoned pueblos. Why, they asked, had their inhabitants left them and moved away? Was there some critical event or events that caused widespread population movements?

Early theories focused on raiding Athabaskans, on intercommunity warfare, and many other simplistic factors such as major environmental change, epidemics, and disruption of Mexican trading contacts (for a summary, see Cordell, 1984). The latest hypotheses argue for frequent, relatively minor rainfall fluctuations before AD 900, with less frequent, but greater variations during the next 250 years. After 1150, the original pattern reappeared. These trends are correlated with changes in hydrological curves, with an increase in water tables between 900 and 1150. If these changes are correctly documented, then the frequent droughts before and after this period may never have allowed farming communities to acquire sufficient food surpluses to sustain large population densities. However, the longer intervals between droughts in the two and a half centuries after AD 900 may have allowed animal and plant populations to recover from previous overexploitation – so good food surpluses could be accumulated in the longer cycles of higher rainfall (Cordell, 1984).

Many complex and interacting cultural and environmental causes may have led to the abandonment of San Juan communities. These might include changes in subsistence strategies, exhaustion of local soils, and changes in amount and distribution of rainfall – to mention only a few factors. The archaeological record implies large-scale regional abandonments, but these, in fact, may not have been abandonments at all, but subtle shifts in local settlement patterns that are often very hard to document centuries later.

Such may have been the case at Chaco Canyon, center of a large, and complex regional system that involved highly organized construction and the labors of many people from widely scattered communities. Some of the areas within the system, including Chaco Canyon itself, may have been so environmentally impoverished that they could not support large resident populations without regional integration and the elaborate roads and other public works that went with it. When the political and social apparatus behind the system collapsed, some dispersal of population was inevitable, for the labor intensive investment that fed them in marginal areas had vanished. Those who remained still continued to hunt, forage, and farm, but within local contexts. There may be an appearance of population decline in the archaeological record, but it may in fact have been one of decentralization, reduced coordination of labor, and major changes in village layout away from the large, formal pueblos of earlier centuries into smaller communities less visible in the archaeological record. There was, then, considerable continuity in Southwestern life, despite major population dispersals and shifts in subsistence strategies.

Late Prehistoric Times
AD 1300 to European contact

Following the abandonments of the late 13th and early 14th centuries, large, aggregated communities began to form in hitherto sparsely populated areas of the Southwest.

Casas Grandes (c. AD 1400). The Casas Grandes area of Chihuahua in northern Mexico lies in relatively high altitude basin and range country, centered on a wide, fertile valley long inhabited by an indigenous,

Casas Grandes, Chihuahua, northern Mexico. (Left) Aerial view showing a ballcourt, lower right, and excavation of room blocks, lower left corner. (Below) Effigy bowl from the site, height 22 cm.

Mogollon-like population (Di Peso and others, 1974). Between AD 1130 and 1300, the beginning of what Charles Di Peso calls the Medio period, the inhabitants of this valley began to congregate in a large settlement known as Paquime (or Casas Grandes). Originally, Charles Di Peso argued for a date between the 11th and 14th centuries for Casas Grandes. This chronology has been replaced by more recent tree-ring dates that assign the heyday of Casas Grandes to the 14th century (Dean and Ravesloot, 1989).

Initially, Paquime consisted of 20 or more house clusters, each with a plaza and enclosing wall. The people lived in single-story adobe houses, with a single water system for the entire settlement. One compound contained rows of rectangular boxes apparently used for breeding macaws for their colorful feathers – pollen analyses have yielded traces of the nesting material, even eggshell fragments, skeletons, and traces of wooden perches were found. Di Peso and others believe that Paquime may have been one of the sources of macaws for Anasazi communities located far to the north.

During the 14th century, the entire community was rebuilt. Paquime phase multi-storied adobe apartment complexes, built of a form of marley concrete that is like clay, now formed the central core of the settlement and housed as many as 2240 people. I-shaped ball courts, stone-faced platform and effigy mounds, a market area, and elaborate water storage systems lay in the public and ceremonial core of the site outside the residential areas in the center. This was a thriving town where many specialist craft activities took place, among them the large-scale production of copper bells, ornaments, and ceremonial axe heads made by the "lost-wax" process, a far from simple procedure. Tons of marine molluscs were turned into trumpets, beads, and engraved or inlaid ornaments.

At the height of its power, Casas Grandes lay at the center of a regional system that covered more than 33,590 sq. miles (87,000 sq. km) and encompassed both the capital itself and satellite communities. Like the earlier Chaco Phenomenon, Casas Grandes did not flourish for long. "Two and one-half generations sat idly by and watched the magnificent city of Paquime fall into disrepair. The artisan-citizens continued to produce an abundance of marketable goods, but civil construction and public maintenance all ceased." Thus does Di Peso describe the decline of Paquime during the Diablo phase. The population of the town apparently increased, but public works were neglected. Some families moved into ceremonial areas and turned them into dwellings. The entire Casas Grandes system fell apart, but it was not until the early 15th century that Paquime was finally abandoned. As far as is known, Casas Grandes was not affiliated with any Mesoamerican state.

Other Areas. In the Rio Grande area and adjacent portions of what is now eastern New Mexico, many famous large and late pueblos have been excavated, some of them considered ancestral communities by modern Pueblo Indian groups. They include Pecos Pueblo, the site where A.V. Kidder carried out his pioneer stratigraphic studies on Southwestern ceramics. There is considerable architectural variation from one site to another, the largest having multiple plazas surrounded by blocks of rooms, one great kiva, and sometimes smaller ones as well. Some of the people in this area may have trickled in from the Chaco and Mesa Verde regions, but there are no signs of mass migrations from those hitherto more densely populated areas.

Some population growth and marked changes in distribution are recorded for the Zuñi area between 1175 and 1275. Many people lived in pueblos at higher elevations, sited to tap watershed runoffs for agricultural purposes. These were mainly villages, which were abandoned between 1275 and 1400, when the population gathered into a few exceptionally large, multi-storied pueblos with as many as 1000 rooms. Room blocks surrounded central plazas, the entire pueblo being encircled by an outer wall. None of these large sites were occupied for long periods of time, although residencies appear to have lengthened after 1400. At European contact in 1540, the Zuñi were living in six or seven large pueblos.

Aggregation of Southwestern populations into large pueblos is recorded from other areas, too, from Tsegi Canyon, Anderson Mesa, where Chavez Pass Pueblo, an ancestral site of the Hopi, lies; Hopi Buttes; and other areas west of Zuñi, from the mountainous area of eastern Arizona near the

Aerial view of Pecos, New Mexico. The Spanish Mission of the 1620s stands at left. Native Americans built the original pueblo here c.1450, a multi-storied quadrangle around a central plaza with 660 living and storage rooms and at least 22 kivas.

Mogollon Rim and within the Gila. Some of these sites contain rock art and kiva murals that are recognizable as part of modern kachina ritual, an important element in Pueblo religion. The Hohokam region also saw major settlement restructuring.

It would be a mistake to think of Southwestern people as typically living in large pueblos during these centuries. Most families may have been affiliated with such a settlement. Throughout the Southwest, isolated farming communities flourished as they always had done, depending on hunting, foraging, and farming for survival, but owing at least some token allegiance to a large social unit centered on a major pueblo.

Further Reading

The following references amplify the general accounts cited in earlier chapters:

Frazier, Kendrick. 1986. *People of Chaco: a Canyon and its Cultures*. W.W. Norton, New York.
A popular account of Chaco for the general reader. Well researched and readable.

Haury, Emil. 1976. *The Hohokam, desert farmers and craftsmen: Excavations at Snaketown, 1964–1965*. University of Arizona Press, Tucson.
Haury's monograph summarizes much of what is known about Hohokam and this important site.

LeBlanc, Steven A. 1983. *The Mimbres People: ancient pueblo potters of the American Southwest*. Thames and Hudson, London and New York.
A lavishly illustrated introduction to some of North America's finest ceramics and the people who made them.

Noble, David G. (ed.). 1984 *New Light on Chaco Canyon*. School of American Research, Santa Fé, New Mexico.
A fine volume of popular essays on Chaco Canyon. Ideal for the general reader.

Rohn, Arthur. 1971. *Mug House, Mesa Verde National Park, Colorado*. National Park Service, Washington DC.
Rohn's monograph contains much valuable information on Mesa Verde as a whole.

PART SIX

THE EASTERN WOODLANDS

*"Outside, some distance from the
lodge, was a meadow of dry grass.
The woman told the man to rub
two sticks together quickly,
holding them in the grass. Soon
sparks flew, the grass caught fire.
Then the woman said, 'When the
sun goes down, you must take me
by my hair and drag me across the
field. After that you may eat.' . . .
When evening came he did as he
had been told. The woman
disappeared, but wherever he had
dragged her, a tall and graceful
plant arose. On it were golden
clusters of grain . . . It was corn,
the friend of all humankind . . ."*

Algonquian Legend

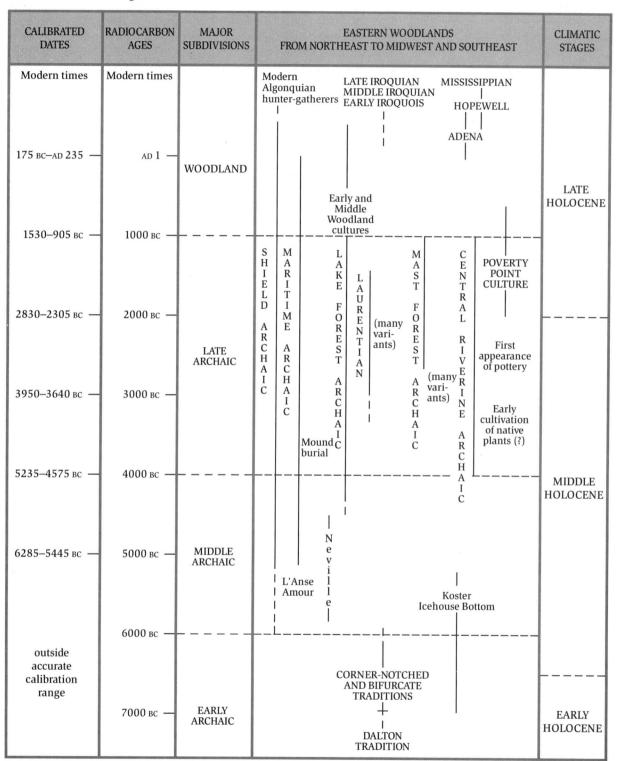

CALIBRATED DATES	RADIOCARBON AGES	MAJOR SUBDIVISIONS	EASTERN WOODLANDS FROM NORTHEAST TO MIDWEST AND SOUTHEAST	CLIMATIC STAGES
Modern times	Modern times		Modern Algonquian hunter-gatherers LATE IROQUIAN MISSISSIPPIAN MIDDLE IROQUIAN EARLY IROQUOIS HOPEWELL ADENA	
175 BC–AD 235 —	AD 1	WOODLAND		LATE HOLOCENE
1530–905 BC —	1000 BC		Early and Middle Woodland cultures	
			S H I E L D A R C H A I C M A R I T I M E A R C H A I C L A K E F O R E S T A R C H A I C L A U R E N T I A N (many variants) M A S T F O R E S T A R C H A I C C E N T R A L R I V E R I N E A R C H A I C (many variants) POVERTY POINT CULTURE	
2830–2305 BC —	2000 BC	LATE ARCHAIC	First appearance of pottery	
3950–3640 BC —	3000 BC		Early cultivation of native plants (?)	
			Mound burial	
5235–4575 BC —	4000 BC			MIDDLE HOLOCENE
6285–5445 BC —	5000 BC	MIDDLE ARCHAIC	Neville	
			L'Anse Amour	
			Koster Icehouse Bottom	
	6000 BC			
outside accurate calibration range			CORNER-NOTCHED AND BIFURCATE TRADITIONS	
	7000 BC	EARLY ARCHAIC	DALTON TRADITION	EARLY HOLOCENE

CHAPTER 16

EARLY AND MIDDLE ARCHAIC CULTURES IN THE EASTERN WOODLANDS

Large hunting territories, long days of tracking bison, caribou, mastodon, and smaller game, seasonal foraging of plant foods – these were the characteristics of free-wandering Paleo-Indian life in the Eastern Woodlands before 8000 BC, until the Ice Age megafauna vanished rapidly. The hunter-gatherers of eastern North America now adapted to progressively warmer and more diverse Eastern Woodlands environments. They turned from big-game to the exploitation of forest mammals like the white-tailed deer, also, increasingly, to nuts and plant foods. We must now examine this important adaptive shift, part of a trend that was to continue for thousands of years in the east. This development was to culminate after 1000 BC in more sedentary lifeways, restricted hunting and foraging territories, and in extensive trading and elaborate mortuary customs. People adapted in many ways, with more-or-less equal efficiency, to different circumstances (Meltzer and Smith, 1986; Neusius, 1986).

This appealing scenario of a gradual shift from big-game exploitation to more generalized hunting and gathering is nothing more than a hypothesis. Preservation conditions at all but a handful of locations militate against the survival of food remains of any kind. Where organic remains do survive, they are in small numbers, barely enough to compile short lists of some of the plant foods that were exploited by the inhabitants. Cumulatively, however, these lists from excavated sites in the 8500 to 6000 BC range hint that the Paleo-Indians' successors were exploiting a broad variety of foods – both forest resources like grey squirrels and nuts, and foods from more grassy environments like white-tailed deer and pioneering seed-bearing grasses (B. Smith, 1986). It seems certain that small game, fish, molluscs, and vegetable foods assumed greater importance in eastern diet after about 8500 BC – characteristics of the so-called Archaic stage (Meltzer and Smith, 1986).

All interpretations of Eastern Woodlands prehistory during the late Early and Middle Holocene are based on this perceived adaptive shift toward more efficient exploitation of woodland environments. Illinois archaeologist Joseph Caldwell identified the trend in 1958: "If there is any overriding pattern to be seen in the history of the East before the establishment of food production as an economic basis, it is in the evidence for increasing efficiency and success in exploiting the resources of the forest" (Caldwell, 1958). He coined the term "Primary Forest Efficiency" to characterize "a degree of settled life ... a more efficient accommodation to life in the

forest" that came into being during the long millennia of the Archaic. Another viewpoint sees the increasing diversity in human diet during the Archaic as possible evidence for stress. It may also have been the case that Eastern Woodland environments as a whole were more productive during the Archaic (Styles, 1981). No one believes the shift was a dramatic one, or that there were large-scale migrations from other areas that brought new populations into the Eastern Woodlands. The basic toolkits used by Archaic people changed but little for thousands of years, except for minor stylistic alterations in ubiquitous stone projectile points.

Projectile Points and the Early Archaic
*c.*8000 to 6000 BC

After about 8500 BC, Clovis-like points gave way to new projectile points throughout the Eastern Woodlands, points derived from earlier fluted designs (B. Smith, 1986; Steponaitis, 1986). We do not know what these stylistic changes mean in cultural terms, but dozens of changing projectile point forms chronicle the Early Archaic societies of the late Early Holocene.

The bewildering array of Early Archaic projectile point finds from the Eastern Woodlands has fascinated archaeologists for generations. "Were we to note all the varieties which suggest themselves, we would be led into a multiplicity of illustrations ... [of] the individual skill and fancies of the respective workmen, the various casualties to which these implements have been subjected ... and the modifications of form consequent thereupon," wrote a frustrated collector, Charles Jones, in his *Antiquities of the Southern Indians* as long ago as 1873. The classificatory confusion lasted until the 1950s, when excavations at a few stratified sites such as Hardaway, North Carolina, and St Albans, West Virginia, yielded the first chronological sequences for these projectile point styles. The deep deposits of the St Albans site yielded no less than 41 stratigraphic levels with each type of projectile point form confined to one or two zones.

In the 1950s, Joffre Coe (1952, 1964) excavated a series of sites in the North Carolina Piedmont. He discovered at once that stratified sites had survived on the alluvial floodplains of the Piedmont. Not only that, but the stratigraphy was sensitive enough that short-term occupations could be identified, something that was well-nigh impossible on the jumbled open sites found on nearby ridges and eroded terraces. Then, he wrote, "the usual hodgepodge of projectile point types are not found – only variations of a specific theme [within an individual occupation layer]." In other words, changes in the features of projectile points were a potential chronological marker over centuries, if not millennia, of human occupation.

Coe excavated four sites – Doerschuk, Gaston, Hardaway, and Lowder's Ferry – and analyzed nearly 66,000 stone fragments from them. In 1964, he used his stratigraphic observations and analyses to identify a sequence of changing projectile point forms that began with the "Hardaway Complex," named after a construction company that had used the site where Hardaway points were stratified. Coe compared the large, thin Hardaway point to "Dalton" points dating to more than 5700 BC found in Tennessee and further west. Palmer, Kirk, Stanly, Morrow Mountain,

(Opposite) Sites and regions of the Eastern Woodlands referred to in Chapters 16-21.

Guilford – Coe traced minute projectile point changes over thousands of years, but unfortunately he obtained no radiocarbon samples from his excavations.

A decade later, Canadian archaeologist James Tuck expanded Coe's work with radiocarbon-dated information from many more sites. He proposed (1974) three Early Archaic horizons in the Eastern Woodlands for the period 8000 to 6000 BC – Dalton (Hardaway), Big Sandy, and Kirk, horizons that could be identified over large areas of the Eastern Woodlands. As Tuck and others pointed out, there was apparently a remarkable uniformity of hunting and gathering culture all the way from Labrador in the north to the Carolinas far to the south, with regional differences reflected in part by minor stylistic variations in projectile points. Even as Tuck was writing, Jefferson Chapman (1975, 1985) was excavating a series of floodplain sites in Eastern Tennessee that added a fourth and later "Bifurcate" horizon to the Dalton-Big Sandy-Kirk tripartite sequence. He also confirmed the basic validity of Tuck's scheme.

There is now general agreement that the 7000 years of the Eastern Woodlands Archaic, from about 8000 to 700 BC, are marked by widespread changes in projectile styles, even if there was considerable local variation (Steponaitis, 1986). This sequence begins with highly varied Early Archaic *side-notched* points that developed from the widespread, earlier Dalton form. Next come *corner-notched* forms, such as the Kirk form, then *bifurcate-base* points, and lastly several *stemmed* forms. The rest of the stone artifact toolkit remained much the same as in Paleo-Indian times, except for the appearance of more varied scraper forms.

The Dalton Tradition
*c.*8500 to ?7000 BC

Dalton points appeared over much of the Southeast in about 8500 BC (Morse and Morse, 1983). They are distinctive artifacts with concave bases with "ears" that sometimes flare outward. These were highly versatile artifacts that served not only as points, but as saws and serrated knives. Archaeologist James Mitchie has used replicas to butcher white-tailed deer and saw up their bones with the tough, saw-like edges. Sometimes the hunters recycled and sharpened the points again and again, turning them progressively into knives, then chisels or scrapers. The Dalton point of the Southeast (called the Hardaway in North Carolina) is known from North Carolina, Illinois, Alabama, and as far north as New England. But the Hardaway has a more triangular shape, with side notches and flaring ears. Both Dalton and Hardaway forms remained in fashion until about 7000 BC, when they gave way to new designs.

This millennium near the close of the Early Holocene saw oak-dominated deciduous forest gradually expanding northward as the ice sheets retreated, replacing spruce and jack pine forests in the Northeast. This northward expansion may have coincided with a gradual adaptive shift toward more intensive exploitation of nuts and other vegetable foods. Thanks to excavations in the Little Tennessee Valley and northeast Arkansas, we know something of the Early Archaic adaptation in the river valleys of the Southeast, an adaptation that may have flourished in many

(Top row) Dalton points, length of largest 5 cm. (Bottom row) Hardaway points, length of largest 5 cm.

different minor variations over much of the region where these points are found.

Brand, Lace, and Sloan. Dan Morse and his Arkansas colleagues (Morse and Morse, 1983) have excavated three important sites that reflect different aspects of Dalton life.

The Lace site lay on a small knoll near the L'Anguille River, in the center of a cluster of smaller Dalton locations. The elevated location was once bordered by sloughs and shallow lakes, an ideal place for a base camp. The main portion of the settlement covered about 1.2 acres (0.5 ha), with some midden accumulation to a depth of as much as 3 ft (1 m), site dimensions that argue strongly for it once having been a base camp.

The Brand site nearby lies on a natural knoll about 2.6 ft (0.8 m) high and 0.25 acre (0.1 ha) in area. Morse excavated five oval Dalton artifact clusters averaging about 125.9 sq. ft (11.7 sq. m). Each contained an

Aerial view of the Lace site, Arkansas (above), and excavations in progress at the nearby Brand site (left).

average of 83 tools, all of them hunting or butchering artifacts like points, knives, choppers, and hammerstones. Morse believes each cluster was left by a single hunter butchering his share of a kill. Each is oriented slightly north of east-west, as if the hunter's back faced the sun or a meat-drying rack straddled the cluster. However, the diversity of tools strongly suggests that the site was occupied by families engaged in a wide range of domestic activities (Schiffer, 1975).

The Sloan site is believed to have been a cemetery. Some 488 Dalton artifacts, 144 of them points, came from a sand dune along the edge of the Cache River floodplain near the northern Mississippi River delta. The artifacts were found in distinctive 6.6 ft (2 m) linear patterns parallel to the dune's long axis. Groups of associated artifacts within the patterns may have been buried in containers. In one case, four Dalton points appeared to have been rolled into a bundle, as hafted points on foreshafts or handles.

Some of the Sloan points were made from cherts from as far away as St Louis, nearly 200 miles (321 km) distant. Unfortunately, only a few bone fragments survived in the dune, but soil tests reveal abnormally high calcium levels, as if skeletons were once present. Morse estimates that between 12 and 25 graves once lay in the sand dune. If his interpretation is correct, Sloan is the earliest known cemetery in the Americas.

Icehouse Bottom and Early Archaic Subsistence

After 8000 BC, Jefferson Chapman tells us (1980, 1985), rains and floods resulting from erosion and runoff from once-frozen slopes of the Smoky Mountains in Tennessee deposited sands and silts down the Little Tennessee River, sediments that formed sand bars, islands, and new bottom lands. The local people soon took advantage of these locations, camping on shallow sand bars that were periodically flooded. The inundations brought down fresh layers of silt and sand that covered abandoned camp sites. The hunters would return to the same location again and again, creating a kind of archaeological layer-cake of Early Archaic and later occupation at such well-known sites as Icehouse Bottom and Rose Island (Chapman, 1973; 1975).

Chapman believes that the people who inhabited the lowest levels of Icehouse Bottom in about 7500 BC, also other base camps, lived in a series of small hunter-gatherer bands who dwelt not only in the Little Tennessee Valley, but moved from there into the Upper Tennessee River drainage and into the southern Ridge and Valley Province of Virginia as well. They were constantly on the move, each band having a base camp or series of such repeatedly used settlements. Icehouse Bottom provided not only comfort and security, but was close to diverse food resources like game and wild vegetable foods (Chapman, 1973; 1985). The base camp was near rock outcrops that yielded fine-grained chert. The people picked up or dug out nodules from the hillside, brought them back home and fashioned them into adzes, points, knives, drills, and other tools used for woodworking, preparing hides, and many other purposes. The camp itself was used by several households, living separately, probably in skin, bark, or matting shelters scattered along several hundred feet of a riverside terrace. Each household had its own hearth, fashioned from red clay brought in from a

Excavations at Icehouse Bottom, Little Tennessee River Valley.

hillside close by. Twenty-nine of the early Icehouse Bottom hearths bore traces of basketry and netting preserved as clear impressions in the fire-hardened clay.

Although preservation conditions at Icehouse Bottom are poor, Chapman believes that hunting and foraging habits changed but little from Early Archaic right into the historic period. The Icehouse Bottom people and their neighbors probably subsisted off white-tailed deer, a meat diet supplemented with black bear and other mammals like elk, fox, opossum, raccoon, squirrel, and rabbit. They hunted turkeys and passenger pigeons, collected box turtles each spring, and also fished. They took suckers as they spawned in the shallow waters of spring, also catfish and drumfish. Freshwater mussels and gastropods were occasionally eaten as supplemental foods.

Wild vegetable foods were as important as game in Icehouse Bottom diet. Hickory nuts were a vital crop each fall, for they yielded crucial fats and protein without any special processing to make them edible. Chapman (1985) quotes the great 18th-century botanist William Bartram, who observed Southeastern Indians harvesting hickory nuts. "I have seen above an hundred bushels of these nuts belonging to one family," he wrote. "They pound them to pieces, and then cast them into boiling water, which, after passing through fine strainers, preserves the most oily part of the liquid: this they call by a name which signifies hiccory milk; it is as sweet and rich as fresh cream, and is an important ingredient in most of their cookery, especially hominy and corn cakes." The Indians would skim off the oil, then the meat, which was mashed, dried, and kept for use in lean months. The cook simply soaked cakes of nut meat in warm water before cooking them. Even the shells were used as fuel – carbonized hickory shells are commonplace in many Eastern Woodlands sites.

The Icehouse Bottom people also gathered acorns, but made less use of them than did their successors. Acorns provide three times fewer calories than hickory, but are rich in fats and carbohydrates that make them a valuable supplement to hickory. However, they have a bitter taste that has to be eliminated by leaching out the tannic acid (Petruso and Wickens, 1984). Many later Indian groups did this by immersing the acorns in boiling water or by passing water through the powdered meat in a basket. The acorn meal was often used to make a form of pastry bread. Walnuts, hazelnuts, and chestnuts were also collected upon occasion, but the most important wild vegetable foods were acorns and hickory nuts (Tallalay, Keller, and Munson, 1984).

Plant foods of many species were abundant near Icehouse Bottom from late spring to late fall, not only nuts but young shoots of green vegetables like pokeweed, fruit such as wild blackberries, strawberries, raspberries, and plums. Occasional roots served as starchy vegetables. Wild vegetable foods were not only eaten fresh but carefully dried for winter use.

The key to the successful exploitation of river valleys such as the Little Tennessee revolved around several critical environmental factors (Chapman, 1985). The diversity of predictable seasonal food resources, both animal and vegetable as well as aquatic, made deliberate scheduling of hunting and foraging a highly adaptive subsistence strategy. Each fall saw the upland forest floors covered with a rich mast, a carpet, as it were, of falling oil-rich nuts and other foods that was a magnet for white-tailed deer and other animals. The same trees yielded bountiful and easily harvested hickories and acorns. Winter and early spring floods often inundated favorite seasonal camps near the rivers. In high flood years, people would move to higher ground, where game was to be found. As the water level fell, they would shift back onto the floodplain and spear fish in shallow pools left by the falling waters. As long as population densities remained relatively small, there was little incentive to exploit anything but a fairly narrow spectrum of animal, plant, and aquatic foods in favored locations.

David Anderson and Glen Hanson (1988) have developed a hypothetical model of Early Archaic settlement within the Savannah River basin, on the South Atlantic Slope. Their model is based on optimal foraging theory, on the assumption that where food resources are homogeneously distributed, foragers will be dispersed, whereas if they are patchy, the optimal distribution for gatherers is to cluster in larger aggregations. They hypothesize that Early Archaic bands living in this area used well-provisioned base camps on the warmer coastal plain during the winter. These were sited within river drainages, close to raw material sources, and placed according to the availability of food resources, including deer, which tended to move in larger groups during winter. In early spring, the deer dispersed and edible plant resources appeared over much of the landscape, first at the coast, then further inland. The people moved out into small, regularly spaced camps, their distribution reflecting the fairly even

David Anderson and Glen Hanson's model of Early Archaic settlement on the South Atlantic Slope. A macroband of some 500 to 1500 people occupied the region. The macroband comprised 8 bands, each exploiting a contiguous northwest to southeast drainage area in a pattern of seasonally shifting camps. Other macrobands occupied adjoining regions.

distribution of food resources. To some extent, the bands were "tethered" to raw material sources, which were irregularly distributed over the landscape. They foraged over the Upper Coastal Plain and the Piedmont during summer. Come fall, the people moved downstream, probably choosing base camp locations that were different from the year before, for resources at those locations were still depleted. Anderson and Hanson believe that between 50 and 150 people lived in each neighboring drainage at the beginning of the Early Archaic, a figure that rose over the centuries, resulting in decreases in annual range as bands fissioned into new groups.

The distribution of Early Archaic bands over the South Atlantic Slope reflected the northwest to southeast flow of most major drainages, from the Appalachians to the sea. Anderson and Hanson believe that, to maintain a viable equilibrium population, bands from three to five drainages had to be in regular contact. They maintained what one might call mating networks both through the movements of individuals and through regular gatherings, probably in fall, reflected by major sites located midway between winter and summer foraging grounds. Anderson and Hanson hypothesize that there was a South Atlantic Macroband of between 500 to 1500 people, perhaps made up of as many as 8 separate groups living in contiguous drainages. Other such macrobands may have lived on all three sides of the region, those to the south and west separated from the South Atlantic Slope by natural geographical barriers. These Early Archaic adaptations were conditioned not only by the local environment, but by biological interaction, population spacing, and restraints of information exchange between neighboring groups. (For a full discussion and an archaeological test of this model, see Anderson and Hanson, 1988.)

Corner-Notched and Bifurcate Traditions
*c.*7000 to 6000 BC

The change from side-notched to corner-notched projectile points may reflect a change in hunting weapons from thrusting spears to lighter weapons propelled by the atlatl, the throwing stick (Chapman, 1985). Corner-notched projectile points form a well-defined Archaic tradition all over the Eastern Woodlands and have been classified into many different local forms, including the well-known Kirk form found over much of the Southeast and further afield (Steponaitis, 1986; B. Smith, 1986).

Icehouse Bottom, Bacon Farm, Calloway Island, and Rose Island in the Little Tennessee Valley all document Early Archaic occupation in the Southeast for a millennium after the end of the Dalton tradition (Chapman, 1973; 1975; 1978; 1979). Jefferson Chapman's meticulous excavations in the 1970s chronicle more than 9000 years of human occupation, beginning in the Early Archaic (Chapman, 1985). The food remains reveal that Icehouse Bottom and the other sites were summer-fall-early winter base camps used regularly for the next 1500 years, perhaps visited as part of a regular seasonal migration pattern. Through the centuries, the way of life changed little, an adaptation very similar to that recorded in earlier times.

Such cultural changes that did occur are reflected in only one category of artifact – stone projectile points/knives. In the lower Tennessee and elsewhere in the east, corner-notched points gave way to bifurcate forms after 7000 BC (Chapman, 1975). These projectile heads have distinctive, bifurcated bases, perhaps a device to increase the lateral strength of the hafted point when cutting and scraping.

The making of bifurcate points in the east continued for about 500 to 700 years. They occur throughout the Eastern Woodlands as scattered finds and in many varieties, named after the sites where they were originally found (Snow, 1980; Steponaitis, 1986). The distribution of bifurcate points extends as far east as the Atlantic seaboard, and south into the oak-hickory-pine forest zone of the South. They are found in the oak-hickory forests of southern Michigan, far into the Northeast and southern Canada, with a western boundary along the eastern edge of the Mississippi River Valley. Chapman (1985) observes that this distribution coincides with the extent of eastern deciduous forests. Perhaps the bifurcated head was an adaptation to hunting certain species of forest game.

(Left) Archaic hunter throwing a spear with an atlatl. (Below) Artist's reconstruction of a camp at Icehouse Bottom c.6500 BC. The hut designs are conjectural.

YRS B.C.

5000 —

5800 —

6300 —

6700 —

6900 —

7000 —

7300 —

a

b

c

d

e

f

g

Stratigraphic profile and radiocarbon chronology at the Icehouse Bottom site. The projectile point styles contained in each of the levels are shown at left: (a) Morrow Mountain I Stemmed; (b) Stanly Stemmed Cluster; (c) Kanawha Stemmed; (d) LeCroy Bifurcated Stem; (e) St Albans Side-Notched; (f) Kirk Corner-Notched; (g) Kirk Corner-Notched.

Bettye Broyles (1971) subdivided the bifurcate points found in her excavations at St Albans, West Virginia, into various distinctive forms, or groups as Chapman calls them. The Rose Island excavations allowed Chapman (1975) not only to place the different groups into stratigraphic order, but also to study the stylistic development of the bifurcate point through the centuries. Four groups of points are stratified within the Bifurcate Point horizon at Rose Island, one of the few sites in the east where many bifurcate specimens are found. The MacCorkle, St Albans, LeCroy, and Kanawha phases are each named after the sites where the point forms were first identified. Chapman believes there was widespread homogeneity in projectile point forms during the Early Archaic, and implies that his Bifurcated phases can be used as chronological markers over the entire distribution of bifurcated points in the east.

The Meaning of Projectile Point Sequences

The Chapman and Tuck style horizons are bolstered by impressive excavations and some radiocarbon dates from widely separated locations. However, it would be a mistake to regard them as rigid, stratigraphic columns of changing artifact styles that can be used over wide areas as precise chronological markers, partly because we lack stratified Archaic sites from many parts of the Eastern Woodlands, and also because of important dating anomalies, especially with later stemmed point forms.

The horizon style sequence has validity in the Southeast, and can also be used in the Northeast, where sites with artifacts dating between 8000 and 6000 BC are rare (Snow, 1980). There are dozens of isolated, surface projectile point finds, hinting at the presence of a complex of lanceolate points in this general region. In addition to some Folsom-like specimens, unfluted points resembling Plano forms from the west are found north of Ohio and into the Great Lakes region, as well as on the Plenge site in New Jersey and in western New York. These points are known to date to at least 8000 BC in the west. Kirk stemmed, serrated, and corner-notched points in the Northeast are contemporary with equivalent Southeastern artifact forms. Despite these matching dates, it is clearly a mistake to think of projectile point forms as precise chronological markers, like the "type-fossils" used by geologists to date geological strata. But they do provide at least a crude way of identifying cultural change over large areas.

Furthermore, the broad geographic similarities between projectile points do not necessarily reflect a homogeneous adaptation to the great environmental diversity of the Eastern Woodlands, nor can they be taken to represent the frontiers of actual social groups. Dean Snow, a Northeastern specialist, has argued (1980) that widely distributed projectile point styles may in fact result from the exchange of finished points between individuals who were maintaining social connections with their kin through reciprocal gifts. So the uniformity of projectile heads may reflect widespread exchange networks, an important way in which far-flung hunter-gatherer bands maintained contact with one another.

Dean Snow argues further (1980) that language may also have played a role in the diffusion of projectile point styles. Between 8000 and 6000 BC, most Easterners lived in small family bands, probably inhabiting well-defined territories that were more constrained than those used by their big-game hunting predecessors. The megafauna had vanished, so people exploited a wider range of food resources, wandering within more restricted areas where, perhaps, seasonal foods assumed greater import-ance. Group territories may have been arenas where neighboring bands came into frequent contact, where every group could understand everyone else's speech. Beyond these familiar frontiers stretched unknown country where other bands lived, people with a multiplicity of basically similar dialects that grew steadily more unintelligible the further one moved from home.

What language did these Early Archaic people speak? Linguists have established that the modern Algonquian and Gulf languages are related in such a way that the relationships must have developed a very long time ago. Gordon Willey (1966) has hypothesized that Early Archaic peoples spoke related Algonquian-Gulf languages throughout the Eastern Wood-lands. This would provide a suitable medium for projectile points to be diffused over a very wide area indeed.

Then there is the issue of individual use of projectile points. A hunter might use different point types against specific prey, or even use one form as a knife, another as a spearhead. One man could make, use, and exchange several projectile points, each of them designed for a special use, but each still having the same overall function, that of serving as a point or knife. Since stone-tipped spears were used for specific subsistence activities, the use of a particular form over a period of time implies that the artifact was well adapted to a well-defined purpose. Thus, it is quite possible that more than one projectile point type was in use in a particular area at one time, each having a different purpose. This would also explain why the distributions of many projectile point forms are discontinuous, sometimes appearing in widely separated locations.

Although, then, there are some broad chronological horizons for Early Archaic projectile point forms, the real problem is to identify the adaptive significance of each type, a task that has barely begun.

Restricted Mobility: Early and Middle Archaic Koster 6500 to 3600 BC

By the beginning of the Middle Holocene in about 6000 BC, the scattered Eastern Woodlands population was relying more and more heavily on the hunting of small mammals, fishing and the harvesting of seasonal plant foods such as pecan and hickory nuts wherever they were plentiful (B. Smith, 1986). The overall population was still very low, with the greatest concentrations of hunter-gatherer bands in areas that offered the greatest diversity of local resources. Now that big-game species had vanished and people were relying on food sources closer to seasonal base camps, the carrying capacities of many less-favored locations may have been reached. This may have left slowly growing hunter-gatherer populations with little option but to lead more circumscribed lifeways, with the greatest occupation densities in resource-rich river valleys where a wide diversity of animal and plant foods were concentrated. In the South Atlantic area, for example, Middle Archaic groups made almost exclusive use of local raw materials, as if rising population densities had restricted their annual ranges (Blanton and Sassaman, 1988). In some favored areas, there was a slow trend towards more permanent settlement in one location, a trend that appears to have accelerated during the 2000 years or so of the Middle Archaic, between about 6000 and 4000 BC.

The famous Koster site in the Illinois River Valley, with its fourteen stratified occupation levels, provides an extraordinary chronicle of human exploitation of a bountiful Midwestern environment from about 7500 BC until AD 1200 (Phillips and Brown, 1983; Struever and Holton, 1979). The first people to camp at Koster were transitory Paleo-Indian visitors. Early Archaic settlement radiocarbon-dated to about 6500 BC came from Horizon 11, a seasonal camp with temporary dwellings that covered about 0.75 acre (0.3 ha). Distinctive St Albans points serve to link Koster 11 technologically to the stratified Archaic site of St Albans itself in West Virginia, while notched specimens are similar to such points found at Graham Cave near the Prairie Peninsula in Missouri. An extended family group of about 25 people returned to the same location repeatedly over the centuries, perhaps to exploit the rich fall nut harvests in the valley. They hunted white-tailed deer and small mammals, caught fish, ate freshwater mussels, and collected hickory and pecans by the tens of thousands, a vital source of high-energy fat. Broken nuts, grinders, and hand stones for preparing vegetable foods lay close to several hearths. Four adults and three infants lay tightly contracted in oval graves, some covered with logs or limestone slabs. The inhabitants also buried three dogs in shallow pits. (The exact date of dog domestication in North America is unknown, but took place during the Early Holocene in the Old World, and may have occurred during the same period in the New.)

The seasonal Early Archaic camp at Koster contrasts dramatically with a substantial Middle Archaic settlement in Horizon 8, radiocarbon dated to between about 5600 and 5000 BC. Computer-generated analyses of the archaeological remains break down Horizon 8 into at least four occupations, each of them the remains of substantial settlements covering 1.75 acres (0.7 ha) or so, occupied on several occasions for a century or more. The houses measured 20–35 by 12–15 ft (6–7.5 by 3.5–4.5 m), their long walls formed by wooden posts up to 10 in (25 cm) in diameter set in trenches about 8–10 ft (2.4–3.0 m) apart. Branches and clay filled the gaps between them. Apparently, there were no end walls. Perhaps they were covered with hides or mats.

The Horizon 8 dwellings were intended for long-term use, perhaps for all, if not most, of the year. The growth patterns of fish scales recovered from the deposits hint that people lived at Koster from late spring through

The Koster site in the Illinois River Valley. Archaeologists study a stratigraphic profile at the site, where fourteen occupation levels have been identified stretching from c.7500 BC to AD 1200.

the summer. In the fall, they gathered freshwater mussels and harvested hickory nuts. Perhaps they abandoned the site during the winter, relying on stored nuts and deer from the uplands for much of their diet. What is striking is that the Middle Archaic inhabitants practiced what many theorists might call optimal foraging strategy, and, presumably, what Caldwell meant by "Primary Forest Efficiency" many years ago. They concentrated on a relatively narrow spectrum of readily exploitable foods, using only small quantities of edible grasses, and virtually ignoring such staples as acorns, black walnuts, hickory, and pecans. It is interesting to note that walnuts and hickory, while highly nutritious, are much harder to harvest, for the shells have to be broken open by hand. Not only that, but walnut tree roots contain a hormone that inhibits growth of other such trees nearby. So walnuts are scattered through the forest, while the easily harvested hickory occurs in dense groves. As long as the Middle Archaic population remained relatively stable, the Koster people could find most of the narrow range of food resources they depended upon within 3 miles (4.8 km) of their settlement.

Analysis of the habitats within a 5 km (3.1 mile) radius of Koster. The site was strategically located to exploit a wide range of environments, from upland forest to bottomland prairie and aquatic habitats (the thick black line running north to south on the left of the diagram is the Illinois River).

BOTTOMLAND PRAIRIE BOTTOMLAND FOREST

UPLAND PRAIRIE UPLAND FOREST

AQUATIC HABITAT

A similar shift from a generalized hunter-gatherer economy to a narrower range of foods can be seen at other Midwestern sites, too. The Modoc rockshelter near the Mississippi in Randolph County, Illinois, lies in a hickory-rich riverine environment about 90 miles (149 km) southeast of Koster (Fowler, M. 1959; Styles and others, 1983). Some 27 ft (8.2 m) of midden accumulation spans human occupations dating from between about 8000 and 2000 BC. The first occupants were general hunter-gatherers, without any particular dietary focus. Early Archaic levels at Modoc show little use of aquatic resources before about 5600 BC, when fish, mussels, and freshwater crayfish assume more importance, just as they did at Koster and other contemporary Midwestern sites like the Rodgers Shelter in central Missouri. The Modoc people exploited many small mammals, including cottontail rabbits, muskrats, and squirrels, but few larger animals. The same emphasis is found at both the Rodgers Shelter and the Graham Cave in central Missouri, but at all locations white-tailed deer become a major food source later in the Middle Archaic, before about 1600 BC (B. Smith, 1986).

At first Modoc was used as a short-term camp. But during the Middle Archaic, selective use of food sources like hickory nuts increased and people used Modoc for longer periods of time. As fish and other bottomland foods came into greater use, Modoc probably became a base camp, used for much of the year. Later it was a place used for more specialized activities, visited when people hunted deer on the nearby uplands and waterfowl in the shallow creeks and ponds nearby.

These changes in Modoc's role may reflect more restricted mobility in many areas during the Middle Archaic, restrictions that may have been the result of climatic change. But, in general, as sites like Koster, Modoc, and Rose Island in Tennessee show, the Middle Archaic saw conservative, seasonal exploitation of the Eastern Woodlands environment – even if we still know little of winter, spring, and summer activities. This seasonal exploitation required at least a degree of careful scheduling to maximize the potential of nut harvests, and to capitalize on the game that fed on the forest mast each fall. In this sense, Caldwell's "Primary Forest Efficiency" was achieved very early in the Archaic, long before Horizon 8 at Koster with its substantial dwellings was occupied.

Riverine Adaptations in the Southeast

In the Southeast, the Middle Archaic witnessed a host of local adjustments to changes in local resource distributions, the catchment areas, if you will, of each band's hunting and gathering territory (B. Smith, 1986; Steponaitis, 1986). There was, however, one universal exception to the local rule: a dramatic increase in the use of riverine aquatic species, which eventually became a major component in the diet of Southeastern river valley populations. The evidence is striking: hundreds of different shallow-water mollusc species are to be found in shell middens along parts of the St Johns, Savannah, Tennessee, Cumberland, and Green rivers (Milanich, 1973 a,b). By about 2500 BC, sea levels in the Southeast were close to those of today. It can be no coincidence that extensive shell middens appear close to Gulf estuaries, marshes, and brackish water sounds between 2200 and

1800 BC. Shell resources were probably exploited even earlier, but the resulting shell middens are under modern sea levels.

Rises in ocean sea levels lowered the gradients of interior rivers and streams, making them more sluggish and perhaps more suitable environments for mussels and bottom fish to flourish. This may have led to a new focus on freshwater aquatic resources in the interior. Such intensification is documented at several well-excavated sites from southern Illinois to northern Mississippi, north of 34°N and west of the Appalachians. Unfortunately, the archaeological evidence for the beginnings of this remarkable phenomenon is obscured by natural disturbance in the lower levels of many valley midden deposits. But there is no doubt that the intensification coincides with the warm Hypsithermal climatic episode. Between about 4500 and 4000 BC, many Midwestern and Southeastern rivers stabilized and accumulated silt in their floodplains. Backwater swamps and oxbow lakes formed. Shallow-water and shoal habitats as well as active streams provided abundant, easily accessible aquatic resources, including fish and molluscs. Thus, aquatic habitats were enhanced. They increased the level of aquatic biomass available for exploitation along long sections of river floodplains.

There is also reason to suspect that changing forest compositions on the uplands tended to impoverish the resource base available on higher ground. Many people have theorized that population growth exploded as a result of the increased exploitation of aquatic food sources, but there is little solid evidence for such an explosion. Bruce Smith (1986) summarizes the situation best when he views the increasing exploitation of river backwaters and shoal areas as "an opportunistic response to the advantageous emergence of a localized, seasonally abundant, dependable, and easily collected resource." This response led to the gradual adoption of sedentary lifeways in many parts of the Eastern Woodlands. Others disagree, and argue that increased population densities forced people to turn to alternative food resources.

Icehouse Bottom in the Little Tennessee Valley and other locations elsewhere in the Southeast document the first 1000 years of the Middle Archaic in this region (Chapman, 1985). Judging from the wide range of projectile point forms, people still relied on hunting for much of their diet, hunting activity that must have concentrated on such solitary animals as the white-tailed deer. But they were probably now exploiting wild vegetable foods, on a more intensive scale than their predecessors. The Icehouse Bottom site has yielded charred nuts as well as nutting stones, also grinding and pounding stones used for processing wild vegetable foods. The inhabitants were fishing, too. Jefferson Chapman found large numbers of water-smoothed river cobbles notched on both sides for securing a line to them. These may have served as net sinkers or line weights, part of large stone traps laid on the shoals of rivers, and became much more common during the subsequent Late Archaic. He had excellent historical analogies. Englishman James Adair spent 40 years in the 18th century living among, and trading with, Indians in the Southeast:

"The Indians have the art of catching fish in long crails, made with cranes and hiccory splinters, tapering to a point. They lay these at a fall of water, where stones are placed in two sloping lines from each bank, till they meet together in the middle of the rapid stream, where the intangled fish are drowned. Above such a place, I have known them to fasten a wreath of long grape vines together, to reach across the river, with stones fastened at proper distances to rake the bottom; they will swim a mile with it whooping and plunging all the way, driving the fish into their large cane pots" (Williams, 1930).

This fishing method was so effective that early white settlers were still using similar stone traps along the Little Tennessee River well into the 19th century.

By 4000 BC, pollen studies document a slight increase in mean annual temperature and a decrease in rainfall. This may have led to lowered water levels in streams, lakes, and rivers in much of the South, perhaps reducing the carrying capacity of the land, for Chapman records fewer sites dating to between 5000 and 3000 BC than are known from earlier millennia of the Archaic. There was still considerable reliance on hunting. The inhabitants of the Eva site in western Tennessee not only took aquatic and vegetable foods, they also ate bear, raccoon, opossum, and turkey. But between about 5200 and 3500 BC, white-tailed deer taken with stone-tipped spears and spearthrowers represented about 90 percent of all the bone from the middens, a similar hunting preference to that in the Midwest (Lewis and Lewis, 1961).

The Issue of Sedentism

Studying the settlement patterns of Early and Middle, let alone better-documented Late, Archaic cultures requires a great deal more archaeological data than is currently available from any part of the Eastern Woodlands. But there are now clear signs from Middle Archaic sites like Koster and Carrier Mills in Illinois that some favored locations were in use for most, if not all, the year (B. Smith, 1986).

Some floodplain midden sites in the Midwest and Southeast have been claimed as probable year-round settlements. The descriptions are loosely cast, for more often they in fact mean permanent to semi-permanent summer to fall, low-water seasonal base camps where many activities took place. Many were located on lower terraces or in low-lying areas that were liable to flooding in late winter and early spring. At that season, goes the argument, everyone moved onto higher ground, to the edge of the valley or onto the uplands. In other words, there was a change from "free wandering" with no particular base camp to "centrally based wandering," a seasonally mobile lifeway that involved returning to the same base location year after year.

This change to centrally based wandering after 4500 BC was not a dramatic shift from earlier habits, but rather involved a slight increase in the length of time spent at summer base camps when water levels were low. During the Early Holocene and early Middle Holocene, the bands ranged up and down regular segments of river valleys with a fairly even distribution of resources. The best way to exploit food sources was to move one's base camp regularly. But when backwaters and oxbows formed after 4500 BC, the biomass level of aquatic resources increased in some well-defined areas to the point where it paid to stay in one place for much longer periods of time, long enough for thick middens to form.

Identifying Sedentary Settlement

In archaeological terms, this change is documented by a change in major site phenomena. Before 4500 BC, Archaic peoples tended to occupy brief, transitory camps widely scattered along floodplain levees and terraces. Their successors often favored the same places year after year, so that midden deposits are now found stacked up on convenient hills or slight rises close to significant backwaters, shellfish beds, or fish spawning grounds. This change does not necessarily mean that the people exploited smaller territories or never visited the uplands. It implies, however, that sedentism, more permanent settlement, was now important.

Identifying sedentism from the archaeological record is far from easy. Many criteria have been used – a greater variety of artifacts in an occupation deposit, the presence of seasonal foods, dense scatters of tools and food remains, an increase in heavy artifacts, even evidence for storage pits. But each of them suffer from major disadvantages, largely because they are so difficult to document in convincing terms.

Two criteria are thought to hint at more sedentary settlement at a number of locations – more substantial dwellings like those at Koster, and cemeteries. Few sites other than Koster have yielded relatively permanent houses. Specially prepared clay house floors occur in Middle Archaic midden sites along the Upper Tombigbee River Valley in Mississippi. These floors were being built before 4300 BC and were apparently swept clean of occupation debris at regular intervals (B. Smith, 1986). The floors were probably reoccupied annually by kin groups during summer and early fall, sheltered with temporary or more permanent brush and timber or hide structures. Unfortunately, there is no means of knowing how long the floors were occupied in terms of weeks, months, or years. But there is evidence of flooding, so the sites must have been abandoned regularly. Sites like Rose Island and Icehouse Bottom in Tennessee offer proof that the same locations were used repeatedly over many years.

Human burials are also a potential measure of sedentary occupation. Early Archaic settlements sometimes yield the bodies of individuals buried within the confines of the camp. But Middle Archaic peoples in the central Mississippi drainage tended to bury the dead quite differently, in formal cemeteries. Their cemeteries usually consist of large, shallow pits that contain burials of up to 40 or more people laid in graves with no particular spacing. Sometimes the pits were dug into natural knolls or bluffs overlooking the valley where people lived. In other cases, the people may even have raised a low, artificial mound above the graves to enhance the visibility of the cemetery. The artifacts or caches of offerings deposited in these cemeteries are usually associated with the grave site as a whole rather than with specific individuals. Perhaps these represent the identity of the kin group that maintained the cemetery. Some such offerings are found with juvenile burials in the cemeteries, as if they were to identify the family and kin group to which the uninitiated young person belonged. Everything points to egalitarian societies in which individual status was unimportant, where leadership and authority were reflected more in age and experience, or skill as a hunter, than in material possessions.

By no means all Middle Archaic burial grounds were formal cemeteries, in the sense that they were maintained purely for the use of members of a specific corporate kin group. Dozens of burials come from sites in the Southeast and Florida, in middens and other occupation or subsistence deposits that may not have been formal cemeteries. The Eva site in western Tennessee, where 118 burials date to between 5000 and 3000 BC, and the well-preserved skeletons from Little Salt Spring in Florida are two examples (Lewis and Lewis, 1961).

The Black Earth site at Carrier Mills in southern Illinois is a rich Middle Archaic midden accumulated over a thousand-year period after about 4000 BC (Jefferies, 1987). The site is remarkable not only for its abundant food remains and many pits for storing, processing, and cooking foods, but for its 154 burials. Since only part of the site was excavated, Richard Jefferies estimates as many as 400 to 500 Middle Archaic people may have been buried at this location over the centuries.

The Carrier Mills burials were mostly individual interments, but as many as four people were sometimes deposited in the same pit. Only 27 percent of the graves contained any form of artifact. There was little to differentiate male or female, and no grave goods that denoted social ranking within Carrier Mills society. Eight individuals, mainly males, had been buried in clay-capped grave pits, as if they were especially important. One 43-year-old man had been buried with a bag or bundle of eagle talons, sections of bear's paw bones, projectile points, a miniature grooved axe, and other objects. Jefferies thinks he may have been a shaman, a man celebrated for his curing skills and ability at communicating with the ancestors.

The Black Earth site at Carrier Mills, southern Illinois: excavations in the Area A midden.

Burials and the Lands of the Ancestors

The sudden appearance of cemeteries and artificial burial mounds near resource-rich river valleys may mark a dramatic change in Archaic life. Douglas Charles and Jane Buikstra (1983) have studied Archaic burial sites in the central Mississippi drainage. They drew on modern studies of sedentary populations to make a basic assumption – that when people start passing vital resources from one generation to the next through lineages and other kin organizations, they will tend to bury their dead in cemeteries. Under this argument, rights of kin groups to use and control vital food resources will be legitimized by popular religion and rituals that reaffirm the kin groups and their rights. One form of this ritualization of inheritance is to reserve a permanent burial area for members of the kin group, a cemetery located on the land the group controls, the land once owned by their ancestors.

Charles and Buikstra used assumptions that had been developed from observations of sedentary farmers. They argued that mobile Midwestern hunter-gatherers like Early Archaic bands did not use cemeteries. However, as early as 4000 BC, their Middle Archaic successors lived in base camps and even year-round settlements that flourished because of the diverse and relatively abundant food resources nearby. Cemeteries on bluffs now appear, overlooking several major Middle Archaic sites in the central Mississippi drainage. Corporate behavior in human societies is actually a form of territorial behavior, a near universal among animals. The

Artist's reconstruction of Middle Archaic life at the Black Earth site. The hunters in the foreground are returning to camp with a deer killed with spears and atlatls, while the people in the background are collecting aquatic plants and fishing in the shallow lake west of the site.

relationship between sedentism, resources inherited through kin organizations, and cemeteries hinges on one reality – that the resources involved are fixed in space, predictable, and sufficiently abundant and diverse that a group can focus its activities around them. If a group wishes to claim rights of ownership and inheritance to these resources, one logical way to do so is through maintaining a corporate cemetery, the ritual home of one's ancestors, the primeval owners of the land. This relationship between cemeteries and the "resource catchment areas" of major archaeological sites has been demonstrated in general terms for Anglo-Saxon cemeteries in England. Similar relationships have been shown to exist for later prehistoric settlements in the central and lower Illinois Valley. Thus, there are good grounds for arguing that sedentism and the appearance of Middle Archaic cemeteries go together as early as 4000 BC in some resource-rich areas.

The argument can be taken even further. With the emergence of fixed territories, perhaps during a warmer and drier period that tended to restrict denser human populations to river valleys, there may have been competition for resources and territories with fixed boundaries for the first time. This competition may have been reflected in sporadic tribal warfare, so far undocumented. But it may also be reflected in a distinctive form of territorial marking: bluff-top cemeteries under low mounds. "Perhaps the most distinctive way to indicate a relationship between a particular group and its inherited rights of access to a particular resource locale is ... to place its ancestors in burial mounds or knolls atop the prairie covered ridges at the edge of the bluff, where they would be clearly visible from the valley floor" (Charles and Buikstra, 1983). They point out that this type of bluff-top location was chosen, and remained in use, for more than 5000 years, until maize agriculture took hold throughout the Midwest. The prominent, bluff-top cemeteries of the Middle Archaic may be seen, then, as monumental structures that served as indicators of hereditary rights to important local resources. Formal cemeteries, and the burial mounds, earthworks, or natural hills associated with them, were to remain a vital element in Eastern Woodlands life for thousands of years, right into historic times in some areas.

It would be a mistake to think of sedentism in this context in the same breath as that of permanent farming villages, for example. There were many variations in the degree and nature of sedentism. A few sites, like Carrier Mills' Black Earth location, may indeed have been fully sedentary settlements, occupied at least by some people for every month of the year. They were situated at prized locations, at a time when the warmer and drier climate of the Hypsithermal concentrated many river valley populations near productive wet environments where there was perennial water and a rich diversity of animal, aquatic, and plant foods. There may have been other groups who divided their time between two base camps, one on the edge of a productive river valley, near upland hunting grounds, the other on the floodplain itself, used when rivers were low. Two processes were under way – increased utilization of floodplain aquatic species, and a long-term trend toward increasingly permanent settlement and carefully delineated group territories, sometimes reflected symbolically in conspicuous cemeteries used over many generations. These were the homes of the ancestors, the true owners of the land.

The Northeast: L'Anse Amour and Neville
*c.*6000 BC and later

Everywhere in the Eastern Woodlands, the Middle Archaic was marked by major, but gradual, changes in hunter-gatherer lifeways. There was more deliberate scheduling of hunting and foraging nutritious, easily acquired "first-line" foods, followed by a slow broadening of the resource base with a wider range of seed and other vegetable foods, and an increasing use of aquatic resources wherever they occurred. The same long-term trends are to be found in the Northeast, although they are still only dimly discerned, owing to a lack of stratified, thoroughly excavated sites. But, for the most part, there was remarkable uniformity of Middle Archaic hunting and gathering culture all the way from Labrador in the north to the Carolinas far to the south, with regional differences reflected in part by minor stylistic variations in projectile points.

With the general amelioration of the climate during the Middle Holocene, it would be logical to expect Northeastern Archaic peoples to be exploiting sea mammals and coastal fisheries. But Atlantic sea levels were still about 30 ft (9 m) lower than today in 6000 BC, so many fishing camps dating to earlier than 3000 BC are now under water and beyond archaeological reach.

L'Anse Amour. Far to the north in Labrador, the land rose as an adjustment to the retreat of massive ice sheets. So some early sites have survived above modern sea levels. At L'Anse Amour, James Tuck found the burial of a 12-year-old child deposited face-down in a 3-ft (0.9-m) deep pit and radiocarbon dated to about 5600 BC (McGhee and Tuck, 1977). The skeleton was associated with an antler toggle harpoon head (Chapter 9) and line holder, a walrus tusk, three quartzite knives, a caribou antler pestle, a bone whistle, some stemmed and socketed bone points and six stone projectile points, and various other artifacts. The grave was covered with a mound of earth and stones, apparently the earliest artificial burial tumulus in North America. Judging from the grave furniture, the L'Anse Amour people probably followed the breeding and migrating patterns of sea mammals and caribou, moving between the coast and interior at different seasons of the year.

Coastal exploitation further south is well documented by dozens of clam and oyster shell middens dating to later than 3000 BC. But some shellfish collectors of 5000 BC camped on steep bluffs well above the waters of the lower Hudson River Valley, so their sites are preserved (Snow, 1980). Unfortunately, there are apparent discrepancies between radiocarbon dates from some of these sites and the projectile points found in them, which are thought to have been in use some 2000 years later, so the dating of at least some of these early middens is in doubt. The base of the Dogan Point shell mound has been radiocarbon dated to about 5000 BC, while layers containing giant oyster shells give readings of between 4500 and 1500 BC. It is likely, however, that more intensive exploitation of coastal shellfish and other marine resources was a later phenomenon.

The Neville Site. Some of the L'Anse Amour stone projectile points resemble those found at the Neville site, close to the Amoskeag Falls on the east bank of the Merrimack River in New Hampshire (Dincauze, 1976). Prehistoric peoples visited the riverside settlement intermittently for more than 8000 years.

The first inhabitants lived in a mixed pine-oak forest environment close to a river that must have swarmed with anadromous fish such as salmon that could be harvested with ease in late spring. This fishery would have been the major attraction of the terrace location, but preservation conditions did not allow the survival of fish bones. However, chemical tests of the occupation layers revealed unusually high mercury concentrations, a clear sign of intensive fishing – mercury compounds existed in ocean fish even before modern industrial pollutants became a factor.

Dena Dincauze has named the first occupation the Neville Complex. The people made characteristic "Neville" stemmed points, bifacial projectile points with carefully shaped tips and symmetrical bodies, clearly intended for piercing. Neville points are found as far north as central Maine, through Connecticut to perhaps as far south as Staten Island in New York. They bear a strong resemblance to the contemporary Stanly stemmed points of the Southeast, and may be considered a variant of this well-known type. Neville points were made between about 5800 and 5000 BC. The remainder of the toolkit included scrapers, perforators, and knives, and rough choppers. At first the inhabitants used local quartz, a technically unattractive raw material, but they eventually became aware of the buff-colored volcanic rhyolite from the Lake Winnipesaukee area of eastern New Hampshire. Dincauze argues that hunting and plant processing were not important activities at Neville – artifacts associated with such work are absent. The location was an important base camp for spring fishing and domestic activities.

Some time before 5000 BC, new projectile point forms appear. The basic toolkit remains much the same, with some minor changes in scraper forms that may reflect a greater range of activities at the camps. By this time, the bands who fished at Amoskeag may have spent most of the year in the same region. In about 3900 BC, they ceased to visit the falls area, for reasons that are still a mystery. Perhaps some minor climatic fluctuation impoverished the fishery.

The Neville site shows that the Middle Archaic people of the Northeast had significant cultural relationships with similar cultures along the Atlantic seaboard and on the Carolina Piedmont far to the south. The stemmed projectile points and flake tools from Neville are directly related to even older Archaic complexes in the Southeast. Dena Dincauze believes that these ancient complexes expanded northward as mixed-oak forests spread into more northern areas during the Early and Middle Holocene.

The Middle Archaic is still so shadowy in the Northeast that we can do little more than speculate about the cultural systems of the period. Neville and other sites may have been base camps where anadromous fish could be taken in large numbers. During the summer and fall, the people may have moved to the shores of freshwater lakes and river valleys where nuts and other plant foods were available, retiring to winter camp sites in the interior, where deer and other game could be taken. Shellfish were a useful food in scarce months. All the evidence points to an ever-broader series of adaptations to local environments, to the emergence of group territories centered around important base camps – a "centrally-based wandering"

Middle Archaic Neville stemmed points from New England, length of one at left 6 cm.

pattern that may reflect more restricted mobility, as it did in many parts of the Midwest and Southeast. Just as in the central Mississippi drainage, the Middle Archaic may have seen more conscious scheduling of seasonal activities and increasing reliance on aquatic resources. And the relative lack of exotic cherts and other materials from distant sources suggests that territories were more restricted and circumscribed by those of others. It was only later that Northeastern cultures broke down this pattern of apparent isolation and developed kin and trade contacts over wider areas.

The Middle Archaic spans an unspectacular period of prehistory, but was of crucial importance in setting the stage for the brilliant efflorescence of human cultures that was to follow throughout the Eastern Woodlands.

Further Reading

Chapman, Jefferson. 1985. *Tellico Archaeology*. University of Tennessee Press, Knoxville.
Chapman's clearly written summary gives an excellent portrait of Archaic life in the Southeast. Strongly recommended for the general reader.

Griffin, James. 1967. "Eastern North American Archaeology: A Summary," *Science* 156:175–91.
A useful basic survey, dated, but an excellent overview of the fundamentals.

Morse, Dan, and Morse, Phyllis. 1983. *Archaeology of the Central Mississippi Valley*. Academic Press, New York.
Excellent on the Dalton and other Archaic developments, focus on northeast Arkansas.

Phillips, James L. and Brown, James A. (eds.). *Archaic Hunters and Gatherers in the American Midwest*. Academic Press, New York.
Wide-ranging technical essays on the Midwestern Archaic that cover a whole spectrum of current research problems.

Smith, Bruce. 1986. "The Archaeology of the Southeastern United States: From Dalton to De Soto, 10,500 to 500 BP," *Advances in World Archaeology* 5:1–92.
This is a definitive synthesis of Southeastern prehistory with an excellent bibliography.

Snow, Dean. 1980. *The Archaeology of New England*. Academic Press, New York.
Snow summarizes the archaeology of the Northeast in a somewhat dated, but provocative, synthesis. Much basic data.

Steponaitis, Vincas. 1986. "Prehistoric Archaeology of the Southeastern United States," *Annual Review of Anthropology* 15:363–404.
Another excellent synthesis that parallels Smith's.

CHAPTER 17

LATE ARCHAIC CULTURES IN THE EASTERN WOODLANDS

"All too frequently, the Archaic peoples, who were greatly diversified culturally through space and time, are treated as if they were a homogeneous array of hunters and gatherers, as though they were *idiots savants* capable only of changing styles of artifacts, producing an occasional nicely ground piece of stone, continuously foraging for a precarious and uncertain subsistence, and in general doing little more than surviving as noble and unspoiled primitives." Howard Winters wrote these words in 1968, rebelling against the simplistic view of Archaic society perpetuated by myopic culture historians. Today, what we know about the complex technology, sophisticated adaptations, and long-distance trade, and emerging mortuary customs of the Eastern Woodlands of 5000 BC belies the long-held stereotypes of earlier archaeologists. These trends toward greater complexity and sophistication accelerated between 4000 and 1000 BC, and afterwards, during a period when the human population of the Eastern Woodlands rose sharply.

The Issue of Population Growth

Prehistoric population growth after 4000 BC coincided with the closing centuries of the climatic optimum that witnessed the final wastage of the Laurentide ice sheet (Delcourt and Delcourt, 1981; 1985; B. Smith, 1986; Steponaitis, 1986). This environmental development opened up vast areas of eastern Canada to caribou and human colonization. Rising sea levels and warming water temperatures along the Atlantic seaboard allowed a steady northward expansion of fish and shellfish habitats. River estuaries were flooded, too, creating far more favorable conditions for anadromous fish migrations in spring or fall. Water levels in the Great Lakes rose also, reducing stream gradients and improving fishing conditions in the now warmer water. Higher sea levels brought more sluggish waters to the Mississippi and other Midwestern and Southeastern rivers, too. Their swampy backwaters, low-lying levees, and lush floodplains became rich and diverse habitats for hunters and foragers. Rising water tables on the Gulf coastal plain established swamps and marshes over wide areas of Florida, while coastal resources were much richer than they had been for thousands of years. Deciduous trees spread north into parts of the once boreal forest-covered Great Lakes region and the Northeast, especially nut-bearing trees like oak, hickory, beech, and chestnut. This increased the amount of plant food available for human consumption in these areas. These changes coincided with a marked increase in human populations throughout the Eastern Woodlands after 4000 BC.

Population Pressure and Resources. How are we to account for this sudden take-off in population densities? Did slow and inexorable rises in population densities trigger technological change and still further increases? Or did environmental change provide conditions for a population explosion? Several possible explanations must be considered.

In 1977, Mark Cohen wrote a long essay he called *The Food Crisis in Prehistory*, in which he argued that human populations have a natural tendency to grow until they reach the carrying capacity limits of their environments. They begin to feel the effects of population pressure – food shortages, territorial disputes, and so on. They respond by experimenting with hitherto unexploited food resources and with their traditional hunting and gathering technology. By adding new, perhaps less palatable, food sources that may take more effort to collect and process, and with more efficient technology, the people overcome their food crisis. Population growth resumes its inexorable course.

The Cohen hypothesis has been criticized by demographic experts, who point out that population growth depends on many complex factors such as environmental change, technology, and social structure, not just on a simple equation of rising population pressure and experimentation with alternatives (B. Smith, 1986). If the hypothesis were to hold true for the Eastern Woodlands, then one would expect to find a gradual increase in the number of archaeological sites between 8000 and 4000 BC, with the occasional appearance of new plant foods, a sudden new dependence on aquatic foods, or improved tools. As we have seen, the limited exploitation of aquatic resources, and more nuts and seeds were added to Archaic diet several millennia before population densities increased around 4000 BC. And the specialized food-processing toolkits and woodworking tools that go with them appear just as early, even if they were in less frequent use. More likely, population growth was a response not only to environmental change, but also to technological and subsistence advances, as well as new settlement patterns.

Population Growth and Sedentism

We have seen how a trend toward more sedentary settlement began during the Middle Holocene, a move that may have coincided with greater aridity and with restrictions on mobility in many areas. More sedentary living may have had a significant impact on many aspects of Archaic life. More permanent base camps allow one to store nuts and other winter foods on a much larger scale than is possible if one is constantly on the move. This creates larger food surpluses, the ability to support more people year-round, and opportunities for kin groups and individuals to play important roles in controlling labor and the redistribution of food and luxury goods.

The technology of storage, using baskets, subterranean pits, perhaps special structures, was greatly enhanced in about 2500 BC by a major technological innovation – the development of waterproof, clay containers in the Southeast (B. Smith, 1986). These earliest North American ceramics appear along the South Carolina coastal plain as early as 2500 BC (Stoltman, 1966). (For Southwestern ceramics, see Chapter 14.) They were unimpressive, shallow clay vessels tempered with plant fibers, modeled on wooden and fiber bowls and trays that had been manufactured for thousands of years. (Temper is the ingredient added to clay to make it bond when fired. All kinds of material are used, everything from fine sand to ground shell or plant fiber.) Nevertheless, pottery-making was a success and had spread to the lower Mississippi Valley by about 1300 BC, perhaps as a result of an extensive steatite trade in the Southeast, a raw material much used for making weights, ornaments, and large containers. At first, pottery-making was an apparently insignificant innovation, for the technology was rudimentary at best. In time ceramics were a major technological advance that provided a highly effective way of storing not only grain and other foods, but also water and valuables. Clay pots and bowls could also hold boiling water, enabling people to process foods like acorns much more readily than they could with fire-heated stones and other age-old devices.

As we noted in Chapter 14, clay vessels are fragile and often heavy, and far from easy to carry from one camp to the next. Large-scale ceramics production could only flourish in more sedentary settlements, such as began fully to develop in the Late Archaic. It should be noted that the invention of pottery-making is not nearly as revolutionary as is sometimes claimed. Any hunter-gatherer who uses open hearths knows that soft earth and clay are baked hard by hot flames and ashes. However, it is hardly advantageous to make clay containers when they are heavier than baskets or skins, and are likely to be broken in transit from one camp to the next.

There were also pervasive long-term economic and social trends toward larger populations. Archaic territories contained a diversity of food resources and raw materials, but there was always something that was lacking – perhaps flint for making projectile points, red ocher for ornamentation, shells, stone for making ground-edged woodworking adzes used in dugout canoe building. Such items had to be sought from elsewhere, either by making a special journey, or by maintaining regular social and economic contacts with groups living closer to the sources of one's needs. Over time, these trading connections assumed ever greater importance in the yearly round. They became a source not only of valued possessions and raw materials traded for food or other commodities, but of social connections and prestige – a way of maintaining diplomatic relations with the outside world. They also affected population densities in indirect ways, especially when the prestige value of exotic objects increased or demand soared. Under these circumstances, more and more hands would be needed to increase the output of food, chert cores, shell ornaments, and other trade goods to meet escalating demand, extra people that had to be supported by additional food surpluses. The intensification of hunting and foraging to meet these demands would lead to population increases – and to the emergence of social ranks based on prestige and social and economic power within previously egalitarian societies.

In archaeological terms, Late Archaic population increases are reflected in much higher site densities. And the greater diversity of local hunting and foraging cultures manifests itself in at least five distinctive regional variants that reflect contrasting adaptations to different environmental zones. They are but generalized archaeological abstractions, identified primarily from projectile point styles and other artifacts, masking a multitude of prehistoric cultures and local adaptations over at least 3000 years.

The Shield Late Archaic
*c.*5000 BC to modern times

As early as 5000 to 4000 BC, the descendants of Paleo-Indian hunters were moving into newly deglaciated lands north of the Great Lakes, into the vast wilderness of the Canadian Shield (J. Wright, 1972). They settled over an enormous area from the north shores of the lakes all the way to the headwaters of rivers flowing into James Bay and Hudson Bay, and far eastward into Quebec and the Maritime Provinces of Canada. There they developed the distinctive Shield Archaic tradition, an adaptation to a country of lakes, rivers, and boreal forest with but sparse game and vegetable resources. The people lived in small bands, mostly near lakes and rivers and close to regular caribou migration routes. They subsisted off caribou and fish, taking other seasonal game such as bear, beaver, moose, and muskrat. The boreal environment provided minimal spring and summer plant foods.

The Shield Archaic was a profoundly conservative adaptation, one that changed but little over many millennia. The earliest projectile point styles are somewhat reminiscent of Plano-like forms from further south, with fairly broad-bladed, notched, corner-removed, or stemmed points appearing later. Heavy duty end and side scrapers, flaked knives and other implements manufactured from exotic flints occur at many sites. For thousands of years, in places right up until European times, Shield Archaic bands flourished in almost complete isolation from the more temperate world to the south. Some Late Archaic copper artifacts like fish hooks and knives occur on Shield sites closer to the Great Lakes, but most of the later boreal forest hunters relied on basically the same age-old Early Archaic technology as their remote ancestors. The sheer vastness and isolation of their harsh, forested wilderness shut off most possibilities of cultural innovation from more sophisticated societies to the south. The Shield Archaic people were probably the ancestors of the Algonquian-speaking hunter-gatherers of the Canadian Shield at European contact.

Maritime Tradition of the Northeast
*c.*6000 to *c.*1000 BC

Three overlapping Late Archaic traditions – Maritime, Lake Forest, and Mast Forest – have been identified over much of the temperate Northeast and east. The oldest identifiable language phylum in this area is Algonquian, a language widely spoken in the Eastern Woodlands at the

Late Archaic traditions of the Northeast.

time of European contact, and thought by some experts to have been in use by at least 8000 to 6000 BC. Linguists have analyzed reconstructed proto-Algonquian words for important animals and plants, especially the tamarisk and beech trees. Since both species were identified in proto-Algonquian, the experts theorize that their distribution coincides broadly with their ancient distribution. Thus, they pinpoint the ultimate homeland of the language as lying in the general area occupied by the Maritime, Lake Forest, and Mast Forest adaptations. Like the Shield Archaic, these three, diverse Late Archaic adaptations were the ancestors of historic peoples encountered by Europeans thousands of years later.

The Maritime Archaic has associations with the "Red Paint People," one of the pervasive myths of North American archaeology, a myth as persistent as that of the Moundbuilders. The Red Paint folk first appeared in archaeological literature in 1912, identified in some red ocher-smothered graves from Maine, a cemetery that seemed quite unlike any known prehistoric Indian find. Fifteen years later, amateur archaeologist Walter Smith published *The Lost Red Paint People of Maine.* He claimed the Red Paint People tribe were drowned when great tidal waves inundated thousands of square miles of a once much larger Maine. It happened that canoe loads of later Indians were paddling around offshore. To their astonishment, they were suddenly deposited on the vacant land. "It would have been the fastest and cleanest population replacement in the history of the world," remarks Dean Snow (1980). A surge of professional research since the 1960s has banished the Red Paint People to the legendary world where they belong. The cemeteries attributed to them belong within the Maritime Archaic tradition.

James Tuck introduced the term Maritime Archaic in 1971 after excavating an important cemetery at Port au Choix, Newfoundland, radiocarbon dated to about 2350 BC (McGhee and Tuck, 1975; Tuck, 1975; 1976). Ninety-nine individuals had been buried in graves sealed with layers of limestone rocks and sandy soil mixed with crushed shell. The dead divided almost equally between males and females, with large numbers of infants and newborns. Everyone had been sprinkled with powdered red ocher, with offerings of tools and weapons accompanying most people, young or adult. The Port au Choix people were buried with slender, bayonet-like spearheads and ground points. They used bone and antler harpoons and bone daggers that were sometimes mounted in antler hafts. Not only the slate bayonets but similar heavy woodworking tools – axes, adzes, and gouges – are also found to the south in Maine. Tuck recovered ground beaver incisors that were once mounted in antler handles and used as knives, bone needles, bone combs, pendants, also carved bird and whale effigies from the cemetery. He believes the Port au Choix people were caribou hunters, who also took sea mammals with their harpoons. They also exploited salmon runs and hunted sea birds, including the now extinct great auk.

The distinctive maritime flavor of the Port au Choix site is repeated at other Maritime Archaic locations along the coasts and rivers of New Brunswick and Maine, through the Maritime Provinces of Canada and along the coasts of Quebec, Labrador, and Nova Scotia that border the Gulf of St Lawrence. This was a sophisticated coastal adaptation, based not only on the exploitation of inshore fish and harbor seal hunting, and on the scavenging of beached whales, porpoise, and black fish, but also on offshore fishing. Swordfish almost never drift ashore, for they are a deep-water fish. But they often sun themselves near the surface off the Maine coast during the summer months. The only way Maritime people could take them was by stalking them in large dugout canoes and spearing their prey with harpoons. Compared with other areas and later millennia in the Northeast, shellfish were relatively unimportant.

Port au Choix, Newfoundland. (Above) Bone comb in the shape of a waterbird. (Below) Bayonet-like dagger.

Inland Maritime tradition sites tend to be located at strategic points on large rivers or on the lower reaches of major tributaries. Caribou flourish on heavy lichen growth, such as grew in the region's pine, hemlock, and spruce forests between about 5000 and 2300 BC. Dean Snow (1980) believes the Maritime people preyed on woodland caribou, easily killed with heavy spears when trapped in water or deep snow. Their hunting methods may have resembled those of historic caribou hunters of Canada's Barren Grounds. They located their camps near established seasonal migration routes and would drive large numbers of animals between converging lines of stone cairns toward lurking hunters, or into water covered with thin ice, where waiting canoes dispatched the trapped beasts. Several inland Maritime sites, among them the Hirundu and Hathaway locations within Maine's Penobscot drainage, are thought to have been anadromous fishing stations.

Everything points to a regular seasonal round. During the summer months, the Maritime people would live at coastal locations, hunting and fishing inshore and offshore in large dugout canoes. Come fall, they would take advantage of bountiful fish runs, hunting caribou inland through the winter until the spring salmon runs began. This was a centrally based wandering system, with, perhaps, somewhat larger band sizes than occurred in earlier times, for the relatively predictable food resources of coast and interior permitted a somewhat higher population density than before. These were skilled ocean hunters with a well-developed religious tradition reflected in careful disposal of the dead. But the graves from Port au Choix and Hathaway show no signs of social ranking.

Almost certainly, the Maritime Archaic evolved from primeval Middle Archaic developments in the region, perhaps drawing some of the maritime elements in its culture from the Sub-Arctic to the northeast, where sea mammal hunting and fishing were long established.

Lake Forest Late Archaic
*c.*3200 to *c.*1000 BC

The Lake Forest Archaic covers a broad cultural continuum of Late Archaic culture associated with the pine and hardwood forests that extend from the Great Lakes into New York State and the St Lawrence Valley (Mason, 1981; Snow, 1980). Lake Forest people who lived to the northeast in the St Lawrence drainage had access to both heavy fish runs in spring and fall, and also to harbor seals who flourished in Lake Ontario and Lake Champlain. Their adaptation may have resembled that of the Maritime tradition. The Lake Forest Archaic was predominantly an inland adaptation, a lifeway that was varied, highly flexible, and based on a multitude of primary and secondary, overlapping food sources. Deer and other mammals medium-sized and small, fish, shellfish, reptiles, water-fowl, ground-running and tree-roosting birds, and all manner of plant foods – all were part of Lake Forest subsistence. Population densities were generally low, except in the most food-rich and resource-diverse areas. The people probably lived in small bands within well-defined territories where they used a regular base camp returned to year after year, but with much seasonal mobility.

The great diversity of the Lake Forest tradition is confusing, even to specialists, partly because of terminological confusion, and also on account of the proximity of its southern boundaries to the dense Late Archaic populations of the Midwest and Southeast. For our broad, descriptive purposes, there are two widely recognized variants which merit more extended discussion: Laurentian, and the Old Copper culture.

Laurentian (3200 to 1400 BC). If there is one phrase that can be used to describe the Laurentian, it is Ronald Mason's (1981) telling "unity within diversity." The term was originally used to describe the Late Archaic culture of northern New York, southern Ontario, and both banks of the St Lawrence into southern Quebec and Vermont, now known to date to between 3200 and 2000 BC (Ritchie, 1969; for history, see Funk, 1988). But the definition was soon found to apply to Late Archaic sites far from this core area, in New England, the Upper Great Lakes, and south into Pennsylvania and New Jersey. So the term "Laurentian" covers a multitude of local variants and adaptations known to specialists under a multiplicity of archaeological labels that may, or may not, bear resemblance to prehistoric cultural reality. In general, however, the Laurentian was a diverse woodland adaptation, based on a wide variety of mammals, wild vegetable foods, and fish. Laurentide subsistence patterns varied with the season and the location, with marked seasonal exploitation of nuts, waterfowl, and other locally plentiful resources.

In archaeological terms, the Laurentian is identified by some characteristic artifact forms, especially the broad-bladed and side-notched Otter Creek point from the Lake Champlain drainage. Related point designs have come from contemporary sites in New England, and far south and west into the Mississippi Valley and Midwest. In all probability, the Otter Creek point developed from earlier Middle Archaic forms used over much of the Eastern Woodlands. Laurentian artisans also made polished atlatl weights known as "bannerstones," chipped-stone gouges and adzes for wood working, and a wide variety of antler and bone points, ornaments, and small tools.

While many artifact forms like scrapers, whistles, and awls are virtually universal, others, such as projectile points, ground-slate tools, and copper objects, appear to have more discrete distributions. In general, ground-slate artifacts and other "northern" tools tend to be more common in eastern Laurentian sites: knives, projectile points, and characteristic semi-circular *ulu* knives, artifacts used by prehistoric and historic Inuit to skin fish and treat sea mammal hides. This technological component of Laurentian culture may have stemmed from the rich Maritime Archaic of the St Lawrence Valley. Artifacts made of native hammered copper from the Great Lakes region are much more common in Laurentian sites to the west, evidence of widespread trade in this metal over a wide area. The Laurentian tradition is made up of diverse technological strands, derived not only from the Maritime provinces of the Northeast, but also from much further afield in the Midwest and south as well.

In New York, Vermont, southern Ontario, and Quebec, the Laurentian is subdivided into three regional phases that overlap in space and time: Brewerton, Vosburg, and Vergennes (Funk, 1988). The Vergennes phase emerged around 3200 to 3000 BC. Vergennes sites are centered in northeast

Laurentian artifacts from New York State. Top to bottom: two side-notched Otter Creek points, a ground-slate ulu, and two perforated bannerstones. Length of longest point c. 12.5 cm.

New York State and in nearby Vermont and southern Ontario. This is the "classic" Laurentian, with a full range of characteristic artifacts, including Otter Creek points. There are some signs of a formative version of the Vergennes dating to earlier centuries. The Brewerton phase of central New York and the Lake Ontario region and the ill-defined Vosburg of the Mohawk and Hudson drainage are broadly contemporary. Neither contain the full range of Laurentian artifacts. They are distinguished by different projectile point forms (for full discussion, see Funk, 1988).

These local variations, and many others, are hardly surprising, for the Lake Forest tradition was a highly adaptable culture that absorbed artifacts and other culture traits from neighbors on every side.

Old Copper Culture (*c.3000 to 2500 BC*). In a few parts of the world, prehistoric peoples used abundant native copper outcrops as a source of "stone" for making artifacts of all kinds without actually smelting the metal. The Lake Superior Basin was one of those regions. Vast outcrops of very pure copper occur on or near the surface along the Brule River in northwest Wisconsin, on Lake Superior's Keweenaw Peninsula, on Isle Royale on the Canadian shore, and on the northern shore of the lake (Mason, 1981). The Indians picked the ore off the surface, or could dig it out with the simplest of tools. For thousands of years, prehistoric peoples made use of this convenient raw material to make artifacts of all kinds, shiny tools and ornaments that were passed from hand to hand over thousands of miles of eastern North America.

No one knows when Archaic people first exploited Wisconsin's copper outcrops, but tens of thousands of Late Archaic metal artifacts have turned up in the eastern part of the state, with outlying finds far into northeast Canada and all over the Great Lakes drainage, also in the east and Midwest. These finds have given rise to a loosely defined western variant of the Lake Forest Tradition – the Old Copper culture, identified by a wide variety of copper implements that bear striking resemblances to Laurentian and Maritime Archaic slate tools. Its type sites are three poorly understood Wisconsin cemeteries – Oconto, Osceola, and Reigh, all disturbed by collectors and industrial activity before investigation. Ronald Mason (1981) dates Old Copper to between about 3000 and 2500 BC. It would be a mistake, however, to think of the Old Copper culture as a rigidly delineated cultural entity. Most likely, it covers a large number of small, diverse hunter-gatherer societies that shared a common copper technology, just as slate artifacts were made in similar ways, and in basically equivalent forms, over much of the Northeast.

Copper projectile points often substituted for stone-tipped weapons. Men hammered out axe and adze blades, gouges, *ulus*, wood splitting wedges, and awls of many forms. Fish hooks and gorges, even gaffs for landing the catch (some dredged from the lake bed in modern fishermens' nets) were fashioned in the shiny metal. The artisans made simple ornaments – tubular and barrel-shaped beads, bracelets, and headdress pieces.

The Lake Superior copper industry had a long and varied history. A large number of western Lake Forest societies exploited the metal and enjoyed its many advantages (Griffin, 1961). In time, word of the shiny metal spread far and wide. Copper artifacts and ornaments passed from hand to hand between close and more distant kin. The further away from the outcrops

Tow spearheads cold hammered from Lake Superior copper. Location unknown.

copper objects passed, the greater the perceived value and prestige associated with them. Over the centuries, extensive trade in copper developed from the Upper Great Lakes far into the east, Midwest, and Southeast. Most of the native copper circulated within the Great Lakes and Laurentian areas, within a radius of about 350 miles (563 km) from the sources. The people living this close to the outcrops used copper for utilitarian objects such as spearheads and adze blades that were used in life and deposited with the dead. Even when used for day-to-day artifacts, copper was a highly esteemed commodity, a shiny material that made "ordinary" artifacts of wood, bone and stone look prosaic. In time, this prized metal became a symbol of social identification both for the living and the dead, who carried their cherished artifacts with them to the world of the ancestors. Outside the 350-mile radius, copper assumed a vastly enhanced prestige value, as something rare and highly prized. The metal was fashioned into ornaments that appear in graves, a clear sign of social prominence carried with one into the afterlife. Lustrous copper artifacts and ornaments were a staple of complex long-distance trading networks that developed all over the Eastern Woodlands between 4000 and 1000 BC. They were also an important element in evolving mortuary traditions, in which grave ornamentation, social ranking, and kin identity played important parts.

Mast Forest Late Archaic (*c.* 2700 to 1200 BC)

Coastal, Piedmont, Mast Forest . . . names for this somewhat ill-defined Late Archaic tradition have proliferated over the years, into what Dean Snow (1980) has called "a thicket of competing abstractions." Whatever the appropriate label, this regional expression extends from the Merrimack drainage of southern New England through coastal drainages as far south as North Carolina and west across the basins of Ohio River tributaries to the southern shores of Lake Erie and into southern Michigan (Funk, 1988). Since it largely coincides with forests with a higher oak tree component, the term Mast Forest is perhaps most appropriate.

As always in the Eastern Woodlands, projectile point forms have played an important role in distinguishing not only between different Mast Forest complexes, but also between Lake Forest and Mast Forest sites. What are potentially more striking, however, are the adaptive contrasts between the two traditions. Mast Forest sites tend to contain more pestles, grinders, and other artifacts for preparing wild vegetable foods, implying that their makers made greater use of nuts, especially acorns. Deer were the major game animal throughout the mast forest, but simple fishing with spears and harpoons was important in rivers and lakes.

Two Late Archaic traditions occur in southern New England under the general rubric of the Mast Forest (Dincauze, 1971; 1975; Ritchie, 1969). The Narrow Point tradition, characterized by points of that name, extended from southeastern New York into southern New England between about 2650 and just after 2000 BC. The better known Susquehanna tradition formed a single cultural province from eastern Pennsylvania to southern Maine and out onto the now-submerged continental shelf. It replaced the

Susquehanna point, length 6.9 cm.

Narrow Point over part of this area and lasted from about 1800 to 1200 BC. The relationships between these traditions and others to the south and west are still little understood, but they are associated with signs of more elaborate burial ceremonies involving cremations and possible multiple burials involving the digging of large pits.

The Mast Forest Archaic includes the famous Lamoka site on the lake of that name, first identified by New York archaeologist William Ritchie in 1932 as part of his Archaic stage of North American prehistory (Ritchie, 1969). Lomoka and related sites lie in the undulating country of west-central New York State, where small bands of hunter-gatherers lived mainly along the tributaries of Lake Ontario around 2500 BC. The Lamoka Lake site itself was probably a base camp used for months on end. It consisted of about 27 houses, a community of perhaps about 150 to 200 people, covered about 0.9 acre (0.4 ha), and formed a midden up to 4.9 ft (1.5 m) deep. The inhabitants lived in rectangular dwellings with up to 215 sq. ft (20 sq. m) of floor space, frames of poles or saplings screwed into the ground and covered with bark, skins, or mats. Acorn-roasting beds up to 49 ft (15 m) long, hearths, and storage pits, also fish- and meat-drying racks, abounded in the settlement.

Most other known Lamoka-related settlements were much smaller and more transitory, reflecting a centrally based wandering system that dispersed the population for much of the year. The hunters used atlatls and spears to take deer, turkey, and passenger pigeons, as well as small mammals of all kinds, staple game animals over much of the Eastern Woodlands at this time. They were also expert fishermen, both with fish spears and with hooks and gorges, as well as nets. Ritchie and others have found enormous numbers of stone fish net weights, also bone net-making artifacts. The Lamoka people also exploited wild vegetable foods in spring, summer, and fall, especially annual harvests of hickory and acorns.

Lamoka toolkits are remarkable for their heavy woodworking tools – hatchets and the characteristic beveled Lamoka adze, perhaps used in canoe building. The people manufactured a wide range of small, narrow-stemmed stone projectile points, small bone tools, and pestles and mortars used for preparing vegetable foods. Many polished-bone or

Lamoka artifacts: (left to right) antler pendant with geometric design; bone dagger; beveled adze; and (above) one side-notched and two stemmed points. Length of adze c. 13.5 cm.

turtle-shell pendants come from Lamoka sites, usually perforated and scored lightly on the edges. Simple geometric designs appear on some of these pendants, artifacts that also occur in Kentucky shell middens. Perhaps the Lamoka people maintained some tenuous connections with groups far to the south.

Like the Maritime Archaic people, the Lamoka hunter-gatherers buried their dead with sedulous care, curled up in a flexed position, although not in cemeteries but in village middens. Occasionally, the bones of the deceased are bundled up, as if they had been collected and buried after decomposition. Their skeletons reveal they were long-headed people, men standing about 5 ft 6 in (168 cm) high, the women slightly shorter. Most graves had red ocher and a few personal possessions like adzes.

Lamoka society was by no means peaceful. Several individuals had been killed by Lamoka-style projectile points still embedded in their skeletons. A few were mutilated after death, then been buried without heads, hands, or feet. Perhaps these people were victims of territorial disputes or of the kind of constant, low-level blood feuding that still smolders on for generations in egalitarian societies throughout the world to this day. Perhaps the Lamoka people practiced sporadic ritual cannibalism, too, for fragments of split and burnt human bone come from some settlements.

The highest Mast Forest population densities may have been near the Atlantic coast. About 2500 BC, a group of Mast Forest people built a stake fish weir on the site of what is now Boylston Street, Boston, on a river bed that is now about 16 ft (5 m) below modern sea level (Conger and others, 1949). Coastal bands like this one probably spent the summer months close to shore, moving inland to hunting camps in the cold season. Shellfish were also an important resource in southeastern New England and along the Atlantic coast. As early as 3900 BC, large oysters were harvested in the Lower Hudson estuary, while the quahog and soft-shelled clam were important New England resources.

Most Mast Forest communities were probably of small size, with occasional larger base camps, like the Bent site on the Mohawk River which covers about 5 acres (2 ha) (Snow, 1980). Six circular post-framed dwellings 30 to 45 ft (9 to 14 m) across, together with a larger, perhaps ceremonial structure, once stood at the Wapanucket 6 site in southeastern Massachusetts. The dwellings had winding, shaped entrances, perhaps for security or to keep out the cold, so the doorways were formed by overlapping walls. They were large enough to house a nuclear family or slightly larger group.

The Mast Forest Archaic shows great regional diversity, with little apparent exchange of exotic raw materials between neighbors. (For a discussion of the Terminal Archaic of the Northeast, see Chapter 21, where these cultures are discussed as background to later prehistory.)

Central Riverine Archaic
c.4000 to 1000 BC

Lamoka Lake and other Mast Forest sites show how higher population densities could develop in areas where plentiful, diverse, and predictable food resources were to be found. The same situation pertained in the major river valleys of the Midwest and Southeast. The Central Riverine Archaic was the most elaborate and well developed of all eastern Late Archaic traditions, for it was centered in and near Midwestern and Southeastern river valleys where both rich deciduous forests and bountiful floodplains provided a superabundance of aquatic, game, and plant foods. The Central Riverine is found in or near the Mississippi, Ohio, Cumberland, and Tennessee valleys, a tradition that developed over thousands of years as rivers stabilized during the Middle Holocene. As we saw in the previous chapter, Early and Middle Archaic occupations at sites like Carrier Mills, Eva, and Koster document the trend toward more sedentary lifeways and ever more efficient exploitation of aquatic and vegetable resources (B. Smith, 1986; Steponaitis, 1986).

Koster (3900 to 2800 BC). Horizon 6 at Koster dates to between 3900 and 2800 BC, a time when people lived there year-round (Phillips and Brown, 1983; Struever and Holton, 1979). The village, part of what is called the "Helton" phase, covered about 5 acres (2 ha), perhaps housing 100 to 150 people. Stuart Struever and his colleagues found six houses, built on sunken earthen floors that were cut like shallow terraces about 18 in (45 cm) into a hill slope. The builders erected rows of stout posts along the long walls, then filled in the gaps between them with woven brush and clay. Apparently they covered the ends with skins, mats, or more brush. Each dwelling covered between 96 and 140 sq. ft (12 to 15 sq. m), sufficient space for a nuclear family.

The food remains from this settlement reveal striking contrasts with earlier Archaic diet in the Illinois Valley. Earlier fishermen had concentrated mainly on fish species that preferred faster-moving river water. Their Horizon 6 successors exploited the shallow backwater lakes and swamps that now abounded near Koster. They speared and netted vast numbers of sluggish, shallow-water fish like bass, buffalo fish, and catfish, species that can be eaten fresh or be dried or smoked for consumption during the winter. Dozens of fish could also be taken by poisoning the water with the chemicals in powdered hickory nut husks, or by driving oxygen-starved fish into pools where they could be scooped up with baskets. One Illinois fisheries biologist has estimated that the Helton occupants of Koster could have taken between 300 and 600 lbs (136–272 kg) of fish flesh per acre every year from backwater lakes that covered hundreds of acres. The same shallow lakes also contained rich mollusc beds that could be used as supplementary food.

Like their predecessors, the Helton people relied on the fall hickory and acorn harvests, as well as black walnuts, pecans, and hazelnuts. But they now exploited many more seed plants, including marsh elder (sumpweed), a swamp-side grass, grinding the seeds with stone pestles and mortars. The hunters took deer and other small mammals, but they now had a new seasonal food – waterfowl that paused to feed and rest on the shallow lakes of the Illinois Valley during spring and fall migrations. The Illinois is on the Mississippi flyway, the narrow migration route used by millions of waterfowl flying north and south to and from their Canadian breeding grounds each year. The Helton people could take hundreds of ducks, geese, and other migrants with bows, or by trapping them with light, weighted

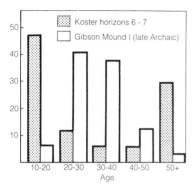

Histogram comparing the preponderance of adolescent and elderly burials in the Koster Horizons 6-7 cemetery with contemporary burials under Gibson Mound, where a much higher proportion were those aged between 18 and 40.

nets cast over sleeping birds, or by using silently paddled canoes to drive them into waiting cages during stealthy dawn raids.

Everything in Koster Horizon 6 points to greater efficiency at food procurement, an efficiency accompanied by the exploitation of a much broader spectrum of animal, aquatic, and vegetable foods. This implies larger food surpluses, surpluses used to feed more people. Enhanced food procurement abilities coincide with more commonplace sedentary occupation, perhaps resulting in part from even more restricted territorial mobility than in the Middle Archaic. But, with more mouths to feed, there may have been food shortages. It cannot be a coincidence that Late Archaic people were now harvesting not only nuts but seed plants, a much broader range of vegetable foods, and also taking opportunistic advantage of migratory birds and other seasonal phenomena.

A small cemetery of eight burials smothered in red ocher came from the edge of the Horizon 6 settlement, most of them men older than 40 years old, who had been crippled by arthritis or serious injury. There were adolescent burials, too, young and old both buried with grinding stones, points, drills, and other day-to-day artifacts. Another cemetery of the same age lay under the later Gibson mound across the river from Koster. This offered a dramatic contrast – not the infirm, but the skeletons of healthy men and women between 18 and 40 years old, associated with more elaborate grave goods. Stuart Struever has argued that these able-bodied villagers may have enjoyed a higher social status than the adolescent and unproductive sick and older people laid to rest at the edge of the settlement.

Koster was abandoned in about 2800 BC, then occupied again about 800 years later by deer-hunting people of the so-called "Titterington" phase from the St Louis area, people who buried prominent members of society with beautiful shell ornaments from the Gulf of Mexico.

Green River Culture (3000 to 2000 BC). To the east, the Green River joins the Ohio River at Evansville, Indiana, part of a floodplain area that offered rich food resources for Late Archaic hunters and foragers. Between about 3000 and 2000 BC, large, stable Indian communities flourished in this part of the Ohio drainage. They remained at, or near, the same locations for centuries, accumulating huge shell middens that were a magnet for early archaeologists, so much so that the term "Shell Midden" Archaic was once coined to describe them (Winters, 1974; W. Webb, 1974). The famous Indian Knoll site in southwestern Kentucky is the best-known location. Excavated by William Webb during the Great Depression, it alone has yielded more than 1000 burials. Collectively, the Green River sites are a mine of information on Late Archaic riverine adaptations of 2500 BC, and on the people who lived there.

Thousands of freshwater shells come from Indian Knoll, Carlston Annis, and other Green River settlements, but they were probably little more than a supplemental food in this resource-rich environment. The dietary staples were both animal (deer and many small mammals) and vegetable. The hunters took game with spears and atlatls. At least 70 Indian Knoll graves contained handles, weights, and atlatl hooks, still lying in place with the wooden shaft decayed away. Shallow-water fish were commonly eaten, but the rich range of vegetable foods is especially striking. Easily stored hickory nuts were the overwhelming favorites, but acorns were also exploited. Less

Atlatl parts from Indian Knoll, Kentucky: handle (left), weight (center), and hook (right).

cyclical in their harvest abundance, acorns may have assumed greater and greater importance during the Late Archaic, partly because they were a more consistent crop than the hickory. Some domesticated squashes appear in the Green River sites, evidence that people were now turning to small-scale horticulture to amplify natural food supplies, also growing gourds as containers.

The Indian Knoll people show a close physical resemblance to those from other Midwestern Archaic cemeteries. Life expectancy was short, only about 18.6 years, compared with the 32.8-year figure from Carrier Mills in southern Illinois, which is even better than that for early 19th-century Americans (Jefferies, 1987). A surprising number of people died violently. Nearly 11 percent of the Indian Knoll skeletons had suffered fractured bones, and at least 23 were associated with stone or antler projectile points that may have been the cause of death. Perhaps these casualties reflect sporadic blood feuding, or even, as some authorities have argued, competition for prized resources. Indian Knoll and other large Green River sites lie in highly favored locations. Perhaps the inhabitants had to defend themselves regularly against those who did not have similar access to such abundant food supplies.

Judging from the Indian Knoll graves, the Green River people lived in a fairly egalitarian society, where everyone owned much the same material possessions. Men were buried with axes, woodworking tools, fish hooks, awls, and stoneworking punches. Women wore bone beads and owned nutcracking stones. One curious funerary anomaly finds male weapons like atlatls occurring with female and child burials. Perhaps, as Nan Rothschild has argued, this phenomenon may mark the beginnings of some form of rank distinction in Late Archaic society, privileges that were inherited and symbolized by prestigious artifacts. Some men and women carried their turtle shell rattles, bone flutes, and shamans' bones with them at death (Rothschild, 1979).

About 4 percent of the Indian Knoll burials yielded exotic objects from afar. Five burials included metal ornaments of Lake Superior copper. Conch shells and shell ornaments such as beads and gorgets, also cups, accompanied 42 skeletons, the *Marginella* and *Olivella* species from the Gulf of Mexico and the southern Atlantic seaboard hundreds of miles away. Both adult men and women owned valuable copper and conch objects, as did infants and children. Some 18,378 disk-shell beads of imported shell came from 143 Indian Knoll graves. Rothschild believes that young people were buried with imported goods because of their kin ties to privileged adults of high status and wealth. Whether such privileges were inherited or acquired by adults during their lifetimes remains unknown.

Round grave burial from Indian Knoll, Kentucky.

The Riverton Culture (1500 to 1000 BC). The Green River culture was, of course, a local adaptation, centered in an area like the Lower Illinois Valley where a great diversity of food resources supported higher than average population densities. There were other such rich areas, too, local culture areas with their own distinctive societies. The Riverton culture of eastern Illinois' central Wabash River Valley flourished between about 1500 and 1000 BC. It was based on a linear territory along about a 40-mile (64-km) length of the central Wabash River in eastern Illinois, with about 10 miles (16 km) between major base camps.

Howard Winters (1968) excavated three large Riverton shell middens in the valley, between 1 and 3 acres (0.4 and 1.2 ha) in area. Judging from the food remains, including migratory birds, each of the sites was occupied at a different season of the year as the people exploited upland and floodplain resources. Riverton itself was a base camp occupied from mid-May to late September. Then the people moved to Swan Island, a temporary autumn camp where foraging was important. During the winter months, until late March, they settled at Robeson Hills, a cold weather settlement on a promontory overlooking the floodplain. There they hunted deer and other mammals, as well as exploiting valley resources. In spring, the hunters returned to Swan Island.

Riverton has sufficiently distinctive artifacts for it to be distinguished from contemporary Late Archaic adaptations elsewhere in the Central Riverine area, from cultures like that centered on Indian Knoll and the Titterington culture of the St Louis region. Where food resources were diverse and abundant, Central Riverine Late Archaic cultures, with their well-demarcated territories, restricted mobility, and relatively sedentary lifeways, were very local phenomena, but societies that depended heavily on social and economic interaction with their neighbors for their survival. Important riverine cultures also flourished in the Tennessee Valley (for a summary, see Chapman, 1985).

Exchange and Interaction

The emergence of social ranking among Late Archaic societies in the east was the culmination of economic and social trends that began at least 3000 years earlier (B. Smith, 1986). By 4000 BC, the diverse hunter-gatherer populations of the Eastern Woodlands were living under very different social conditions from those enjoyed by their remote ancestors. Each group lived in its own territory, under much more "closed" social conditions, where territorial boundaries and relations with neighbors were more rigidly defined than they had been in Paleo-Indian times. This greater degree of closure is reflected in much greater regional variation in artifacts and stylistic traditions, especially after about 2000 BC. Under these new economic and social circumstances, relationships with neighbors assumed much greater importance. Such relationships would take many forms – informal bartering of fine-grained rocks, occasional communal hunts and ceremonies, more formal gift exchanges, and ever-shifting political and social alliances based on obligations of kin and reciprocity between individuals. As time went on, the manipulation of social alliances, and the barter and exchange that went with them, led to enhanced concerns with prestige and social distinction, to more complex social orders.

Not that social change was rapid, for the archaeological record reflects a profound, inherent conservatism reflected not only in artifacts and choice of base camps, but in burial customs, subsistence patterns, and inter-band relationships as well. Few eastern societies of 1000 BC were much larger than a few hundred souls, and even those that were, were still predominantly egalitarian in their social organization. But there were far-flung relationships based on networks of reciprocal social obligations and the symbolism of gift-giving associated with them.

As we have seen, long-distance exchange of prized materials such as marine shells and copper appeared for the first time in the middle South between about 5000 and 4000 BC and escalated gradually over the next 3000 years. Exotic materials of all kinds passed from band to band, over enormous distances – Lake Superior native copper and hematite, Atlantic and Gulf Coast sea shells, galena from the Upper Mississippi Valley, jasper from eastern Pennsylvania, chalcedony and black slate from Canada, cherts, hornstones, and other fine-grained rocks for ornaments and tool-making from all over the Midwest and east (B. Smith, 1986). All these

Prized materials were exchanged over vast distances in the Eastern woodlands. Marine shells, one such material, are seen here in use as receptacles for a luxury drink at a council meeting of Florida Indians in this engraving by Theodore de Bry (1591).

materials were exchanged between individuals and groups, passed "down the line" from settlement to settlement, valley to valley through informal exchange networks that evolved and maintained an essential continuity over thousands of years. The range of exotic materials is astounding. The Koster people, at the time a small group, were receiving copper, galena, sea shells, Arkansas bauxite, fluorspar from southern Illinois, and chert from many regions of the Midwest well before 2000 BC (Struever and Holton, 1979).

These precious materials circulated in raw and finished form. As the distribution of copper objects from the western Great Lakes shows, trade objects in any form appear to have assumed a greater prestige value the further away from the source they were exchanged. *Busycon* shells from Florida were made into axe blades and gouges by those who collected them or who lived close inland. But the groups far in the interior who received precious shells placed a quite different value on the same material. Shell ornaments and necklaces had prestige value and a highly specific social context; a social context which, as yet, is still dimly understood (Goad, 1980).

After 5000 BC, people invested more labor in fashioning socially valued artifacts and ornaments like finely ground "bannerstones," delicate slate ornaments and weapons, and steatite gorgets and bowls. Finely incised bone points are found widely along the eastern seaboard and in Midwestern valleys. There are signs, too, that access to some precious materials was carefully controlled. Huge caches of fine chert preforms are found in Maritime Archaic and Laurentian graves, as if the value of these trade commodities was deliberately manipulated.

Some groups living in areas where different trade networks intersected may well have exploited their strategic locations and become middlemen in long-distance trade. It is possible, for example, that the Green River people exploited the opportunities of both the copper trade from the northwest and the shell exchange from the south and southeast.

Within this context of regular social gatherings and exchanges, a modest degree of social differentiation based on reciprocity may have emerged in Late Archaic society. This may have been nothing more than a degree of ranking between younger and older members of society, or perhaps the emergence of one kin group as the "ranking" lineage, the one from whom social and ritual leaders traditionally came. Judging from increasingly elaborate mortuary customs, both kin-based and individual social ranking took place within a context of increasing ritual elaboration, in which exotic objects and fine ornaments played a major part. Cemeteries themselves assumed a special significance, often placed, as we have seen, on elevated ground, sometimes beneath low, artificial mounds.

By 1000 BC, social differentiation is well documented by the grave goods found in Central Riverine Archaic graves at Indian Knoll, in Riverton and Titterington sites, and other cemeteries (B. Smith, 1986). This differentiation was nothing dramatic, for it was still firmly based in age-old kin ties and reciprocity.

Anthropologists have long recognized the importance of reciprocity in hunter-gatherer societies, obligations between individuals that place the common good ahead of personal interest. Such reciprocity must have been characteristic of all early North American societies, however unsophisticated: their survival depended upon it. But, under conditions of more sedentary settlement, higher population densities, and regular contacts between neighboring groups, some form of emerging social ranking based on reciprocity is almost inevitable.

We can only speculate as to how this occurred. One possible scenario might go something like this – some individuals, perhaps respected shamans or elders, leaders of a particular lineage, might assume roles as ritual and social mediators in newly sedentary societies. They were the people who arbitrated disputes and controlled relations with neighboring, and sometimes perhaps competing, groups. It was they who gave gifts to influential neighbors and participated in formal gift exchanges, who became traders, people with reciprocal obligations that extended to other individuals and kin leaders living near and far. It was they, too, who were responsible for internal reciprocity, for redistributing food, essential raw materials, and luxury goods through the community. Some of these people were better at trading, at dealing with allies and enemies, at attracting the loyalty of kinspeople and followers. They had the quality of being able to persuade people to work for them, hunting, fishing, and gathering, perhaps digging out chert and blocking it into preforms. Social and ritual arbitrators, skilled diplomats and acquisitors, these individuals became the leaders of the ever more complex human societies of the Eastern Woodlands after 1000 BC (B. Smith, 1986).

The Poverty Point Culture
1700 to 700 BC

These slow, incremental culture changes did not affect every region of the Eastern Woodlands in the same ways. Many groups continued to live much as they had in earlier millennia, even if they exploited nut harvests more intensively and stored small, starchy seed crops for later use. In some areas, they deliberately cultivated sunflowers, marsh elder, knotweed, and other indigenous wild plants in small gardens. But no heavy dependence on cultivated foods developed, for there may have been so many edible species that there was no compelling reason for them to become overwhelmingly important. It was only much later, during the first millennium AD, that maize, and, later, bean cultivation, revolutionized subsistence in the Eastern Woodlands.

The Poverty Point culture of the Lower Mississippi Valley and adjacent Gulf Coast offers a dramatic contrast (Gibson, 1974; 1980; Walthall, 1980; C. Webb, 1977). More than 100 Poverty Point sites form ten regional discrete clusters within natural geographical boundaries, each apparently grouped around a regional center that belongs within the Poverty Point culture. The earliest Poverty Point sites date to about 1700 BC, forming the earliest component in a cultural sequence that lasted for 1000 years.

The Poverty Point site itself lies on the Macon Ridge overlooking the Mississippi floodplain, near the confluences of six rivers. This was a strategic point to trade up and downstream, to receive exotic materials that came downstream, not only along the Mississippi, but the Arkansas, Red, Ohio, and Tennessee rivers as well. The Poverty Point settlements became a natural location for exchanging raw materials and finished products, artifacts made of a remarkable variety of exotic materials – argilite, slate, copper, galena, jasper, quartz, and steatite were only a few of the tool-making materials at the site, some of them from as far as 620 miles (1000 km) away. This may have been the kind of social environment in which individual leaders first came into prominence, for there is strong reason to believe that the leaders of Poverty Point not only exported and imported a wide range of commodities, but that they redistributed them to regional centers within their own culture area.

Poverty Point itself with its great earthworks is a remarkable contrast to the humble base camps that characterized most of the Eastern Woodlands at the time. Six concentric semi-circular earthen ridges divided into segments average about 82 ft (25 m) wide and 9.8 ft (3 m) high. They are set about 131 ft (40 m) apart, each capped with midden and fill deposits in places over 3.2 ft (1 m) deep. The significance of these earthworks is a complete enigma, beyond a suspicion that they are connected with astronomical observations. To the west lies an artificial mound more than 66 ft (20 m) high and more than 660 ft (200 m) long. A person standing on this mound can sight the vernal and autumnal equinoxes directly across the center of the earthworks to the east. This is the point where the sun rises on the first days of spring and fall.

The Poverty Point habitation area covers about 494 acres (200 ha). Built between about 1000 and 700 BC, Poverty Point took more than 1,236,007 cu. ft (35,000 cu. m) of basket-loaded soil to complete, an organized building effort that would not be undertaken again in North America for another millennium. One authority has calculated that 1350 adults laboring 70 days a year would have taken three years to erect the earthworks. Estimates of as many as 600 dwellings housing between 4000 and 5000 people may be somewhat optimistic, but even at a third that size, Poverty Point is a unique, and still little understood, phenomenon. (Theories that the site owes much to Mexican influences, from the Olmec civilization of the Mesoamerican lowlands, are now discounted.)

The Poverty Point people enjoyed the same general adaptation as other Central Riverine societies, exploiting wild vegetable foods and fishing in nearby oxbow lakes, as well as cultivating bottle gourds and squashes. The major centers appear to have been sited near natural escarpments, close to unusually bountiful floodplain swamps and oxbow lakes, and to upland hunting grounds. But we still know nothing about the internal organization of the site, nor about the relationship between those who lived at the great settlement and the dozens of smaller communities and the regional centers associated with them.

Over 2000 years later, the Natchez Indians of the lower Mississippi lived in ranked societies that distinguished between privileged nobles and chiefs and common people. They were dual societies, that is to say they were organized into moieties, halves associated with two cardinal directions. Individuals of one moiety married partners of the other moiety. J.L. Gibson (1980) analyzed 19,000 artifacts from Poverty Point, and found different artifact groups on the northern and southern sides of the site. This, he claims, is evidence for similar social organization two millennia earlier. Perhaps, too, the Poverty Point leaders followed another Natchez rule: nobles not only married commoners, but commoners from the other moiety. Gibson believes that the limited distributions of stone pipe bowls,

Poverty Point, Louisiana. (Left) Artist's reconstruction. The artificial earthworks cover 1 square mile. (Below) Aerial view of Poverty Point toward the northwest.

red jasper beads, and zoomorphic pendants in the Poverty Point earthworks are evidence of social differentiation, ornaments associated with prominent people and no one else, but this hypothesis is at best an intelligent guess, based on historical analogy.

Many questions about Poverty Point remain unanswered. Did people from throughout Poverty Point territory contribute labor to the great earthworks, or were they merely the work of the actual inhabitants? What were the social and political relationships within the Poverty Point culture? How were goods redistributed, and who were the leaders who organized the vast communal efforts needed to build earthworks, organize trade, and control the local exchange of goods throughout the Poverty Point area? How did they control the loyalties of the hundreds, if not thousands, of people who erected and used the great earthworks? Excavations at the greater center, and outlying sites have barely begun. At present, Poverty Point stands as an isolated and enigmatic phenomenon, but as a prophetic symbol of cultural developments that were to emerge in the remaining millennia of eastern prehistory that lay ahead.

Further Reading

In addition to the references for Chapter 16:

Jefferies, Ron. 1987. *Carrier Mills*. Center for Archaeological Investigations, Carbondale, Illinois.
  This important monograph describes important Middle and Late Archaic settlements. Strongly recommended.

Mason, Ronald J. 1981. *Great Lakes Archaeology*. Academic Press, New York.
  Mason's synthesis is an admirable regional survey of the northern parts of the Eastern Woodlands.

Muller, Jon. 1986. *Archaeology of the Lower Ohio Valley*. Academic Press, New York.
  Analysis of a major culture area in the Midwest, with a focus on cultural process and basic data.

Neusius, Sarah W. (ed.). *Foraging, Collecting, and Harvesting: Archaic Period Subsistence and Settlement in the Eastern Woodlands*. Center for Archaeological Investigations, Carbondale, Illinois.
  Essays that focus on subsistence issues, and amplify the general account given here.

Struever, Stuart, and Holton, Felicia. 1979. *Koster: Americans in Search of their Prehistoric Past*. Anchor Press, New York.
  Popular account of a major Midwestern site. Vivid reconstructions of prehistoric life, and rich in provocative interpretation. Strongly recommended for the beginning reader.

CHAPTER 18

EARLY WOODLAND AND THE ADENA COMPLEX

After 1000 BC, Eastern Woodlands societies embarked on a complex, multi-faceted trajectory of cultural change and elaboration, culminating in the brilliant efflorescence of the Mississippian cultural tradition in the closing centuries of prehistoric times. But these two-and-a-half millennia, the so-called "Woodland" period, saw no dramatic wars of conquest or major economic revolutions. The Adena, Hopewell, Mississippian cultural traditions, and their equivalents in other regions of the east, stemmed not from military campaigns or major population movements, but from the culmination of long-term adaptive and cultural trends that had emerged during the Archaic, some of them before 4000 BC. These trends are simply enumerated – more intensive exploitation of diverse food sources in highly localized environments, a move toward more sedentary living and better-established territorial boundaries, more intensive exchange of scarce materials, and the emergence of more complex social orders.

At the very beginning of the Woodland, three important innovations took hold in many eastern societies – pottery manufacture, deliberate cultivation of native plants, and interment under funerary mounds. Each was to have an important impact on human life.

Pottery and the "Container Revolution"

As we saw in Chapter 17, crude clay vessels appeared along the South Carolina coastal plain by 2500 BC (Stoltman, 1966). Fiber-tempered clay vessels appeared in the Lower Mississippi Valley by about 1300 BC, perhaps as a result of a related trade in steatite from north Georgia and Alabama, a prized material for making containers and such artifacts as atlatl weights, cooking stones, or net weights. Indeed, some clay vessels resemble what may be steatite prototypes (Jenkins, 1982; Griffin, 1967).

Thick, grit-tempered pottery spread, or was being made, all over the Eastern Woodlands between 2500 and 500 BC, from the Mississippi to New England, and from the Ohio to the St Lawrence Valley. It is still not clear whether the new technology spread from one area of origin, for a good case can be made for an indigenous development of cord-marked and grit-tempered pottery in the Northeast. Everywhere, the potters used simple methods, building up vessel walls with coils of clay, then thinning them out and welding the coils by paddling the sides with an anvil held inside the pot. Most ceramic containers had wide mouths and flat to rounded bases. The paddle anvil was often wrapped with cords, creating cord-markings on both inside and outside of the vessel. Many Early Woodland pots have been described as crude flower-pots, heavy and clumsy containers that took some time to make and were difficult to carry around.

Bruce Smith (1986) has described the introduction of pottery, and an apparently widespread trade in gourds, as a "container revolution" in the Eastern Woodlands. As eastern societies became more sedentary, he argues, their new lifeway enabled them to manufacture and use vessels that were too easily broken by societies on the move. Pots must have played an important part in more intensive exploitation of wild seed crops. For instance, experiments have shown that pottery did allow more efficient processing of hickory nuts, and probably other species, where crushing and boiling increases the amount of nutmeats processed in one hour at least tenfold (Taladay, Keller, and Munson, 1984). The earliest eastern pottery is thick walled and easily broken when heated. Perhaps it was associated with the preparation and eating of raw or roasted seeds (Braun, 1983; 1989). It was only later that thinner-walled vessels came into use, pots that were more break resistant when heated. The greater demand for waterproof containers may be associated with a major, and in the long term revolutionary, development in the Eastern Woodlands after 2000 BC – the development of highly efficient seed collection systems and the deliberate manipulation of native plants, a process that led to full domestication of several indigenous plant species.

So Bruce Smith's "container revolution" is part of a much broader set of cultural developments in the east that began during the Archaic and continued to unfold right up to European contact and beyond.

Cultivation of Native Plants

By 1500 BC, every human population in the Eastern Woodlands relied heavily on wild vegetable foods, and usually on a relatively small constellation of plants for most of its vegetable diet. When these plants were in short supply, the people turned to a wide range of secondary food sources. (For useful essays on early food production, see Keegan, 1987.)

This strategy works well in areas where there is plenty of territory to exploit – people can forage alternative patches of staple foods. The hunter-gatherers probably overcame food shortage stress by covering large distances, by possessing knowledge of potential food sources over wide areas. But what happened if population growth or social conflict, or just inadequate food supplies, restricted peoples' ability to feed themselves by exploiting large territories? They could forage for less preferred food plants, increase the energy expended collecting food and processing it and exploit alternative food sources like, say, acorns, that required a great deal more effort to prepare – or they could cultivate certain native annuals that flourished in disturbed habitats, *provided* the disturbed habitat was maintained by deliberate human intervention.

In the Eastern Woodlands, these three strategies were adopted by many Late Archaic groups faced with restricted territory owing to population growth and other factors. Richard Ford (1985) believes that food production began as a result of deliberate cultural responses to changing conditions. First, people faced with inadequate food supplies turned to intensive harvesting of small, starchy nuts. Although these are lower in calories and require much more work to prepare, they can fulfil nutritional requirements and allow people to remain within restricted territories (Petruso and Wickens, 1984; Taladay, Keller, and Munson, 1984). Ford believes this may have been the first step toward effective food production.

This scenario can be developed further. As populations increased, territories became smaller, alternative collecting areas became inaccessible. Many homelands were inadequate to supply basic nutritional requirements even of a stable population. Inevitably, the people turned to new food-getting strategies. They could rely on generations-old kin ties, reciprocal ties that ensured everyone shared food supplies. They could trade for basic foodstuffs with more fortunate neighbors or take up residence with relatives to obtain food in times of need. They would also use technological solutions, developing more effective food storage systems to tide them over lean months. Some groups also used their food-gathering technology to clear natural vegetation, to create space within their territories where they could cultivate several food species.

These Late Archaic strategies were effective for many centuries, being progressively adopted by many groups throughout the east after about 2000 BC. The strategy of small-scale cultivation worked well for centuries. It was much later, after about AD 700, that the cultivators intensified their efforts, modifying the landscape on a large scale to maximize the environmental requirements of a single plant species – maize. This was true farming, clearing large tracts of forest to eliminate competing vegetation and to increase sunlight, sometimes building earthen or stone terraces to conserve precious soil. At this point, domesticated maize, and later beans, both non-natives, as we saw in Chapter 14, replaced crop yields from native plant communities, even cultivated ones.

To what extent stress actually played a role in early cultivation in the Eastern Woodlands is unknown. Most current thinking focuses on the relationship between human groups and the plants and plant communities associated with them (Crites, 1987; B. Smith, 1987; Watson, 1988). Under these arguments, stress was not a primary cause of plant domestication. Human groups created and sustained a disturbed habitat that transported seeds of a wide variety of plants from their natural floodplain and upland niches into their local, and disturbed, habitat. These were casual and unintentional activities, with plant and animal populations, including Archaic groups, tied together in a series of opportunistic adaptations to changes in the structure and composition of floodplain ecosystems. A whole set of interacting variables, among them the establishment of human base camps, produced a significant change in floodplain ecosystems. These ecosystem changes allowed some of the floodplain plant species to occupy, and evolve within, newly disturbed habitats. A number of on-going selective pressures acted on these plants within these disturbed habitats that were clearly related to human activities. These were unintentional activities, not the result of deliberate human actions. Some of these pressures may have increased seed production in sumpweed, gourds, and other plants, also have reduced dormancy periods and also enhanced the ability of species to occupy disturbed ground. All of these pressures would have set plant evolution in a direction that increased their economic potential and their attractiveness as human food sources. All humans would have done to achieve this was to sustain a disturbed habitat and to tolerate species with economic value.

At some point, humans would have begun to categorize some of these plants as useful, others as mere weeds. They may have started to discourage the weeds to encourage the spread of economically useful plants, thereby managing natural stands of the latter. This simple process of encouraging, intervening, and deliberately planting harvested seeds, even on a small scale, marked the beginnings of deliberate cultivation – if sustained in the longer term. At this point, automatic selection within the affected plant population begins, with minimal effort by human beings. Their casual efforts at encouragement result in an ever more dependable and abundant, easily monitored local food resource. Thus, human land clearance and genetic changes in plants may have been a major factor in the emergence of horticulture in eastern North America (for full discussion, see B. Smith, 1987).

This plausible scenario is supported by rapidly accumulating archaeological evidence from Late Archaic and Woodland sites throughout the Eastern Woodlands (for a summary, see Ford, 1985; B. Smith, 1987). Late Archaic groups in the Eastern Woodlands cultivated a variety of plants, among them sunflowers, sumpweed, and goosefoot, but also gourds and squashes, long before they turned to maize agriculture.

Gourds and Squashes. Gourds (*Cucurbita pepo*), the forerunners of not only modern gourds, but squashes and pumpkins, are recorded in eastern North America before 2000 BC, more than 1000 years before any other native domesticates appear in archaeological sites.

In fact, a Texas gourd, *Cucurbita texana*, may be a surviving wild North American variety of *C. pepo* that was once widely distributed elsewhere in the north, but has now vanished. Perhaps, botanist Charles Heiser theorizes (1985), it once flourished in the very habitats that humans chose for their settlements. They eliminated it by excessive harvesting and hybridization with domestic forms.

C. pepo was probably first domesticated for its seeds rather than its bitter flesh and thin rind that is of little use for containers (for an extended discussion, see B. Smith, 1987). In contrast, the bottle gourd (*Lagenaria siceraria*) is ideal for containers in its domesticated form. Originally an African native, it appears to have floated across to the Americas, perhaps to Brazil, thousands of years ago, long before it was domesticated. Bottle gourds are known from Mexico at least as early as 7000 BC, and perhaps spread into North America as a weed following moving human populations. Whether they arrived in domesticated form or were tamed in the east quite independently is still a completely open botanical question (Heiser, 1985; B. Smith, 1987). The earliest record in the Eastern Woodlands comes from the Phillips Spring site in Missouri at *c.*2300 BC, but it is not known if this is a domesticated specimen.

If Mexican forms of gourds, pumpkins, and squashes were introduced into North America, which route did they follow to the Eastern Woodlands? As long ago as 1948, veteran archaeologist Alex Kreiger drew attention to

The white-flowered bottle gourd,
Lagenaria siceraria *(far left), with*
immature fruit (left).

botanical theories that had these and other Mexican traits diffusing into North America through a Texas "corridor." This route, sometimes called the "Gilmore corridor" after the botanist who first described it in the 1930s, is a direct, and easily traveled, route to the east. As Dee Ann Story has recently pointed out (1985), Archaic populations on the coastal plain were very mobile before about 2500 BC, capable of interacting over large areas, conditions that were ideal for the spread of cultigens, especially plants that could be used as containers. Theoretically at any rate, the Gilmore route would be a logical one. Unfortunately, areas like the all important Guadalupe drainage that runs into the south-central Texas coast and lies along the proposed route, are still little explored. Nor are there any dated occurrences of early squash or gourd from Texas sites.

Sunflowers and Indigenous Plants. A number of indisputably native plants were domesticated in North America in Archaic times (Heiser, 1985; B. Smith, 1987). The wild sunflower (*Helianthus annuus*) was widespread in the west and became a favorite food source. It was introduced into central and eastern regions in prehistoric times and was apparently domesticated there, perhaps by about 1500 BC, both for its seeds and its dye and oil. The Jerusalem artichoke (*Helianthus tuberosus*) is widely distributed in eastern North America, and may have been domesticated – the evidence is uncertain.

Perhaps the most common domesticated native plant is sumpweed or marsh elder (*Iva annua*), a lake- and river-side oily-seeded plant that flourished in eastern river valley bottoms. David and Nancy Asch have studied this little-known native for years, documenting it from flotation samples taken at the Koster site and other locations in the Midwest's Illinois River Valley (Asch and Asch, 1978; 1985). As early as 3800 BC, in Koster's Horizon 6, sumpweed comprises 40 percent of seed samples. This may be the result of harvesting wild growth, for none of the achenes (hard seeds) show signs of selection for domesticated forms. The Asches have measured achenes from dozens of Archaic sites and believe that domestication was well under way by 2000 BC. Thereafter, cultivation may have been sporadic in Illinois, but sumpweed was an important component in horticultural activities in Kentucky during the first millennium BC (Yarnell, 1978; B. Smith, 1987).

Goosefoot (*Chenopodium berlandieri*) was one of a series of small, starchy seeds that were an important component in Illinois Early, Middle and Late Woodland subsistence (Asch and Asch, 1985; B. Smith, 1984). The other species were knotweed (*Polygonum erectum*), maygrass (*Phalaris caroliniana*), and little barley (*Hordeum pusillum*). Goosefoot was probably a minor food in west-central Illinois during most of the Archaic, recorded from Koster by at least 6500 BC. It was extensively exploited and probably domesticated by Late Archaic Titterington people in the Midwest in about 2000 BC (Asch and Asch, 1985). Goosefoot was definitely cultivated in Illinois by Early Woodland times (Smith, 1984), and was a major food in Kentucky after 1500 BC.

Knotweed was economically important in the Upper Mississippi and Illinois Valleys, but was apparently little exploited before Middle and Late Woodland times. Maygrass is a southern wild species that assumed much greater economic importance after 2000 BC. Apparently it was intentionally propagated, with seeds being planted in fall or late spring. A cold resistant species, maygrass was grown considerably north of its natural range. Two or three weeks later, in the early summer, and at a time when no other cultivated foods were available, people could harvest little barley. However, the grain was hard to separate from the stalks, but how the people did this is unknown (Asch and Asch, 1985).

Lastly, tobacco (*Nicotiana* sp.) seeds have been recovered from a Middle Woodland context at the Smiling Dan site in Illinois, dating to about AD 250. Tobacco is not a native North American plant. It is thought to have been introduced from Mexico and was widely cultivated throughout the east at European contact (Yarnell, 1978). Many pipes occur in eastern sites, but they do not necessarily document tobacco smoking. People smoked hemp and many other substances as well.

Thanks to the development of the highly effective flotation method for collecting seed samples from archaeological sites thousands of years old, we can now be certain that some Late Archaic and many Early Woodland people were cultivating several highly productive native plants by 500 BC. However, the domestication of these indigenous species did not lead to a total dependence on agriculture, or to anything even remotely like it. Until about AD 800, agriculture was a way of producing valuable supplemental foods, of amplifying food supplies by enhancing wild crop yields, of helping feed locally dense hunter-gatherer populations. It was only with the introduction of maize in the first millennium AD that agriculture became the major means of subsistence in the Eastern Woodlands (Watson, 1985.)

Early Woodland: Burial Mounds and the Adena Complex
before 1000 BC to AD 100

Many Archaic burials and cemeteries testify to the great symbolic importance of death and funerary rituals in eastern life. These mortuary rites assumed increasing complexity and importance during the Late Archaic, when the first small burial mounds appear. Some communities buried their dead in low, natural ridges overlooking river valleys and at other strategic locations. As we have seen, some groups used low, artificial mounds, perhaps as territorial markers, kin-based burial grounds that were respected by neighbors.

Adena and Glacial Kame culture areas.

A similar special concern for the dead appears in other parts of the Eastern Woodlands well before 1500 BC. Mound burials commemorated the Maritime Archaic dead in Labrador as early as 3500 BC, while Glacial Kame Late Archaic groups living between southern Ontario and Indiana around 1500 to 1000 BC interred the departed in the summits of low hills of glacial gravel. Tools and exotic ornaments of copper and sea shell lay with the dead in these natural tumuli. From using natural ridges and hills, it was but a short step to erect small artificial mounds in strategic places, which served the same symbolic purposes – perhaps to mark territory and commemorate kin affiliations.

The idea of building earthworks was nothing new, witness the great earthen banks at Poverty Point in Louisiana, but it did involve the cooperative labors of many families over considerable periods of time, people to dig and pile up basketfuls of earth by the thousand, not only individual families but entire villages, perhaps gatherings of close kin or several neighboring communities. Judging from what we know of Late Archaic and Early Woodland subsistence, hunting, foraging, and cultivation were family activities, but activities that sometimes involved exchange of vital commodities between neighbors near and far. These same exchange networks may have helped foster elaborate communal burial cults involving the interment of kin group members and perhaps the commemoration of lineages and ancestors.

During Early Woodland times, and especially after 500 BC, burial mounds were an important part of mortuary ceremonialism from the western Appalachians to the Mississippi Valley, and north into Wisconsin and Michigan (Griffin, 1978). But the most marked ceremonialism is found in the so-called Adena complex of the central Ohio Valley.

A typical artifact of the Glacial Kame culture was the sandal-sole gorget, such as this example with an animal cut in relief. Length 18 cm.

Adena is not so much a culture as a ceremonial complex, perhaps best described as the climax of the Early Woodland (Muller, 1986). Adena has been identified from Indiana's Whitewater River Valley in the west to Pittsburgh in the Upper Ohio Valley in the east, and from the Blue Grass region of the Licking and Big Sandy and Kanawha Rivers in the south and east, to the upper reaches of the Scioto and Muskingum of Ohio in the north (Griffin, 1978).

Most Adena sites are burial mounds, perhaps once numbering 300 to 500 in the heartland (W. Webb and Snow, 1945; W. Webb and Baby, 1957; Dragoo, 1963). During Early and Middle Adena, in the last centuries before Christ, burial mounds and funerary customs were still simple (Dragoo, 1964). The people started with a small mound that covered the burial of a single person in a shallow, elliptical pit lined and covered with bark. Sometimes the burial lay in a house, at other times in an open area within the village. As more and more burials were added to the tumulus, it grew in size. Sometimes the dead were cremated, sometimes entire bodies were deposited in the mound. Occasionally the mourners simply deposited a bundle of bones, as if the body had been exposed on an open platform until the flesh decayed – or perhaps the dead person died away from home and the bones were brought back for burial. In some cases, only a few parts of the body were buried in the mound, as if the corpse had been dissected before burial.

Early and Middle Adena burials were often sprinkled with powdered red ocher, sometimes with yellow ocher, graphite, or manganese dioxide in small amounts. Apparently, grieving relatives painted the corpse with red ocher paint as well. They prepared the paint on crude stone tablets, convenient thin slabs of limestone, sandstone, and other rocks. Some of the tablets are deeply grooved by the rubbing of pieces of hematite. There are few signs of any social distinction between individuals, as if society was still basically egalitarian.

At first Adena mourners buried the dead with mostly utilitarian objects, artifacts such as flint blades, drills, scrapers, stone axes and adzes, also simple bone tools. These appear to have been the personal possessions of the deceased. The dead wore strings of small copper beads, shells, including some large marine gastropods, and occasionally bone. Some people owned quadrilateral slate or copper gorgets with concave sides. The most distinctive grave artifacts were tubular pipes, fabricated from clay-stone or very fine-grained silicate in straight or cigar-shaped tubes with a blocked end. Such pipes are common in the Upper Ohio Valley.

Late Adena, dating to about 2000 years ago, saw sweeping changes in burial customs, changes reflected in far more elaborate mound interments. The Robbins Mound in Kentucky was one of many Late Adena sites where simple graves gave way to large burial chambers or enclosures that contained one or more bodies. These structures lay on, or beneath, house floors, often circular houses with thatched walls and wood post frames that were burned down before the mound was built. Perhaps the structures were used to expose the dead for long periods of time.

Many Adena bodies were painted with bright pigments, attended with offerings of food and valuable artifacts. Sometimes people erected a canopy over the grave and surrounded it with a log platform. Occasionally, the mourners applied paint to the bones, as if the bodies were exposed long

Cross-section and plan of an
Adena burial from the Wright Mound,
Kentucky.

Cutaway reconstruction of a
restored Adena structure that may
have had a mortuary function.
Postmold plan at the left.

0   8 ft

0   2.5 m

enough for the flesh to decay completely. Subsequently, the grave was buried under a large earthen mound. Some mounds were used again and again, with more log tombs being added to an existing tumulus, until it reached vast dimensions. Some of the largest and most elaborate are found in the central Ohio Valley, like the famous Grave Creek mound at Moundsville, West Virginia, which was originally over 67 ft (20 m) high, with a volume of nearly 2.47 million cu. ft (70,000 cu. m).

The Late Adenans sometimes built circular earthen enclosures near their burial mounds. These "sacred circles" may have been the meeting places for the kin group using the associated tumulus (W. Webb and Snow, 1945). Perhaps the individuals buried in log tombs in the mounds were important kin leaders. Sometimes, the sacred enclosures occur in groups of two to eight, as if the people were divided into formal social units such as clans.

As treasure hunters discovered generations ago, Late Adena burials carried a rich variety of grave goods with them, especially the individuals interred in log tombs. Some important burials were interred with a long-clean skull, often laid on the lap. One such find at the Cresap Mound in West Virginia bore a slight polish, as if it had been treasured and handled regularly for some time. Mark Seeman (1988) has shown beyond reasonable doubt that these were "trophy skulls," perhaps the heads of enemies or revered ancestors.

Although fine flint blades, awls, and other utilitarian objects like drills were still deposited with the dead, there were many more distinctive ornaments in the graves. These included copper bracelets and finger rings. There were crescents and sheets fabricated from North Carolina mica, some marine shells, adzes, and other items from Lake Superior copper. There were many forms of gorgets and distinctive atlatl weights. Pipe designs were far more elaborate than earlier Adena forms, with carved animal effigies coming into fashion for the first time. Tubular Ohio pipestone pipes were exchanged as far away as Ontario, New England, and Maryland. The stone tablets used for preparing ocher were now much more carefully prepared, sometimes adorned with zoomorphic or animal designs, including carrion crows (W. Webb and Baby, 1957). Some other characteristic grave goods include large, leaf-shaped spearheads and knives, often made of bluish grey hornstone from Indiana or Illinois, artifacts sometimes found in caches. Perhaps such point collections were exchanged as gifts. Small triangular points made of local materials are

(Below) Adena stone effigy pipe in the shape of a human, from the Adena Mound, Ross County, Ohio. Height 20 cm. (Below right) Adena platform effigy pipe in the image of a dog, from Neward, Ohio.

Two engraved stone Adena tablets. About half-size.

often found in Early Woodland cemeteries, artifacts often made of chert and apparently exchanged over long distances. They occur from Wisconsin and Illinois all the way to New England. Carved bird effigies known as "birdstones," and "boatstones" replace the bannerstones of the Late Archaic. Finely made three-quarter grooved axes and adzes were widely used for woodworking.

Several Late Adena mounds have yielded wolf palates, each carefully trimmed, with the upper and lower incisors removed, so that they could be worn in a man's mouth. William Webb and Raymond Baby (1957) made an ingenious reconstruction of this form of mask, with the skin of the wolf head fitting over the head. The great 19th-century painter George Catlin depicted similar masks being worn by western Indians. Puma and other animal masks may also have been used. Some of these artifacts may have been shamans' masks, or they may have been used in rituals that depicted the symbolic relationships between familiar animals and different clans.

As James Griffin (1978) has pointed out, "Adena" is a convenient archaeological term that covers dozens of local Early Woodland cultures in the Eastern Woodlands, cultures that were contemporary, often close neighbors, and interacting with one another continuously. After 500 BC, many local cultures flourished in the Midwest and Southeast, cultures

Birdstones, such as this example from Milwaukee, may have served as atlatl weights.

remarkable for their diverse artifacts, widespread trading contacts, and burial ceremonialism. They are distinguished one from another by pottery styles and other artifacts and the details need not concern us here (see Griffin, 1967; 1978; Muller, 1986).

There is considerable artifact diversity among these societies, reflected in many local pottery styles. Once enough Adena village sites have been excavated, it may be possible to associate individual communities, or groups of settlements, with individual mound complexes (Dragoo, 1963). Most Early Woodland settlements were small, perhaps consisting of no more than a dozen or so houses (Muller, 1986). People lived in relatively cramped dwellings, but the villagers occasionally built larger structures, capable of holding as many as 40 people. As far as we know, Late Archaic subsistence patterns continued into the Early Woodland, with locally intensive exploitation of wild vegetable foods, and deliberate cultivation of native plants. In most respects, Early Woodland material culture, subsistence patterns, and settlement distributions resemble those of the Late Archaic communities that were either contemporary with, or before, them. The greatest differences are those of mortuary custom.

Everyone now agrees that the distinctive, elaborate, and varied Adena burial traditions developed from Late Archaic roots, perhaps in the Ohio Valley. The Early Woodland was a time of accelerating culture contacts over wide areas, contacts that brought Ohio pipestone from the lower Scioto Valley to Lake Huron and the upper St Lawrence Valley, copper from Lake Superior deep into the Ohio Valley, and sea shells from the Gulf Coast deep into the Midwest. In some areas, local population densities rose. There were Adena sites along every major tributary stream of the Ohio River from southeastern Indiana to central Pennsylvania by 2000 years ago, with great concentrations of burial mounds in some well-defined areas – the Scioto Valley of south-central Ohio, the Kanawha River in West Virginia, and around Cincinnati, Ohio, to mention only three. Perhaps these reflect a tendency toward concentration within tribal territories.

Inter-regional Exchange

If there is one characteristic beyond elaboration of burial customs that distinguishes Early Woodland from Late Archaic traditions, it is a gradual intensification of local and inter-regional exchange. This process of intensification reached its apogee during Middle and Late Woodland times, and has fascinated archaeologists for many years (Brose, 1979; Braun, 1986).

As population densities rose and group territories became more and more defined and circumscribed, styles of projectile points and other artifacts appear to display more local variation, as if they became "stylistic boundary markers" (Brose, 1979). There are some precedents from studies of modern societies in New Guinea and elsewhere to show that such "markers" develop within single cultural and ecological zones where several groups are in partial competition for the same resources. Ethnic boundaries develop as a result, as ways of reducing the dangers of unwanted confrontation by clearly delineating rights of access to different resources (Barth, 1975). Thus, considerable variability in projectile point styles in northern parts of the Eastern Woodlands after 1000 BC may reflect a trend toward better defined local territories, and toward more formal exchange mechanisms that structured the bartering of essentials and prestigious luxuries from area to area in a web of reciprocal obligations and formal gift-giving. It is noticeable that a similar elaboration of projectile point traditions is not found further south, where seasonal contrasts are much less marked, and there are not such highly localized and short-lived abundances of food resources.

At about the same time, too, the first signs of more elaborate traditions appear in the northern woodlands – overlapping sets of burial traditions, ways of treating corpses, of depositing them, constructing graves. These Early Woodland complexes were highly localized – Adena was one, Red Paint in the Northeast another. They flourished alongside dozens of Late Archaic communities that still lived as they had done for centuries.

As territorial boundaries became more marked and interaction between neighbors increased, so membership in social groups assumed much greater importance, for it was these lineages and clans that controlled access to food and other resources. It is probably no coincidence that the Early Woodland sees a continuing trend toward at least semi-sedentary settlement, with people living at one base location for many months on end. This may have helped foster a growing sense of corporate identity, an identity reinforced by regular burial ceremonies at earthworks where important clan leaders and others were buried for many generations. And in areas like the northern woodlands, where the Late Archaic adaptation was often precarious, different groups were probably careful to maintain rights of access to resources located outside their own territories, as a form of "insurance" in lean years when frosts or other natural phenomena decimated local foods. In other words, people used social processes to maintain exchange networks to handle not only food, but to maintain access to resources of restricted distribution at a distance.

Judging from living societies, the main participants in such exchange systems would have been lineage leaders, individuals honored at death with special artifacts, funeral ceremonies, and adorned with the ceremonial items that recognized their social role and importance and that were their right. Thus, burial rites assumed great importance in Early Woodland life. They validated not only group identity on a regular basis, but commemorated the status of prominent kin leaders. These individuals were those who organized community work efforts by clan members when needed – to erect burial mounds, construct earthworks, and to carry out other projects that were to the collective benefit. Everyone who participated received gifts of redistributed food and other goods. And the highly prized status goods such as mica sheets, copper ornaments, and carved pipes buried with clan leaders not only proclaimed their social standing, but maintained their high prestige by vanishing below the ground when their owner died.

This is a convincing model for Early Woodland subsistence, exchange, and burial ceremony, one that contains mechanisms for both fostering inter-group relationships and for ameliorating food shortages. As David Brose argues (1979), such a system provided increasing social and economic stability, reinforced trends toward sedentary living and specialized exploitation of local resources, and probably led to population increases.

In a sense, these developments merely accentuated the pressures they evolved to reduce, for their very success permitted higher levels of population growth, growth that in turn triggered additional responses – more ranked and well-integrated social systems that replaced the more flexible ones of earlier times. David Brose believes that there was what he calls a "trajectory" of long-term cultural change. These changes first developed in areas where there was maximal pressure or very low potential carrying capacity. The more closely integrated social systems emphasized rank within individual lineages, rank validated by exotic objects of great prestige from afar and by seasonal ceremonies when all the members of lineages, from near and far, came together to reinforce their social identity and common goals. About the time of Christ, this trajectory of cultural change led to far more elaborate social institutions and ceremonial life during the Middle Woodland.

Further Reading

In addition to the references for the previous chapter:

Ford, Richard I. (ed). 1985. *Prehistoric Food Production in North America.* University Museum of Anthropology, University of Michigan, Ann Arbor.
An edited volume of articles on crop domestication, a useful synthesis of a rapidly moving field.

Keegan, William F. (ed). 1987. *Emergent Horticultural Economies of the Eastern Woodlands.* Center for Archaeological Investigations, Carbondale, Illinois.
Essays on various aspects of plant domestication, including genetic factors.

Webb, William S. and Baby, R.S. 1957. *The Adena People no. 2.* Ohio Historical Society, Columbus.

Webb, William S. and Snow, C.E. 1945. *The Adena People.* University of Tennessee Press, Knoxville.
Still authoritative accounts of the Adena Complex. Most recent literature is in scientific journals.

See also the references for Chapter 19.

MIDDLE WOODLAND AND THE HOPEWELLIAN

The term "Middle Woodland" is sometimes used to refer to the period between about 200 BC and AD 400 when most of eastern North America was dominated by the Hopewell culture, a name derived from the name of a farm in Ross County, Ohio (Griffin, 1967). The Southeast was home to a great variety of sophisticated hunter-gatherer societies during these same centuries, societies that regularly cultivated native plants.

The Hopewell Culture
*c.*200 BC to AD 400

Hopewell stands out as a remarkable cultural phenomenon in many ways, both for its flamboyant burial customs and for its complex exchange networks that traded both raw materials and finished artifacts over vast areas of North America (Brose and Greber, 1979). Hopewell earthworks in Ohio assumed enormous proportions, sometimes clusters of mounds and enclosures that covered many acres. These were the "forts" and "tumuli" of the lost civilizations described by Moundbuilder cultists in the 19th century (Silverberg, 1968).

The Hopewell culture flourished over much of the Midwest, but achieved its greatest elaboration in the Ohio Valley. The Scioto Valley near Chillicothe is the center of Hopewell development in Ohio. Elaborate mounds and spectacular geometric earthworks enclose from 10 to hundreds of acres (4 to many hectares). There are other centers of Hopewell earthworks and tumuli near Marietta and in southwestern Ohio (Griffin, 1967). These clusters of Ohio Hopewell were clearly the foci of important religious, political, and economic activities. Hopewell influence extended far from its Midwestern homelands. Many contemporary societies from eastern North America are known to have shared mortuary customs, ritual and religious beliefs, and artifact styles with the Ohio Hopewell.

Origins

There can be little doubt that much of the Ohio Hopewell originated in the Adena tradition. Olaf Prufer once went as far as to remark (1964) that "one might say that Ohio Hopewell minus the elaborate ceremonial and

A Hopewell man wearing earspools and pendants of beaten native copper, and pearl beads of freshwater shellfish. Reconstruction in the Field Museum of Natural History, Chicago.

artifactual trappings would not be much different from Adena." In general, he is probably right, for Adena has a long history in the Ohio Valley, as well as respectable antecedents in the Late Archaic of the Midwest and Northeast. Prufer believed, however, that the explosion of Hopewell ceremonial and trading activity resulted from this older tradition merging with some newly introduced ideas, perhaps even being the consequence of population movements. He hypothesized that these new ideas, or people, arrived in Ohio from southern Indiana and the Midwest.

At about the same time as Hopewell traits emerge in the Ohio Valley, they also appear in southern Illinois. Since some of these features may be slightly earlier in the west, one could argue that Hopewell originated in Illinois and spread or diffused into Ohio – but this is little more than speculation.

Whatever the ultimate origins of the Hopewell, anyone who reviews its complex archaeological manifestations has to synthesize a number of regional variations on the Hopewell tradition, each of them with their own pottery styles and local environmental adaptations. All these regional expressions have in common a number of highly characteristic artifact styles and exotic raw materials. The latter include copper, marine shells, mica, and obsidian, also such items as shark and alligator teeth, meteoric iron, and many other commodities. The finished objects common to each area include cymbal-like copper ear spools, copper breast plates, obsidian artifacts, marine shells used as containers, and mica sheets cut into geometric and representational forms. There are plain and effigy platform pipes, clay human figurines, and special pottery vessels, especially small jars, known in both Illinois and Ohio as "Hopewell Series." All of these commodities and artifacts were obtained through complex exchange networks, sometimes called the "Hopewell Interaction Sphere." This exchange zone flourished from as early as 100 BC to about AD 300 to 500.

As long ago as 1958, Joseph Caldwell identified a number of regional traditions throughout the Eastern Woodlands in Early Woodland times and later. These he distinguished on the basis of pottery forms and decoration, each of them also remarkable for distinct ecological adaptations as well. These regional traditions formed an important part of Caldwell's basic thesis about Eastern Woodlands prehistory – that both Archaic and Woodland peoples achieved greater efficiency in the exploitation of forests, and in so doing became more and more diverse and specialized in their adaptations (Caldwell, 1958). The Hopewell traits found in these traditions are all found in restricted locales, but with varying degrees of participation in the interaction sphere.

Hopewell artifacts. (Above left) Clay figurine depicting a man, possibly a shaman, with a topknot hair style. From an unknown location in Ohio. (Top right) Raven or crow cut from native sheet copper, with a freshwater pearl for an eye. From an unknown location in Ohio, length 38 cm. (Above) Sheet mica depiction of the claws of a bird of prey. Unknown Ohio location, length 28 cm. (Far left, and left) Four clay bird-effigy smoking pipes. Locations unknown, height of tallest 6 cm.

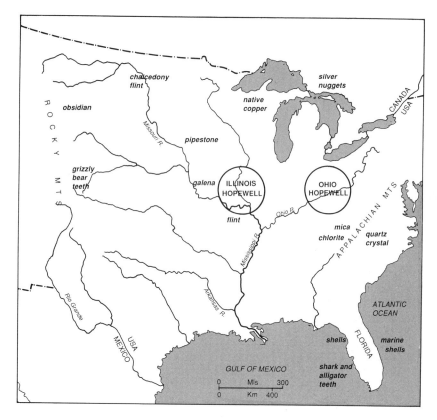

Hopewell exchange zone. Indicated here are the far-flung sources of materials that were exchanged.

Hopewell Exchange Systems

The Hopewell exchange zone, and local imitations of it, cover most of the Eastern Woodlands, from the Southeast into southeastern Canada (Seeman, 1979a). Within this vast area, local societies participated in exchange to a highly variable degree, with the greatest activity along major waterways (Brose and Greber, 1979). Judging from Ohio burials, the amount of non-local raw material acquired by some Hopewell trading parties reached impressive proportions (Griffin, 1967). They obtained native copper from the Lake Superior region, silver from the same place, and also from deposits near Cobalt, Ohio. Mica, quartz crystal, and chlorite came from the southern Appalachians. The exchange networks handled large marine shells from the Florida east coast, and smaller maritime shell species from the Southeast and Florida Gulf Coast. Galena cubes came from northwestern Illinois or Missouri, nodular flint from Illinois and Indiana. Neutron activation studies on Hopewell obsidian reveal sources as far away as the Yellowstone Park area of the Rocky Mountains, while chalcedony came from the Knife Fork area, North Dakota, and southern Manitoba.

Most of these exotic materials were obtained by people living in major trading and manufacturing areas. They then converted them into finished artifacts or ornaments that were often exported through local and regional exchange networks. For example, copper artifacts may have been exported from Ohio as far afield as Tennessee and the Deep South, and from New

York to Iowa and Missouri. Characteristic Hopewell platform pipes fabricated from Ohio pipestone are found from New York State west to Wisconsin and Iowa, and as far southwest as Hardin County, Illinois.

Two "core areas" are marked by high concentrations of Hopewell-style finished goods – the Mississippi and Illinois river valleys in Illinois, and the Scioto and Miami valleys in southern Ohio (Braun, 1986). Each of these two areas, the one to the east, the other to the west, stands at the center of a large, inter-regional exchange network. In time, they overlapped with one another, but they never lost their own identities (Struever and Houart, 1972). Hopewell exchange outside the Ohio/Illinois area is sharply reduced, but there are important clusters of exchange activity represented by the Copena culture of Alabama, and in Florida (Seeman, 1979a).

These regional exchange systems had been functioning in one form or another since at least 4000 BC. Not that they flourished uninterrupted. There is good reason to believe that the networks went through constant cycles of expansion, then dissolution, with ever-changing geographic ranges. What did happen, however, was that the *scale* of the networks grew, with a broad trend toward more complex exchange systems as time went on. The diversity and number of distinctive, but similarly styled, artifacts handled along the networks increased over the centuries, as did the complexity of the social hierarchy that controlled the circulation. Thus, the Hopewell may have developed as a result of common evolutionary processes that developed over much of the Eastern Woodlands in the centuries immediately before the Christian era.

Subsistence and Reciprocity

Hopewell burial customs and earthworks are so spectacular that generations of archaeologists have concentrated their efforts on excavating mounds and other conspicuous monuments, at the expense of humbler settlements. So we still know little of Hopewell subsistence, settlement patterns, or daily life. According to Yerkes (1988), Ohio Hopewell settlements were probably small hamlets, occupied for only part of the year. Illinois Hopewell people did, however, live in some much larger villages, and mounds tended to be associated with some of them (Asch and others, 1979). Where adequate settlement data is available, the intensification of exchange activities appears to coincide with some major changes among the participating populations. In some areas, they tended to congregate in large river valleys near major waterways, often settling in more sedentary, nucleated settlements, as if mobility was no longer a major factor in daily life.

In western Illinois, David Braun has observed much larger house floor areas and an increase in the capacities of cooking vessels. And in the same area, flotation samples reveal a dramatic increase in the cultivation of native plants, as if there was major intensification of subsistence activities. In an ingenious calculation, Braun uses the thinner walls of domestic pottery after 200 BC to argue for major innovations in cooking practices, perhaps reflecting new ways of preparing such foods as starchy seeds for much more concentrated populations (Braun, 1985).

The overall expansion of trading activity may, therefore, reflect a contemporary rise in local population densities, decreased mobility, and increasing complexity in subsistence activities. But why did this expansion take place? As in previous periods, a major element was reciprocity, social obligations outside the narrow compass of household and community that led to the reciprocal exchange of food and other goods over large areas, the exchange serving as a form of "savings account" against lean years (Ford, 1974; Brose, 1979). At the center of these transactions were local leaders, the individuals who negotiated exchanges and maintained contacts with neighboring communities. In some areas, like Ohio's Scioto Valley, people may have moved into concentrations of settlements where more coordinated decision-making was possible. These may have been the places where more aggressive leaders, people some anthropologists call "Big Men," acquired political and economic power and prestige through their expertise at gift exchange, through acquiring loyal followers among their fellow kin.

Who were these special individuals? Bruce Smith (1986) believes they were important people, who accumulated wealth through shrewd exchanges and reciprocal gifts, attracting to themselves groups of loyal followers, whose labor and loyalty were rewarded with regular sharing of food and other wealth.

The notion of trade, reciprocity, and "Big Men" is associated with the researches of two anthropologists. The first is Bronislaw Malinowski, who studied the celebrated *kula* ring trade of the Trobriand Islands of the southwestern Pacific. The other is Marshall Sahlins, who studied isolated island communities in the same general area. He found these islands were linked by the ties formed by entrepreneurs, who exchanged symbolic gifts and acted as political and economic brokers in egalitarian, autonomous societies. They were, as Sahlins picturesquely writes, "a shunting station for goods flowing reciprocally between their own and other like groups of society" (Sahlins, 1972).

Smith believes that the "Big Man" model is appropriate in the river valleys of the Southeast, places where communities were interdependent, yet isolated. The gift-giving and social transactions reinforced friendly feelings between neighboring communities and enhanced the prestige of each "Big Man." They, in turn, redistributed goods to their followers. As time went on, these leaders would compete with one another in competitive displays of wealth and prestige, both in life and death, taking their symbols of individual power with them to the grave. "Big Men" were opportunists, people who took advantage of ever-changing circumstances, whose status was highly individual, never inherited, and always volatile, vanishing the moment they were interred. Their grieving followers would continue to live as they always had until another kinsman emerged as a new leader, a new "Big Man." The separation of occasional, more richly decorated burials in Southeastern mounds may, then, reflect the commemoration of "Big Men" in death with the symbols of prestige and wealth they had accumulated while living.

The inter-community ties fostered by such individuals can never have been permanent, never particularly strong. The archaeological record for the Hopewellian culture and for contemporary Southeastern societies seems to mirror such ever-changing small-scale chiefdoms. The tangible signs of successful "Big-Man-ship" only survive in richly decorated burials and distinctive mortuary customs.

Hopewell was never a widely distributed, uniform culture, in the sense, say, that Maya civilization extended over a vast area of Mesoamerica. Rather, it was a local phenomenon, with greatly differing degrees of flamboyance and elaboration in Illinois, Ohio, and other areas – and the Hopewell style, characterized by elaborate burial customs and distinctive artifact and art styles, was diffused over a vast area of eastern North America through a maze of local and regional exchange networks. Along these routes, too, may have flowed distinctive religious beliefs that served to give scattered kin groups a sense of common identity.

Hopewell Exchange and Artifact Standardization

Hopewell exchange networks covered such a large area that many archaeologists have thought of this trade as a relatively unified system of transactions, carried out over enormous distances (Prufer, 1964; Struever and Houart, 1972). They argue that many pipes, small clay jars, copper ear spools, and other artifacts display remarkable stylistic similarity, as if they were traded as part of a well-organized exchange system that also handled raw materials over large distances.

These theories tend to pre-date detailed analyses of the distribution of different exotic artifacts and raw materials. It turns out that each style of finished artifact and each raw material has a distinct and unique distribution (Griffin, 1965; Griffin and others, 1970; Braun and others, 1982). Furthermore, these new studies have shown that many exotic raw materials tended to move directionally, in what Braun (1986) calls a "preferential" way. Perhaps they were collected by small parties of people from Hopewell core areas, who journeyed many miles to collect a stock of raw material for local manufacture back home. In contrast, the exchange of finished artifacts appears to have been a more local phenomenon, presumably on a reciprocal basis.

How are we to account for the standardization of artifact style over enormous distances? It is not enough to invoke such explanations as a small number of specialists who created prestigious artifacts, or to argue for a broadly unifying symbolism of individual authority – in any case close analysis of the exchange networks does not bear such theories out. Rather, we should think in terms of networks of cooperation and interaction between close and more distant neighbors that developed out of local pressures. In time, these exchange relations developed their own language, as it were, a set of exchange tokens with easily recognized designs and style that evoked similar meanings between scattered groups of people who shared at least some broad, philosophical ideas about the world.

It is difficult to prove the validity of this hypothesis, but there are some telling clues, especially from a distinctive form of Hopewell ceremonial ware found in many burial mounds. This pottery comes in the form of small, squat jars that are quite distinct from local pottery forms. Wherever it is found, the ceremonial ware has a thickened, vertical rim and is adorned with bands of cross-hatched lines, punctuations, and body decoration in curvilinear, geometric, or bird-motifs, depicting raptorial or spoon-billed species.

Hopewell ceremonial vessel from the Marksville site. Roulette motif outlines the design incised into the clay. Height c. 11.4 cm.

These distinctive vessels appear in the lower Mississippi, in the central Missouri, and the lower Illinois valleys. The same avian motifs are found on stone, bone, copper, and shell in western Illinois and southern Ohio. Perhaps, believes David Braun (1986), the same symbols were used in several regions at the same time. They indicated not necessarily the exchange of actual artifacts, but a decorative imagery that communicated a broadly similar ritual message in many different, widely separated areas.

We tend to think of Hopewell exchange in terms of exotic, prestigious artifacts and materials, but in fact both the exchange mechanisms and the reasons for trading assumed many forms (Goad, 1979). Local exchange would have involved such prosaic items as foodstuffs, day-to-day raw materials, transactions that evened out local shortages between neighbors. Long-distance trade may have had nothing to do with feeding households and scattered villages (Griffin, 1965). It was an increasing need for exotic goods such as copper objects or marine shells that differentiated social status that led to regional and longer distance exchange.

Sharon Goad (1979) has examined historic Indian trails and trade routes in the Southeast and believes that Middle Woodland exchange moved along similar kinds of trails, the mechanism of exchange being a form of reciprocity. In the Southeast, for example, Goad believes copper, galena, and other Midwest and Great Lakes items entered the region through northern centers such as Wright and Roden in Alabama, and Tunacunnhee in northwestern Georgia. Exotic objects from the north are rare in the Southeast, as if these northern centers were obtaining some exotics from the north and not passing them far into the Southeast. Most Middle Woodland trade in the Southeast appears to have been regional, with regional networks overlapping with their neighbors and sometimes transporting artifacts and especially raw materials over longer distances.

Hopewell exchange is best seen as an intricate patchwork of regional exchange systems, each of which developed to satisfy local needs and obligations, using long-established trails and trade routes that changed constantly over the centuries. Over these myriad trails traveled symbolic exotica and fine artifacts with intense ritual and social meaning, items that linked widely distributed Hopewell centers with a broad semblance of ritual and cosmological unity that was but superficial, hiding a bewildering diversity of Middle Woodland cultural traditions.

Hopewell Mortuary Customs

We know more about Hopewell burial customs than about any other aspect of the Middle Woodland, largely because most excavators have concentrated on spectacular mounds and earthworks, and on the multiplicity of decorated Hopewell graves found in them (for useful essays, see Brose and Greber, 1979). Unfortunately, many of these excavations took place before the advent of rigorous scientific methods, and still more remain unpublished, the artifacts scattered in museums throughout the Midwest.

The most spectacular burial mounds come from the Ohio Valley. At Hopewell itself, a mound complex near Chillicothe, 38 mounds lie within a rectangular enclosure covering 110 acres (45 ha). Other mound groups are as impressive. The Seip Mound is 30 ft (9 m) high, 250 ft (76 m) long, and

150 ft (46 m) across, after Hopewell itself the largest tumulus of all. The average size of Ohio mounds is about 30 ft (9 m) high and some 100 ft (30 m) across, with a volume of about 500,000 cu. ft (14,000 cu. m). Each represents over 200,000 man-hours of earthmoving using the simplest of stone-bladed tools and baskets.

Like their Adena predecessors, Hopewell monuments were erected inside sacred earthworks, but earthworks on a much more imposing scale. At Mound City, Ohio, for example, 24 mounds lie within an enclosure covering 13 acres (5.2 ha). A vast complex of circles, square, and octagon linked by avenues encircles the burial mounds at Newark, Ohio, the entire mortuary landscape covering 4 sq. miles (6.4 sq. km).

The Great Serpent Mound in Ohio is a celebrated example of the Hopewell earthwork builder's art, perhaps a symbolic representation of an important lineage buried within its confines. With tightly curved tail, the earthen serpent wriggles with convoluted folds for 1254 ft (382 m) along a low ridge, its open jaws enclosing an oval burial mound. We are lucky that the Great Serpent survives. A century ago, the coils were ravaged by pot hunters and eroded by grazing cattle. Harvard archaeologist Frederick Putnam managed to persuade a group of Boston ladies to raise funds to purchase and restore the earthwork before it was too late (Fagan, 1977).

(Above) The Ohio Mound City complex consists of several mounds within an enclosure.

(Below) Aerial view of the Great Serpent Mound, Ohio.

Cross-section and perspective view of the Hopewell WH6 burial mound, with multiple burials.

Hundreds of burials have been excavated from these and other Hopewell earthworks by both treasure hunters and archaeologists. More than 1150 individuals have come from the major Ohio mounds groups alone, buried in many different ways. More than three-quarters of scientifically studied burials were cremated, with, apparently, only the elite being deposited intact into the ground. Hopewell mourners used both burial crypts and charnel houses. The former were large boxes constructed for the storage of the dead and their grave goods. They were simple structures sunk into the ground and covered with heavy roofs, often built on isolated high-spots clear of the settlement. Crypts were maintenance free, and apparently served as corporate facilities for a single community (Brown, 1979).

Charnel houses were designed both to shelter the dead and the burial activities associated with them. The bodies of the deceased were subjected to considerable preparation, preparation that may have reflected the status of the dead. These structures and the rituals associated with them required much more effort by the communities associated with them. Both cremated individuals and entire corpses were placed in large charnel houses with thatched roofs and substantial post frames. Once the charnel houses had fulfilled their role, they were burnt to the ground and an earthen mound erected over them (for a detailed discussion of crypts and charnel houses and their possible significance, see Brown, 1979).

The elite in Hopewell society were buried in log-lined tombs within the charnel houses, accompanied by far richer grave ornaments than anything found in Adena burials. A young man and woman buried together in the main mound at Hopewell wore copper ear-spools, copper breast plates, and necklaces of grizzly bear teeth. The woman went to her grave wearing thousands of freshwater pearl beads, and copper-covered wooden and stone buttons. Both had artificial copper noses. A log tomb within the Seip mound yielded four adults and two children deposited with thousands of freshwater pearls, copper tools, and ornaments of mica, silver, and tortoise shell. Some of the men in the mounds may have been expert artisans, like an individual from Hopewell buried with 3000 mica sheets and 198 lbs (90 kg) of galena. Another was an expert obsidian worker, buried with hundreds of stone fragments.

Hopewell mounds contained not only richly decorated burials but catches of exotic objects, many of them obtained from long distances away. The mourners deposited copper axes, cut-out silhouettes of birds, fish, claws, and human heads or hands in copper or mica, flint and chlorite discs, finely polished stone atlatl weights and beautiful effigy pipes. There were engraved human bones, painted fabrics, occasional clay figurines depicting bare-breasted women in belted skirts, men in loincloths.

We know almost nothing about Hopewell funerary rituals, for archaeological traces of such activities have not been preserved, except for frequent scatters of broken animal bones associated with the charnel houses, perhaps the remains of meals consumed nearby. Our only analogies are far-removed at best, and come from European-influenced Southeastern societies of centuries later.

Charnel houses were in widespread use in the Southeast at European contact, some of them restricted in use to the elite. Those of the Choctaw, however, were accessible to all members of society. Choctaw chiefs were often buried in a special house, but there were others for everyone else, probably controlled by different kin groups (Swanton, 1931). Among the Choctaw, the dead were placed on covered platforms in the open with special food offerings. When the flesh had decomposed some months later, the deceased's relatives called in fellow clan members, priestly specialists who defleshed the bones and placed them in a chest. A communal feast followed, a ceremony when the bones were deposited in the charnel house. The burial remained in the charnel house for some time, commemorated at regular ceremonies and feasts. Eventually, sometimes when the charnel house was full, the bones were ceremonially removed and interred. The regular feasts associated with mortuary ceremonies and charnel houses may have served a practical role in Choctaw society, to ensure redistribution of game meat and other foods throughout society, to compensate for periods of scarcity, perhaps to stimulate production.

Superficially, Choctaw burial customs seem to parallel those found under Hopewell mounds quite closely (Seeman, 1979b). Both sets of customs involved a sequence of exposure, defleshing, sometimes cremation, redepositing of the dead in charnel houses, and reinterment in burial mounds. If the animal bones found under many Hopewell mounds are the remains of meals, then mortuary customs may also have provided a context for redistribution of food supplies. But there are significant differences as well. Hopewell people relied more heavily on cremation, placed great importance on exotic artifacts and materials in burial furniture, and destroyed their charnel houses when they were full.

To suggest that Hopewell and Choctaw burial customs were identical, that one can use historic custom in a straightforward manner to interpret mortuary remains from much earlier times, is the height of folly. Rather, as

MOUND OF EARTH BUILT OVER SACRED ENCLOSURE

CREMATION AND BURIAL IN A SACRED ENCLOSURE LATER COVERED BY A MOUND OF EARTH

Two stages in Hopewell mound building. First, the people cremate a body and bury it within a sacred enclosure. Funerary offerings are placed on altars at right front and upper right. Then the mourners heap up basketloads of earth over the burial to form a mound. From an exhibit in the Field Museum of Natural History, Chicago.

Mark Seeman argues (1979b), Hopewell charnel houses may have served as a catalyst for local chieftains to manage food resources, not only the increasing yield from native plant gardens, but also game meat, food that flowed into the charnel house as offerings and was redistributed at feasts and other ceremonies. Perhaps, too, local Hopewell leaders were reinforced in their political and ritual authority, for, as is well known from societies all over the world, chiefdoms obtain their political power from their spiritual authority, perhaps, in this case, an authority intimately associated with game animals, the wild creatures depicted so frequently in Hopewell art and commemorated with dance masks and other artifacts.

It should be stressed, however, that Hopewell is a phenomenon rather than a widespread culture with finite boundaries. There may have been ritual and exchange links between neighboring population concentrations in Ohio, Illinois, and further afield. The underlying culture was always local, displaying a variety of adaptations and local variations, many of them in communities that had never seen a Hopewell earthwork or given support to a "Big Man."

Woodland Adaptations in the Southeast
*c.*500 BC to AD 400

There were significant differences between mainstream Hopewell culture and contemporary societies to the south and east, despite regular trading contacts between the Midwest and Southeast. The great diversity of Southeastern society after about 500 BC is reflected in a proliferation of new pottery styles and in many local adaptations. Potters experimented with decorative motifs, new vessel forms, and many different clay tempers. These included grit, limestone, and sand, as opposed to the vegetable fibers used in earlier times. Southeastern archaeologists have used these many variations to chronicle different local cultures across the Southeast. Unfortunately, however, many of their ceramic samples for the four centuries after 500 BC come from shallow sites with a high prevalence of mixed occupation levels (Muller, 1986; B. Smith, 1986).

Coastal Adaptations. The long, low-lying coastal strip along the south Atlantic coast from North Carolina to Florida's St John River was exploited by numerous hunter-gatherer bands, who camped on higher ground close to salt swamps, marshes, freshwater estuaries, and lakes. These people are known to us mainly from shell middens, which give the impression that they subsisted almost entirely off oysters and clams. In fact, closer examination reveals a much broader-based economy, one that took advantage of the remarkable diversity of the marshes and coasts. The people took deer and other terrestrial animals, also fish, shellfish, and a wide variety of nuts, seeds, and other plants (Byrd, 1976; Milanich and Fairbanks, 1980). In all probability, too, these coastal peoples cultivated some native plants, including gourds and squashes (B. Smith, 1986).

All the hunter-gatherers did was to graft the planting and harvesting of some native plants onto a long-standing marsh and coastal adaptation. (There are isolated occurrences of maize from the Southeast as early as AD

200, but these do not represent widespread corn agriculture (B. Smith, 1987).) By AD 1, many coastal communities were small, semi-permanent villages linked to seasonally occupied camps along the shore and close inland.

Along the northeast Gulf of Mexico coast, the so-called Deptford people lived in small villages of about 5 to 10 families, spaced about every 10 miles (16 km) along the coast. During the winters, the 60 or so people in each village appear to have dwelt in oval-shaped houses with internal hearths about 22.9 by 32 ft (7 by 10 m) across, occupying smaller, open oval structures during the summer months (Milanich and Fairbanks, 1980). This was by no means a uniform settlement pattern, for there were many smaller, often short-term coastal and inland camps.

River Valley Adaptations. Much interior settlement in the Southeast concentrated along the banks of large and small rivers. Many communities consisted of small- or medium-sized villages that were occupied for much, if not all, the year. Some covered as much as 1.5 acres (0.6 ha). As on the coast, many groups used both summer and winter dwellings, often within the confines of the same settlement (Milanich, 1973a,b).

These interior populations show clear cultural links to earlier Archaic traditions. Dramatic changes in subsistence were, however, under way by 500 BC. By this time, people living north of the evergreen forest zone were exploiting annual nut crops more intensively, especially acorns, less heavily used in earlier times. Perhaps this increased reliance on nuts and acorns was the result of improved processing technology that enabled people to process large numbers of acorns – well-made ceramic vessels that permitted large-scale boiling of the harvest to leach out toxic tannic acids. The process itself was nothing new, for Archaic peoples had boiled nuts in laboriously manufactured steatite vessels. In fact, such containers may have been more effective, but clay pots were easier to manufacture, and with reasonably careful use were very durable (Walthall, 1980; B. Smith, 1986).

Many interior sites of this period reflect another important technological advance – much better storage facilities. Many communities now used deep, circular storage pits, perhaps lined with woven fiber or bark, to store their surplus gathered and cultivated foods. These resources they consumed during the scarce winter months, while dwelling in more permanent winter villages. Improved storage may have selected for more sedentary settlement and an investment in the extra labor needed to erect more substantial, permanent dwellings that were used for years on end.

Just as in Archaic times, the river valley populations traded a wide variety of exotic and more prosaic commodities up and down local rivers. The Hopewell exchange systems extended into the Southeast, indeed some of the societies that were originally part of these systems continued to flourish after more northerly centers in Illinois and Ohio went into decline. Fine-grained chert, copper, marine shells, mica, and steatite were handled through these exchange networks, with a few artifacts such as tubular pipes from northeastern Tennessee. These may testify to occasional fleeting contacts with populations living north of the Ohio River. There are no signs of elaborate mortuary cults throughout the Southeastern interior during these centuries, nor of extensive moundbuilding.

Mounds and "Big Men" in the Southeast
AD 1 to 450

Between AD 1 and about 450, two important cultural developments emerged in the Southeast. First, mortuary customs became far more elaborate. Second, there are now signs that some individuals achieved greater social and political importance among what had been egalitarian societies. There was still basic cultural continuity from earlier centuries, a continuity reflected in great variations in settlement size and the persistence of ancient lifeways from Archaic and Early Woodland times.

These four-and-a-half centuries saw the construction of hundreds of low, oval or circular earthen burial mounds throughout much of the Southeast. Superficially, all these tumuli looked much the same, but their interiors reflect considerable diversity of burial custom. Many mounds contain no less than two dozen burials, perhaps a way of commemorating the common social affiliation of the kin buried in them. Others yielded but a few interments.

When excavating burial mounds, it is not enough just to examine the core of the earthwork and the central burials. One has to excavate the surrounding areas, the original land surface, too, to search for information on the funerary activities and rituals that took place before the mound itself was built. Only a few Southeastern excavations have probed more than mound cores, but it seems that many communities laid out their dead in charnel houses. When sufficient corpses had accumulated, or after a specified period, the people gathered for public funeral ceremonies. Judging from the great variety of interments found in the mounds, the initial treatment of the dead varied considerably. Some corpses were defleshed and merely the bones buried. Others were deposited in tightly flexed postures.

The Crooks Mound in eastern Louisiana witnessed at least six episodes of burial activity, with the dead being deposited in almost equal proportions as flexed interments and disarticulated skulls or bone bundles. It is as if a nearby charnel house was emptied periodically (Brown, 1979). Sometimes, a few individuals were given special treatment, occasionally deposited in rock- or log-lined tombs, or on special platforms under the mound (B. Smith, 1986). Some burials in special pits or even wooden dugout canoes were separated from other interments, as if they were individuals of special importance. Often, one or two people were given preferential treatment by being buried in special graves, accompanied by many more grave goods, prestigious items like copper pan pipes, ear-spools, or breast plates.

The Hopewell Decline
after AD 400

The intricate Hopewell exchange systems endured in the Midwest until about AD 400. Then the networks collapsed, inter-regional art styles broke down, and moundbuilding by entire communities was interrupted. One has an impression of overall disruption, but a disruption that is still little understood, partly because chronological information is imprecise.

Many theories have been advanced to explain this sudden decline. One is population growth resulting from an increase in maize agriculture, and competition for patchy natural resources. Thus, when the limits of population carrying capacity were reached, raiding rather than exchange became a viable way of obtaining access to more resources. This hypothesis suffers from the objection that there is no evidence of fighting or tribal conflict from Hopewell sites. We also know that maize was first cultivated widely in about AD 800, long after the Hopewell decline.

The Hopewell decline is thought by some to be linked with unchecked population growth resulting from the replacement of the age-old atlatl and spear with a revolutionary new technology, that of the bow and arrow. Atlatl weights do indeed disappear from the archaeological record in about AD 400, and small stone points, perhaps from arrows, appear at Illinois sites dating between AD 400 and 600 (Muller, 1986). But did the enhanced firepower of the bow result in greater hunting success and decimation of game herds, also a rise in warfare, perhaps hinted at by fortifications at some Ohio sites? Again, there is nothing but speculation to fall back on.

There is good evidence for a trend toward colder climatic conditions all over the world in about AD 400 (Delcourt and Delcourt, 1981). This cooler weather might have affected yields of nuts and other wild resources, thereby disrupting the exchange networks of the Midwest. It is interesting to note that long-distance exchange continued to flourish in the Southeast long after the more northerly Hopewell centers were in decline.

These hypotheses are relatively simple in their explanations, as opposed to those that argue for long-term cultural processes (Braun, 1986). Two main long-term theories hold the stage, theories that complement one another. The first argues that the trend toward more intensified agriculture was fueled by highly successful inter-regional exchange and the changes of leadership that were reinforced by such activities. Horticulture became so successful that the ecological incentives for long-distance exchange, for reciprocal gift-giving, were removed – there was much less variation in resource availability between local areas, so ample food was available closer to hand. By the same token, local leadership by talented individuals became much less important.

The second hypothesis is a variation on this theme. Any form of agriculture may increase the carrying capacity of the land, but it carries serious risks with it owing to variations in rainfall and other natural phenomena from one year to the next. There is a higher risk of famine, of catastrophic shortages among much denser populations. The best strategies for minimizing such risks are those of developing food storage systems, diversifying the crops planted and growing them in different, considerably separated fields, and by developing reciprocal ties with kin living outside the immediate local area.

These sort of strategies appear to have developed among Hopewell communities over much of the Midwest during the Middle Woodland. Much of Hopewell exchange may have been based initially on competition, on individuals vying for prestige and success, rather than on the need to provide for mutual assistance in scarce times. Thus, goes the argument, long-distance exchange networks and personal prestige became less important as maize cultivation became more important, more intensive, and more successful.

It is very difficult to marshal archaeological evidence in support of either of the last two theories, simply because the processes they analyze do not survive readily in the archaeological record. David Braun points out (1986; 1989) that the widespread incorporation of distinctive Hopewell decorative motifs into domestic pottery at dozens of localities throughout the Midwest after AD 200 *may* reflect a rising importance in domestic orientation. At the same time, he argues that pottery styles show greater consistency between different localities, as if economic and social ties between neighboring communities became increasingly long-term. In other words, the Hopewell decline was not, in fact, a decline at all, but simply the long-term consequence of social processes that had begun centuries earlier. The collapse of the Hopewell interaction sphere was the symbolic, social, and economic consequence of interaction between large numbers of similarly organized local communities, scattered over thousands of square miles of the Eastern Woodlands.

The centuries between AD 450 and 800, the date when maize agriculture came into widespread use in the Southeast, have often been characterized as a period of Late Woodland decline, of "rather uninspiring self-sufficient horticultural societies" (Belovich and others, 1982). In fact, more sophisticated excavations, surveys, and mound investigations are revealing clear signs of gradual population growth, continued inter-community exchange, and increasing cultivation of native plants by sedentary peoples in river valleys and along Southeastern sea coasts. These developments were to culminate in a series of remarkable riverine cultures after AD 800, in the great Mississippian tradition of the South and southern Midwest. We examine the Late Woodland antecedents of the Mississippian and the Mississippian itself in the next chapter.

Further Reading

In addition to earlier references:

Brose, Davis S. and Greber, N'omi. (eds.). 1979. *Hopewell Archaeology.* Kent State University Press, Kent, Ohio.
    The proceedings of a Hopewell conference, the papers in this volume cover the entire spectrum of the subject and are often definitive. Comprehensive bibliography.

Caldwell, Joseph R. and Hall, Robert (eds.). 1964. *Hopewellian Studies.* Illinois State Museum, Springfield, Illinois.
    Invaluable essays on all aspects of the Hopewell problem. Somewhat outdated, but still very useful.

CHAPTER 20

MISSISSIPPIAN CLIMAX

Over 6000 years of continuous, gradual cultural evolution in the Midwest and Southeast culminated in one of North America's most brilliant achievements – the Mississippian tradition. With its great centers and myriad smaller communities, this complex patchwork of chiefdoms large and small flourished for about six centuries, up to European contact and beyond. The Mississippian's ultimate cultural and social roots lie in much earlier Archaic and Woodland cultures that flourished long before maize agriculture became widespread in the great river valleys of the Eastern Woodlands (B. Smith, 1986; Steponaitis, 1986).

The Weeden Island Culture
AD 200 to c.1000

Perhaps the best known of the many cultures that flourished in the Late Woodland Southeast is the Weeden Island culture, which arose among the prehistoric peoples who lived among deciduous and mixed pine forests, near lakes, rivers, and wet prairies on the Gulf coastal plain between Florida, Alabama, and Georgia about two centuries after Christ (Milanich and others, 1984).

Characteristic Weeden Island pottery appears in about AD 200, and may have developed out of earlier Swift Creek ceramic traditions in the Apalachicola-Chattahoochee valleys on the Alabama-Georgia border. Weeden sites extend into western parts of northern Florida and as far west as the Tombigbee River in Alabama along the Gulf coast and into the interior. An early Weeden Island I period lasted from about AD 200 to 700, Weeden Island II from 700 to between 900 and 1000, each distinguished by characteristic pottery styles (Willey, 1949). Gordon Willey's surveys revealed many more Weeden Island II sites, occupied over a relatively brief two-century span, perhaps reflecting population increases resulting from the adoption of maize agriculture. About AD 900 to 1000, Weeden II developed *in situ* into local forms of Mississippian culture at many locales, to the point that it might legitimately be called "proto-Mississippian" (Milanich and others, 1984). Some Weeden II communities may have survived in parts of northern Florida into the 15th century. The Weeden people were surrounded by other Late Woodland cultures, among them the Troyville and Coles Creek developments of the low-lying Mississippi and

Louisiana coast, and the St Johns culture to the southeast that developed continuously from Middle Archaic times right into the historic eastern Timucuan groups encountered by both Spanish and French explorers in the 16th century.

Weeden Island is part of a long evolutionary continuum that started right back in Paleo-Indian times, continued through the Archaic and Woodland, and culminated in the Mississippian. As populations increased during Late Archaic and Early Woodland times, the inhabitants of the Southeast developed more complex settlements and more elaborate forms of social organization as adaptations to higher population densities. Jerald Milanich and his colleagues argue that by AD 200, lineages and other forms of social status were well established among all Southeastern peoples. At times, too, even more complex forms of social organization may have appeared for brief periods – witness Poverty Point (Chapter 17). All these economic, social, and ideological changes culminated during the three centuries after AD 700, among Weeden II and related cultures.

Weeden Island has developed as an archaeological construct over more than a century and is a far more complex culture than might superficially appear. William Sears (1956) excavated the Kolomoki site in Georgia, excavations that led him to draw parallels between the social organization and ceremonial life of the Kolomoki Weeden Island peoples and the Natchez and other historic peoples in the Southeast. He pointed out that there was a sharp dichotomy between the sacred and the secular in these societies. In the case of the Hopewell and Mississippian, there was great uniformity in ceremonial paraphernalia, mound construction, and even in settlement hierarchies throughout much of the Southeast and Midwest. Yet there were numerous local variations in secular life, in economic conditions, technology, and other traits – to the point that the Weeden Island culture can be interpreted in several ways. On the one hand it is an ever-changing, secular pottery complex that occurs at most village sites through Weeden Island territory. On the other, it is a sacred, ceremonial complex, that may have developed from earlier Hopewell-like belief systems and religious usages. This complex may have revolved around elaborate mortuary rituals centered on low, platform mounds used as bases for charnel houses, the residences of important men, and for preparing bones for burial. The nature of this complex was illustrated dramatically at the McKeithen site in northern Florida (Milanich and others, 1984).

The McKeithen site is a village with three low platform mounds, none more than 6 ft (2 m) high (for platform mounds, see below). It was a horseshoe-shaped settlement encompassing three mounds with a central plaza, the village and its extensive middens being open to the west-north-west. Excavations showed the site was occupied between AD 200 and 700 during Weeden Island I. The three low platform mounds had been constructed at about the same time, between AD 350 and 475, during the period of densest occupation and highest population – radiocarbon dates cannot tie down the date for the tumuli more accurately. About AD 475, the structures on the mound platforms were burnt and removed, and the mounds capped. The village was still occupied after that date, but its importance as a center declined.

The exact position of the McKeithen mounds was planned to allow the rising sun at the summer solstice to be observed from the summit of one of

*Weeden Island culture.
(Above left) Plan of the McKeithen mounds. The three mounds form an isosceles triangle. The perpendicular, formed by a line from mount B to the triangle base, points towards the position of the rising sun at the summer solstice. (Above) Weeden Island Red pedestaled duck effigy from Kolomoki Mound D. Height 34 cm.*

Weeden Island Punctated bowl, from Carter Mound 1.

the mounds, the three earthworks forming an isosceles triangle. Each mound began as a low platform, then structures with walls supported by vertical posts were erected on top of two of them. One was probably a residence or temple, inhabited by an individual, probably a religious specialist, who was later buried in it. He was a man in his mid- to late thirties, and buried with a small, triangular stone projectile point in his hip (this does not seem to have been the cause of death). The body had been exposed for some days, then buried in an extended position, perhaps wearing a headdress of animal and human bone. A ceramic turkey vulture's head from an effigy pot lay less than 3 ft (1 m) from the head. The building on the mound was burnt down over his grave.

The structure on the second mound was probably a charnel house. The third platform mound was topped with a pine-post screen, and the area behind it was used to inter and exhume burials. This may have been where the bones of the dead were cleaned before being taken over to the charnel house. There they were stored until buried under the cap of the completed mound. Together, the mounds formed part of a complex mortuary process, presumably supervised by the man buried in the temple or residence. He may also have kept track of the yearly calendar, of the summer solstice. Mortuary activities may have ceased with the death of this important individual. The structures were burnt down, the mound platforms capped with clean sand.

Platform mounds of the general type found at Kolomoki and McKeithen are found in Florida, Georgia, Tennessee, Alabama, and Mississippi. Most date from AD 150 to 400, a few as late as AD 750. Their design was probably related to the burial ceremonies conducted on them. Occasionally, the people added additional burials as the mound was being built, some complete interments, others in the form of bone bundles or even single skulls. Some scholars believe these were the burials of slaves and retainers sacrificed at the death of the important personage under the mound. Sometimes the mourners deposited caches of elaborate clay vessels in the mounds, many of them ceremonial pots in the shape of humans, birds, or animals. They were punctured with holes through the base, some of them before they were even fired. (For a fascinating discussion of the process of moundbuilding and its significance, see Schnell and others, 1981.)

Brenda Sigler-Lavelle (in Milanich and others, 1984) predicts that each Weeden Island village or lineage had a religious practitioner, an individual who provided a link to the supernatural. This person probably had special social status, was a true "Big Man" for the time when he was active, and was supported by members of his lineage, who were buried in the communal burial mound. Burial in such a tumulus was an affirmation of lineage membership, and ensured that ritual obligations occurred at central locations. The individuals who carried out these rituals had an exalted status in society, positions that enabled them to develop outside contacts, to manipulate long-distance trade, to acquire some political power. Individual villages like McKeithen could assume great importance in inter-lineage activities for a short period of time, while their "Big Man" was at the height of his powers.

The social organization characteristic of McKeithen and other Weeden Island sites appears to have lain somewhere between the basically egalitarian structure of Archaic hunter-gatherers and the chiefdoms characteristic of later Mississippian society. Between AD 700 and 1000, village centers like the abandoned McKeithen and their religious specialists assumed ever-greater importance as maize agriculture and harvest rituals became more central features of Southeastern life. Over these centuries, the social, political, and ideological institutions of later Weeden Island agricultural communities and their contemporaries evolved into those associated with the Mississippian.

Between AD 800 and 1000, more intensive maize agriculture appeared over a broad area of the interior Southeast from the central Mississippi Valley to the western Appalachian piedmont (Steponaitis, 1986). Rectangular houses built with wall trench foundations and shell-tempered pottery are now characteristic of small settlements throughout this large area, both classic features of later Mississippian culture. Shell temper was an important innovation, for it allowed the manufacture of more durable and larger vessels, also enhanced the qualities of local clays, so potters could construct a wider range of forms. It is hardly surprising that this new artifice spread far and wide within a short time (Steponaitis, 1984). But the underlying catalysts for the brilliant flowering of Mississippian culture after AD 1000 were the widespread adoption of maize cultivation throughout the Eastern Woodlands after AD 800, and the efflorescence of sacred ceremonial complexes that led to the emergence of numerous powerful chiefdoms throughout the Southeast.

As we saw in Chapter 14, maize cultivation began in the Southwest during the first millennium BC. The maize pool in that region was highly diverse (Ford, 1985; B. Smith, 1987), and a small-cob 12- and 14-rowed race of hard flint maize, sometimes called "North American pop," was the first to spread across the southern Plains into the Southeast by the fifth century AD. This form was dominant before AD 1000, when it gave way to eight-rowed, hardy Maiz de Ocho, the form that became a staple over much of the Midwest and Eastern Woodlands. Flotation samples from eastern sites document a transition from sporadic occurrences of maize to intensive cultivation after about AD 800. For example, a Late Woodland occupation at Koster East in west-central Illinois dating to about AD 620 contains but one occurrence of maize, whereas a later one of about AD 830 contains 24 percent maize (Asch and Asch, 1984).

Beans (*Phaseolus vulgaris*) were introduced into the Eastern Woodlands in about AD 1000 (Ford, 1985), and were not in common use until Late Mississippian times, after AD 1200. Beans provided an important protein source for Eastern Woodlands peoples, as they did elsewhere in the Americas (Chapter 14).

It was the widespread cultivation of maize and beans that helped foster higher population densities, larger food surpluses, and more complex political and social organization in the closing centuries of prehistoric times in eastern North America. Most likely, the shift to maize agriculture was the result of stress largely precipitated by population pressure (Steponaitis, 1986). However, Steponaitis qualifies this observation (personal communication, 1989) by remarking that there was no land shortage in the Southeast at this time, for there were many unoccupied river valleys. Perhaps, in some senses, the population pressure was socially induced, conceivably by warfare. Growing population densities brought people to the point where the high start-up costs of clearing land were worth it. Begun initially to create more supplemental foods, the new agriculture transformed the landscape in such ways that hunting and foraging provided much less food for energy expended than maize cultivation. Within a short time, an entirely new economic pattern came into being.

Defining the Mississippian

With the exception of maize, and later bean, agriculture, there was nothing dramatically new in the way Eastern Woodlands people lived in the late first millennium AD. It was just that the diversity and intensive scale of river floodplain adaptations reached new heights.

The Mississippian adaptation appeared more-or-less simultaneously across much of the Southeast by AD 900 (B. Smith, 1978). It developed in river valleys large and small, often expanding up small tributaries of major waterways. This restriction of Mississippian populations to floodplains was not only because of easily cultivable alluvial soils. For thousands of years, river valley peoples had adapted to low-lying environments where locally concentrated aquatic, game, and vegetable resources were abundant. Fertile agricultural soils formed bands within these same valleys, providing additional diversity of food resources in traditional homelands.

A constant supply of water-borne nutrients helped these floodplain areas sustain a rich biomass of animals and plants, and resulting high human population densities. The Mississippians who lived in these environments developed complex, yet very flexible adaptations, which involved exploiting fish, migratory waterfowl, terrestrial game (deer, raccoon, and turkey), nuts, fruits, and berries, and seed-bearing native plants. They selectively exploited these optimum energy sources within the floodplain ecosystem and deliberately destroyed the natural vegetation on preferred soils to grow maize, beans, squash, and some native plants.

Just as important, local topography, the amount of spring flooding and summer drain off, and location relative to migratory waterfowl flyways, were of critical importance for people maximizing their floodplain habitats. As a result, fish and waterfowl together may have contributed at least half of the total protein intake of Mississippian populations living along the bottomlands of the great river, in places where oxbow lakes and abandoned channel meanders were plentiful. Add to this effective cultivation of nutrient-rich soils fertilized by regular floods, and it is safe to claim that the Mississippians enjoyed a unique adaptation in the Eastern Woodlands (Nassaney, 1987).

Bruce Smith (1978) uses the term Mississippian to define prehistoric populations living in the eastern deciduous woodlands from AD 800 to 1500 "that had a ranked form of social organization, and had developed a specific complex adaptation to linear, environmentally circumscribed floodplain habitat zones." This definition has the advantage of not being too rigid, and it allows for great differences in social organization and ideology from one local area to the next. And there is abundant evidence of great variation in social complexity, with major centers like Cahokia in the so-called American Bottom near the modern city of St Louis at one end of the spectrum, and hundreds of small, local centers and minor chiefdoms at the other. (For a discussion of a minor Early Mississippian center, see Schnell and others, 1981.) The discussion of the Mississippian which follows gives, at best, a general impression of this remarkable, and highly diverse, cultural tradition.

Subsistence

It is difficult to know how important hunting was in Mississippian life. Apart from waterfowl and fish in favored areas, the game species from many sites include such familiar species as deer, but many of them were animals that would prey regularly on growing maize fields.

Wild plant foods were of vital importance to Mississippian communities, especially the rich nut harvests of fall. In bountiful years, nuts would provide enough food to feed a much higher population density than actually lived even in the most favored locations. By the same token, and judging by modern experience, good agricultural years could yield far more than the 19th-century average for the United States of about 22 bushels an acre (1320 kg/ha), a figure close to current worldwide production counts (figures quoted from Muller, 1987). In the so-called Black Bottom area of the Lower Ohio Valley in which the well-known Kinkaid site lies, there were an estimated 1482 acres (600 ha) of occupied agricultural land in Mississippian times (Cole, 1951). With yields like this, an average maize year could support some 2000 people, about double the maximum population estimated for the region (Lafferty, 1977).

Woman grinding maize: a stone effigy pipe from Spiro Mound, Oklahoma. Height 25 cm.

Bountiful yields in good years meant good living, but yields from both fields and nut trees varied dramatically from year to year. The bottomlands of the Mississippi and Ohio rivers flood regularly in the spring, and can be subject to inundation as late as July. These floods are irregular, but not infrequent, making farming on such lands a high-risk proposition even today. It was no coincidence that many Mississippian communities and their gardens were concentrated on fertile, well-drained ridges, or on nearby terrace soils that were never flooded, even if the risk of drought was higher. Almost certainly most villages maintained fields both in high-risk flood areas and on higher ground. Here other factors came into play – crop diseases spreading through closely placed gardens and build-up of weeds and pests resulting from repeated cropping of the same land.

This meant that most Mississippian communities lived with the constant threat of food shortages. The people dwelt in permanent settlements, so they could not adopt the age-old strategy of shifting base when local resources were in short supply. In some locations, there may have been occasional episodes of extreme stress. A series of complex studies of some Mississippian burials reveal stress lines on limb bones (known as Harris lines) and other clear signs of cyclical stress, some of which were probably caused by dietary factors (Buikstra and others, 1986).

What strategies, then, could prevent starvation in lean years? Most of the time, the household served as the primary production unit, and was a self-sufficient entity. But at least once or twice a decade the yields of gardens and trees were probably insufficient, creating a real need for vital, supplemental resources – and for social mechanisms to minimize the risk of famine.

Each household may have cultivated a mosaic of several gardens, situated in separate environmental zones. People short of food could rely on kinspeople living in other areas for seed and rations, knowing that one day they might have to reciprocate in kind. Or a community or kin group could stockpile surplus food from one year for use in lean times. Several of these strategies required some form of coordination, either through kin leaders or on a larger scale (Muller, 1987).

Some groups may have even gone so far as to maintain communal granaries under the control of a local chieftain, like those observed among the historic Muskogean Indians of the Southeast by the 18th-century botanist William Bartram:

"There is a large crib, or granary, erected in the plantation, which is called the king's crib; and to this each of the family carries and deposits a certain quantity, according to his ability or inclination ..." This, wrote Bartram, was a "public treasury" "to which every citizen has the right of free and equal access, when his own private stores are consumed; to serve as a surplus to fly to for succour; to assist neighboring towns, whose crops may have failed ..." The chief, Bartram tells us, had the task of distributing "comfort and blessings to the necessitous" (Bartram, 1853).

This account treats of a people who were under strong European influence. But Jon Muller (1987) believes that the practice had evolved from earlier, prehistoric custom. The emergence of an elite within Mississippian society may, then, have been a way of mitigating risks for households and entire villages. These leaders were the people who oversaw the stockpiling of food supplies, who ensured that cultivated lands were maintained in different environmental zones, so that chances of crop failure were much reduced. Some of these strategies could be operated through ties of kin and reciprocity, but only up to a certain point of scale. At times, food shortages may have been such that entire regions had to cooperate with one another, cooperation requiring organized leadership and coordination in a more formal way (Muller, 1987). At the center of these mechanisms of reciprocity and cooperation lay complex local and long-distance exchange systems, developed in various forms over many centuries.

Low-Level Chiefdoms

Most Mississippian exchange took place at the household level, the domestic unit that organized and scheduled food gathering and production. Apparently, however, Mississippian communities were grouped into larger political and social units, headed by local chieftains, individuals who probably rose to prominence as "Big Men," just as their predecessors had done for centuries. These low-level chiefdoms, with an emerging elite, where in some places elite status may have been passed from one generation to the next, perhaps functioned as a way of balancing the distribution of vital foods and raw materials. The Mississippian elite may have used valuable, exotic artifacts as a means of rewarding their loyal followers and strengthening their political power, just as their humbler predecessors had done (B. Smith, 1986).

Many exotic objects are found in Mississippian burials, with the result that archaeologists have tended to describe all such interments as those of "high-status" individuals. This is a dangerous assumption, for most burial excavations have concentrated on centrally located, "high-status" cemeteries, often places where a much greater variety of artifacts occurs anyhow. Were, then, such exotic objects as shell cups, engraved shells, and other fine artifacts badges of rank, or merely trade objects that were widely distributed in societies that showed little social or material distinction between commoner and elite?

Mississippian exchange networks linked hundreds of communities large and small, mainly with local transactions. Production of artifacts of every kind was a dispersed activity throughout Mississippian territory, with exotic objects and raw materials finding their way into the hands of artisans even in the smallest villages. For instance, sea shells were exchanged over vast areas of the Southeast. The complete shells were turned into ornaments and often engraved with distinctive designs by specialists. The motifs executed by different individuals can be recognized in many cases (Phillips and Brown, 1978).

Only two commodities may have involved some degree of specialized production – chert and salt (Muller, 1987). Chert from the famous Union County quarries in Illinois may have been quarried by local, part-time

Sea shells were traded over vast areas of the Southeast in Mississippian times. (Below left) Conch shell engraved with an abstract face from Arkansas. (Below) Conch shell engraved with a flying shaman, from Oklahoma.

specialists. Much of it was turned into stone hoes, exchanged and used throughout the northern Lower Mississippi Valley. Salt production assumed much greater importance as maize cultivation took hold in the Southeast, for farmers have to supplement their diet artificially with salt. Cake salt was manufactured at a limited number of places. According to 18th-century French explorer Le Page du Pratz, people would come from long distances to make salt at locations like Great Salt Spring near the Saline River in southeast Illinois (Le Page du Pratz, 1758). There may have been some centers of local production, but at best this was probably a part-time activity, involving work parties from communities at a distance.

As far as we can tell, person-to-person bartering or gift-giving and formal redistribution were the only means of exchange of goods and commodities in Mississippian society. This means that the great diversity of Mississippian communities were not organized along highly formal, rigid social class lines. We cannot argue, for example, that Mississippian chieftains employed specialists to convert exotic raw materials into prestigious artifacts to reward their followers. The kinds of production were little more complex than those found in earlier Woodland societies, although the elite may have stimulated the development of part-time specialization (Muller, 1987). In other words, every family, every household was involved in agricultural production and food procurement. There were no "non-producers," such as one finds in early state-organized societies such as those at Teotihuacan, Mexico, and in Maya society. Nor, as far as is known, were there any full-time traders, who specialized in long-distance exchange and nothing else.

Mississippian communities were relatively autonomous, exchanging and producing goods and commodities through age-old ties of kin and reciprocal obligation. Judging from historic accounts, the more elite members of society may have been involved in the storage and redistribution of grain. Apparently these stockpiles could reach impressive proportions. We know this because in later centuries, early European explorers like Spaniard Hernando de Soto and his conquistadors were able to loot considerable quantities of stored grain from Southeastern villages on occasion.

Much grain redistribution activity may have taken place at formal ceremonies. As late as the 17th century, Southeastern communities from many miles around would congregate for feasts and dances, at which people would barter goods, share food, and reaffirm ties with other villages and individuals. These major ceremonies may have been sponsored by important individuals, to enhance their prestige and acquire influence. This was one of the few ways in which they could consolidate their authority, for there appears to have been no way in which they could restrict their followers' access to desirable goods or commodities (Muller, 1987).

A Question of Scale: Cahokia and Moundville

The prehistoric societies that are loosely classified under the label "Mississippian" flourished over a wide area of the Midwest and South, enjoying complex adaptations that varied widely from one location to the

Map showing the main Mississippian groups and locations of some key sites.

next (B. Smith, 1978). Most Mississippian communities were small, many of them grouped into a multiplicity of chiefdoms that were probably in a constant state of political flux as the followings of important individuals waxed and waned, chiefs died, alliances were forged and fell apart, and new people came into prominence. But there are some Mississippian centers that appear to have nurtured more complex social and political structures. The most famous of these are Cahokia in the American Bottom on the Mississippi River opposite St Louis, and Moundville in Alabama. These centers raise important questions about the complexity of Mississippian society, about the political organization of the most elaborate of all North American prehistoric cultures.

Cahokia. The American Bottom is a pocket of low-lying river floodplain along the Mississippi from the confluence with the Illinois River near Alton, Illinois, as far south as Dupo, Illinois. The Bottom is only about 25 miles (40.2 km) from north to south and 11 miles (17.7 km) wide at its greatest extent. It was formed by the meanderings of the Mississippi and Missouri river channels over the flatlands, forming swamps and oxbow lakes in its abandoned channels. The result was an environment of exceptional diversity, rich in aquatic resources, game, and vegetable foods, a floodplain with fertile soils lying on the borders of several ecological zones. It was here that Cahokia flourished, with probably the focus of the highest prehistoric population north of Mexico (Milner, 1990).

At the height of its power, between AD 1050 and 1250, Cahokia extended over an area of more than 5 sq. miles (13 sq. km) (Fowler, M., 1969; 1978). Some 2000 acres (800 ha) of this vast area were covered with dwellings, housing perhaps as many as 30,000 people. The inhabitants lived in pole-and-thatch houses clustered along a central east-west ridge. Several residences per acre was the rule, the same building site being used again and again over the generations. The dwellings vary greatly in size, perhaps a reflection of different social status. They may have been grouped in clusters, each associated with mound and plaza complexes, subdivisions of the community.

The Cahokia people erected more than 100 earthen mounds over the centuries, mounds of various sizes, shapes, and functions in an apparently carefully planned layout. Most of them cluster along the central ridge of the site, the driest higher ground in the vicinity. They are grouped around a series of what must have been open plazas. The most extensive grouping lies around Monk's Mound, the largest earthwork built by the prehistoric North Americans.

Monk's Mound rises in four terraces to a height of 100 ft (30.4 m), measures 1037 by 790 ft (316 by 240 m), and covers 16 acres (6.4 ha). The people heaped up more than 21,700,000 cu. ft (614,478 cu. m) of earth to erect this huge construction. Monk's Mound is more than twice the size of any other mound, so the large building that once stood on its summit must have been the focus of the entire community. Some of the largest mounds at Cahokia were laid out in two rows on either side, with a plaza area

Cahokia mounds, c. AD 1100. The 100-ft (30.4-m) high Monk's Mound dominated the site, with many smaller mounds and houses surrounding it. Trading and major public ceremonies took place in the central plaza. A log stockade protected the central precincts, with a solar calendar at the far left. Maize gardens surrounded Cahokia, and water supplies came from Cahokia Creek and small lakes that formed in borrow pits dug to quarry clay for moundbuilding.

Cahokia. (Left) Aerial view of Monk's Mound, the largest prehistoric earthwork in North America. It was built in stages from AD 900 to 1200. (Below) Artist's impression of the central Cahokia mound complex in its heyday, looking across the Grand Plaza to Monk's Mound.

apparently lying immediately to the south. Most of these were platform mounds where important public buildings or elite residences once stood. The conical mound south of Monk's Mound was one of the burial tumuli, and perhaps charnel houses where high-status people were laid out, then interred (Fowler, 1978). A large log palisade with watchtowers and gates enclosed the 200 acres (80.9 ha) of the central area. It was rebuilt at least four times. Melvin Fowler believes this was either a defensive wall, or designed to isolate people of high status from commoners.

We do not know if Cahokia was occupied all at one time, but it was a large, complex site as early as AD 900, during the so-called Fairmount phase. The population appears to have reached its maximum a century and a half later, during the two centuries of the Sterling and Moorehead phases. Cahokia was long abandoned by the 17th century, when Europeans first penetrated the St Louis area.

There is a temptation to think of Cahokia as a large prehistoric town, even a city, with vast public works erected by a huge urban workforce. However, these estimates are no longer considered valid, because of the lack of precise chronological controls over mound excavations at this site and elsewhere.

No question, Monk's Mound is an impressive monument by any standards. Its earthen contents would have taken a theoretical 370,000 work days to accumulate. There would have been additional work days for carrying the soil and spreading it out evenly. This entire task, theoretically, would take 2000 people under 200 days to complete! In practice, Monk's Mound was built in fits and starts, in stages that would occasionally require heavy labor investments, perhaps for one or two years. So this vast complex is misleading in terms of population, for many fewer people may have built it over a considerable period of time (Muller, 1987). There may have been as few as 500 people living within the central area of Cahokia, with the remainder of the population dispersed over the nearby floodplain. Indeed, the extensive hinterland around Cahokia may have played an important role in determining the size of the earthworks.

Some figures from the smaller Mississippian center at Kinkaid in the Lower Ohio Valley tend to confirm the Cahokia calculations, theoretical as they may be. There, the people piled up some 3,284,246 cu. ft (93,000 cu. m) of earth in mounds of various kinds. This construction did not take place all at once, but extended over some five centuries between AD 900 and 1400 (Lafferty, 1977). For working purposes, Robert Lafferty assumed that it took about two to three hours to pile up a cubic meter of earth, and that people worked about as hard as today. He calculated that it would have taken between 37,200 and 55,800 individual work days of five hours to build the Kinkaid earthworks. Thus, a population of 500 people would have completed them in 74 to 112 days, if they had undertaken the work continuously. Over five centuries, it could, theoretically, have taken 500 people 28 different four-day festivals to erect the mounds.

All of this means little in practical terms, for there are many intangible variables that could have affected long-term construction plans. The point is that large-scale moundbuilding does not necessarily imply dense Mississippian populations, however imposing the earthworks. Everything points to dispersed village populations, but populations who cooperated regularly in important rituals, moundbuilding activities, and in trade.

Cahokia was the center of a still little-documented hierarchy of lesser settlements. Four sites nearby cover more than 124 acres (50 ha), and boast of several mounds. Five still smaller settlements each surround a single tumulus. More than 40 small hamlets and farmsteads have been recorded in the Bottom, most covering only a few acres (Fowler, M., 1978).

This hierarchy may reflect a more complex political order than that elsewhere in Mississippian territory. There is striking evidence for elaborate burial customs in Mound 72 at Cahokia. Melvin Fowler (1974) records a male burial laid out on a platform of 20,000 shell beads. This was an important man, for he was accompanied by three high-status men and women buried nearby. About 800 arrowheads, copper and mica sheets, and 15 polished stone disks used in a spear-throwing game lay with these skeletons, perhaps those of close relatives sacrificed at the funeral. Nearby were the bodies of four decapitated men with their hands cut off. More than 50 young women aged between 18 and 23 were buried in a pit close by. Fowler suspects they were strangled to death.

Moundville. Cahokia was by far the largest Mississippian community, but its power declined after AD 1250 when other large towns achieved prominence. Moundville lies by the Black Warrior River in west-central Alabama and flourished between AD 1250 and 1500. The site with its 20 large platform mounds covers more than 300 acres (121.5 ha) (Steponaitis, 1983). The mounds delineate a rectangular plaza of about 79 acres (32 ha), some supporting public buildings or residences for important individuals, a few associated with skull caches, with a sweat house and charnel structure lying just outside the southern side of the plaza. Mound B is the highest, with an altitude of about 56 ft (17 m). Higher-status people lived, and were buried, east of the mounds on the eastern side of the plaza. The three sides of the site away from the river were protected by a bastioned palisade during some of Moundville's history. As at Cahokia, hundreds of people lived within the general site area, perhaps as many as 3000 souls. Altogether 3051 burials have been excavated at Moundville, with the highest-status interments lying in the mounds. People of lesser status were buried in the major village areas along the northern boundary of the site (Peebles, 1978; 1979; Peebles and Kus, 1977).

Moundville's complex history began with the West Jefferson phase of AD 900 to 1050, when the inhabitants of the Black Warrior drainage lived mainly in small settlements, with only a few larger communities, of which the Moundville location was one (for a more detailed summary, see Peebles, 1978; Steponaitis, 1983). These can be described as villages, none constructed mounds, and the people relied mainly on hunting and gathering, also limited agriculture. Each village was a more-or-less permanent settlement, a base for a yearly cycle of economic activities (Welch, 1981), and society was probably egalitarian.

The Moundville I phase lasted from 1050 to 1250, when the local people came to rely much more heavily on maize agriculture. Up to 60 percent of the seeds from this phase are from corn. While wild plants were much less important, game meat and fish were still staples. The first ceremonial centers appear, larger sites, most with a single pyramidical mound – flat-topped structures associated with a mortuary area. These centers may signify the existence of low-level chiefdoms.

*Moundville, Alabama. (Right)
Location of the site and neighboring
Mississippian mounds. (Below)
Changing settlement patterns in the
Moundville area. Moundville itself rose
to dominance in Phases II and III (AD
1250 – 1500), before disappearing as a
significant center in Phase IV (after
1550).*

MAJOR SETTLEMENTS IN THE
CENTRAL BLACK WARRIOR
VALLEY A.D. 900-1600

multiple mound center
single mound center
settlement

N

0   5   10   15km

WEST JEFFERSON PHASE

MOUNDVILLE I PHASE

MOUNDVILLE II PHASE

MOUNDVILLE III PHASE

MOUNDVILLE IV PHASE
(ALABAMA RIVER PHASE)

MOUNDVILLE III PHASE

- burial/gravelot – moundville III
- burial/gravelot – moundville III or alabama river
- mound – definite

escarpment

0 125 250 m

Moundville, Alabama. (Left) The site at its peak, with 20 mounds built around a central plaza on the south bank of the Black Warrior River. (Below) Slate palette from Moundville incised with a hand-and-eye motif within two entwined horned rattlesnakes. Diameter 32 cm.

Moundville phases II and III lasted from AD 1250 to 1500. Moundville itself now assumed much greater size and importance, with between 5 and 14 mounds standing around its plaza. During Moundville III, the site assumed its final form, with 20 mounds. Most of the inhabitants of the drainage lived not in small villages but in dispersed hamlets, at a time when social ranking at Moundville reached its peak. This is reflected in elaborate mortuary rites and many mound burials of the elite, while some people outside Moundville were interred in small cemeteries near local centers. During these three centuries, Moundville stood alone as a major regional center, presiding over a series of local centers of roughly equal size, all with one mound, and over hundreds of tiny hamlets. Most Moundville settlements were located on ecotones, places where several distinct ecological zones, like, for example, wooded uplands and floodplain meadows, intersect. They lay at places where the people could combine agriculture with intensive hunting and gathering. The animal bones from Moundville and other major, contemporary sites like Etowah in Georgia and Spiro in Oklahoma, are mostly from deer and turkey, as if the hunters were concentrating their efforts on a few, readily accessible species. Almost certainly the Black Warrior Valley was under Moundville's political control.

Vincas Steponaitis (1978) studied the Moundville settlement data with its two-tiered hierarchy of major and minor centers and residential sites. Detailed burial studies confirm that the highest status individuals were interred only at Moundville itself, with some members of the elite being buried at the minor centers. Given Moundville's large size with its 20 mounds, it appears that political power was highly centralized, drawing on tribute and labor from centers as far as nearly 45 miles (72 km) away. Steponaitis assumes that those minor centers closest to Moundville paid more tribute, simply because transport costs were lower. He calculated that a distance of about 9 miles (14.5 km) was about the maximum for large-scale tribute gathering on a regular basis without serious difficulties in transporting supplies and enforcing assessments.

Cahokia, Moundville, Etowah, Georgia (Larsen, 1971), and Spiro, Oklahoma (Brown, 1971), were large, complex communities, ruled by high-status individuals of great political, social, and religious influence. Steponaitis (1978) has called them "Complex Chiefdoms."

Complex Chiefdoms

The simplest chiefdoms are single-level societies, where the chief is but a part-time administrator, who still farms the land. The chief is self-suffici-ent. He does not live off tribute and other foodstuffs supplied by his followers. He is expected to be a generous kinsman, who redistributes most goods back to other members of society. Under these circumstances, there is a balanced flow of goods between different levels of the community, with reciprocity playing an important part in society (Steponaitis, 1978).

More complex chiefdoms have two or even three tiers of political hierarchy. Nobles are clearly distinct from commoners and do not usually engage in any form of agricultural production. Thus, the higher-status members of society consume most of the goods that are passed up the hierarchy as tribute. Reciprocal obligations are fulfilled by the nobles carrying out ritual or secular services that only they can perform. They may also make token, symbolic redistributions of food and other goods.

In two- or three-tiered chiefdoms, higher-ranking chiefs have control over a number of lesser-ranking individuals, each of whom control specific territory or a social unit. Political control rests on the chief's ability to maintain access to a sufficiently large body of tribute, passed up the line by lesser chiefs. They in turn collect from those below them, from communities close to their own center. At the apex sits the most powerful chieftain of all.

What were the dynamics of such polities? The debate about the evolution of chiefdoms has raged unabated for decades, with a chiefdom being defined somewhat loosely as "a centralized polity that organizes a regional population in the thousands" (Earle, 1989). Some degree of inherited social ranking and economic stratification appears to go with such chiefdoms.

The formation of any complex political organization like a chiefdom requires that a leader create ties of loyalty to his person, by controlling peoples' labor in ways that cause them not to move away. Thus social and technological changes are needed to organize large numbers of people at close quarters. So the leader has been thought of as a "manager." Thus, he was an entrepreneur who succeeded in making his position hereditary under circumstances where a variety of factors, including population growth and economic change, were creating conditions favorable to such political consolidation.

More recent research is focusing on the political processes that lead both to the creation and maintenance of chiefdoms. There are many ways of doing so. Chiefs can use naked force, make people indebted to them through feasting or by improving the distribution and availability of food supplies. They can encourage circumscription, forge external ties with neighbors, and seize control of all production and distribution of wealth. They can control long-distance trade, even become masters of the forces of the supernatural (Steponaitis, quoted by Earle, 1989).

All of these strategies for seizing control depend, of course, on the willingness of the population at large to accept them. In the case of the

Symbol of a hierarchical society? A warrior decapitates a victim on this Mississippian stone effigy pipe from Spiro Mound, Oklahoma. Height 25 cm.

Mississippian, increasing control of long-distance exchange, especially in exotic, prestigious goods, and the use of this wealth to control local labor may have been important catalysts for political change. There is every indication that Mississippian chiefs used the exotic, and highly valuable, objects they received from outside as symbols of their legitimacy, of their special relationship to supernatural powers that were theirs alone to control. This form of ideological governance is vulnerable to the uncontrollable forces of long-distance exchange, so stability was achieved by linking the exotic objects used in major ceremonies with ceremonial architecture, and with land ownership. Thus, the great earthworks of Cahokia, Moundville, and other centers were a way of fostering bonds between the people and the elite, between one community and another.

There are no signs that Mississippian chiefs exercised strict economic control over commoners. It is as if local populations were "drawn into sociopolitical systems in part by 'smoke and mirrors' " (Earle, 1989). This was a religious ideology that was based on notions of centrality, a centrality symbolized by large ceremonial structures and by exchanges of exotic objects of great symbolic value.

Under these circumstances, Mississippian chiefdoms were fragile institutions, the end-products of a constant process of balancing economic interdependence, ideology, and force. These chiefdoms were in a constant state of change, as centers of power changed, some chiefdoms collapsed, and others nearby rose in their place. Local and regional conditions changed frequently, fueled by the competitive political dynamics that are so characteristic of chiefdoms everywhere – societies with few high-status positions. In the long-term we face a formidable task – explaining the rise of complex chiefdoms in Mississippian society will mean understanding not only local political conditions, but the shifts in long-distance exchange networks, and ideologies over much larger areas as well.

The Mississippian was no political and social monolith, with important rulers maintaining absolute authority over vast areas of the Midwest and South. Rather, hundreds of local societies large and small, fall under the general category "Mississippian." They enjoyed an infinite variety of local adaptations to a very diverse resource base, and varied greatly in their dependence on maize and bean agriculture. Long-distance exchange networks brought a degree of cultural continuity to the entire vast area, and there was some common religious tradition among many of them, reflected in widely used art styles and abiding ritual symbolism. The people lived under dozens of chiefdoms large and small, many of them virtually egalitarian, others, like Cahokia, highly complex, powerful political and social units. But these complex chiefdoms still depended heavily on kin ties and notions of reciprocity to function properly. With their regular feasts and elaborate ceremonies, Mississippian chiefs validated their authority in vivid, symbolic ways, well aware that their power depended on a fine line between coercion and reciprocity.

Religion and ceremonial may have been an important means by which Mississippian chiefs asserted their authority. This cedarwood mask, perhaps worn by a shaman, has shell inlay and antlers carved in imitation of those of a deer. From Spiro Mound, Oklahoma. Height 29 cm.

Mississippians and Mesoamericans

Cahokia is a startling sight to someone used to the relatively small scale of prehistoric North American communities. Even today, the great earthworks

Mississippian Southern Cult. The belief systems of the late prehistoric peoples of the Southeast were closely tied to local political and social organization. The people depicted complex symbols on clay vessels, stone, copper, and shell objects. The meanings of many of these symbols elude us, but they include "weeping eyes," birds, serpents, skulls, and hand, motifs that may be associated with ancestor rituals. As in many agricultural societies around the world, these ancestral ties reaffirmed social status. Serpents were also associated with the fertility of crops and the soil. (Above) Shell head with weeping eye and other facial decoration, height 6 cm. (Opposite page): (Above, left and right) Weeping eyes appear on this pottery human effigy vessel and embossed copper face. (Below left) Shell disk with crested woodpeckers, from Sumner County, Tennessee. Diameter 8.5 cm. (Below right) Shell gorget depicting a flying shaman with a death's head in one hand and a ceremonial mace in the other. Diameter 10 cm.

are awe-inspiring, surrounded as they are by the urban sprawl of East St Louis. It is hardly surprising that earlier generations of scholars speculated about possible connections between Mississippian sites and the complex states and civilizations of Mexico to the south. Certain features of Mississippian architecture, and a distinctive art tradition known as the Southern Cult, caused them to suspect Mesoamerican influence at Cahokia and other large centers.

Larger Mississippian communities enjoyed a more-or-less standardized layout. Their inhabitants built platform mounds and capped them with temples and the houses of important people. These mounds were arranged around an open plaza, while most families lived in thatched dwellings sometimes clustered close by. Advocates of Mexican influence point out that this arrangement of temple mounds is a familiar one in Mexico, beginning with the Olmec and other primeval lowland societies before 1000 BC and reaching its culminating elaboration at Teotihuacan, Tikal, Copán, and the Aztec capital, Tenochtitlán. Mesoamerican civilizations relied on an intricate, intensely symbolic, and highly complex religious cosmology, commemorated with elaborate public ceremonies centered in large plazas. Did the distinctive Mississippian architecture, cosmology, art, and religious symbolism derive from such a foreign cosmology? Did maize and bean cultivation diffuse from Mexico, with corn agriculture coinciding with a population movement and new cosmologies from civilized lands in Central America? The answers must come, not from chance resemblances between architectural traditions that appear to have originated indigenously in both places, but from art styles revealed on Mississippian artifacts, artifacts of the so-called Southern Cult.

A generation ago, it was not unusual for archaeologists to refer to the Mississippian as a series of state-organized societies, each centered on a major ceremonial complex like Cahokia or Moundville (Brown, 1976; Muller, 1989). Mississippian cemeteries and mound centers contain finely made pottery and other artifacts that bear elaborate decoration and distinctive artistic motifs. These artifacts include axes with head and shaft carved from a single piece of stone, copper pendants adorned with circles or weeping eyes, shell disks or gorgets showing woodpeckers, rattlesnakes, elaborately decorated clay pots and effigy vessels, copper plates, and engraved shell cups adorned with male figures in ceremonial dress (Phillips and Brown, 1978).

When the themes and motifs on these objects were compared over wide areas of the Southeast, not only from classic Mississippian centers like Etowah, Georgia, and Moundville, Alabama, but also from Spiro mound in Oklahoma, part of the related Caddoan moundbuilding culture, they were found to have many features in common (Brown, 1971). These distinctive elements were thought to link sites from the Atlantic and Gulf coasts to others far inland, in distant eastern Oklahoma and on the borders of the lower Ohio Valley. Not only that, but the representations and symbols were thought to display a strong Mexican influence. These elements included small copper masks depicting long-nosed gods, and preoccupations with wind, fire, sun, and human sacrifice. Some of these themes are reminiscent of Mesoamerican artifacts, to the point that some scholars have argued they were brought to Mississippian country by professional Mexican merchants, the famous *pochteca*.

Today, any Mexican connections are discounted, for, as many experts have pointed out, the styles and themes of the Southern Cult resemble those of earlier Eastern Woodland societies much more closely than anything from Mexico. The arrival of maize and beans over a period of many centuries hints at sporadic and indirect contacts with the south, but the introduction of these plants was a far from major symbolic or mythical event. Everything points to both Mississippian architecture and cosmology being an indigenous North American development.

The oldest art objects of any complexity found in the Eastern Woodlands are found in Early and Middle Woodland sites. These can be shown to have general connections with the basic themes of Southern Cult art. Such themes include widespread use of bird symbolism, "weeping eyes," and circles and crosses. They appear to have been common to all eastern societies, themes that were used, refined, and developed as new traditions and beliefs arose.

Was there such a phenomenon as the "Southern Cult" at all? When originally defined in the 1930s, it was based on artifacts found at the major centers. Now we have access to hundreds more finds, many from lesser Mississippian communities. We know now that it would be totally misleading to think of a single, closely defined artistic horizon that extended across the South and Southeast after AD 900. Nor can one argue that such a highly varied artistic tradition reflects a unifying religious faith over a large area. In fact, quite distinct cultural and artistic phenomena have been lumped together under the Southern Cult label. It is true that some motifs, and the widespread distribution of raw materials like sea shells, do serve to link many local artistic complexes. But used as a general label, the "Southern Cult" gives a misleading sense of cultural unity among a myriad of local societies with every kind of adaptive strategy imaginable.

Jon Muller (1989) believes the Southern Cult label should be reserved for a 13th-century complex of shared motifs, themes, and finished goods exchanged over a wide area. Few distinctive stylistic elements tie together the Cult. They include bi-lobed arrows, striped poles, and fringed aprons, as well as raccoon hindquarters. Even these elements are still ill-defined. How much unity was there within the Southern Cult area in the 13th century? Muller argues that there were both similarities and differences between the many exchange and artistic traditions of the Southeast in late prehistoric times. These exchange networks that handled copper, sea shells, and finished goods such as shell gorgets, had been in place for thousands of years before the 13th century. In time, the common basic cosmology of the Southeast showed some fundamental similarity over thousands of square miles. But the regional art styles of the "Southern Cult" were linked more by centuries-old exchange links than by true stylistic resemblances (Knight, 1986).

It is doubtful, then, that there was ever a "state religion" in the Southeast. Rather, the "Southern Cult" reflects a complex, highly variable set of religious mechanisms that supported the authority of local chieftains. Undoubtedly, some of the ceremonial artifacts associated with the Cult served as badges of rank and status. And the religious beliefs behind Mississippian society had their ancestry in far earlier tradition and ritual intimately connected with the symbolic world of millennia of earlier human experience.

Natchez, Coosa, and the 16th Century

By the time European traders and explorers reached the Mississippi Valley, Cahokia was long past its apogee. The great center had reached the zenith of its political and economic power by AD 1250. New construction ceased in the 14th century and the site was abandoned by 1500. Moundville was also past its apogee, but still an important center. Nevertheless, numerous chiefdoms existed in the Mid-South and Southeast right up to European contact, and beyond. Some of them, like Moundville and Natchez, are quite well known through archaeological investigations (Hudson and others, 1985). Etowah, an important center in Georgia, was the hub of an important chiefdom before the 16th century (Larsen, 1971). Still others, like the little-known chiefdom of Coosa, are being reconstructed by combining archaeological data and early historical records.

Natchez. The Natchez chiefdom on the Lower Mississippi is especially well known, both from archaeological investigations and from observations by French explorers. The Natchez may have descended from a prehistoric cultural tradition known as the Plaquemine that brought elements of Cahokia culture into the local Coles Creek culture in about AD 1150 (Fiedel, 1987). They were still building earthen mounds in the 17th century, when French explorers first visited them. Decimated by European diseases, they numbered some 3500 people in 1700. They lived in at least six districts (earlier nine), each controlled by local chiefs. The entire tribe was ruled by the Great Sun, a paramount chief, and his younger brother, Tattooed Serpent, who was war chief. The Great Sun and Tattooed Serpent lived in the political capital, the "Grand Village" as the French rather grandiloquently called it, a scatter of about nine houses and a temple built on the summit of an earthen mound. Most Natchez families lived in small hamlets dispersed over the countryside (Swanton, 1911).

Every month, the Great Sun received tribute from his own people and local chiefs at regular feasts. "These feasts are normally undertaken when the great chief has a need of some provisions ... which they place at the door of his cabin in a heap the last day of the feast," wrote a French observer. Another remarked that the feasts were to thank the chief "for the benefits he has sent men."

In the year 1720, French explorer Le Page du Pratz (1758) spent some time living among the Natchez. He found himself in a rigidly stratified society, headed by a chieftain also known as the Great Sun. His relatives were known as Suns, and served as important officials. Under them were Nobles (Honored Men) and commoners, known to the elite as "Stinkards." The Great Sun was a despot with absolute power. Only a few chosen priests and the Great Sun could enter the temple where a sacred fire burned day and night. But the Great Sun, and all members of the elite had to marry commoners. The only other way a Stinkard could achieve Honored rank was through prowess in warfare. When the Great Sun died, his wives, relatives, and servants accompanied him in death. Natchez society was apparently a complex, tiered chiefdom.

Coosa. Hernando de Soto and his conquistadors traversed the Southeast in 1539–41, and recorded sketchy impressions of the chiefdoms they

The French explorer Le Page du Pratz witnessed the funerary rites of the Natchez Chief Tattooed Serpent in 1720, a rare firsthand account of Mississippian ritual. The dead man was carried on a litter to his temple, high on an earthen mound. There he was buried with his wife and retainers, who had been strangled beforehand.

encountered. They were impressed with the wealth of Cofitachequi, but found more food in Coosa, a powerful chiefdom based on what is now known as the Little Egypt site near Carters, Georgia (Hudson, C., and others, 1985; Milanich and Milbrath, 1989). Little Egypt boasts of three mounds and was occupied from *c.*1400 to 1600. Its deposits contained pottery types associated with the Lamar culture, and with the Mississippian Dallas and Mouse Creek phases. Historical accounts describe Coosa not as a town but as a series of communities separated by fertile gardens. After leaving Coosa, de Soto and his men marched for two days in the rain, to another large settlement named Itaba, thought to be the Etowah site. There is a Lamar component at Etowah and European artifacts have been found there. By careful correlation of historical records and archaeological sites, Charles Hudson and his colleagues have been able to establish the broad outlines of Coosa, and have associated the three subdivisions of the chiefdom with different archaeological phases identified by pottery styles and other artifacts.

Research of this type has hardly begun, but there is clearly a considerable potential for identifying specific, archaeologically identified cultures and chiefdoms with documented polities in early Spanish records. It should also be possible to trace connections between prehistoric chiefdoms and their much altered 18th- and 19th-century descendants (Hudson, C., and others, 1985). We will return to Coosa and other 16th-century chiefdoms when we examine the impact of European contact on the interior Southeast in Chapter 21.

Further Reading

In addition to earlier references:

Brown, James A. (ed.). 1971. *Approaches to the Social Dimensions of Mortuary Practices*. Society for American Archaeology, Washington DC.
Some of the essays in this volume are concerned with Mississippian mortuary practices.

Milanich, Jerald, Cordell, Ann S., Knight, Vernon J., Kohler, Timothy A. and Sigler-Lavelle, Brenda J. 1984. *McKeithen Weeden Island: The Culture of Northern Florida AD 200–900*. Academic Press, New York.
A comprehensive analysis of the Weeden Island culture, which is fundamental to understanding Mississippian origins.

Schnell, Frank T., Knight, Vernon J. Jr, and Schnell, Gail S. 1981. *Chemochobee: Archaeology of a Mississippian Ceremonial Center on the Chattahoochee River*. University Presses of Florida, Gainesville.
This site report is remarkable for its description of a Mississippian ceremonial center and accompanying moundbuilding.

Smith, Bruce D. (ed.). 1978. *Mississippian Settlement Patterns*. Academic Press, New York.
Authoritative papers on Mississippian topics, especially site distributions and hierarchies.

Steponaitis, Vincas P. 1983. *Ceramics, Chronology, and Community Patterns*. Academic Press, New York.
A study of Moundville ceramics that ranges widely over the development of this important site.

CHAPTER 21

ALGONQUIANS AND IROQUOIS

"Their food is whatever they can get from the chase and from fishing; for they do not till the soil at all ... In the month of February and until the middle of March, is the great hunt for beavers, otters, moose, bears ... and for the caribou, an animal half ass and half deer. If the weather then is favorable, they live in great abundance, and are as haughty as Princes and Kings; but if it is against them, they are greatly to be pitied, and often die of starvation ..." (Pierre Biard, 1616, quoted by Snow, 1980).

"When we went further inland we saw their houses, which are circular in shape, about fourteen to fifteen paces across, made of bent saplings ..." (Giovanni da Verrazzano, 1524, quoted by Snow, 1980).

"Their food is generally boiled maize, or Indian corn, mixed with kidney-beans, or sometimes without. Also they frequently boil in this potage fish and flesh of all sorts, either new taken or dried, as shads, eels, alewives or a kind of herring, or any other sort of fish. Also they mix with the said potage several sorts of roots ... also several sets of nuts or masts ..." (Daniel Gookin, 1674, quoted by Snow, 1980).

Seventeenth-century sailors' accounts of coastal Indians of the Northeast are a palimpsest of impressions, accurate and inaccurate, tantalizing and confusing. By this time, coastal peoples in the Northeast had been in contact with Europeans for some time, sporadically trading beaver furs with occasional coasting ships – to the point that the Pilgrims were greeted at Plimoth Rock by an Indian named Samoset, who said, "Welcome Englishmen!" (For a detailed account of Northeastern societies at contact, see Snow, 1980.) The annual round of summer fishing and foraging in the Northeast, of winter caribou and moose hunting and forest trapping, still flourished as it had for thousands of years, ever since Archaic times. We must now unravel the complicated ancestry of these Northeastern societies, deep in prehistory. To do so, we must retrace our steps back into the Late Archaic and examine the primeval cultures of the region.

Algonquians and Iroquoians

People living in coastal drainages between Nova Scotia and North Carolina were Algonquian speakers. They are grouped into the Eastern Algonquian language group, isolated from their western and northern relatives by an intrusive block of Iroquoian and other languages in the interior.

The ultimate origins of Algonquian are still a mystery, but a form of this language probably goes back far into prehistory, to a time when prehistoric cultures in the Eastern Woodlands were far more widespread and generalized than they were in later times. Both Algonquian and Gulf languages from the Southeast may, perhaps, be descended from a common group of related dialects once spoken throughout the Eastern Woodlands before 4000 to 3000 BC.

The Northern Iroquoian languages form the most important barrier between the coastal Algonquian speakers and those to the west. They form an insulating block between coast and far interior all the way from central Pennsylvania through New York State and down the St Lawrence Valley to the Gulf of St Lawrence in Canada. Every linguistic expert agrees that the Iroquoian language distribution represents an ancient intrusion of a different linguistic group into the Northeast, a group later associated with the powerful Iroquois confederacies that dominated a vast region between the St Lawrence and into New York at European contact. Fierce warriors, shrewd traders, and very sophisticated negotiators, the Iroquois were to play a dominant role in the Northeast to the very end of the Colonial period and beyond.

A central question in Northeastern prehistory is to establish when Iroquois speakers first spread into their present homelands, and to identify them in the archaeological record. To do this requires examining Late Archaic cultures in the Northeast, for the roots of Iroquois culture probably lie deep in prehistory.

Terminal Archaic
1650 to 700 BC

Throughout the Eastern Woodlands, rivers large and small were arteries that flowed through the centers of Archaic territories. They provided not only aquatic resources and sustenance for the animal and plant populations on their banks, but vital communication arteries between widely scattered hunter-gatherer populations. The higher ground between the river valleys served as boundary land, sometimes remote, sometimes traversed by narrow trails, often serving as little more than a place where neighbors might hunt and collect wild vegetable foods. In the Archaic Northeast, one can think of these higher lands as buffers between different population concentrations. And these population concentrations were controlled in large part by the carrying capacity of the land during the leanest months of the year.

For thousands of years, prehistoric populations in the Northeast were nearly stable, at levels below the carrying capacity of the land. Population growth was slow. Dean Snow (1980) has estimated that no more than 25,000 people lived in New England before 8000 BC, and only between 158,000 and 191,000 in AD 1600. He calculates an average growth rate of 0.0002 percent over these 9600 years, with occasional periods of rapid increase and sometimes catastrophic decline. In contrast the world population increase rate has been as high as 0.018 percent in recent years. This primeval population spacing lasted for thousands of years, only beginning to break down during the last six centuries before European colonization. By this time, the introduction of new storage technologies and of horticulture had allowed higher population densities in many parts of the Northeast.

After 1650 BC, the Archaic communities of the Northeast enjoyed a diverse, and carefully scheduled, hunting and gathering lifeway. This "Terminal Archaic" spanned 10 centuries, until about 700 BC, a period marked by long-distance trading of chert, soapstone, and other stone materials, and by the widespread use of carved soapstone bowls, also broad and narrow "fishtail" stone projectile points. Many local cultural traditions flourished during this period (for full discussion, see Snow, 1980).

Susquehanna and Orient. The so-called Susquehanna tradition of New York, Pennsylvania, and neighboring areas flourished during the earlier centuries of the Terminal Archaic (c. 1650–1320 BC), a widespread tradition marked by a variety of broad projectile points that may also have doubled as knives. The Susquehanna is more of a tradition of point manufacture than an actual cultural complex.

The Orient replaced the Susquehanna in the New York region and is characterized by long, narrow points with fishtail-shaped bases that persisted in use during later Woodland cultures as well. Oval and rectangular soapstone bowls with flat bottoms and lug handles that appear to have been copies of wooden prototypes came into widespread use, especially in larger base camps, artifacts also used by Susquehanna people. These heavy cooking vessels were apparently highly prized, traded widely, and enjoyed long lives. The use of these heavy vessels foreshadowed pottery manufacture after 700 BC.

Orient fish-tailed point, length c. 11 cm.

Susquehanna and Orient flourished alongside Mast Forest and Lake Forest Archaic societies in many areas, with much human settlement concentrated near rivers and coasts. The millennia-old traditions of cremation continued. There were some population movements from New York and southern New England into more northern areas. These population movements and the population growth that may have attended them are still little understood. William Turnbaugh among others (1975) has invoked a general warming trend and the stabilization of sea levels as possible factors favoring the expansion of Terminal Archaic cultures.

There is strong evidence for general cultural continuity in economic and social life over much of the Northeast from early in Archaic times, if not earlier (Trigger, 1985). Until after AD 800, we have insufficient evidence to argue that there was continuity in native populations as well.

Early Horticultural (Woodland) Societies in the Northeast
c. 700 BC to AD 1000

Dean Snow has coined the term "Early Horticultural" to cover the 1700 years of prehistory immediately following the Terminal Archaic in the Northeast. He argues for the use of this term on the grounds that Early and Middle Woodland are very hard to define. We use it here both for simplicity's sake and also because it highlights the most important cultural innovation during this period – horticulture.

Pottery-making and simple horticulture appeared in many Northeastern societies in the late first millennium BC, but the moment of appearance varied greatly. The overall population of the Northeast may have increased, as well as the number of small bands scattered in territories of widely differing size in river drainages, near lakes, and along sea coasts. The increasing use of pottery may signal a trend toward more sedentary lifestyles over the centuries. Small cooking pots with pointed bases, decorated with stamped and cord-marked patterns and manufactured with simple coiling techniques, were in common use throughout the Great Lakes region by about 500 BC. Further south, in New York State, the Meadowood phase provides strong hints of cultural influences from both earlier and contemporary cultural traditions.

Meadowood Phase (?c.700 BC to ?300 BC). Meadowood sites occur throughout west and central New York State and into the Mohawk drainage to the west. The many Meadowood communities were probably anchored by larger base camps, some of them, perhaps, semi-permanent settlements close to places where goosefoot and other native plants were cultivated. The resulting stores of native seed helped tide the people over the lean months.

There are strong indications that the Adena, and later, Hopewell trade networks extended into parts of the Northeast and into Meadowood country. The Meadowood people fabricated their characteristic points and blade blanks from Western Onondaga chert, also clay imitations of Adena tubular stone pipes. Copper ornaments, slate gorgets, birdstones, and boatstones from Ohio – these and many other grave goods hint at Adena cultural influence that went far beyond simple trade and exchange.

Meadowood cemeteries often cluster on low, natural hills, just like Glacial Kame burials in earlier centuries. The graves were closely packed together, the bodies usually cremated, but not always immediately after death. The mourners lined the burial pits with bark, laying out the cremated remains in red ocher-sprinkled shrouds. Projectile points and luxury items were usually buried with the dead, some of them obtained through trade networks that extended far into the Midwest.

Meadowood phase. Left to right: side-notched projectile point; expanded-base drill; birdstone; and stone gorget. Variable scale.

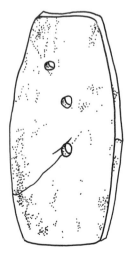

In time, these exchange activities brought Adena mortuary practices from their Ohio homeland to the Northeast, practices reflected in later burial mounds containing Adena-style log-lined graves and characteristic artifacts such as tubular pipes, birdstones, and boatstones. Such tumuli are scattered across southern Ontario, New York, and parts of southern and western New England, also in the Delaware drainage. Gary Wright has argued that a far-flung ideological system sustained later Hopewell exchange networks in the Midwest and far afield. The same may also be true of the Adena mortuary complex, which lasted in parts of the Northeast from the mid-first millennium BC for seven centuries (Snow, 1980).

The centuries between 700 BC and AD 1000 saw a great variety of early horticultural societies developing throughout the Northeast (Snow, 1980). Many of these societies were contemporary with the Hopewell tradition of the Midwest, but Hopewell exchange networks never penetrated far into New England.

In southern New England, early horticultural societies combined cultivation of native plants with hunting, gathering, and shellfish collecting. Their basic adaptation had primeval roots in the Mast Forest Late Archaic of earlier millennia, but there is increasing regional variation after 700 BC. In some areas, winter hunting camps lay close to small streams and ponds in the back country. Shellfish collecting and maize cultivation were important summer activities near the coast. During the Terminal Archaic, ocean temperatures were warmer than today, so the people exploited bay scallops, oysters, and quahogs, shellfish that are sensitive to cold water. In contrast, early horticultural societies lived by colder seas and relied more heavily on the soft clam (*Mya arenaria*) in some areas.

Maine and northern New England societies were using pottery some time before the Christian era, considerably later than peoples to the south. They never became cultivators, remaining hunters, foragers, and shellfish collectors. Some of the coastal populations lived in substantial, semi-subterranean pit dwellings. These oval-shaped houses were between 11.4 and 13.1 ft (3.5 to 4 m) long, with a sunken hearth near the entrance and elevated sleeping benches along the walls. Apparently, they were conical, wigwam or tipi-like structures excavated partially below ground level for additional warmth and insulation (Sanger, 1979). Judging from animal bones, many coastal aboriginal peoples dwelt in pithouse communities for fall, winter, and spring, perhaps moving inland during the summer to take salmon, alewife, shad, and eels from streams and lakes.

The same basic lifeway persisted among a great diversity of Northeast coastal populations in the coastal Northeast up to and beyond European contact in the 16th and 17th centuries AD.

Iroquois Origins

The great 19th-century historian Francis Parkman (1823–1893) devoted his life to chronicling the long conflict between England and France in North America. He interpreted this conflict in purely European terms, for the movements of Indian populations were, he thought, merely aimless migrations across a vast, sparsely inhabited continent (Parkman, 1867).

The Iroquois, Huron, and other American Indian groups in the Northeast were seen as part of a vanishing past, as "more akin to the forests in which they lived and the animals they hunted as competitors for control of North America" (Trigger, 1985).

Theories. It was anthropologists who first became interested in the origins of the Iroquois speakers of the St Lawrence lowlands. There was no archaeological data on the early Iroquois, so they relied on oral traditions and linguistic connections for tracing their origins (for a history of research, see Trigger, 1985). Originally, they believed the St Lawrence Valley was the homeland of all Iroquoian-speaking people, but these and related theories were abandoned about three-quarters-of-a-century ago, with the discovery of archaeological sites quite different from those of historical Iroquois groups.

At the same time, linguists found close ties between Iroquois and Cherokee, the language spoken in the southern Appalachian region of the southeastern United States. This led to an influential theory that had the Iroquois arriving in their northern homeland from the south (Parker, 1916). This hypothesis persisted for generations, despite the discovery of early Iroquois societies with strong Algonquian features. Instead of arguing that these attributes were the result of an indigenous origin, scholars assumed they were modifications resulting from contact between invading Iroquois and indigenous Algonquian cultures.

It was not until the late 1930s that archaeologists began to speculate that Iroquoian culture might have developed among a population already living in the Northeast. No ancestral version of Iroquois culture was known from the Southeast, nor were there any signs of their northward migration in the Ohio Valley. It was Richard MacNeish who formally rejected the migration theory in a classic monograph published in 1952. He examined historical Iroquois pottery and traced its origins far back into prehistoric times, to the local Middle Woodland societies that archaeologists had hitherto assumed to be those of Algonquian speakers. MacNeish stressed local lines of development, an approach that has led to complex studies of evolving Iroquois settlement patterns, changing subsistence strategies, and burial practices (Trigger, 1985).

Recent, almost total, excavations of the Draper and Nodwell Iroquois settlements in Ontario have documented the remarkable diversity of Iroquois culture, changing subsistence patterns, and social organization (J. Wright, 1974; Finlayson, 1985; Warrick, 1984). There is now widespread agreement that Iroquois-speaking cultures have local roots deep in prehistoric times – the problem is to identify them in the archaeological record.

Middle Woodland and Iroquois Origins. At least three broadly contemporary Middle Woodland cultures flourished in the St Lawrence lowlands during the first millennium AD, each defined by differing artifact and pottery styles. Each of these cultures was the work of several neighboring bands. They interacted with one another, but it is not clear just how ethnically distinct they were. The Laurel culture flourished in northern Ontario, parts of Manitoba, Michigan, and Minnesota (J. Wright, 1967), the Saugeen in southwestern Ontario. The best known is the Point Peninsula culture of central and eastern southern Ontario, with variants in southern Quebec and upper New York State. All are variations on the same adaptive theme.

There was a general continuity in subsistence and social life in the St Lawrence lowlands from as early as Paleo-Indian times right up to the historic era. These three Middle Woodland cultures reflect this continuity, with a small, and widely scattered, indigenous population living in small bands, each with their own territory. The people were exploiting game, aquatic, and plant resources ever more efficiently, and some groups may even have been cultivating native plants. (The earliest record of maize is in about the seventh century AD (Trigger, 1985).)

During spring and summer, these small groups would congregate into larger concentrations of between 100 and 300 people at river- and lake-side fishing stations. These were the times when important burial ceremonies took place in cemeteries close to the fishing camps, when marriages were held, ceremonies enjoyed, exotic artifacts and raw materials exchanged. At Rice Lake in southern Ontario, important leaders were buried under earthen mounds with Hopewellian artifacts, probably obtained from Hopewell exchange networks for silver nuggets brought to the lake from northern Ontario (Spence, 1982).

This annual pattern of establishing friendly ties with neighbors was adaptive, in that it ensured that hunting, fishing, and foraging were not disrupted by warfare. It also made it possible for people to shift from one band to another as populations rose and fell, but it is uncertain whether men or women remained with their home bands upon marriage (Trigger, 1985). The climate was so harsh that there was never a sufficiency of food resources in one area to allow year-round, sedentary settlement. So the congregated bands had to scatter into small family groups during the long winter months to hunt forest game.

The historic Algonquians of central Ontario enjoyed such an annual coming together. There were chiefs among them, often hereditary leaders from certain families, who were without formal political power, yet able to resolve conflicts during the summer months when tiny bands became a concentrated population of more than 100 people (Cleland, 1982). Perhaps the Middle Woodland peoples of southern Ontario had similar chiefs, the antecedents of the peace chiefs who were to emerge among later Iroquois groups (Trigger, 1985).

Thanks to MacNeish's pioneer work, most archaeologists assume that Iroquois-speaking people have lived around the lower Great Lakes for a long time. James Tuck (1977), James Wright (1984), and others believe the Iroquoians go back to Archaic times, and had their origins among societies which flourished before 2000 BC. Others argue that the arrival of the Iroquoians coincides with the earliest appearance of the Late Archaic Lamoka culture in New York State, in at least 2500 BC, a culture, which, as we have seen, has ties in common with Archaic cultures in the Southeast (Haviland and Power, 1981). Dean Snow believes (1980) that the Iroquois arrived with the Terminal Archaic Lake Frost Island culture, the ancestor, he says, of both the Meadowood and Peninsula Point Middle Woodland cultures. Whatever the minor disagreements, there appears to be general consensus that the Iroquois appear in the archaeological record of the Northeast at least as early as the Middle Woodland, perhaps earlier.

Language. Linguistic research has come a long way since the pioneer days of the late 19th century. In recent years, both Cherokee and Iroquois languages have been subjected to intense scrutiny, and are believed to have separated from one another between 2000 and 1500 BC, during the Archaic (Lounsbury, 1978). The same authority believes that Iroquois speakers lived for a long time in central New York, north-central Pennsylvania, and perhaps northeastern Ohio. Then some groups spread south, and to the immediate north and west.

Complex lexical studies of Iroquoian have isolated a whole series of clues that place these languages in an environmental setting very similar to that of the northeastern Eastern Woodlands today, while skeletons from as early as Middle Woodland times display anatomical features very similar to those of historic populations (Molto, 1983). Earlier migration theories thought of the Iroquois as possessing a very different, horticultural culture quite unlike that of the indigenous Algonquian hunter-gatherers (Parker, 1916). Current hypotheses envisage small migrating groups of Iroquois-speaking newcomers who spread northward into the St Lawrence lowlands from the south, during the late Middle Woodland period, perhaps earlier. These immigrants enjoyed much the same form of culture as the indigenous Algonquians. It was only after they settled in their new homelands, bringing some cultural innovations with them, as well as a widely adopted language, that the distinctive features of the Iroquois lifeway developed (Trigger, 1985).

Early Iroquois
AD 1000 to 1300

Around AD 1000, warmer climatic conditions pertained in northern latitudes. As we saw in Chapter 1, it was these conditions that brought the Norsemen across chilly seas to Iceland, Greenland, and to Labrador. The growing season for both crops and wild plants was now longer. This may have attracted population movement from the south into hitherto uncultivable areas like the St Lawrence Valley. The six centuries that followed were ones of profound political and economic change, of slowly rising population densities and intense conflict.

For thousands of years, Northeastern populations had been centered on major lakes, estuaries, and waterways. Canoes and water travel were still important, but farmers now made increasing use of overland trails that connected tracts of cleared land and large villages (Snow, 1980). These were the centuries, too, when the Iroquois moved into the lower St Lawrence Valley, where Europeans were to encounter them in the 16th century.

Princess Point and Glen Meyer. The earliest signs of this Iroquoian culture appear in southwestern Ontario, represented by the Princess Point and Glen Meyer cultures. The dating of these two cultures is still uncertain, but some Princess Point sites are as early as AD 800, if not earlier, and Glen Meyer may be some two centuries later (Trigger, 1985). Early Princess Point summer camps were located on river flats, by sheltered inlets or tributary streams, uncomfortable places in winter and frequently inun-

Princess Point typical cord-decorated potsherd rims.

dated in spring. The Iroquoians may have grown maize and fished at these sites during the warm months, dispersing to hunt during the winter (Stothers, 1977).

Early Iroquois summer villages may have held between 100 and 400 people, families living in small, multi-family dwellings with hearths arranged down the center. These houses appear to have been rebuilt many times, with families living on either side of the hearths. Such dwellings were nothing new, for they are known to have been constructed back in Middle Woodland times (Brose, 1970).

Maize itself appears to have spread north from the Midwest some time in the mid-first millennium AD – the exact date of its arrival is uncertain. Despite the introduction of this important new staple, the general pattern of Iroquois life remained basically unchanged, with the people remaining in one place during the growing season. Perhaps the new food surpluses generated by farming allowed the people to remain in their summer settlements much later into the fall. Initially, the new crop may have served as a valuable supplemental food to wild plants or dried fish, for the stored grain could help reduce the risk of starvation during the harsh winter months. Furthermore, maize could be planted in areas near summer fishing camps where nut trees did not grow, and wild rice never flourished. Thus, it added a new, reliable dimension to Iroquois diet.

Princess Point and Glen Meyer were, in many respects, a continuation of Middle Woodland hunter-gatherer life, with the addition of maize agriculture. And if these bands were still exogamous, the custom of marrying outside the band would have resulted in the rapid spread of both maize horticulture and pottery-making from one group to the next (Trigger, 1985).

Owasco. To the south, in the Mohawk drainage and Finger Lakes region of upper New York State, the Owasco tradition emerged at about the same time, a very similar culture of small, loosely related communities of Iroquois people. But already there were signs of considerable cultural diversification and of more nucleated settlements. For example, the Maxon-Derby site near Syracuse, NY, lies on the terrace of a large stream and covers about 2.4 acres (1 ha) (Ritchie and Funk, 1973). Seven houses were excavated, one of them almost square, others more elongated, one an oblong dwelling measuring 26 by 59 ft (8 by 18 m). House design was far

Maxon-Derby site, New York State: eastern end of House C, with wooden markers indicating outlines of the structure.

from standardized, but evolving toward the well-known Iroquois long house design that was used everywhere in later centuries.

Early Owasco summer settlements were used for many months, but by AD 1200 earthworks and palisades protect some villages, such as the Sackett site near Canandaigua. There the ditch and palisade enclose an elliptical area 203 by 242 ft (62 by 74 m) (Ritchie and Funk, 1973). By 1250 most major villages were palisaded, and maize, beans, and squash cultivation had assumed major importance in the subsistence economy. It is interesting to find a much higher incidence of tooth decay among Owasco populations at about this time, perhaps as a result of a higher carbohydrate content in the diet.

The fortified villages and increasing importance of overland trails coincide with the emergence of warfare and an important element in Iroquois life. Owasco cemeteries have yielded skeletons riddled with arrow points, while scattered human bones have come from village middens. No longer were the dead buried under mounds. Most people were deposited in cemeteries, fully clothed with few, if any, grave goods, for a trend toward less elaborate burial ceremonies had begun centuries earlier.

Middle Iroquoian
AD 1300 to 1350 or later

Throughout the Early Iroquoian period, most communities still only numbered a few hundred souls at the most favorable times of the year, just as they had done in Middle Woodland times. Some of the people, especially the elderly, may have lived in the same settlements year-round, but society was still organized in bands in the form of localized matrilineal clans. Each band had its own leader, was exogamous, and identified with a group of totemic animals. Intermarriage was an important way of cementing good relations with neighbors, but by the same token, there appears to have been little long-distance exchange of ceremonial goods, perhaps a reflection of less flamboyant burial customs (Trigger, 1985). Biologically, the southern Ontario Iroquois population was very homogeneous before AD 1350, as if there was considerable movement between one group and another. Since there is considerable pottery diversity over this area during these centuries and women are the potters, each community may have been matrilineal, with the men taking up residence with their wives and their kin after marriage.

Although we still know little about the rate of cultural change in Early Iroquoian times, there is good reason to believe that maize agriculture assumed increasing importance in Iroquois culture as time went on, either because of the introduction of better strains or because of rising population densities (Trigger, 1985). Maize agriculture may have been one of the factors behind the dramatic changes in Iroquoian life throughout the St Lawrence lowlands and in the Mohawk drainage during the 14th century.

The Middle Iroquois period may have lasted only a half-century or so, between AD 1300 and 1350, although some believe it lasted longer (Trigger, 1985; Wright, 1966). Apparently, it began first in southwestern Ontario, the cultural transitions spreading rapidly eastward to Iroquois groups to the east. This half-century or more saw the Iroquois living in much larger communities and becoming heavily dependent on maize farming. For example, two or three Glen Meyer communities near London, Ontario, now joined into a single, large settlement along a creek. Here they were much further away from productive acorn forests, but close to heavier soils that were hard to cultivate but less vulnerable to drought conditions (Pearce, 1984).

Some of the largest Middle Iroquois settlements now covered more than 4.9 acres (2 ha). More families lived in the same dwelling, longer houses that were built closer together and sometimes parallel to one another in groups. Perhaps these groupings coincided with related matrilineages or individual clans. Placing long houses closer together may have been a labor-saving device to reduce the amount of palisading needed to protect larger villages (Noble, 1969). By 1400, some of the largest Iroquois settlements regularly housed as many as 1500 people, with far more elaborate village plans, large work areas, and even garbage disposal zones (Warrick, 1984).

But larger settlements brought new pressures to Iroquois society. A community of 1500 people consumed enormous quantities of firewood, to say nothing of construction lumber. Agricultural land was soon cleared and exhausted, so these large settlements had to shift location more frequently than smaller ones. The men spent more and more time clearing land or in communal construction work. Nevertheless, a few Iroquois settlements achieved populations of more than 2000 people, about six clan groups. But factionalism may have strained dispute-resolving mechanisms to the limit and prevented large villages from lasting long. The largest known settlement is the Draper site in Ontario, which covered 19.76 acres (8 ha) and housed between 2000 and 3000 people for a few decades in the 15th century (Trigger, 1985).

Changes in the Social Order. These larger villages may have resulted from clusters of scattered communities coming together, perhaps for mutual protection. As these settlements developed, hitherto dispersed clans came into much closer proximity, with a much greater potential for serious disputes, factional quarrels, and other disruptions. Bruce Trigger (1985)

Artist's reconstruction of the Draper village, Ontario, at its largest.

believes the Iroquois now instituted more formal village councils made up of representatives from each clan. Among the historic Iroquois, these offices were hereditary among individual families in each clan. Just as among historic tribes in the Southeast, there may have been separate chiefs (*sachems*) for war and peace.

Peace chiefs kept a pulse on public opinion, settled domestic disputes, organized community works, rituals and ceremonies, and negotiated with others. War chiefs had more limited powers. They organized and led war parties, dealt with prisoners, and killed suspected witches. Both offices were sources of prestige rather than power, for no chief had the authority to do anything more than act as a spokesman. His family had to work hard to provide the additional food that enabled him to extend hospitality to other people in the village and to strangers. Since there was no fixed law of primogeniture, relatives would compete with one another for the succession, vying to prove their prowess as generous hosts, brave warriors, and expert hunters (Trigger, 1969). Among Iroquois groups living north of Lake Ontario, the solidarity of each community was now celebrated with the elaborate Feast of the Dead, a ceremonial reburial of those who had died while a village was inhabited carried out before the settlement was moved to a new location.

Warfare and Cannibalism. Warfare became an important factor in Iroquois life during the 14th century. Many communities were now elaborately fortified, but others were still undefended, close to navigable waters, not away from them as became the rule in later, more turbulent, centuries. But cannibalism appears for the first time – in the form of split, cut, and cooked human bones found in Iroquoian sites throughout southern Ontario (Wright, 1966).

The consumption of human flesh was not a matter of obtaining extra protein, but an intensely symbolic act. Among the Aztecs and other Mexican civilizations, prisoners of war were sacrificed in elaborate public ceremonies, on altars located on high places. The victim was stretched across the altar, his heart ripped out in view of the sun, the body tumbled down the pyramid, dismembered, and parts consumed in private rituals (Fagan, 1984). This symbolic act, the ritual of human sacrifice and the consumption of human flesh, may have diffused north from Mexico, just as maize and other crops did (Trigger, 1969). In time, the idea of this kind of ceremony reached the northern Iroquois. They waged war, at least in theory, to avenge the killing of kinsfolk by outsiders. The warriors would capture someone from the group who did the killing as a replacement for the victim. Or they would kill him, bringing his head or scalp home as a trophy. Male prisoners were often slain in elaborate sacrifices to the sun, women and children usually permitted to live.

Why did warfare suddenly assume such importance after 1300? Some theories argue that cooler and drier climatic conditions now led to more frequent droughts and food shortages, so that Iroquois groups living on the sand plains of southwestern Ontario and on New York's cool Allegheny Plateau may have moved away from their homelands in search of moister, more fertile soils. The result may have been more competition for prime farming land and other strategic resources (Warrick, 1984). However, population densities among the Iroquois were still low and there was more agricultural land available than people to occupy and cultivate it. Neighboring groups could have fought over hunting rights, but why go to war over deer, when the game population may have, in fact, increased with so much cleared agricultural land to graze on?

Perhaps warfare was closely connected with the quest for personal prestige (Trigger, 1985). As time went on, the basic tasks of hunting, fishing, and forest clearance, once great tests of a man's ability to support his family through the winter, became more collective tasks carried out by larger groups. Individual resource and prestige had once come from skill in the chase, but now this activity was no longer a way of acquiring individual prestige. Women, as the farmers, were now accounting for more food and were the dominant social lineages. Thus, men had to prove themselves and their worth. John Witthoft (1959) believes that warfare replaced successful food getting as the avenue to male prestige. Disputes between neighboring groups may have proliferated as the young men sought every excuse to wage war – perhaps to the point that every community had some enemies.

Bruce Trigger develops the Witthoft theory still further. Perhaps, he argues, this led to a situation where some neighboring villages combined for self defense, resulting in much larger settlements. Fortified Middle Iroquois communities may have first developed in western Iroquois country, where the people had long fought with the Central Algonquians, then come into use over the entire region, resulting in major changes in local society. For generations, the Iroquois had maintained close ties between scattered communities by men or women marrying into neighboring villages. With larger settlements, the need for such marriage customs was reduced, so the ties were severed, ties that helped reduce conflict between neighbors. About the only alternative was to settle disputes by force.

Horticulture, especially maize agriculture, assumed ever greater importance in prehistoric Iroquois life. Much agriculture is women's work, and larger communities depended heavily on their crops. Perhaps the men felt threatened, and turned to warfare as a means, not only of acquiring prestige, but also captives, who were sacrificed to the sun, the symbol of fertility and life. Thus, argues Trigger, the men assumed a prestigious role in a society that was becoming more and more sedentary and agricultural.

The Emergence of Tribes. After 1400, differences in pottery styles, burial practices, and house types chronicle major divisions between Iroquois groups living north of Lakes Ontario and Erie, while other archaeological "cultures" now define groups ancestral to historic tribes to the south. For example, between 1450 and 1475, a small and a much larger village near Syracuse, New York, deliberately settled within a few miles of one another to form the Onondaga nation. James Tuck was able to show that the larger village had itself been formed by the amalgamation of two smaller ones (Tuck, 1971). Similar fusions took place all over Iroquois country, with relatively dense local populations clustering in specific areas, separated from one another by largely uninhabited country. Periodic population movements and regroupings were much more frequent in Ontario to the north, perhaps because the people lived in environments close to the northern limits of large-scale maize cultivation and sedentary settlement was much harder.

These new tribal grouping resulted in greater social complexity in Iroquois life. Tribal councils emerged as an extension of village ones, designed to regulate life on a larger scale. Complex clan ties cut across village and tribal boundaries, clans identified by their totemic animals (Fenton, 1978). Among the historic Iroquois, some of these clans grouped themselves into associations, phratries, that organized much of ceremonial life, including funerals. There were medicine societies, too, societies that cured the sick and carried out curing rituals. All these complex mechanisms helped maintain links between expanding, and increasingly complex, Iroquois societies.

Why did large Iroquois settlements and tribes form? Some large communities may have controlled important resources and exchange networks. But warfare may have been the major factor in forging large communities and political alliances. And when a village reached its maximum practicable size, the inhabitants expanded into new communities, forming confederacies, tribes, and other associations. These settlement clusters depleted natural food resources more rapidly, making the people more dependent on horticulture. The constant political maneuvering and warfare led to more elaborate fortifications in the 16th century, villages with multiple palisades, earthworks, and massive tree-trunk ramparts.

Late Iroquoian
AD 1400 to European contact and later

Sometime before the end of the 16th century, neighboring Iroquois tribes in both Ontario and New York came together in loosely knit, larger associations, confederacies aimed at reducing blood feuding and warfare between close neighbors. The common link between them was an agreement to settle grievances by other means than bloodshed. A confederacy council of headmen from member tribes gathered occasionally for ceremonial feasts, conferences, and to adjudicate disputes and set reparation payments if called for. At European contact, the major Iroquois tribes were the Huron, Erie, Tobacco, and Neutral in the north, and, to the south, the famous League of the Iroquois, made up of the Five Nations: Seneca, Cayuga, Onondaga, Oneida, and Mohawk.

When did the Iroquois League and other confederacies come into being? Some scholars believe that they were the result of external pressures caused by the arrival of Europeans, that they were the way in which the Iroquois resisted the foreigners and traded effectively with them (Tooker, 1964). These confederacies were then further strengthened by the fur trade.

In fact, they probably formed many generations earlier. The Iroquois confederacies were made up of people who enjoyed similar culture and language, and used the same political institutions. Under such circumstances, confederacies may well have been adaptive, unlike historically known alliances between quite different groups with no cultural ties that sometimes formed to resist European encroachment in other areas, only to fall apart shortly afterward. Bruce Trigger (1976) believes that the Iroquois

Map showing Iroquois groups in historical times.

Iroquois 18th-century wampum belt. Location unknown

confederacies were a logical extension of complex, long-term forces that had much earlier replaced small hunting bands with larger groups, then with tribes. The confederacy was adaptive in that it allowed groups to legislate against unnecessary blood feuding, while still maintaining individual cultural and political identity in their dealings with others. The arrival of Europeans and their fur traders created a new, highly volatile political situation, in which it was clearly an advantage for neighbors to be linked in close alliances. Since the Iroquois already enjoyed confederacies, it would have been an easy matter to strengthen them in response to new circumstances.

For generations after the Iroquois League was formed, the Five Nations were greatly feared by the Huron and the Algonquin. The Iroquois themselves symbolized their League as a vast long house that stretched from west to east. The Seneca were the "Keepers of the Western Door," the Mohawk the "Keepers of the Eastern Door." The Onondaga were in the center, the "Keepers of the Council Fire." They were also "Keepers of the Wampum Belts" (for a full description of the League, see Tooker, 1978).

Both the Iroquois and the Algonquians of the Northeast strung white and purple or black shells into strands and complex belts named after the Algonquian word "wampum." The woven dark and white designs on these belts symbolized all manner of transactions – major events, treaties, and agreements. One Onondaga chief kept the treaty wampum for the Five Nations. It was he who knew the patterns and what they meant. Eventually wampum became a form of currency when Europeans arrived, but the beads were hard to manufacture even with iron drills and were soon replaced with cheap glass trade beads from overseas.

At European contact, all Iroquois-speaking peoples depended heavily on horticulture, with fishing also a vital part of the subsistence economy. Among the Huron of the north and the Seneca, horticulture – corn, beans, squash, and sunflowers – may have provided up to 80 percent of the diet. The northern Iroquois lived in fortified villages, in elm tree bark-covered long houses shared by many families. They dwelt on either side of the central hearths. Unlike the Algonquians, the Iroquois were matrilineal, with the children living with their mother's clan. Each long house group was a subdivision of the matrilineal clan, for sisters with their husbands and children shared a common dwelling. The men, who cleared the land, hunted, fished, traded, and built houses and fortifications, were warriors, and moved into the long houses of their wives at marriage. The women grew, weeded, and harvested crops, and tended the children.

With its confederacies and tribes, Iroquois society was governed highly effectively. Their political organizations seem precarious, based as they were on decisions made by a network of tribal and community councils, in situations where consent was needed on the part of all concerned. But, in fact, they were highly effective in suppressing blood feuds among populations numbering as many as 20,000 souls, and at coordinating at least a degree of diplomatic policy toward outsiders.

The northern Iroquois were unified by many common religious beliefs and ceremonial practices. But above all they were remarkable not for their material culture, but for the sophistication and finesse of social

Smoking a native tobacco in a zoomorphic pipe. Reconstruction of Iroquois life at the Keffer site, Ontario.

relationships. The Iroquois respected individual dignity and self-reliance. They looked down on public displays of emotion or open quarrelling, considered politeness and hospitality toward one another and toward strangers fundamental to correct social behavior. As later events were to show, these warlike and astute people were more than a match for the European fur traders and missionaries who settled among them.

In the year 1534, French master mariner Jacques Cartier sailed past Newfoundland and up the great St Lawrence River. Bad weather had his ships taking shelter in Gaspe Bay at the mouth of the river, where he encountered about 300 men, women, and children (Trigger, 1976). They wore only skins and loin cloths, fisherfolk with few possessions. The men shaved their heads except for a topknot tied into a knot with leather thongs. Cartier was unimpressed with what he called the "sorriest people in the world," people who had no furs to trade. But the French took the trouble to compile a word list, the earliest record of Iroquois language ever made. From this moment on, the Iroquois were destined to undergo catastrophic cultural change, as a result of economic factors operating far over the eastern horizons of the Atlantic, in distant Europe.

Further Reading

Snow, Dean. 1980. *The Archaeology of New England*. Academic Press, New York.
  This comprehensive survey is now somewhat dated, but still laden with good data and original ideas.
Trigger, Bruce. 1972. *The Children of Aataentsic: A History of the Huron People to 1660*. 2 vols. McGill-Queen's University Press, Kingston and Montreal.
  — 1985. *Natives and Newcomers*. McGill-Queen's University Press, Kingston and Montreal.
  Bruce Trigger's elegant and thorough studies are definitive accounts of Iroquoian archaeology and history. The serious reader need look no further for authoritative analysis.
Tuck, J.A. 1971. *Onondaga Iroquois Prehistory*. Syracuse University Press, Syracuse, NY.
  A thorough study of changing settlement patterns in late Northeastern prehistory.

PART SEVEN

AFTER COLUMBUS

"It is terribly important that the 'small things forgotten' be remembered. For in the seemingly little and insignificant things that accumulate to create a lifetime, the essence of our existence is captured . . ."

JAMES DEETZ, *In Small Things Forgotten*, 1977

CHAPTER 22

THE ARCHAEOLOGY OF EUROPEAN CONTACT

For more than 12,000 years the native Americans occupied the vast tracts of North America undisturbed. During these long millennia, they developed a huge diversity of responses to a bewildering array of natural environments. The trajectory of cultural change through these millennia was usually gradual, sometimes dramatically rapid, as was the case, for example, when maize and bean cultivation took hold in the Southeast. But the momentum of continual change, of fine-tuned cultural adaptation, was never disrupted. Then, in the year 1492, Christopher Columbus landed in the Indies. Now began the last, and perhaps least understood, chapter of native American history – five centuries of catastrophic and disruptive cultural change in the face of an inexorable European presence.

Until recently, surprisingly few archaeologists had paid attention to this important period of native American history, a period that lies, for the most part, outside comprehensive documentary records. When such records are available, they are concerned almost entirely with European affairs, the indigenous people merely serving as a backdrop for events considered important in Western minds. It is only recently that the full potential of archaeology as a source of historical information during the contact period has come to the fore. This interest has been furthered in response to the Columbus Quincentennial (Thomas, 1989), and also because of a growing realization that excavated evidence provides a unique window into the daily lives of everyday people, who are often as anonymous in the historical record as their predecessors are in the prehistoric (Bass, 1988; Baudry, 1987; Deetz, 1977; Nöel Hume, 1969).

Archaeology offers the best chance for students of the past to examine cultural change in all societies, whether simple or complex, over long periods of time. Of no period of North American prehistory is this more true than of the 15th to 18th centuries AD, when the full impact of European contact fell upon indigenous society. Any form of cultural contact, however fleeting, is a two-way process, with often lasting impacts on both cultures involved (for a useful discussion, see Trigger, 1985). The European perspective on the exploration and settlement of North America is relatively well documented, but the effects of these developments on native American societies of the day are still little understood. This subject is, of course, an enormous one, and we can but summarize some of the major issues here. They revolve around a set of interconnected, fundamental questions. First, what was the effect of exotic European infectious diseases introduced at

(Opposite) Excavations in progress at the Santa Catalina de Guale mission church, St Catherine's Island, Georgia. This project, directed by David Hurst Thomas of the American Museum of Natural History, has been one of the major recent field projects in post-contact North American archaeology. See pages 445-447.

Sites of the eastern United States referred to in this chapter.

contact on the indigenous population? Second, what were the short- and long-term results of direct and indirect contacts between European and native American cultures, in material, social, and political terms?

The Issue of Disease and Depopulation

No one knows exactly when a European infected with smallpox or another exotic disease first landed in North America. Some very early explorers may have carried the disease and infected some local, isolated populations, but the epidemics may have died out without infecting wide areas. Whenever infectious diseases did arrive, the effects on the native American population were devastating.

Why were there no New World counterparts for European diseases? Perhaps the parasites were killed off by arctic temperatures as tiny founder populations migrated into the New World thousands of years ago. More likely, primeval population densities were too low. The survival of acute diseases depends on sustained contact between infected individuals, such as occurs in densely populated, sedentary settlements. North America, and even to some extent Mesoamerica, lacked the densely packed, urban settlements of the Old World. It was there that bacterial and viral diseases became fixed in urban populations.

In epidemiological terms the turning point was 1519, when a Spanish conquistador infected with smallpox landed at Vera Cruz, Mexico. The conquistadors had some immunity to the disease, but the Indians did not. In months, smallpox spread like wildfire from the coast to the highlands. The first pandemic hit the Aztec capital in 1520. Indians died by the thousand. Other unfamiliar diseases, including influenza, measles, and typhus, ravaged the Mexican population during the next century. The population of Mexico has been estimated at 11 million in 1519. A mere 20 years later, it was under 6.5 million, by 1607 less than a fifth of that of a century earlier. Similar massive demographic catastrophes occurred throughout the Americas. For example, more than 310,000 Indians lived in California at the time of Spanish colonization in 1769. Coastal populations fell from about 72,000 to 18,000 by 1830. By 1900, the total number of California Indians was 20,000, less than 7 percent of the pre-contact population (Cook, 1978).

The nature and timing of Indian population declines has sparked great controversy among historians, anthropologists, and prehistorians, a debate that focuses on three fundamental issues. First, how large was the human population of North America at contact, and how great was the subsequent decline? Second, when exactly did the decline take place relative to the first census counts? Third, what role did infectious diseases play in the decline?

The great Berkeley anthropologist Alfred Kroeber and others argued that exotic diseases played a relatively minor role in the early decades after contact. But they agreed that aboriginal populations declined after *sustained* European contact. Under this rubric, the earliest historical census counts do not represent decimated populations. Thus, North American Indian populations were relatively small at contact, Kroeber (1939) estimating a figure of about 0.9 million people. This was a static view of such cultures at contact, the so-called "Ethnographic Present."

In contrast anthropologist Henry Dobyns (1983) and historical demographers Sherborne Cook and William Borah (1976) assume that infectious diseases attacked even isolated populations decades, if not centuries, *before* actual physical contact between Europeans and Indians and before historical records began. Thus, even the earliest post-contact census counts reflect populations reduced by as much as 95 percent from pre-contact highs. This has led Dobyns (1983) to propose North American population figures as high as 18 million, a dramatic contrast to the very conservative Kroeber figure.

Archaeologist Ann Ramenofsky (1987) has recently evaluated these two contrasting approaches using archaeological evidence. Ramenofsky points out that both new multi-disciplinary researches and a much more complete archaeological record than that at Kroeber's disposal show beyond all reasonable doubt that there was constant cultural change not only throughout prehistoric times, but over the critical centuries of European contact as well. Thus, she argues, patterns of archaeological change in populations can be evaluated independently of ethnographic or historical records. This is important, for such attempts as have been made to develop population estimates have been based invariably on modern analogues, so that conservative figures based on some form of "ethnographic present" come into play. It is hardly surprising, then, that population estimates have been conservative.

Ramenofsky has measured population change by using comprehensive settlement data, data that is completely independent of ethnographic and historical records. She examined a single, testable archaeological hypothesis: "Did native Americans experience a population collapse immediately following contact with Europeans, but predating written records and sustained colonization?" Her study is based on three regions: the lower Mississippi Valley, central New York, and the middle Missouri Valley. Although she had to contend with sampling biases, a lack of quantitative data on house or settlement size, and gaps in regional coverage, she was able to discern some general patterns of considerable significance. In the lower Mississippi Valley, both historical and independent archaeological data identified an unambiguous and precipitous decline of aboriginal populations in the 16th century – after the De Soto expedition and before the French colonized the valley in the late 17th century.

The New York data came from the Finger Lakes region, the area inhabited by the Five Nations of the Iroquois at the beginning of the historic period. Had Iroquois populations and cultural systems remained constant right up to the American Revolution or had epidemics radically altered Iroquois society in the 16th or 17th centuries? Ramenofsky's calculations of settlement area and house roof area suggest that the Indian population was considerably reduced by the 17th century, but the exact date of the decline is in doubt. Historical descriptions of Iroquois society support and extend the archaeological record of collapse in these centuries with their chronicles of drastically reorganized settlements and the final breakdown of multi-family dwellings and fortified settlements. Historical descriptions of the Five Nations are those of populations developing new adaptive strategies, partly as a result of diminishing numbers.

The middle Missouri Valley sample was from the Northern Plains area, where European contact began in 1540 and colonization in the 18th century. Did exotic diseases cause catastrophic depopulation with colonization or during the two preceding centuries? Again, the archaeological data, mostly from large river basin surveys, was sufficient to reject the 18th-century hypothesis. Ramenofsky's settlement calculations suggest a decline at least a century earlier, perhaps coinciding with the appearance of European trade goods in the region. But again, the data are ambiguous as to the exact timing of the population loss, which may have occurred as early as the 16th century, before any significant numbers of trade goods appeared in the area.

In all three areas, archaeological data tend to confirm Dobyns' theory, derived from other sources, that demographic catastrophe *preceded* the major influx of Europeans by decades, perhaps in some areas by centuries. Ramenofsky estimates the pre-contact native American population of North America at about 12 million, a more conservative figure than Dobyns, but much higher than that espoused by Kroeber and his contemporaries.

Any study of cultural change among American Indian societies after European contact must be undertaken against a background of massive population decline that persisted in some areas until the 19th century. From the anthropological and archaeological point of view, these declines are important in that they confirm that the so-called "ethnographic present," the carefully compiled record of native American society after contact, is not necessarily a close mirror of pre-contact society. All of these societies, whether or not they had sustained physical contact with Europeans, had already undergone major change and readjustment long before they were studied by modern scientists. These changes are only now being studied closely by archaeologists.

The Onondaga of the Five Nations: Continuous Redefinition of Culture

In 1535, Jacques Cartier wintered on the banks of the St Lawrence River, and sustained contact between European and American Indians began in the Northeast for the first time. This contact was fueled in large part by the profits to be derived from the international fur trade. A century later, this relationship emerges into the full light of history, by which time both local European and Indian society had changed considerably (for a brilliant analysis, see Trigger, 1976; 1985).

The overall thrust of events is well known, but many details of the changes undergone by Iroquois society are a mystery. James Bradley (1987) has studied the Onondaga, the group who emerged as the core of the Five Nations confederacy in the 17th century. For a start, the degree of influence was not necessarily even. For instance, at first the cultural patterns of the French colonists were shaped more strongly by their Iroquois neighbors than the other way round. The Onondaga's response to the French was that of a society that was perfectly capable of coming to terms with European culture.

The Onondaga's first response to Europeans was within the context of their existing cultural beliefs and values. They craved iron axes, for example, but viewed them from their own cultural perspectives. The people were selective in their response to European culture. They chose exotic artifacts for both ideological and utilitarian reasons. For at least 3500 years, they had acquired a series of indigenous, rarely occurring substances such as sea shell, native copper, and other raw materials, associated with life-enhancing, life-restorative "power" (Bradley, 1987). Initially, the Onondaga may have thought of Europeans as alien beings, as the traditional keepers of these powerful substances. The French often bartered mirrors, metal objects, and glass beads and other baubles, artifacts that tended to reinforce the perception of them as people from another world. The few European artifacts found on proto-historic Onondaga sites are restricted to a few categories – copper sheet, iron objects, and glass beads. These substitutes for earlier exotica appear to have become the substances of "power" during the 16th century.

During the late 16th and early 17th centuries, the ideological basis for Onondaga selection waned, as utilitarian preferences came to the fore. This may have been due to greater availability of European artifacts, to the point that they lost value and prestige. Ideological considerations were still important, for there is reason to believe that the categories of artifact with "power" associations were expanded to include new categories such as glazed ceramics and glassware. After the founding of a Jesuit mission in 1655, Christian symbols such as rings, medals, rosary beads, and other artifacts entered the spiritual arena.

By the late 16th century the Onondaga were using European copper and iron for many more utilitarian artifacts, using and re-using them until they were completely worn out. Iroquois sites of the 16th and 17th centuries contain both copper kettles and iron axes, artifacts sought not necessarily as objects, but also as sources of raw materials. Onondaga metalworkers then used these materials to fashion traditional Onondaga artifacts. Thus, the initial impact of European goods was conservative, not revolutionary, for the way in which they were used promoted traditional cultural patterns, not their change. European materials were accepted, not because they were

The recycling of a copper kettle by the Onondaga: (a) the iron handle is removed and ground into an awl; (b) heavier gauge material from the lug is scored and cut into triangular projectile points. At the same time, sheet metal from the body of the kettle is turned into (c) a knife blade; (d) a tubular bead; (e, f) a conical bangle or pipe bowl liner; and (g) a pendant.

superior, but because they made sense in an opportunistic, flexible culture both in spiritual and utilitarian terms (Fenton, 1978).

The Onondaga's response to their first century of exposure to European culture was one of continuity as much as change, the change being gradual rather than catastrophic in nature. In the case of the Onondaga, and many other societies, Bradley believes that the first evidence of cross-cultural change will be in areas of a culture where it is most useful and least threatening to the existing cultural order.

Despite smallpox epidemics and other disruptions, the Onondaga still retained their basic cultural values and beliefs in the mid-17th century, living in a culture where European artifacts and materials had been grafted onto traditional society. After 1655, circumstances changed profoundly, for European contacts increased dramatically. Jesuit missionaries were in residence, a French settlement was nearby, and the Onondaga's European neighbors were increasingly aggressive. The archaeological record now shows more hybrid artifact forms, more blending of European and native culture. This increased blending is reflected in wampum, one of the major mediums of exchange between native and newcomer.

Wampum had been important in pre-contact days, but it assumed much greater significance to the Iroquois as a whole in the early 17th century. Wampum beads strung into belts became common, since they were now a commodity of major importance both to Europeans and Iroquois. To the former, the wampum belt was a valuable medium of exchange for use in the fur trade. The Dutch in particular were quick to seize on the possibilities of wampum, for they had long experience of shell as a trade item when buying slaves in faraway Africa. The same company was incorporated for fur trading in North America, turned to the same currency, and soon realized the potential of wampum. It was probably they who developed the notion of belts as a widespread, informal currency in a medium that had important cultural significance not only to the Five Nations. To the Iroquois, shell was a source of power, wampum life-enhancing and restoring, an important element in rituals that served to console close relatives of a deceased and to raise up another person to fill the void. The Onondaga were the keepers of wampum for the Five Nations, so it was of great importance to them as an emblem of diplomacy not only between Indians, but with Europeans as well.

The Iroquois confederacy of Five Nations had been formed as a means of redressing grievances among its members. Not that this prevented constant bickering among them, many of the tensions resulting from the differing trading opportunities that were available to different tribes. These quarrels, constant warfare, and devastating epidemics, so weakened the Iroquois that they were almost destroyed. But in the late 1660s the Onondaga used their diplomatic talents to restructure the Confederacy, redefining its workings so that the organization would act as the diplomatic front for all the Five Nations. The Five Nations now presented a more united front. This led to a series of treaties and alliances in 1677, agreements that stabilized and balanced the competing interests of the English colonies, which had supplanted French settlers to the southeast, the Five Nations, and other tribal groups. To the English this Covenant was a legal document, and to the Iroquois a set of social and political obligations that bound participants together to minimize differences between them. The Covenant with its diplomatic expertise, with its treaties expressed in terms of wampum belts and intricate rituals, was a product of long-drawn-out acculturative processes that saw Onondaga culture transformed not only in material ways, but in response to new external realities, which, ultimately, they were sometimes able to exploit to their advantage.

Joseph Latifau's depiction of Iroquois leaders gathered to recite the laws of the Five Nations (1724). At the base is an enlarged view of the wampum belt, from which they "read" these laws.

The initial impact of European contact fell hardest, of course, on American Indian societies living near coasts or major waterways such as the St Lawrence or the Lower Mississippi. As European settlement spread, some coastal groups were conquered and employed as agricultural laborers. Others, in California, were forcibly resettled under deliberate "reduction" policies that brought them into the Spanish mission system, where the friars could more easily control both the process of conversion, and the economic life associated with it (Spicer, 1962). For several centuries, however, aboriginal groups living in the more distant interior largely avoided sustained contact with explorers, colonists, or missionaries, even if their economic, political, and social systems underwent drastic modification as a result of devastating epidemics.

The entire process of culture change as a result of European contact is still little understood. For the purposes of the remainder of this chapter, we focus on the Southeast, where systematic research into the interactions between Spaniard and American Indian has been most intense.

The Archaeology of De Soto

Hernando de Soto's foray through the Southeast in 1539–1543 is a terrible baseline in North American history, famous not only for its brutality, but for its legacy of smallpox and other diseases that decimated Indian populations, triggered long-term massive political and social change, and undoubtedly had profound psychological effects on Southeastern society. But what of the material remains of this extraordinary incursion? Until about 15 years ago, it seemed that De Soto and his force had passed through the Southeast without leaving an archaeological signature behind them. Part of the problem was that no one knew what to look for – 16th-century artifacts were largely a closed book even to historical archaeologists. However, the collaboration of archaeologists, anthropologists, and historians has produced significant results, and three possible locations where traces of De Soto, or at least very early Spanish contact, survive (Milanich, 1987; Milanich and Milbrath, 1989).

Recent excavations at Tatham burial mound in Citrus County, Florida, have yielded large numbers of Spanish artifacts, including metal, glass beads, and armor fragments. More than 70 Indians had been buried in a mass grave in the tumulus, perhaps victims of an epidemic. Some bodies exhibit wounds from sword cuts (Mitchem and Hutchinson, 1987). Tatham dates to before 1550.

Even more dramatic discoveries come from the Coosa River in northwestern Georgia, from the King site that was once a frontier village of the Coosa chiefdom, visited by the Spaniards in the 16th century (Hudson, C. and others, 1985). King was a fortified settlement, whose dwellings surrounded a central plaza. Several Spanish artifacts came from the excavations, including a 16th-century basket-hilt sword manufactured in either Germany or northern Italy. Even more important, one of every five of the burials from the excavations exhibited fatal slashing wounds on legs

The chief of Coosa greets De Soto and his army in this early 18th-century engraving. In the background the chief is carried on a ceremonial litter preceded by trumpet blowers.

and head that could only have been inflicted by long-bladed European swords, as opposed to Indian weapons – arrows and spears that would make puncture wounds. The victims were young women, also middle-aged males and females. No children or men of the warrior class were among the dead. Since Southeastern Indians usually killed warriors and captured women, the case for Spanish killing is even more compelling.

Of the three Spanish expeditions that penetrated Coosa in the 16th century, only De Soto's could have reached the King site. Wherever he went, De Soto took slaves, women for sexual purposes and others as carriers – the very segment of the King population that lay in these graves. Perhaps these people mounted a desperate resistance against enslavement, or violence stemmed from a Spanish attempt to extort or steal food from the village when the warriors were absent. The bones bear puncture and gnaw marks from opossums and rats, as if they lay in the open for a while before being interred by the survivors. The village may never have recovered from De Soto. It was abandoned by 1575 (Blakely, 1988).

From October 1539 to March 1540, Hernando de Soto and his 600 conquistadors set up winter camp at the major Apalachee town of Anhaica, which lies today under downtown Tallahassee, Florida (Ewen, 1989). Anhaica was a sizeable settlement with 250 dwellings and other structures. The Apalachee abandoned their town to their unwelcome visitors, but harassed the Spaniards constantly. Calvin Jones, and later Charles Ewen, have excavated a small portion of the encampment, attempting to establish the dimensions of the camp and uncovering two circular wattle-and-daub Indian dwellings. The site has yielded five early 16th-century Spanish and Portuguese coins, Apalachee artifacts, and considerable numbers of Spanish artifacts and ceramics. This is hardly surprising, since we know that De Soto was resupplied from his ships in Tampa Bay. There were a fragment of a crossbow bolt, numerous European glass beads, and pieces of Spanish chain mail, also datable 16th-century imported majolica pottery. The chain mail fragments are of particular interest, for it was at Anhaica that the conquistadors discovered that chain mail was no protection against Indian arrows and turned to quilted cloth coats instead.

The search for further traces of De Soto's expedition continues, and the debate about his exact route still rages. These controversies are of more than academic interest, but the real issues surround not the events of the expedition itself, but the long-term consequences of his passage. And these consequences, still archaeologically little known, were to be momentous.

Artist's illustration of Spanish chain mail from the Martin site, Tallahassee, Florida, the Anhaica village where the De Soto expedition spent the winter of 1539–40.

Culture Change in the Southeastern Interior

Marvin Smith (1987) has studied a portion of the interior Southeast centered on the Georgia and Alabama piedmont, in an attempt to measure the extent of early post-contact cultural change. European contact began in this region with the De Soto expedition of 1540. Both exotic diseases and foreign trade goods percolated into the area during the following century, this early period of indirect contact ending with the arrival of English settlers from Virginia and South Carolina in the 1670s. Smith points out that the situation in this region was very different from that, say, of the Five Nations of the Iroquois, where the people were in sustained, direct contact with Europeans for generations. Here the contact was indirect. Acculturation of the type found among the Onondaga, for example, did not take place, yet there were major changes in population density and settlement patterns, to say nothing of political and social institutions.

The 16th-century Southeast was a land of flourishing and often complex chiefdoms with high levels of military organization. These presided over dense populations often housed in substantial settlements. The people were ruled by an elite, their lives governed by complex religious beliefs and elaborate rituals (C. Hudson, 1976). Like most chiefdoms of this complexity, there were several layers of hierarchy. In Smith's research area, the chiefdom of Ocute consisted of a capital with five mounds (the Shoulderbone mound group), two other multiple mound sites, two single mound centers, and many villages and smaller settlements. This densely inhabited "province" was surrounded by a large buffer zone of unoccupied land (Smith and Kowalewski, 1980). By analyzing the routes taken by De Soto and other early Spanish explorers, Smith and his colleagues have been able to identify many 16th-century polities and actual named settlements, identifications that are the baseline for examining population decline and political restructuring during the century that followed.

Throughout much of the late 16th and early 17th centuries, the Southeastern interior remained unknown territory, although plenty was happening around the periphery. The Spanish mission system spread along the Georgia coast, through northern Florida, increasing both knowledge of foreigners and indirect contacts through the years. When English visitors first reached Cofitachiqui in South Carolina, a settlement visited by De Soto in 1540, it was still an important place. Its inhabitants were well aware of the Spanish, of a land to the west with bells and friars, and of people who rode on great deer (horses). The Cherokee of the Tennessee Valley were well equipped with firearms, brass pots, and kettles by 1673. French explorers entering the lower Mississippi from the Great Lakes region reported encounters with Indians armed with muskets, who also possessed glass bottles, iron axes, and other European goods, obtained from a coast said to be 10 days away. Peaches, chickens, and watermelons had spread widely from village to village (Sauer, 1980). These material changes were symptoms of much more profound alterations in Indian life.

Marvin Smith approached the problem of measuring cultural change from several archaeological angles. First, he established chronologies based on stylistic changes in categories of easily dated European trade goods that were exchanged with native peoples all over the world. This methodology, employed successfully in the Northeast, and often called the "Iroquois Methodology," works well where there is continual, sustained contact, as there was in the fur trading areas (Wray and Schoff, 1953). But in the Southeast the contacts were more complicated and less constant, the flow of European goods resulting not only from occasional direct trade, but from such diverse sources as slave trading, looting of shipwrecks, and through native middlemen. Intricate exchange routes had criss-crossed the Southeast since Archaic times: they were still in use and many exotica undoubtedly traveled along them.

In the Southeast, many of the earliest trade goods were quickly consumed as prestigious grave goods. Smith's seriations of European goods found in archaeological sites chronicle long-term changes. From 1525 to

1565 aboriginal culture was little affected by exotic influences, although European goods were buried with the elite, who controlled the supply. Native copper associated with the Southern Cult was still in use. Between 1565 and 1600, native copperworking was in decline, but other traditional crafts with important ritual associations such as shellwork were still common and important. After 1600, the pattern changed, as imports became more common and were no longer restricted to elite burials. Perhaps this reflects the breakdown of powerful chiefdoms. At any rate, more common artifacts, like iron axes, became more utilitarian possessions – just as they had in the Northeast. Only native ceramics remained unchanged. Between 1640 and 1670, firearms were in use, and English artifacts appeared more common, as if trade networks now extended to the Northeast.

These material changes took place against a background of massive depopulation resulting from epidemics. The chroniclers of the De Soto expedition make it clear that diseases introduced by earlier coastal visitors preceded the conquistadors into the interior. At the village of Talomeco in South Carolina, hundreds of bodies were stacked up in four of the houses. Evidence of epidemics from later decades is abundant. Sir Francis Drake's men contracted a highly contagious form of fever, perhaps typhus, in the Cape Verde Islands, and carried it ashore when they attacked the Spanish settlement at St Augustine, Florida, in 1586 (Crosby, 1972). Hundreds of Indians living nearby soon died of the same disease. And Thomas Hariot noted that the English settlers at Roanoke, in the colony of what was then called Virginia (now North Carolina), soon infected the local people. "Within a few days after our departure from everies such townes, people began to die very fast, and many in short space" (Crosby, 1972).

Without question these later coastal epidemics entered the interior, resulting in massive depopulation, perhaps killing as many as 90 percent of some village populations (Smith, 1987). Not only that, but the survivors probably suffered severely from starvation, especially if epidemics struck during periods of planting or harvest. The processes of depopulation may have been so rapid and devastating that ancestral traditions and much of indigenous culture may have been swept away in a few short months. The loss, in particular, of religious and genealogical lore is especially devastating to a traditional society, for such elements are an important element in helping people adjust to a new culture (Smith, 1987; Trigger, 1976). In the Southeastern interior, such a loss may have led to the fragmentation of hitherto powerful chiefdoms into much smaller, less centralized societies, and to population movements. In archaeological terms, Smith believes that the epidemics and general social disruption may be reflected in a rapid increase in multiple burials during the 16th century, as is documented in sites of the Mouse Creek culture of eastern Tennessee and in the King site of northwestern Georgia, with graves dating to the period between 1525 and 1565. A visitor to the Arkansas people in 1698 remarked that "not a month had elapsed since they had rid themselves of smallpox, which had carried off most of them. In the village are now nothing but graves, in which they were buried two together, and we estimated that not a hundred men were left" (Philips and others, 1951). Settlement sizes shrank, too, witness the Toqua site in Tennessee. This fortified mound center was occupied from about 1215 to 1620. The earliest village covered some 420,000 sq. ft (39,018 sq. m) with dispersed houses. Later, between 1350 and the early 16th century, the occupied zone shrank to 210,000 sq. ft (19,509 sq. m). Around 1580–1600, the fortified area shrank to as little as 180,000 sq. ft (16,727 sq. m), a much smaller settlement in which three multiple burials were found (Smith, 1987).

The strongest evidence is for political breakdown, for there is ample historical documentation that the large and powerful chiefdoms encountered by De Soto had been reduced to dozens of small-scale societies that were to band together to form the Creek Confederacy in the early 18th century. These small societies were ruled by *mikos*, little more than village headmen. The fall of the chiefdoms was closely linked not only to epidemics, but to the severe loss of the manpower that peopled the hierarchical provinces of the Southeast. Archaeologically, the decline can be documented by a virtual cessation of mound building, known to have been a chiefly activity. In Smith's research area, no new mounds were built after about 1600. Some mound centers were abandoned, and there was a widespread trend during the 18th century toward more dispersed village settlements (L. Wright, 1981).

The hierarchical settlement patterns of larger centers and a well-defined ranking of lesser settlements were apparently abandoned during the 16th century, a loss well documented in the Wallace Reservoir area and Oconee drainage area of Georgia (Smith and Kowalewski, 1980). By the early 17th century, the copper axes and spatulate axes, as well as other sumptuary goods symbolic of chiefly power, were no longer in use, as if such powers had eroded dramatically. Decimated, without the support of their traditional beliefs, the societies of the interior were left in a state of cultural impoverishment. By virtue of their remoteness from the coast, they had not been exposed directly to Spanish, French, and English culture and Christianity, as they were after 1673. Ultimately, the drastic cultural changes of the previous 130 years put the Indians in a position to accept more easily elements of European culture in the years that followed, when acculturation truly began. It was not until the 18th century that the peoples of the Southeast came together in the Creek Confederacy, a response to armed invasions by northern Indian groups, and to raids by European slave traders.

Text-aided Research: The Archaeology of La Florida

Historical archaeology, sometimes called text-aided archaeology, has been defined as "the archaeology of the spread of European culture throughout the world since the 15th century and its impact on indigenous peoples" (Deetz, 1977). The peoples it studies do not necessarily have to be literate, indeed only a minority of, say, early Spanish settlers or English colonists could write. But this minority wrote about the others and kept at least sketchy records of them. They sent reports to the homeland, recorded births, marriages, and deaths, kept tax rolls, laid out and administered tiny settlements according to regulations promulgated by distant monarchs. These records complement the archaeological record – the artifacts of literate and non-literate people living often simple lives, of different classes or ethnic groups with often quite distinctive artifacts, of Europeans interacting with native Americans. The material remains of their myriad existences chronicle the historical realities of recent centuries of North American history in ways that no official living at the time would consider worth recording. Historical archaeology provides fascinating perspectives not only on the European settlement of North America, but on the cultures of various major immigrant groups, and on every economic class of emerging American society, including the native Americans confronted by the newcomers.

Historical archaeology has assumed significant proportions in North America, both because of culture resource management and ardent historic preservation activities, and because most North Americans can identify more closely with historic sites from the recent past than they can with the prehistoric achievements of native American societies. In its early days, historical archaeology was restricted to selected, important sites such as forts, major missions, and the residences of major historical figures. Much excavation was conducted at the behest of architectural historians. In the past quarter-century, however, perspectives have changed. Both archaeologists, and to a lesser extent historians, have realized that archaeology gives access to a very broad range of human behavior, not only spoken, but preserved in the form of material remains (Deetz, 1977; Nöel Hume, 1969; Schuyler, 1977). Much recent work, especially that concerned with the so-called Spanish Borderlands, has what can only be described as an anthropological orientation. This focus concentrates not only on material remains, but on the processes of interaction between different population groups.

What have been called the Spanish Borderlands were, in fact, an ever-shifting frontier on the margins of the vast Spanish Empire in the Americas. This northern boundary of New Spain was never fixed, and always changing, a part of New Spain where there was constant interaction between settlers and native Americans, between long-established indigenous societies and aggressive newcomers. Ultimately, the borderlands stretched from St Augustine, Florida, in the east to San Francisco, California, in the west. The processes of interaction and cultural change associated with them began with European contact, with the Ponce de Leon expedition in the east, with Fray Marcos de Niza in the Southwest, and with Juan Cabrillo's voyage up the California coast in 1542. They ended with the Mexican Revolution of 1821.

The complicated history of this vast area has long been studied by historians, but only recently by archaeologists. Inevitably, the historical picture has been burdened with offensive stereotypes and simplistic interpretations, some due to the intellectual and social climate of the times in which they were written, others the result of the limitations of documentary evidence. As David Hurst Thomas has pointed out, the objective perspective of text-aided archaeology is adding a new balance, new insights to the historical record. Nowhere are these perspectives more exciting than in La Florida, the Hispanic Southeast. (For comprehensive perspectives on contact between Europeans and American Indian societies, see Thomas, 1989, which deals with Spanish borderlands in the west, and subsequent volumes to cover other parts of the country).

Shortly after Columbus landed in the Indies, Spanish explorers extended their king's domains through the Caribbean, into Mexico, and into South

America. They also explored much of the Gulf and Atlantic coasts of North America, the lands named La Florida by Ponce de Leon in 1513 (Chapter 1). La Florida was far from wealthy and attracted few Spanish settlers until 1565, when Pedro Menéndez de Aviles overran a French colony near present-day Jacksonville, Florida, and founded two settlements – St Augustine and Santa Elena, the latter on Parris Island, South Carolina (South and others, 1980). The local Indians exercised such pressure against Santa Elena and its forts that it was abandoned by 1587, two years after Sir Walter Raleigh's colony was established in Virginia to the north.

St Augustine enjoyed a strategic position, located as it was close to the point where Spanish treasure fleets turned offshore with the north-flowing Gulf Stream that brought them up from the Indies. No less than 21 percent of the royal defense budget was spent in La Florida between 1564 and 1577, with resulting heavy ship traffic in and out of St Augustine, ships that brought provisions and other necessities as well as military reinforcements, missionaries, and settlers.

Sixteenth-century St Augustine was a tiny settlement, a small mission and presidio. By the end of the century, about 425 people living in 120 households dwelt in the town (Deagan, 1980; 1983). Only about 30 percent of them included women, and only half of those were Spanish. The rest were Indian wives or concubines. The garrison was plagued with flood, fire, and hurricanes, plundered by Sir Francis Drake in 1586. A member of his crew drew a map of the town, showing nine blocks of single-story, thatched structures with board walls (Manucy, 1985). Many earlier dwellings were made of wattle and daub. St Augustine survived and served as the capital of La Florida until 1702, when the British besieged its Castillo de San Marcos for six weeks. Eventually the defenders fled, after burning the wooden buildings of the town to the ground. This time, the colonists replaced them with masonry buildings, as the town expanded in the first half of the 18th century.

Kathleen Deagan and a team of archaeologists have investigated 18th-century and earlier St Augustine on a systematic basis since 1977 (Deagan, 1983), combining historic preservation with archaeological excavation. Excavating the 18th-century town has proved a difficult task, partly because the entire archaeological deposit for three centuries is only about 3 ft (1 m) deep at the most, and has been much disturbed. Nevertheless, the excavators have recovered dozens of barrel-lined trash pits, and the foundations of 18th-century houses built of tabby, a cement-like substance of oyster shells, lime, and sand. The builders laid foundations of oyster shell or tabby in footing trenches that were the shape of the intended house. Then the walls were added. The tabby floor soon wore out, so another layer of earth was added and a new floor poured on top.

The St Augustine excavations were highly informative, and showed that the layout of both St Augustine and Santa Elena was highly structured, rigidly organized, and very conservative. This is hardly surprising, since it was established by 16th-century government ordinances. Households and their barrel-lined wells were laid out at 50 ft (15.2 m) intervals, the streets on a grid pattern. Exactly the same rigid and conservative layout persisted into the 18th-century. Only building materials changed. Every time the town grew, the expansion followed the original blueprint. Archaeology

a. SOUTH ELEVATION

SMOKE HOLE

b. END ELEVATION

12'

PALLET

CHEST

8'

A··B

HEARTH

FUEL→

STOOL

FOOD JARS

C. PLAN

Sketch plan and elevations of a 16th-century thatched structure for a common settler in St Augustine, Florida.

Spanish 16th-century majolica ware recovered by Kathleen Deagan in her St Augustine excavations.

The stereotyped image of the Spanish colonists. Throwing Indians to the dogs, by G. Benzoni, 1594.

confirms what one might suspect from historical documents. The colonists maintained their "Spanishness," which was based on standards set elsewhere, partly as an adaptive strategy to survive within the Spanish colonial system. Local environmental and social factors led to some modification of the Spanish pattern, especially at the domestic level, where intermarriage may have introduced new foods and domestic artifacts into many households (Reitz and Scarry, 1986).

For generations, a pervasive attitude and mythology characterized the Spanish colonists as cruel, bloodthirsty, lustful, and responsible for the decimation of native American populations (Maltby, 1971). This stereotypical "Black Legend" has long been discredited, but it is interesting to note that the objective eye of historical archaeology has documented considerable differences in the ways in which Hispanic-American and Anglo-American cultures developed in North America (Thomas, 1989). Spanish colonial sites contain many more imported and native American ceramics than British settlements of the same period. The vigorous Spanish ceramic tradition resulted from many factors, not only a flourishing export trade but from the custom of subjugating native populations through mechanisms that bound their labor to Spanish masters. Most Spanish settlers were males, and the incorporation of local women into their households brought native ceramics into their settlements. By the time St Augustine was founded, the Spanish had developed a means of interacting with the local population that was based on religious conversion, intermarriage, and tribute (which was later abandoned). The Spaniards integrated themselves physically with local populations, while still maintaining detailed, rigid, and highly legalistic classifications of people by race. In contrast, British colonists based their interactions with Southeastern populations on trade, warfare, slavery, and servitude. There was some intermarriage on the frontier, but there were more English women in English colonies. Archaeology reveals far fewer native American artifacts and influence in such sites.

There are other differences, too. At St Augustine, the settlers buried their trash in abandoned wells. In a hot climate where food spoils rapidly and fish was commonly eaten, this is a sensible precaution. Many British settlers were far more casual, tossing their trash on the ground around their dwellings (for discussion, see Deagan, 1983; South, 1977). Judging from the St Augustine excavations, Spanish colonists lived in a structured and highly organized social environment, an environment reflected by a tightly patterned material record. The pattern was conservative, in contrast to that recorded by James Deetz (1977) in New England, where an English rural tradition was soon replaced by local adaptations developed by people living not within a structured empire, but in almost complete isolation.

Spanish Missions in the Southeast

Only four Franciscan friars served the spiritual needs of all of La Florida in 1584. They spent most of their time ministering to the needs of the Spanish colonists of St Augustine and Santa Elena, activities that left them with little time to missionize among the local Timucua Indians, let alone the Guale to the north. Three years later, hostile Guale forced the abandonment of Santa Elena, so Spanish headquarters were moved to St Catherine's Island off the Georgia coast. The island with its Mission Santa Catalina de Guale represented the northernmost extension of Spanish influence along the Atlantic coast for most of the 17th century. The Mission was to flourish until it was abandoned after a British attack in 1680.

Santa Catalina de Guale was part of a large mission system in the Southeast (Thomas, 1988). By the mid-17th century as many as 70 Franciscans served approximately 25,000 Indians in a chain of 38 missions throughout La Florida. This extensive mission network compares with the 50 or so stations that were operating in the Southwest under the direction of 26 friars, and the 650-mile (1046-km) long chain of 21 Franciscan missions in Alta California with their 60 friars that were serving as many as 18,000 Indians in 1830. The California and Southwestern missions are relatively well known. Many of them are still places of worship for substantial congregations. In contrast, those of Spanish Florida are largely forgotten, despite their numerical and strategic importance three centuries ago. Hispanicized native Americans disappeared from La Florida as it came under British rule in 1763. The missions themselves soon fell into disrepair. They were modest structures, constructed of mud and sticks, sometimes of "flimsy board and thatch." They were easily set afire, sometimes blown over by hurricanes, or inundated by floods. Hardly any of 16th- or 17th-century La Florida's buildings survive, so mission archaeology assumes particular importance in the Southeast.

According to historical accounts, the 16th-century Mission Santa Catalina de Guale consisted of but a church and a friary. Its 17th-century successor, built after the original was burnt down in 1597, was a square, fortified compound with palisades 193 ft (59 m) on a side and a central, shell-covered plaza. The compound protected the church, friary, the kitchen and garrison. Construction was probably simple, the buildings being held up with tree-trunks, then covered with wattle and daub. David Hurst Thomas of the American Museum of Natural History is using archaeological survey and excavation to amplify vague historical records, and to throw detailed light on mission and Indian life during the Spanish period (Thomas, 1988). Thomas used a battery of sub-surface testing methods not only to locate the major features of the mission, but to develop a baseline library of geophysical signatures for such sites. This archaeological record is a growing archive of resistivity signatures, radar profiles and so on, characteristic of different buried features such as palisade walls and cemeteries that will guide future researches at this and other comparable sites. At Mission Santa Catalina, soil resistivity surveys defined the shape, orientation, and extent of unexcavated buildings such as the friary and a series of contemporary Indian buildings, while proton magnetometer surveys provided information on lengths of clay walls, located a well, also the well-preserved church and kitchen. Cross-cutting, ground-penetrating radar profiles helped define the layout of palisades and bastions surrounding the central mission plaza. This remote-sensing approach had several advantages. It was much cheaper than large-scale excavation, enabled sample trenches to be positioned accurately, and provided valuable information about unexcavated portions of the mission. Careful test excavations based on the remote-sensing program exposed specific structures, many of which have since been excavated in detail.

The church was constructed with a single nave, a rectangular building 65.5 ft (20 m) long and 36 ft (11 m) wide. The wattle-and-daub façade supported a pointed gable and a thatched roof. Pine planking and wattle formed the whitewashed side walls, which may have been adorned with ornate metal panels. The sanctuary was planked, and elevated slightly, with a sacristy on the left side facing the altar. Thomas even recovered some wheat grains from this room, perhaps part of the grain used to bake the flatbread used for the Eucharist (Thomas, 1988). A plaza surfaced with white seashells about 50 ft (15 m) on each side lay in front of the church. It was once enclosed with a low wall. Aerial photographs even revealed a worn pathway across to the doorway.

About 400 to 450 Christianized Guale Indians were buried under the nave and sanctuary, their graves associated with religious paraphernalia, rare majolica vessels, glass trade beads, and other artifacts. After examination, they are being reburied in reconsecrated ground at the Mission.

The Friary complex lay across the main plaza from the church. The first such wattle-and-daub structure was about 52 ft (16 m) long and 23 ft (7 m) wide. This was burnt down by the Guale in 1697, and replaced with two structures, one for the friars, the other a separate kitchen. The friars lived in small, sparsely furnished rooms, built around two central enclosures.

Like St Augustine, Mission Santa Catalina was the product of a rigid and highly conservative society, built along strict architectural specifications. By the same token, too, the American Indians who lived at these missions lived regimented lives where everything, including space, was organized by alien blueprint (Thomas, 1988).

St Catherine's Island, Santa Catalina de Guale mission church undergoing excavation, June 1982. The foundations of the single nave are visible as a dark outline.

Anglo-American Culture: Martin's Hundred and New England

To the north, the English had founded Jamestown in 1607, which soon became an important trading center with tentacles that stretched far into the Southeast and included regular forays for slaves. The *Mayflower* anchored off Plimoth in New England in 1620. Forty-four years later, English colonists took New York from the Dutch, ending over 50 years of Dutch influence over fur trading in the Northeast. Even further north, the French had settled along the St Lawrence, where they dominated the fur trading activity in that region. Their fur traders and explorers had spread throughout the Great Lakes during the 17th century, while Marquette and Joliet descended the Mississippi Valley in 1673. La Salle followed in their footsteps and even tried to colonize the Texas coast. By 1700, the peoples of the Eastern Woodlands were surrounded by what Marvin Smith (1987) calls an "ever-tightening noose of the European presence." Dutch, English, French, and Spanish – each group had different, competing interests that exerted severe pressure on Indian groups often hundreds of miles away from actual direct contact with the foreigners. The dynamics of these pressures, of Indian responses to the European presence, are still little understood. It is only recently, indeed, that historical archaeologists have begun to define the distinctive Anglo-American culture of the British colonists, in Virginia, New England, and elsewhere.

Martin's Hundred. Late in 1618, 220 settlers were shipped from England to settle 20,000 acres (8000 ha) of uncultivated land named Martin's Hundred, facing the James River in Virginia (Nöel Hume, 1982). The settlers built what proved to be a short-lived community that included a small, palisaded fort for protection against Spaniards and Indians and a fledgling settlement named Wolstenholme Towne. This was little more than a hamlet of timbered and thatched houses, a settlement of some 30 to 40 people. At first the local Indians were friendly, but on 22 March 1622 they attacked the James River settlements without warning. Half the Martin's Hundred population was massacred or taken hostage. The survivors eked out a precarious existence for a few more years, but virtual starvation and contagious diseases eventually wiped them out. Wolstenholme Towne was almost forgotton for 350 years.

In 1970, Ivor Nöel Hume, then resident archaeologist at Colonial Williamsburg, was searching for vanished outbuildings, belonging to a colonial plantation in process of restoration. To his surprise, he uncovered 17th-century postholes, pits, and graves – the remains of Wolstenholme Towne (Nöel Hume, 1982). The excavations that followed explored an area of 2 acres (0.81 ha), a jigsaw of post holes, old tree holes, pits, and other long-decayed timber structures. The wooden fort was found to have covered 10,000 sq. ft (929 sq. m). Excavated in its entirety, it was four-sided, of trapezoidal shape, about 83 by 130 ft (25.2 by 39.6 m), with a stout watchtower at the southeast corner and a bastion at the southwest. This once held a cannon, aimed toward possible Spanish ships in the James River. Nöel Hume estimated the palisade was about 7.7 ft (2.3 m) high, with a clay-filled platform behind.

The dwellings were built of wattle, daub, and thatch, some of them built over large cellars as much as 30 ft (9 m) in diameter. In a piece of brilliant archaeological and historical detective work, Ivor Nöel Hume used historical records to show how impecunious farmers would start by living in cellar-like underground houses that they lined with timber and bark, floored with planks, erecting a roof and eaves above ground. A fragment of twisted gold thread and an iron cannonball enabled him to track down the owner of one dwelling through census records and sumptuary laws. It was one William Harwood, once the headman of the tiny settlement.

Excavations like Martin's Hundred are complicated jigsaws of archaeological and historical clues, testimony to the enormous complexities of

Iron helmet of 1622 from the Martin's Hundred excavations.

The wooden fort of Wolstenholme exposed during Ivor Nöel Hume's Martin's Hundred excavations.

historical archaeology. The Martin's Hundred finds took Nöel Hume as far afield as Germany, Ireland, England, and Bermuda, in search of such esoteric information as the design of 17th-century coffin lids and the pathology of cleaver wounds on murder victims.

New England. "The personalities of prehistory will remain forever nameless and without faces. Dynamic and charismatic personae have peopled the stage of history ... But in our not knowing them on personal, individual terms lies a great asset, for the true story of a people depends less on such knowledge than on a broader and more general familiarity with what life was like for all people." Thus does James Deetz (1977) distill the essence of historical archaeology. Archaeologists are concerned with the broad sweep of cultural change, with basic human motivations and behavior. By studying the material remains of the past, it records not the deeds of a select, literate elite, but the lives of members of society as a whole – of minorities, merchants, native Americans, and, above all, of the humble folk and their settlements long forgotten.

The tiny ship that anchored in Plimoth harbor in December 1620 brought a small group of settlers to New England to an unfamiliar land. But they brought with them a clear image of the culture they were going to recreate in their new homeland. It was a culture identical to that in distant England, a form of rural society that had strong roots in the Middle Ages. The colonists were mainly simple artisans and farmers, plain folk who used a familiar cultural blueprint to hack out farms in the more extreme climate of New England. For more than 40 years, New England colonial culture was essentially a copy of that of simple, rural England. Deetz (1977) has pointed out that the earliest colonial houses in the Northeast show considerable resemblances to English rural architecture, and have no surviving counterparts. Some of the Plimoth colony dwellings were thatched long houses, subdivided into several rooms, built on massive sills rather than foundations. There was considerable architectural diversity reflecting the many homelands of their builders. By 1660, large numbers of colonials had never been to England, and more distinctive, local architectural styles began to develop.

Deetz and others have used such artifacts as New England gravestones and earthenware to document Anglo-American culture in the 17th century (Dethlefsen and Deetz, 1966). The latter were of great importance when he excavated the foundations of a large house 50 ft (15.2 m) long and 30 ft (9.1 m) wide on an island in Wellfleet Bay on outer Cape Cod. The numerous artifacts included imported pottery and glassware that dated the house to c.1670 to 1740. They included very large numbers of clay pipe fragments and eating and drinking utensils, while one cellar contained a whale vertebra and a harpoon. The tavern – it could be nothing else – lay on a remote, high bluff overlooking a place where shoals of small blackfish whales were often to be seen. The location was ideal for whalers to gather and wait for their prey.

We cannot possibly survey the full range of discoveries made by historical archaeologists in North America in the space available, but several recent projects will serve to highlight what this important facet of archaeology does best – documenting the lives of humble men and women going about their daily lives.

The Black Experience and Archaeology

Historical archaeology in America has, until recently, mainly been concerned with the study of the dominant, European culture. Once it dealt mainly with architecture, artifacts, and settlement patterns, often as part of the process of reconstructing elegant country houses and colonial settlements (Silberman, 1989). With a new emphasis on social history in the 1960s, some scholars became aware of the great potential of archaeology for documenting much of the unrecorded experience of plantation life and slavery. Early excavations focused on plantation sites in the coastal regions of Georgia and South Carolina (Singleton, 1985). Artifacts from such excavations reveal that from 1740 to 1790, the African heritage was still relatively strong in slave communities. This legacy was systematically devalued by slave-owners between 1790 and 1861, and perpetuated during the tenant farming period that followed emancipation. Recent excavations in Virginia, South Carolina, and Texas have turned up additional examples of artifacts like clay pipe bowls that bear motifs with uncanny resemblances to ideo- and cosmo-grams from West Africa (Silberman, 1989).

This search for African heritage is but part of researches into Afro-American history. Excavations are in progress in black communities such as Fort Mose, Florida, just north of St Augustine, the earliest free black town in North America, a place where escaped slaves sought sanctuary under Spanish rule.

Thomas Jefferson's estate at Monticello, Virginia, employed as many as 200 slaves. Jefferson was not only a politician, a philosopher, and an archaeologist, but a major landowner as well. His estate is carefully preserved for the modern visitor as an embodiment of Jefferson's times, but it is easy to forget that it looked very different in his lifetime. Again, the objective eye of the archaeologist has yielded significant information about the anonymous slaves who toiled on his estate (Kelso, 1986).

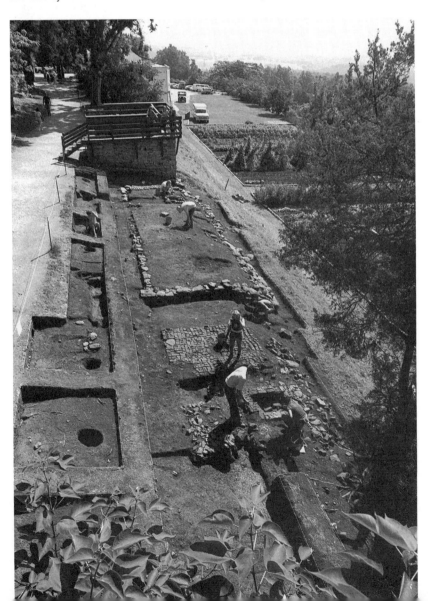

Monticello, Virginia. Excavations in progress of the Storehouse and Smokehouse/Dairy.

Some of Jefferson's slaves lived along Mulberry Row, the access road to Monticello, a road lined with 19 artisans' and laborers' dwellings, workshops, and storage buildings. William Kelso excavated this area, a task materially assisted by Jefferson's meticulous records. A slave working at Monticello could expect to live in a variety of dwellings, perhaps something as small as a 12 by 14 ft (3.6 by 4.26 m) log cabin with a dirt floor with wooden chimney, or in a much larger stone house, 34 by 17 ft (10.3 by 5.18 m), complete with stone and brick fireplace neo-classical façade and elevated pediment. One visitor to Monticello observed with justification that "the outhouses of the slaves and workmen . . . are all much better than I have seen on any other plantation . . ."

The occupants of Mulberry Row were somewhat more privileged than many of their fellow slaves on the estate, and certainly than those elsewhere (Kelso, 1984). There was probably a social hierarchy among them, and some of the ceramics found in the dwellings were of quite fine quality. Many of the beef and pork bones were poorer cuts of meat, less meaty portions that were used to make stews. It is interesting to note that slave sites on coastal plantations in Florida and Georgia have yielded many more bowls than planters' or overseers' houses, as if stew was a staple diet. There are signs that domestic trash was brought in from the main house to be picked over. Numerous buttons came to light, thought to be from discarded clothes that were made into heavy quilts.

All these excavations are helping redefine the relationship between modern Afro-American communities and those of the past, offering accurate depictions of slave life to replace the often-trivial depictions of many modern restorations.

Ships and Shipwrecks

Lakes, rivers, and other waterways were the highways of early European America, highways where thousands of humble, illiterate Americans spent their lives in quiet anonymity. Occasionally, a well-preserved shipwreck offers insights into their lives, and into the ships they manned.

In 1976, a group of archaeologists recovered a small 18th-century cargo boat from shallow water at Brown's Ferry, South Carolina (Albright and Steffy, 1979; Steffy, 1988). Such boats were the short-haul freighters of North America two centuries ago – sailed, poled, and rowed from one obscure waterway to another. They carried people, animals, and cargo, abandoned by a river bank or lake shore to sink forgotten at the end of their useful lives. The brick-filled Brown's Ferry boat lay at a favorite river dumping ground, covered with all manner of rubbish, including the remains of a horse-drawn buggy. More than two-thirds of the hull survived. Once the bricks were removed, a few artifacts including a beer mug, glass bottles, and a quadrant recovered, the hull was lifted from the river bed in a specially designed iron frame. Ship historian and modelmaker J. Richard Steffy pieced together the design of the boat from the actual timbers, from archival research, and from intelligent conjecture. The coaster was 50 ft 6 in (15.4 m) long on deck, with a beam of about 14 ft (4.2 m), a heavy, flat-bottomed vessel that enabled her to operate in shallow water and load from river banks. She was rigged with two masts, perhaps with a simple

Model by J. Richard Steffy of the small 18th-century cargo vessel recovered at Brown's Ferry, South Carolina.

spritsail rig. The crew lived at both ends of the boat, with the galley stove forward of the foremast. The double-ended vessel had oak frames, pine planks, and was repaired and recaulked at least once. This humble craft, built by rural shipwrights and launched without ceremony, sank with a full load of bricks during her last voyage, a boat whose whole life depended on tides and currents. Her forgotten wreck gives the historian and archaeologist insight not only into ancient ship design and construction, but into the daily life of her crew more than two centuries ago.

The Brown's Ferry ship is only one of numerous historic wrecks now being revealed by underwater archaeology in North America. For example, the Ronson ship, unearthed in the heart of New York City, was an old vessel when she was condemned some time before 1750. She was filled with rubble and pressed into service as cribbage for a wharf along the local waterfront. This was another humble craft, this time an ocean carrier about 100 ft (30.5 m) long, used for long-hauling of all manner of cargoes (Steffy, 1988).

Special stern-wheelers with exceptional shallow draft plied the upper sections of such rivers as the Missouri and the Colorado during the 19th century. Many served as supply boats for military posts and mines, carrying not only people, but stores of every kind. The 161-ft (49-m) long *Bertrand* was one such vessel, wrecked on the Missouri River after striking an underwater obstruction on 1 April 1865. She was located under 26 ft (8 m) of water by treasure hunters, then investigated under the aegis of the National Park Service in 1968–69. The overlying silt was removed by dragline, high pressure hose, and by hand. The lower portion of the hull up to the main deck was exposed, enabling the excavators to make detailed plans of the vessel. They also recovered almost 2,000,000 artifacts, among them foodstuffs, clothing, agricultural and mining supplies, medicines, liquor, and many types of domestic ware. There was ammunition for the Army's 12-pound (5.4-kg) mountain howitzers for their local garrisons, even crates of personal effects. This is the only large-scale excavation of a river steamboat of any kind, and the *Bertrand*'s contents tell us much about the mining and frontier economy of mid-19th-century North America. The local effects of this wreck were considerable, for her cargo was no less than 13 percent of the entire tonnage shipped to Fort Benson in 1865 (Simmons, 1988).

Mines and Miners

Western history is replete with images of rugged mining camps, peopled by individualists, small pockets of civilization surrounded by wilderness (Hardesty, 1988). The 19th-century Nevada mining frontier consisted of many such communities, islands of outsiders who brought their own social and cultural environment with them. These centers were controlled, financed, manned, and supplied from outside, from major business centers in America and Europe. As archaeologist Donald Hardesty points out, they were linked in a real sense to the world economic system of the day, through information networks that expanded fast with the completion of the transcontinental telegraph in 1860, bringing established Victorian values and additional capital to the mines. Supply networks linked to the world economic system transported supplies and mined ore, networks like the one that brought the *Bertrand* up the Missouri River in the upper Midwest. The same mines were linked into a complex migration network that brought miners from all over the United States, also from Asia and Europe, to remote Nevada communities.

Mining activity in Nevada is well documented through contemporary records, but archaeology adds valuable dimensions, by observing buildings, trash dumps, and ruined mines in a three-dimensional context of time and space – the same context used to study prehistoric sites. Archaeology and history collaborate best in the study of 19th-century mining technology, residential settlements, and individual households. Hardesty points out that only the archaeological record survives to document the layout of most smaller Nevada mining settlements. Most were little more than strips of houses along tracks, or clusters of buildings around mines and crushing mills.

The ethnically diverse Shoshone Wells mining camp in the Cortez Mining District was settled in 1863, reached a considerable size in the early 1880s, and was still occupied by Chinese and a few Italian immigrants as late as 1902. It provides a fascinating example of how text-aided archaeology can document ethnic neighborhoods. The existing archaeological site consists of 50 hut sites, most arranged into five clusters, each a distinctive neighborhood. One cluster of 22 adobe, dugout, and wood frame houses lay along a road on the valley floor. The artifacts associated with these houses are predominantly Anglo-European and Anglo-American or Chinese. Another cluster consists of four stone houses on the hillside above the other groups. These contain Italian artifacts such as Italian bitters bottles, and may have been the dwellings of Italian wood cutters mentioned in historical records.

Mine owner Simeon Wenban's house cluster contained Victorian artifacts such as fine French porcelain that reflected a much higher social status. Written records describe the mine owner's residence as a two-story redwood building standing in an irrigated lawn and garden. Wenban had trouble with his "turbulent and riotous" Cornish and Welsh miners, so he replaced them in the early 1870s with cheaper and less quarrelsome Chinese laborers. They lived along the road, and in the deep ravine below it. Their houses contain Chinese brownware, commonly used for food containers, opium tins and a pipe, gaming pieces, also European glassware, bottles that once contained beer, champagne, and other drinks.

The importance of Shoshone Wells is that it gives an example of how a combination of archaeological and historical records can provide insights into the great variability among 19th-century mining communities. The archaeological study of mining provides a way of relating what Hardesty calls (1988) "the settlement," the archaeological record of houses and other structures, to "community," the actual people who lived in it. And such studies are invaluable when examining mining camps that were predominantly male, made up of people of very cosmopolitan origins living in a society where individualism and minding one's own business were the social norms.

The W.C. Hoff General Store, San Francisco. One link in the mining economic system was San Francisco. The California Gold Rush of 1849 brought a flood of humanity from all corners of the globe to the then obscure village that was San Francisco, a bayside settlement with less than 1000 permanent residents. Within three years it was a sprawling boomtown of hotels, bars, cheap rooming houses, and stores, many of them built on piles off the original shoreline. There were regular fires, culminating in the great waterfront fire of 3 May 1851 that virtually destroyed the town, including William Hoff's general hardware store. Hoff himself abandoned his collapsed store to the mud and set up shop elsewhere.

The remains of his once prosperous shop were covered with landfill and forgotten until 1986. Then excavations at the corner of Sacramento and Battery Streets probed 15 ft (4.5 m) below modern street level and recovered much of Hoff's stock buried in wet mud (Pastron, 1988). Hoff's Store was a remarkable snapshot of Gold Rush days, of clothing, furniture, medicines, firearms, construction tools and mining implements from the 1840s. It was a chronicle, not of the spectacular and the unusual, but of the humble and mundane, of kegs of nails, work boots, and Chinese porcelain. There were bottles of champagne and jars of imported olives alongside barrels of salt pork, dried beans, and cheap whisky. Army surplus goods including carbines, powder flasks, and lead shot accompanied many a miner into the interior. There were toilet sets and patent medicines. It is with sites like this that historical archaeology is often at its best, providing a wealth of information about daily life in North America as recently as the late 19th century.

San Francisco has yielded a rich archaeological record, including the remains of a Chinese fishing village located on Rincon Point, where both fishermen and shipwreckers working on abandoned Gold Rush ships dwelt. Excavations have revealed rice and opium bowls, medicines, and both Chinese and Euro-American artifacts. Judging from the large numbers of small ceramic crucibles, some of the inhabitants may have been in contact with mining claims in the Sierra Nevada. The Rincon Point finds reveal a community engaged in varied, and sometimes innovative, economic activites, spurred by the need to maintain the highest possible degree of economic self-reliance (Pastron, 1989). This quest for self-reliance is a reflection of the threatening and intolerant social climate of the day.

Eighteenth-Century Annapolis and the Archaeology of Gardens

Text-aided archaeology not only chronicles the lives of both rich and poor, of 19th-century urban black neighborhoods in eastern cities, of Southern slave plantations and Chinese fisherfolk in the Far West, it can throw light on prevailing social attitudes of past centuries (Schuyler, 1977). For example, archaeologists from the University of Maryland have worked closely with historians on a citywide exploration of the Historic District of Annapolis (Leone and Potter, 1984). Annapolis enjoys a high level of historic preservation because the city escaped the Civil War and the Industrial Revolution and did not undergo any urban renewal until the 1950s. Many buildings and the archaeological record have been preserved, and archaeology has played an important part in the preservation process. Over the years, the excavators have investigated an 18th-century tavern, a printshop, several private residences, the site of a formal garden and three properties first occupied about 1690. Bottles, cups, and plates dating to that decade came from the bottom of the excavations of the Governor Calvert House (Yentoch and McKee, 1987), followed by intricate occupation layers, including a timber house of the early 1700s. Governor Calvert's brick house, whose first floor now forms part of a modern hotel, was subsequently built on the same site in the 1720s. Most of this structure was drastically rebuilt in the 19th century, but the original walls were preserved within the Victorian building. The excavations also revealed a brick heating system for channeling hot air to a greenhouse. This was partially torn up in the 1760s and filled with domestic refuse before being covered over by an addition to the 1720 house. The refuse proved a rich treasure trove of historical information, for it included animal bones, fish scales, pins, buttons, hair, pieces of paper, and cloth. The Calvert House enabled the archaeologists to recover complete layers of Annapolis history virtually intact.

The Annapolis research has far wider objectives than just historic preservation, however (Leone, 1984). Mark Leone and his colleagues work

Annapolis. Plan produced by Mark Leone's research team showing how the Carroll House gardens were carefully terraced to enhance distant views and to bolster the civil and social authority of the owners.

with broader anthropological concerns, which involve two basic premises. One is that space between buildings is as significant as the structures themselves. Managed landscapes can enhance the appearance of a house, more land may betoken greater wealth or social standing. The second is that landscape helps to generate social life as well as reflecting it, research that has caused them to focus not only on houses, but on the gardens that surround them – on the premise that 18th-century gardens were important ways of creating social status and power (Leone and others, 1989). By using soil coring, topographical surveys, and family records and photographs, Leone's research team were able to reconstruct the gardens of the Charles Carroll residence, which covers 2 acres (0.8 ha). Their surveys showed that the garden had been designed with terraces that enhanced both the house and distant views, using optical illusions such as terraces, also path and flowerbed lines. The archaeologists' topographic map brought all the variations and hidden secrets of the Carroll garden together, and showed how clever landscape design was used to bolster the civil and social authority of the owners, a central part of the 18th-century gentleman's self-definition in Annapolis.

The Annapolis excavations are but one example of the great potential of text-aided archaeology in achieving a more balanced, objective view of our remote and more recent past. For more than 12,000 years, human beings have settled in North America, adapted to its many environments, and interacted with one another within its boundaries. It is well that all of us, members of one of the most ethnically diverse societies on earth, understand some of the processes that have created this diversity, and shaped the way in which we live. It is not enough merely to look at American history through European glasses, through ethnocentric spectacles based on historical documents and what can be myopic sources. As James Deetz urges (1977): "Don't read what we have written: look at what we have done." Our understanding of one another, and of ourselves, will be infinitely more perceptive as a result.

Further Reading

Bass, George (ed.). 1988. *Ships and Shipwrecks of the Americas*. Thames and Hudson, London and New York.
Underwater archaeology in the Americas described by some of the leading authorities. A beautifully illustrated volume.

Deagan, Kathleen. 1983. *Spanish St Augustine*. Academic Press, New York.
This superb case study of a Spanish settlement sets a trend for such work in the future.

Deetz, James. 1977. *In Small Things Forgotten*. Anchor Books, New York.
Deetz' charming essay on historical archaeology captures the essence of the subject.

Milanich, Jerald, T. and Milbrath, Susan. 1989. *First Encounters*. University of Florida Presses, Gainesville.
A superb popular account of European-Indian contact in the Southeast.

Nöel Hume, Ivor. 1969. *Historical Archaeology*. Alfred Knopf, New York.
A general description of the methodology, with a strong East Coast emphasis. Strongly recommended for beginners.

—— 1982. *Martin's Hundred*. Alfred Knopf, New York; Gollancz, London.
One of the classics of historical archaeology. A beautifully written archaeological detective story.

Singleton, Theresa. 1985. *The Archaeology of Slavery and Black Plantation Life*. Academic Press, Orlando, Florida.
Essential reading for anyone interested in Afro-American archaeology.

Thomas, David Hurst. 1988. *St Catherines: An Island in Time*. Georgia Endowment for the Humanities, Atlanta.
A popular account of the Mission Santa Catalina de Guale researches, which is ideal for the beginning reader.

—— (ed.). 1989. *Columbian Consequences, vol 1: Archaeological and Historical Perspectives on the Spanish Borderlands West*. Smithsonian Institution Press, Washington DC.
The first of three edited volumes commemorating the Columbus Quincentennial – the articles are of varied quality, but many of first-rate importance.

Bibliography

This Bibliography makes no pretence at being complete, and represents only a small proportion of the references used to research and write this book. The sources that follow, together with the Guides to Further Reading at the end of each chapter, will, however, enable the reader to delve more deeply into the highly complex and diffuse literature of North American archaeology.

Ackermann, Robert. 1982. "The Neolithic-Bronze Age cultures of Asia and the Norton Phase of Alaskan Prehistory," *Arctic Anthropology* 19(2):11–38.

Adovasio, James. 1980. "Yes, Virginia, it really is that old: A reply to Haynes and Mead," *American Antiquity* 45:588–595.

——— 1982. "Meadowcroft Rockshelter 1973–1977: A synopsis," in J.E. Ericson and others (eds.). *Peopling of the New World*. Ballena Press, Los Altos, California, pp.97–131.

——— 1984. "Meadowcroft Rockshelter and the Pleistocene/Holocene Transition in South-West Pennsylvania," in Hugh Genoways and Mary Dawson (eds.). *Contributions in Quaternary Vertebrate Paleontology of the Carnegie Museum of Natural History* 8.

——— and Donahue, J. and Stuckenrath, R. 1990. "The Meadowcroft Rockshelter Radiocarbon Chronology 1975–1990," *American Antiquity* 55(2):348–354.

Agogino, G. 1969. "The Midland Complex – Is it valid?" *American Anthropologist* 71:1117–1118.

Aigner, Jean. 1970. "The Unifacial, Core, and Blade Site on Anangula Island, Aleutians," *Arctic Anthropology* 7(2):59–88.

Aikens, C.M. 1966. *Fremont-Promontory-Plains Relationships* ... University of Utah Anthropological Papers 82.

——— 1967. "Plains Relationships of the Fremont Culture: A Hypothesis," *American Antiquity* 32:198–209.

——— 1970. *Hogup Cave*. University of Utah Anthropological Papers, 93.

——— 1978. "The Far West," in Jesse D. Jennings (ed.). *Ancient Native Americans*, W.H. Freeman, San Francisco, pp.131–182.

——— 1982. "Archaeology of the Northern Great Basin: an overview," in David Madsen and James O'Connell (eds.). *Man and Environment in the Great Basin*, Society for American Archaeology, Washington DC, pp.139–155.

——— 1983. "The Far West," in Jesse D. Jennings (ed.). *Ancient Native Americans*, W.H.

Freeman, San Francisco, pp.149–201.

——— and Madsen, David. 1986. "Prehistory of the Eastern Area," in Warren D'Azevado (ed.). *Volume 11 Great Basin, Handbook of North American Indians*. Smithsonian Institution, Washington DC, pp.149–160.

Albright, A.B. and Steffy, J.R. 1979. "The Brown's Ferry Vessel, South Carolina," *International Journal of Nautical Archaeology* 8:121–142.

Ames, K.M. 1981. "The evolution of social ranking on the Northwest Coast of North America," *American Antiquity* 46:789–805.

Anderson, David, and others (eds.). 1982. *The Mattasee Lake Sites*. National Park Service, Atlanta, Georgia.

Anderson, David G, and Hanson, Glen T. 1988. "Early Archaic Settlement in the Southeastern United States: A Case Study from the Savannah River Valley," *American Antiquity* 53:262–286.

Anderson, Douglas D. 1968. "A Stone Age Campsite at the Gateway to America," *Scientific American* 216(8):24–33.

Antevs, Ernst. 1948. "Climatic Changes and Pre-White Man," in "The Great Basin with Emphasis on Glacial and Postglacial times," *University of Utah Bulletin* 38(20), Biological Series 10(7), pp.168–191.

Asch, David, and Asch, Nancy. 1978. "The Economic Potential of *Iva annua* and its Prehistoric Importance in the Lower Illinois Valley," in Richard I. Ford (ed.). *The Nature and Status of Ethnobotany*, Museum of Anthropology, University of Michigan, Ann Arbor, pp.300–341.

——— 1985. "Prehistoric Plant Cultivation in West-Central Illinois," in Richard I. Ford (ed.). *Prehistoric Food Production in North America*, Museum of Anthropology, University of Michigan, Ann Arbor, pp.199–203.

Asch, David, and others. 1979. "Woodland Subsistence and Settlement in West Central Illinois," in David S. Brose and N'omi Greber (eds.). *Hopewellian Archaeology*. Kent University Press, Kent, Ohio, pp.80–85.

Atwater, Caleb. 1820. "Description of the Antiquities Discovered in the State of Ohio and other Western States," *Transactions and Collections of the American Antiquarian Society* 1:105–267.

Bamforth, Douglas. 1988. *Ecology and Human Organization on the Great Plains*. Plenum, New York.

Bandelier, A.F. 1881. "Report on the Ruins of the

Pueblo of Pecos," *Papers of the Archaeological Institute of America* 1:37–133.

Bareis, C.J. and Porter, J.W. (eds.) 1984. *American Bottom Archaeology*. University of Illinois Press, Urbana, Illinois.

Barley, D. 1980. *Marpole: Anthropological Reconstructions of a Prehistoric Northwest Culture Type*. Occasional Paper 8, Department of Anthropology, Simon Fraser University, Burnaby, B.C.

Barnett, H.G. 1955. *The Coast Salish of British Columbia*. University of Oregon, Eugene.

Barth, Frederick. 1975. *Ritual and Knowledge among the Baktama of New Guinea*. Yale University Press, New Haven.

Bartram, William. 1853. "Observations on the Creek and Cherokee Indians (1789)," *American Ethnological Society Transactions* 3,1.

Bass, George. (ed.) 1988. *Ships and Shipwrecks of the Americas*. Thames and Hudson, London and New York.

Baumhoff, M. 1963. "Ecological determinants of aboriginal California populations." *University of California Publications in Archaeology and Ethnology* 49(2):155–236.

——— 1978. "Environmental Background," in R.F. Heizer (ed.). *Volume 8 California. Handbook of North American Indians*. Smithsonian Institution, Washington DC:16–24.

——— and Heizer, R.F. 1965. "Postglacial climate and archaeology in the Desert West," in H.E. Wright and D.G. Frey (eds.). *The Quaternary of the United States*. Princeton University Press, Princeton, NJ, pp.697–707.

Beadle, G. 1981. "The Ancestor of Corn," *Scientific American* 242(1):96–103.

Beaudry, Mary C. (ed.) 1987. *Documentary Archaeology in the New World*. Cambridge University Press, Cambridge.

Bednarik, R.G. 1989. "On the Pleistocene Settlement of South America," *Antiquity* 63(238):101–111.

Belovich, S.J. and others. 1982. "Archaeological Survey at George Andrews Lake and Chattahoochee River," *Archaeological Research Reports of the Cleveland Museum of Natural History* 37.

Benninghoff, W.S. 1968. "Biological Consequences of Quaternary glaciations in the Illinois region," in Robert E. Bergstrom (ed.). *The Quaternary of Illinois*. University of Illinois Press, Urbana, Illinois, pp.70–77.

Berry, C.F. and Berry, M.S. 1986. "Chronological

and conceptual models of the Southwest Archaic," in Carol J. Condie and Don D. Fowler (eds.). *Anthropology of the Desert West: Essays in Honor of Jesse D. Jennings*. Department of Anthropology, University of Utah, pp.253–327.

Betancourt, J.L. and Van Devender, T.R. 1981. "Holocene vegetation in Chaco Canyon, New Mexico," *Science* 214:656–658.

Bettinger, R.L. 1987. "Archaeological Approaches to Hunter-Gatherers," *Annual Review of Anthropology* 16:121–142.

Bettinger, R.L. and Baumhoff, M.A. 1982. "The Numic Spread: Great Basin Cultures in competition," *American Antiquity* 47:485–503.

———— 1983. "Return dates and intensity of resource use in Numic and PreNumic adaptive strategies," *American Antiquity* 48:830–834.

Bickel, P. McW. 1978. "Changing sea levels along the California coast: Anthropological implications," *Journal of California Archaeology* 5:(1):6–20.

Bielawski, E. 1988. "Paleoeskimo Variability: The Early Arctic Small-Tool Tradition in the Central Canadian Arctic," *American Antiquity* 53(1):52–74.

Binford, L.R. 1968. "Post-Pleistocene adaptations," in Sally and Lewis Binford (eds.). *New Perspectives in Archaeology*. Aldine, Chicago, pp.313–342.

———— 1978. *Nunamiut Ethnoarchaeology*. Academic Press, New York.

———— 1983. *In Pursuit of the Past*. Thames and Hudson, London and New York.

———— 1986. "In Pursuit of the Future," in David Meltzer, Don Fowler, and Jeremy Sabloff (eds.). *American Archaeology Past and Future*. Smithsonian Institution Press, Washington DC, pp.459–479.

———— and Chasko, W.J. Jr. 1976. "Nunamiut demographic history: a provocative case," in Ezra Zubrow (ed.). *Demographic Anthropology: Quantitative Approaches*. University of New Mexico Press, Albuquerque, pp.63–144.

Binford, S.R. and Binford, Lewis R. (eds.) 1968. *New Perspectives in Archaeology*. Aldine, Chicago.

Birket-Smith, Kaj. 1929. *The Caribou Eskimo*. Report of the Fifth Thule Expedition 1921–1924:5. Glydenclalski Boghandel, Nordisk Forlag, Copenhagen.

Biswell, H.H. 1967. "The Use of Fire in Wildlife Management in California," in S.V. Ciriacy-Wantrup and J.J. Parsons (eds.). *Natural Resources: Quality and Quantity*. University of California Press, Berkeley, pp.71–86.

Blakely, Robert. (ed.) 1988. *The King Site: Continuity and Contact in Sixteenth-Century Georgia*. University of Georgia Press, Athens.

Blanton, D.B. and Sassaman, K.E. 1988. "Pattern and Process in the Middle Archaic of South Carolina," in A.C. Goodyear (ed.). *Papers in Honor of Robert L. Stapleton . . .* Institute of Archaeology and Anthropology, University of South Carolina, Columbia, SC.

Blevins, B.B. and Joiner, C. 1977. "The archaeological survey of Tijeras Canyon," in Linda S. Cordell (ed.). *The 1976 excavation of Tijeras Pueblo, Cibola National Forest, New Mexico*. US Department of Agriculture, Forest Service Southwest region, Albuquerque, pp.126–152.

Blitz, John H. 1988. "Adoption of the Bow in Prehistoric North America," *North American Archaeology* 9(2):123–145.

Boas, Franz. 1905–1909. "The Kwakiutl of Vancouver Island," *Memoirs of the American Museum of Natural History* 8:307–515.

Borah, W. 1976. "The Historical Demography of Aboriginal and Colonial America: An Attempt at Perspective," in W.H. Denevan (ed.). *The Native Population of the Americas in 1492*. University of Wisconsin Press, Madison, pp.13–34.

Borden, C.A. 1975. *Origins and Development of Early Northwest Coast Culture to about 3000 BC*. Archaeological Survey of Canada, Mercury Series 45, Ottawa.

Bradley, James. 1987. *Evolution of the Onondaga Iroquois*. Syracuse University Press, Syracuse.

Braun, David P. 1983. "Pots as Tools," in James Moore and Arthur Keene (eds.). *Archaeological Hammers and Theories*. Academic Press, New York, pp.107–134.

———— 1985. "Ceramic Decorative Diversity and Illinois Woodland Regional Integration," in Ben A. Nelson (ed.). *Decoding Prehistoric Ceramics*, Southern Illinois University, Carbondale, Illinois, pp.128–143.

———— 1986. "Midwestern Hopewellian Exchange and Supralocal Interaction," in Colin Renfrew and John Cherry (eds.). *Peer Polity Interaction and Sociopolitical Change*. Cambridge University Press, Cambridge, pp.117–126.

———— 1989. "Coevolution of Sedentism, Pottery Technology, and Horticulture in the Central Midwest, 200 BC-AD 600," in W.F. Keegan (ed.). *Emergent Horticultural Economies of the Eastern Woodlands*, Southern Illinois University, Carbondale, Illinois, pp.153–182.

Bray, W. 1988. "The Paleoindian Debate," *Nature* 332:107.

Brose, David S. 1970. *The Summer Island Site: A Study of Prehistoric Cultural Ecology and Social Organization in the Northern Lake Michigan Area*. Case Western Reserve Studies in Anthropology 1.

———— 1979. "A Speculative Model of the Role of Exchange in the Prehistory of the Eastern Woodlands," in David S. Brose and N'omi Greber (eds.). *Hopewellian Archaeology*, Kent University Press, Kent, Ohio, pp.3–8.

———— and Plog, Stephen. 1982. "Evolution of 'Tribal' social networks: theory and prehistoric North American evidence," *American Antiquity* 473:504–525.

Brose, D.S. and Greber, N. (eds.) 1979. *Hopewellian Archaeology*. Kent University Press, Kent, Ohio.

Brown, J.A. 1976. "The Southern Cult Reconsidered," *Midcontinental Journal of Archaeology* 1,2:115–135.

———— 1979. "Charnel Houses and Mortuary Crypts: Disposal of the Dead in the Middle Woodland Period," in David S. Brose and N'omi Greber (eds.). *Hopewellian Archaeology*, Kent University Press, Kent, Ohio, pp.211–219.

Broyles, B. 1971. *Second Preliminary Report: the St Albans site. Kanawka County*. West Virginia Geological and Economic Survey.

Bryan, A.L. (ed.) 1978. *Early Man in America from a Circum-Pacific Perspective*. Archaeological Research International, Edmonton, Alberta.

———— (ed.) 1986. *New Evidence for the Pleistocene Peopling of the Americas*. Center for the Study of Early Man, Orono, Maine.

Bryant, Vaughn, and Holloway, Richard (eds.) 1985. *Pollen Records of Late-Quaternary North American Sediments*. American Association of Stratigraphic Palynologists Foundation, Dallas, Texas.

Buikstra, Jane E. and others. 1986. "Fertility and the Development of Agriculture in the Prehistoric Midwest," *American Antiquity* 51:528–546.

Byers, D. 1954. "Bull Brook – a fluted point site in Ipswich, Massachusetts," *American Antiquity* 19:343–351.

Byrd, K.M. 1976. "Tchefuncte Subsistence: information obtained from the excavation of the Morton Shell Mound, Iberia Parish, Louisiana," *Southeastern Archaeology Conference Bulletin*, 19.

Caldwell, Joseph R. 1958. *Trend and Tradition in the Prehistory of the Eastern United States*. Illinois State Museum, Springfield, Illinois.

Campbell, J.M. (ed.) 1962. *Prehistoric Cultural Relations between the Arctic and Temperate Zones of North America*. Arctic Institute of North America. Technical Paper 11, Montreal.

Carlisle, R. (ed.) 1988. *Americans before Columbus: Ice Age Origins*. Ethnology Monographs 12, Department of Anthropology, University of Pittsburgh.

Carlson R. 1970. "Archaeology in British Columbia, new discoveries." *BC Studies* 6–7.

———— (ed.) 1983. *Indian Art Traditions of the Northwest Coast*. Archaeology Press, Simon Fraser University, Burnaby, BC.

Cassidy, Francis. 1965. "Fire Temple, Mesa Verde National Park," in Gordon Vivian and Paul Reuter (eds.). *The Great Kivas of Chaco Canyon and their relationships*. School of American Research Monographs 22, pp.73–81.

Castetter, E.F. and Bell, W.M. 1942. *Pima and Papago Indian agriculture*. University of New Mexico Press, Albuquerque.

Chagnon, N. 1970. "Ecological and Adaptive Aspects of California Shell Money," *Annual Report of the UCLA Archaeological Survey* 12:1–25.

Chapman, Jefferson. 1973. *The Icehouse Bottom site 40MR23*. Department of Anthropology, University of Tennessee, Knoxville.

———— 1975. *The Rose Island site*. Department of Anthropology, University of Tennessee Knoxville.

———— 1978. *The Bacon Farm site and a buried site reconnaissance*. Department of Anthropology, University of Tennessee, Knoxville.

———— 1979. *The Howard and Calloway Island sites*. Department of Anthropology, University of Tennessee, Knoxville.

———— (ed.) 1980. *The 1979 Archaeological and Geological Investigations in the Tellico Reservoir, Eastern Tennessee*. Department of Anthropology, University of Tennessee, Knoxville.

———— 1985. *Tellico Archaeology*. University of Tennessee Press, Knoxville.

Chard, C.S. 1974. *Northeast Asia in Prehistory*. University of Wisconsin Press, Madison.

Charles, D.K. and Buikstra, J.E. 1983. "Archaic Mortuary Sites in the Central Mississippi Drainage: Distribution, Structure, and Implications," in James Phillips and James Brown (eds.). *Archaic Hunters and Gatherers in the Midwest*. Academic Press, New York, pp.117–145.

Childe, V.G. 1956. *Piecing Together the Past.* Kegan Paul, London.

Chuing, Tang, and Pei, Gai. 1986. "Upper Palaeolithic Cultural Traditions in North China," *Advances in World Archaeology* 5:339–364.

Cinq-Mars, Jacques. 1978. "Bluefish Cave I: a late Pleistocene eastern Beringian cave deposit in the northern Yukon," *Canadian Journal of Archaeology* 3:1–32.

Clark, D.W. 1966. "Perspectives in the Prehistory of Kodiak Island, Alaska," *American Antiquity* 31:356–371.

——— 1974. "The Earliest Prehistoric Cultures of Kodiak Island, Alaska: 1971 Fieldwork, Preliminary Report." *Arctic Anthropology* 11(1):41–46.

Clark, J.G.D. 1954. *Star Carr.* Cambridge University Press, Cambridge.

Claussen, C.J. and others. 1979. "Little Salt Spring, Florida: A unique underwater site," *Science* 203:609–614.

Cleland, C.E. 1982. "The Inland Shore Fishery of the Northern Great Lakes: Its Development and Importance in Prehistory," *American Antiquity* 47:761–84.

Coe, Joffre. 1952. "The cultural sequence of the Carolina Piedmont," in James B. Griffin (ed.). *Archaeology of the eastern United States.* University of Chicago Press, Chicago.

——— 1964. "The formative cultures of the Carolina Piedmont," *Transactions of the American Philosophical Society,* 54,5.

Coe, M., Snow, D. and Benson, E. 1986. *Atlas of Ancient America.* Facts on file, New York and Oxford.

Cohen, Mark. 1977. *The Food Crisis in Prehistory.* Yale University Press, New Haven.

Cole, Fay-Cooper. 1951. *Kincaid.* University of Chicago Publications in Anthropology, Chicago.

Coles, J.R. 1973. *Archaeology by Experiment.* Heinemann, London.

Colinvaux, Paul. 1980. "Vegetation of the Bering Land Bridge revisited," *Quarterly Review of Archaeology* 1:18–36.

Collins, H.B. 1937. "Archaeology of St Lawrence Island, Alaska," *Smithsonian Miscellaneous Collections* 96,1.

——— 1940. "Notes and News: Arctic," *American Antiquity* 5:234.

——— 1956. "Archaeological Investigations on Southampton and Coats Islands, Northwest Territories," *National Museum of Canada Bulletin* 142:82–113.

Collins, M. and Dillehay, T. 1986. "The implications of the lithic assemblage from Monte Verde for Early Man studies," in Alan L. Bryan (ed.). *New Evidence for the Pleistocene Peopling of the Americas.* Center for the Study of Early Man, Orono, Maine, pp.339–355.

Condie, C. and Fowler, D.D. (eds.) 1985. *Archaeology of the Desert West: Essays in Honor of Jesse D. Jennings.* University of Utah Press, Salt Lake City.

Conger, P.S. and others. 1949. "The Boylston Street Fishweir II," *Papers of the Robert S. Peabody Foundation for Archaeology* 4,1.

Cook, S.F. 1976. *The Populations of the California Indians 1969–1970.* University of California Press, Berkeley.

——— 1978. "Historical Demography," in R.F. Heizer (ed.). *Volume 8 California. Handbook of North American Indians,* Smithsonian Institution, Washington DC, pp.91–98.

——— and Borah, W.W. 1960. "The Indian Population of Central Mexico 1531–1610," *Ibero-Americana* 44, Berkeley.

Cordell, Linda S. 1979. *Cultural Resources Overview of the Middle Rio Grande Valley, New Mexico.* US Government Printing Office, Washington DC.

——— 1984. *Prehistory of the Southwest.* Academic Press, New York.

Cox, S.L. 1986. "A re-analysis of the Shoop site," *Archaeology of Eastern North America* 14:101–170.

——— and Gumerman, George J. (eds.) 1989. *Dynamics of Southwest Prehistory.* Smithsonian Institution Press, Washington DC.

Crites, D. 1987. "Human-Plant Mutualism and Niche Expression in the Paleoethnobotanical Record: A Middle Woodland Example," *American Antiquity* 52:725–740.

Croes, Dale. 1988. "The significance of the 3000 BP Hoko River Waterlogged Fishing Camp in our overall understanding of Southern Northwest Coast Cultural Evolution," in Barbara Purdy (ed.). *Wet Site Archaeology,* Telford Press, Caldwell, NJ.

——— 1989. "Prehistoric ethnicity on the Northwest Coast of North America: An evaluation of style in basketry and lithics," *Journal of Anthropological Archaeology* 8:101–130.

——— and Blinman, E. (eds.) 1980. *Hoko River: a 2500 year-old fishing camp on the Northwest Coast of North America.* Laboratory of Anthropology, Report of Investigations 58.

——— and Hackenberger, S. 1988. "Hoko River Archaeological Complex: Modeling prehistoric Northwest Coast Economic Evolution," *Research in Economic Anthropology,* Supplement 3:19–85.

Crosby, A.W. 1972. *The Columbian Exchange.* Greenwood Press, Westport, Connecticut.

Currey, D.R. and James, S.R. 1982. "Paleoenvironments of the Northeastern Great Basin and Northeastern Basin Rim Region: A Review of Geological and Biological Evidence," in David Madsen and James O'Connell (eds.). *Man and Environment in the Great Basin,* Society for American Archaeology, Washington DC, pp.27–52.

Cushing, Frank. 1882–3. *My Adventures in Zuñi.* American West, Palo Alto (1970 edition).

Damas, David (ed.) 1984. *Vol 5 Arctic. Handbook of North American Indians.* Smithsonian Institution, Washington DC.

D'Azevado, Warren (ed.) 1986. *Vol 11 Great Basin. Handbook of North American Indians.* Smithsonian Institution, Washington DC.

Deagan, K. 1980. "Spanish St Augustine: America's first melting pot," *Archaeology* 33(5):22–30.

——— 1983. *Spanish St Augustine.* Academic Press, New York.

Dean, J.S. and Ravesloot, J.C. 1989. "The chronology of cultural interaction in the Gran Chichimeca," in *Culture and Contact: Charles C. Di Peso's Gran Chichimeca.* Amerind Foundation, Dragoon, Arizona.

Deetz, James. 1977. *In Small Things Forgotten.* Anchor Books, New York.

Delcourt, H.R. and others. 1985. "Quaternary palynology and vegetational history of the southeastern United States," in V.M. Bryant and R.G. Holloway (eds.). *Pollen Records of Late Quaternary North American Sediments,* American Association of Stratigraphic Palynologists Foundation, pp.1–37.

——— 1986. "Holocene Ethnobotanical and Paleoecological Record of Human Impact on Vegetation in the Little Tennessee River Valley, Tennessee," *Quaternary Research* 25:330–349.

Delcourt, P.A. and Delcourt, H.R. 1981. "Vegetation maps for eastern North America," *Geobotany* 11:123–165.

——— 1983. "Late Quaternary vegetational dynamics and community stability reconsidered," *Quaternary Research* 19:265–271.

Dethlefsen, Edwin, and Deetz, James. 1966. "Death's Heads, Cherubs, and Willow Trees: Experimental Archaeology in Colonial Cemeteries," *American Antiquity* 31:502–510.

Deuel, Thorne. 1935. "Basic cultures of the Mississippi Valley," *American Anthropologist* 37:429–445.

Dewhirst, J. 1980. "The indigenous archaeology of Yoquot, a Nootkan Outside village," *National Historic Parks and Sites Branch, History and Archaeology* 39, Ottawa.

Dillehay, T. 1988. "How New is the New World?" *Antiquity* 62:94–97.

——— and Collins, M. 1988. "Early Cultural Evidence from Monte Verde, in Chile," *Nature* 332:150–152.

Dincauze, Dena. 1971. "An Archaic Sequence for southern New England," *American Antiquity* 36:194–198.

——— 1976. *The Neville Site: 8000 years at Amoskeag.* Peabody Museum, Harvard University, Cambridge, Mass.

——— 1984. "An Archaeo-Logical Evaluation of the Case for Pre-Clovis Occupations," *Advances in World Archaeology* 3:275–323.

Di Peso, Charles C. and others. 1974. *Casas Grandes: a fallen trading center of the Gran Chichimeca.* Amerind Foundation, Dragoo, and Northland Press, Flagstaff, Arizona.

Dobyns, Henry. 1983. *Their Numbers Became Thinned.* University of Tennessee Press, Knoxville.

Dragoo, D.W. 1963. "Mounds for the Dead: an analysis of the Adena Culture," *Annals of the Cargenie Museum,* 37.

Dumond, Don E. 1968. "On the Presumed Spread of Slate Grinding in Alaska," *Arctic Anthropology* 5(1):82–91.

——— 1971. "A Summary of Archaeology in the Katmai Region, Southeastern Alaska," *University of Oregon Archaeological Papers,* 2.

——— 1978. "Alaska and the Northwest Coast," in Jesse D. Jennings (ed.). *Ancient Native Americans.* W.H. Freeman, San Francisco, pp.43–94.

——— 1982. "Trends and Traditions in Alaskan Prehistory: The Place of Norton Culture," *Arctic Anthropology* 19(2):39–52.

——— 1987. Rev. (ed.). *The Eskimos and Aleuts.* Thames and Hudson, London and New York.

Dunnell, R. 1980. "Evolutionary Theory and Archaeology," *Advances in Archaeological Method and Theory* 3:38–99.

——— 1982. "Science, Social Science, and Common Sense: the Agonizing Dilemma of Modern Archaeology," *Journal of Anthropological Research* 38(1):1–25.

Earle, T.K. 1989. "The Evolution of Chiefdoms," *Current Anthropology* 30(1):84–88.

Elston, Robert G. 1982. "Good Times, Bad Times: Prehistoric Culture Change in the Western Great Basin," in David Madsen and James O'Connell (eds.). *Man and Environment in the Great Basin*, Society for American Archaeology, Washington DC, pp.186–206.

——— 1986. "Prehistory of the Western Area," in Warren D'Azevado (ed.). *Vol.11. Great Basin. Handbook of North American Indians*, Smithsonian Institution, Washington DC, pp.135–148.

Ericson, J.E. 1977. "Egalitarian Exchange Systems in California: A preliminary view," in Earle, T.K. and Ericson, J.E. (eds.). *Exchange Systems in Prehistory*. Academic Press, New York, pp.109–126.

Ewen, C.R. 1989. "Apalachee Winter," *Archaeology* 42(3):37–41.

Fagan, B.M. 1977. *Elusive Treasure*. Charles Scribners, New York.

——— 1984. *The Aztecs*. W.H. Freeman, New York.

——— 1987a. *The Great Journey*. Thames and Hudson, London and New York.

——— 1987b. *In the Beginning*. 6th ed. Scott, Foresman-Little, Brown, Glenview, Illinois.

——— 1989. *People of the Earth*. 6th ed. Scott, Foresman-Little, Brown, Glenview, Illinois.

Fages, P. 1972. *A historical, political, and natural description of California by Pedro Fages (1775), Soldier of Spain*. Ballena Press, Ramona, California.

Farwell, R.E. 1981. "Pit houses: prehistoric energy conservation?" *El Palacio* 87(3):43–47.

Fenton, W.N. 1978. "Northern Iroquoian cultural patterns," in Bruce G. Trigger (ed.). *Vol. 15 Northeast. Handbook of North American Indians*. Smithsonian Institution, Washington DC, pp.296–321.

Ferguson, W.M. and Rohn, A.H. 1987. *Anasazi Ruins of the Southwest in Color*. University of New Mexico Press, Albuquerque.

Fiedel, Stuart J. 1987. *Prehistory of the Americas*. Cambridge University Press, Cambridge.

Finlayson, W.D. 1985. *The 1975 and 1978 Rescue Excavations at the Draper Site: Introduction and Settlement Patterns*. National Museum of Canada. Mercury Series 130.

Fish, P.R. and Fish, S.K. 1977. "Verde Valley Archaeology: Review and Perspective," *Museum of Northern Arizona Research Paper* 8.

Fish, S.K. and Fish, P.R. (eds.) 1984. *Prehistoric Agricultural Strategies in the Southwest*. Arizona State University, Tempe, Arizona.

Fisher, Robin. 1977. *Contact and Conflict: Indian-European Relations in British Columbia 1774–1890*. University of British Columbia Press, Vancouver.

Fitzhugh, W.W. 1976. "Environmental factors in the end of the Dorset Culture: a marginal proposal for Hudson Bay," in Moreau Maxwell (ed.). *Eastern Arctic Prehistory: Paleoeskimo Problems*. Society for American Archaeology, Washington DC, pp.139–149.

——— 1980. "Preliminary Report on the Torngat Archaeological Project," *Arctic* 33:585–606.

——— and Crowell, Aron (eds.) 1985. *Cultures in Contact: The European Impact on Native Cultural Institutions in Eastern North America, AD 1000–1800*. Anthropological Society of Washington Series, Smithsonian Institution, Washington DC.

——— (ed.) 1988. *Crossroads of Continents*. Smithsonian Institution Press, Washington DC.

Fladmark, Knud E. 1971. "A Preliminary Report on Lithic Assemblages from the Queen Charlotte Islands, British Columbia," in R.A. Smith and J.W. Smith (eds.). *Early Man and Environments in Northwest North America*, University of Calgary Archaeological Association, Calgary, pp.117–136.

——— 1975. *A Paleoecological Model for Northwest Coast Prehistory*. National Museum of Man, Ottawa, Mercury Series 51.

——— 1983. "Times and Places in Environmental Correlates of Mid-to-Late-Wisconsinian Human Population Expansions in North America," in Richard Shutler (ed.). *Early Man in the New World*. Sage Publications, Beverly Hills, California, pp.13–42.

——— 1989. "Early Prehistory of the Queen Charlotte Islands," *Archaeology* 32(2):38–45.

Flannery, Kent V. 1973a. "Archaeology with a Capital A," in Charles Redman (ed.). *Research and Theory in Current Archaeology*, J. Wiley Interscience, New York, pp.337–354.

——— 1973b. "The Origins of Agriculture," *Annual Review of Anthropology* 2:271–310.

Ford, J.A. 1952. "Measurement of some Prehistoric Design Developments in the Southeastern States," *Anthropological Papers, American Museum of Natural History* 44,3.

——— and Willey, G.R. 1941. "An Interpretation of the Prehistory of the Eastern United States," *American Anthropologist* 43(3):325–363.

Ford, Richard I. 1974. "Northeastern archaeology: past and future developments," *Annual Review of Anthropology* 3:385–413.

——— 1981. "Gardening and Farming before AD 1000: patterns of prehistoric culture north of Mexico," *Journal of Ethnobiology* 1(1):6–7.

——— (ed.) 1985. *Prehistoric Food Production in North America*. Museum of Anthropology, University of Michigan, Ann Arbor, Michigan.

Fowler, C.S. 1982. "Settlement Patterns and Subsistence Systems in the Great Basin: The Ethnographic Record," in David Madsen and James O'Connell (eds.). *Man and Environment in the Great Basin*. Society for American Archaeology, Washington DC, pp.121–138.

——— 1986. "Subsistence," in Warren D'Azevado (ed.). *Vol 11 Great Basin. Handbook of North American Indians*. Smithsonian Institution, Washington DC, pp.64–97.

Fowler, D.D. and Jennings, J.D. 1982. "Great Basin Archaeology: A Historical Overview," in David Madsen and James O'Connell. *Man and Environment in the Great Basin*. Society for American Archaeology, Washington DC, p.105–120.

Fowler, Melvin. 1959. *Summary Report of Modoc Rock Shelter*. Illinois State Museum, Springfield, Illinois.

——— (ed.) 1969. *Investigations in Cahokia Archaeology*. Illinois Archaeological Survey, Urbana, Illinois.

——— 1974. *Cahokia: Ancient Capital of the Midwest*. Addison-Wesley Publishing Company, Menlo Park, California.

——— 1978. "Cahokia and the American Bottom: Settlement Archaeology," in Bruce D. Smith (ed.). *Mississippian Settlement Patterns*, Academic Press, New York, pp.455–478.

——— and Hall, R.L. 1972. *Archaeological Phases at Cahokia*. Illinois State Museum, Springfield.

Frazier, Hendrick. 1986. *People of Chaco: A Canyon and its Cultures*. W.W. Norton, New York.

Fredrickson, D.A. 1973. "Early Cultures of the North Coast Ranges, California." PhD dissertation, University of California, Davis.

Frison, G.C. 1971. "The Buffalo Pound in Northwestern Plains Prehistory. Site 48CA302." *American Antiquity* 36:77–91.

——— 1973. "The Wardell Buffalo Trap 48SU301: Communal Procurement in Post-Altithermal Populations in the Northwestern Plains," *University of Michigan Anthropological Papers* 46:11–20.

——— 1974. *The Casper Site*. Academic Press, New York.

——— 1978. *Prehistoric Hunters of the High Plains*. Academic Press, New York.

——— and Bradley, B.A. 1981. *Folsom Tools and Technology at the Hanson Site. Wyoming*. University of New Mexico Press, Albuquerque.

——— and Stanford, D. (eds.) 1973. *The Agate Basin Site: a record of the Paleo-Indian occupation of the Northwestern High Plains*. Academic Press, New York.

——— and Todd, L.C. (eds.) 1987. *The Horner Site*. Academic Press, New York.

——— and Wilson, M. 1975. "An Introduction to Bighorn Basin archaeology," *Wyoming Geological Association 27th Annual Field Conference Guidebook*, pp.19–35.

Funk, R.E. 1988. "The Laurentian Concept: A Review," *Archaeology of Eastern North America* 16:1-42.

Galinat, W.C. 1985. "Domestication and Diffusion of Maize," in Richard I. Ford (ed.). *Prehistoric Food Production in North America*. University Museum of Anthropology, University of Michigan, Ann Arbor, pp.245–282.

——— and Campbell, R.G. 1967. "The diffusion of Eight-Rowed Maize from the Southwest to the Central Plains," *Massachusetts Agricultural Experiment Station Monograph, University of Massachusetts, Amherst*.

Gardner, W.M. 1974. "The Flint Run Complex: Pattern and Process During the Paleo-Indian to Early Archaic." *Occasional Publications of the Catholic University of America, Washington DC*, pp.5–47.

——— 1976. "Paleo-Indian to early Archaic: continuity and change in Eastern North America during the Late Pleistocene and early Holocene," in James B. Griffin (ed.). *Habitats Humaines Anterieurs a L'Holocene en Amerique*. IX Congres Union International des Sciences Prehistoriques et Prothistoriques, pp.19–46.

——— 1977. "The Flint Run Paleo-Indian Complex and its implications for eastern North American prehistory," *Annals of the New York Academy of Sciences* 288:257–263.

Geist, Otto W. and Rainey, F.G. 1936. *Archaeological Excavations at Kukulik, St Lawrence Island, Alaska*. Miscellaneous Publications of the University of Alaska, Fairbanks, 2.

Gerasimov, M.M. 1935. "Excavations of the Palaeolithic Site of Mal'ta," *Investia Gosudarstvennoy Akademii Istorii Material 'noy Kultury* 118:78–115.

Gerow, B.A. 1968. *An Analysis of the University Village Complex with a reappraisal of Central California Archaeology*. Stanford University Press, Palo Alto.

Gibson, J.L. 1974. "Poverty Point, the first Native American Chiefdom," *Archaeology* 27:96–105.

——— 1980. "Speculations on the origin and development of Poverty Point Culture," in J.

Gibson (ed.). "Caddoan and Poverty Point Archaeology," *Bulletin of the Louisiana Archaeological Society* 6:321–348.

Giddings, J.L. 1960. *Ancient Men of the Arctic.* Alfred Knopf, New York.

——— 1964. *The Archaeology of Cape Denbigh.* Brown University Press, Providence, R.I.

Gladwin, W. and Gladwin, H.S. 1931. "Some Southwestern Pottery Types, Series II," *Medallion Papers* 10, Globe, Arizona.

Glassow, M.A. 1972. "Changes in the Adaptions of Southwestern Basketmakers: a systems perspective," in Mark Leone (ed.). *Contemporary Archaeology*, Southern Illinois University, Carbondale, pp.289–302.

——— 1978. "The Concept of carrying capacity in the study of culture process," *Advances in Archaeological Method and Theory* 1:32–48.

——— 1979. "An evaluation of models of Inezeño Chumash subsistence and economics," *Journal of California and Great Basin Archaeology* 1(1):155–161.

——— 1980. *Prehistoric agricultural development in the northern Southwest: a study in changing patterns of land use.* Ballena Press Anthropology Papers 16, Socorro, New Mexico.

——— Wilcoxon, L. and Erlandson, J. 1987. "Cultural and Environmental Change during the Early Period of Santa Barbara Channel Prehistory," in Geoff Bailey and John Parkington (eds.). *The Archaeology of Prehistoric Coastlines*, Cambridge University Press, Cambridge, pp.64–77

Goad, S. 1979. "Middle Woodland Exchange in the prehistoric southeastern United States," in David Brose and N'omi Greber (eds.). *Hopewellian Archaeology*. Kent University Press, Kent, Ohio, pp.239–246.

——— 1980. "Patterns of Late Archaic Exchange," *Tennessee Archaeologist*, 5:1–16.

Gould, R. (ed.) 1978. *Explorations in Ethnoarchaeology.* University of New Mexico Press, Albuquerque.

Goss, James A. 1977. "Linguistic Tools for the Great Basin Prehistorian," in Don D. Fowler (ed.). *Models and Great Basin Prehistory: A Symposium.* Desert Research Institute, University of Nevada, Reno, 12.

Grant, Campbell. 1965. *Rock Paintings of the Chumash.* University of California Press, Berkeley.

Grayson, Donald. 1982. "Toward a History of Great Basin Mammals during the Past 15,000 years," in David Madsen and James O'Connell (eds.). *Man and Environment in the Great Basin.* Society for American Archaeology, Washington DC, pp.82–101.

Greenburg, J. 1987. *Language in the Americas.* Stanford University Press, Palo Alto.

——— and others. 1986. "The Settlement of the Americas: A Comparison of the Linguistic, Dental, and Genetic Evidence," *Current Anthropology* 27:477–497.

Griffin, James B. 1946. "Culture Change and Continuity in the Eastern United States," in F. Johnson (ed.). *Man in Northeastern North America.* Robert S. Peabody Foundation for Archaeology, Andover, Massachusetts, pp.37–95.

——— 1961. "Some correlates of climatic and cultural change in eastern North American prehistory," *Annals of the New York Academy of Sciences* 95(1):710–717.

——— 1965. "Hopewell and the dark black glass," in James Fitting (ed.). "Papers in Honor of Emerson F. Greenman," *Michigan Archaeologist* 11:115–155.

——— 1967. "Eastern North American Archaeology: A Summary," *Science* 156:175–191.

——— 1978. "The Midlands and Northeastern United States," in Jesse D. Jennings (ed.). *Ancient Native Americans,* W.H. Freeman, San Francisco, pp.221–280.

——— and others. 1970. *The burial complexes of the Knight and Norton Mounds in Illinois and Michigan,* Museum of Anthropology, University of Michigan, Ann Arbor.

Guidon, N. and Delibrias, J. 1986. "Carbon–14 Dates Point to Man in the Americas 33,000 years ago," *Nature* 321:769–771.

Gumerman, George. 1984. *A View from Black Mesa.* University of Arizona Press, Tucson.

Gunnerson, James. 1969. "The Fremont Culture: a study in cultural dynamics on the northern Anasazi frontier," *Papers of the Peabody Museum of Archaeology and Ethnology* 59(2).

Guthrie, R.D. 1982a. "Paleoecology of the large-mammal community in interior Alaska during the Pleistocene," *American Midland Naturalist* 79:346–363.

——— 1982b. "Mammals of the Mammoth Steppe as Paleonevironmental Indicators," in David Hopkins and others (eds.). *Paleoecology of Beringia.* Academic Press, New York, pp.307–326.

Hardesty, D.L. 1988. *The Archaeology of Mining and Miners: A View from the Silver State.* Society for Historical Archaeology, Pleasant Hill, California.

Harp, E.J. 1961. "The Archaeology of the Lower and Middle Thelon, Northwest Territories," *Arctic Institute of North America Technical Paper* 11.

——— 1962. "The culture history of the Central Barren Grounds," in J.M. Campbell (ed.). *Prehistoric Cultural Relations Between the Arctic and Temperate Zones of North America.* Arctic Institute of North America, pp.69–75.

——— 1976. "Dorset settlement patterns in Newfoundland and southeastern Hudson Bay," in Moreau S. Maxwell (ed.). *Eastern Arctic Prehistory: Paleoeskimo Problems.* Society for American Archaeology, Washington DC, pp.119–138.

——— 1978. "Pioneer Cultures of the Sub-Arctic and the Arctic," in Jesse D. Jennings (ed.). *Ancient Native Americans.* W.H. Freeman, San Francisco, pp.95–129.

——— and Hughes, D.R. 1968. "Five prehistoric burials from Port au Choix, Newfoundland," Baker Library, Dartmouth College, *Polar Notes* VIII:1–47.

Harper, K.T. 1986. "Historical Environments," in Warren D'Azevado (ed.). *Vol. 11 Great Basin. Handbook of North American Indians.* Smithsonian Institution, Washington DC, pp.51–63.

——— and Alder, G.M. 1970. "The Macroscopic Plant Remains of the Deposits of Hogup Cave, Utah, and their Paleoclimatic Implications," in C.M. Aikens, *Hogup Cave,* Anthropological Papers of the University of Utah, 93:215–240.

Harrington, J.P. 1942. "Culture Element Distributions XIX: Central California coast," *Univerity of California Anthropological Records* 7:1–146.

Harrison, W.M. and Harrison, E.S. 1966. "An archaeological sequence for the Hunting People of Santa Barbara, California," *UCLA Archaeological Survey Annual Report 1965–1966*: 1–89.

Haury, E.W. 1950. *The Stratigraphy and Archaeology of Ventana Cave.* University of Arizona Press, Tucson.

——— 1957. "An alluvial site on the San Carlos Indian Reservation, Arizona," *American Antiquity* 23:2–27.

——— 1976. *The Hohokam, desert farmers and craftsmen: excavations at Snaketown 1964–1965.* University of Arizona Press, Tucson.

Haven, Samuel. 1856. *Archaeology of the United States.* Smithsonian Institution, Washington DC.

Haviland, W.A. and Power, M. 1981. *The Original Vermonters. Native inhabitants: Past and Present.* University Press of New England, Hanover, NH.

Hayden, Brian. 1981. "Research and Development in the Stone Age: Technological Transitions among Hunter-Gatherers," *Current Anthropology* 22(5):519–548.

——— 1982. "Interaction Parameters and the Demise of Paleo-Indian craftsmanship," *Plains Anthropologist* 27:109–123.

Hayes, Alden C. 1981. "A survey of Chaco Canyon," in A.C. Hayes and others (eds.). *Archaeological Surveys of Chaco Canyon, New Mexico.* National Park Service Publications in Archaeology, Washington DC, 18A:1–68.

——— and others. 1981. *Archaeological Surveys of Chaco Canyon.* University of New Mexico Press, Albuquerque.

Haynes, Vance. 1966. "Elephant Hunting in North America," *Scientific American* 214(6):104–112.

——— 1975. "Pleistocene and recent stratigraphy," in F. Wendorf and J. Hester (eds.). *Late Pleistocene Environments of the Southern High Plains.* Fort Burgwin Research Center Publications 9:576–596.

——— 1980. "Paleo-Indian Charcoal from Meadowcroft Rockshelter: is contamination a problem?" *American Antiquity* 45:582–587.

——— 1982. "Were Clovis Progenitors in Beringia?" in David Hopkins and others (eds.). *The Paleoecology of Beringia,* Academic Press, New York, pp.383–398.

——— 1987. "Clovis Origins Update," *The Kiva* 52:83–93.

Heiser, Charles B. 1985. "Some Botanical Considerations of the Early Domesticated Plants North of Mexico," in R.I. Ford (ed.). *Early Food Production in North America.* University Museum of Anthropology, University of Michigan, Ann Arbor, pp.57–72.

Heizer, R.F. 1964. "The western coast of North America," in Jesse D. Jennings and Edward Norbeck (eds.). *Prehistoric Man in the New World.* University of Chicago Press, Chicago, pp.117–148.

——— and Elsasser, A.B. 1964. "Archaeology of Hum–67: the Gunther Island site in Humboldt Bay, California," *University of California Archaeological Survey Reports* 62:1–122.

——— and Hester, T.R. 1978. "Great Basin Projectile Points: Forms and Chronology," *Ballena Press Publications in Archaeology, Ethnology, and History* 10.

——— and Napton, L.K. 1970. "Archaeology . . . as seen from Lovelock Cave, Nevada," *University of California Archaeological*

Research Facility Contributions 10(1).
—— and Whipple, M.A. (eds.) 1971. *The California Indians: A Source Book*. University of California Press, Berkeley.

Hester, J.J. 1975. "Paleoarchaeology of the Llano Estacado," in F. Wendorf and J. Hester (eds.). *Late Pleistocene Environments of the Southern Plains*. Fort Burgwin Research Center Publications, 9:247–256.

Hester, T.R. 1973. "Chronological Ordering of Great Basin Prehistory," *University of California Archaeological Research Facility Contributions* 17.

Hodder, I. 1982. *Symbolic and Structural Archaeology*. Cambridge University Press, Cambridge.

Hoffman, J.J. 1953. "Comments on the use and distribution of tipi rings in Montana, North Dakota, South Dakota, and Wyoming," *Montana State University Anthropological and Sociological Papers* 14.

Holmes, W.H. 1903. "Aboriginal Pottery of the Eastern United States," *Bureau of American Ethnology, 20th Annual Report*, Washington DC.

Holtved, E. 1954. "Archaeological investigations in the Thule District (Part 3): Nugdlit and Comer's Midden," *Medelelser om Greenland 146: CA Reitzels Forleg, Copenhagen*.

Hopkins, David O. and others (eds.) 1982. *Paleoecology of Beringia*. Academic Press, New York.

Hudson, C. 1980 *The Southeastern Indians*. University of Tennessee Press, Knoxville.

Hudson, C. and others. 1985. "Coosa: A Chiefdom in the Sixteenth-Century Southeastern United States," *American Antiquity* 50:723–737.

Hudson, T. and Blackburn, T. 1983. *The Material Culture of the Chumash Interaction Sphere*. Ballena Press, Socorro, New Mexico.
—— and others (eds.) 1978. *Tomol: Chumash watercraft as described in the ethnographic notes of John P. Harrington*. Ballena Press, Socorro, NM.
—— and others. 1979. "Solstice observations in Native California," *Journal of California and Great Basin Archaeology* 1(1):38–63.
—— and Underhay, E. 1978. *Crystals in the Sky: An Intelletual Odyssey involving Chumash astronomy, cosmology, and rock art*. Ballena Press, Socorro, NM.

Hunter-Anderson, Rosalind. 1987. *Prehistoric Adaptation in the American South-West*. Cambridge University Press, Cambridge.

Husted, W.M. 1969. *Bighorn Canyon Archaeology*. Publications in Salvage Archaeology 12.

Hutchings, S.S. and Stewart, G. 1953. "Increasing Forage Yields and Sheep Production on Intermontaine Winter Ranges," *US Department of Agriculture Circular 925*, Washington DC.

Ingstad, Anne. 1977. *The Discovery of a Norse Settlement in America*. Universitetsforlaget, Oslo.
—— (ed.) 1985. *The Norse Discovery of America*. Norwegian University Press, Oslo.

Irwin, H.T. and Wormington, M. 1970. "Paleo-Indian tool types on the Great Plains," *American Antiquity* 325:24–34.

Irwin-Williams, C. 1967. "Picosa: the elementary Southwestern culture," *American Antiquity* 32:441–456.
—— 1968. *Archaic Culture History in the Southwestern United States*. Eastern New

Mexico University Press, Portales.
—— 1973. "The Oshara Tradition: origins of Anasazi culture," *Eastern New Mexico University Contributions to Anthropology* 5,1.
—— 1979. "Post-Pleistocene archaeology 7000–2000 BC," in Alfonso Ortiz (ed.). *Vol. 9 Southwest. Handbook of North American Indians*, pp.31–42.
—— 1980. 'Investigations at Salmon Ruin: Methodology and overview," in C. Irwin-Williams and P.W. Shelley (eds.). *Investigations at the Salmon site: the structure of Chacoan Society in the northern Southwest*. Eastern New Mexico Press, Portales, pp.107–170.
—— and others. 1973. "Hell Gap: Paleo-Indian Occupation on the High Plains," *Plains Anthropologist* 19:40–53.

Jefferies, R. 1987. *Carrier Mills*. Southern Illinois University Press, Carbondale, Illinois.

Jefferson, Thomas. 1797. *Notes on the State of Virginia*. J. Stockdale, London.

Jenkins, N. 1982. *Archaeology of the Gainesville Lake Area: Synthesis*. Office of Archaeological Research, University of Alabama, Birmingham.

Jennings, J.D. 1957. *Danger Cave*, University of Utah Anthropological Papers, 27.
—— 1964. "The Desert West," in J.D. Jennings and E. Norbeck (eds.). *Prehistoric Man in the New World*. University of Chicago Press, Chicago.
—— 1966. *Glen Canyon: A Summary*. Department of Anthropology, University of Utah.
—— (ed.) 1978a. *Ancient Native Americans*. W.H. Freeman, San Francisco.
—— 1978b. *Prehistory of Utah and the Eastern Great Basin*. University of Utah Anthropological Papers 98.
—— 1986. "Introduction," in Warren D'Azevado (ed.). *Vol. 11 Great Basin. Handbook of North American Indians*, Smithsonian Institution, Washington DC, pp.113–119.
—— 1987. *The Prehistory of North America*. 3rd ed. Mayfield, Palo Alto.
—— and Norbeck, E. 1955. "Great Basin Prehistory: A Review," *American Antiquity* 21:1–11.
—— and others. 1980. *Sudden Shelter*. University of Utah Anthropological Papers 103.

Johnson, A. and Earle, T.K. 1987. *The Evolution of Human Societies*. Stanford University Press, Palo Alto.

Johnson, E. and Halliday, V.T. 1980. "A Plainview Kill–Butchering locale on the Llano Estacado – The Lubbock Lake Site," *Plains Anthropologist* 25:89–111.

Jordan, R.H. 1978. "Introduction," *Arctic Anthropology*, 15:1–8.

Judd, N.M. 1954. "The Material Culture of Pueblo Bonito," *Smithsonian Miscellaneous Collections* 124.
—— 1964. "The Architecture of Pueblo Bonito," *Smithsonian Miscellaneous Collections* 147(1).
—— 1967. *The Bureau of American Ethnology*. University of Oklahoma Press, Norman.

Judge, W.T. 1984. "New light on Chaco Canyon," in David Noble (ed.). *New Light on Chaco Canyon*. School of American Research Press, Santa Fé, pp.1–12.

Kaplan, Lawrence. 1965. "Beans of the Wetherill Mesa," in D. Osborne (ed.). *Contributions of

the Wetherill Mesa Archaeological Project*. Society for American Archaeology, Washington DC, pp.153–155.

Keegan, William F. (ed.) 1987. *Emergent Horticultural Economies of the Eastern Woodlands*. Center for Archaeological Investigations, Carbondale.

Kehoe, T.F. 1960. "Stone tipi rings in north-central Montana and the adjacent portion of Alberta, Canada. Their historical and archaeological aspects," *Bureau of American Ethnology Bulletin* 173. Anthropological Papers 62:421–473.

Kelly, R.L. and Todd, L.C. 1988. "Coming into the country: Early Paleoindian hunting and mobility," *American Antiquity* 53:231–244.

Kelso, W.M. 1984. *Kingsmill Plantation 1619–1800*. Academic Press, New York.
—— 1986. "Mulberry Row: Slave Life at Thomas Jefferson's Monticello," *Archaeology* 39(5):28–35.

Kidder, A.V. 1924. "A contribution to the study of Southwestern Archaeology, with a preliminary account of the excavations at Pecos," *Papers of the Southwestern Expedition. Phillips Academy* 1. Yale University Press, New Haven.
—— 1927. "Southwestern archaeology conference," *Science* 68:489–491.
—— 1931. "The Pottery of Pecos (Vol. 1)," *Papers of the Southwestern Expedition. Phillips Academy* 5. Yale University Press, New Haven.

King, C.D. 1971. "Chumash inter-village economic exchange," *Indian Historian* 4(1):31–43.
—— 1978. "Protohistoric and historic archaeology," in R.F. Heizer (ed.). *Vol. 8 California. Handbook of North American Indians*. Smithsonian Institution, Washington DC, pp.58–68.
—— 1984. *The Evolution of Chumash Society: A Comparative Study of artifacts used in social system maintenance in the Santa Barbara Channel region*. University of California, Santa Cruz. Microform.

King, T.F. 1970. "Archaeological problems and research in the Coast Miwok area," *Treganza Anthropological Museum Papers* 6:32–81.
—— 1974. The evolution of status ascription around San Francisco Bay," in L.J. Bean and T.F. King (eds.). "? Antap: California Indian political and economic organization," *Ballena Press Anthropological Papers* 2:35–54.

Kirk, Ruth. 1975. *Hunters of the Whale*. William Morrow, New York.

Kirk, R. and Szathmary, E. (eds.) 1985. *Out of Asia: Peopling the Americas and the Pacific*. Journal of Pacific History, Canberra, Australia.

Knight, V.J. 1986. "The institutional organization of Mississippian Religion," *American Antiquity* 61:675–687.

Knudsen, R. 1983. "Organizational Variability in Late Paleo-Indian Assemblages," *Washington State University Laboratory of Anthropology. Report of Investigations* 60.

Knuth, Eigil. 1967. "Archaeology of the Musk Ox Way," *Contributions du Centre d'Etudes Arctiques et Finnoscandinaves* 5.

Kornfeld, M. and Todd, L.A. (eds.) 1989. *McKean/Middle Plains Archaic*. Occasional Papers on Wyoming Archaeology 4.

Kroeber, A.L. 1916. "Zuni Potsherds," *Anthropological Papers of the American Museum of Natural History* 18(1):7–37.
—— 1939. *Cultural and Natural Areas of Native North America*. University of California

Publications on American Archaeology and
Ethnology 38.
Kroeber, T. 1965. *Ishi in Two Worlds*. University of
California Press, Berkeley.

Lafferty, R. 1977. *The Evolution of Mississippian
Settlement Patterns and Exploitation
Technology in the Black Bottom of Southern
Illinois*. PhD dissertation, Southern Illinois
University.
Lamb, S.M. 1958. "Linguistic Prehistory in the
Great Basin," *International Journal of
American Linguistics* 24(2):95–100.
Landberg, L.C.W. 1965. *The Chumash Indians of
Southern California*. Southwest Museum
Papers 19.
Larsen, Helge. 1968. "Near Ipiutak and Uwelen-
Okvik," *Folk* 10:81–90.
–––––– and Rainey, F. 1948. "Ipiutak and the
Arctic Whale Hunting Culture,"
*Anthropological Papers of the American
Museum of Natural History* 42.
Larsen, L.H. 1971. "Archaeological implications
of social stratification at the Etowah site,
Georgia," in J.A. Brown (ed.). *Approaches to
the Social Dimensions of Mortuary Practices*.
Society for American Archaeology, Washington
DC, pp.58–67.
Lawton, H.W. and others. 1976. "Agriculture
among the Paiute of Owens Valley," *Journal of
California Anthropology* 3(1):13–50.
LeBlanc, S.A. 1983. *The Mimbres People: ancient
pueblo potters of the American Southwest*.
Thames and Hudson, London and New York.
Lekson, S.H. and others. 1988. "The Chaco
Canyon Community," *Scientific American*
259(1):100–109.
Leone, Mark. 1984. "Interpreting Ideology in
Historical Archaeology: the William Paca
Garden in Annapolis, Maryland," in D. Miller
and C. Tilley (eds.). *Ideology, Power, and
Prehistory*. Cambridge University Press,
Cambridge, pp.25–35.
–––––– 1986. "Symbolic, Structural, and Critical
Archaeology," in David Meltzer and others
(eds.). *American Archaeology Past and Future*.
Smithsonian Institution Press, Washington DC,
pp.415–438.
–––––– and Potter, P.B. 1984. *Archaeological
Annapolis*. Historical Annapolis Inc,
Annapolis, Maryland.
–––––– and others. 1989. "Power Gardens of
Annapolis," *Archaeology* 42(2):34–40.
Le Page du Pratz, Antoine S. 1758. *Histoire de la
Louisiane*. 3 vols. Paris.
Lewis, J. 1973. *Patterns of Indian Burning*.
Ballena Press, Socorro, NM.
Lewis, T.M.N. and Lewis, M.K. 1961. *Eva: An
Archaic Site*. University of Tennessee Press,
Knoxville.
Libby, Willard. 1955. *Radiocarbon Dating*.
University of Chicago Press, Chicago.
Lipe, William D. 1978. "The Southwest," in Jesse
D. Jennings (ed.). *Ancient Native Americans*.
W.H. Freeman, San Francisco, pp.421–494.
Lister, Robert H. and Lister, Florence C. 1981.
*Chaco Canyon: Archaeology and
Archaeologists*. University of New Mexico Press,
Albuquerque.
Lobdell, John E. 1986. "The Kuparuk Pingo site: A
northern Archaic hunting camp on the Arctic
Coastal Plain, North Alaska," *Arctic* 39(1):47–
51.
Lounsbury, F.G. 1978. "Iroquoian Languages," in
Bruce Trigger (ed.). *Handbook of North

American Indians. vol 15*. Smithsonian
Institution, Washington DC, pp.334–343.
Lynch, T. 1990. "Glacial Age Man in South
America?" *American Antiquity*. 55(1):12–36.

MacDonald, G.F. 1968. "Debert: a Paleo-indian site
in central Nova Scotia," *Anthropology Papers*
16, National Museum of Canada, Ottawa.
MacNeish, R. (ed.) 1970. *The Prehistory of the
Tehuacan Valley*. University of Texas Press,
Austin.
Madsen, D.B. 1979. "The Fremont and the Sevier:
Defining Prehistoric Agriculturalists North of
the Anasazi," *American Antiquity* 44:711–722.
–––––– 1980. "Fremont Perspectives," *Utah
Division of State History Antiquities Section
Selected Papers* 7(16).
–––––– 1982. "Get it where the Gettin's Good: A
Variable Model of Great Basin Subsistence of
Settlement Based on Data from the Eastern
Great Basin," in David Madsen and James
O'Connell (eds.). *Man and Environment in the
Great Basin*. Society for American Archaeology,
Washington DC, pp.207–226.
–––––– 1983. "Black Rock Cave Revisited," *Utah
Bureau of Land Management. Cultural
Resource Series* 14.
–––––– 1985. "Great Basin Nuts: A Short Treatise
on the Distribution, Productivity, and
Prehistoric Use of Pinyon," in C. Condie and D.
Fowler (eds.). *Anthropology of the Desert West*,
University of Utah Press, Salt Lake City, pp.110–
125.
–––––– and Lindsay, L.W. 1977. "Backhoe
Village," *Utah Division of State History
Antiquities Section Selected Papers* 4(12).
–––––– and O'Connell, James (eds.) 1982. *Man
and Environment in the Great Basin*. Society
for American Archaeology, Washington DC.
Madson, R.G. 1989. *"The Locarno Beach Phase
and the Origins of the Northwest Coast
Ethnographic Pattern,"* in A.B. Onat,
*Development of Hunting-Fishing-Gathering
Maritime Societies of the Pacific*, Volume 3.
Circum-Pacific Prehistory Conference Reprint
Proceedings, Washington State University,
Pullman, Washington, Part 2C.
Malouf, C. and Conner, S. 1962. *Symposium on
Buffalo Jumps*. Montana Archaeological
Survey, Memoir 1.
Maltby, W.S. 1971. *The Black Legend in England:
The Development of Anti-Spanish Sentiment*.
Duke University Press, Durham, NC.
Mangelsdorf, Paul. 1974. *Corn: Its Origin,
Evolution, and Improvement*. Harvard
University Press, Cambridge, MA.
Manucy, A. 1985. "The Physical Setting of
Sixteenth-century St Augustine," *The Florida
Anthropologist* 38(1–2):34–53.
Marquandt, W. and Watson, P.J. 1983. "The Shell
Mound Archaic of Western Kentucky," in J.L.
Phillips and J.A. Brown (eds.). *Archaic hunters
of the American Midwest*. Academic Press, New
York, pp.323–332.
Marshall, M.P. and Doyel, D.E. 1981. *An Interim
Report on Bi Sa' ani Pueblo, with notes on the
Chacoan Regional System*. Navajo Nation CRM
Program, Window Rock, Arizona.
Martin, P.S. 1967. "Pleistocene Overkill," in P.S.
Martin and H.E. Wright (eds.). *Pleistocene
Extinctions: The Search for a Cause*. Yale
University Press.
–––––– 1973. "The Discovery of America,"
Science 197:969–974.
–––––– and Klein, Richard (eds.) 1984. *A

Pleistocene Revolution*. University of Arizona
Press, Tucson.
Martin, Paul S. 1979. "Prehistory: Mogollon," in
Alfonso Oritz (ed.). *Vol. 10 Southwest.
Handbook of North American Indians*.
Smithsonian Institution, Washington DC,
pp.61–74.
–––––– and Plog, F. 1973. *The Archaeology of
Arizona*. Doubleday/Natural History Press,
Garden City, NY.
Marwitt, J. 1970. *Median Village and Fremont
Culture Regional Variation*. University of Utah
Anthropological Papers 95.
–––––– 1986. "Fremont Cultures," in Warren
D'Azevado (ed.). *Vol 11 Great Basin. Handbook
of North American Indians*, Smithsonian
Institution, Washington DC, pp.161–172.
Mason, R. 1981. *Great Lakes Archaeology*.
Academic Press, New York.
Mathiassen, T. 1927. "Archaeology of the Central
Eskimos, the Thule culture and its position
within the Eskimo culture," in *Report of the
Fifth Thule Expedition 1921–1924*.
Glydenclalski Boghandel, Nordisk Forlag,
Copenhagen.
Matson, R.G. 1989. "The Locarno Beach Phase
and the Origins of the Northwest Coast Pattern,"
manuscript in press.
Matthews, J.V. 1982. "East Beringia during Late
Wisconsin Time: A Review of the Biotic
Evidence," in David Hopkins and others (eds.).
Paleoecology of Beringia. Academic Press, New
York, pp.127–152.
Maxwell, M.S. 1960. "An archaeological analysis
of eastern Grant Land, Ellesmere Island,
Northwest Territories," *National Museums of
Canada Bulletin* 180:20–25.
–––––– 1973. *Archaeology of the Lake Harbor
District, Baffin Island*. Archaeological Survey of
Canada, Mercury Series Paper 6, Ottawa.
–––––– 1976a "Pre-Dorset and Dorset Artifacts:
the view from Lake Harbor," in M.S. Maxwell
(ed.). *Eastern Arctic Prehistory: Paleoeskimo
Problems*. Society of American Archaeology,
Washington DC, pp.58–78.
–––––– (ed.) 1976b. *Eastern Arctic Prehistory:
Paleoeskimo Problems*. Society for American
Archaeology, Washington DC.
–––––– 1980. "Dorset site variation on the
southeastern coast of Baffin Island," *Arctic*
33:505–516.
–––––– 1985. *Prehistory of the Eastern Arctic*.
Academic Press, New York.
McCartney, A.P. 1977. *Thule Eskimo Prehistory
Along Northwestern Hudson Bay*.
Archaeological Survey of Canada, Mercury
Series 70.
–––––– 1979. "Archaeological Whale bone: a
northern resource," *University of Arkansas
Anthropology Papers* 1, Fayetteville.
–––––– 1980. "The Nature of the Thule Eskimo
Whale Bone," *Arctic* 33(3):517–541.
–––––– 1984a "Prehistory of the Aleutian
Region," in David Dames (ed.). *Vol. 5 Arctic.
Handbook of North American Indians*.
Smithsonian Institution, Washington DC,
pp.119–135.
–––––– 1984b. "History of native whaling in the
Arctic and Subarctic," in H.K. Jacob, and
others (eds.). 1984. *Arctic Whaling*,
Archaeological Center, Groningen, Netherlands,
pp.79–112.
–––––– 1988. "The Cape York Meteorite as a
Metal Souce for Prehistoric Canadian Eskimos,"
Meteorics 23(3):288.

——— and Mack, D.J. 1973. "Iron Utilization by Thule Eskimo," *American Antiquity* 38:328–339.

——— and Savelle, J.M. 1985. "Thule Eskimo Whaling in the Central Canadian Arctic," *Arctic Anthropology* 22(2):37–58.

McCluskey, S.C. 1977. "The Astronomy of the Hopi Indians," *Journal for the History of Astronomy* 8(2):174–195.

McDonald, J.N. 1981. *North American Bison.* University of California, Berkeley.

McGhee, R. 1970. "Speculations on climatic change and Thule culture development," *Folk* 11–12:172–184.

——— 1976. "Paleoeskimo occupations of Central and High Arctic Canada," in M.S. Maxwell (ed.). *Eastern Arctic Prehistory: Paleoeskimo Problems,* Society for American Archaeology, Washington DC, pp.15–39.

——— 1978. *Canadian Arctic Prehistory.* National Museums of Canada, Ottawa.

——— 1979. *The Paleoeskimo occupations at Port Refuge, High Arctic Canada.* Archaeological Survey of Canada, Mercury Series 92, Ottawa.

——— 1982. "Norsemen and Eskimos in Arctic Canada," in E. Guralnick (ed.). *Vikings in the West.* Archaeological Institute of America, Chicago, Illinois, pp.38–52.

——— 1984. "Contact Between Native North Americans and the Medieval Norse: A Review of Evidence," *American Antiquity* 49:4–26.

——— and Tuck, James A. 1975. *An Archaic Sequence from the Strait of Belle Isle, Labrador.* Archaeological Survey of Canada, Mercury Series 34.

——— 1977. "An Archaic Indian burial mound in Labrador," *Scientific American* 235(5):122–129.

McGregor, J.C. 1941. *Southwestern Archaeology.* John Wiley, New York.

McKern, W.C. 1939. "The Midwestern Taxonomic Method as an Aid to Archaeological Study," *American Antiquity* 4:301–313.

NcNett, C.A. (ed.) 1985. *Shawnee Minisink.* Academic Press, New York.

NcNitt, Frank. 1957. *Robert Wetherill: Anasazi.* University of New Mexico Press, Alburquerque.

Mehringer, P.J. 1977. "Great Basin Late Quaternary Environments and Chronology," in D.D. Fowler (ed.). *Models and Great Basin Prehistory: A Symposium.* Desert Research Institute, University of Nevada, Reno, Publications in the Social Sciences 12:113–167.

——— 1986. "Prehistoric Environments," in Warren D'Azevado (ed.). *Vol 11 Great Basin.* Handbook of North American Indians, Smithsonian Institution, Washington DC, pp.31–50.

Meighan, C. and Haynes, C.V. 1970. "The Borax Site revisited," *Science* 167:1213–1221.

Meldgaard, J. 1962. "On the Formative Period of the Dorset Culture," in J.M. Campbell (ed.). *Prehistoric Relations between the Arctic and Temperate Zones of North America.*

Meltzer, David. 1983. "The Antiquity of Man and the Development of American Archaeology," *Advances in Archaeological Method and Theory* 6:1–51.

——— 1988. "Late Pleistocene Human Adaptations in Eastern North America," *Journal of World Prehistory* 2(1):1–52.

——— 1989. "Why Don't We Know When the First People came to North America?" *American Antiquity* 54:471–490.

——— and others (eds.) 1986. *American Archaeology Past and Future.* Smithsonian Institution Press, Washington DC.

——— and Mead, J.I. (eds.) 1985. *Environments and Extinctions: Man in Late Glacial North America.* Center for the Study of Early Man, Orono, Maine.

——— and Smith B. (eds.) 1986. "Paleo-Indian and Early Archaic Subsistence Strategies in Eastern North America," in Sarah Neusius (ed.). *Foraging, Collecting, and Harvesting: Archaic Period Subsistence and Settlement in the Eastern Woodlands.* Center for Archaeological Investigations, Southern Illinois University, Carbondale, pp.3–32.

Milanich, J.T. 1973a. *The Southeastern Deptford Culture: a preliminary definition.* Florida Department of State, Tallahassee.

——— 1937b. "A Deptford Phase house structure, Cumberland Island, Georgia," *Florida Anthropologist* 26:105–118.

——— 1987. "Hernando de Soto and the expedition in La Florida," *Miscellaneous Project Report Series* 32. Florida State Museum, Gainesville.

——— and Fairbanks, C. 1980. *Florida Archaeology.* Academic Press, New York.

——— and others. 1984. *McKeithen Weeden Island: The Culture of Northern Florida, AD 200–900.* Academic Press, New York.

——— and Milbrath, Susan (eds.) 1989. *First Encounters.* University of Florida Presses, Gainesville.

Milner, George R. 1990. "The Late Prehistoric Cahokia Cultural System of the Mississippi River Valley: Foundations, Florescence, and Fragmentation," *Journal of World Prehistory* 4(1):1–44.

Mitchell, D.H. 1971. "Archaeology of the Gulf of Georgia area: a natural region and its cultural types," *Syesis* 4, Supplement 1.

Mitchem, J.M. and Hutchinson, D.L. 1987. "Interim Report on archaeological research at the Tatham Mound, Citrus County, Florida: Season III," Miscellaneous Project Series. Florida State Museum, Gainsville.

Mochanov, Yuri A. 1977. *The Most Ancient Stages of the Human Settlement of Northeast Asia.* Science Press, Siberian Division, Novosibursk.

Molto, J.E. 1983. *Biological Relationships of Southern Ontario Woodland Peoples: The Evidence of Discontinuous Cranial Morphology.* Archaeological Survey of Canada, Mercury Series 117, Ottawa.

Moore, J.A. and Keene, K.S. (eds.) 1983. *Archaeological Hammers and Theories.* Cambridge University Press, Cambridge.

Moratto, M.J. 1984. *California Archaeology.* Academic Press, New York.

Morgan, Lewis H. 1877. *Ancient Society.* Henry Holt, New York.

Morison, Samuel Eliot, 1971. *The European Discovery of America. Vol 1: The Northern Voyages.* Oxford University Press, New York.

Morlan, Richard. 1980. *Taphonomy and Archaeology in the Upper Pleistocene of the Northern Yukon Territory: A Glimpse into the Peopling of the New World.* National Museum of Man, Ottawa.

Morse, Dan, and Morse, Phyllis. 1983. *Archaeology of the Central Mississippi Valley.* Academic Press, New York.

Morss, N.M. 1931. "The Ancient Culture of the Fremont Sevier in Utah," *Papers of the Peabody Museum of American Archaeology and Ethnology,* Cambridge 12(3).

Morton, Samuel. 1839. *Crania Americana.* J. Dobson, Philadelphia.

Muller, Jon. 1986. *Archaeology of the Lower Mississippi Ohio River Valley.* Academic Press, New York.

——— 1987. "Salt, chert and shell: Mississippian Exchange and Economy," in E. Brumfiel and T.K. Earle, *Specialization and Exchange and Complex Societies.* Cambridge University Press, Cambridge, pp.10–21.

——— 1989. "The Southern Cult," in Patricia Galloway (ed.). *The Southeastern ceremonial complex: Artifacts and Analysis.* University of Nebraska Press, Lincoln, pp.11–26.

Muller, W.R. 1966. "Anthropological Linguistics in the Great Basin," in Warren D'Azevado and others (eds.). *The Current Status of Anthropological Research in the Great Basin.* Desert Research Institute, University of Nevada, Reno, Social Sciences Publications 1.

——— and others. 1971. "A Lexicostatic study of Shoshoni Dialects," *Anthropological Linguistics* 13(4):142–164.

Müller-Beck, Hans-Jurgen. 1982. "Later Pleistocene Man in Northern Eurasia and the Mammoth-Steppe Biome," in David Hopkins and others (eds.). *Palecology of Beringia.* Academic Press, New York, pp.329–352.

Nassaney, Michael S. 1987. "On the Causes and Consequences of Subsistence Interactions in the Mississippi Alluvial Valley," in William Keegan (ed.). *Emergent Horticultural Economies of the Eastern Woodlands.* Center for Archaeological Investigations, Southern Illinois University, Carbondale, pp.129–151.

Nelson, Nils C. 1916. "Chronology of the Tano Ruins, New Mexico," *American Anthropologist* 18(2):159–180.

Nelson, R.K. 1969. *Hunters of the Northern Ice.* University of Chicago, Chicago.

Neusius, S.W. (ed.) 1986. *Foraging, Collecting, and Harvesting: Archaic Period Subsistence and Settlement in the Eastern Woodlands.* Center for Archaeological Investigations, Southern Illinois University, Cabondale.

Noble, David (ed.) 1984. *New Light on Chaco Canyon.* School of American Research Press, Santa Fé, New Mexico.

——— 1985. *Mesa Verde National Park.* School of American Research Press, Santa Fé, New Mexico.

Noble, W.C. 1971. "Archaeological Surveys and Sequences in Central District Mackenzie, Northwest Territories," *Arctic Anthropology* 8(1):102–135.

Noël Hume, Ivor. 1969. *Historical Archaeology.* Alfred Knopf, New York.

——— 1982. *Martin's Hundred.* Alfred Knopf, New York, Gollancz, London.

O'Connell, James. 1967. "Elko Eared/Elko Corner-Notched Projectile Points as Time Markers in the Great Basin," *University of California Archaeological Survey Papers on the Great Basin Archaeology* 70. Berkeley.

——— 1975. "The Prehistory of Surprise Valley," *Ballena Press Anthropological Papers 4.* Ramona, California.

——— and others. 1982. "Some Thoughts on Prehistoric Archaeology in the Great Basin," in David Madsen and James O'Connell (eds.). *Man and Environment in the Great Basin,* Society for American Archaeology, Washington DC, pp.227–240.

O'Laughlin, Thomas C. 1980. "The Keystone Dam Site and other Archaic and Formative Sites in northwest El Paso, Texas," *Publications in Anthropology*. University of Texas. El Paso.

Osborn, A.J. 1983. "Ecological Aspects of Equestrian Adaptations in North America," *American Anthropologist* 85:563–591.

Parker, A.C. 1916. "The Origin of the Iroquois as Suggested by their Archaeology," *American Anthropologist* 18:479–507.

Parkman, Francis. 1867. *The Jesuits in North America in the Seventeeth Century*.

Pastron, Allen G. 1988. "Bonanza from Old San Francisco," *Archaeology* 41(4):32–40.

———— 1989. "Golden Mountain," *Archaeology* 42(4):49–53.

Peebles, C. 1978. "Determinants of settlement size and location in the Moundville Phase," in Bruce Smith (ed.). *Mississippian Settlement Patterns*. Academic Press, New York, pp.369–416.

———— 1979. *Excavations at Moundville 1905–1951*. Museum of Anthropology, University of Michigan, Ann Arbor.

———— and Kus, S. 1977. "Some archaeological correlates of ranked societies," *American Antiquity* 42(3):421–448.

Petruso, K.M. and Wickens, J.M. 1984. "The Acorn in Aboriginal Subsistence in Eastern North America," in P.J. Munson (ed.). *Experiments and Observations of Aboriginal Wild Plant Foods Utilized in Eastern North America*. Indiana Historical Society, Indianapolis, pp.360–378.

Phillips, J.L. and Brown, J.A. (eds.) 1983. *Archaic Hunters and Gatherers in the American Midwest*. Academic Press, New York.

Phillips, P. 1970. "Archaeological Survey in the Lower Yazoo Basin, Mississippi 1945–1955," *Papers of the Peabody Museum of Archaeology and Ethnology* 60.

———— and Brown, J. 1984. *Pre-Columbian Shell Engravings from the Craig Mound at Spiro, Oklahoma*. 2 vols. Peabody Museum of Archaeology and Ethnology, Harvard University.

———— and others. 1951. "Archaeological survey in the Lower Mississippi alluvial valley, 1940–1947," *Peabody Museum Papers*, 25.

Plog, Fred. 1974. *The Study of Prehistoric Culture Change*. Academic Press, New York.

———— 1983. "Political and economic alliances on the Colorado Plateau, AD 400–1450," *Advances in World Archaeology* 2:289–330.

Plog, S.E. 1980. *Stylistic variation in prehistoric ceramics: design analysis in the American Southwest*. Cambridge University Press, New York.

Pope, S.T. 1923. *Hunting with the Bow and Arrow*. James H. Barry, San Francisco.

Porter, S.C. 1988. "Landscapes of the Last Ice Age in North America," in R. Carlisle (ed.). *Americans before Columbus: Ice Age Origins*. Department of Anthropology, University of Pittsburgh, Pittsburgh, Pennsylvania, pp.1–24.

Powell, S. 1983. *Mobility and Adaptation: the Anasazi of Black Mesa, Arizona*. Southern Illinois University Press, Carbondale.

Powers, W.R. and Hamilton, T.D. 1978. "Dry Creek: A Late Pleistocene human occupation in central Alaska," in A.L. Bryan (ed.). *Early Man in America from a Circum-Pacific Perspective*. Archaeological Research International, University of Alberta, Edmonton, pp.72–77.

———— and Hoffecker, John. 1989. "Late Pleistocene Settlement in the Nenana Valley, Central Alaska," *American Antiquity* 54(2):263–287.

Prufer, Olaf. 1964. "The Hopewell Complex of Ohio," in R. Caldwell and R.L. Hall (eds.). *Hopewellian Studies*, Illinois State Museum, Springfield, pp.35–84.

Ragir, S.R. 1972. "The Early Horizon in Central California prehistory," *University of California Archaeological Research Facility Paper* 15.

Rainey, F.G. 1941. "Eskimo Prehistory: The Okvik Site on the Punuk Islands," *Anthropological Papers of the American Museum of Natural History* 37(4):443–569.

Ramenovsky, A. 1987. *Vectors of Death: The Archaeology of European Contact*. University of New Mexico Press, Albuquerque.

Rasmussen, K. 1931. "The Netsilik Eskimos: social life and spiritual culture," *Report of the Fifth Thule Expedition 1921–1924*:8. Glyndendalske Boghandel Nordisk Forlag, Copenhagen.

Ravesloot, J. and Dean, J.S. 1989. "The Chronology of Cultural Interaction in the Gran Chichimeca," Unpublished seminar Paper at the Amerind Foundation, Dragoo, Arizona.

Redman, Charles L. 1978. *The Rise of Civilization*. W.H. Freeman, San Francisco.

Reher, C.A. 1974. "Population Study of the Casper site bison," in George Frison (ed.). *The Casper Site*. Academic Press, New York, pp.231–240.

———— and Frison, G.E. 1980. "The Vere Site, 48CK302, a Stratified Buffalo Jump in the Wyoming Black Hills," *Plains Anthropological Memoirs* 16.

Reitz, E.J. and Scarry, M.C. 1986. *Reconstructing Historic Subsistence with an Example from Sixteenth-Century Spanish Florida*." Society for Historical Archaeology, Glassborough, N.J, Special Publication Series 3.

Renfrew, C. and Bahn, P. 1991. *Archaeology: Theories, Methods, and Practice*. Thames and Hudson, London and New York.

Ritchie, W. 1969. *Archaeology of New York State*. Natural History Press, Garden City, New York.

Ritchie, W.A. and Funk, R.E. 1973. *Aboriginal Settlement Patterns in the Northeast*. New York State Museum and Science Service Memoir 20, Albany.

Rohn, A.H. 1971. *Mug House, Mesa Verde National Park, Colorado*. National Park Service, Washington DC, Archaeological Research Series 7D.

———— 1977. *Cultural Change and Continuity on Chapin Mesa*. Regents Press of Kansas, Lawrence.

Roosa, William. 1965. "Some Great Basin Fluted Point Types," *Michigan Archaeologist* 11(3–4):89–102.

———— 1977. "Great Lakes Paleoindian: the Parkhill Site, Ontario," in Walter Newman and Bert Salwen (eds.). *Amerinds and Their Paleoenvironments in Northeastern North America, Annals of New York Academy of Sciences* 228:349–354.

Rothschild, N.A. 1979. "Mortuary behavior and social organization at Indian Knoll and Dickson Mounds," *American Antiquity* 44:658–675.

Rountree, H. 1989. *The Powhatan Indians of Virginia*. University of Oklahoma Press, Norman.

Rudenko, S.I. 1961. *The Ancient Culture of the Bering Sea and the Eskimo Problem*. Translated by Paul Tolstoy. Arctic Institute of North America, Toronto. Translations from Russian Sources 1.

Rutter, N.W. 1980. "Late Pleistocene History of the Western Canadian Ice-Free Corridor," *Journal of Canadian Anthropology* 1:1–8.

Sahlins, M. 1972. *Stone Age Economics*. Aldine, Chicago.

Sanger, D. 1979. "The Ceramic Period in Maine," in D. Sanger (ed.). *Discovering Maine's Archaeological Heritage*. Maine Historic Preservation Commission, Augusta, pp.99–115.

Sauer, C.O. 1954. "Comments to "Gatherers and Farmers in the Great Southwest"," *American Anthropologist* 56(4):529–560.

———— 1980. *Seventeenth Century North America*. Turtle Island, Berkeley.

Savelle, J.M. and McCartney, A.P. 1988. "Geographical and Temporal Variation in Thule Eskimo Subsistence Economies: a model," *Research in Economic Anthropology* 10:21–72.

Sayles, E.B. 1936. "Some Southwestern Pottery Types, Series V," *Medallion Papers*, Gila Pueblo, Globe, Arizona 21.

———— 1983. "The Cochise Culture Sequence in Southern Arizona," *Anthropological Papers of the University of Arizona* 42.

———— and Antevs, E. 1941. "The Cochise Culture," *Medallion Papers* 25.

Schell, D.M. 1983. "Carbon–13 and Carbon–14 abundances in Alaskan aquatic organisms: delayed production from peat in Alaskan food webs," *Science* 219:1068–1071.

Schiffer, M.B. 1975. "Some further comments on the Dalton settlement pattern hypothesis," in M. Schiffer and J. House (eds.). *The Cache River Archaeological Project*. Arkansas Archaeological Survey, Fayetteville, pp.103–112.

Schledermann, P. 1979. "The "Baleen Period" of the Arctic whaling hunting tradition," in Alan McCartney (ed.). *Thule Eskimo culture: an anthropological retrospective*. National Museum of Man, Ottawa, Mercury Series 88:134–148.

———— and McCullogh, K. 1980. "Western elements in the early Thule culture of the eastern High Arctic," *Arctic* 33:833–842.

———— 1987. *Formation Processes of the Archaeological Record*. University of New Mexico Press, Albuquerque.

Schledermann, Peter. 1990. *Crossroads to Greenland: 3000 Years of Prehistory in the Eastern High Arctic*. Arctic Institute of North America, Calgary.

Schnell, F.T. and others. 1981. *Cemochechobee: Archaeology of a Mississippian Ceremonial Center on the Chattahoochee River*. University Presses of Florida, Gainesville.

Schultz, C.B. 1943. "Some Artifact Sites of Early Man in the Great Plains," *American Antiquity* 8:242–249.

Schuyler, Robert L. 1977. "The spoken word, the written record, observed behavior, and preserved behavior: the contexts available to the archaeologist," *Conference on Historic Sites Archaeology Papers* 10:99–120.

———— 1979. *Historical Archaeology: A guide to substantive and theoretical contributions*. Baywood, Farmingdale, NY.

Sears, W. 1956. *Excavations at Kolomoki: final report*. University of Georgia Press, Athens.

———— 1973. "The sacred and the secular in prehistoric ceramics," in D. Lathrap and J.

Douglas (eds.). *Variations in Anthropology: essays in honor of John McGregor*. Illinois Archaeological Survey, Urbana, pp.31–42.

Seeman, M.F. 1979a. *The Hopewell Interaction Sphere: the evidence for Interregional Trade and Structural Complexity*. Indiana Historical Society, Indianapolis.

—— 1979b. "Feasting of the Dead: Ohio Hopewell Charnel House Ritual as a Context for Redistribution," in David Brose and N'omi Greber (eds.). *Hopewellian Archaeology*. Kent University Press, Kent, Ohio, pp.39–46.

—— 1988. "Ohio Hopewell Trophy-Skull Artifacts as Evidence for Competition in Middle Woodland Societies circa 50BC-AD350," *American Antiquity* 53:565–577.

Shafer, H.J. 1982. "Classic Mimbres phase households and room use patterns," *The Kiva* 48(1–2):17–38.

Sharer, R. and Ashmore, W. 1987. *Archaeology: Discovering Our Past*. Mayfield, Palo Alto.

Shaw, R.D. and Holmes, C.E. 1982. "The Norton Interaction Sphere: Selected Papers from a Symposium," *Arctic Anthropology* 19(2).

Shepherd, Anna O. 1954. *Ceramics for the Archaeologist*. Carnegie Institute of Washington Publications, 609.

Shipley, W. 1978. "Native Languages of California," in R.F. Heizer (ed.). *Vol. 8 California. Handbook of North American Indians*. Smithsonian Institution, Washington DC, pp.80–90.

Shutler, R. and others. 1974. "The Cherokee Sewer site (13CK405)," in Dale R. Henning (ed.). *A Preliminary Report of a stratified Paleo-Indian Archaic site in northwestern Iowa*. Journal of the Iowa Archaeological Society 21.

Silberman, N.A. 1989. "The Black Experience in America," *Archaeology* 42(5):62–72.

Silverberg, R. 1968. *Mound Builders of Ancient America: the archaeology of a myth*. New York Graphic Society, Greenwich, Connecticut.

Simmons, A.A. 1984. *Archaic Prehistory and Paleoenvironments: the San Juan Basin, New Mexico*. University of Kansas Museum of Anthropology, Lawrence.

—— 1986. "New Evidence for the Early Use of Cultigens in the American Southwest," *American Antiquity* 51:73–88.

Simmons, J.J. III. 1988. "Steamboats on Inland Waterways: Prime Movers of Manifest Destiny," in George Bass (ed.). *Ships and Shipwrecks of the Americas*. Thames and Hudson, London and New York, pp.189–206.

Singleton, T.A. 1985. *The Archaeology of Slavery and Plantation Life*. Academic Press, Orlando.

Smith, B.D. (ed.) 1978. *Mississippian Settlement Patterns*. Academic Press, New York.

—— 1984. "Chenopodium as a Prehistoric Domesticate in Eastern North America: Evidence from Russell Cave, Alabama," *Science* 226:165–167.

—— 1986. "The Archaeology of the Southeastern United States: From Dalton to de Soto, 10,500 to 500 BP," *Advances in World Archaeology* 5:1–92.

—— 1987. "The Independent Domestication of Indigenous Seed-Bearing Plants in Eastern North America," in William F. Keagan (ed.). *Emergent Horticultural Economies of the Eastern Woodlands*. Center for Archaeological Investigations. Southern Illinois University, Carbondale, pp.3–48.

Smith, E.A. 1983. "Anthropological application of optimal foraging strategy: a critical review," *Current Anthropology* 24:625–651.

Smith, M.T. 1987. *Archaeology of Aboriginal Culture Change in the Interior Southeast*. University of Florida Presses, Gainesville.

—— and Kowalewski, S.A. 1980. "Tentative Identification of a prehistoric 'province' in piedmont Georgia," *Early Georgia* 8:1–13.

Smith, S. 1977. *Method and Theory in Historical Archaeology*. Academic Press, New York.

—— 1980. *The Discovery of Santa Elena*. Institute of Archaeology, University of South Carolina, Columbia.

Snow, Dean. 1980. *The Archaeology of New England*. Academic Press, New York.

Snow, Dean and Forman, W. 1976. *The Archaeology of North America*. Viking, New York (published in Britain as *The American Indians*. Thames and Hudson, London).

Soffer, O. 1984. *The Upper Palaeolithic of the Central Russian Plain*. Academic Press, New York.

South, Stanley. 1977. *Research Strategies in Historical Archaeology*. Academic Press, New York.

—— and others. 1988. *Spanish Artifacts from Santa Elena*. South Carolina Institute of Archaeology and Anthropology.

Spaulding, A.C. 1953. "Statistical Techniques for the Discovery of Artifact Types," *American Antiquity* 18:305–313.

—— 1973. "Archaeology in the Active Voice: The New Anthropology," in Charles Redman (ed.). *Research and Theory in Current Archaeology*. John Wiley Interscience, New York, pp.337–354.

Spence, M.W. 1982. "The Social Context of Production and Exchange," in J. Ericson and T. Earle (eds.). *Contexts for Prehistoric Exchange*. Academic Press, New York, pp.173–197.

Speth, J.D. 1983. *Bison Kills and Bone Counts*. University of Chicago Press, Chicago.

Spicer, E.H. 1962. *Cycles of Conquest*. University of Arizona Press, Tucson.

Spier, L. 1917. "An Outline for a Chronology of Zuni Ruins," *Anthropological Papers of the American Museum of Natural History* 18,3.

Sproull-Thomson, J. 1979. "Recent Studies in Thule art: metaphysical and practical aspect," in A.P. McCartney (ed.). *Thule Eskimo prehistory: an anthropological perspective – National Museum of Man, Ottawa*, Mercury Series 88:485–494.

Squier, E.G. and Davis, E.V. 1848. *Ancient Monuments of the Mississippi Valley*. Smithsonian Institution, Washington DC.

Stanford, D. 1976. "The Walakpa Site, Alaska," *Smithsonian Contributions to Anthropology* 20.

—— 1978. "The Jones-Miller Site: An Example of Hell Gap Bison Procurement Strategy," in L. Davis and M. Wilson (eds.). "Bison Procurement and Utilization: A Symposium," *Plains Anthropologist Memoir* 16:90–97.

Stark, B.L. 1986. "Origins of Food Production in the New World," in David Meltzer and others (eds.). *American Archaeology Past and Future*. Smithsonian Institute Press, Washington DC, pp.277–322.

Steffy, J.R. 1988. "The Thirteen Colonies: English Settlers and Seafarers," in George Bass (ed.). *Ships and Shipwrecks of the Americas*. Thames and Hudson, London and New York, pp.107–128.

Steponaitis, V. 1978. "Location theory and complex chiefdoms: a Mississippian example," in B.D. Smith (ed.). *Mississippian Settlement Patterns*. Academic Press, New York, pp.417–453.

—— 1983. *Ceramics, chronology, and community patterns: An archaeological study at Moundville*. Academic Press, New York.

—— 1984. "Technological Studies of prehistoric pottery from Alabama: Physical properties and vessel function," in S.E. van der Leuw and A.C. Pritchard (eds.). *The Many Dimensions of Pottery*. Ven Giffen Institute, University of Amsterdam, pp.79–122.

—— 1986. "Prehistoric Archaeology in the Southeastern United States 1970–1985," *Annual Review of Anthropology* 15:363–404.

Steward, J. 1938. "Basin-Plateau Aboriginal Sociopolitical Groups," *Bureau of American Ethnology Bulletin* 120.

—— 1941. "Culture Element Distributions, XII: Nevada Shoshone," *University of California Anthropological Records* 4(2):209–360.

—— 1943. "Culture Element Distribution XXIII: Northern and Gosuite Shoshone," *University of California Anthropological Records* 8(3):263–392.

—— 1955. *A Theory of Culture Change*. University of Illinois Press, Urbana.

Stoltman, J. 1966. "New Radiocarbon Dates for Southeastern Fiber Tempered Pottery," *American Antiquity* 31:872–873.

—— 1978. "Temporal Models in Prehistory: An Example from Eastern North America," *Current Anthropology* 19(4):703–746.

Storck, P.L. 1984. "Research into the Paleo-Indian occupations of Ontario: A Review," *Ontario Archaeology* 41:3–18.

Story, D. 1985. "Adaptive Strategies of Archaic Cultures of the Gulf Coastal Plain," in R.I. Ford (ed.). *Early Food Production in North America*. Museum of Anthropology, University of Michigan, Ann Arbor, pp.19–56.

Stothers, D.M. 1977. *The Princess Point Complex*. Archaeological Survey of Canada, Mercury Series 58, Ottawa.

Strong, W.D. 1935. "An Introduction to Nebraska Archaeology," *Smithsonian Miscellaneous Collections* 93, 10.

—— 1940. "From History to Prehistory in the Northern Great Plains," *Smithsonian Miscellaneous Collections* 100:353–394.

Struever, S. (ed.), 1971. *Prehistoric Agriculture*. Natural History Press, Garden City, NY.

—— and Holton, F. 1979. *Koster: Americans in Search of the Prehistoric Past*. Anchor Press, NY.

—— and Houart, G. 1972. "An analysis of the Hopewell Interaction Sphere," in E. Wilmsen (ed.). *Social Exchange and Interaction*. University Museum of Anthropology, Ann Arbor, pp.47–80.

Stuart, D.E. and Gauthier, R.P. 1981. *Prehistoric New Mexico: background for survey*. New Mexico Historic Preservation Bureau, Santa Fé.

Styles, B.W. 1981. *Faunal Exploitation and Resource Selection: Early Late Woodland Subsistence in the Lower Illinois Valley*. Northwestern University Archaeological Program Scientific Paper 3.

—— and others. 1983. "Modoc Rock Shelter Revisited," in J.L. Phillips and J.A. Brown (eds.). *Archaic Hunter-Gatherers in the American Midwest*. Academic Press, New York, pp.261–297.

Suarez, B.K. and others. 1985. "Genetic Variation in North American Populations: The Geography of Gene Frequencies," *American Journal of Physical Anthropology* 67:217–232.

Swanton, J.R. 1911. "Indian Tribes of the Lower Mississippi and adjacent coast of the Gulf of Mexico," *Bureau of American Ethnology Bulletin* 43.
——— 1931. "Source material for the social and ceremonial life of the Choctaw Indians," *Bureau of American Ethnology* 103.

Talalay, L. and others. 1984. "Hickory nuts, walnuts, butternuts, and hazelnuts: Observations and experiments relevant to their aboriginal exploitation in Eastern North America," in P.J. Munson (ed.). *Experiments and Observations on Aboriginal Wild Plant Food Utilization in Eastern North America.* Indiana Historical Society Prehistoric Research Series 6(2):338–359.
Taylor, W.E. 1956. "A description of Sadlermiut houses excavated at Nature Point, Southampton Island, NWT. *National Museum of Canada Bulletin* 62:53–99.
——— and Swinton, G. 1967. "Prehistoric Dorset Art," *The Beaver* 298:32–47.
Thomas, David H. 1970. "Artiodactyls and man in the prehistoric Great Basin," *Center for Archaeological Research, Davis, Publication* 2:199–208.
——— 1981. "How to classify the projectile points from Monitor Valley, Nevada," *Journal of California and Great Basin Archaeology* 3(1):7–43.
——— 1982. "The 1981 Alta Toquima Village project: A Preliminary Report," *Desert Research Institute Social Sciences Technical Report Series* 27.
——— 1983. *The Archaeology of Monitor Valley 1. Epistemology, 2. Gatecliff Shelter.* Anthropological Papers of the American Museum of Natural History 58, Pt. 1 and 59, Pt. 1.
——— 1985. *The Archaeology of Hidden Cave, Nevada.* Anthropological Papers of the American Museum of Natural History, 61, Pt. 1.
——— 1988. *Mission Santa Catalina de Guale.* Anthropological Papers of the American Museum of Natural History, 63.
——— 1989. *Columbian Consequences, vol. 1 The Spanish Borderlands.* Smithsonian Institution Press, Washington DC.
——— and Bettinger, R.L. 1976. "Prehistoric piñon ecotone settlements of the Upper Reese River Valley, central Nevada," *American Museum of Natural History Anthropological Papers* 53(3):263–366.
Toll, H. and others. 1980. "Late ceramic patterns in Chaco Canyon: the programmatics of modeling ceramic exchange," in R.E. Fry (ed.). *Models and Methods in Regional Exchange.* Society for American Archaeology, Washington DC, pp.95–118.
Tooker, Elizabeth. 1964. *An Ethnography of the Huron Indians, 1615–1649.* Bureau of American Ethnology, Bulletin 190, Washington DC.
Trigger, Bruce G. 1969. *The Huron: Farmers of the North.* Holt, Rinehart, and Winston, New York.
——— 1976. *The Children of Aataentsic: A History of the Huron People to 1160.* 2 vols. McGill-Queens University Press, Montreal.
——— 1985. *Natives and Newcomers.* McGill-Queens University Press, Montreal.
Tuck, James A. 1970 "An Archaic Indian Cemetery in Newfoundland," *Scientific American* 222(6):112–121.
——— 1971. *Onondaga Iroquois Prehistory: A Study in Settlement Archaeology.* Syracuse University Press, Syracuse, NY.
——— 1974. "Early Archaic Horizons in eastern North America," *Archaeology of Eastern North America* 2(1):72–80.
——— 1975. "Prehistory of Saglek Bay, Labrador: Archaic and Paleo-Indian occupations," *Archaeological Survey of Canada Publications* 34.
——— 1976. *Newfoundland and Labrador Prehistory.* National Museums of Canada, Ottawa.
——— 1977. "A Look at Laurentian," *Researches and Transactions of the New York State Archaeological Association* 17(1):31–40
——— 1984. *Maritime Provinces Prehistory.* Archaeological Survey of Canada, Ottawa.
Turner, Christy. 1984. "Advances in the Dental Search for Native American Origins," *Acta Anthropogenetica* 8(1,2):23–78.
——— 1986. "The First Americans: The Dental Evidence," *National Geographic Research* 2:37–46.
——— 1987. "Telltale Teeth," *Natural History* 96(1):6–10.

Upham, Steadman. 1982. *Politics and Power: an economic and political history of the Western Pueblo.* Academic Press, New York.
——— and others. 1987. "Evidence concerning the origin of Maize de Ocho," *American Anthropologist* 89(3):410–419.

Van Devender, T.R. and Spaulding, W.R. 1979. "Development of vegetation and climate in the Southwestern United States," *Science* 204:701–710.
Vega, Garcilaso de la. 1951. *The Florida of the Inca.* University of Texas Press, Austin.
Vivian, Gordon. 1979. "The Hubbard site and other tri-wall structures in New Mexico and Colorado," *National Park Service Archaeological Research Series 5*, Washington DC.
——— and Mathews, T.W. 1965. "Kin Kletso, A pueblo III community in Chaco Canyon, New Mexico," *Southwestern Monuments Association, Technical Series 6*, Globe, Arizona.
Vivian, Gwinn R. 1974. "Conservation and Diversion: water-control systems in the Anasazi Southwest," in Theodore Downing and McGwire Gibson (eds.). *Irrigation's Impact on Society.* University of Arizona Anthropological Papers 25:95–112.
——— 1988. "Kluckholhn Reappraised: the Chacoan System as an Egalitarian Enterprise," *Journal of Anthropological Research* 45(1):101–113.
——— 1990. *The Chacoan Prehistory of the San Juan Basin.* Academic Press, Orlando, Florida.

Wahlgren, Erik. 1986. *The Vikings and America.* Thames and Hudson, London and New York.
Wallace, W.J. 1978. "Post Pleistocene Archaeology," in R.F. Heizer (ed.). *Vol 8 California. Handbook of North American Indians.* Smithsonian Institution, Washington DC, pp.462–470.
Walthall, J.A. 1980. *Prehistoric Indians of the Southeast.* University of Alabama Press, Birmingham.
Warren, C.N. 1967. "The San Dieguito Complex: A review and hypothesis," *American Antiquity* 32(2)168–185.
——— and True, D.L. 1961. "The San Dieguito Complex and its place in California prehistory," *UCLA Archaeological Survey Annual Report* 1960–1961:246–338.
Warrick, Gary. 1984. *Reconstructing Ontario Iroquoian Village Organization.* Archaeological Survey of Canada, Mercury Series 124:1–180.
Waters, Michael R. 1986. "The Geoarchaeology of Whitewater Draw," *Anthropological Papers of the University of Arizona* 45.
Watson, P.J. 1985. "The Impact of Early Horticulture on the Upland Drainage of the Midwest and Midsouth," in R.I. Ford (ed.). *Early Food Production in North America.* University Museum of Anthropology, University of Michigan, Ann Arbor, pp.73–98.
——— 1988. "Prehistoric Gardening and Agriculture in the Midwest and Midsouth," in Richard Yerkes (ed.). *Interpretations of Culture Change in Eastern Woodlands During the Late Woodland Period.* Department of Anthropology, Ohio State University, pp.39–67.
Wauchope, R. 1972. *Lost Tribes and Sunken Continents.* University of Chicago Press, Chicago.
Webb, C.M. 1977. "The Poverty Point Culture," *Geoscience and Man* 17:1–73.
Webb, W.S. 1974. *Indian Knoll.* University of Tennessee Press, Knoxville (new edition).
——— and Baby, R.S. 1957. *The Adena People no. 2.* Ohio Historical Society, Columbus.
——— and Snow, C.E. 1945. *The Adena People.* University of Tennessee Press, Knoxville.
Wedel, Waldo. 1938. "The Direct-Historical Approach in Pawnee Archaeology," *Smithsonian Miscellaneous Collections* 97,7.
——— 1953. "Some aspects of human ecology in the central Plains," *American Anthropologist* 55(4):499–514.
——— 1961. *Prehistoric Man on the Great Plains.* University of Oklahoma Press, Norman.
——— and others 1968. 'Mummy Cave: Prehistoric record for the Rocky Mountains of Wyoming," *Science* 160:184–186.
Welch, p. 1981. "The West Jefferson Phase: Terminal Woodland Tribal Societies in West Central Alabama," *Southeastern Archaeology Conference Bulletin* 24:81–83.
Wendorf, F. and Hester, J. (eds.) 1975. *Late Pleistocene environments on the Southern High Plains.* Fort Burgwin Research Center Publication 9.
——— and Kreiger, A.D. 1959. "New Light on the Midland Discovery," *American Antiquity* 25:66–78.
——— and Reed, Erik. 1955. "An alternative reconstruction of northern Rio Grande prehistory," *el Palacio* 62(5–6):131–173.
West, F.H. 1981. *The Archaeology of Beringia.* Columbia University Press, New York.
Whalen, N.M. 1975. "Cochise site distribution in the San Pedro River Valley," *The Kiva* 40(3):203–211.
Wheat, J.B. 1972. *The Olsen-Chubbock Site: A Paleo-Indian Bison Kill.* Society for American Archaeology, Washington DC.
Wilcox, David R. 1985. "The Teipiman Connection: A model of Mesoamerican-Southwestern Interaction," in Randall H. McGuire and Francis Joan Mathier (eds.). *Ripples in the Chichimec Sea.* Southern Illinois University Press, Carbondale, pp.86–94.
Willey, G.R. 1949. "Archaeology of the Florida Gulf Coast," *Smithsonian Miscellaneous Collections* 113.

———— 1953. "Prehistoric Settlement Patterns in the Virú Valley, Peru," *Bureau of American Ethnology Bulletin* 155.

———— 1966. *Introduction to American Archaeology. Vol.1: North America*. Prentice Hall, Englewood Cliffs, NJ.

———— and Phillips, P. 1958. *Method and Theory in American Archaeology*. University of Chicago Press, Chicago.

———— and Sabloff, J.A. 1980. *A History of American Archaeology*. 2nd ed. W.H. Freeman, San Francisco.

Williams, S.C. (ed.) 1930. *Adair's History of the American Indians*. Watauga Press, Johnson City, Tennessee.

Williams, S. and Brain, J.P. 1983. "Excavations at the Lake George Site, Yazoo City, Mississippi, 1958–1960," *Papers of the Peabody Museum of Archaeology and Ethnology* 68.

Williamson, R.A. 1981. "North America: A Multiplicity of Astronomies," in Ray A. Williamson (ed.). *Archaeoastronomy in the Americas*. Ballena Press, Los Altos, California, pp.61–80.

———— 1984. *Living the Sky*. University of New Mexico Press, Albuquerque.

Wills, W.H. 1989. *Early Prehistoric Agriculture in the American Southwest*. School of American Research, Santa Fé, New Mexico.

Wilmsen, E. and Roberts, F.H.H. 1978. "Lindenmaier 1934–1974. Concluding Report on Investigations" *Smithsonian Contributions in Anthropology* 24.

Winterhalder, B. and Smith E. (eds.) 1981. *Hunter-Gatherer Foraging Strategies*. University of Chicago Press, Chicago.

Winters, H. 1968. *The Riverton Culture: a 2nd Millennium occupation in the Central Wabash Valley*. Illinois State Museum, Springfield.

———— 1974. "Introduction," in W. Webb, *Indian Knoll*. University of Tennessee Press, Knoxville, pp.v-xxvii.

Witthoft, J. 1952. "A Paleo-Indian site in eastern Pennsylvania: An early hunting culture," *Proceedings of the American Philosophical Society* 96:464–495.

———— 1959. "The Ancestry of the Susquehannocks," in John Witthoft and W.F. Kinsey, III, (eds.), *Susquehannock Miscellany*. Pennsylvania Historical and Museum Commission, Harrisburg, pp.19–60.

Wittlaufer, B.N. 1955. "The Mortlach Site in the Besant Valley of Central Saskatchewan," *Anthropological Series No. 1, Department of Natural Resources, Regina*.

Wobst, H.M. 1974. "Boundary Conditions for Paleolithic Social Systems: A Simulation Approach," *American Antiquity* 39:147–177.

Wormington, Marie. 1955. "A Reappraisal of the Fremont Culture," *Proceedings of the Denver Museum of Natural History*, 1.

———— 1957. *Ancient Man in North America*. Denver Museum of Natural History.

Wray, Charles F. and Schoff, Harry L. 1953. "A Preliminary Report on the Seneca Sequence in Western New York," *Pennsylvania Archaeologist* 22:53–63.

Wright, H.E. (ed.) 1983. *Late-Quaternary Environments of the United States. Vol 2: the Holocene*. University of Minnesota Press, Minneapolis.

Wright, J. 1972. *The Shield Archaic*. National Museum of Man, Ottawa.

Wright, J.L. 1981. *The only land they knew*. Free Press, New York.

Wright, J.V. 1966. *The Ontario Iroquois Tradition*. National Museum of Canada, Bulletin 210.

———— 1967. *The Laurel Tradition and the Middle Woodland Period*. National Museum of Canada, Bulletin 177.

———— 1984. "The Cultural Continuity of the Northern Iroquoian-Speaking Peoples," in M.K. Foster and others (eds.). *Extending the Rafters: Interdisciplinary Approaches to Iroquoian Studies*. State University of New York Press, Albany, pp.283–299.

Wylie, A. 1985. "The Reaction Against Analogy," *Advances in Archaeological Method and Theory* 8:63–111.

Yamura, K. 1979. "On the origin of Thule culture as seen from the typological studies of toggle harpoon heads," in A.P. McCartney (ed.). *Thule Eskimo prehistory: an anthropological retrospective*. Archaeological Survey of Canada, Ottawa, Mercury Series 88:474–484.

Yarnell, R.A. 1978. "Domestication of sunflower and sumpweed in eastern North America," in R.I. Ford (ed.). *Early Food Production in North America*, University Museum of Anthropology, University of Michigan, Ann Arbor, pp.285–299.

Yellen, J.E. 1977. *Archaeological Approaches to the Present: Models for Predicting the Past*. Academic Press, New York.

Yerkes, R.W. (ed.) 1988. *Interpretations of Culture Change in the Eastern Woodlands during the Late Woodland Period*. Department of Anthropology, Ohio State University, Columbus.

Young, S.B. 1982. "The vegetation of Land-Bridge Beringia," in David Hopkins and others (eds.). *Paleoecology of Beringia*. Academic Press, New York, pp.179–194.

Illustration Credits

Index and Glossary